D0925798

Displaced Persons

DISCARD

DISCARD

DISPLACED PERSONS

The Literature of Exile from Cicero to Boethius

Jo-Marie Claassen

```
R  O  M  A
O        M
M        O
A  M  O  R
```

The University of Wisconsin Press

To my mother, and in memory of my father

Published in the United States of America by
The University of Wisconsin Press
2537 Daniels Street
Madison, Wisconsin 53718-6772
www.wisc.edu/wisconsinpress/

First published in 1999 by
Gerald Duckworth & Co. Ltd.
61 Frith Street
London W1V 5TA
Tel: 0171 434 4242
Fax: 0171 434 4420
Email: duckworth-publishers.co.uk

All rights reserved. No part of this publication may be reproduced,
stored in a retrieval system, or transmitted, in any form or by
any means, electronic, mechanical, photocopying, recording or
otherwise, without the prior permission of the publisher.

© 1999 by Jo-Marie Claassen

Libraray of Congress Cataloging-in-Publication Data

Claassen, Jo-Marie.
    Displaced persons : the literature of exile from Cicero to
Boethius / Jo-Marie Claassen.
        p.   cm. – (Wisconsin studies in classics)
    Includes bibliographical references and index.
    ISBN 0-299-16640-6 (cloth: alk. paper). – ISBN 0-299-16644-9
(pbk.: alk. paper)
    1. Exiles' writings, Latin—History and criticism. 2. Cicero,
Marcus Tullius–Criticism and interpretation. 3. Ovid, 43 B.C.–17
or 18 A.D.–Criticism and interpretation. 4. Seneca, Lucius
Annaeus, ca. 4 B.C.–65 A.D.–Criticism and interpretation.
5. Boethius, d. 524–Criticism and interpretation. 6. Latin
literature–History and criticism. 7. Exiles—Rome–History.
8. Narration (Rhetoric) 9. Rhetoric, Ancient. I. Title. II. Series.
PA6018.E95C58 1999
870.9′920691–dc21   99-29892

Printed in Great Britain

Contents

Contents

Preface

ROMA *ibi tibi sedes – ibi tibi* AMOR;
ROMA *etsi te terret et iste* AMOR,
ibi etsi vis te non esse – sed es ibi,
ROMA *te tenet et* AMOR.   *(Anon)*

At Rome you live – at Rome you love;
From Rome that Love may you affright,
although you'd leave, you never move,
for Love and Rome both bar your flight.

This book offers a discussion of reactions to exile in the Roman world by five authors, four of whom wrote in Latin, one in Greek. It will in passing touch on many other exiled personages and many aspects of exile, not least being the strong desire evinced by most to be back in Rome. The above little piece of doggerel, culled from a collection of Latin palindromes found on the Internet (Enzinger 1998), although clearly stressing erotic *Amor* as the complement of *Roma*, may be taken as the *Leitmotiv* of this book. The grammatically objective genitive in the phrase *amor Romae* ('love of Rome') informed almost every page of the literature which I have chosen to treat together as 'the literature of exile'. Love of Rome was experienced subjectively as the overriding reason for discontent at being elsewhere by most of the exiled authors included in this study. To list exceptions to this rather simplistic statement would be to crowd the whole work into this Preface, and therefore I shall leave that aspect to unfold in the body of the work.

The book has been long in the making, and has undergone various Teresias-like, if not quite Protean, metamorphoses since its humble beginnings as a D.Litt. dissertation on Ovid's exilic poetry (1986). It first developed into an excursive discussion on 'the exilic genre' (completed in 1989), and finally it became this more popularly-aimed study of the emotions and literary reactions of five exiled personages from the Roman literary world. Along the way it spawned a paper (read at the 11th Pacific Rim Roman Literature Seminar, University of Natal, Durban in June 1997) entitled '*Amor-Roma et Augustus*: did Ovid have the last laugh?' and various articles. These have appeared in four scholarly journals. Thanks to their editors and anonymous referees for their contribution to my heightened insights. These papers were in their turn re-integrated into the fabric of the work, and have therefore undergone more revision since their publication under the following titles:

'Exile, death and immortality: voices from the grave', *Latomus* 55.3 (Brussels, 1996) pp. 577-90.
'Dio's Cicero and the consolatory tradition', *Proceedings of the Leeds International Latin Seminar* VIII (Leeds, 1996) pp. 29-45.
'Cicero's banishment: Tempora et mores', *Acta Classica* 35 (Pretoria, 1992) pp. 19-45.
'The Consolatio Philosophiae of Boethius: pagan tradition and Christian innovation', *UNISA Medieval Studies* 4 (Pretoria, 1991) pp. 177-95.

Sincere thanks to Prof. Victoria E. Pagán and Prof. Jeffrey Wills, readers for the University of Wisconsin Press, for their valued criticism and detailed comments, which reached me only after the final proofreading and indexing had been completed. Unfortunately not all their suggestions could be incorporated at this late stage. Deference to the advice of Professor Wills would have entailed a large-scale reworking of parts of the book. A better book may have resulted, but it would have been a different book from this one. I was sorry to be unable to incorporate Professor Pagán's biblio-graphical suggestions and apologise to my readers for not having noted them in the first place. Like Ovid at the Northern ends of the Roman earth, I can merely offer as *recusatio* the observation that these escaped me in my various peregrinations to the Western world from the modern 'ends of the earth' that is the new South Africa.

I am obliged to many persons (in all the senses of the word 'person', as these senses will become apparent as the other main feature of this work): from the Division of Research Development at the University of Stellenbosch, to a number of host Universities in Britain, Italy, Canada and the US (whose library facilities I consulted at various times), to Prof. Bert van Stekenlenburg (who made me produce a dissertation in haste to be reworked at leisure), to Prof. Peter Green (whose sense of humour often put me on the right track), to Prof. Wolfgang Haase (who first suggested the generic treatment of exilic literature), to Prof. Susanna Morton Braund (whose thorough scrutiny and valuable comments made this a better book), and to Deborah Blake of Duckworth (who accepted her recommendation and treated both author and book with great kindness) and to my friend Prof. Elaine Fantham of Princeton University (now *emerita*, whose valued suggestions saved me from numerous errors), to colleagues and clerical staff at the Department of Classics, Stellenbosch University (for help during various stints of study leave), to Maridien Schneider, an exemplary assistant (for support in countless ways), and, finally, to the four persons who give me a sense of place, Piet, Carol, Daan and Karin – home is where the heart is.   J.M.C.
Stellenbosch

Introduction

Banishment, displacement and the return of the exiled constitute a consistent world-wide modern phenomenon, which ranges from the wanderings of Vietnamese boat-people and the unfortunate victims of the continued Hutu-Tutsi power struggles of the African Rift Valley, to the exile and return of Imelda Marcos, or, in recent Southern African history, of various members of SWAPO and the African National Congress. Exile is a political act. Political change sometimes, but not always, brings return. The UN Council for Refugees in December 1997 reported that world-wide some 22 million displaced persons have no hope of return to their home countries, and a further 25 million are internally displaced. Articulate exiles, when removed from the theatre of power, often, but not always, resort to writing.

This book is mainly about displaced persons in the Roman world and the various means of literary sublimation that individual exiles found for the feeling of social and political isolation that they experienced. Exile as an ancient sociological phenomenon was twenty years ago thoroughly treated by Grasmück (1978), whereas Doblhofer a decade later (1987) chose to concentrate on the literary expression of *Heimatferne* (homesickness). Grasmück concentrates, as I do, on the literary reworking of their emotional experience by Cicero, Ovid and Seneca. He stresses the concept of exile as an illness for which sublimation of some kind acts as a cure. These two works are in German. Recently Gareth Williams has published two works in English on Ovid, his *Banished Voices* (1994) and, on the *Ibis*, his *The Curse of Exile* (1996). Peter Green's Penguin translation, *Ovid: The poems of exile* (1994) offers an excellent introduction and commentary, embodying recent scholarship. Two editors have produced recent editions of Cicero's exilic writings, Rita Degl' Innocenti Pierini, a critical edition of his letters from exile (1996), D.R. Shackleton Bailey a translation of and commentary (1991) on his speeches after his return. Degl' Innocenti Pierini's *Tra Ovidio e Seneca* (1990b) meticulously traces intertextual relationships.

This book in no way seeks to supersede these works, but intends to complement them. Its thrust is literary, but it will encompass a certain amount of sociological and historical material. It will start, as does Doblhofer, with Cicero, but it will take the line through to the virtual end of the

1

Classical era, with a study of aspects of the consolatory tradition in the Christian writer Boethius.

My literary-critical approach is largely conventional, with, however, eclectic attention to modern literary theory, particularly in analysis of narrative strategies employed by our various authors. The title I originally coined for the book was too much of a mouthful for my editor to accept, and so I bowed to her superior wisdom. What appears on the cover and title page is an adaptation of my original *Persons, personae and personalities in exile: the literature of exile from Cicero to Boethius*. The time spanned by the literature under consideration is close on five centuries. The personages included in chronological order between Cicero (106-43 BC) and Boethius (fl. AD 480–524) are the 'a-political' (but in fact highly political) poet Ovid (42 BC – c. AD 17) and two politically-minded philosophers, Seneca the Younger (c. AD 4 – 65) and Dio Chrysostomus (c. AD 40-50 – c. 110). Four of these personages shared almost the same cultural milieu. The date of death of the first member of each consecutive pair and the birth of the next virtually overlapped, forming a continuum. It will become apparent that, although separated from them by several centuries, Anicius Manlius Boethius had, both in intellect and in circumstances, a spiritual affinity with the other four. This study concentrates on the political and social isolation of these persons, each formerly powerful in a particular sphere, and their attempts either to sublimate their consequent powerlessness or to find new ways of wielding power, chiefly by literary means. It will therefore concentrate on works from these authors' own pens.

The term *persons* is of crucial importance here, paradoxically involving both the precision and the vagueness currently implied by its manifold, almost Protean, uses in modern life. The major persons featured are all men, despite the modern genderless connotation given the word – we have no material written by exiled Roman women, and relatively little on them (although the two Juliae, respectively the daughter and granddaughter of the emperor Augustus, appear in passing in discussion of Ovid's fate). Discussion will be literary, and literary influence (or intertextual allusion), chronologically traceable from one exiled personage to the next, will need to be noted, but *Quellenforschung* is not the major object of the work. Of importance is rather the manner in which each exile experiences his condition and the way in which his reaction is put into words.

The work is divided into four 'Stages', each comprising two or more *Chapters*. These are subdivided into topical *Sections*. My approach will be diachronic, and topics will, where feasible, be explored chronologically as they impinge on each of the persons discussed. The main ordering principle of the study hinges, however, on a second and relatively precise meaning of *person*: *grammatical person*. Discussion will start, after initial placement and taxonomy, with the *third grammatical person*, that is, narratives about exiles, 'he' or 'they' (the *First Stage*). This aspect will, however, receive the least emphasis, as a more discursive treatment would

2

require a different, historiographic-analytical approach, which is not the aim of this work. Discussion of narrative techniques and focalisation will largely aim at setting in place a social, cultural and political framework for the treatment of second person outreach and first person utterances by the five main protagonists.

In the *Second Stage*, then, discussion will focus on the *second grammatical person*, that is, on dialogue (especially letter-writing as dialogue at remove) between the exile and another, a 'you-and-I' situation. A major difference in focus within this mode depends upon whether the interlocutor or the addressee is the person exiled. When the non-exiled interlocutor is the producer of the text, the major emphasis will be on the formal tradition of consolation, 'you-in-exile'. In the case of Seneca the emphasis is, however, on the exile himself as consoler, 'I-in-exile advise you-at-Rome'. Two further and divergent aspects colour discussion of address by an exile to a non-exiled second person: attack and invective or appeal for aid, 'you-at-Rome have harmed / must help me-in-exile'. In this mode focalisation shifts subtly from the deeds or misdeeds of the second person to the needs and sufferings of the first person, leading naturally to the third stage, consideration of the 'isolated I', the *first person* in exile. By far the longest section of the work, then, will be devoted to study of utterances in which the *first grammatical person* predominates (*Stages Three* and *Four*). Here the isolating effect of exile is prominent – discussion will concentrate on what is essentially monologue. *Stage Three* concentrates on the individual and particular, *Stage Four* on our protagonists' universalising of the particular, through the power of their poetry.

A further grammatical aspect beside *person* is frequently involved in the consideration of exilic writings, i.e. *tense*. Exiles either look to the *past*, describe their *present*, or express hopes for a better *future*. Focalisation of time depends on whether the exile has returned safely, and is looking back on his exiled state, or whether, still in exile, he is looking back at happier days, enunciating the impressions of a miserable present, or hoping for future return.

Psychologically justifiable solipsism is the chief feature of the second person discussion of exile. It also produces the most intense poetry. Consideration of exilic poetry in the main involves Ovid's poems from exile, but also the effusions of Cicero, Seneca and Boethius. In the last stage, then, I discuss the poetry of exile by these four personages. This poetry partakes of all the features of tense and aspect involved above. Each of these displaced persons is creating a *poetic persona*. This *persona* may or may not differ radically from the authorial *personality* to be discovered in his other works. The potential of slippage between the 'authorial I' of the empiric author as creator of a work and the 'subjective I' of his creation, the *poetic persona*, will receive due attention throughout.

'Exile' throughout means 'exile from Rome'. Our first two exiles, Cicero and Ovid, were Latin-speaking Romans. Seneca was the son of a naturalised Spaniard. Boethius was a Roman in the service of the Ostrogothic ruler of Rome. My theme is unashamedly 'Roman' in its fixing of parameters, but, as with most other aspects of the ancient world, many spillovers from the Greek world informed the thought of our Latin-speaking protagonists. Only one of the exiles was a Greek, but Dio Chrysostomus, too, was expelled from Rome – a Rome in which the Stoic philosophy had become virtually synonymous with subversion. Dio of Prusa, a Greek philosopher exiled from Rome by a Roman emperor, wrote in Greek about his experience of exile in a Romanised Hellenistic world. Greek philosophers could and often did exert influence at Rome on behalf their native cities, but it was exile from Rome that coloured Dio's perception of loss of a spiritual home. He later was allowed to return to the cultural hub that Rome had become for many Greeks during the first century of imperial rule.

The last of our protagonists, Boethius, Roman consul under an Ostrogothic emperor, was both exiled from Rome and imprisoned (at Pavia), as the result of political machinations by enemies at court. His contemplation of exile gains in poignancy as a form of both external and internal exile – in prison he felt himself alienated from all he had ever been, and he needed to rediscover a lost philosophical strength in order to ensure his spiritual survival. The chronicle of his spiritual journey, a supreme example of the power of the human mind to transcend temporal vicissitudes, offers a fitting conclusion to the study at hand. Boethius is important for his obvious use of the literary precedents set by his four exiled predecessors, as well as his literary debt to almost the whole of the Classical *corpus*.

It must be emphasised at the outset that the literary effusions under consideration are, with the exception of Cicero's private letters, literary artefacts, with their own deliberate programme of self-presentation by each author. Cicero's rewriting of his exile by hindsight in various speeches and in his poetry (6.1, 7.2 and 8.1) shares in this authorial deliberateness. Inclusion of his informal letters in a work purporting to study the 'literature' of exile may be criticised on various fronts, not least that it contributes to Cicero's notoriously 'rough treatment by the press'. Yet his private letters from exile are important for their very ingenuousness and for their evidence of the kind of inner turmoil which is both experienced and stylised by his successors. His letters to exiled contemporaries will be seen (Section 3.1.1) to reflect a long tradition of consolation, which he could not make his own when he himself was banished.

An unashamedly large part of this study (particularly Chapters 4, 5 and 7 and almost all of the *Fourth Stage*) will be devoted to the poet Ovid, simultaneously the most mysterious of our displaced persons and the most transparent. Before him, Cicero's self-revealing but largely ingenuous effusions had set the tone for exilic writings about exile. After him, Seneca and Dio were working with a specific ancient tradition, also consciously followed by Boethius (Chapter 3). Ovid's exilic writings took over Cicero's emotional tone and consciously recreated his own reactions to displace-

4

ment into an art form without parallel in ancient literature. His poetic precedents will in the end be discussed as the major influence that still works to colour modern readers' perceptions as to the nature and characteristics of the literature of exile in the ancient world, the topic of this work.

To take the scheme of the book in order: Chapter 1 will set the scene, whereafter we shall progress from narrative (Chapter 2) through exilic outreach (Chapters 3 and 4) to invective (5); Chapters 6 and 7 will be devoted to our protagonists' concentration on themselves, with particular attention to what we may term first person narrative, retrospection and introspection – reasonably objective focus on the exiled 'I'; Chapters 8 and 9 will concentrate on exilic poetry – almost wholly subjective focus on the exiled 'I'. Chapter 8 will treat of the generic range within the poetry of exile, and Chapter 9 will conclude this study with an analysis of Ovid's poetic contribution to the generic tradition, and intertextual allusion to this tradition in the poetry ascribed to Seneca and Boethius. An Epilogue will return to the issues of person, *persona*, personality and genre raised in the Introduction and Chapter 1.

THE FIRST STAGE

TYPES AND TALES

Preamble: Setting the Stage and Priming the Canvas

My first two chapters will set the stage, the first with a consideration of the nature of exile as a political tool, the second with third person narratives of exile (both starting and ending with discussion of particular aspects of the *myth of exile*).

In Chapter 1 the political nature of exile in the ancient world and the relationship between exile and power (and exile and literature) will first be explored (1.1, 1.2). Sources and generic types will be considered (1.3). This includes discussion of the formal aspects of the consolatory tradition (1.4 and 5). After this attention will be paid to the major subjective contributors to our view of exile in the Roman world, Cicero (1.6) and Ovid (1.7 to 9). Discussion of Ovid and his 'invention without parallel', the essential fictionalisation of his experiences (1.9), leads naturally to the next chapter, consideration of exile in myth and history, that is, third person narrative, starting with narrative fiction.

Chapter 2 has a double function, both to provide a synoptic narrative background for the literary figures that feature throughout, and to consider aspects of third person narration as a literary phenomenon. It therefore opens with a subsection featuring discussion of narrative strategies (2.1.1), leading to tales of exile in myth and literature (2.1.2 and 3). Emphasis is on third person narrative. Instances considered here (Medea, Aeneas, Orpheus and Orestes, as well as dispossession within Vergil's pastoral world) are all appropriate to the issue of the displaced person within the geographical outreaches of the Mediterranean, the canvas upon which our picture of dispossession will be painted. As will become clear in the course of the book, these mythical outcasts very largely became the prototypes upon which historical outcasts fashioned themselves in the stylised presentations of self (in both second person outreach and first person introspection) which inform the larger part of this work.

Next follows consideration of political exile in historical context, first in the Greek world (2.2.1) and then in the Roman (2.2.2). These, too, serve as historical paradigms for the stories of our major protagonists. Two versions of Cicero's exile, as narrated respectively by Dio and Plutarch (2.1.3), are compared, in order to distinguish the narrative emphasis of each author. The next two subsections briefly consider the temporary exile or permanent banishment of some historical figures under Augustus: Agrippa and Tiberius, the two Julias and some of their lovers (2.2.4), in the end concentrating on the poet Ovid (2.2.5).

Next comes a brief overview of exile and power relations in the first century. Tiberius withdrew voluntarily to Capri, seemingly yielding his power (2.2.5), but thereafter emperors retained their power, and it was various philosophers that were sent into retreat, Seneca for an apparent sexual misdemeanour (2.2.6) and others for opposition to the imperial regime (2.2.8). My discussion then leaps over several centuries, to consider Boethius' exile and imprisonment (2.2.9). The chapter ends with a consideration of the manner in which, with Ovid, historical narrative partakes of the elements of myth (2.3).

1

Exiled Persons

1.1 Exile, power and sublimation

Exile is a basic aspect of *la condition humaine* looming large in literature, both ancient and modern. Exile is a condition in which the protagonist is no longer living, or able to live, in the land of his birth. Exile may be either voluntary, a deliberately decided-upon protracted journey to or stay in a foreign country, or involuntary, merely the result of circumstances, such as an offer of expatriate employment, with little hardship to the protagonist. It may, however, be enforced. Enforced exile frequently results from a major difference of political allegiance between the most powerful in the state and the person being exiled. Very often such exiles are the helpless victims of extraneous circumstances such as protracted war, but sometimes the exiles are themselves political figures, exiled because of their potential threat to the political well-being of their opponents. In the modern world, helpless victims abound, but international law no longer allows a state to get rid of potentially disruptive citizens by sending them away from its territory. It does acknowledge the right of potentially dangerous citizens to leave voluntarily and seek political asylum elsewhere, often to pre-empt imprisonment in their home country. Such exile is essentially still enforced.

The fact of exile depends on perception. Removal from the *patria* (homeland) may offer little or no hardship to either voluntary or involuntary exiles; enforced exile usually brings the kind of hardship addressed in the literature of exile, especially in autobiography.

These differences were recognised by Roman law, where no injunction against the exiling of its citizens was in existence, and where no neighbour states could object to becoming a haven for politically or criminally unacceptable former Roman citizens. In a society that had no extensive prison system, criminal justice knew of only two punishments for major crimes: exile or death. Enforced exile was an acknowledged tool in the exertion of criminal justice as well as in politics. Exile in the ancient world was, as today, a major political tool and as such it was often employed by the powerful to reduce the power of their most feared opponents. Roman political life in the last century of the Republic and in the early empire was by definition centred in the capital and mere removal from the hub of political activity would reduce an exiled politician's power to virtually nothing. Their physical presence was required if politicians wished to stand for office. Their daily presence at the early-morning *salutationes* (formal visits by clients) of the great was imperative if aid were to be forthcoming. A person under political threat lost virtually all power of salvation if he was forced to leave Rome.

The same could not, however, be said about an exile's literary power. Cicero after his return from banishment in 58 BC was politically a spent force, but his literary works after his return comprise some of the most important aspects of his contribution to Western thought. After his recall from exile to become tutor to the young prince Nero, the younger Seneca regained all the power he had lost, if only for a time. By voicing his own view of his situation in the context of consoling others in bereavement, Seneca gave an interesting new angle to an established literary genre, the convention of writing consolations to an exile. By doing so, he was practising what he preached, for the major method of sublimation suggested to exiles within this tradition was literary activity. Dio Chrysostomus, a Greek philosopher, stands somewhat apart from the more overtly political Romans, but he appears to have been an influential Greek within his Roman setting, and when he was allowed to return, he continued to use his voice for the benefit of his compatriots.

Boethius,[1] one of the last of the literary figures of Classical Rome, or perhaps the earliest of the versatile 'Renaissance men', had, in the turbulent days of sixth-century Ostrogothic power struggles, risen to the highest rung possible at Rome, and had fallen, together with his Gothic overlord. His excursive reworking of the many strains of a by then extremely complex literary tradition is by no means an epilogue or dying whimper, but stands as a monument to the tradition of sublimation of exilic discomfort by literary means.

In this company of politicians and philosophers, the poet Ovid (exiled to Tomis on the Black Sea ostensibly for a literary *faux pas* but more likely for involuntary involvement in political intrigue against the emperor Augustus) stands apart, yet his exile shows certain affinities with those of the others. We do not know whether Ovid continued at the time to wield the same kind of literary influence *in absentia* that he had wielded while still in Rome. Yet his powerful poetic voice has continued to speak over the centuries. The power of Ovid's exilic writings is a major theme in this book.

Ovid is largely responsible for the creation of a *myth of exile*. Ovid's exilic poems, while ostensibly giving a view of 'real exile' in the 'real world', manage to universalise the exilic psyche. Exile is given a mythical, universal dimension by its recurrence as *Leitmotiv* in ever-shifting facets of psychological isolation, but also of psychological redemption by means of poetry.[2]

In the Roman world, exile and death were closely related. Because exile frequently served as pre-emption of or substitute for the death penalty, it was often portrayed in literature as the virtual equivalent of death. Yet even in banishment, intimations of immortality often served to lighten some exiles' lot. Such sublimation will receive emphasis in the final chapter of this book.

1.2 Exilic and generic taxonomies

Exile was defined in Roman law as *ciuitatis amissio* (loss of citizenship).[3] An intricate web of rulings covering the various vicissitudes attendant upon public or imperial disfavour is an indication of the prevalence of varying degrees of dislocation in the political life of Roman citizens. Incompatibility of citizenship meant that a Roman settling elsewhere automatically lost his Roman citizenship. Conversely, foreigners coming to Rome could receive citizenship if they were under Roman patronage.[4] Change of domicile was known as *solum vertere* (best translated as 'change of location'). Loss of civic status was immediate only if it was a case of *solum vertere exilii causa* (change of location because of exile), involving escape from capital condemnation[5] or if the sentence imposed was *interdictio aquae et igni* (prevention from enjoying the privileges of water and fire).[6] Loss of Roman citizenship commenced only on arrival at the imposed destination. A Roman *exsul* could take up local citizenship. A freedman returning to his country of origin automatically lost his Roman citizenship, through *postliminium* (cross-border movement). *Relegatio* meant enforced removal from Rome, with retention of full citizenship.[7] Voluntary exile was frequently undertaken to pre-empt the capital punishment decreed by *abrogatio* (annulment) of the civic rights of the accused.[8] Only after the *Lex Tullia de ambitu*, a law which was passed during Cicero's consulship in an attempt to curb corruption at the hustings, was exile officially designated as a penalty for political malfeasance.[9]

So much for the nature of exilic displacement. What of the nature of exilic literature? Such literature comprises writings *about* exile and exiles (mythical, historiographical or factual), *on* exile (philosophical and moralistic or psychological), *to* an exile (comfort and advice) or *from* an exile (frequently covering all the above, but autobiographically coloured).[10] Exile as topic has featured incidentally in narrative literature of various kinds from Homer onwards, and the tales of their exile and return feature in the biographies of some of our various protagonists, and in Roman historiography. These narratives will be discussed only briefly in a work whose main focus will be on subjective exposition of the emotions, whether vicarious sympathy or subjective misery, of the various authors involved. Their works represent, as may be expected, a great variety of generic types, ranging from epic, elegiac and lyric poetry to informal and formal epistolography and formal essays or diatribes. Exilic narrative features, as narrative most often does, verbs in the third person. In the case of some sort of address, whether epistolary or rhetorically-coloured persuasion (as, particularly, in consolatory works) or deliberation (in philosophical musings on exile, often presented as conversation with a notional second party), second person verbs predominate.

Naturally, in the case of autobiography, verbs in the first person predominate. A common factor among our second person writers on exile is not so much the *fact* of their exile as the *status* of the individual exile. In the ancient world, both enforced exile and voluntary exile undertaken for political reasons involved the powerful or potentially powerful, and these were also the persons who wrote about their own exile; perhaps because the educated (and therefore both potentially most powerful and potentially most exile-prone) were the most articulate. An autobiographical writer of exilic literature was often the vocal or literary representative of a 'silent majority', articulating the experiences, hopes, fears and longings of a large section of the Mediterranean world of his time.

Exilic literature clothes psychologically similar content in a wide spectrum of traditionally separate generic forms: in poetry, a variety of metres, and in prose, epistolography with its subgenre the *consolatio* 'or consolation to an exile', rhetorical works of various kinds, philosophical dialogue, Menippean *satura* (a mixture of verse and prose, not necessarily satirical) and historiography.[11]

The letter as *sermo absentis* (conversation with an absent friend) is perhaps the single most important exilic form, implying, as it does, that the addressee is the other in a dialogue. Here the personality or reaction of the addressee, whether 'real' or 'imagined', is almost as important as that of the exile.[12] 'Real', or private, letters may be distinguished from 'literary', or public, 'letters', of which some are in metrical form. The most extensive body of exilic literature is Ovid's collection of poems from exile. A large number are epistolary and ostensibly private, but were clearly intended by the author for publication – public literature masquerading as private correspondence. The 'real' audience as opposed to the ostensible addressee must be taken into account.

The question may be posed whether we are justified in grouping these diverse generic modes into a single unit – whether it makes literary sense to speak about 'exilic literature' as a single body of work, and whether this group may in any way be considered as a single genre. What would the ancients have thought? No ancient theorist set out primarily to specify the contents or characteristics of a particular genre, but came to a definition while discussing a related topic.[13] Exilic literature is perhaps not a genre of the same order as, for instance, drama or epic (convenient categories acknowledged by most modern Classicists in their understanding of the nature of genre), yet it does form a topical unit. Ancient theorisers may possibly not have acknowledged such a topical unit as a literary genre, but the concept *gênos* – *genus* – genre has undergone some changes in the course of twenty-five centuries of literary theorising.

Today the term genre is considered as of less importance than the complex relationship between *author*, *text* and *reader*. The text is no longer considered to have status only as representative of a genre, but it is designated in various, sometimes conflicting, ways as either an autonomous unit that creates its own meaning, or as a system of signals that must be reconstructed anew by each reader, or must be decoded in order to find the authorial purpose, or which may be deconstructed to create meaning, or to find its intertextual message.[14]

Ancient practitioners of various genres seemed sometimes to be aware of the need for intertextual decoding. For Conte (1994: 137), 'intertextuality is ... the very condition of literary legibility'. Charles Segal in his *Introduction* to Conte's work (1994) points out that genre is 'the mediating term between a literary work and the various cultural discourses and social functions within which literature operates', while Conte himself (1994: 35) considers genre as 'the sign of an active tension between virtuality and its actualisation'. An author chooses a particular 'model of the world' that emerges as what Conte terms 'partial *transcodification*' of values. He points out (1994: 47) that the co-presence in a text of diverse elements creates 'a tension that menaces a genre's constitution'. This 'menace subverts the genre into another' – that is the essence of the type of deconstruction of generic convention we shall find in Ovid.[15]

Modern literary theories diverge widely in approach, but many have interesting parallels with ancient theories. One of the most useful of these modern theories relates to the empirical author's visualising of his potential audience. The importance of the audience is central to modern reception theory, and the mediating role of the reader is paramount in modern semiotics.[16] Due cognisance will be taken below of the ideas of modern theorists such as Umberto Eco on the centrality of the reader in decoding texts as signals, and on the relationships between empirical and model readers and their reciprocal relationships with the empirical and model authors of the works they read. Eco (1994: 15-17) postulates an 'empirical reader', the person in the act of reading, and a 'model reader' the notional audience at which the 'empirical author' pitches his material. This reader, in turn, by a continuous interpretative process mentally creates the 'model author' who has made the text into what is discovered in this process.[17]

We need, however, to relate or contrast these *personae* with the ideas of ancient theorists in order to give ourselves a certain generic base (that would have been understood by our authors) for interpretation in contemporary context of the texts to be examined in this study, with full awareness that generic taxonomy is also a readerly process.

Horace, in his *Ars Poetica*, while emphasising both *authorial purpose* and the importance of the audience or reader as *receptor*, crystallised the generally held ancient understanding of generic convention, characterising genre by both *metre* (*medium*) and *content* (*object*). Here he followed a Roman precedent: for Varro, style and content could not be

13

divorced.[18] The Horatian view offers a justification for my thematic approach to ancient texts. Horace was following Aristotle's emphasis on *object of presentation* as criterion. Aristotle's division of prose into epideictic, deliberative and forensic genres (*Rhet.* 13, 1-6) is a recognition of the role of the *receptor* (recipient) or audience in the labelling of *genre*.[19] His third and fourth criteria were *mode* and *manner* (of which more below),[20] and these also influenced later Hellenistic approaches, which fixed in turn on *medium*, *object* and *manner* of presentation.[21] The Alexandrian generic criterion of *metre* presumed analysis of *medium* of presentation. Their division of prose into historiography, rhetoric and philosophy was tied to *manner* of presentation, that is, literary style.[22] The Alexandrian *topical* division ignored metre and reverted to the Aristotelian 'object' in a wider sense, concentrating on the *circumstance* in which the protagonist is presented. Here the *purpose* of the poet in composing a work acts as generic criterion.[23]

All literary forms which treat of exile may therefore, according to the criterion of circumstance, be combined in a generic study of 'the *literature of exile*'. Yet this *topical* canon, containing divergent literary forms, cannot further be characterised in Horatian or Aristotelian terms: the literature of exile is not confined to a single *mode* (prose or poetry) nor a single *manner* of presentation (narrative or dramatic, descriptive or autobiographical). Its study entails *manner* of presentation, *object* of presentation, and the *audience* or reader as *receptor*.[24]

Various modes of presentation (traditional genres such as historiography, letters, and poetry – epic, lyric, elegy) occur in the literature I have classified as 'exilic'. Modern narrative theories have interesting points of similarity with the above ancient categories. Study of manner of presentation entails study of style and stylistic devices, but may also be equated with, among others, the modern narratological concepts of *focalisation*, *narrative time* and *narrative space*, all aspects which will feature in Chapter 2.

The ancient approaches all focus on the authorial function, whether of style or of intent. This study will in passing frequently comment on style as an authorial function, but it will also apply the Horatian (and Alexandrian) generic criterion of *purpose* or *aim* in an attempt to analyse authorial intent, more specifically, the notional audience ('model reader') for whom an author writes. 'Authorial purpose' as a concept has become increasingly suspect in post-modern literary criticism. 'Intentionalism' is at present considered a critical solecism, but Galinsky (1997) sensibly comments that use of a particular medium (or choice of genre) must still be ascribed to an author's intentional choice. Such a concession leaves the door open for a return to informed speculation about authorial intent, even while partially conceding to the post-modern concept of the intangibility of the author, who, at best, is seen as no more than a construct of the informed reader's mind.

14

1. Exiled Persons

According to some modern theorists, it is equally dangerous to speak of *a* or *the* reader, as a case may be made out in the study of most texts for a shifting series of readerly actions and therefore for a shifting series of aims by a shifting series of both empirical and notional authors of these texts. Particularly in autobiographical texts *the area of reception* envisaged by our exiled authors is of importance and the question to ask is *who they saw as their readers*, both notional and empirical.[25] Focus will be on the feelings of the writer (in any one of a series of implicit manifestations), but also of the notional or model reader as envisaged by the writer.

In such an excursive study, reference will be made in passing to very many works. Particular attention will be paid to those illustrating the exile of the two most prolific writers about their own exile, Cicero and Ovid. Treatment of each aspect will be diachronic, where possible, but with chronology subservient to considerations of *person* and *genre*. What follows below is an attempt to give a brief account of the field to be covered in greater detail in subsequent chapters. Emphasis will be on the variety of canonical 'generic forms' (modes of presentation) featured in the topical material which according to my definition may be included under the term 'exilic literature'. The rest of this chapter will therefore serve as a diachronic overview of key themes. Using the tripartite structural arrangement based on grammatical persons which I have set as the ordering principle of the book, I shall review, in that order, material in which third, second and, finally, first person verbs predominate, and discuss a representative sample from each.

1.3 Tales of exile: legal, historical and literary sources

Our Roman legal sources on exile are late, and codify practices which developed and had became institutionalised in the centuries since Rome's beginnings.[26] There is ample evidence of a narrative nature from earlier historical and literary sources. Stories about exile abound. Livy (1.59.11-60 and 2.2.2) construes the banishment of the Tarquins as 'exile', and composes 'letters' from them to nobles in Rome, pleading their cause.[27] Republican Rome featured many notable exiles, such as Caeso Quinctius, the son of Cincinnatus (Livy 3.2), Gaius Servilius Ahala (4.14) and Camillus (7.1.10). Plutarch considered the careers of Camillus and Coriolanus, the exiled Roman general who reluctantly betrayed his native city to the Volscians, as worthy of comparison with their Greek counterparts, Themistocles and Alcibiades.[28]

Capture by an enemy meant loss of civil status in Rome. The consular Regulus, a Roman general in the first Punic War, who, after eight years in Carthaginian captivity agreed to lead a deputation to Rome to sue for a peace he considered disgracefully favourable to the enemy, voluntarily chose to protract his loss of civil status rather than to advocate capitulation. He returned to torture and death in Carthage, the Carthaginian

15

mission unattained. Regulus became enshrined in the Roman imagination as the embodiment of civic loyalty.[29] Similarly, the flight into exile and triumphant return of Marius, only to end in premature death during his seventh consulate, also became a frequently exploited literary *topos*.[30] Cicero, for instance, employs the example of Marius in a variety of ways, depending upon his audience – before the Senate Marius becomes a dangerous demagogue who got his just deserts; before the people he is a fellow-hero from Arpinum, the victim of aristocratic treachery.[31]

Cicero's discussion of exile as a philosophical phenomenon (*Tusc.* 5.107), lists as involuntary exiles Greek philosophers who never returned to their native cities, including his friend Posidonius. Their 'exile' may perhaps merely have been voluntary removal to a cultural centre. The century preceding the Ciceronian era had produced many noble Roman exiles, who frequently resorted to temporary or permanent settlement in the provinces, often in the East, particularly Rhodes and Mytilene.[32] Opimius, the consul of 122 BC, acquitted after the death of Gaius Gracchus, was nevertheless condemned, some ten years later, for intriguing with Jugurtha.[33] He died in exile at Dyrrachium, much later Cicero's place of banishment. Opimius' contemporary Metellus Numidicus, frequently cited by Cicero, went into voluntary exile to Rhodes rather than acquiesce in the agrarian reforms of Apuleius Saturninus and Glaucia.[34] Rutilius Rufus, exiled after 88 BC, was the first to devote the involuntary *otium* (leisure for study) resulting from enforced retreat from public life both to philosophic writing and to self-exoneration while composing a contemporary Roman history. The accusation against Rutilius was intrigue with the enemies of Rome. Unhelpfully brief fragments of his apology survive, of which none, except possibly Diomed. 1.374, appears to refer to his exile.[35]

The exile, or, rather, banishment of Cicero therefore had many precedents. His own thundering accusation of Catiline appears to end somewhat lamely as an appeal 'to remove himself from within the walls of Rome'. Voluntary withdrawal into exile, often a pre-emptive for possible capital punishment decreed by *abrogatio* (annulment) of civic rights, would here have shown up the conspirator's guilt.[36] When Cicero himself fled from Rome in 58 BC, he was following this convention, with a predictable result.[37] The two matters are closely related, for it was Cicero's decisive voice in the Senate's decision to impose the death penalty on the remaining conspirators without a ratification by the commons that gave his enemies a handle against him.

For Cicero all retreat from the capital was exile of a sort, and he was almost ludicrously miserable when he was at last forced to take up the proconsulate of Cilicia, long after his return from exile and some twelve years after the end of his term of office. He carried out his duties conscientiously, as witness the humorous letter to Caelius, referring to his administration of the province ('only the panthers complain that they don't get justice', *Fam.* 2.11), his reports to the Roman people, and to Cato.[38]

16

1. Exiled Persons

The details of Cicero's exile are clear enough, but his attitude to this momentous event is complex. An 'unauthorised' but 'truer' version of Cicero's exilic autobiography is reflected in the letters from exile, written mostly to Atticus.[39] Later the returned exile propagated an 'official version' by means of 'heroic hindsight', the mythicising of his exile in various declamations, rewriting his own history in heroic terms, as I hope to show in Chapters 6 and 7.[40]

The story of Cicero's exile (58-57 BC) is narrated in the third person by Plutarch, Dio Cassius and Aulus Gellius, but as the historians themselves largely depended on the prolific author's own writings, the overview that follows below is largely based on the letters. The story is offered here as an example of how an objective exilic tale may be reconstructed from various sources, including the protagonist's own subjective missives. Individual authors' narrative treatment of the story will be discussed in Chapter 2.

Cicero's letters are the major source for historical study of the last years of the lives of both Cicero and Julius Caesar, and are of particular importance for the author's second person observations on their relationship.[41] The events leading to Cicero's banishment read like a catalogue of the forces of retribution mustering against a man intent on self-destruction. Towards the end of his consulship in 63 BC Cicero allowed Cato to manoeuvre him into acquiescing in the death of Catilina's fellow-conspirators. In the political climate of 63 not all at Rome shared Cicero's own enthusiasm for this feat.[42] Soon after, Cicero earned the undying hatred of the aspirant tribune Clodius by his role in refuting Clodius' alibi for his masquerade as a female flute player in the Bona Dea scandal that resulted from Clodius' unsuccessful attempt to seduce Caesar's young wife Pompeia (for which Caesar divorced her). Clodius' peccadillo was seized upon by his enemies as an opportunity to undermine his influence in Rome, particularly to separate him from his still real influence in the Senate. A letter from Cicero to Atticus on 25 June 61 (*Att.* 1.13.3) gives, with salacious amusement, the details of the Bona Dea affair.

Clodius was eventually acquitted, perhaps because Caesar famously refused to testify. It suited Clodius to concentrate his reciprocal *invidia* ('anger' rather than 'envy') on a single senator, and Cicero, being a *novus homo* or 'new man', the first of his family to attain senatorial rank, was easily sacrificed (largely by neglect) by the Senate to become the scapegoat and focal point of Clodius' increasing demagoguery.[43] This was the time when Caesar sealed a political alliance with Pompey and Crassus, which effectively abrogated the Roman system of political checks and balances, and put all political power into their hands. The feeling between Cicero and Clodius was in 59 largely overshadowed by senatorial unease over the triumvirs' encroachment of power. Cicero retired to Antium. The triumvirs were gaining in popular appeal.[44] Clodius, scion of an ancient patrician family, retained their favour just long enough to be supported in his *traductio ad plebem* (change to plebeian status), which facilitated his political ambition to become tribune. In *Ad Atticum* 2.15.2 Cicero admits to a certain grudging admiration of the way Clodius could use the triumvirs for his purposes, and then discard them.

Having achieved the tribunate, early in 58 BC Clodius passed four major laws, the last of which was aimed at revenge. The first three were not as 'revolutionary' as Cicero chose to present them later. Reinstatement of the right of association, abrogated six years previously, revived erstwhile *collegia* (voluntary associations of a political nature, guilds) and established new ones, potentially useful political tools.[45] Popularity was bought by providing for gratis grain rations, already heavily subsidised, and therefore no real threat to the public *fiscus* (treasury).[46] An amendment to the *lex Aelia Fufia* restricted magisterial powers, safeguarding the assembly against political abuse of religious sanction, and limited the powers of the censor.[47]

There was a stronger element of popular feeling against Cicero than he liked to acknowledge. After Clodius' bill *de capite civis Romani* (about the life of a Roman citizen), interdicting from fire and water anyone who had executed a citizen without trial, Cicero put off his brave front and tried to gain support as suppliant, the whole Senate going into traditional mourning with him. When this proved useless, he fled precipitately (Plut. *Cic.* 31). The triumvirs supported Clodius' measures by inaction, largely because they themselves were concerned to safeguard rulings that they had enacted in 59, and could not afford to alienate a powerful tribune.[48] According to Dio Cassius (38.17.1) Clodius even managed to manoeuvre Caesar at a *contio* (public gathering) into giving the plebs his opinion, of necessity negative, of the execution of citizens without popular trial.

A second bill *ut M. Tullio aqua et igni interdictum sit* (that Marcus Tullius be denied water and fire) officially sanctioned as banishment Cicero's voluntary withdrawal.[49] Clodius could legally attach Cicero's property. This second bill merits attention in the first of the hasty notes dispatched to Atticus by the southward-bound fugitive (*Att.* 3.1).[50] He went where he knew he would be received by friends willing to brave prosecution for harbouring an *exsul*. Perhaps he was tending vaguely towards Sicily, which was close enough to Italy for rapid recall, and potentially congenial (*Planc.* 95, 96). He turned eastward, however, staying in turn with those friends who were prepared to flout the decree of interdiction of water and fire which had followed the first decree. The early letters (*Att.* 3.1 to 3.5) indicate nothing of this. Cicero wanted to reach Atticus at Epirus, hoping for his friend's continued support and real aid. En route to Brindisi from Vibo he noted from a copy of the bill that it stipulated banishment beyond four hundred Roman miles. Even Malta would have been too close.

Flight over the Adriatic came next, and an anxious fifteen months or so were spent at the house of his patient friend Cn. Plancius at Dyrrachium.

The distraught Cicero could not so much as decide whether or when to leave Dyrrachium in order to join Atticus in Epirus. Anxious letters discuss the triumvirs' every move, exhorting Atticus to greater efforts on the exile's behalf, bewailing past mistakes and minutely analysing every report of political movement at Rome.

When after more than a year the political climate changed, and it suited the triumvirs, particularly Pompey, and also the Senate, who probably saw in Clodius an increasing threat to their power, Cicero was recalled, more by default than by the universal acclaim he so fondly extolled. That his journey from Brindisi to Rome resembled a triumphal march need not be doubted, but this should rather be ascribed to the notorious fickleness of mob mentality than to a conscious popular vindication of Ciceronian rectitude.

Cicero never regained the power he had enjoyed toward the end of his consulate in 63. After initially inveighing against the consuls of the year 58, Piso and Gabinius, as subservient functionaries of his arch-enemy Clodius, the major author of his downfall, he was later forced even to abjure revenge, and on one occasion to defend Gabinius, the man he regarded as instrumental in his exile.[51]

Our other exiles receive brief narrative treatment in extant sources. The exile of Ovid, Seneca and Dio Chrysostomus will feature with that of Boethius in later chapters, under discussion of different thematic aspects. In the case of the poet Ovid, there are no contemporary sources (other than his own writings) which refer to his exile, so that the reality or possible fictionality of his exile has become a major point of discussion for some critics.[52] Seneca's victimisation under Gaius and Claudius receives brief narrative treatment in Dio Cassius (59.19 and 50.8), and a passing reference in Tacitus, *Annales* 12.8.[53] These will not be discussed in detail here. Dio is our major source on his own life. In addition there exist a brief summary in Philostratos' *Lives of the Sophists* (1.7, pp. 486-8) and an exchange of letters between the younger Pliny and Trajan (*Epp.* 10.81-2) on Pliny's investigation of accusations of peculation levelled against Dio by fellow Prusians, in which the philosopher is vindicated.

1.4 The consolatory tradition

As the third-person exilic histories of our five major protagonists will be treated in some detail in Chapter 2, we may leave them for the moment, to consider one of the basic aspects of second person address as it related to exile. A considerable part of the second person literature of exile concerns itself with a particular type of philosophical discourse, the *consolatio ad exulem* (consolation offered to an exile).

Ancient philosophy was concerned with the examination of all aspects of the human condition, including the moral implications of exile. Such discussion frequently took the form of conversation with and exhortation of the exile, in which, naturally, verbs in the second person would carry the main thread of argument, with narrative sections merely providing illustration. When an exile himself addressed the problem, either for self-consolation, or for the sake of apologetic self-justification, second person verbs predominated. The basic question was whether exile influences the striving for moral happiness, and discussion largely concentrated on the question of whether exile is evil, neutral, or positively good.

The relationship between exile and death in Greek and Roman history is important for understanding the development of this literary subgenre; voluntary exile or suicide frequently pre-empted the imposition of the death penalty. It was no great step therefore when philosophy began to equate exile with death.[54] Discussion of exile as an evil followed much the same train of argument as discussion of the problem of death.

When it moved from the purely academic to the personal, discussion of death was usually adapted to the need to console the living after bereavement. For example Cicero in his *Tusculan Disputations* mustered the full force of his philosophical knowledge to find comfort after the death of his daughter Tullia. So too, personal discussion of exile, when not couched as apologetic autobiography, came frequently to mean consolation to those living in exile. Such a *consolatio* could be offered as dialogue, in a letter, or, less personally, in a philosophical essay or diatribe.[55] In letters, as in dialectic *consolatio*, focus on the exiled figure requires verbs in the second person, imperative forms, and other concomitants of dialectic.[56]

The development of what became a separate philosophical genre, reflections on exile, cannot be fully traced.[57] Bion and Ariston of Chios were the probable initiators of the genre, which can be reconstructed by comparing common elements in the surviving fragments of Teles (*fl. c.* 242-227 BC),[58] Musonius Rufus (*c.* AD 30-110)[59] and Favorinus (*c.* AD 80-90 – *c.* 150) with the more extensive *consolationes* of Seneca and Plutarch. There is very little material extant from before the first century AD.[60] The collection of apophthegms made for his son (perhaps in the fifth century AD) by Johannes Stobaios offers some consolatory fragments, notably from Teles (ed. Hense p. 21ff.). Large parts of Favorinus' speech survive. Dio Chrysostomus (*Or.* 13) summarises the tradition in his speech on his own exile.[61]

The ideal of sagacious self-sufficiency is much wider than the concept of the exiled sage, but is one of the most important features of consolation in exile. The Stoic Stilpo of Megara (*c.* 380-300 BC), refusing Ptolemy Soter's invitation to go to Egypt after the plunder of Megara, retired to Aegina. Demetrius, son of Antigonus, while attempting to restore Megara and make restitution to its inhabitants, asked Stilpo for a list of his lost possessions. Stilpo denied having lost anything, 'as he still retained his eloquence and knowledge' (Diog. Laert 2.113).[62] In Plutarch's version (*Demetr.* 9.5)[63] Stilpo replies negatively to Demetrius' query about whether he had been robbed, 'for I saw no one carrying away knowledge'. Stilpo acknowledged as true Demetrius' boast that he was leaving the Megarians their city in freedom, for 'Demetrius had not left the people of Megara a single slave'. This is an early example of the central argument of consolation in exile: that man needs but little on earth, and what he most needs, he carries with him.

Cicero, writing to the exiled Trebianus in September 46 (*Fam.* 6.10.4), gives a clear analysis of what is required of a letter to an exile: it may contain a promise of aid, offer advice, or give comfort. The tradition of consolation for death or exile clearly had a single literary paradigm.[64] The letters of consolation written by Cicero to various exiled friends during the years 52-45 BC closely follow the pattern of consolation offered Cicero himself by Servius Sulpicius Rufus (*Fam.* 4.5) after the death of Tullia early in 45 BC.

Cicero received more than one consolatory letter after his daughter's death. Sulpicius, writing in March 45, seems to follow a set pattern of *topoi*, starting with the problem of offering consolation when the author of the letter is himself saddened. Sulpicius offers cold comfort, an apparent adaptation of the concept that death precludes future misery: as the state itself is lost, he says, private grief is small, set against the public woe, and Tullia is well out of it. The ruins of the great cities of Greece offer *exempla* illustrating the brevity of life. Set against the vast universe, the loss of a *mulierculae anima* (the life of a mere woman) is no great thing; death awaits all. Tullia had enjoyed a full life, had seen her father crowned with high office, and, novel comfort in straitened times: she was dying *with* the Republic. Cicero must be like a doctor, willing to cure himself, and although time does alleviate grief, it is better to put away grief consciously, for her sake, but also so as not to appear to be mourning the Republic. This latter comment is practical advice in dangerous times.

These arguments appear, with slight variation, in all the extant consolatory literature. Sometimes one aspect receives more emphasis, sometimes another. Cicero himself was perfectly aware of the conventional aspects of consolatory epistolography, but was not always capable of following its precepts. *Fam.* 5.13, perhaps written in 45, thanks Lucius Lucceius for a consolatory letter, and attests to brave and philosophical acceptance of his troubles,[65] but this fortitude was not to last. By May 45, Lucceius is writing to Cicero to take him to task for continued, excessive mourning, and for staying away from the city (*Fam.* 5.14). Cicero's replies to both Sulpicius and Lucceius (*Fam.* 4.6 and 5.15) exhibit a psychological attitude not yet ripe for comfort: he has lost the only comfort left to him after his political desolation, and, as he admits to Lucceius, recourse to literary pursuits works not as *medicina perpetua* (a permanent panacea), but only as temporary oblivion from pain. This all too human reaction stands in stark contrast to the philosophical exhortation Cicero had offered to 'Titius', otherwise unknown[66] about a year before: humanity is subject to the *tela fortunae* (the slings and arrows of Fortune) and as the

21

loss of a child lies within the course of nature, and is small in contrast to the present perils of the State, 'Titius' must take comfort; death, whether offering oblivion or eternal consciousness, is a blessed state, serving to save individuals from temporal troubles. 'Titius' should forestall the normal relieving effect of the passage of time by active pursuit of philosophy.

1.5 Elements of the consolatory genre and their application

In time Cicero as bereaved father composed not only his *Tusculan Disputations* as a means of comforting himself, but he also composed a formal *consolatio*, now lost. Van Wageningen in 1916 attempted to reconstruct, by means of collation of fragments, a conjectural *consolatio*, to compensate posterity for its loss.[67] Van Wageningen's synthesis of various testimonia with fragments from the *Tusculan Disputations* was adapted to the framework of two of Plutarch's *consolationes*, to his friend Apollonius on the death of his daughter (*Mor.* 102A-121F) and to his own wife, on the death of their baby daughter (*Mor.* 608B-612B).[68] This reconstruction was met not uncritically,[69] but it offers a useful paradigm. Van Wageningen argues that Cicero and Plutarch appear to follow a common tradition, whereas Seneca's *Consolatio ad Polybium* follows a different tradition, or was perhaps more extensively influenced by Seneca's Stoicism to employ a less rigorous ordering system of argument.[70]

Whatever Van Wageningen's faults, with similar analysis, also using Plutarch as our model, we may deduce what would traditionally have been the essential elements of a formal *consolatio ad exsulem*. Plutarch, writing late in the first century AD, composed a *consolatio* to an exile from Sardis, probably living in Athens, perhaps Menemachus of Sardis, obviously a *relegatus* ('relegated' – banished but with the retention of his property) free to travel, but not to return home.[71] A suggestion that the exile should choose a new city indicates that the relegation was *in perpetuum*, for acceptance of a new citizenship would have meant loss of the old.[72]

The essay has four major divisions: exhortation to exhibit a rational attitude toward exile; the argument of the universality of the human condition and the uncertainty of Fortune; a practical discussion of suitable places for the exile to visit; and finally, refutation of arguments that exile is evil. The whole has much in common with Cynic-Stoic *consolationes* to the bereaved. These elements recur regularly in consolations addressed to individual exiles.

Cicero's varied literary *corpus* includes a vast collection of letters, some obviously written as public statements or 'open letters', others private and intimate. Some letters were addressed to Cicero's exiled friends at various times during the vicissitudes of the last days of the Republic, offering consolatory arguments. All these are genuine, private letters, for which the term *primary epistle* may be coined. These will be discussed in Chapter 3. So, during the last years of the Republic, Cicero frequently offered consolatory arguments to exiled friends, but during his own exile he was himself too miserable to draw comfort from them.

When the whole spectrum of generic forms available to the exiled poet is considered, it appears strange that Ovid, when exiled to the ends of the Roman earth, Tomis on the Black Sea, availed himself so little of what until then had been the major form of exilic literature, philosophical comfort.[73] Ovid's playful attitude towards philosophy disappears in the poems he wrote from his place of exile, *Tristia* ('sad songs') and *Epistolae ex Ponto* ('Letters from the Black Sea').[74] As will become clear during the course of this study, the subjective focus of his exilic works and the lack of reciprocation from his correspondents precluded any extensive recourse to the consolatory genre, which in a great degree depended on a certain balanced objectivity and focus on the second person as recipient of a particular missive. Ovid's exilic poems, although often cast as 'letters' and therefore by definition reflecting the principle of dialogue, more often than not appear as a one-way *sermo absentis* (conversation with an absent friend). He reaches out to friends at Rome, but we hear very little about any form of reply. For these poetic letters we may coin the term *secondary epistle*.

Ovid's frequent railings at Fortune seem to indicate some familiarity with aspects of the consolatory tradition, and the apotheosis of his Muse as his chief source of comfort shows him practising what is frequently preached to the exile: literary sublimation.[75] Yet he in no way attempted to spell out any consistent system of philosophical comfort to himself. Ovid, as a poet, not a philosopher, subscribed to no consistent philosophical system, only occasionally adapting *topoi* from philosophy to suit the exigencies of a particular poem.[76] His philosophic doctrines tend to vary with his mood.

So Ovid practises self-consolation, but he seldom preaches it, writing only one consolatory 'letter' from exile, *Ex Ponto* 4.11, to his friend Gallio, on the loss of his wife.[77] Its focus is on the bereaved widower, but even here first person self-interest predominates over the second person as object of commiseration, as may be seen in the opening lines (1, 2):

> *Gallio, crimen erit vix excusabile nobis,*
> *Carmine te nomen non habuisse meo.*

> Gallio, it'll be a crime that I could hardly be forgiven for if I didn't have you as the title to my song.

A variety of typically Ovidian ploys suit the poem to the words. Gallio's name appears at the head of the poem, in the opening place that popularly would give a poem its title, but both lines of the opening couplet end on words referring to the exile, *nobis* and *meo* ('to us' – poetic plural for 'me' – and 'my'). Hyperbaton in the pentameter separates noun and possessive adjective, *carmine ... meo (within my ... song). The split phrase suitably and graphically embraces the personal pronoun te* (you) as well as the exile's reference to the addressee's *nomen* (name) as the name of the song.

The body of the poem refers in great detail to the services formerly rendered to the exiled poet by his recently bereaved friend. At verses 11, 12 the poet 'refuses' to employ the commonplaces of consolation when he at last does attempt to comfort his friend on the loss of his wife. *Praeteritio* (emphasis by means of an ostensible refusal to emphasise) of these very commonplaces invokes the 'healing influence of time' and the 'need for timely consolation, or none at all'. Even this refusal to utter conventional comfort is a commonplace, and the poet is aware of it. That irony is intended, is not impossible.

A last consideration (vv. 21, 22), that the bereaved may already be happily remarried by the time the letter reaches him, emphasises the distance of Tomis from Rome. The comment may also be offering a subtle criticism of the Julian laws which forced widowers to remarry in almost indecent haste. This may be a new angle on the *topos* of abandoning grief before it abandons the mourner, but more to the point is that even in this very particular kind of outreach to a second person there is more about the poet as exiled protagonist than about the emotions of his bereaved friend. The poem largely functions as an illustration of the single-minded misery experienced by the exile.

Here we encounter a typical aspect of second person exilic literature: its tendency toward solipsism. In the case of Seneca, again an exiled protagonist comforting an addressee at Rome, the focus also shifts from the bereaved recipient of consolation to the exile himself as philosopher, but also as 'the departed'. Lucius Annaeus Seneca is known for his extremely successful contribution to the Romanising of Stoic philosophy and his less successful guidance of the youthful excesses of his charge, the emperor Nero. His series of philosophical discussions, the *Epistolae morales*, couched in the form of letters to a young friend, Lucilius, penned in the period after his fall from that emperor's good graces, frequently reflect his preoccupation with the basic ills of humanity, of which exile is one. His works from an earlier period of disgrace, before the imperial accession of Nero, show us an interesting picture of philosophical fortitude, which some critics would rather interpret as cowardly and time-serving. In a series of three consolations, to his friend Marcia, the daughter of Cremutius Cordus, to his mother Helvia, after the death of his own son,[78] and to Polybius, a freedman of the emperor Claudius, at whose instigation Seneca had been relegated to Corsica, we get an extensive and personalised reworking of the declamatory genre of consolation to the bereaved.

Of these, the *Ad Helviam* and the *Ad Polybium* must be classed as 'exilic literature' by virtue of the fact that they were written by Seneca while in exile on Corsica. In the case of the *Ad Helviam* the exhortation is aimed not so much at consoling a grandmother for the loss of an infant grandson than at consoling a mother, for the loss, by exile, of a son. The diatribe bears all the hallmarks of a typical *consolatio*. The flattery of the emperor Claudius contained in the letter to his freedman has been castigated as servile, or excused, as redolent of hidden irony.[79]

Dio Chrysostomus of Prusa discusses the consolatory tradition in his oration on his own exile (*Or.* 13). In the case of Dio, the literary tradition, which at least on the ostensible level always involved interlocutor and protagonist, has been adapted to focus solely on the protagonist. The oration lies generically within the category of *consolatio*, but in our division of topics according to grammatical person, it will be treated in Chapter 6 as an example of self-revelatory second person discourse. Dio artlessly recounts his own personal examination of the problems of exile, and offers an apparently dispassionate account of his fluctuations of emotion, his search for philosophical solace, and the triumph of his own good sense over his perception of misery. Dio's report on his own exile is an illustration of *consolatio*-in-action, whole-hearted philosophical adoption of his own creed.[80] As a dispassionate autobiographical narrative, the report is couched in the first person, and verbs are in the past tense. Like a recovered patient reporting on a past illness, the returned exile enumerates his symptoms and describes the cure. Yet this report, too, is a literary creation, and the narrating self is also a conscious creation.

Finally, after the lapse of over four centuries, we come to Boethius.[81] He was, like Cicero, also an ex-consul.[82] While in exile at Pavia and awaiting the consummation of his death sentence, he writes an autobiographical *Consolatio Philosophiae* in which he chronicles his own fall from philosophical grace, and his re-conversion to the tenets of a personified Philosophia. Boethius applies self-consolation in the guise of a personified *alter ego* and an opponent of the 'false strumpet' Fortune. This is the figure of Dame Philosophy, who calls him back to a contemplation of the truth, once familiar, which he had temporarily lost in his exilic misery, while awaiting death. By this means the thought of his exile and certain death become bearable to him.[83] Like Dio, Boethius is a recovered patient describing a past illness. Boethius' self-consolation is all the more remarkable because he effected the cure and regained his philosophical self-sufficiency, having achieved neither his freedom nor a return to Rome and to his former state. By using Philosophia as interlocutory mouthpiece, Boethius achieves both the second person objective remove of consolatory address and the first person subjective involvement of autobiographical narrative.[84]

Boethius, writing in the sixth century AD, has produced a work which marks both the chronological and the intellectual culmination of the consolatory tradition.[85] Boethius was a Christian philosopher writing in a Christian era. Yet the *Consolatio Philosophiae* appears to follow the tradition of Classical consolatory literature, without wholly conforming to it. Equally, however, Christian precedents do not seem to have been strongly influential. The *Consolatio* is confessional, but it smacks more of the self-approbation and consciousness of rectitude which permeates the writings of the exiled pagans Cicero, Ovid or Seneca the Younger, than of the self-denigration and awareness of sin expressed in its famous Christian predecessor, the *Confessiones* of Augustine. The tone of Boethius' *Consolatio* is self-denigratory only with regard to the protagonist's temporary loss of philosophical fortitude. The author never appears to intend depicting himself as a prototype 'original sinner' in the Christian sense.

In form, Boethius' *Consolatio* is Menippean, being a mixture of prose and verse, with the lyric sections offering condensed comment on the subject matter of the prose sections. In content the work bears no relationship to the Menippean satirical genre, as represented by Seneca's *Apocolocyntosis* (or 'Pumpkinification of Claudius') or the *Satyricon* of Petronius. Just as it was Lucretius' Epicurean intention to sweeten the rim of the cup of philosophy by means of the honey of poetry, so Boethius' poetic interludes sweeten the teachings of his apparition.[86] In a sense, the poems work as a crutch to hold up the errant philosopher's wavering spirit long enough for the medicine of philosophy to complete the healing process. There is a close topical connection between each prose-verse pair. It is noticeable that, in the first book, the lyric passages precede prose exhortations; in subsequent books they serve to sum up or epitomise what has gone before. As the pupil becomes stronger in his willing return to dependence on his mentor, the philosophical passages grow longer and the poetry plays a less prominent role.[87]

Like Cicero, Boethius' importance as philosopher lies not so much in his originality, as in his faculty of synthesis. Coming as it does at the end of a long line of historical and literary precedents, Boethius' *Consolatio* offers little new in its philosophical content. The Classical antecedents for the philosopher's mélange of arguments are for the most part identifiable.[88] Problems are mostly related to structure and form, and to the philosophical thrust and pagan colouring given them by an author known for his Christian persuasion.[89] The concept of God as a benign, omnipotent and omniscient Being is not overtly Christian, underlying as it does much of pagan philosophical thought. The fact that Boethius makes use of apparently non-Christian content has been a source of much discussion, but will be touched on only in passing in the pages that follow.

Although exile and imprisonment were the springboard of Boethius' *Consolatio*, in a sense this work is not wholly exilic. It combines the philosophical approach to exile and death more fully than does Seneca's *Ad Helviam*, and in the end it serves to vindicate the power of philosophy to uphold the human spirit in any untoward situation.[90] The personified Philosophia does for Boethius what his Muse does for Ovid. Both sustain the exile's spirit, and offer the assurance of immortality.

1.6 Cicero on his own exile: generic variations

So already in our discussion of three exiled philosophers and the exiled poet we have seen that second person address very often shades off into first person solipsism. We now turn to the personage most versatile in his writings about exile, and yet closely involved in every nuance of his exilic experience. The consular Marcus Tullius Cicero was a prolific writer. His *corpus* is varied: polished versions of declamations spoken on legal or political matters, philosophical writings, fragments of his poems, and a large body of his letters reflecting the details of his life, including the circumstances of his exile. Few displacements have been so consistently and self-revealingly documented by the exile himself as Cicero's experience of banishment in the years 58 to 57 BC.[91] At different stages he utilised virtually all the generic forms for which he had by then become famous to document one or another aspect of his troubles.

Cicero was probably banished as the result of political manoeuvring on many fronts, but ostensibly for his part in the death of the Catilinarians. The details have been touched upon above, and do not need to be repeated here.[92] Cicero's fluctuations of attitude to his banishment can be read in what may be termed 'Cicero's exilic *corpus*', which comprises letters, speeches and poems.

Cicero may be seen as the unconscious creator of the autobiographical genre 'complaints from exile'. Its characteristics are partly anti-consolatory, partly a reflection of Roman social and political convention. Appeals for aid, thanks, and recriminations alternate with calls for spiritual rather than material relief, and an end to pain (*Att.* 3.7).[93] Although he frequently acknowledges receipt of letters, the impression is of a drawn-out monologue, not conversation. Cicero is the 'exiled I', the centre of a dislocated universe where the hub is out of kilter. His correspondents exist only as sounding boards for his misery. Although discovery of his self-revelatory letters caused the Italian humanist Petrarch great distress, readers at the end of the twentieth century are less inclined toward blind hero-worship of the ancients, and therefore are less shocked when the humanity of a protagonist such as Cicero is revealed in his own writings.

Cicero's total exilic *corpus* gives a complex view of the psychological make-up of the exiled consular, but very little factual or political detail about the years 58 and 57 BC. Continued political manoeuvring by friends and foes alike, in Rome and elsewhere, is documented in twenty-seven of Cicero's letters to Atticus, and a handful of letters to his family and brother. A picture emerges of his increasing anxiety as the prospect of exile loomed larger, the inevitability of his personality clashes with powerful figures who could have saved him, had they so wished, his doubts and fears during exile, and his hopes for a change in the political climate in Rome. Strangely, however, there is little about the practical, day-to-day arrangements of exile, the disposal of his effects, availability of domestic comforts and the selfless care provided by his friend Plancius, in whose house at Dyrrachium Cicero spent most of his exile.

Pure solipsism is reflected by the predominance of first person verbs and pronouns. Verbs in the second person, implying the other half of '*sermo absentis*', the addressees of his many letters from exile, are important only in their subjective relation to the exile. On occasion he employs third person narrative to portray the villainy of those who had brought him down.

The letters, written almost as a journal at the height of his troubles, reflect Cicero's daily fluctuations of hope, despair, misery and grief. They attest to his first fears of impending danger, and portray the almost day-by-day history of his seventeen months in banishment and his near-hysterical obsession with self, bewailing past mistakes and minutely analysing every report of political movement at Rome. Cicero's letters appeal for aid, mourn his altered state, and finally record his triumphant recall.[94] The focus is on the author: important verbs are in the first person, possessive adjectives *meus* and *noster* abound; the banished man is wrapped in a self-imposed cocoon of misery.[95] Elizabeth Rawson (1975: 114-18) dismisses his letters from exile as hardly reliable evidence of anything but the state of his mind, which, she guesses, was 'very likely near a real nervous breakdown'. We shall discuss the letters in Chapters 3 and 4.

In subsequent chapters we shall be concerned with other aspects of Cicero's presentation of self, always in an antagonistic tension with those persons whom he saw as the architects of his doom. Invective against enemies, or against ineffectual friends, follows his recall, and history is rewritten. A noble and heroic philosopher, who bravely bore all vicissitudes,[96] emerges from the various speeches of thanks on his recall, delivered before the Senate and people, and from Cicero's appeal before a religious board to have his property returned and deconsecrated in the speech about his house (*De domo sua*).[97]

The self-sufficient and courageous figure that emerges from the retrospective speeches held immediately after Cicero's return, and in defence of Sestius, bears as little relation to Cicero at Dyrrachium, as the consuls of the year 58, Piso and Gabinius (who had allowed the decree of banishment to take effect), bore to the monstrous embodiments of vice portrayed by the returned exile in his speeches of bitter invective against his persecutors by default, for which see Chapter 5.[98] As will be seen in Chapter 6, Cicero simultaneously presents his public with a romanticised version of the sorry details of loneliness and hurt pride which speak from his exilic correspondence.[99]

The literary treatment of his consulate had been initiated earlier by Cicero himself, when the possibility of impeachment first loomed. In what may be deemed a third aspect of his perception and consequent portrayal of his own banishment, Cicero later turns to the embellishment of history in autobiographical commentaries (in both Latin and Greek) meant as the basis for excursive historical works by his friends Lucceius and Posidonius. In *Ad Atticum* 2.1, *c.* 3 June 60 BC, he reports on Posidonius' reaction to his brief *commentarium* in Greek, which he had hoped Posidonius would expand into a full scale history; its thoroughness, he said, had left Posidonius *deterritum*. Similarly, he is puzzled (*Att.* 1.16) that his friend the poet Archias did not want to celebrate his consulate in verse. He decides to do so himself, after completing his own Greek prose version (*Att.* 1.19 and 1.20, March to June 60). He resorts to epic poetry, as the most suitable vehicle for the establishment of a 'myth of the banished hero and the return of the Saviour of the Republic'. We shall return to these in Chapter 8.

1.7 Protean Ovid

Ovid's eloquent and extensive literary output is the most complex part of the whole exilic corpus, looming large as its single most important aspect, and a proportionate part of this study will be devoted to it. It truly is *sui generis*. No other contemporary sources refer to Ovid's exile. The playful love poet Publius Ovidius Naso in some way transgressed the social, political or literary rulings of emperor Augustus and as punishment he was banished from Rome in AD 8 or 9. In his exilic poetry two reasons are given for his punishment: *carmen* and *error* – his poetry, which did not fit in with the Augustan new morality, and some dubious mistake, never specified, into which the poet unwittingly fell. That the *error* was solely political is the most popular current theory.[100] Wielders of power did not usually waste a potent political tool on the merely frivolous. Augustus' sterner measures of repression were usually employed against serious opponents, such as contemporary political pamphleteers.

Ovid was relegated to Tomis on the Black Sea (or *Pontus*, to give it its Latin name). The town is usually identified as Constanza, a Milesian Greek settlement on a small Pontic peninsula. Its hinterland is the Dobroudja, a flat stretch of coastal Romania bounded on the west and north by the coils of the Danube, and on the south-east by the Black Sea itself. In this bleak area the urbane poet spent the last years of his life, yearning for a recall that never came.[101]

So the exiled Ovid, during a conjectural ten-year period, from his relegation in AD 8 or 9 until his death in about 17, produced nine books of purportedly autobiographical poetry, and one of invective, as well as probably at that time also polishing the *Metamorphoses* (fifteen books on mythological figures who underwent change of kind, interwoven with aspects of imperial Rome)[102] and reworking his *Fasti* (a selective mélange of cult and myth relating to the first six months of the Roman calendar, now increasingly viewed as deliberately subversive).[103]

Three overtly exilic works (altogether comprising ten books of elegiacs) offer a multi-faceted view of the psychology of exile, but give less real information on the literal, physical aspects of Ovid's exile than is often thought. The five-book *Tristia* (literally, Sad Songs) chronicles the journey into exile, the first years at Tomis, and the exile's inner turmoil. The *Epistolae ex Ponto* (Letters from the Black Sea), four books of personal verse epistles to friends in Rome, depict the last years of the exile's life.[104] Ovid's focus is mainly on the exile, but a secondary figure looms over all the exile's utterances – the person who exiled him. Only *Tristia* 2 is overtly addressed to Augustus, but its focus is reciprocally on the exiled poet, his former innocence and his present misery. The reader is left with a strongly negative picture of the emperor Augustus as the wielder of absolute political power.[105]

Roman readers are presented with the fears of a Roman exile living in a sham state of peace. The non-existence of the *pax Augusta* (peace brought by Augustus) is suggested by the exile's fears and on occasion explicitly stated.[106] In the Pontic area there is no peace, and no hope for such. Throughout the eight to ten years of Ovid's exile the town of Tomis is depicted as being in a perpetual state of siege.

The five books of *Tristia* and four of *Epistolae ex Ponto* combine to lift the exile to an heroic plane. With these he composed an extraordinary poem of invective, the *Ibis*, a literary effusion based on a Callimachean prototype, in around the year 12. The *Ibis* is a single long poem, ingeniously construed by Williams (1996) as representing the 'manic phase' in the poet's portrayal of the depressive debilitation of exile. The poem offers a strange mélange of curses directed at an unknown enemy of which the climax is to be doomed to spend a wasted life, like the poet, in the bosom of the savage Getae and Sarmatians. Yet here, as in the poems that purport to be letters, the focus is less on the second person, the unknown enemy (perhaps even the emperor who exiled him) than on the exile himself and his emotions – in this case vituperative and virulent hatred.

Ovid's exilic oeuvre appears as a digest, in a variety of modes, of all possible reports on the physical and mental condition of an exile,[107] a unique and Protean answer to a unique literary challenge – to convey feeling at removal and to transcend space and time in an essentially 'one-way' attempt at communication.[108] For Ovid, writing poetry that no one can read 'is like dancing in the dark' (*Pont.* 4.2.33, 34), and yet he continues to write.[109]

The autobiographical elegies show the exile's emotional life in almost day-by-day shifts of hope and despair. The pervasive topic of a rudderless victim wandering over land and sea, driven by an angry god, shows the exiled poet as an Odysseus-Aeneas, *fato profugus* (driven forth by fate), and Augustus as the angry god, a composite Poseidon-Neptune-Hera-Juno-Jupiter, more powerful than any one of these powerful personages.[110] In the whole of the collection Ovid draws himself in larger-than-life terms, creating a composite of all mythical and factual exiles that suffered debilitating isolation before him. By creating the 'myth of exile', Ovid sets a paradigm for the literary treatment of the hopes, fears and vicissitudes of political displacement. Hereby he fixed many of the conventions of exilic poetry, for example the stereotyped bleakness of the place of exile, the metaphor of exile as death, and the mythologising of the central, lonely figure of the exile.

1.8 Multiple 'I's': a 'truth' stronger than fiction

The literary myth of exile is not wholly Ovid's creation. It is the perfection of a literary form established by Cicero, whose subjective depiction of his banishment and return served to elevate the orator in his own eyes to a similar, mythic plane. Yet Cicero's friends replied to his broken pleas. What raises the exiled Ovid to a higher mythical plane is the silence that greets his outreach. Ovid takes the next logical step in the equation of exile with death. He sings in a 'voice from beyond the grave', while showing us that the 'living' in Rome are mute. His readership is clearly wider than his non-responsive friends at Rome. He interacts with a posterity, his 'model reader', to use Umberto Eco's term, which needed time to develop.[111]

The fictionalisation or mythicising of exile in ostensibly autobiographical literature points the problem of the subjective 'I' as narrator and the objective 'I' as topic of narration, and the question of 'sincerity' as function of style rather than objective truth.[112] When a male poet's first person 'narrator' is female, the problem is simple. The poet and, say, Dido in *Her.* 7, are not factually identical.[113] When Ovid imitates Cicero's letters from exile, both creative poet and suffering narrator are male. Immediately to the reader's perceptions they appear conflated. Because Cicero's exile was 'factual', Ovid's poetic depiction of his exile is also accepted as 'fact', but with Ovid the personalities of poet and exile do not always coincide. I have consistently (Claassen 1986-1998) chosen to differentiate three *personae*: *poeta*, a jocular poet who fell foul of the emperor; *exsul*, a suffering exile, who happened to be a poet; *vates*, a speaker of 'divine truth' (what we today would call 'psychological realism') about the emotional life of the second personage of the series, while as narrator often fudging the realities of both the first and second.[114] Perhaps above these we should postulate a fourth *persona*, the creative artist who draws his readers into the world of the first three personages, and leaves them to discover and enjoy the intricacies of his art.[115] The subjective 'I' is no less an element of this invitation; Ovid the Protean creative artist invites his readers: 'come and see the picture which *I in my great ingenuity* have painted'.

Analysis of aspects of time can work in the understanding of such multiple personalities. We can date the historical fact of displacement of Ovid-the-poet with a fair degree of accuracy to between AD 8 and 9. The heroic exile lives in a 'timeless now' in a mythical world of complete isolation. The psychological realist as poet-in-exile creates this fictional picture of timelessness, interspersed with flashbacks to a Roman present where 'real time' progresses, and to a Roman past where things may or may not have happened as he depicts them. The creative poet (who also is all three of the others) works from about AD 8 to 17 to create the body of work that we call 'Ovid's exilic oeuvre'. It has taken almost two thousand years of accumulated reading (of which the record of the first few centuries is lost) for a series of readerships as second person addressees to develop their divergent reactions to the inviting 'I' that has induced them both to grasp the timeless psychological misery of the exile and to appreciate his endlessly creative ways of depicting his displacement at the time when he himself was living through such an experience. This he does by means of wide-ranging generic experimentation.

1.9 Ovid's invention without parallel

Ovid is a complex and subtle poet. With him, genre has always been subjected to interesting conflations and adaptations. In matters of style Ovid did not keep even to the larger generic distinction of epic and elegiac, but purposely fused them.[116] Generic innovation is a feature of Roman literature. Ovid's *Amores* (Love Poems) exhibit a development from earlier elegy, as Vergil's *Georgics* developed from Lucretian didactics, and, by a logical next step, these then led to the *Ars Amatoria* (Art of Love), an eroto-didactic collection that was almost certain to evoke Augustus' moral ire. The *Metamorphoses* transferred 'collective epic' to Rome from Greek collections of epyllia, much as Vergil adapted pastoral from the Greek. The epistolary form of Ovid's earlier *Heroides* (Daughters of Heroes) was an 'invention', as Lucilius 'invented' the satiric genre, relating it to aspects of an earlier Roman tradition.[117] The *Tristia* and *Epistolae ex Ponto* appear as an invention without parallel, but one may assume some extant 'earlier traditions' as points of departure.

Subsequent chapters will deal with many aspects of the style of the creative artist. Here, to tie in with our initial discussion about the generic nature of the *corpus* of exilic literature, I offer a brief discussion of Ovid's exilic poems as 'an invention without parallel'. In his exilic corpus the creative artist indulges in complex generic experimentation, but always based on precedent, some his own. Such intertextuality appears inevitable, stemming as it does from ancient literary convention.[118] The basic questions are which generic subclassifications have been conflated, and whether a consistent artistic personality emerges as a single voice, speaking in subgenres, or whether each subgenre reveals its own consistent voice-of-the-artist-for-the-moment. That means that we need to discover the degree to which the creative artist is consistent or whether his 'vatic' personality is also a *persona* which he adapts at will. This latter question cannot be answered wholly here, but should be kept in consideration throughout.

Ovid's allusive use of his literary sources is not limited to verbal, metrical or conceptual echoes, but includes reworking and inversion of conventional *topoi*, generic adaptation and auto-imitation.[119] Of interest is which of his predecessors the poet chooses for allusion, and why, or to what effect. The conventionality, for example, of Ovid's storm poetry indicates how much he remained, even in exile, part of the society that rejected him. Auto-imitation in the exilic works may proclaim a related aspect. The exiled poet is showing the emperor that his own former apparent *nequitia* (jocular naughtiness) is congenital rather than deliberately subversive.

Particular characteristics of different genres and their different proponents are adapted to the exilic mode. Apart from the more obvious elegiac precedents (to be discussed in Chapter 8), Vergilian strains from epic and *Georgics* blend to give Ovid's picture of exile its transcendental dimension.[120] Literary allusion works to increase the weight of meaning of a particular phrase, verse or concept, carrying an additional body of meaning into a given poem, either in support of the emotional effect of the context, or as a counterpoint that ironically undercuts or inverts the emotional statement. Much of Ovidian allusion appears unconscious, or is allusive at second hand through the mediation of echoes by his predecessors of still earlier writers. The poet often amplifies a borrowed concept out of context, for humorous effect. For example, his ingenuous self-exculpation from the accusation of having written unsuitably erotic material rewrites the famous first lines of Vergil's *Aeneid, Arma virumque cano ...* (Of arms and the man do I sing ...) with a wickedly funny travesty: *et tamen ille tuae felix Aeneidos auctor/ contulit in Tyrios arma virumque toros* (and your own favourite author of the *Aeneid* – he of blessed memory – he tossed both arms and the man into an Eastern marriage bed!). Such conscious parody works retroactively, either to complete a concept, adding one more logical facet, not fully explored by the poet's predecessor, or to comment, by hindsight, on the effect or originally serious thrust of the model.[121] Choice of an unusual author or genre for deliberate allusion or imitation indicates an unusual intention. Here he is questioning both Augustus' literary and his moral values. Imitation, however, is not necessarily parodic or critical, but can involve simple thematic or topical borrowing. It can also be 'counter-parodic', involving the restoration of a phrase, verse or concept to a more 'elevated' new context. Some self-imitation may be the result of a deliberate restitution of potentially offensive *double entendre* by deflection into a 'single' meaning.[122]

The epistolary precedents for Ovid's exilic poems correspond to the precedents for his *Heroides*. Letters feature in epic, tragedy and comedy. Some fragments of early Greek love letters survive, also later philosophic-didactic letters of Plato and Epicurus. Ovid would have known epistolary treatises by Varro, Cicero's voluminous correspondence, in particular his letters from exile, and the epistolary satires of Lucilius and Horace.[123] Propertius' 'letter from Arethusa' (Prop. 4.3), is probably the earliest 'Herois'-type, and the monologue by Cynthia's ghost (4.7) shows some of the characteristics of attempted outreach toward a distant lover, which the Ovidian heroines exhibit. This, and the famous Cornelia-elegy, the 'queen of elegies' (Prop. 4.11) may have prompted the idea of 'letters from beyond the grave', central to much of Ovid's exilic elegy. The Cornelia-elegy reflects the ethic of Roman married love, offering a paradigm of rectitude to the exiled *lusor amorum* (love's gamesman). Even its political and personal character may have prompted Ovidian emulation, as it offered a vehicle for outreach to Augustus, who probably figured largely as real recipient in the imagination of the author of ostensible 'letters' to his wife and friends.[124]

The humorous possibilities of inversion of all previous and divergent poetic strains by means of the unifying device of a 'fiction of exile' were considered by Janssen (1951) and, more recently, by others, to lie behind what they consider to be sheer literary invention, a new direction for Ovid's Protean ingenuity to explore.[125] Self-imitation by inversion is perhaps the most recurrent motif. Elegiac misery where the exile is an *exclusus amator* (excluded lover) knocking at death's door suggests the *Amores*. Excursions into literary history in *Tristia* 2 shade into the didactic stance of the *Ars Amatoria*.[126] The formerly cynical *praeceptor amorum* (teacher of love) is now the ardent and desolate lover of his wife, who in her turn is a devoted *univira* (once-married spouse) like the paragon, the empress Livia, in whose constant praises the existence of her first husband, the biological father of Augustus' 'sons', is conveniently forgotten by the exile. Topics, tales and characters common to either the *Fasti* or the *Metamorphoses*[127] reappear in the exilic poetry, but, above all, the *Heroides*, letters of longing written by desolate women to the men who left them behind, seemed to call for their complement, letters from a male protagonist to the person who sent him away.

To Janssen and his intellectual successors the exilic poems appeared as the logical next step for a poet who had tried everything more than once. Janssen's argument was, however, based on a gullible acceptance of one of the patently fictitious features of the myth of exile, the poet's claims to debilitation of his powers of expression.[128] A much more acceptable explanation for the notion of exilic fiction would be that the poet associated himself to such a degree with his works, that when his poetry (often playfully referred to as his 'child', e.g. in *Tr.* 3.3) was banned from public circulation at Rome, he pretended to have been banned himself. Attractive as these theories are, there is, however, little chance that they could have been correct.

Had Ovid's exilic poetry been a playful fiction, that would still not have detracted from the art whereby the creative poet could combine his previously adapted generic experimentation such as erotodidactics and elegiac lament[129] into a new and ostensibly 'serious' mode, an invention without parallel. The exile's 'seriousness' is often undercut just sufficiently to suggest a second, and often a third, level of meaning.[130]

These and related topics will recur consistently in discussion of Ovid's exilic poetry and the stylised portrait of heroic exile that he paints with his pen. However, we need now to return to the wider aspect of narrative about displaced persons in the Eastern Mediterranean which is the canvas upon which many pictures of exile are painted. The next chapter will start, appropriately, with a discussion of fiction *par excellence* – the presentation of exile in myth. That will imply consideration of third person narrative, thereby initiating our exploration of persons, *personae* and personalities in exile.

2

The Third Person: Exilic Narrative

2.1 Myth and literature

2.1.1 Narrative strategies

Any study of authorial narrative, i.e., literature in which third person verbs predominate, needs to acknowledge the existence of a host of modern theories about what narrative is and what it does, and to show awareness of a vast and sometimes contradictory array of terminology variously coined and divergently understood by their authors. It is not my intention to venture too deep into this minefield. I shall rather use whichever term suits my analytical purpose, while at the same time indicating what I understand this term to mean.[1]

The first aspect of narrative that we need to consider would be its material, that is, what is told. Contemporary narrative theorists assume a basic difference between 'story', a sequence of interrelated events, and 'plot', an individual narrator's arrangement of those events, in which order, structure, emphasis and style all contribute meaning, and where 'focalisation' (the point of departure or perspective from which events are narrated) is central to understanding the emotional appeal of a tale.[2] Discussion of exilic narrative, if undertaken chronologically, should logically start with what for the ancients was their earliest history, their tales of gods and heroes, that is, it should start with myth. One of the most baffling characteristics of myth, however, is that it is all *story*, while its *plot* is incidental and can differ in each retelling. Each version is as valid as any other.[3] Hence my coupling of 'myth and literature'. We need to consider the manner in which individual authors retell the same stories.

Structuralists consider that the individual elements of myth (those pieces which individual authors can rearrange to make up their plots) may be considered as more important even than the basic story, i.e., than their simple interrelated sequence.[4] These pieces ('mythemes') may be seen as representative of basic oppositions, love and hate, life and death, youth and age, nearness and distance. These oppositions may be used as thematic organisers in a study of myth as an attempt to rationalise the irrational. They may equally serve to organise a view of myth as a generalisation of the particular; in the words of Segal (1971:37), 'myth provides the means of posing and clarifying questions of human existence'.

2. The Third Person: Exilic Narrative

2.1.2 Mythical narratives

Exile is a frequent mythical theme.[5] Gods and heroes could experience exile. Apollo was exiled from heaven for a time.[6] Treatment of the myth of Orestes throughout ancient literature concentrates on the theme of his dispossession and alienation from the *patria* (fatherland) as well as the conflict of filial loyalties. Heracles found his lack of a *patria* a boon, boasting 'I am not an Argive or a Theban for I don't belong to any one city: any fortress in Greece is my home'.[7]

In the sense that myth treated of heroic figures, the mythical depiction of exile, like historical exile, involved the powerful or potentially powerful. Alcmaeon, attempting revenge on his father Amphiaraus for the death of his mother, hears from the Delphic oracle that he will be safe from the Furies on land not yet in existence when his dying mother uttered her curse: an alluvial island at the mouth of the Achelous. Plutarch interprets the story as representing escape from political turmoil.[8]

The existence of the title *Zeus Zenios* (Zeus, god of strangers) is interpreted by Plutarch (*Mor.* 605A) as proof of the prevalence of exile as part of the human condition, and that exile can be positive. That exile of an individual could lead to greater universal happiness speaks from the myths of Theseus, Cadmus and Dionysus.[9] Yet the dark side of exile is more frequent in literature.[10] Polyneices, interrogated by Jocasta on the evils of exile, lists misery, lack of free speech, the overbearing attitude of a powerful opponent, expectancy rather than realisation of hope, lack of friends, uselessness of high birth, hunger, dependence on strangers.[11] Jocasta recoils from her son's enforced foreign marriage.[12] Xenophobia is an aggravating factor.

Myth is the stuff of epic, and in both primary and secondary epic (traditional versus literary epic) mythical exile looms large. Epic narrates the great deeds or great sufferings of heroic beings with monolithic propensities for good or ill, aided or persecuted by often unpredictable, morally inferior but physically superior and immortal, divine beings. Odysseus has Athena as divine helper; Poseidon dogs his journeying with single-minded malevolence.

The theme of the exile's lamenting the loss of his native land was established by Homer in his *Odyssey* (1.48-59) and recurs frequently throughout ancient literature.[13] Odysseus was, however, a special case: his wanderings tended toward home, even though he was at one stage commanded by Teiresias to carry his oar inland until he met 'people who did not know the sea' (*Od.* 11.119ff.). The treatment of the exile by the Phaeacians established a norm of hospitality.[14] As will be shown below, Ovid frequently portrays himself as an Odysseus, while stressing that his wanderings take him away from home, rather than toward it.

In Roman treatment of myth, exile also features prominently. Homer's archetypes were taken over and transformed by Vergil, while preserving

37

the Greek characters, the system of apparent composition by 'word blocks' or '*formulae*' and the tragic and human dimensions of his protagonists. The wanderings of Aeneas are perhaps non-typical, for his exile has a fixed purpose: he is tending towards a 'new fatherland'. He is aided by Venus, his divine mother; Juno persecutes him throughout eleven books; in the twelfth she, too, is reconciled with the future ancestor of the Roman imperial line. On his journeys Aeneas' path is, however, frequently crossed by expatriates: Dido (*Aen.* 1-4), Mezentius (8.492; 10.689-952), who kills Acron (10.719-31) and Mimas (702-6), respectively a Greek and a Trojan exile, Metabus (11.541ff.), Menoetes, killed by Turnus (12.517-20) and Aeolus the Trojan (12.542-7). Metabus and Mezentius are political exiles. Metabus' exile strongly influenced the life and death of his daughter Camilla. Evander, too, is a king in exile (8.307-560).[15] In *Aen.* 10.433-6 Lausus and Pallas, exiled sons of exiled kings, oppose each other in battle. For both, *Fortuna negarat/in patriam reditus* (Fortune had denied any return to the fatherland ...); this is the essence of exile.[16]

Vergil very consciously refers to the exile of his hero at key points in his epic narrative. The famous opening speaks of the hero as *fato profugus* (driven forth by fate, *Aen.* 1.2). Vergil's use (following Homer) of flashbacks as epic device turns impersonal narrative into first person reminiscence, which is still apposite here in our review of myth. Book 3 of the *Aeneid* starts with a second phase in the hero's tale of Troy's unhappy fate, and within the first sentence we have *diversa exilia et desertas quaerere terras / auguriis agimur divum ...* (we are driven to seek various places of exile and desert lands ..., *Aen.* 3.4-5).

Aeneas' exile will in the end bring about a positive result (*Aen.* 2.293-5). In contrast, the exiled Helenus and Andromache, widow of Hector, now ruling the domain of Achilles' son Neoptolemus at Buthrotum in Epirus (*Aen.* 3), are pathetic. Andromache is continually haunted by memories of Hector; Helenus is tragic in his attempt to recreate Troy (*Aen.* 3.336) and in his partial vision of the future (*Aen.* 3.389-432).[17] This is the curse of exile.[18]

The exile of Dido, before she meets Aeneas, is creative, turning Carthage into a new *patria*; but the end of her romance with Aeneas takes more than her life; she is portrayed as having lost all creative drive, her energies driven into a self-defeating vortex of psychological introspection. Paradoxically, Aeneas reverses his own tragic exile into a positive search for a new fatherland, at the expense of Dido's loss of creativity and in the end, of her life. Significantly, Vergil's narrative, when depicting Dido's agonised rumination on alternatives, turns to the first person. Dido even desperately asks of herself *Iliacas igitur classis atque ultima Teucrum / iussa sequar?* (Should I then follow the Trojan fleet and obey their every command?, *Aen.* 4.537-8) and she contemplates going into a new exile, as a sailor's hanger-on. When she dies, her tortured spirit struggles to free itself of its mortal coil until the goddess Iris is sent to cut it loose in terms reminiscent of the Roman legal formulae used in the manumission of slaves: *Hunc ego Diti / sacrum iussa fero teque isto corpore solvo* (I take this by sacred order of Dis and free you from that body of yours, *Aen.* 4.702-3). In the final position of line 705 the verb *recessit* (her spirit departed) closes the book, clinching Vergil's third person narrative with emphasis on the last action that could be ascribed to Dido – a retreat into death as the ultimate exile. Paradoxically, in the Underworld Dido is reunited with her husband and it is Aeneas who is left an empty-handed suppliant as she turns away. Aeneas' descent to the Underworld is, like Odysseus', a necessary narrative device, but it also represents the ultimate dispossession.

Vergil expends almost two hundred lines (*Aen.* 6.268-450) on Aeneas' slow journey through the Underworld – a living exile passing through an ultimate existential experience – before the hero descries Dido, *recens a vulnere* (recently arrived after her dreadful wounding, 450). He recognises her only when he is almost upon her. Vergil's choice of verbs and his stress by position on the noun *umbras* (shadows) and adjective *obscuram* (hidden) indicate the uncertainty Aeneas experiences at this vision:

> quam Troius heros
> ut primum iuxta stetit agnovitque per umbras
> obscuram, qualem primo qui surgere mense
> aut videt aut vidisse putat per nubila lunam   (Aen. 6.451-4)

The Trojan hero recognised her dimly through the gloom only when he stood next to her, like someone who sees, or thinks that he sees, the moon rising through the clouds.

In the relationship of Dido and Aeneas Vergil has epitomised the pathos of psychological alienation as well as the pathos of physical exile. Paradoxically, Dido's exile is over. She ignores Aeneas' pleas, and turns to the spirit of her former husband, waiting for her in the gloom:

> Illa solo fixos oculos aversa tenebat
> nec magis incepto vultum sermone movetur
> quam si dura silex aut stet Marpesia cautes.
> tandem corripuit sese atque inimica refugit
> in nemus umbriferum, coniunx ubi pristinus ille
> respondet curis aequatque Sychaeus amorem   (Aen. 6.469-74)

She turned away and kept her eyes on the ground and she was no more moved when he started speaking to her than if she stood there as a hard oak or Marpesian rock. At length she collected herself and fled from him as his enemy, into the shadowy wood where her first husband Sychaeus returned her caresses and equalled her love with his own.

Aeneas has no such comfort. He is doomed to wander on through life until he completes his god-given mission to found a new nation. That tale will not concern us further here. We now turn to the consideration of the narration of a tale that combines the same elements of a hero's travel to the Underworld, his unsuccessful meeting with his beloved, who had died a violent death, and his fate to continue journeying on earth.

In *Metamorphoses* 10, Ovid portrays Orpheus' journey to the Underworld and his empty-handed return in terms deliberately reminiscent of Vergil, but in a totally different manner and with a totally different thrust. Intertextual allusion acknowledges the older author, but works to point contrast.

Orpheus loses his bride to death from a snake bite. We are not given her name, but may be expected to remember it from another intrusive reminiscence, to Vergil's own version of the story from *Georgics* 4.453-527. After first having given due place to the usual mourning practices, *Quam satis …/ deflevit vates* (and when the singer had appropriately lamented her, *Met.* 10.11, 12), Ovid's hero accomplishes the downward journey in four lines (10-14). He strides into the abode of Persephone and Dis and proceeds to address the king and queen of the Underworld in a dramatic monologue. His diction is rapid and staccato, the argument simultaneously patronising and casuistic:

> *Vicit Amor! supera deus hic bene notus in ora est*
> *an sit et hic, dubito. sed et hic tamen auguror esse.*   (*Met.* 10.26-7)

Love won through! This god is well known on the shores above. Whether he is here too, I doubt. But I tell it as a divine truth that he is here too.

Neither Persephone nor her husband are meant to remember the author's own previous narrative (*Met.* 5.385-550) of lust and rapine that led to her becoming Queen of the shades. All is love and light in Tartarus, and if it be not, the speaker wills it such. The perspicacious model reader is meant to recognise a Vergilian allusion, this time to *Eclogue* 10.69: *Omnia vincit Amor: et nos cedamus Amori* (Love conquers all; let us too give way to love!).[19] Ovid is capping Vergil: the perfect *vicit* (has conquered) denotes an accomplished fact: Orpheus' love has won his bride back. He triumphantly calls out her name. But this victory is not narrative fact, only the speaker's assertion, and by verse 57 Orpheus has lost his bride for the second time. Before this denouement, he has charmed the bloodless wraiths to tears, and has suspended by his song the catalogue of traditional tortures in Tartarus that Vergil narrates at length in detailed horror (*Aen.* 6.548-627). Ovid's catalogue of temporarily reprieved sinners encompasses five lines of rapid review.[20] The Queen relents and calls Eurydice. The description of their journey back (50-7) again evokes Vergil's Dido. Eurydice goes past newly dead shades, *umbras … recentes* (48), her step slowed by the snake-bite, *passu de vulnere tardo* (with slow pace because of her wound,

49). The narrative slows down to the equivalent of filmic 'slow motion',[21] and the road is designated in terms familiar from Vergil: *Carpitur adclivis per muta silentia trames, / arduus, obscurus, caligine densus opaca* (the steep path is undertaken in mute silence, arduous, secret and thick with dense fog, 52-3). Proportionally the longest part of the narrative is devoted to Eurydices' lingering lapse back into the shades.[22] Orpheus' amazement at this 'second death' (*gemina nece*, 64) merits an eight-line Homeric comparison – to the emotions experienced by any wanderer through Hell at seeing the three-headed dog and all the other horrors that had previously left the hero unmoved. Retroactive ring composition slowly reprises the first casually elided journey, now at last accentuating its danger and horror.

Like Aeneas, Orpheus is doomed to go back to the world of the living, alone in his quest, but singing still.[23] The narrative articulation of the *Metamorphoses* lends itself to accentuating through narrative space the duration in time and spatial length of the singer's lonely journey. His exile seems, however, to be voluntary, and his loneliness not unalloyed. Ovid returns to Orpheus only at the beginning of the next book (11.1-66), six hundred and fifty-three lines after we have been told that many women had been in love with him, but that many had been saddened by his rejection of their advances (82). In the three lines that end this first episode Ovidian humour partly undercuts the pathos of the tale by his bland and non-judgmental narration of the tradition that Orpheus was the 'first pederast'. This fact, then, leads to the singer's death, when the Ciconian women (significantly designated *nurus*, brides, 11.3) in their Bacchic fury recognise in him a *contemptor* of women (7) and stone him to death. The first stone is deflected by his music and lies at his feet 'like a suppliant', but when the women drown his sweet music with their raucous sounds, the singer and his song fall victim to their rage. Orpheus' wandering is over, but his disembodied tongue babbles on until its head sinks into the Hebrus, whose banks echo the mournfully dying lullaby:

> *Flebile nescio quid queritur lyra, flebile lingua*
> *murmurat exanimis, respondent flebile ripae.*   (*Met.* 11.53)

The mournful lyre complains of I know not what; the mourning tongue lifelessly murmurs on; the river banks mournfully reply.

Ovid's treatment of another of the great tales of exile bears consideration. The myth that stands out as epitomising all the despair and alienation attendant upon exile is the tale of Medea. The barbarian princess gave up home and fatherland to aid the hero of the Argo, first to gain the Golden Fleece, and then successfully to evade her father's pursuit. Her life as Jason's wife changed into that of an exiled outcast when she was repudiated so that her husband could marry into the royal house of

Corinth. The despair that led to Medea's destruction of her own children is an extreme example, but may still be seen as typical of emotional reaction to exile. Awareness of betrayal and loss accompanied an historical Cicero into exile no less than it moved his mythical psychological prototype to a bizarre act of vengeance.

Ovid seems to have a particular affinity for this exiled heroine. Ovid's lost drama *Medea* has been the object of much speculation. One of his monologues from deserted women (*Heroides* 12) portrays her inner anxieties. Other literary treatments of the myth extensively portray the anxieties and psychological terror caused by deliberate psychological withdrawal from an exiled protagonist by the object of her affection.[24] Euripides' drama shows that by abandoning Medea, Jason turned her voluntary physical exile into involuntary mental and emotional exile, leading to total psychological displacement and dispossession. The lost Ovidian drama, we may conjecture, would perhaps similarly have stressed this emotional debilitation.

Ovid's depiction of Medea in the *Metamorphoses* (7.1-424) seems deliberately to choose to stress aspects of the tale which are glossed over in other literary treatments. Intertextual reminiscences of Apollonius' *Argonautica* 3 are very noticeable here, but Apollonius Rhodius depicts what is essentially an adventurous romance with a 'happy ending', with only vague hints of the forebodings of doom that his readers would be expected to pick up. Ovid seems to be combining the Euripidean and Apollonian versions into a new plot, which borrows aspects of each. In a recent article, Thalia Papadopolou (1997) has shown that both Euripides (*Medea* 1021-55) and Apollonius Rhodius (*Argonautica* 3, 772-801) make use of what she terms 'interior monologue', a form of 'stream of consciousness' writing later made famous by Virginia Woolf. Ovid seems to do the same. Ovid expends sixty lines on Medea's inner debate on whether she should risk voluntary exile in pursuit of her demented love (Ovid's version of Apollonius' 'interior monologue' referred to by Papadopolou), six lines relating the perfidious blandishments whereby Jason gained the herbs that ensured his safe achievement of his mission, and fifty-eight lines of dramatic narrative recounting Jason's threefold confrontation: with the brazen bulls, with the soldiers that sprang from the ground, and the dragon that guarded the Golden Fleece.

Their flight from Colchis bearing the Golden Fleece is condensed into two and a half lines (in which Medea is designated a 'second trophy' (*spolia altera*, 7.157),[25] whereafter the narrative lingers for upwards of a hundred and thirty lines (158-293) over Medea's efforts to prolong the life of her father-in-law, Aeson. This is a set-piece of narrative description that stresses her horrific supernatural abilities. Ovid's Medea is a fully-fledged witch. First travelling in a fiery sun-chariot to cull herbs from the mountain tops, Medea prepared a ghastly potion with which she renewed the blood in Aeson's veins. Her use of the sun-chariot is familiar from

Euripides, but also serves to prepare readers for her later escapes, first from the daughters of Pelias and then from a vengeful Jason. Ovid is as it were preparing, by means of an intertextual 'prequel' (the term used by Hinds 1993: 40 about *Her.* 12), a rationale for Euripides' *deus ex machina*, the divine intervention of Helios.

Next Ovid tells in great detail how Medea used her magic to trick the daughters of Pelias, Jason's wicked uncle, into killing their father on the pretext that she would renew his life in a similar fashion (294-349, fifty-five lines). The 'impiously pious' daughters turned away their gaze as they repeatedly slashed at their father, reprising Apollonius' Medea, who had similarly averted her gaze when Jason hacked at Absyrtus. Medea's escape from the sisters' wrath offers the poet the opportunity to relate in an equally long passage (350-403) a second magic flight over the mountain tops, and to encapsulate various myths by linking them to the places over which Medea flew.

The story of her betrayal by Jason and her terrible revenge, the entire plot of Euripides' drama, is reduced to four lines (404-7). By this time the dragons have become virtually passé as she once again sets off, an event that had formed the climax of the Euripidean plot. Medea's life at Athens is narrated in twenty-two lines (404-24) as another example of her wickedness; Theseus, the son of her champion Aegeus, is nearly poisoned by her hand, after which Medea fades from the tale, which quickly moves on to recount a Minoan threat to Athens.

The poet has by his selection of emphasis (signalled by the relative length accorded different parts of the story) chosen to round out the picture drawn by Euripides and Apollonius. At Colchis Medea is the love-sick woman, torn by conflicting emotions, going, like her Apollonian counterpart (*Arg.* 3.842), to the altars of the moon-goddess, protectress of witchcraft, for aid in her decision whether she should betray her father and go into willing exile with Jason. This is reminiscent of Vergil's Dido, who, herself, owes a debt to Apollonius' Medea. The circular intertextual allusion is strengthened by, for instance, an evocation of both Dido's obsessive religiosity in *Aen.* 4.56 (*aut ante ora deum pinguis spatiatur ad aras*, 'or before the countenance of the gods she travelled back and forth to the laden altars') and Aeneas' journey to the Underworld in the famous *Ibant obscuri ...* (They went, shadowed over ...,*Aen.* 6.268). Ovid combines the first word of the latter with the last word of the former, in *Ibat ad antiquas Hecates Perseidos aras* (She was on her way to the ancient altars of Hecate, child of [the Titan] Perses, *Met.* 7.74). The connotation is sinister. She worships a Medusa-like figure, and her act of worship almost stiffens her resolve, but it melts at the sight of Jason, and Medea is reduced to the status of a blushing virgin, easy victim to the hero's smooth tongue and easy promises (85-94).

Fear of the high seas at first holds Medea back, but the thought of lying on board ship safe on her 'husband's' breast spurs her on (67). Conscience reminds her of the wickedness of her contemplated action. The god of love (here merely designated as *Cupido*, one word representing the fully-rounded portrait of the mischievous boy-god that Apollonius sketches at *Arg*. 3. 10-66, 275-86) is nigh defeated. Love is on the point of flying off (73) when Jason persuades her with promises of marriage to give in (89-94). In this version Ovid leaves out both Euripides' version involving Medea's horrific mutilation of her small brother's body and Apollonius' stress on the guilt she shares with Jason for the murder of an adult Absyrtus. Once in Corinth, Medea is presented as powerful in her control over her magic powers, and Ovid again seems to avoid portraying Medea's despair when Jason decides to repudiate her.

The effect of the whole is rather like that of a modern popular journal or Sunday paper that 'fills in' readers on the salacious or horrific background of some notorious figure whose misdeeds have been reduced to over-reported pulp. Yet in, but apart from, Ovid's narrative, the myth appears to have a life of its own, and those aspects of the story not mentioned by the poet are as palpably there as the aspects that he chooses to stress. Ovid's plot assigns a reasonable narrative connection to events treated as given in earlier versions of the myth. He shows Medea's herb-gathering absence after the death of Pelias (350-93) as giving Jason the opportunity to choose a new bride, and in rapid narrative gives the gist of Euripides' dramatic plot, adding as moralistic comment (402) that Aegeus' 'marriage to Medea' was the only dubious act of his entire life. The poet's frequent employment of a censorious tone and editorial comment in the extended narrative sections seems to invite his readers to react against it and to recall both the fall from innocence of Apollonius' 'scarlet woman' (on whom more below) and the pathos of Euripides' rejected heroine – and of his own, from her monologue in *Heroides* 12. It takes an enlightened re-reader (Winkler's concept, 1985: 10-13) to question why the fearless pilot of a fiery chariot should at all have feared the high seas – why she did not, in fact, invoke the chariot to facilitate her escape with her 'first husband'.

The epistolary monologue that is Medea's 'letter' to Jason (*Her*. 12) fills in the narrative. It is a creative reworking of Euripides' drama (perhaps also Ovid's own), about which Hinds comments (1993: 39) that the dramatic heroine does not 'come quietly' when entering elegy. Most of the letter is taken up with the past.[26] Although this is second person narrative, Medea in her 'now' (after her repudiation by Jason, but before the murders of their sons and his new bride) recounts the thoughts and deeds of herself 'then' with an impersonal distance between her present self and the young girl that she had been before she met him, who did not know his true nature: *Tunc ego te vidi, tunc coepi scire, quis esses* (Then I saw you, then I began to know who you were, 31). A vast gulf lies between her innocent self and the knowledgeable self she subsequently became. Over a hundred lines are devoted to a detailed account of the events at Colchis (1-112). The deserted wife is reminding her faithless husband of her past services to him. Intertextual reminiscences of Apollonius are very noticeable. The fate of her brother Absyrtus is again glossed over, whether the Euripidean version, where she had a direct hand in the slaughter of a child, or the Apollonian, where she contrived to trap him (as the adult leader of the expedition sent by her father against Jason). In Apollonius, Jason strikes him down, and, dying, Absyrtus smears his sister's gown with his own red blood, thereby showing her up as the prototypic 'scarlet woman'. Here the omission works as convincing evidence of the sister's feeling of guilt (113-16). The death of Pelias is recounted in three lines, and the faithless Jason is reminded that this horrific deed, too, was done for his sake (129-31). The last part of the poem moves to the future tense, with threats which the informed reader can understand and interpret correctly: that the new bride will be engulfed in fire (180), that Medea will use a knife to good effect (181). The ultimate irony lies in her projected fear that a wicked stepmother will harm the boys (188). The reader knows (as does Medea) that no stepmother can do more to harm her sons than she will herself. The concluding lines alternate between pathos and veiled threats, ending with a return to a state of not knowing: *Nescio quid certe mens mea maius agit* (212, translated by Isbell, 1990: 113, 'I do not know for certain what is in my soul'). The resonances set up between Ovid's treatment of the myth in these two works convey a powerful image of great and mysterious powers curdled into evil through great suffering. Each version gains dimension by being read with the other.

In the poems written from his own exile Ovid thrice alludes to the myth, once in a context that serves to depict the essential horror and alienation of exile.[27] At *Tristia* 3.8.1-4 the exile wishes that he, too had a fiery chariot with which to flee the Pontic shore, and reminds himself (and his readers) that Augustus, like the great Sun-god, is powerful enough to give him wings, should he so wish (*Tr.* 3.8.15-16). The next poem turns this positive reminiscence into an ominously negative evocation of the dreadful murder that all the previous narratives had so studiously skirted. Ovid's derivation of the name of Tomis from the Greek *temnô* (I cut, *Tr.* 3.9.5-6), referring to the 'cutting up' by Medea of her brother in order to delay her father as she and Jason fled across the Black Sea, was part of the tradition.[28] Ovid's poem begins with the factual statement that Tomis was established as a colony by the people of Melitus. A parenthetical *quis crederet?* (who would believe this? v. 1), together with a series of visually evocative literary devices, suggests that the local Greek culture is decadent.[29] Archaeological evidence shows a vastly different picture,[30] but the introduction to this poem sets the atmosphere for the fanciful and horrific aetiological connection of the name of the city with a deed of inhuman cruelty.[31] A lookout sees approaching sails (11). Medea knows this, and knows (*conscia*, fully aware, 15) what she is about to do. She casts about and her eyes fall on her brother (*lumina flexa*, 22) in a verse evocative of her eyes 'fixed on' Jason at *Met* 7.87. For Medea, to see is to do.[32] Without further ado she undertakes the grisly deed (25-8), arranging up the pieces on a rock in grim sequence, first the boy's pale hands, and then his bloodied head, to ensure their father's being delayed by the sight (29-30). The last couplet (33-4) completes the picture: the name of the place, 'Tomis', comes from the Greek word for dismembering.[33] Here at last the narrative is completed and the whole picture falls into place. Exile brings unredeemed horror. The poet purposely wishes to horrify his Roman readership.

In *Pont.* 3.3 Ovid returns to the Medea-myth, but here the context is ribald. This is one of the few instances of extended narrative in the exilic poems. A mock-solemn tone moves into comedy and back to spurious solemnity. It presents a tale within a tale: the exile tells his patron and friend, Fabius Maximus,[34] about a dream he had or an apparition that approached him: a bedraggled and sorry-looking 'Amor', exhausted and dishevelled from his long flight, had come from Rome to visit him, had exonerated him from all blame in the matter of morality and had prophesied future happiness, especially after Tiberius' projected triumph. The debilitated Amor explained (79-80) that he had visited the region once before, when inspiring the Phasian maiden. In a subtle play on the fact that the Latin word *docere* (to teach) takes two accusatives, of animate pupil and inanimate topic, Amor (the topic of the didactic *Ars Amatoria* which had supposedly caused his ruin) is personalised and berated by the poet as an ungrateful pupil, a non-Achilles to his non-Chiron, or a non-Numa to his non-Pythagoras (vv. 43-4). This is a typically playful Ovidian conceit, which has wrested every possible nuance from the situation. Intertextual allusion calls for the reader to remember both Apollonius' description (*Arg.* 3. 275-86) of the flight of the quiver-bearing Eros, intent on transfixing the young Medea's heart, and Medea's near-dismissal of Cupido at *Met.* 7.73, only prevented by the timeous arrival of Jason.

Apart from his use of the Medea-myth in his exilic poems, Ovid tells one other tale of exile, using double focalisation. The narrative of the Orestes-myth is placed in the mouth of an old Getic man (*Pont.* 3.2.43-98). The poet's first focus is on illustrating the value he places on friendship. He reports hearing the tale of the friendship of Orestes and Pylades in the land of the Taurians,[35] as it was told by a local. It is a tale of exile and safe return. The tale is in fact a reprise of Euripides' *Iphigeneia among the Taurians*.[36] Pylades stood by his friend when Orestes was looking for his sister. When both were captured and about to be sacrificed, the priestess (the lost sister, not yet recognising her brother) suggested one should stay to die, the other take the news back home to Greece. The barbaric Artemis celebrated in this cruel countryside is a far cry from a gentle Roman 'Diana the Huntress'. Her reeking altar is sprinkled with the blood of human sacrifice (vv. 53-4). The friends vie with each other to be the one to die:

2. The Third Person: Exilic Narrative

Ire iubet Pylades carum periturus Oresten;
hic negat, inque vices pugnat uterque mori.
extitit hoc unum, quo non convenerit illis:
cetera par concors et sine lite fuit   (Pont. 3.2.88)

Orestes, determined to die, bids his dear friend Pylades go. He refuses and in turn each strives to be the one to die. This was the only thing that ever happened in which the two did not agree: for the rest they were one of heart and never quarrelled.

Of interest here is the poet's manipulation of tense. The narrative verbs are in the present; comment in a gnomic aorist. The tale continues in similar vein. While the friends go on arguing the priestess scribbles a note (*exarat*: ploughs [in wax], v. 90). In the next couplet (91-2) imperfect verbs indicate continuous action, with an interjection in the imperative mood:

ad fratem mandata dabat. cuique illa dabuntur
(humanas casus aspice) frater erat

She was giving a message to her brother. And the man to whom she was giving the message (just regard the lot of humanity!) – he was her brother!

After the scene of recognition, events move rapidly and are narrated in the historic present, as before, but the tale ends with a gnomic present; their love made these friends famous, says the old man, *in Scythia magnam nunc quoque nomen habent* (in Scythia even now they still have a great reputation, 96). Even in a place of horror some timeless tales of love and bravery persist – and a narrative 'now' gives the exile hope.

2.1.3 From myth to history: pastoral dispossession

Half-way in the spectrum of Roman literature between the narration of myth in epic poetry and the prosaic relation of events as 'history' lies pastoral poetry as evocation of timeless aspects of the human condition writ small. The narrow focus of pastoral and the apparent limiting of its field of interest (framing) serve paradoxically to concentrate the reader's attention on the larger implications of the topics of which it treats. Roman pastoral is suffused with quasi-historical evocations of exile. The years of unrest at the end of the Republic brought about dispossession and exile to rural Italy, especially to areas which had supported the losing side. Vergil's first and ninth *Eclogues* reflect a painful, living reality, after the appropriations of land for resettlement of veterans.[37] Pastoral from Theocritus onward has offered a view of the complexity of life by reduction to a stylised simpler mode. The generic characteristics of pastoral and most versions of myth (whether epic, lyric or dramatic) differ widely, but there is a certain coincidence of narrative style, what Eco (1994: 117f.) calls a 'fictional protocol', particularly with respect to portrayal of time, both duration and

47

designation. Myth and pastoral share what in Australia could be termed 'dreamtime', a timeless present, which shifts back and forth along an endless line of 'nows'.

The Vergilian *Eclogues* appear redolent of languid timelessness, sunshine and shade, and a nature that harmonises with simple humanity. They also feature Roman politicians, including Cornelius Gallus (before his fall from grace) – and both the happy recipient of Augustan clemency of *Ecl.* 1 and the sadly dispossessed and displaced persons of 1 and 9. Politics provide a counterpoint to the restful ambience. Real time intrudes into dreamtime. At Tomis Ovid depicts marauders surging across the ice-bound Danube, dragging captive local inhabitants, who cast longing backward looks at their wretched homes (*Tr.* 3.10.55-66). This pathetic picture takes the Vergilian theme of dispossession through war one step further. As with Vergil, who had earlier reminded the Romans of the terrible price of conquest, the Ovidian pastoral vignette carries a political message: the Augustan peace cannot guarantee the safety of all nations. Continuing dispossession of both the formerly powerful and the permanently powerless is shown as grim reality. It is typical of the sensibility of both poets to choose to focus on the dispossession of the powerless resulting from the actions of the powerful. Vergil through pastoral and Ovid through his creation of the myth of exile offer views that diverge from the Augustan myth of Golden Age peace and prosperity.

2.2 Political exile in historical context

2.2.1 Exile in the Greek world

Cicero, writing to Lucceius (*Fam.* 5.12) refers to the pleasure afforded by reading of the exile and return of Themistocles.[38] To him it is a 'natural drama, with its own acts and scenes'. The exilic material to hand in Roman literature reflects not only its own literary precedents, but also the phenomenon of exile as a very real factor in Greek life. The spectacular exiles of history acted both as *exempla* in literature and as paradigms in life.

Political exile normally meant not only the thwarting of political ambition but often worked as the focal point of potential unrest. Dio Chrysostomus (*Or.* 13.6) refers to exiles returning to wage war against 'popular governments and despotism', considering it an honour to 'fight unto death on their native soil'. From the mythical beginnings of Athenian democracy, Greek insistence on the curbing of excessive power, particularly by banishment of the powerful, played a part in Athenian political life. Paradigms abound: Cleisthenes, the instigator of the practice of ostracism, was one of its first victims.[39] Solon's travels were perhaps voluntary exile, undertaken when he saw Peisistratos established as tyrant at Athens.[40] Diogenes Laertius quotes a 'letter' from the tyrant to Solon: 'If you had known what I was like, you would perhaps have tolerated me ... come home, be my friend!' The reply was unmoving: 'How can I return and seem to approve of you?' Such, then, was voluntary political exile by the powerful. The Peisistratids and Alcmaeonids moved in and out of Athens and Athenian political focus, each in turn wielding power by exerting decrees of exile on their opponents.[41] The mixture of sex and politics appears in all ages to be a heady one, liable to lead to exile of the protagonists; the expulsion of Peisistratos' son Hippias in 510 BC, three years after the violent death of Hipparchus, may be traced to an explosive love affair.[42]

Other Greek cities had their measure of exiles. Herodotus' *Histories* abound with tales of displacement. The legendary Croesus was host to the fugitive Adrastus, before he himself was advised by the god Apollo to seek exile. At Corinth similar tales obtain; none more horrific than that of the dynastic machinations of the tyrant Periander.[43]

Long after Themistocles' enforced exile to a series of host cities and his final settlement under the Persian Artaxerxes,[44] the brilliant but unstable Alcibiades thrice underwent self-imposed exile, on his return vindicating his retreat as 'counter-espionage' tactics.[45] His power, both potential and real, accompanied him in all the vicissitudes of exile. The historian Thucydides was exiled to Skaptê Hylê on Chalcidike for his participation in the command at Amphipolis, a case of punishment for the unsuccessful wielding of power. Thucydides shows admirable restraint in the reportage of these events, where he appears clearly as the victim of mismanagement by his colleague Eucles.[46] His sole comment on his twenty years of exile was that it gave him a clearer view of the events of the Peloponnesian war, enabled as he was to associate with both sides and therefore to produce a more objective history. Later Xenophon could represent the *Anabasis* (Return Expedition) of the Greek mercenaries under his leadership (who had been stranded after the death in battle of the Persian prince who had hired them) as a glorious Odyssean return from exile, but his retirement to Scillus may have been enforced, punishment for his participation in the expedition of the Ten Thousand.[47]

Philosophers wielding intellectual, rather than political, power, fell equal victim to the vagaries of Fortune. Socrates, facing death as the ultimate exile, chose to acquiesce in his sentence rather than disobey the laws of his native city by attempting escape. Cicero (*Tusc.* 5.108) typified Socrates as a 'Cosmian', at heart no exile, *Mundanum – totius mundi se incolam et civem arbitrabatur* (A world citizen – he thought of himself as inhabitant and citizen of the whole world).[48]

Plato's vicissitudes entailed circuitous exile. He was the son of an Athenian settler in Aegina, who, with others, had been expelled by the Spartans (Diog. Laert. 3.4). Later, during his attempt to educate the notorious tyrant of Syracuse, he was enslaved in Sicily by Dionysius and handed over to be sold in the market on Aegina, where he stood to forfeit his life as the 'first Athenian to return'. He would then have been the indirect victim of political machinations in which he had had no part. Plato was acquitted because of his status as a philosopher, or, in another version, perhaps ransomed (*id*. 3.18-20). Two more voluntary journeys to Sicily brought no more signal success (*ibid*. 23). The life story of Diogenes the Cynic attracted many apocryphal accretions. After an initial banishment from Pontus, he apparently was twice sold into slavery.[49] The wanderings of Aristotle (384-322 BC) were complex, and included periods in Macedon and Chalcis, where he died.[50] Plutarch, *Mor*. 603C, claims that Aristotle simply preferred Macedon. Theophrastus (*c*. 370-286 BC) was banished for a year, following a proposal that no philosopher should preside over a school except by permission of the Boulê.[51] So the careless flaunting of intellectual power could also provoke a decree of exile.

Cicero (*Tusc*. 5.107), discussing exile, cites as involuntary exiles a long list of philosophers who never returned to their native cities. The list is representative of the various schools of Greek philosophy: the Old Academy: Xenocrates, Crantor; the Middle Academy: Arcesilas, Lacydes; the Peripatetics: Aristotle and Theophrastus; the Old Stoa: Zeno, Cleanthes; the Middle Stoa: Chrysippus, Antipater; the New Academy; Carneades, Clitomachus; contemporary New Academicians: Philo, Antiochus; and, finally, the two Stoics best known in the Roman world, Panaetius and Cicero's friend Posidonius.[52] The fact of their 'exile', perhaps only removal to another cultural centre, seems to have loomed large in Cicero's consciousness. Jerome (*Ep*. 60.5.2) quotes some of these in a context which indicates them as sources for Cicero's lost *consolatio*.[53] Of these names, Plutarch, in a similar list, [54] cites Aristotle, Theophrastus, Zeno, Cleanthes and Chrysippus, to whom he adds: Straton of Lampsacus, Glycon from the Troad, Ariston from Ceos, Diogenes 'from Babylon', Antipater from Tarsus, and Archelaus, who left Athens for Babylon.

These diverse examples indicate interstate mobility as a normal way of life in the Greek world, and show the importance of enforced exile as a means of dampening overt exercise of power.[55] We need to turn to the Roman world for a view of voluntary exile as a means of escape for the powerful from political retribution by powerful opponents, and for the continued use of enforced exile as a political tool.

2.2.2 Exile in the Roman world

In Chapter 1 we noted the paradigmatic status accorded Regulus, hero of the First Punic war, who chose to return voluntarily to Carthage as a prisoner of war after urging the Romans to continue hostilities. He had been sent by the Carthaginians to sue for peace and had agreed to return if his mission remained unaccomplished. Regulus' exile features extensively in Roman literature.[56] Silius Italicus, in his epic on the Second Punic War, used the Vergilian narrative technique of historic encapsulation ('flash back') in order to give pride of place to the Roman hero from the

2. The Third Person: Exilic Narrative

First Punic War. The episode begins at *Punica* 6.117, after the battle of Lake Trasimene. Serranus, the son of Regulus, encounters a former companion of his father, who graphically describes the events leading up to Regulus' slow death (545). Half the passage (vv. 140-285) is devoted to a suitably epic encounter with a monstrous snake (also featured in Livy's eighteenth book, as reported in the *Periocha*). Silius' depiction of the onslaught of the gigantic reptile evokes Vergil, particularly *Aeneid* 2. The soldier's narrative of the battle of Bagrada against the Spartan Xanthippus is predictably heroic, with Regulus triumphant in the midst of battle (302-38). Only a perfidious simulated retreat, reminiscent of Hannibal's later strategy at Cannae, can daunt the hero (327-36). Regulus is captured and later sent with a Carthaginian contingent to parley for peace.

Capture in war would result in automatic loss of Roman citizenship, or *capitis deminutio* (literally 'diminishment of his head', better translated as 'reduction to minor status'). Regulus is fully aware of his loss of civic status. Even in Rome, he continues to act like an exile; ignoring the pleas of the senate and his family, he keeps to the quarters allocated to the Punic embassy, retains Carthaginian dress (389-409), and prevents the Roman consul from being polluted by the touch of his own disgraced hand (399-400). His aspect and mien are more than human; the poet is hard put in his narrative to reconcile his depiction of the nobility of his hero's carriage with the Roman convention that an exile or the condemned would be attired in mourning garb. Again Vergil is invoked. The resultant picture portrays a 'Charon' ennobled by his very squalor:

> *humana maior species erat; horrida cano*
> *vertice descendens ingentia colla tegebat*
> *caesaries, frontique coma squalente sedebat*
> *terribilis decor atque animi venerabile pondus*   (*Pun.* 6.426-9)

His appearance was greater than human: tousled grey hair hanging down from his white crown covered his tremendous neck and a fringe stuck to his dirt-encrusted forehead as a frightful indication, suited to the venerable gravity of his intention.[57]

The author contrasts the hero's degraded exterior with the gravity of his purposeful decision. Focus is on outer appearance as opposing symbol of inner nobility. Silius is portraying the ideal Stoic sage, ennobled by the ultimate trial of his fortitude.[58] Earlier than Silius, Horace (*Carm.* 3.5.13-56) chose to emphasise the steadfastness and nobility of Regulus' decision, rather than his physical appearance. Here focus is on outer action as symbol of inner intention. The exile leaves voluntarily, deliberately aware of the fact of his *deminutio capitis*:

Displaced Persons

Fertur pudicae coniugis osculum
parvosque notos ut capitis minor
  ab se removisse et virilem
    torvus humi posuisse voltum
donec labantes consilio patres
firmaret auctor numquam alias dato
  interque maerentes amicos
    egregius properaret exsul.   (*Carm.* 3.5.41-52)

It is said that he rejected the kiss of his chaste wife and the children so well
known to him, as one who had lost his civic status, and that he turned aside
his face, looking at the ground, until he, as instigator of the plan that never
else would have been given, could strengthen the resolve of the hesitant city
fathers, until he could hurry away from amongst his mourning friends, an
exile not from the common herd.

The Punic antagonist, virtual hero of the *Punica*, Hannibal himself, was
also finally an exile at the court of Prusias of Bithynia.[59] His exile, too, soon
became an heroic prototype for the literary treatment of exile, as in
Juvenal's famous exposition, *Sat.* 10.147-67. Measured on a scale, the
satirist asks, what would Hannibal be worth? – *Expende Hannibalem: quot
libras in duce summo invenies?* (Weigh Hannibal: how many pounds would
you find in the greatest of leaders?). The implication is that the hero is
negligible. Emphasis is on the powerlessness of the once-powerful:

> *exitus ergo quis est? o gloria! vincitur idem*
> *nempe et in exilium praeceps fugit atque ibi magnus*
> *mirandusque cliens sedet ad praetoria regis,*
> *donec Bithyno libeat vigilare tyranno.*

What is his end? O glory! Even he is undoubtedly vanquished and flees
headlong into exile, and there, as a great and remarkable suppliant, he sits
at the door of the king's palace, until it should please the Bithynian king to
get up in the morning.

The century preceding Actium produced many noble Roman exiles.
Losers in a series of continuing power struggles frequently resorted to
temporary or permanent settlement in the provinces, more often than not
in the East, particularly Rhodes and Mytilene.[60] Opimius, the Consul of
122 BC, acquitted after the death of Gaius Gracchus, was nevertheless
condemned, some ten years later, for intriguing with Jugurtha.[61] He died
in exile at Dyrrachium, the place from which Cicero later was to send his
most abject pleas, and whence he finally returned in triumph. Opimius'
contemporary Metellus Numidicus, frequently cited by Cicero, went into
voluntary exile to Rhodes rather than acquiesce in the agrarian reforms of
Appuleius Saturninus and Glaucia.[62]

Often such retreat was unconstitutional. The flight into exile and
triumphant return of Marius, only to end in premature death during his

seventh consulate, became a frequently-exploited literary topic.[63] Cicero celebrated the popular hero in a youthful epic poem of which fragments survive.[64] The virtuous Rutilius Rufus, exiled after 88 BC, was the first Roman exile to devote the involuntary *otium* ('leisure to dally in studies') resulting from enforced retreat from public life both to philosophic writing and to self-exoneration, while composing a contemporary Roman history. The accusation against Rutilius was, once more, intrigue with the enemies of Rome. As we have noted above, unhelpfully brief fragments of his apology survive, of which none appears to refer to his exile.[65]

Exiled nobles, such as L. Aemilius Paullus,[66] sometimes preferred the intellectual life of Greece and chose to remain even after a turn of the political tide in their favour. Similarly, Cicero's correspondent T. Pomponius Atticus was a voluntary exile, but for intellectual rather than political reasons.[67] Exile by no means always diminished politicians' power. The consular Memmius, Lucretius' patron, accused of bribery (54 BC), went into exile to Athens, where he acquired a dilapidated house, reputed once to have belonged to Epicurus. The Epicureans turned to Cicero, who in July 51 BC wrote a polite appeal to Memmius, recommending that the great man reconsider his apparently high-handed decision to demolish the building. The appeal is a model of circumspect deference to palpable power. Cicero is careful to state that he is in accord with the Epicurean Patro, head of the sect, in all except doctrine.[68] This letter highlights the problems of correspondence with an exile: a matter that could quite easily have been cleared up in conversation has to be treated with great circumspection in its written form. This also explains the efficacy of exile as a political tool. Where Roman civic life depended hugely on personal contact, as in the daily *salutationes* (morning visits by clients who would then accompany a great man to the Forum) loss of daily intercourse and visual contact meant loss of a vital aspect of political power.

Memmius in exile is twice more the object of Ciceronian intervention. During 50 BC he is asked to allow the artist C. Avianus Evander to continue working as sculptor in a shrine dedicated to the Memmian family (*Fam.* 13.2), and in the next letter, Cicero recommends a certain A. Fufius to Memmius' attention. Here is a clear case of displacement of power to a new sphere, rather than real curtailment of power. Memmius has apparently acquired a new set of power lines in Athens, probably more pecuniary than political.

Exile did not always bring freedom from political pressure. Cicero's *Pro Flacco* defends the young Flaccus, prosecuted by Laelius. Laelius' *subscriptor* (second signatory to the document of accusation) was the young Appuleius, a graecised Roman, whose father, C. Appuleius Decianus, had been living in exile for the past thirty years, and who had formerly prosecuted Flaccus' father. In the tradition of *ad hominem* argument, Cicero exploits this ancient quarrel and portrays the Appuleii as decadent

Romano-Greeks who oppressed all decent Greeks in Asia by means of underhand business dealings.[69]

A sad case of exile, with an unhappy ending, is that of the noble Marcellus, a political opponent of Julius Caesar, who betook himself to voluntary exile on that haven for Roman political refugees, Mytilene on the island of Lesbos.[70] In letter after letter Cicero urged Marcellus to return, pardon having been granted him by the dictator. It is for this pardon that Cicero thanks Caesar profusely in the *Pro Marcello*. However, before Marcellus reaches Rome, he is embroiled in an argument with P. Magius Cilo. Servius Sulpicius, writing from Athens, has the sad task of telling Cicero about the death of his friend, as the victim of a sordid quarrel about money.[71] Chapter 3 will return to the fate of Marcellus.

2.2.3 Cicero in exile: two narratives

The most thoroughly documented case of exile in the ancient world was that of Cicero.[72] For third-person narrative of the event, we turn to Dio Cassius (47.8.3-4, 11.1-2) and Plutarch (*Cic.* 48-9). Differences in narrative mode between the two authors result partly from the different ancient generic traditions within each was writing, Dio as historiographer and Plutarch as moralistic biographer. In the ancient generic tradition both would have been concerned with adding rhetorical colour of some kind, what moderns would perhaps term 'fictionalising' of historical fact.[73] Each manipulates the basic story line into a 'plot', the details of which receive differing emphases or focalisation. The two authors' differing narrative strategies therefore merit comparison. In what follows particular attention will be paid to 'narrative time', the device whereby emphasis is modulated by alternately speeding up and slowing down of narration of consecutive events.

Both our authors wrote considerably later than the events they narrate, and it is generally thought that Cicero's letters may have been Dio's major source.[74] Plutarch in particular inclines to relay gossip as if it were fact, nor does he always have his facts straight, tending even to misquote matters verifiable from the *Letters*.[75] Plutarch's interest lies in character as source of action and reaction. His narrative techniques have much in common with the modern cinematic techniques of 'slow motion' and 'zooming'. His narrative framework sets the scene with a rapid review of a series of Cicero's verbal gibes aimed at political opponents, such as his calling Marcus Aquinius (whose two sons-in-law had been exiled) 'Adrastus', after the mythical king of Argos who gave his two daughters in marriage to Tydeus and Polyneices, both exiles from their native cities (Plut. *Cic.* 27.2). Plutarch sees Cicero's misplaced sense of humour as the major reason for the tide of public opinion turning against him, and follows (28) with the racy story of Clodius' intrusion on the secret rites of the *Bona Dea* held at

Caesar's house, clearly an abridged version of Cicero's equally racy account in *Att.* 1.13.3 of Clodius' attempt on the virtue of Caesar's wife.

Plutarch's next paragraph begins with the statement that 'Cicero was a friend of Clodius whom he had found most helpful and protective during the Catilinarian affair' of 63 BC. This relationship was soured, says Plutarch, by the fact that Cicero's evidence broke Clodius' alibi when he was charged with sacrilege. Here Plutarch ascribes to Cicero an uxorious acquiescence in the wishes of his wife Terentia, who, he says, was jealous of Cicero's relationship with Clodius' sister. More than a page in the Loeb edition is then devoted to gossip about the siblings and another page to further aspects of Cicero's acerbic humour (29), after which follows in less than a page a rapid review of the laws whereby Clodius won the favour of both people and Senate, his manipulation of Caesar and Cicero into mutual mistrust, and of Caesar into concurring in a general condemnation of Cicero's decisive part, some four years earlier, in the death in the Catilinarians.

Several years' activities are condensed into the compass of a few lines, narrative space thereby working to speed up the reader's perception of the passage of real time. All this reads most persuasively, until one compares Plutarch's version with the fairly complete collection of Cicero's letters of the era, which, in their day-by-day reflection of his reaction to changing events, give a different picture of the deeds of the various protagonists, and his own emotions and reactions.[76] For example, Plutarch claims (30.2-3) that Cicero insinuated himself into Caesar's favour in order to get an invitation to accompany him to Gaul in 59, after which Clodius tricked him by first allaying his fears by blaming Terentia for their rift, and that Clodius then made his move (when Cicero felt so much at ease that he annoyed Caesar by declining the invitation, 30.4), openly leading those that taunted Cicero when he appeared as suppliant. Cicero's letter to Atticus (2.18.3), reporting Caesar's offer, shows none of these nuances, but indicates Cicero's uncertainty about whether to accept an invitation apparently voluntarily extended to him by Caesar.

So much for Plutarch's narration of events. Dio's history shows equally interesting use of various narrative strategies, in particular both abbreviation and extension of narrative space to convey either a quick passage of time, or, conversely, slow emphasis. The *Bona Dea* affair is condensed into two sentences, erroneously turning attempted seduction into fact, for the moment ignoring Cicero's role in destroying the perpetrator's alibi (Dio 37.45.1, 2), but stressing Caesar's refusal to prosecute the reputed adulterer. Clodius' trial and acquittal merit half a page in the Loeb edition, with oblique reference (37.46.1-3) to the gossip about his reputed incestuous relationship with his sisters (embroidered more fully by Plutarch, *Cic.* 29.3-4). As Dio is writing a 'History of Rome' and not a biography, he expends the rest of Book 37 and the beginning of the next book, about twenty-one Loeb pages in all, on the actions of the major political and military players of the era, including the political and financial arrangement between Caesar, Pompey and Crassus that became known as the First Triumvirate. The major focus is on Caesar, but when Cicero re-enters the narrative (at 38.9.2), almost a page (paragraphs 9.2 to 10.1) is expended on discussing the rumour that Cicero and Lucullus had plotted to kill Caesar and Pompey, for which there is no evidence in Cicero's letters. It may be argued that Cicero would not have been likely to have revealed such a plan, had it existed, to Atticus, but, again, the tone of his letters of the era indicates none of this.

Dio next gives as the major reason for the triumvirs' animosity towards Cicero his defence of his former consular colleague Antonius against a charge of complicity in the Catilinarian plot, in which defence he launched a personal attack on Caesar. Almost a page (38.11) is expended on an analysis of Caesar's devious thought processes, and the way in which he would take revenge in a manner that would enhance his reputation for clemency. Two paragraphs (12, 13) are then devoted to a secret appeal to Clodius by Caesar, on the grounds that formerly, when offered the opportunity, he, Caesar, had not accused Clodius of adultery. Caesar now wanted aid in getting his revenge on Cicero, and the author then recounts the manner in which Clodius carried this out. No mention is made of personal animosity between Clodius and Cicero.

Now Dio seems to be using Plutarch as his main source. He trots out the claim that Cicero antagonised many by his acerbic wit (without citing examples). Clodius was gaining in popularity by means of the laws he promulgated, instituting a corn dole (corn had formerly been heavily subsidised), reviving the right of association in *collegia* and safeguarding freedom from arbitrary censure for all the orders. These three issues are dealt with in a sentence, but the next issue merits four sentences, comprising almost a page in the Loeb edition.[77] Caesar during his consulship enacted laws by himself, ignoring the feeble attempts of his colleague Bibulus to stop these by his almost daily claims that the auguries were unfavourable. Dio does not mention this fact, but explains that no popular voting could be done if the sky-divination was unfavourable. This measure Clodius circumvented by enacting the rule that omens were not to be taken from the sky on days when the people were about to vote on any public measure. Dio construes this as pre-emption of a possible strategy by Cicero, if faced by prosecution, to prevent his being brought to public trial. It could more happily be seen as an attempt to prevent a recurrence of the kind of arbitrary enactment indulged in by Caesar.

Dio's following chapter relates a further aspect of Clodian trickery – he avers that Clodius next struck a bargain with Cicero, promising that he would not indict him, in exchange for tacit support of his measures (14.2), after which Clodius enacted the general law interdicting from water and fire all those who had put citizens to death without the condemnation of the people. This law did not name Cicero, but the consular was suitably anxious, and, at first merely putting off his senatorial toga, went about seeking advice. Paragraphs 14 and 15 give the impression that Caesar and Pompey were in collusion, giving conflicting advice in order to get Cicero to destroy himself, Caesar then suggesting the judicious retreat to Gaul, and Pompey urging him to stay and fight it out. Little of this emerges from correspondence of the time.

Dio's chronology is clearly suspect, and his assigning of motives open to criticism. Cicero's anticipation of a successful rebuttal of the insinuations against him is carefully drawn, and the action slows in Paragraph 16 to describe the deeds and recount the individual opinions of all the major role players, so that the reader gains an impression of a slow movement over several months, from Clodius' first promulgation of the law (14.4) toward a great denouement, the coming into effect of the law (17.5), quickly followed by Cicero's precipitate departure. Three sentences rapidly sketch the confiscation of his property, the razing of his house and the passing of the personal decree against him (17.6-7). The author's use of alternately slowed and accelerated narrative time is the most obvious device that Dio uses to portray the uncertainties of the era. Focus is almost exclusively on Clodius and his machinations, Cicero, Caesar and Pompey all together appearing as only minor players.

Cicero's recall is related in a few sentences (30.1-3) and Dio ascribes this recall wholly to a falling-out between Pompey and Clodius. The twelve intervening chapters are devoted to an interesting imaginary conversation between Cicero and a philosopher, which leans much more heavily on literary tradition than on historical fact. This retarding narrative device works as the literary predecessor of a film close-up, but the focus is more on the imaginary interlocutor than on the supposedly major protagonist. As the representation of a conversation, however, it does not form part of the third person *corpus* under present discussion, and it will be treated at length in Chapter 3.

2.2.4 Exile under Augustus: Tiberius, Julia's lovers, and the poet Ovid

There soon followed more years of strife. Pompey died in Egypt, a fugitive from his erstwhile friend, the now all-powerful Caesar. After the death of Caesar, judicious retreat to their provinces by Brutus and Cassius took them from the hub of danger. Antony's virtual enslavement in the toils of the Egyptian queen was construed by the young Octavian as a voluntary retreat that admirably suited his increasingly powerful opponent. He exploited Antony's withdrawal to the East for his own ends. Antony played into Octavian's hands by virtually repudiating his wife, Octavian's sister (Plut. *Ant.* 53.1). Her journey to the East with supplies and gifts and a hand-picked band of two thousand men to help her husband aroused her rival's jealousy, so Plutarch says, and led to her being sent back. This offered her brother an excuse to open active hostilities. After Actium, a period of relative calm descended on the empire and Octavian, as Augustus, wielded power almost alone.

Subsequently, Augustus' lieutenant Agrippa and his stepson Tiberius in turn retreated into apparently voluntary exile. Agrippa's journey to the East in 23, after Augustus' recovery from fever and the return of the seal he had entrusted to his friend, has been construed as self-imposed exile, the result of Agrippa's pique at the favouring of the young Marcellus, Augustus' nephew and son-in-law. It is true that Agrippa stayed at Mytilene, a favourite haunt of political exiles, until after the death of Marcellus. Agrippa's return to favour and marriage to Augustus' daughter Julia ended only with his death, after which Augustus arranged for her to marry Tiberius, the elder son of his wife Livia.

We hear of few exiles under Augustus, until the commencement of Tiberius' first self-imposed exile, to the island of Rhodes. Syme (1974) surmises it was prompted by anger at Augustus' too-rapid promotion of the two sons of Agrippa and Julia, whom he had adopted. Augustus had then to depend upon others to command his legions until the boys became suitably of age. These others were men of Ovid's age group, among them the P. Quinctilius Varus (*consul* 13 BC) who lost the legions after a German ambush in the Teutoberger Woods in AD 9, Paullus Fabius Maximus (*consul* 11 BC), Ovid's patron and friend, and Julia's lover Iullus Antonius (*consul* 10 BC), and others, later involved in the conspiracy of the elder Julia.[78] Julia was exiled in 2 BC 'for flagrant immorality', perhaps for an otherwise covered-up political plot against her father, and her lovers, reputed or real, were put to death or forced into exile for conspiracy, *maiestas*.[79]

On 5 February, 2 BC the emperor was accorded the title *pater patriae* (father of the fatherland), on the proposal of Messalla Corvinus, Ovid's literary patron, who under show of Republican independence acquiesced in the new order, hailing Augustus as the saviour of the state. The years 2 BC to AD 8 saw many changes, among others Tiberius' return from exile in 4, the final reorganisation of Augustus' dynastic arrangements and of his relationship with the Senate. The exile of various personages near to the Imperial throne followed: in 8 the younger Julia shared her mother's fate, and her presumed lover Silanus was allowed to go into voluntary exile. The coincidence of sexual and political misdemeanours, an accusation of the former acting as a cover-up for the latter, thrived in the dangerous atmosphere of the Imperial Palace.[80]

A curious set of coincidences links Ovid and the exiled members of Augustus' family: first, the publication of Ovid's major amorous works coincided with or came soon after the disgrace of the elder Julia; his relegation to Tomis came after the disgrace of her daughter. The political interpretation of Ovid's exile stems from this, although it was never explicitly connected with it by the poet himself, except in vague hints.

Opinion is divided on the relationship between sex and politics in the affair.[81]

With Ovid, the tenor of his creative life caused his downfall. In the general imperial euphoria the misdemeanours of both Juliae had struck a wrong note, and so had the publication of Ovid's flippantly erotic works. His exile cannot be interpreted as pre-emptive in a potential power-struggle, nor was he the inadvertent prey of power-hungry contenders.[82] Ovid's exile marks the beginning of a new phase in the story of exile: the wielding of literary power, and attempts at its suppression.

2.2.5 Ovid at Tomis

The poet is our major source on the details of his life: Publius Ovidius Naso was born in 43 BC in the Paelignian town of Sulmo. The young Ovid, sent to Rome for his education, soon rejected all aspiration to public office, and devoted himself to poetry.

Ovid's autobiographical poem, *Tristia* 4.10, is an unusual document in that it gives far more personal details than customary in autobiographical narrative. As its verbs are mainly in the first person, it does not warrant full discussion here, but the lines on his initiation into a public career and his manner of composition are worth noting. He recounts almost impersonally, as if talking about someone else:

> *Curia restabat: clavi mensura coacta est;*
> *maius erat nostris viribus illud onus.*
> *nec patiens corpus, nec mens fuit apta labori,*
> *sollictae fugax ambitionis eram,*
> *et petere Aoniae suadebant tuta sorores*
> *otia, iudicio semper amata meo.*   (*Tr.* 4.10.35-40)

Only the Senate was left: the broad stripe (on my toga) became narrow; but that burden was too great for my powers. My body couldn't stand it; my mind wasn't suited to the job; I was becoming a refugee from worrisome ambition, and the Muses (lit. Aeonian sisters) were urging me to seek the safe haven of dalliance in studies, my favourite occupation, always suited to my taste.

In this passage only three words refer directly to the writer – *nostris, meo* and *eram. Nostris* is the poetic plural equivalent of *meo* (my). The only volition the young Ovid displayed in public office was to initiate flight – the imperfect *eram* can most readily be interpreted as inchoative, 'I was becoming' *fugax* (a refugee). For the rest, the narrative is strangely impersonal. Strategic placement gives emphasis to key terms and word-order supports meaning. Public office loomed over the young man, and it was an intolerable burden. *Curia* (the senate house) stands menacingly at the head of the first couplet, which ends with *onus* (burden). *Chiastic hyperbaton* (splitting of a phrase) separates the comparative *maius*, 'too great', from *onus*, framing *nostris viribus* (my powers) thereby giving a visual impression of the unwilling young man threatened on either side by the burdens of office, indicated only by the impersonal report that the striped garment of his youth had been supplanted by the white toga of a senator. Even his turning to poetry was less a matter of choice than of grateful acceptance of coercion; the Muses were forcefully persuading him to turn toward the leisure afforded by study.

This passage confirms the impression in an earlier couplet. He had tried, the poet says, to write in prose, but:

> *Sponte sua carmen numeros veniebat ad aptos*
> *et quod temptabam dicere versus erat*   (*Tr.* 4.10.25-6)

By itself the song kept coming out in a suitable metre, and what I tried to *say*, became a verse.

Here the imperfect *veniebat* seems best translated as iterative, 'kept coming'. It is significant, however, that the poet does not show his youthful self as working over-hard at his prosaic efforts, for the subject here is *carmen* (a song). The poet was a helpless victim in the grasp of metre, trying to 'say (*dicere*) a song out loud'. No wonder it became a verse. It never was anything else. That is the joke of all verse narrative, delicately pointed in this case, by the reportage, also in verse, of his father's condemnation of such activity:

> *Saepe pater dixit 'studium quid inutile temptas?*
> *Maeonides nullas ipse reliquit opes'.*   (*Tr.* 4.10.21-2)

My father often said 'Why do you try such useless studies? Even Homer himself did not leave any wealth'.

The joke hinges on the reader's appreciation of the repetition of **dic* (say), the smooth metrics of the couplet (his father is also 'saying in verse') and the reader's evaluation of what constitutes riches. We are led to deduce that Homer's literary legacy was 'wealth' of a superior kind – also in the eyes of an emperor that encouraged epic in celebration of his own regime.

Ovid began composing seriously at about 25 BC,[83] and produced five books of elegiacs, the *Amores*. Around 16 BC the poet produced the *Epistolae Heroidum*, a book of romantic elegy entirely new in concept and execution: fifteen verse epistles purporting to be from heroines of myth to the men who had abandoned them. These dramatic monologues are remarkable for their psychological delineation and their kaleidoscopic handling of time and space – as we noted in discussion of Ovid's treatment of the Medea-myth. Psychological alienation is portrayed as stemming from physical displacement. The heroines' graphic narrative of past action and prophetic 'vision' of future events encapsulate time, overcoming the static nature of monologue. Distance is bridged by each heroine's visionary conceptualisation of her beloved's peregrinations.

A three-book edition of the *Amores* was published in about 2 BC, followed in AD 2 by the *Ars Amatoria*, which purported to teach 'what everybody knows': the art of dalliance. The *Remedia Amoris* was no attempt at restoring morals presumably led astray by the *Ars Amatoria*, but a humorous palinode. Apparently almost concurrently the poet had embarked on the *Metamorphoses*, the fifteen books of pseudo-epic, which had myth as topic and physical change as connecting theme, starting with the creation of the universe and ending with the apotheosis of Julius Caesar and a prophecy of a similar celestial future for Augustus. Its last lines triumphantly assert the power of poetry to confer immortality on the poet, and defiantly challenge Envy, *Livor edax*.[84]

At some time during AD 8 or 9, the decree of relegation fell on the popular poet, then engaged in 'national' elegy. The *Fasti* purported to have been a reworking of the whole Roman religious calendar, in twelve books, a book per month. Only January to June have survived, or were ever completed.[85] The poet did not abandon this work when he left Rome, although he says that he attempted to burn the 'incomplete' *Metamorphoses*. Both these works show signs of reworking during his exile.

No other contemporary sources refer to Ovid's exile. We have only the evidence of his exilic poetry. He gives two reasons for his punishment: *carmen* and *error* (a song and a mistake). *Carmen* has generally, following the poet's own interpretation in, for example, *Tr.* 2.239-50, been taken to refer to the *Ars Amatoria* (and possibly the *Remedia*) whose flippancy and generally amoral tone violated all that Augustus had envisaged with his programme of cultural uplift and the promulgation of the *lex de adulteriis coercendis* (law pertaining to the limitation of adultery) and the *lex Julia de maritandis ordinibus* (law about the obligation resting on members of the various orders to marry). These had come into effect by 17 BC, making adultery a civil offence, and were intended to encourage marriage and family life. Instead of advocating marriage and the advantages of setting up a conjugal establishment, Ovid's amatory works gave a cold-blooded and racy view of the kind of *otium* (leisure for dalliance – in love as well as in books) enjoyed by the fashionable Roman world. That it was possibly near the truth about contemporary society probably added to its unpopularity with the ageing emperor.[86] The ostensible reason for his punishment, reported by the poet as having been advanced by Augustus, was the 'immoral tone' of these works. The discrepancy in time between their publication and the poet's relegation appears inexplicable.[87] It is generally assumed that the *error* was political and that Augustus would not have wasted the full weight of his displeasure on so frivolous an offence as irreverent poetry.

Ovid was sent to Tomis, so he tells us. Ancient Tomis is usually identified as Constanza, a Greek city situated about 60 km from the mouth of the Ister, or Danube.[88] Here the most urban of Roman poets spent his last ten years. And here he must have died in about AD 17. There is no contemporary record. The earliest allusion, other than the poet's own exilic works, to both the fact and place of banishment, is in Pliny the Elder, *Nat. Hist.* 32.152, referring to the *Halieutica*, ascribed to Ovid, as follows: *his adiciemus ab Ovidio posita animalia, quae apud neminem alium reperiuntur, sed fortassis in Ponto nascentia, ubi id volumen supremis suis temporibus inchoavit* ... (to these we add the animals listed by Ovid, which are found in no other author, but appearing by chance in the Black Sea, where he began this book at the end of his life ...). Pliny does not name Tomis but speaks in general terms of the area.[89] Tacitus makes no mention of the poet's death, nor does the younger Seneca, who was the brother of the adopted son of one of Ovid's ostensible correspondents, Junius Gallio, and who otherwise quotes Ovid frequently, and was himself exiled. This silence has sparked off much controversy.[90] Jerome, *Chronica*, Olymp., 184, 199, dates Ovid's death and burial at Tomis to AD 17.[91]

2.2.6 Tiberius on Capri

Tiberius' second period of self-imposed exile, from AD 27 until his death, appears as inexplicable as the exile of Ovid. His is a case of voluntary retreat by a supremely powerful man, to a not-so-remote island, whence his power, perhaps unwillingly undertaken, was wielded as efficiently as at the hub of empire.[92] Tiberius' historically well-documented sojourn on Capri merits and has received detailed study elsewhere. There is, however, no excursive autobiographical material from which to draw a fully rounded picture. Most of his letters from Capri, as for instance reported by Tacitus (*Ann.* 4.69-70), were impersonal indictments.[93] Both Tiberius' reasons for retreat and his emotions in seclusion (which may perhaps have greatly differed from the morose brooding traditionally ascribed to him) can only give rise to vague conjectures. From Capri came instructions such as his famous repudiation of Seianus in a *verbosa et grandis epistula* (wordy and influential letter, Juv. *Sat.* 10.72) and at Capri he held one of his heirs, his dead brother's grandson, Gaius, virtual prisoner, refusing to choose between him and his own grandson, Tiberius Gemellus. It was left to the Senate, instigated thereto by the praetorian prefect Macro, to elect Gaius emperor. Gaius had won Macro's favour at Capri, so that in the end his enforced seclusion had stood the younger man in good stead.

2.2.7 Seneca the younger on Corsica

Seneca managed to survive the bloodthirsty years of Gaius' imperial rule,[94] when many fled the absolute power wielded by an emperor who acted like a corrupt and apparently demented despot, but soon after Claudius' generally benign succession, the philosopher succumbed, probably as a result of the intriguing of another powerful figure, the empress Messalina. For the details of Seneca's exile we have the evidence of his own *consolationes*,[95] and the narrative of various historians.[96] Seneca appears to have been exiled in AD 41, the first year of Claudius' rule, and recalled in 49, after the marriage of Claudius and Agrippina. The details of Seneca's life before exile emerge from passing allusions in his works. He had been married, and probably widowed, before exile, and was the father of two, perhaps three, children, one of whom had died in the arms of its grandmother Helvia some three weeks before its father was exiled, and ten days after the accession of Claudius.[97]

Seneca was accused of an adulterous relationship with the young Julia Livilla, niece of the emperor. Apparently the senate condemned him to death, but the emperor changed the sentence to *deportatio* under military guard to the island of Corsica (*Dial.* 11.15.2). This was a more severe form of banishment than the relegation imposed on Ovid. Seneca's political career was effectively ended, but he departed for Corsica with Stoic fortitude. After the deaths of the two imperial princesses, the charge was changed to *incerto crimine*, technically an indication of a 'not proven' judgement.

Parallels with Ovid's situation indicate the possibility of political intrigue, but there is little to go on. That an apparently recently bereaved widower and father would seek comfort in the arms of a politically dangerous princess seems dubious, but not inconceivable. Sexual misdemeanours frequently offered a cloak for more serious political errors which it did not suit the imperial accusers to reveal, but with Seneca nothing can be proved. Judging from the possibly peripheral involvement of the philosopher in the Pisonian conspiracy, Seneca's penchant for political intrigue was apparently not strong, and at this stage of his career, unlikely. Seneca's consistent consciousness of innocence, whatever the charge, may indicate the possibility of deliberate 'framing' by an opponent.[98]

Meinel (1972) argues for personal animosity against Seneca on the part of Messalina, and the charge, involving the philosopher and the princess, as a golden opportunity to incapacitate both a rival and a personal enemy.[99] Dio Cassius (60.8.5) shows the princess as the principal victim, and Seneca as almost casually embroiled.

The picture of the philosopher that emerges from Tacitus' *Annales* is well-rounded, but subtle; some have considered it incomplete.[100] On the possible reasons for Seneca's exile, Tacitus is silent. We have only a brief allusion: after the marriage of Claudius to Agrippina, the latter recalled Seneca and had him appointed to a praetorship, judging that his literary reputation would ensure her popularity, and planning to use him as a tutor for her son Lucius Domitius Ahenobarbus. Seneca was believed to be devoted to her, and could be counted upon to bear a grudge against Claudius for having been exiled by him (*Ann.* 12.8). Dio also fixes upon Seneca's reputed 'devotion' to Agrippina, which he construes as a full-blown affair (Dio 54-58). That there was animosity toward Claudius and that it must have rankled in the mind of the philosopher is borne out by the existence of the *Apocolocyntosis*, which can safely be imputed to Seneca. The gauche panegyric on the deceased emperor, written by Seneca and delivered by Nero before an amused Senate, is evidence, probably, not of ineptitude, but of calculated irony on the part of its author.[101] This evidence prompts critics to find less than full candour in the exile's fulsome references to Claudius in the exilic *consolatio* addressed to his secretary *ad libellis*.[102]

Dio's portrait of Seneca is fraught with inconsistencies. Occasional aphoristic comment does less than justice to the complexities of Seneca's situation in the imperial periphery. The picture that emerges is of a dullard who 'neither learnt from the Julia episode, nor from his period of exile, and foolishly did not fear the redoubtable Agrippina'.[103] Inconsistencies may be ascribed to the scope and method of composition of Dio's monumental work, use of sometimes inconsistent sources, his annalistic approach and his concomitant inability to draw wide-ranging conclusions, moving as he does from notable episode to notable episode, in which the exigencies of sustained narrative are the major criterion.[104] Dio's comments on the 'craven attitude' of Seneca before Messalina, and before Claudius' freedman, 'about whom he wrote a book', apparently refer to the *Consolatio ad Polybium*. As Seneca is nowhere in any of his writings explicit about the reasons for his exile, the ancient historian had no more to go on than the modern researcher.

The *Consolatio ad Polybium* probably dates from the first months of exile, and the *Consolatio ad Helviam* from soon after, within the first ten months of exile. Seneca apparently had a good library on the island, and devoted himself to study, also apparently undertaking some *leviora studia*, the 'anonymous' poetry which by subject matter can be connected to him, perhaps also discussion of poetics.[105] His literary reputation was unimpaired by his exile. This was perhaps the main reason for Agrippina's choice of the philosopher as mentor to her son. The rest of Seneca's career is not of concern here, although his retirement from court life after his fall from grace may be construed as a form of semi-voluntary exile.

2.2.8 The Stoics of the first century AD

We have seen displacement as essentially a political act. Few in Republican Rome were persecuted for their beliefs. Yet practitioners of strange cults were on occasion removed from Rome. The most famous episode was the banning in 186 BC, by official *senatus consultum*, of the Bacchic cult, recounted in Livy 39.8ff., and commemorated on an inscription (*CIL* 1² 581), after the revelation of their apparently unsavoury practices by a young courtesan who was accorded citizen status as a reward for her efforts.[106] Rawson (1985: 316) considers that the banishment from Rome in 139 BC of 'Chaldaei' was typical of Roman conservative reaction to foreign cults, and is not evidence of their power or potential power in the state.[107] Their occult art was seen as a threat to the *mores maiorum*. Cato Maior did not want even his bailiff to be familiar with them. At various stages Jews were regarded as a potential source of trouble, and were banished. Under Claudius there was a general exodus. The missionary Paul at Corinth enjoyed the hospitality of Aquila and Priscilla, a Jewish couple exiled from Rome under Claudius (*Acts* 18.2). The couple accompanied him to Ephesus (*ibid.* 26), apparently later returning to Rome, as may be deduced from the subsequent inclusion of their names in a greeting to believers in Rome (*Romans* 16.3). Later they again feature in the missionary's letter from Rome to his young assistant (2 *Tim.* 4.19). Their mobility may perhaps be ascribed to the exigencies of commerce in the pursuit of their trade as tent makers, rather than to continued persecution.[108]

In the first, settled years of Flavian rule, it could have been expected that displacement would no longer be a factor. Yet in the second half of the first century AD, under the apparently benign Vespasian no less than under his more problematic son Domitian, the republican ideal appears to have been fostered particularly by the adherents of Stoicism, which coloured their opposition to the powerful. This seems to have led to suspicions against the Hellenistic teachers of prominent Roman Stoics.[109] Their 'power' was the ephemeral 'power' of potential thought control, but as such, it was frequently curbed by the imposition of exile. Sometimes the emperors could hardly help themselves; opposition, however tenuous, had to be deflected. Such action turned the emperors into paradigms of oppression.[110] Under Vespasian, Rubellius Plautus and his mentor Musonius Rufus were both exiled. Musonius, who had previously been banished and had returned, retreated to the island of Gyaros.[111] His pupil Epictetus of Hierapolis was deported from Rome to Nicopolis in 89, relegated when Domitian banished all philosophers. There he established a school.[112]

The development of a didactic genre of 'memorial' or 'tyrannicide' literature, commemorative pamphlets, and even the minutes of trials, offered intellectual fare to the opposition, and a basis for imperial action. Even voluntary retreat was construed as criticism, on the argument that 'he who flees, condemns'.

Two letters of Pliny the Younger, referring to the women married or born into the house of the Paeti, offer a brief narrative showing the influence of Stoic teaching about freedom. Arria, married to Caecina Paetus, became famous for taking the initiative in their double suicide under Claudius, first stabbing herself and then handing the dagger to her husband with the words *Non dolet, Paete!* (it doesn't hurt, Paetus). In *Ep.* 3.16 Pliny narrates various incidences of Arria's bravery, including her following (in a small fishing smack) the ship in which her husband was being taken captive to Rome after his participation in the Illyrian rebellion of Scribonianus. This was a case of a wife returning with her exiled husband to captivity in Rome. Pliny recounts her scathing repudiation of the wife of Scribonianus, who had turned evidence against him. Their daughter, also an Arria, chose not to die with her husband Thrasea Paetus, for the sake of her little daughter Fannia (Tac. *Ann.* 14.34.2) but was banished under Domitian (Tac. *Agr.* 45.1), returning under Nerva. Her daughter Fannia exhibited a similarly independent feminine spirit, which, Pliny somewhat uncomfortably acknowledges, was nobler than the subservience of the masculine elite of the time.

There is a discernible series of linkages between the philosopher-exiles of the first century AD; Musonius Rufus was the mentor not only of Rubellius Plautus, but also of Thrasea Paetus, Borea Soranus, the younger Seneca, Euphrates of Tyre, Epictetus, Dio Chrysostomus and his own son-in-law Artemidorus.[113] Artemidorus was removed to the Roman suburbs. One Demetrius the Cynic, perhaps a follower of Musonius, perhaps his opponent, who was exiled by both Nero (AD 66) and later, after a return, by Vespasian (71), warned that 'wisdom had become a crime'.[114] His 'ranting' had aroused the emperor's anger.

Dio Chrysostomus of Prusa had apparently been relegated some seven years earlier. He had been implicated in a conspiracy, perhaps of the emperor Domitian's relatives, Junius Rusticus (Mommsen) or Flavius Sabinus, the father-in-law of Titus (von Arnim).[115] Dio was interdicted from Rome, Italy and his native Bithynia, and spent his years of exile, like an Odysseus, wandering from place to place. There was a practical reason for not settling: not having taken up citizenship elsewhere, Dio could, after his recall by Nerva, once again resume his full rights as a Roman citizen, and could use his considerable influence for the betterment of his city Prusa.[116] Dio's orations 'On Kingship' (*Orr.* 1-3) did much to establish Trajan's reputation as the 'good king'.[117] Evidence for Dio's exile and Odysseus-like wanderings is largely autobiographical, and will be dealt with in Chapter 6.[118]

Stoic opposition to imperial rule continued. Dio Chrysostomus' pupil Favorinus of Arelate was reputed to have been of the third generation of Stoic exiles; perhaps he merely wrote on exile.[119] Favorinus quarrelled with Hadrian and retreated, perhaps to Chios. The circumstances of Hadrian's quarrel with Favorinus, the 'hermaphrodite from Gaul', appear rather obscure, but offer insight into the invidious position in which the expression of even mild dislike of an opponent put Roman emperors, from Augustus onward. Favorinus himself considered it a mark of particular favour that he could survive a difference of opinion with Hadrian. Dio Cassius (69.3.4-6) avers that Hadrian did not like Favorinus.[120] The latter certainly did quarrel with an Ionian fellow-Stoic, Polemo, a favourite of the emperor. According to Philostratos (I.8) Hadrian, who was dabbling in philosophy 'merely to lighten the affairs of state' was taken aback by the Athenians' serious reaction to Favorinus' mild reluctance to carry out a liturgy placed upon him. After the Athenians had overturned a statue of

2. The Third Person: Exilic Narrative

Favorinus 'as if he were the emperor's bitter enemy' he was apparently exiled. Favorinus' reaction to this was suitably philosophical: 'Socrates would have much preferred an overturned statue to hemlock'. No details of the exile itself are known, but the fragments from his treatise attest his interest in, perhaps personal experience of, exile as a moral phenomenon.[121]

These historically verifiable figures are linked in a strange narrative recounting the marvellous life of Apollonius of Tyana. Apollonius was a rather shadowy figure, perhaps a friend of Musonius Rufus. Philostratos' *Life of Apollonius* (written in the third century, c. AD 220) is a romance, marginally historical, perhaps based on the memoirs of an even more shadowy 'Damis', perhaps also a deliberate pagan antidote to the popularity of the Christian gospels and *Acta*. Apollonius, a miracle-worker and virtually divine figure, was the prototype voluntary exile, travelling as far as India and Egypt.[122] He is depicted as in contact with a series of emperors, some of whom travelled to meet him and to take his advice on how to rule wisely.[123] The narrative gives an interesting view (especially 7.9-32-9ff.) of the hazards run by philosophers in their opposition to what they observed as 'tyranny', when Apollonius was apparently called to testify against Nerva and Orfilus.[124]

The chief interest of the work for our present purposes is the ingenuity with which the largely fictitious tale is made to fit in with verifiable historical events. Apollonius' travels took him from Tyana to Antioch, through Babylon, Nineveh and Ecbatana, into India and Nepal, then back via Babylon, Nineveh, Antioch and Seleucia, to Cyprus, thence to Ionia, including Ephesus, Smyrna, Pergamum and Troy, then Lesbos, Athens and Crete, to Rome under Nero, whence he was banished in 66, along with other philosophers. He then journeyed to Spain, Africa and Sicily and back to Greece, including Chios and Rhodes, then to Alexandria (where Vespasian travelled to meet him), and down the Nile to Ethiopia. Next the emperor Titus summoned him to come to Tarsus, whence he travelled back to Egypt, and then to Italy, in time to criticise Domitian bravely to his face, to be tried and acquitted, and then to leave for Greece and Ionia.

Much of what Apollonius experiences seems to be based on traditions of autopsy, travellers' tales and ethnographic descriptions, interspersed with tales of monsters and miracles, and of his wisdom in interpreting these as portents,[125] and signs of extreme veneration by all the monarchs he meets. He is portrayed as having seen the death of Domitian in a vision at the very moment of its occurrence, after which he sent Damis to Rome and miraculously disappeared.[126] To readers familiar with the *Acts of the Apostles*, Apollonius seems to be reprising the journeying of Paul of Tarsus, while recreating the miracles of Christ. Apollonius is the romantic pagan counterpart set up as a rival to both Christ and his adventurous follower.

2.2.9 Boethius at Pavia

The narrative of exile would be incomplete without reference to the life of the Christian polymath Anicius Manlius Severinus Boethius, who again is our major source for his own history.[127] Boethius, born late in the fifth century AD, stands on the periphery of the classical world, in a sense one of the initiators of mediaeval scholarship.[128] Boethius was a true Roman statesman, fully as dedicated to study as to public duty. Although a Christian, he was instrumental in the tradition of Greek philosophy to the modern Western world.[129]

Boethius was from a noble family, had been consul himself, and had seen his two sons entering together into the consulate (by now a largely honorific position) under the Ostrogothic king Theodoric. He composed the *Consolatio Philosophiae* in 519 after falling from favour, perhaps because of his support of the 'wrong side' after the clerical and political schism between East and West in 484. Boethius had been arrested, condemned and relegated to Ticinum, modern Pavia. The senate confirmed Theodoric's condemnation of the ex-consul. He was finally put to death in 524 or 525, as were his father-in-law Symmachus and the pro-Eastern Pope John I. Here too displacement served to nullify the power of those who were seen as a threat by the even more powerful.[130]

2.3 History into myth: Ovid's exilic mythologising

Before his death Boethius shows himself comforted by the philosophical truths from which he had felt totally alienated in his initial misery after his fall from grace. Significantly, a central poetic interlude (3.m.12) in his *Consolatio Philosophiae* recounts the tale of Orpheus and Eurydice, a tale of alienation and loss. As Curley (1987) and Martindale (1993: 6-10) emphasise, the hermeneutics involved in translation and imitation of his predecessors add resonances to any earlier version of the same material. Literary intertextuality works as a manner of commenting upon his predecessors.

As will be shown below (Chapter 9) Boethius had started his consolation with an Ovidian lament (1.m.1) after which he resolutely moved away from anything remotely Ovidian. His prose sections had shown the sufferer consistently strengthened by Dame Philosophy, to the point of being able to abandon his poetic crutches. This final poem of Book 3 harks back to Boethius' Ovidian model. The last verse shows Orpheus unable to rescue his wife from Hades, incapacitated by the very emotion, romantic love, that had sent him to look for her. Curley evokes the tradition that has seen Orpheus as the conventional poetic archetype in Latin literature, and interprets this as a statement of the ultimate incapacity of verse to convey truth. For Boethius, the failure of Orpheus as singer signals the failure of poetry (including his models, both Vergil and Ovid) to sustain him *in extremis*. In the judgement of Boethius, Ovidian 'truth' apparently pales before the 'truth of philosophy'.

But what was this Ovidian truth? We have seen Ovid's literary treatment of the myth of Orpheus, told with typically Ovidian elegance, showing the singer as a stranger, doomed to wander until he meets his death at the hands of the Ciconian women. Ovid's own displacement is treated in similar fashion. Ovid's known predilection for generic mixture allows his ostensibly autobiographical exilic works to be interpreted as heroic narrative written in the elegiac metre, an 'elegiac epic' of sorts. Ovid the creative poet takes up and transforms the day-to-day vicissitudes of his own exile into the stuff of myth, employing both primary and secondary themes. Augustus becomes the vengeful god. Ovidian use of myth and the conventions of epic helped to form the conventions of exilic literature,[131] a literary codification of the psychological reactions to exile of earlier exiles, such as Cicero. Ovid's self-portrait as a mythological figure will form a large part of the discussion of his poetry in subsequent chapters; as 'third-person narrative' it need feature only briefly in this chapter, in the context of discussion of his myth-making processes.

Ovid's solipsism means that the greater part of the exilic poetry is focused on the first person. True third-person narrative is comparatively rare. Some narration occurs, usually in elaborate ecphrases. Examples are the evocation of Tiberius' triumph (*Pont.* 2.1, 3.4) and the taking of Aegisos (*Pont.* 4.7.25-52), with epic features such as the larger-than-life dimensions of the obstacles overcome by the heroic Vestalis in this poem.[132] Aegisos had been taken by an enemy and Vestalis, the Romanised Ligurian prince, as representative of Rome, had come to its aid, probably as centurion in an army under Vitellius.[133] Ovid's descriptions are epic in their dimensions. The citadel reached into the clouds; enemy arrows poured down like rain; stones fell like hail. The hero was a veritable Ajax, treading over a mountain of corpses, setting an example to equally valorous underlings, winning through for Rome. This is history mythologised.

Tiberius' triumph (possibly for a victory engineered by Germanicus)[134] is first predicted in the ridiculous dream-sequence in *Pont.* 3.3 (discussed above, p. 46) and should therefore not be taken very seriously. It is then briefly described in 3.4. While purporting to serve as a further elaboration of the triumph prophesied in 3.3, this next poem has an apologetic tone which contrasts with the 'dream sequence' of its predecessor *Ex Ponto* 3.4 is addressed to Rufinus, as a *recusatio*, begging pardon for the 'poor quality' of a poem written on Tiberius' triumph.[135] If such a poem ever existed, it is now wholly lost, but it is possible that the second half of the poem (vv. 87-105) *is* the promised 'triumph poem'. In its entirety 3.4 wavers between humility, tearfulness and pathos, and attempts to sound ingratiating and conciliatory. The poet's mock-recusatory stance is not wholly convincing, and his description of the triumph is undercut by the reader's memory of the bathos, in the previous poem, of the 'prophetic' figure of 'Amor' with its bedraggled feathers, that had incongruously proclaimed that this triumph would take place.[136] A final apostrophe addresses the empress Livia, enjoining her to rejoice in her son's triumph and giving a small cameo-like evocation of a typical Roman triumph (vv. 95-110):

> *perfida damnatas Germania proicit hastas.*
> *iam pondus dices omen habere meum.*
> *crede, brevique fides aderit. geminabit honorem*
> *filius, et iunctis, ut prius, ibit equis.*
> *prome, quod inicias umeris victoribus, ostrum:*
> *ipsa potest solitum nosse corona caput ...*   (*Pont.* 3.4.97-102)

Perfidious Germany is renouncing her accursed weapons; soon you will admit that my prophecy has weight; believe me, proof will soon be to hand. Your son will double his honours and ride as before behind a yoked pair of horses. Bring out the triumphal purple to put round his shoulders; the laurel wreath is quite capable of recognising that familiar head ...

It is all very predictable; the victorious general will carry a jewelled shield, a personified and dishevelled figure of the Rhine will be followed by prisoners of war. Even here the narrator cannot keep to the third person, and involves both his ostensible addressee and the imperial family with frequent apostrophe or imperative verbs. More interesting is the subtext of the two poems, taken together: the poet's allusions to the familial relationships of the various actors in the triumphal procession.[137] The poet assumes familiarity in his readership with the intricacies of Augustus' system of serial adoption. The various imperial adoptions are apparently ignored, and therefore, paradoxically, are accentuated in readers' consciousness. The concatenation of allusions gains a strange tone when read with his *reductio ad absurdum* of the Caesars' claim to divine ancestry; the exile had shown 'Amor' as Tiberius' great-uncle (*Pont.* 3.3.62). Tiberius is uncomfortably aligned with his 'great-uncle's' vindication of the errant poet.

To the degree that we have distinguished creative poet ('empirical author', *Erzahler-Ich*) and suffering exile ('topic of the first person narrative', *Ich-Erzahlung*) we may see Ovid's pervasive first person narrative as a form of impersonalised mythologising. Each allusion to a mythical hero recalls an encapsulated tale. In that sense the exilic poems have an extensive subtext of untold narratives that relate to dispossession and alienation. The topic of wandering over land and sea, driven by an angry god, shows the exiled poet as a lonely Odysseus-Aeneas, *fato profugus* (driven forth by his fate), as in *Tristia* 1.5.64: *me profugum comites deseruere mei* (my companions deserted me as I was driven forth).[138] The tie with Troy is subtly spelt out in the evocation of the exile's last night at Rome, *Tristia* 1.3.26: *haec facies Troiae, cum caperetur, erat* (just so was the appearance of Troy when it was taken). The wailing of the household evokes *Aeneid* 4.667-71 and so turns the departing poet into a 'departed Dido'. In this he is perhaps following the example already set by Cicero, whose grief at his own departure and later pride in his return is portrayed in both intimate correspondence and public orations as greater than any that had ever gone before.

Ovid's use of Penelope, Laodamia and Medea as illustrative material in his exilic poetry ties these poems to his earlier *Heroides*. Of the ostensible writers of Ovid's pathetic letters of desolation, three, Dido (*Her.* 7), Ariadne (10) and Medea (12) are women who left their homes and their *patriae* (home countries) to follow a perfidious lover. In contrast, Penelope (*Her.* 1) writes as the wife of an exile, offering a focus, both literal[139] and figurative, for her exiled husband in his hopes of return. Ovid's Penelope differs in important respects from the exemplary Homeric paragon. She is a woman of feeling and character, but the creator-poet allows her to comment on Odysseus' exilic fidelity; his pursuit of the return journey was not always single-minded. Penelope is aware of the psychological as well as physical alienation involved in exile. As the poem is a monologue cast as a 'letter', it rightfully fits into discussion of second person outreach, but we may imagine that the poet's conception of his heroine in *Heroides* 1 continued to colour his use of Penelope as *exemplum* in the exilic poems.

Imagery in which Ovid depicts his wife as a simultaneous Penelope, Andromache, Evadne and Laodamia (*Tr.* 1.6.19-22; 5.14.35-40, in various combinations), shows him by implication as a *Ulysses multipatiens* (long-suffering Odysseus), a Hector, the victim of epic anger, a Capaneus struck by lightning[140] and a Protesilaus, the first to fall at Troy.[141] Explicit portrayal of himself as Capaneus turns his wife into an Evadne, by implication, then, ready to leap into the same fire that has engulfed her hapless spouse (*Tr.* 4.3.63, *Pont.* 3.1.51). An aberrant view of some of these paragon wives in the fabric of the poet's thought colours the exile's attitude towards his own wife. Intertextual allusion to his earlier treatment of these women directs the reader towards the possibility of multiple interpretations of any particular instance. For example, Ovid's Laodamia in *Her.* 13 knows of the prophecy that the first Greek to set foot on shore will be the first to fall at Troy, yet she urges Protesilaus to hurry and engage the war so that he may return to her. She is in fact urging him to his own death, as will be apparent to those familiar with the myth (which ends with her sharing her husband's death, through suicide).[142] Throughout the poem Laodamia's blind obsession with death is apparent. Ovid's wife is apparently being equally blindly urged towards civic suicide, a sharing of the poet's exile, so often equated by him with 'living death'.

Compression, inversion and retrogression of time are narrative devices central to epic. Ovid gives mythological and epic weight to time. Three years' passing (*Tr.* 5.10.3, 4) feels like the 'ten years of the Trojan siege'. Exile as the final metamorphosis ties the poet firmly into the tradition of his own special epic convention.[143] Long monologues are frequent in the

Metamorphoses, often by a character on the point of death. In the exilic oeuvre, imagery equating exile with death is pervasive, and Ovid's auto-biographical poem, *Tristia* 4.10, functions as such a monologue.

Tristia 4.10 firmly turns the poet's 'history' into 'myth'. It is a hymn to his Muse, the resourceful goddess that aids him in withstanding every onslaught of blind fate and the powerful figure that manipulates it. In sum, the exiled Ovid is an epic hero; he, too, has a divine guardian. She does not waft him in a cloud off the battlefield, but appears to him in many guises. His Muse remains his constant guide. She wafts him from his frozen exile to the balmy slopes of Helicon:

> *Gratia, Musa, tibi: nam tu solacia praebes;*
> *tu curae requies, tu medicina venis.*
> *tu dux et comes es, tu nos abducis ab Histro,*
> *in medioque mihi das Helicone locum* (*Tr.* 4.10.117-20)

Thanks, o Muse, to you: for you offer solace; you come as my rest from care, as medication. You are my leader and companion, you waft me away from the Ister and give me a place in the midst of Helicon.

As always, Ovid the poet can have it both ways. He is simultaneously a Hesiod, inspired to sing on the slopes of the Muses' Mount, recounting the momentous battles of men and gods, and the godlike hero of these very battles, a victimised exile. He is a displaced person, but at the same time a larger-than-life, eternal survivor, sustained by the most powerful goddess of all.[144] That this creative force worked to sustain all five of our major protagonists will become evident in the chapters that follow.

THE SECOND STAGE

THE SECOND PERSON:
EXILIC OUTREACH

Preamble: On the Nature of
Second Person Exchange

Discussion so far has been concerned with narrative, the presentation of the facts and circumstances of exile, implying a predominantly objective, third person focus, or, if the narrative is autobiographical, concentrating on the actions of the protagonist and his antagonists. Reportage is reflective. Shift of focus from third to second person implies personal interaction between the exile and another, 'at home' in a safe haven. The term 'second person' implies just that; apart from the external reader that takes up a document to read, there are always at least two *personae* internally involved in such literature, 'speaker / writer' and 'addressee'. This means that the second person literature of exile essentially portrays dialogue, with at least one of the personages involved experiencing some form of displacement.

Dialogue between an exile and another in most cases involves a spatial remove, which (in the era before the telephone and 'real-time' exchange on the Internet) brings with it a temporal remove. Time is needed for the contribution of each participant to reach the other. Such dialogue may be 'conversation' or 'monologue', that is, it may be cast in letter-form, implying half of an interchange, or it may comprise formal rhetorical address, essentially soliloquy, but fixed on the other as focus of interest. In both cases focus is on the exile's needs. Depending on whether the speaker or writer is the exile or the one at home, this focus involves either appeal for aid, or the offering of spiritual or material comfort. It may also involve reproach or invective.

The most common type of second person exilic dialogue is the letter, which may be formal or informal.[1] The letter is essentially *sermo absentis*, a conversation with an absent friend. Quintilian (9.4.19f.) differentiates between the rigid and closely textured diction of oratory and the colloquial fluidity of the language of speech and letter-writing. Degrees of formality may produce letters that are close to informal speech, and others that verge on the careful formulation of oratory. Tone may vary from playful to serious, and the letter may convey facts or serve as an indication of the writer's mood. Traditionally the epistolary form, whether serious or playful, serves to convey information, to offer comfort or aid, or merely to entertain, largely in the manner of social intercourse. Focus may be on either the wants and needs of the addressee or on the deeds or emotions of the writer.

Letter-writing, then, is a form of conversation at one remove. This remove involves both space and time. The most important factor is the consciousness, with both author and recipient, that communication of a reciprocal nature is taking place. The letter-writer deliberately creates 'half a conversation', and the recipient looms large in his mind. This fact underlies the frequent occurrence of the vocative and other means of apostrophising, imperative forms, and verbs in the second person, colloquialisms, questions, assumed questions and replies.

The two most important formal aspects in letter-writing are the grammatical persons (implying both *personae* and personalities) and the convolutions of time involved. The empirical author writes in his own present, and the empirical reader reads at any subsequent time (obviously, with reading of classical authors there may be a lapse of up to two millennia). This is, however, of less importance than the notional persons and the notional time involved in both the writing and the subsequent reading of such a letter. First we must postulate an ostensible or notional 'letter-writer', sometimes coincidental with and sometimes opposed to the empirical author; in 'mock letters' such as Ovid's *Heroides* 13, for instance, the 'writer' is a fictitious Laodamia. The ostensible or notional 'reader' is someone other than the 'model reader' of narrative discourse; this is the *addressee* implicit within any document that has the characteristics of direct address. In the case of *Heroides* 13 the addressee is a mythical Protesilaus – perhaps, but not necessarily, already dead at the notional time of writing, the ostensible writer's epistolary *now*. For this type of letter I have coined the term 'secondary epistle'.

In the case of Cicero's letters, empirical author and letter-writer coincide. Likewise Cicero's correspondents, say Atticus or his brother Quintus, are both model reader and addressee.[2] These letters, for me, represent the 'primary epistle'. With the exiled Ovid the *personae* multiply. The poet as empirical author has created the exile-as-letter-writer, addressing missives to ostensible addressees, but writing for publication to a wider readership, his 'model readers' (which may have included Augustus himself). In his poetic revelation of the inner anguish of exile we may see Ovid as 'model author', applying all the intricacies of his still playfully ironic style to create a picture of exilic resilience in adverse circumstances.[3] Oscillations of Ovidian *personae* and personages involved result in oscillations between primary and secondary epistle. Part of the charm of Ovid's exilic poetry lies in the challenge offered his readers (in all aspects of readership we have so far considered, and perhaps more) to interpret these oscillations.

Aspects of time are equally complex. We may assume, particularly with reference to Ovid's secondary epistles (his literary letters from absent heroines) a notional or 'epistolary' *now*, which is a 'present' for the letter-writer, and a similar *then*, which is the notional future time at which the letter-writer imagines her addressee as reading the missive. From that perspective, his present is past, and the reading time is a new present. The letter-writer keeps a double focus on time continuously in mind, as she imagines her addressee as a future interlocutor, while anticipating the potential questions or comments of this interlocutor (for whom, remember, her present is past, and whose present is her future). The intervening time is then envisaged from the letter-writer's perspective as a 'future perfect', which will have become simple past by the time the addressee reads the letter. Both common past and distant future partake of this shifting focus, becoming pluperfect and either continuous present or immediate future. Sometimes simple (aorist) past becomes 'perfect', with its connotation of continued effect.

In Chapter 2 we saw Ovid's Medea writing at a *now* located just before she starts her revenge. Most verbs are in the past; the letter is largely narrative, but dire warnings of her uncertain future actions are couched in the future indicative or potential subjunctive. Aspects of time are important. It is unclear when this letter will be read by Jason, perhaps in that exiguous interval between its completion and the act of revenge, but perhaps only after the murders have been committed. From the perspective of the empirical reader,[4] familiar with Euripides' version,[5] the moment is already fixed when the potential future of Medea's threats becomes actualised as a horrible perfect that will continue to reverberate in Jason's consciousness.[6] Uncertainty lies in interpretation: are Medea's threats to be interpreted by the empirical reader (us, today) as dire warnings that Jason ignored to his cost, or are we to imagine that he will have read them only after the deed, when the full dramatic irony of her words will at last explain to him her motive for killing their children? The creative author has left the choice of interpretations to his model readership, whose judgement of Jason will be affected by this interpretation.

With Laodamia's letter (*Her.* 13), we have seen the heroine writing in her *now* while the heroes are still waiting for a breeze to take them to Troy. Her warnings to her husband occur in the present (or near future) of imperative verbs; she tells him about her emotions at his departure in the perfect and again uses the imperative to urge him to hurry. Here the reader's awareness of the outcome serves to point the irony of her outpourings: the more Protesilaus will hurry, the sooner both notional writer and notional reader will die.

The following three chapters will consider various forms of outreach to a second person, starting with consideration of informal and formal adaptations of the genre of *consolatio ad exulem* (Chapter 3) and continuing with appeal (Chapter 4) and invective (Chapter 5). Ovid (sections 4.3 to 4.8), Seneca (3.2.3) and Boethius (3.2.4) are all engaged, in various ways, in formalising exilic 'dialogue'. Cicero's letters will be seen (3.1, 4.2) as not quite fitting into the pattern of deliberate literary artifice followed by our other authors, but even in his rejection of the consolatory tradition (3.1.2) we shall meet him as aware of such a tradition (3.3). His externalisation of the blame for his downfall in various speeches (5.1, 5.2) will appear as in its way as obsessive as the vitriol poured forth by Ovid in his *Ibis* (5.3), but far less subtle than what may be interpreted as Ovid's *controversia* against Augustus (5.4).

3

Comfort in Exile

3.1 Cicero

3.1.1 Cicero's informal consolatory letters to exiles

What I have termed 'primary epistle' are those letters where model and empiric writers coincide, as do model and empiric readers, and where later readers were involved only as secondary consideration or by mere chance. Without long reference to the debate on the editing and publication of Cicero's letters, let us turn to these as good examples of primary epistle.[7] In a letter to his friend Curio, Cicero points out that there are four kinds of letters: those bringing news, those offering social intercourse at a distance, those discussing serious issues, and finally, those admonishing or advising a friend.[8] In this category falls the genre of consolatory admonishment to the bereaved or to those in exile.

Even before Caesar's final ascendance the turbulent politics of the last years of the republic saw many fluctuations of power, and the formerly powerful often had to find temporary or even permanent refuge outside Rome. Advice to friends in exile was the frequent object of the correspondence of Cicero's later years. These informal letters, while clearly functioning as *sermo absentis* (conversation with an absent friend), fall largely in the category of exhortation or advice. They differ in length, but all may be seen to subscribe to the formal tradition of consolatory literature. We saw in Chapter 1 that the formal parts of a typical *consolatio ad exulem* comprised four elements: exhortation to rationality, acceptance of the uncertainty of Fortune, discussion of alternative places of refuge, and refutation of arguments that exile is bad.

The year 56 BC provoked the earliest of these letters from Cicero to friends in exile: *Ad familiares* 5.17, to P. Sittius, the 'king-maker', a voluntary exile at the court of the Mauretanian king.[9] Cicero had been back in Rome from his own term of displacement for about a year, but his position was very uncertain and he was at the mercy of the factions that had banded against him. The existence of this letter, in which Cicero assures a former Catilinarian of his efforts on behalf of the exile and his son, is indicative of the extent to which political alliances fluctuated at the time, although it appears that already in the year following Cicero's consulship he had been sure enough of Sittius' innocence (or of his own potential for success) that he had represented Sittius in a civil case relating to the retention of his property in Italy. Its interest for us lies in its informal use of the elements of traditional *consolatio ad exulem*:

> ... *ne hoc quidem praetermittendum esse duxi, te ut hortarer rogaremque ut et hominem te et virum esse meminisses, id est, ut et communem incertumque casum, quem neque vitare quisquam nostrum nec praestare ullo pacto potest, sapienter ferres et dolori fortiter ac fortunae resisteres cogitaresque et in nostra civitate et in ceteris quae rerum potitae sunt multis fortissimis atque optimis viris iniustis iudiciis talis casus incidisse.* (*Fam.* 5.17.3a)

> I did not think that I should omit urging and begging you to remember that you are both a human being and a man, facts which imply that you should philosophically bear the uncertainty and unpredictability of that chance which none of us can in any way foretell and also that you should bravely bear and stoutly resist pain and misfortune, and also to keep in mind that both in our and other powerful states such a lot has befallen many illustrious men through the passing of unjust verdicts.[10]

Although the second person verbs and pronouns focus clearly on the recipient, it is not difficult to read an awareness of his own recently-ended exile and his present precarious position into Cicero's words, pointed by the telling *nec quisquam nostrum* ('and no one of us') which may be read in the political context of the time as far more specific than the 'us' denoting common humanity. Cicero appears to have in mind himself and Sittius and like-minded members of the Senate (the *boni* – good men – of many of his speeches).[11] His point is further personalised and adapted to the present circumstances of writer and recipient (most plausibly the exclusive 'us' referred to above) with the further *illud utinam ne ve<re> scriberem, ea te republica carere in qua neminem prudentem hominem res ulla delectet!* (I wish that it wasn't true to write that you are at present doing without a political situation in which nobody with any sense is at all happy about anything, 3b).

Next we have a letter written in 52 BC (*Fam.* 5.18), to Fadius, one of the tribunes of 58 BC who had worked for Cicero's recall.[12] Such a proof of friendship required reciprocation, here by brief formal consolation. The letter clearly complies with the characteristics of the tradition. Eighteen lines in Shackleton Bailey's edition serve to cover the basics: the inability of the comforter to offer comfort in hard times, exhortation toward philosophical fortitude, and admonition that the exile should count his blessings in comparison with the general debilitation of the state (a typically Ciceronian adaptation of the *topos* of the universality of misfortune and changes of fortune as inherent in the human condition), the greatness of Fadius' loss in his loss of the City. Finally, Cicero assures Fadius that his exile will soon be over (a prophecy that came to fruition some seven years later). Fadius' 'blessings' include the fact of sentence of exile on a relatively slight charge.

3. Comfort in Exile

After this letter, Cicero's exiled correspondents were much more clearly on the opposing side in the great convulsion of the state following Caesar's crossing of the Rubicon. After 49 BC, during the stormy years of Caesar's dictatorship, and particularly after Thapsus, exile became a way of life to many. The Pompeians were in disarray, and, after a miserable wait on the outskirts of power, for months virtually cowering at Brindisi, Cicero had safely returned to Rome. He was trying manfully to blend tactful acquiescence in Caesar's ascendance with concern about the dictator's policies, while maintaining his own political independence. His own family life was in disarray. During this period he experienced several momentous upheavals in his personal life, including the return of his pregnant daughter to her parent's home, her consequent divorce from Dolabella, Caesar's lieutenant, the birth and death of her little son, Cicero's own divorce from his wife of thirty years, his subsequent marriage, the death of his daughter, and his subsequent second divorce. Often money matters preoccupied his interest in the letters to his faithful confidante Atticus – in the end three sets of dowries occupied his attention, the payments of two of which kept falling due while the return of the third (from his ex-son-in-law, the Caesarean Dolabella) was unpredictable.[13] None of these matters comes to the fore in the consolations Cicero during this time wrote to friends in exile. One can almost imagine the beleaguered consular sitting in the ruins of his private life, watching what to him were the ruins of his public life, and grinding out letters of comfort to men who were no worse off away from Rome than he was in the City itself.[14] If these letters often seem perfunctory and stale, it should come as no surprise.

A predictable pattern of consolation and advice is discernible in most of these letters to friends away from Rome. Beside the almost obligatory 'misery of the letter-writer himself', which makes consolation difficult, the themes we have identified in the letter to Fadius predominate: private grief is small against public woe, exile is preferable to watching in person the debilitation of the state, the addressee's woes are temporary, the exile must count his present blessings, particularly the kindness of family, friends and children; the blows of Fortune are part of the human condition; public life is experiencing a convulsion which will end an era; death will bring relief; the exile must undertake literary studies as a means of curing grief; time brings change; the addressee must work for his own relief by a conscious moral effort; a consciousness of innocence and rectitude brings inner comfort.[15]

Cicero's advice is not always consistent, being adapted to the apparent needs of each individual. His exhortation of Cn. Domitius Ahenobarbus to resort to philosophy may be an attempt to keep Ahenobarbus from suicide.[16] Mescenius Rufus, formerly *quaestor* under Caesar, but now a Pompeian awaiting news of Thapsus, and probably forbidden to enter Rome,[17] is exhorted to bear *funditus aversam fortunam* (the fact that his lot was fundamentally convulsed) bravely, and even to pray for death.

79

Rome is frequently contrasted with the victim's place of exile: exile is a lesser evil than being present to watch the Republic crumble. This consideration did not comfort Cicero during his own exile. *Fam.* 4.15, written at some time in 46 BC, offers Cn. Plancius (his host during Cicero's own banishment) the cold comfort that he must realise that all in the state are sharing a common danger. He should not shy away. Marcellus is also exhorted to return and continue his 'spiritual exile' in the city itself (*Fam.* 4.7, 4.8, 4.9, on which more below), whereas Torquatus and Aulius Caecina are comforted with the thought that they are 'well out of it' – to hear about the miseries of the state is less painful than to see its daily ruin (6.1, 6.4, 6.5, 6.6). Caecina is advised to stay near Rome for easy recall (6.8) whereas Toranius is similarly advised about the island of Corcyra (6.20).[18]

In September 46 BC Cicero was employed in writing a whole series of exhortations. The Pompeian, P. Nigidius Figulus (*Fam.* 4.13), who later died in exile, [19] is given a picture of Cicero's own despair and concomitant inability to produce suitable words of consolation; Nigidius can think of better arguments himself. His personal woes will soon end, those of the Republic will not. Cicero exhorts Nigidius to turn to study for comfort, while also undertaking to conciliate Caesar on Nigidius' behalf. In the same month a letter congratulates Ampius Balbus (*Fam.* 6.12) on his restitution of civil rights and return to Rome. The letter contains details of Cicero's efforts to order the exile's domestic affairs. The last paragraphs refer to consolatory letters written by Cicero during Balbus' exile, and to Balbus' consistently admirable fortitude, exhorting him to turn to historiography, literature being the only safe resort in troubled times.

Other letters written in September 46[20] refer to the duty of a friend to offer comfort or aid. All combine practical details with praise of the exile's fortitude, bolstered by his philosophical pursuits. Cicero's optimistic assurance that Trebianus' exile would soon end, as Caesar was becoming more lenient, was justified by events. In June 45 another letter reassures Trebianus about his property and congratulates him on his restitution. Typically Ciceronian egoism adds piquancy: the writer is gratified by his friend's thanks, and appeals to him to make his gratitude known, particularly to their common friend, the philosopher Siro.

Caesar in the end pardoned all exiles who had left Rome after Pompey's ascendance (except Milo, convicted for killing Clodius and ineffectively defended by Cicero). He was clearly also inclined towards clemency for those who had actively opposed him during the civil war. We meet Fadius (the paradigmatic consoled exile of 52) again in *Fam.* 7.27 (early in 45) apparently safely back in Rome, but now bitterly reviled by Cicero. This is the most vicious letter in Cicero's whole collection. Shackleton Bailey surmises *ad loc.* that Fadius' request for a loan had been turned down by the impecunious Cicero, and his negative reaction to this had prompted the consular's outburst. Reflection on the vicissitudes of Cicero's private life at the time will perhaps suggest to readers a more personal reason than is generally admitted for the otherwise inexplicable outburst – sheer exasperation. As so often, the nature of letters as *sermo absentis*, of which half is lost, preclude any final solution to this puzzle.

Three sets of consolatory letters each tell an interesting tale. We may read more of Cicero as the writer than of the recipient in the first of the series, four letters to the Pompeian Aulus Manlius Torquatus, dating from January 45 (*Fam*. 6.1, 6.3, 6.4, 6.2, in that order, so Shackleton Bailey). He was in exile in Athens, later perhaps in Italy, still outside Rome. These informal letters purport to be consolatory, with features common to the formal consolatory genre. All three are clouded with pessimism, illustrating the *topos* of the difficulty of consoling another when the consoler himself is unhappy. The letters stress Torquatus' philosophical fortitude, his awareness of some present blessings, the common danger to the state felt by all in opposition to the present *status quo*, the community of pain in being separated from loved ones, and the consolatory force of time. The first letter analyses in some detail Cicero's own previous forebodings about the bloody direction politics would take after 49 (6.1.5) and he expresses concern about Torquatus' debilitated mental state (*ibid*. 6). Cicero candidly admits that in similar circumstances, literature did little to relieve his own misery. The last of the series is extremely pessimistic and ends with a morbid, rather than philosophical, desire for death to relieve his present woe. The consoler cannot console.

Next we have a series that hinges on the poetics of both consolatory and conciliatory composition, three letters, dated late 46 to January 45, from Cicero to Aulus Caecina, exiled to Sicily (in order, *Fam*. 6.6, 6.8, 6.5), and one from Caecina himself (*Fam*. 6.7). He was a Pompeian, from Etruscan stock, who had been pardoned by Caesar, but had not been allowed to return to Italy. The letters discuss an apparently abject *Liber Querellarum* (Book of Lamentations), written by Caecina in exile, of which Caesar has taken no notice. Caecina had apparently formerly written a polemical pamphlet against Caesar (Suet. *Iul*. 75.5). Caecina is now by turns hopeful and fearful that the book of complaints will come to Caesar's attention. A long ironical essay (*Fam*. 6.6) analyses the temper of the times in 'Etruscan' augurial terms (2-9). The clemency of Caesar 'augurs' well; the analysis takes the place of *illa consolatione qua facile fortem virum sustentarem* (that consolation with which I should easily sustain a brave man, 12). A paragraph of rapid *praeteritio* (emphasis by ostensible passing-over) lists the commonplaces of consolation which Cicero should have offered Caecina, but did not: the comfort that lies in consciousness of rectitude, exhortation to philosophical acceptance of Caecina's lot, consolation in literature and *exempla* to show the universality of the human lot, *Levat enim communis quasi legis et humanae condicionis recordatio* (the remembrance of a virtual law of community in the human condition relieves one's pain.)

Caecina's elaborate and somewhat hesitant reply admits: *meus error*

*exsilio corritur, cuius summa criminis est, quod armatus adversario male-
dixi* (My mistake is being corrected by exile, that mistake of which the
most serious point of accusation is that I cursed an adversary when I was
myself armed, *Fam.* 6.7.1).[21] He elaborates on the characteristics of eulogy
and invective, and the problem of how to mollify a great man (2-4). He
appeals to Cicero to help by editing his book, but not to publish it,
complaining that in these things his son is useless (5). He is conscious of
being a nuisance: *nisi forte aut in miseria nimis stulte, aut in amicitia
nimis impudenter tibi onus impono* (If I am not acting too stupidly in my
misery, then by stressing our friendship I am acting too presumptuously
when I impose a burden on you, 6). Cicero replies kindly; *Ad Familiares*
6.8 encloses a copy of a letter of recommendation to Furfanius, governor of
Sicily; in 6.5 Cicero assures Caecina that he is careful not to leave the book
lying about, expresses gratitude for Caecina's past kindness when he,
Cicero, was in exile, and sets the father's mind at ease about his son,
promising aid to the whole family. Caecina apparently was ultimately
pardoned by Caesar.[22]

The last of the three sets of letters ends tragically. The series *Ad
Familiares* 4.7-12 reflects the story of M. Marcellus. We have four letters
from Cicero to Marcellus and one reply, all from early 46, and a letter to
Cicero from Servius Sulpicius (*Fam.* 4.12) from May 46. The consular
Marcellus, after opposing Caesar's 'debauchment of the constitution', had
chosen to retreat to Mytilene rather than to seem to condone it.[23] Like
Rutilius Rufus, who had taken refuge on the same island, he was clearly
setting himself up as the philosophical sage. Voluntary exile was his way
of taking a stand against Caesar. His friends worked for his recall. Later
Caesar's free pardon of Marcellus gave rise to Cicero's extravagant eulogy
of Caesar in the speech *Pro Marcello*.[24] The embarrassment now was that
the freely pardoned opponent refused to accept that pardon and was
maintaining his Stoic opposition in solitary grandeur on the island. Cicero
himself had by now developed some sort of working relationship with
Caesar, and it was in his interest that Marcellus should return.

Marcellus appears to have been rather short tempered, and Cicero's
letters breathe the soul of tact, and are clearly aimed at mollifying the
great man, by showing himself as one of mind with Marcellus. First person
plural verbs predominate in 4.7, as Cicero analyses his and Marcellus'
attitude to the civil war: *non enim iis rebus pugnabamus quibus valere
poteramus, consilio, auctoritate, causa, quae erant in nobis superiora, sed
lacertis et viribus, quibus pares non eramus. victi sumus igitur; aut, si vinci
dignitas non potest, fracti certe et abiecti* (We were not fighting with the
weapons with which we might have prevailed – policy, prestige, cause. In
these lay our superiority; but we fought with brute force, in which we were
outmatched. So we were vanquished, or if moral standing cannot be
vanquished, at any rate broken and cast down, 2b, trans. Shackleton
Bailey 1978). This is philosopher speaking to philosopher with an exclu-

sive 'we'. Next comes praise of Marcellus' noble stance, followed by a plea to modify that stance. The focus is on the second person, but the interests are those of the writer.

Letters 4.7 to 4.10 have a single thrust: that Marcellus should return, that it is safer to live under Caesar's benevolence at Rome than danger-ously in opposition to him elsewhere, that, even if death is preferable to exile, to die at home is the greatest boon, that the alienated spirit can endure 'internal exile' better in the bodily comfort of home, that it is better to watch the ruin of the state than to hear about it, that matters would have been no different under Pompey, and that Marcellus has a duty to his *patria orbata* ('the fatherland, robbed [of its most valuable son]', *Fam.* 4.9). Cicero stresses that continuation of exile in its turn robs the great man of the benefit and use of his own private possessions, and in the end he seems to urge the predominance of private affairs over public.[25] The letters are worded carefully; Marcellus is a great man, but has a somewhat prickly personality.[26] Philosophical appeal can be used to turn the tables on the would-be Stoic stage. In *Ad Familiares* 4.9.4 the philosopher is reminded in terms of a Diogenes, whose pride was reputed to have 'shone through the holes in his tattered clothing', that he should beware that continued spurning of Caesar's clemency should not appear as excessive pride.

Marcellus' reply (*Fam.* 4.11) shows that Cicero has prevailed: Marcellus' devotion to philosophy had sustained him happily in Greece; devotion to the state was now drawing him home. The letter is equally formal, and significant in what it does not say. Of the usual consolatory aphorisms he was in no need: Marcellus shows his correspondent that he had been satisfied with his lot. Gratitude is limited to gratitude for Cicero's friendly concern, not for his successful intervention, a subtle difference. A final letter comes as a shock: Servius Sulpicius, governor of Achaea, writes in May 45 from Athens to tell Cicero of Marcellus' death; a certain Magius Cilo, a member of his circle, had fatally stabbed him, perhaps in a quarrel about money.[27] Sulpicius had arranged for the cremation of Marcellus' body in the gymnasium of the Academy, [28] as befitted a Roman nobleman and a philosopher. So died the only truly philosophical exile in the Ciceronian epistolary collection.

3.1.2 *Cicero's letters from exile as 'anti-consolatio'*

Cicero himself when in exile was no such philosopher.[29] Despite his obvious familiarity with the consolatory tradition, which may be deduced from the above overview of his own occasional use of its *topoi* in the last years of the Republic, during his own earlier banishment in 58-57 BC, Cicero could draw no comfort from his familiarity with the tradition. In his letters from exile Cicero exhibited those psychological aspects which all philosophical effort aims at dispelling, even begging his friend Atticus *not* to try to console him. More than one of Cicero's letters from exile follow the ordered pattern of philosophical discussion of exile, and formal consolation, as may be deduced from the above, but in a negative vein.

A long letter from Thessaly, written in August 58 (*Att.* 3.15) offers a complete palinode of the normal *consolatio*, interspersed with references to matters of practical importance. The consolatory role of a friend is acknowledged in the first sentence: *accepi Idibus Sextilibus quattuor epistulas a te missas* (I have received the four letters you sent on 17 August). A detailed reply to these letters follows, two of which clearly had adapted consolatory *topoi* to Cicero's circumstances.

On the 'need for a rational attitude', Cicero comments that he has no opportunity in exile for exercising the rational faculty. If Atticus is missing Cicero, what, does he imagine, are Cicero's feelings at having lost all? Recapitulation of his losses would mean that Cicero himself was 'reopening his own wound'. This medical imagery (continued later with *meis vulneribus*, 'through my wounds'), is followed by a catalogue of ills: no one before has ever lost so much; counting his blessings is a futile exercise, for the thought of past happiness augments present misery. The usual assumptions about exile and loss, for instance, that passage of time will alleviate pain, are untrue, for *Dies autem non modo non levat luctum hunc, sed etiam auget* (no day, however, alleviates this mourning of mine, but even increases it, 2). About half a page of discussion of political connections follows (3), after which Cicero turns to the contemplation of future happiness, when Fortune will *aliquando* (someday) restore him to his friends and *patria*.[30] He promises then to be a better friend to Atticus (4).

Consciousness of rectitude is tempered by consciousness that Cicero has been his own greatest enemy, and brought much of his misery upon himself by short-sighted political action and reaction (4a). The *topos* that the faults of mankind are to be ascribed 'not to Zeus but to themselves' is turned here into a convoluted accusation-cum-exoneration of Atticus for having at the time advised Cicero to flee instead of making a stand. He himself should have remained firm, Cicero says, which would have led either to freedom or to death (4b).

Cicero touches on disenfranchisement in his examination of the circumstances which led to the decree of exile, blaming his friends and himself for their blindness in not having ignored Clodius' first bill, and for having gone into mourning when it was passed (5). Cicero's concern, in a series of questions about his property and house, negates the *topos* of the universality of the human condition. For him, there can be no true restitution without recovery of his property: *sin autem spei nihil est, quae est mihi vita?* (but if there is no hope [of that], then what sort of a life have I got?, 6a). He ignores consolatory *topoi* such as 'world-citizenship' and man's adaptability through self-sufficiency. A severely practical discussion of the place of exile follows: Cicero wants to stay close to Rome in the hope that events may develop favourably, but desires seclusion on Atticus' estate *ut neque videam homines, quos nolim, et te, ut scribis, videam* (so that I don't have to see any people I don't want to, and may see you, as you write, 6b). He does not attempt to cite the traditional criticisms of exile as an evil but his attitude is negative throughout the letter. For Cicero life away from Rome is no life at all.[31]

The close of the letter again criticises Atticus for bad advice. Cicero blames himself and his friend: *ego proditus, inductus, coniectus in fraudem omnia mea praesidia neglexi, totam Italiam mire erectam ad me defenden-dum destitui et reliqui, me meos mea tradidi inimicis inspectante et tacente te* (I was betrayed, deceived and tricked and neglected all my normal resources, I deserted and left behind an Italy wonderfully prepared to defend me and I handed over myself, my people and my things to my enemies while you watched and said nothing, 7a). This was voluntary exile of a despicable sort, and Cicero blames himself for having allowed Atticus to allow him to rush to his own ruin, *exitium* (7b). The *topos* of exile or death as the pre-emption of an unhappy future is inverted into the idea that pre-emption of possible ruin brought misery.

Cicero throughout remains very conscious of his loss of a good reputa-tion. Consciousness of past achievements is confined to the hope that Atticus may in some way achieve Cicero's restitution to some sort of social and political power. He laments: *qui fui, et qui esse potui, iam esse non possum* (What I was and what I could have become I now no longer can be 8a). This letter, like others written by the exile while in the depths of despair, is our only evidence of any attempt by Cicero at creativity in exile, the traditional staple of advice to an exile. Cicero's literary activity is limited and querulous.

In short, Cicero in exile does not display the philosophical ideal of the soul's creation of its own happiness by the practice of virtue. He can be comforted only by complete restitution; his friend must not try to comfort him with an offer of anything less (7b). A contrite rider follows: Cicero hopes that his friend will realise that he blames himself most (8b).

3.2 Formal consolation

3.2.1 Formal characteristics of consolatio ad exulem

It is this kind of letter which has, over the centuries, given rise to much negative criticism of Cicero as man. It is said that in the early Italian Renaissance Petrarch could hardly credit that he was reading the master's own words; in this century Carcopino (1951: 4-32), ascribed the publication of the correspondence to an enemy of Cicero. Dio Cassius, an author relatively near in time to the consular, dealt with a perhaps generally felt disquiet by composing an arguably fictitious 'dialogue' between the exiled Cicero and a somewhat elusive 'Philiscus *tis anêr*'. In a famous passage (38.18-29) Dio lays his dialogue in the mouths of the exiled Cicero and

'Philiscus', otherwise unknown, a former acquaintance whom he meets again in Macedonia, and who offers him consolation.[32]

Dio presents Philiscus as engaging the exiled Cicero in conversation. The dialogue appears to refute *Ad Atticum* 3.15, point by point.[33] It must be remembered that Dio Cassius is an historian, writing within the historiographic tradition. Dio's inclusion of an 'actual conversation' is typical of the difference between ancient biography and ancient historiography, between Plutarch's narrative of Cicero's exile (discussed above in Chapter 2) and the dramatic presentation of events that ancient historiography required. Dio normally exploits the historiographical convention of including speeches or dialogue in his narrative, to convey character, whereas Plutarch tends rather to moralise.[34]

Before we move to consideration of this consolatory conversation, some general points need to be made. The origins of the subgenre, the formal *consolatio ad exulem*, have been discussed in Chapter 1 and its characteristics recurred briefly in the discussion of informal consolation earlier in this chapter. Analysis of another example of formal consolation will give us a basis for comparison. I shall therefore start by comparing Dio's dialogue with a consolation to an exile by Plutarch (*Mor.* 599A-607F).[35] Stress will be on the manner in which Dio adapts the tradition to his topic.

Traditionally the formal consolation most often is cast as rhetorical diatribe, where the 'speaker' carries the intellectual burden of the argument, but involves a second person as the object of his outreach. The illusion of conversation is then mostly maintained by means of apostrophe and rhetorical questions, as well as assumed questioning by the addressee.[36] Plutarch's 'epistle', following the form of his other moral essays, is a declamatory monologue, addressed to the exile, but, by virtue of its publication, also pitched at a wider 'model readership'. Predominance of second person verb forms, imperatives and assumption of arguments to be countered, creates the effect of dialectic. Dio's 'discourse' between 'Philiscus' and Cicero, after its initial conversational introduction, is in fact also an intellectual monologue (where one *persona* carries the burden of thought) fitted with the trappings of dialectic exchange. Dio has therefore made explicit the normally implicit dialectic characteristics of diatribe, with monologue becoming assumed dialogue (very much in the manner of informal epistolography discussed above).

3.2.2 Comparison of Dio and Plutarch

Plutarch's epistle on exile and Dio's imaginary dialogue, although separated by more than a century, both come towards the end of a long tradition.[37] Dio Cassius is writing at the beginning of the third century.[38] Plutarch's consolation stems from the troubled first century. Both authors cover the same subject matter, and, even where the order differs, there are more similarities than differences in their manner of presentation. The direct influence of Plutarch on Dio need not necessarily be assumed.[39] They have as common factor the essential elements of formal exilic *consolatio*, which they adapt to the situation in hand.[40] These we have identified above in relation to Cicero's informal letters.[41] These are: the necessity of exhibiting a rational attitude to exile, the universality of the human condition as subservient to Fortune, discussion of places of exile, and discussion of exile as neutral, and not an evil.

The exordium of each work has a similar content: Plutarch's traditional analysis of the duty of a friend is reflected in Dio's conversational opening: 'Philiscus' pretends to act like a friend lightening a physical burden (38.18.1-4). Cicero is chided for his faint-hearted prostration (38.18.5). This parallels Plutarch's disquisition on a friend's duty to help the sufferer to examine his problem (*Mor.* 599A).

Both authors use medical imagery, the protagonist's suffering in each case being portrayed as a 'curable disease'. Both exhort the exile to submit to rational arguments: he must know that his pain stems from his perception of woe, not from fact.[42] 'Cicero' in this conversation shows himself more aware than in any of his exilic letters that he is not acting the exiled sage. He desires to partake of the 'medicine of philosophy' (38.19.1). The first step, so 'Philiscus' tells his eager disciple, is to 'count his blessings': his good health and the means with which to enjoy it (38.19.2).[43] 'Cicero's' rejoinders outline his inner feelings of dejection. Dio's portrayal of Cicero's awareness of misery (38.20-1) is not only historical, but also traditional, and clearly parallels the stuff of Plutarch's various assumptions about exile. Philiscus demolishes these in terms similar to the conventional arguments against the assumption that exile is an evil that we find in Plutarch (600B). 'Philiscus' exhorts the exile to find comfort in his own proven sagacity. His sense of justice should enable him to bear like a philosopher what Fortune (Tychê) brings (38.22.1, 2).[44]

Dio shows 'Philiscus' adapting a commonplace of exilic literature *ad hominem*, in his emphasis on Cicero's own responsibility for ordering his life and his role in bringing banishment upon himself (38.22.2-4).[45] This is in the vein of Plutarch's argument that it is not Zeus, but man himself that orders his lot (600D).

'Cicero' does not accept everything his friend offers him, but discourses on disenfranchisement and the other disadvantages of exile. These observations 'Philiscus' counters with traditional arguments about the universality of the human condition. The idea of world-citizenship may be based on the fact of man's adaptability and the frequency of voluntary exile (38.23). A fuller form of this argument may be found with Plutarch: not only is the world man's natural habitat, but the world itself is so small a speck in the universe that any one spot on it is very close to any other. The man who realises the advantage of enforced migration can choose a place suited to his temperament (600E – 601F).

Conventionally the next topic is choice of suitable places of retreat.

Plutarch's essay follows the usual discursive pattern. He discourses at length on choice of place, including islands traditionally associated with exile, such as Gyaros or Cinaros.[46] With this comes the argument that happiness is to be attained by the sequestered life,[47] free from civic duties[48] with time enough for study (602C-603F).

Plutarch next refutes negative views of exile as an evil: argument from cosmology refutes the idea of 'fixed stars being less happy than wandering planets' (*Mor.* 604B). Banishment from one city means access to all, freedom to travel, freedom to write (604C-F). Dio's dialogue is much less discursive on this point. 'Philiscus' limits his discussion of choice of destination to the suggestion that Cicero should find a remote retreat on the coast where he may enjoy his new-found *otium* (a reference, perhaps, to Cicero's Tusculan villa).[49] Dio's philosopher shows himself to be such with extensive reworking of the *topos* of creativity in exile. The creation of an own ambience for a happy life is illustrated with *exempla* from Greek and Roman history (38.26.3-27.3). Like Xenophon and Thucydides, Cicero should devote himself to farming and historiography (38.28.1). These two *exempla* are clearly from the common corpus of consolatory *topoi*, and also occur in Plutarch (605C), as well as Philistus, Timaeus, Androtion and Bacchylides.

The close of the traditional *consolatio ad exulem* could differ widely, and was usually most closely adapted to the circumstances of the addressee's life. Plutarch's peroration, for instance, quotes Empedocles on 'life as an exile from heaven' (607D, E).[50] As the soul has come from elsewhere, life is a 'journey' and the soul, imprisoned in the body, is free, wherever it may be going, to the extent to which it practises virtue and wisdom and thereby creates its own happiness.

Dio's choice of the consolatory tradition for the basis of historical elucidation may perhaps be ascribed to the fact that Cicero himself features within this tradition as one of the archetypical exiles. Plutarch, writing just over a hundred years after the famous consular's death, when refuting the idea that loss of fame is attendant upon exile, chooses as one of his *exempla* Cicero himself: which is better, to be the persecutor Clodius or the persecuted Cicero, he asks his friend (605E).[51] The *topos* of such 'active vs. passive' preference recurs with Dio's 'Philiscus': Cicero has attained the high office of consul; no second consulship is needed to add to his fame. The ultimate question is whether Cicero would prefer to be himself, alive but banished, or whether he would rather be a Marius or a Corvinus, whose multiple consulships did not keep them from death, the common lot of humanity (38.28.4).[52]

Dio is therefore writing from the perspective of an historian, even while making use of philosophical material. The use of dramatic irony was not precluded in the ancient conception of the limits of the historiographer's brief. He can therefore, with authorial hindsight, portray 'Philiscus' as employing a final, effective argument: the thought that present banish-

ment may pre-empt future ills of a more drastic nature. 'Philiscus' suggests that exile now may offer the pre-emption of a worse fate:
decapitation, and abuse of the ex-consular's grisly remains by all who pass
it by in the Forum (38.29.2, 3). Emphasis on 'all, man and woman' subtly
evokes Cicero's known fate and the role of Fulvia, widow of Clodius, and
wife of Antony, whose revoltingly feminine mutilation of the once-eloquent
tongue of the enemy of both husbands with a *fibula* (pin) is well-attested.[53]
'Philiscus' argument is obviously a *vaticinium post eventum* (prophecy
after the event) based Dio's awareness of Cicero's end, but it is equally part
of the tradition of commonplaces refuting the idea of exile as an evil, as
used, for instance, by Plutarch in his discussion of Euripides' *Phoenissae*.[54]

Dio's Cicero accepts the philosopher's cogent arguments and is greatly
comforted. If we had had only this passage from Dio Cassius as source, and
did not have Cicero's own letters from exile at hand, nor any other ancient
accounts (e.g. Plut. *Cic.* 32.5, where the exiled consular is likened to 'an
unhappy lover, yearning towards Italy')[55] we should have formed a totally
different picture of Cicero's demeanour in exile.[56] No downcast Roman
politician, but a self-sufficient Roman sage, in full control of his emotions,
and sustained by a centuries-old Greek tradition, strides from the scene,
presumably to take up those Greek philosophical studies conventionally
employed by the exiled to while away a time of enforced *otium* (leisure for
study) when removed from the hub of their Roman universe.

The peroration of Plutarch's consolation takes a different direction from
that of Dio: he quotes Empedocles on 'life as an exile from heaven' (607D,
E).[57] This exile ends with death, but as the soul has come from elsewhere,
life is a journey and, while on earth, the soul, imprisoned in the body, is
free wherever it goes, to the extent in which it practises virtue and wisdom
and thereby creates its own happiness. This concept, central to exilic
consolation, is illustrated by Ovid's use of his poetry as a means to escape
a miserable present, by Seneca's self-sufficiency in exile, and by Boethius'
composition, in exile, of the *Consolatio Philosophiae*, but only the Cicero
of Dio's fiction is in such control.

3.2.3 Senecan consolatio

With Seneca we come to the formal Latin adaptation, in form as well as
thrust, of the long Greek tradition of consolation. There are three *consolationes* in Seneca's collection of *Dialogues*. Strictly speaking, these are, like
Dio's 'conversation between Cicero and Philiscus', monologues dressed as
dialogue, or, better, rhetorical *suasoriae* (persuasive oratory) masquerading as formal letters.

The title *Dialogues* has traditionally been attached to Seneca's collection of ten treatises of which these three consolations comprise numbers
4, 9 and 10. The title implies no more than a technical attribution of
remarks to a speaker.[58] In terms of second person outreach the title may

rather be justified by remarking that Seneca's treatises generally involve the 'model' reader in the process of their creation, by use of direct address, apostrophe, assumed questioning and argument, whereas these three consolations very specifically are 'letters', with a single person as addressee and ostensibly as both 'empirical' and 'model' reader. As letters, however, they seem to fall half-way between what I have chosen to term 'primary' and 'secondary' epistle, for they appear to have been written for publication, which immediately involves a nuancing of the model readership involved. Griffin (1976: 21-2) suggests tentatively that these formal letters were very clearly written for consumption by a wider audience than purported by their author. It is generally agreed that the publication and the popularity of these works, two of which were written during Seneca's exile, could have served as an incentive for his recall.

With Seneca the link between exile and death is strong, for two of his *Consolationes* are exilic only in the sense that they were written by an exile to comfort the bereaved. These are, as we have noted above in Chapter 1, his mother Helvia, after the death of his own son, and Polybius, a freedman of the emperor Claudius, who lost a brother. The consolation, for the loss of a son, addressed to his friend Marcia, the daughter of the Stoic martyr Cremutius Cordus (who had committed suicide under Tiberius rather than be subservient to Seianus),[59] had set Seneca's pattern for extensive and personalised reworking of the declamatory genre of consolation to the bereaved. It probably dates from before Seneca's exile.[60] The *Consolatio ad Polybium* probably dates from the first months of his exile, and the *Consolatio ad matrem Helviam* from soon after, perhaps within the first ten months of exile.[61]

Seneca is famous for his adaptation of Stoic philosophy to Roman life. Yet all three consolations have a partly non-Stoic thrust. These strongly persuasive and pragmatic diatribes are coloured eclectically.[62] All clearly fall within the consolatory tradition. Each in some way relates to exile, the *Ad Marciam* more indirectly than the other two. Seneca also exhibits awareness of the tradition in his *Letters to Lucilius*, composed after his withdrawal from the court of Nero. In *Epistulae* 63.14 he confesses to being less able to apply consolatory tenets about the limiting of mourning in his own life than to carry on a discourse about them, a very human admission that many readers have wished Cicero could also have made.

The *Ad matrem Helviam de consolatione* ostensibly treats of the death of Helvia's grandchild, Seneca's infant son,[63] who had died some three weeks before its father was exiled, soon after the accession of Claudius, but Seneca's exile is its main topic. Here the exiled sage is the one offering consolation to a bereaved relative. Exhortation is aimed not so much at consoling a grandmother for the loss of an infant grandson than at consoling a mother, for the loss, by exile, of a son. The diatribe bears all the hallmarks of a typical *consolatio*. Seneca appears here, appropriate to the convention that equates exile with death. His consolation is, as it were, 'a voice from the dead', in the manner of Propertius' Cornelia elegy, and also as Ovid portrayed himself in exile.

Edwards (1997), following Griffin (1976: 3-5) stresses how little Seneca reveals of himself in his ostensibly personal letters to Lucilius. Griffin (1976: 412) quotes Abel's warning against the kind of 'positivism' that seeks to read an author's known outer circumstances into a text[64] and in her turn warns against the opposite kind: absolute belief in the 'truth' of circumstances portrayed in a literary effusion. Abel offered structural analysis as a viable alternative to both historicist and historical analysis. Present literary-critical methods tend largely to avoid both extremes, and the critic may concentrate on various other aspects, including 'deconstruction of the referential structure of Senecan language'.[65] For the moment I shall try to avoid both positivism and deconstruction, and like Abel, begin with a structural analysis.

The structure of Seneca's two exilic declamations bear comparison with that of the consolation of the bereaved Marcia,[66] the antecedents of which may be sought in Cicero's *Tusculan Disputations*.[67] The three *consolationes* follow a similar pattern. Here, in spite of the traditional title of the collection, there is no great pretence at dialogue. As elsewhere, Seneca appears conscious of his Ciceronian sources, while consciously rejecting the conversational mode, in favour of deliberate didacticism.[68] The declamatory framework of a conventional *suasoria* (set-piece of persuasive oratory) is personalised by reference to the addressee, who is, in each case, the protagonist in need of consolation. As may be expected, verbs in the second person, imperatives and, in the case of the two female addressees, feminine forms of adjectives and participles predominate.

The first 'dialogue', to (or rather, *with*, Marcia) has, demonstrably, eight sections: (1) exordium: initial *captatio benevolentiae* (soliciting of the addressee's favour) followed by an explanation of the author's approach; (2) then, in explicitly unusual order, two *exempla* of reactions to grief, respectively positive and negative, by Livia and Octavia, the wife and the sister of the emperor Augustus; (3) a linking section containing Stoic commonplaces on the immutability of Fate; (4) general precepts on the tempering of grief, conventionality of excessive grief, deliberate pre-emption of the assuagement of time, the predictable fickleness of *Fortuna*,[69] the externality of possessions, birth as the first step towards death, and the mutability of life;[70] (5) particular precepts relating to Marcia: on her bereavement, on the community of fellow sufferers, with historical *exempla* of Stoic acceptance of bereavement of offspring, on the even-handedness of *Fortuna* and the universality of the human condition; (6) a second linking section showing that grief is unnecessary for the living and futile for the dead; (7) particular precepts relating to Marcia's attitude: a refutation of the idea of death as evil, allusions to Fate's allotment of time and place, her son's freedom from future ills, his past achievements, and discussion of the ills of life, including exile, imprisonment and suicide.

Then follows an excursus on the suicide of Marcia's father according to Stoic precepts, by abstention from food. Next, a *laus mortui* ('praise of the deceased') ends with Stoic affirmation of the immortality of the soul. (8) The *peroratio* is couched as a *prosopopoeia* (appearance in person) by Cremutius Cordus himself, exhorting Marcia to contain her grief, to endure good and bad as *Fortuna* grants it, to keep mortality in mind, and to realise that the whole universe will end in a cyclic conflagration.[71]

The whole is a stylised set-piece, a show-piece of the tradition of consolation to the bereaved. Much of it is familiar from Cicero's correspondence. Its major thrust is Stoic, but Academic and Peripatetic influence is discernible, especially in its concession to the emotions, as are the threads of consolatory discourse from Chrysippus, Crantor and Antiphon, as we have so far established them, as well as aspects of Cynic and Epicurean thought. Seneca's language is striking and poetic. Dunn (1989) discusses the last line of the dialogue as a virtual dactylic hexameter, with verbal echoes from both Vergil, *Aeneid* 6.637, Anchises' revelation of the future to Aeneas, and Ovid, *Metamorphoses* 15.456-8, the words of Pythagoras to Numa. In the context of the appearance of a father-philosopher to reveal a glorious truth to his pupil-progeny, Cremutius and Marcia appear as a suitable third to the these literary pairs. That this is no 'letter', nor even a private exhortation in the form of a declamatory monologue, sets the stage for our reception of the other two *consolationes*. The *Ad Marciam* could very well have served, too, after the fall of Seianus, to set up its empiric author as a *persona* with strong connections with all who opposed or fell victim to Tiberius' praetorian prefect, the man who had driven Cremutius to suicide and caused his books to be burnt.[72]

Life in the early empire, as we have seen, was fraught with danger to those on the periphery of power. At some time after the composition of the *Ad Marciam*, Seneca was exiled on the count of a reputed affair with Claudius' niece Julia Livilla. He was to spend some seven years in all on Corsica. We may assume that it was in Seneca's interest to proclaim his innocence. The *Consolatio ad Polybium*, which purports to console the emperor's freedman (and the official in charge of petitions, including petitions for recall of an exile) on the death of a brother, has been castigated as servile, or excused as redolent of hidden irony.[73] Its relationship with the philosopher's exile is perhaps tenuous, and its consolatory content largely predictable and conventional, except for its greater stress on application to public duties instead of the more conventional advocacy of literature. It appears as a unique form of *captatio benevolentiae*, a pretext for adulation of Claudius. Yet it is important not only as an example of consolation to the bereaved, but for its exposition of the public duty of both the emperor and his freedman, whom Degl' Innocenti Pierini (1990b: 235-40) designates an effectual *alter ego* of Claudius.

The *Ad matrem Helviam de consolatione* is clearly exilic.[74] The *Ad Marciam* offers a structural paradigm, accentuating another aspect of exilic literature: the consistent equation of exile with death. The *Ad Helviam* is essentially a voice from beyond the grave, coming to comfort the bereaved. It is an admirable example of a formal *consolatio*, but one that combines comfort for exile with comfort after bereavement. In other words, we may combine the two usual consolatory schemata: *deceased – bereaved – comforter* and *comforter – exile*, but instead of five, only three persons are involved: the dead baby, who features as a minor focal point (virtually a lay figure), the grieving mother, both bereaved of the baby and bereft of her son, and the exile, who is the comforter of his mother in both capacities, but also, as the 'major deceased', a 'voice from the grave'. Novelty lies in the exile being the comforter, the one at Rome the bereaved. He is also the presumably suffering victim. A further novelty lies in the fact that this victim is the person that demonstrates Stoic *apatheia* (freedom from passion). The modern reader may be allowed here to see Seneca the playwright-actor at work, manipulating an intricate set of *personae* and slipping on one mask after the other. In the analysis that follows, we shall use the name 'Seneca' for all the *personae* that the empirical author has assumed, with due awareness that his creative pen has produced for us a multifaceted portrait of a benign and self-sufficient personality, behind which the creative author may sometimes allow his readers to glimpse his method, but seldom his mood.[75]

This complicated scene is set and the consolation is formally exact. Seven sections may be distinguished: exordium, *exempla*, precepts relating to Seneca (as the 'deceased'), a linking section, precepts relating to Helvia (as the 'bereaved') and a peroration.[76] The exordium comprises paragraphs 1-3, but inverting the order of subsections found in the *Ad Marciam*: an outline of his approach (1, 2) is followed by the *captatio benevolentiae*, which portrays Helvia not as a 'judge', but as the victim, or better, veteran of many attacks by Fortuna (3). If Helvia intends to sit in judgement on Fortuna, Seneca, as the advocate for the defence, will show that she has no case against Fortuna. Helvia has experienced good and bad fortune, and she acts as her own *exemplum*. She has in turn lost her mother, stepmother, uncle and husband, and three grandchildren, the last the infant, Seneca's child, whose death is the ostensible occasion of this missive. Her fortitude in bearing all other losses will act as *exemplum* for her now. As veteran she has learnt to suffer. Seneca will conquer her grief by showing her that she has no reason to be wretched (4.1).

This leads naturally to the precepts relating to Seneca himself, the exile as 'deceased'. Seneca's ordering of precepts differs from those of Plutarch and Dio Cassius, and also from his *Ad Marciam* and *Ad Polybium*. First, the exile reassures his mother that he is not unhappy (4.2) – perhaps not yet the perfect sage, but learning from the philosophers that externals are unimportant, and that one should expect only one constant from Fortuna: that she is inconstant (5). Next, exile as a 'change of place': he discusses in turn islands, voluntary exile, and migration, with examples of each (6.7).

Next, the problem of the universality of the human condition (which includes human mortality); self-sufficiency lies in internalisation of virtue; *exempla* are cited (8-11.6). Then follows the central argument against exile as 'an evil': the body needs but little, while the soul is free (11.7-13.6). Seneca's argument, that fame does not die with the ending of mortal life (13.7), is closer to the persuasion of the poets[77] than it is to the arguments of Plutarch, Dio Cassius and Boethius on the relativity, and consequent negligibility, of fame.

A linking passage (14) corresponds exactly with a similar link in the *Ad Marciam* (19.3), and also in the *Ad Polybium* (9). The philosopher asks his mother whether she is mourning for herself in losing him as her stay and support, or whether her unhappiness is for her son as an exile. This leads to precepts relating to Helvia. Again she serves as her own *exemplum*: she had previously been separated from him for long periods of time, and had borne this separation well. She was in any case independent of spirit and generous: giving to her offspring rather than attempting to receive from them. He exhorts her to grapple with Fortuna, first of all, predictably, by limiting her mourning (15-16.6). *Exempla* of virtuous women follow, suitable for the mother of an exile: Cornelia, mother of the Gracchi, was brave in all adversity; Rutilia followed her son Cotta into exile, and did not mourn at all when he was killed (16.7).

Seneca next advocates study as a means of assuaging grief; he advises his mother to apply herself to her studies, deploring the short-sightedness of her husband (his father) in not encouraging her in the pursuit of a liberal education (17) but considering her able of application even now. The consolation of philosophy can become the spiritual property of the bereaved mother of an exile as much as it can comfort the exiled sage himself. Finally, he exhorts her to count her blessings in the persons of her other sons, her grandchildren and her sister (18, 19). The sister acts as a final *exemplum* of courage in adversity, of modesty while the wife of a public official in Egypt, of bravery in bearing up under shipwreck and in salvaging for burial the corpse of her husband, who had drowned in the storm. This personal and pathetic detail of storm and shipwreck is very different from the cosmic vision of universal conflagration in the mouth of 'Cremutius Cordus' at the end of the *Ad Marciam*.

The *Ad Helviam*, even more than the *Ad Marciam*, offers an unusually detailed view of the lifestyle and interests of Roman women of the elite and the attitudes of their menfolk to them, but that is not the point of the present analysis. Nor, apparently, was the idea of comforting his mother the sole incentive for Seneca's composition of the work. By the very formality of this *consolatio* Seneca has signalled that his portrait of the artist as a happy man is a conscious construct, a public statement. In all his letters (which were clearly written for publication) Seneca was notoriously reticent about the details of his own life.[78] No biography can be composed from the few self-revelatory fragments in Seneca's epistles, for he treats of public matters. Only sometimes these public matters become metaphors for his inner life. And here, it seems, his inner life is offered as a metaphor for his public image: the *persona* that emerges here is of a man more involved in philosophy than in either politics or amorous dalliance.

The peroration is short, personal and optimistic: 'think of me often, know that I am happy and realise that I have leisure for my studies' (20). The stylised 'advantages of exile' as advocated by Dio Cassius' stock philosopher here take on the vigour of a personal communication. The exile is very much the self-sufficient sage, actively engaged in the exercise of the kind of self-consolation that Cicero advocated to others, but could not achieve himself. The cheerful autobiographical tone of the closing paragraph of this diatribe, which for the rest focuses mainly on the addressee as protagonist, is striking for its apparently candid thrust and tone. It is easy to imagine that Helvia must have been much consoled by the reception of the document, for the positive aspects of the peroration give a clear picture of Seneca as the self-sufficient exiled sage, speaking 'from beyond the grave', and practising in exile what he preaches to the 'bereaved' in Rome.[79]

It then takes an effort of will to realise that this 'dialogue' is in fact a public document, composed by an empirical author in exile, pitching his work as an ostensible comfort for his mother as first 'empirical reader' at Rome, but with a wider 'model readership' clearly envisaged, and that this reading public will in its turn reconceptualise the 'model author' (whose apparent openness here is an exception within his literary oeuvre). A closer look at the last sentences will demonstrate the degree to which this *is* a public (and poetic) document, as well as the degree to which it is not completely appropriate to consider the work as second person outreach. The *Ad Helviam* reflects a more subtle solipsism than Cicero's non-altruistic advice to exiles. It is nevertheless more concerned with the exile as *persona* than it is with the recipient as person.

The exile assures his mother that she can rest easy, for his mind is peacefully employed in happy occupations. He then launches into a *laus animi* (praise of the mind) in terms reminiscent perhaps of Cicero's *Dream of Scipio*, but even more directly of Lucretius' *Laus Epicuri* (praise of Epicurus, *De Rer. Nat.* 3.1-30). The mind, he says, ranges free and wide, examining this and sampling that, now thinking of geographical placement of lands, and then of the courses of rivers, understanding meteorological manifestations and at last bursting forth in an understanding of the Divine, and of its own indestructible nature: *aeternitatis suae memor in omne quod fuit futurumque est uadit omnibus saeculis* (while remembering its own immortality it ranges over all that ever was and ever will be in all ages, 20.2b). This prose hymn, in the climactic final position occupied by the Stoic vision of cyclic conflagration in the *Ad Marciam*, is contrived from many strands, not least being the stuff always recommended to an exile to while away his time: geographical and mete-orological research.[80]

The *Consolatio ad Polybium* may also be read as a document that creates its model author as a palpable *persona* within the text. Again second person outreach serves, however subtly, as a means of focusing upon the exile as protagonist. Yet it depicts, in its final paragraph, the exiled sage as mentally debilitated by his exile: Seneca had written this *consolatio* 'as well as he could' with a mind 'dulled and rusted', presumably by exile (18.4). Only in this passing allusion, and in an otherwise inexplicable excursus on Claudius, the author of his exile, does the exilic nature of the diatribe appear. Irony has been read into the document, which is redolent with what appears to modern readers as unctuous obsequiousness. Griffin (1976: 416) is worth quoting on the problem: 'Pliny and Tacitus understood the realities of despotism better than to see irony where it was painful to see flattery'. Ahl (1984a) shows that it was not always impossible for severe criticism of the powerful to masquerade as praise. Now, fifteen years after Ahl, in a literary-critical era dominated by reception theory, study of hermeneutics and the role of each reader in re-creating the text, the debate is more open than ever.

Part of the problem lies with the assumptions of readers of today, assumptions about consistency, as well as assumptions about the function ascribed by the ancients to a particular text. By this I mean not so much ancient authorial intention as ancient hermeneutics. The modern reader has difficulty in reconciling the generally accepted portrait of a stammering semi-spastic (as portrayed by Seneca himself in the *Apocolocyntosis*) with the paragon of eloquence, erudition and sagacity eulogised in the central sections of this diatribe. Tacitus reports (*Ann.* 13.3) that the Senecan eulogy written for the youthful Nero to pronounce on his deceased stepfather Claudius provoked laughter in the Senate.[81] The *Ad Polybium* appears less than candid, even disingenuous, in its eulogy of the emperor when still alive. However, even a sage in exile may be excused for resorting to flattery of the powerful to improve his civic lot.[82] Edwards (1997) stresses Seneca's assumption of sometimes conflicting roles both in his literature and in his life, and assumes that his interest in drama enabled him consistently to dissimulate on various levels. She reads from this a deep tension between the philosopher's urge to identify himself in his writings and the diplomat's desire toward impenetrability.

Significantly, Seneca, who supposedly had the means to suppress any of his writings that he deemed unworthy, apparently at no time made an effort to suppress this document, purposely including it in his published 'Dialogues'. Dio Cassius (61.10.2) appears to suggest that he suppressed an earlier version, addressed to the empress Messalina and other freedmen at Claudius' court. It will be remembered that Seneca was recalled at the behest of Messalina's successor as empress, Agrippina, Claudius' niece. Griffin (1976: 415) argues that suppression of a published document would have been difficult, and that the *Ad Polybium* may have been the document in question. Its opening sections are missing, and may well have contained Messalina's name. The tension between the attitude evinced toward Claudius in the *Ad Polybium* and in the *Apocolocyntosis* may perhaps be explained by assuming that Seneca may have tried to redirect a negative interpretation of his apparent obsequiousness in the earlier work by taking an opposite stance in the *Apocolocyntosis*. Griffin (pp. 133, 217) cites examples from the *Apocolocyntosis* of deliberate self-parody of the *Ad Polybium*. These may have served either to redirect readers' earlier interpretation of the text, or to have redirected the thrust of the earlier document itself.

The *Consolatio ad Polybium* has essentially the same structure as the *Ad Marciam*, without the equivalent of the first two sections of the *Ad Marciam*. The diatribe starts somewhat abruptly with a series of Stoic commonplaces on the relativity of the lifespan of cities against the perpetuity of Nature; even this universe is mortal; man cannot complain against Fate, for he is subject to Nature. The philosophical thrust is eclectic, with a non-Stoic, possibly Ovidian, equation of *Fortuna* ('Chance') with *Fatum* ('the fixed lot of humanity', 'God's will', 'Fate'). A section on the immutability of Fate repeats arguments from the *Ad Marciam*. Manning (1981: 27) argues that the *Ad Marciam* offers a 'defence' of *Fortuna* before Marcia as 'judge'. Similarly, paragraphs 2-3 of the *Ad Polybium* appear as Polybius' indictment of *Fortuna*, preparatory to Senecan defence.

We have seen that Seneca deliberately changed the 'usual order' for consolatory argument in the *Ad Marciam*. Here the order is presumably 'normal': a *laus mortui* (praise of the deceased) follows the indictment of *Fortuna* in this section (2, 3), next follow general precepts, precepts relating to Polybius (4-8), and a linking section which explores subjectivity and objectivity in grief (9). Then follow precepts relating to the deceased: death is no evil, the bereaved must remember past happiness (9.5-11). The long central section (12-14) exhorts Polybius in adulatory tones to draw his comfort from his patron Claudius. It may have been ironically meant. The passage represents an interpolation, within a consolation to one of his freedmen, of a *captatio benevolentiae* of the emperor Claudius. It appears to have been prompted by the exile's desire to return. Its overly servile tone is not untypical of the genre of 'appeal to the powerful'.[83]

After this excursus follows a series of exemplary heroes (15, 16), corresponding to the Stoic *exempla* in *Ad Marciam* 14-16. At this stage, therefore, Seneca has resumed his precepts relating to the bereaved. These end with the injunction to Polybius to concentrate on his studies, starting with easy composition,[84] and progressing to the writing of a *laus mortui* (18.1-4). The *peroration* predictably ends with the reiteration of the Stoic call for a reasonable control of grief, memory of past blessings, and reminiscence (18.5-8).

The concluding paragraph (18.4), corresponding to Cremutius Cordus'

97

cosmic vision of impending conflagration in the *Ad Marciam*, and the *laus animi* in *Ad Marciam* 20, stands in stark contrast to the other two conclusions. The exile apologises for the quality of his work, explaining, as noted above, that his mind was 'dulled and rusted' in exile. Instead of a grand vision of future aeons, we are presented with a morbid picture of a debilitated exile.[85] Without falling into either of the positivist traps adumbrated by Griffin (1976: 412), it is safe to comment that the tone of the work is tempered by an explicit exposition of the consciousness of the exile, as *persona*, of his own innocence and rectitude. He is appealing not for mercy, but for justice.

The last sentence combines a consolatory *topos* (the inability of the consoler to console when he himself is burdened) with poetic language redolent of the poet Ovid in exile;[86] the writer can scarcely express himself in Latin, as he is surrounded by barbarous growlings in an uncouth tongue:

> ... *cogita, quam non possit is alienae uacare consolationi, quem sua mala occupatum tenent, et quam non facile Latina ei homini uerba succurrant, quem barbarorum inconditus et barbaris quoque humanioribus grauis fremitus circumsonat.*

> ... just think how someone hardly has leisure to console another if he is himself held fast by miseries, and with what difficulty Latin words come to someone around whom a howling resounds, deep-seated in barbarity and unpleasing even to more civilised barbarians.

This lugubrious passage closely mirrors in a negative vein the positive concluding paragraph of the *Ad matrem Helviam* (20.1, 2) in content, but its tone is reversed. It is a *recusatio pro hebetatione animi* (literary excuse based on the dullness of the mind). Instead of the wide-ranging penetration of an Epicurean mind exploring all things, we are presented with the Lucretian prototype of humankind, grovelling down-trodden in the dust of his own misery.

We need to compare this portrait with the poems that can very plausibly be ascribed to our author during this exile on Corsica (Chapter 9) in order to discover other facets of the artist's many *personae*, designated by Edwards (1997: 33) as '[a] Senecan self ... multiple, fragmented and riven with conflict'. In both the *Ad Polybium* and the *Ad Helviam*, then, we see a conscious artist, fully accomplished in the consolatory tradition, using the tradition in a novel way. Its novelty is threefold: the exile is the one who reaches back to Rome; second person outreach is a cover for apparently non-solipsistic solipsism; the line between exile and death is virtually obliterated. Our last example will be an author standing on the brink of the final obliteration of that line, but very much in control. This author exploits second person outreach even more subtly, creating a new set of shifting *personae*.

3. Comfort in Exile

3.2.4 Boethius: Consolatio Philosophiae

Boethius, exiled and imprisoned at Pavia in the sixth century AD, as the victim of factional differences between Eastern domination and Roman subservience, writing his *Consolationes Philosophiae* while awaiting death, has produced both the chronological and the intellectual culmination of the Classical tradition of consolatory literature.[87] The *Consolatio Philosophiae* of Boethius has, as we have seen, a vast generic tradition behind it, both philosophical and literary. The consolation, Menippean in form but not spirit,[88] comprises five books of alternating prose and verse, with lyric sections offering condensed comment on the subject matter of the prose sections. Its texture is densely allusive, with a rich intertextuality that works as the learned Boethius' means of reflecting his own reception of a vast array of literary material. In form it is cast as a conversation between the exiled author and the apparition of '*Philosophia*' that comes to comfort him in his dejected state.

The *Consolatio Philosophiae* is autobiographical in the sense that the author casts himself as the protagonist, but throughout it is presented in the form of a 'dialogue', [89] here not so much Socratic dialectic, but, as with Dio Cassius' 'Philiscus' discourse, declamation cast as conversation. The protagonist acts as object of interrogation, and personified Philosophy expounds a segmented philosophic monologue. Lerer (1985) has argued that the silences are as important as the words, particularly the increasing silence of the protagonist who is shown as tacitly and gradually absorbing the tenets of philosophy until he can again show evidence of its mastery.[90]

In an elaborate five-volume *consolatio* it is to be expected that the thread of argument would be much more elaborate than in a shorter work, yet the traditional four rhetorical sections may be discerned.[91] Boethius' *Consolatio Philosophiae* is, however, not conventional, neither in its consolatory aspect nor as dialogue. In contrast to the self-sufficient construct presented by Seneca in his *Ad Polybium*, which degenerates into servility and misery, it portrays the initial alienation between an erstwhile philosopher and the truths he has lost, and his gradual re-adoption of these life-giving tenets. His despair is equated with sickness, which Philosophy proceeds to heal.[92]

Boethius' intricate use of grammatical persons is a main feature of the work. He simultaneously exploits mutually exclusive literary advantages inherent in the first person immediacy of autobiography and the second person urgency of exhortation. Here Boethius differs from, for instance, Augustine's use in his *Confessions* of second person invocations of the Deity, which intersperse his autobiographical narrative. Boethius' separate first person interrogator (*Philosophia* as authoritative 'I') still focuses on the protagonist himself as the exhortatory 'you'. First person confessional 'I' and second person exhortatory 'you' refer to the same character – the exiled philosopher who has lost his philosophical vision. The confessional 'I' narrates his fall from grace and recovery in first person preterite narrative; the exhortatory 'you' is often silent, or answers hesitatingly, while Philosophy brings him by a dialectic process to rediscovery of inner strength.

The *Consolatio* as dialogue[93] has as chief participants the exile and Dame Philosophy, but there are various other personae: the Muses, who are banished by Philosophy, and Fortune, who is presented in consistent contrast with Divine Providence, but is shown by Dame Philosophy as having done no more to the sufferer than she has done before to countless others. Above and within the words of *Philosophia* hovers the Deity, not of necessity the Christian God, but the God of philosophy, mysterious and transcendent, standing outside time and space, perfect in omniscience and infinite in self-sufficiency, yet in charge of the life of the sufferer, a fact that he in his misery has forgotten, and which *Philosophia* leads him to recall.

Curley (1987: 352) considers that the *Consolatio* transcends the limits of the genre, and sees the concept of 'the remedy being chosen as appropriate to the condition of the patient' as the only motif clearly taken from the consolatory genre. He stresses (p. 355) the 'peculiar texture of the *Consolatio*' as an indication of generic manipulation of a high order. As presentation of a 'self' in exile, more clearly than in Senecan consolation, it shows the *auctor* as *actor* (Winkler's term). Both *auctor* (creative author) and *actor* ('self as character in a drama') demonstrate a familiarity with Greek philosophic tradition, of which the *auctor* remains in firm control while he shows the *actor* regaining the control he had lost just before the first dramatic scene is opened with an elegiac lament.[94]

This elegiac lament ends with the telling line, *qui cecidit, stabili non erat ille gradu* (whoever has fallen, never stood on a firm step, 1.m.1.21). About thirty lines of prose serve to place the *auctor* as *actor* within the scene as the singer of the elegy just ended, and to describe the wonderful epiphany of Dame Philosophy. So the work starts in the first person, moves on to narrative, and then shifts into second person outreach. The reader gradually becomes aware of a crowded stage; Philosophy's first words are not addressed to the hapless victim, but ask of an unidentified fourth person, *Quis ...has scenicas meretriculas ad hunc aegrum permisit accedere quae dolores eius non modo nullis remediis fouerent, uerum dulcibus insuper alerunt uenenis?* (Who ... allowed these play-acting harlots near this patient, who will not only cosset his sorrows with remedies that are none, but also feed him with poison on top of that? 1.pr.1.30-2). The 'harlots' in question are the Muses of poetry and song. So it was not the victim singing a dirge by himself; the Muses had supported him in expressing his misery.

The Muses are virtually whipped off the stag and flee, never to reappear. *Philosophia* takes over care of the patient, and initially she applies the self-same remedy as had the discredited mistresses of song. She does not address the prisoner directly, but sings a dirge that mourns his fall into self-pity and the loss of that freedom that his mind once enjoyed.[95] Only at the beginning of the second prose section does Dame Philosophy at last address the despondent prisoner: *'Tunc ille es' ait, 'qui nostro quondam lacte nutritus educatus alimentis in uirilis animi robur euaseras?'* (So you are the man who was formerly suckled on my milk and brought up to manly strength of mind with my nourishment? 1.pr.2.3-5). The terrified prisoner is dumb-struck. A series of questions elicits no answers. It is to be noted that these serve as 'stage directions' for the visualisation of the scene: *'Agnoscis me? Quid taces? Pudore an stupore siluisti? Mallem pudore, sed te, ut video, stupor oppressit'* ('Do you recognise me? Why do you stay quiet? Did you keep mum from shame or from stupidity? I should prefer it to have been from shame, but as I see it, stupidity fell upon you', 1.pr.2.7-9). Personified *Philosophia* then wipes the tears from his eyes, and the re-education of the lapsed philosopher begins.

Personification of philosophy enables the author to make concrete the traditional consolatory idea that rational thought and conscious adaptation of the will helps the exile to bear all that Fortune brings. *Fortuna* ('Chance') is similarly personified, as the antagonistic third person, standing in contrast to Philosophy, intent on breaking down the resistance of the sage. Books 1 and 2 carry an exhortation of the exile toward rational acceptance of the buffeting of Fortune and realisation of the universality of Nature and of the human condition. Philosophy points out that Boethius' *real exile* lies in the fact that he has deserted her, in his subjection to the miseries that have assailed him. The place of final resort is heaven as the dwelling of Philosophy, the exile's spiritual home. This place can be sought and found, even in prison. Book 3 amplifies the content of the first two books, explaining how the wise man can oppose *Fortuna* in a rational manner.

For Boethius, there is a clear distinction between *Fortuna* and *Fatum*, concepts often blurred in Ovid and Seneca. The fourth book presents *Fatum* as divine action, perceived in its orderliness by all human reason, God's dynamic presence in the world.[96] This book addresses the problem of understanding evil and suffering by treating Boethius' exile as victimisation at the hands of evil men. It concentrates on a philosophical topic also addressed by Plutarch (*Mor.* 605E), the preferability of passive victimisation to active persecution. Boethius' argument runs that wickedness causes more unhappiness to its perpetrator than to its victim. Books 4 and 5 together comprise an extensive refutation of the concept of exile as an evil. Discussion centres on perception of the nature of Evil and Good, reaction to the so-called 'unfairness of Fate', and the ultimate vindication of the rule of Good in the superiority of the mind of the sage, which consciously strives toward a perfect knowledge of God.

Boethius, then, while differentiating between *Fortuna* and Fate, reconciles the problem of the prescience of God versus the rule of Fate, a problem not confined to exile. Its solution, spelled out in the last two books, is couched in terminology common in the consolatory genre: God is time-less and perceives all time from without, as in a single moment. So he knows what humankind will choose, and is even aware of changes of mind lying in the future of any individual. The concept of past, present and future encompassed in a single point of view underlies the argument, frequent in consolatory literature, that man's life is but an instant against the expanse of time, and its concomitant, that the world is but a dot within the universe.[97]

Although the work is cast in the conversational framework of first and second person exchange, its major thrust is autobiographical retrospection, and we shall return to it in Chapter 6.

3.3 The Protean tradition

We have seen that the consolatory tradition, although an apparently fixed genre with well-defined *topoi*, offered a rich spectrum of possibilities for adaptation. Where the notion of 'second person outreach' seems to have stood central to its beginnings, the tradition in the hands of the mainly Latin authors that we have considered had a distinctly and consistently double focus, on both the writer as first person and on the second person as object of the exchange. Only in the most clearly fictional account of the philosopher's interlocution of the exiled Cicero do we have the virtual disappearance of the 'speaker' as a *person* in own right. 'Philiscus' serves merely as a mouthpiece for presentation of traditional *topoi*. For the rest, whether Cicero as concerned politician is offering consolation to exiled friends, or Seneca as exile is reaching back to Rome, focus is divided between the concerns of the writer and the addressee. In the case of Boethius we find a creative author consciously dividing his view of himself (or the view which he chooses to project of the character that he terms 'myself') into a 'second person' *persona* of himself as the downtrodden outcast that is addressed by the 'first person interlocutor', a *persona* which he created from the abstract tenets of Greek philosophy. By distributing these roles, and by intricate use of second person narrative and variation of tense, Boethius has given a subtle and layered overview of the thought processes involved in the application of the consolatory tradition as self-therapy, and he has shown this tradition as alive, adaptable and efficacious.

4

From You to Me: Exilic Appeal

4.1 Bridging the divide

Aulus Caecina, writing to Cicero (*Fam.* 6.7) in December 46 BC about the possibility of bringing his self-exculpatory *Liber Querellarum* to Caesar's attention, touches on the central problem of writing from exile: the exile's first instinct is to exculpate himself, and that is potentially dangerous. Caecina is conscious of having sinned no more (and probably even less) than many others. Self-exculpation is, however, tantamount to accusation of the powerful figure who brought about the exile. Inveighing against the antagonist will not work, and is dangerous. Any form of apology carries the danger of misconstruction. If the exile's aim is to write an appeal for remission of sentence, subservience clothed in eulogy is the best approach.[1] Relatives (in Caecina's case, his son) are useless, for they have little political power; Caecina's only hope of support is Cicero himself, to whom he appeals for judicious services as editor and publisher. Cicero's various replies to Caecina are soothing and calculated to allay the exile's fears, while giving evidence of practical aid.[2]

Traditionally, both public and private consolations offered to exiles advocate literary studies as best occupation in exile: philosophy will comfort the exile, literature will amuse him. The exile who wishes to produce auto-centred prose has various options: personal letters to family and influential friends, chronicling the vicissitudes of his journey and seclusion, and appealing for comfort or aid; public letters of a similar nature, in which he publishes apologetic appeals to the wielder of power;[3] autobiography, rewriting history in a manner to arouse public opinion in his favour; invective against the initiators of his exile. The latter course was potentially dangerous, but possible for a returned exile, as Cicero shows in various speeches. The returned exile can, as did Dio Chrysostomus in his 13th oration, merely give a sober account of both his feelings and his actions whilst in exile.

In Chapter 3 we saw that even the apparently most selfless outreach from a comforting friend to the second person as addressee still closely involves focus on the writer or speaker as first person. When the displaced person is the writer, whether ostensible or empirical, and whereas displacement by definition involves alienation from the familiar, solipsism is perhaps unavoidable. The tendency towards self-dramatisation appears as a basic characteristic of most 'first person' exilic literature, which is frequently couched in the epistolary mode, but in some cases is adapted to other literary forms, particularly to poetry.

The first function of exilic epistle is to bridge the divide that separates the exile from those at Rome. Such a bridge very often serves to channel appeals for aid to a second person, safely at Rome. Such appeal is directed at the powerful. This power may lie in the political sphere, but it may also be psychological, the ability to give comfort. Aspects of such comfort-giving were explored in Chapter 3. This chapter will consider exilic outreach to a second person, with emphasis on appeals for practical aid. Our first example will be Cicero, where we shall consider the relatively small *corpus* of letters to his friend Atticus and his wife and family that date from his precipitate flight from Rome, and his miserable eighteen months at Dyrrachium.

Poetic letters are usually auto-centred in the sense that the first person is their major focus, even in 'mock letters' such as Ovid's *Heroides*. For these I have coined the term 'secondary epistle', but the terminology is in a sense inadequate. Where the creative (empirical) author and the ostensible (notional) writer coincide, we are closer to 'primary epistle' (as represented by Cicero's missives from exile). A positivist stance (acceptance of the 'literal truth' of the artist's poetic projection) will tempt the empirical reader to interpret as 'primary' poetic secondary epistle (as represented by Ovid's exilic poetry). This problem will receive due attention.

The exiled Ovid, during a conjectural ten-year period, until his death in about AD 17, produced nine books of purportedly autobiographical poetry, which, while serving all the functions outlined above, lifted the exile to an heroic plane. By creating the 'myth of exile', Ovid has created a paradigm for the literary treatment of the hopes, fears and vicissitudes of exile.[4] The empirical reader needs consciously to decide whether (or distinguish the degree to which) these secondary epistles at all conform to the characteristic of letter-writing as *sermo absentis* (conversation with an absent friend) as we defined it in our previous chapter. The greater part of the chapter will therefore concentrate on Ovid's poems from exile as appeals, to his friends, his wife, the emperor, and finally, to posterity – to us as his ultimate 'model readers'. Stress will be laid on the manner in which the creative author manages to dupe his wider readership into accepting these literary effusions as primary epistles to which they have been given privileged access. Here the terms 'internal' and 'external' audiences will prove useful.

We have seen that Roman political life offered many examples of greater or lesser fortitude in exile. Not all resorted to appeal of any kind. The paradigm of Stoic resistance to the vicissitudes of his lot that we have encountered so far, Cicero's correspondent, the Pompeian Marcellus, had an earlier parallel in Rutilius Rufus, for Cicero the great example of fortitude in exile. His career is worth examining briefly as a backdrop to the abject misery portrayed in Cicero's appeals to his correspondents. Rutilius Rufus, at his trial for corruption in 92 BC, remained conscious of his own integrity and innocence, and defended himself, says Quintilian (11.1.12), in an almost Socratic manner, refusing to resort to appeal, merely offering 'the truth' (Cic. *De Or.* 1.53.229).[5] He later refused all Sulla's appeals for him to return to Rome from exile from Smyrna, after leaving Mytilene.

Even during his public career, Rutilius had been devoted to literature.[6] During exile, Rutilius wrote treatises on grammar and lexicography and a contemporary Roman history, perhaps his own memoirs, perhaps an autobiography; the few extant fragments are not very clear.[7] This is consistent with Rutilius' demeanour at his trial, where his philosophical endurance caused him to accept contumely with equanimity. He did perhaps compose a self-exculpatory essay in Greek to repudiate allegations of collusion with Mithridates.[8] The Stoic Posidonius of Apamea, who visited him frequently in exile, was a major factor in the early establishment of the tradition of Rutilius as the ideal Stoic sage, demonstrating that tranquil self-sufficiency in exile with which philosophy arms her adherents (Cic. *Off.* 3.2.10). A fragment quoted by Charisius (1. p. 125 K) indicates his steadfastness: *P Rutilius de vita sua II 'Animo' inquit 'constante'* (P. Rutilius said about Book 2 of his autobiography 'With constant mind ...').[9]

So Rutilius appears as the willing Stoic martyr, free from complaints, appeals or self-justification. Cicero in exile is very different, as will be seen below. Private letters (to Atticus) and more formal letters (to his wife and family) attest to his first fears of impending danger, portray the almost day-by-day history of his seventeen months in exile and his near-hysterical obsession with self. His letters appeal for aid, deny finding comfort in literature or anything else, but finally record his triumphant recall. Cicero, no less than Ovid, romanticised his exile into an heroic myth, but to do so, he resorted to a variety of genres and modes. The cumulative picture will emerge over time, as we look in turn at Cicero's various generic excursions in the chapters that follow. Here we shall concentrate on Cicero's letters from exile as appeal to the second person in a dialogue at remove.

4.2 Cicero's letters of appeal

Cicero, in exile, demonstrates in his private letters to Atticus that the letter is truly *sermo absentis*, outreach by the author, as first person, to his reader as second person. Writing to Atticus from Tres Tabernae on 18 April 59 BC in the gloomy prologue to his exile (*Att.* 2.12), Cicero explains that a letter from Atticus, then at Rome, gives him a far better insight into life at

Rome than any tête-à-tête conversation with Curio. Most of Cicero's exilic letters fall outside the four categories ascribed to epistolography by Cicero himself: they convey very little factual information, are not entertaining, decry philosophy and seldom encourage their recipient. The focus of these letters is solipsistic, exhortation from the exile to his correspondent at Rome to do something about the exile's invidious position.[10]

Even before the decree of exile, Cicero's letters of 60 and 59 reflect a growing unease. His correspondents merely serve as sounding boards. At first, the general state of the Republic is of greater concern than any danger threatening his person, real as it is: *mortem et eiectionem quasi maiora timemus, quae multo sunt minora* (I fear death and banishment, which are much smaller, as if they are greater [than the danger to the Republic], *Att.* 2.18.1). His fears, so far, are for the general good, and he himself feels brave: *Non lubet fugere, aveo pugnare* (I don't want to flee – I'm spoiling for a fight! *ibid.* 3). He is aware of Clodius' threats, and proposes to bear them 'with the greatest dignity'. Caesar's somewhat surprising offer of an appointment to a legateship to Gaul would have saved both Cicero's person and his face, but it was refused. He still relished fighting back (*Att.* 2.19.5).

In 60, when storm clouds had already started gathering, Cicero idly contemplated going to Egypt 'to get away from this part of the world where people are tired of me and to come back when they have begun to miss me a little'. One important consideration impeded him: *Quid vero historiae de nobis ad annos DC praedicarint? Quas quidem ego multo magis vereor quam eorum hominum, qui hodie vivunt, rumusculos* (But what will history tell about me in six hundred years' time? For I fear *that* more than the petty tales of people now still alive, *Att.* 2.5.1). Cicero's regard for the judgement, not only of history, but also of his contemporaries, gains in importance in his own perceptions, and eventually appears as a fixation.

In the latter part of 59 concern about the actions of the triumvirs, cautiously designated as *eos, qui tenent omnia* (those men who hold all the power [that threaten to engulf the state]), alternates with a growing concern about Clodius, who threatens 'now violence, now a law suit' (*Att.* 2.22.1). By this time Cicero is willing even to resort to arms (*Q.Fr.* 1.2.66). Every movement of the Clodian plot and counter-plot is reported in guarded language. The author's moods swing with every letter. In October he confesses *prorsus vitae taedet* (I'm really tired of living, *Att.* 2.24.4). Appeal begins to loom in his consciousness and is reflected in his outreach. He begins to view his literary friends as a potential source of political support, which he tries to gain through praise of their scholarly efforts. The polymath Varro is his chief target, and his request to Atticus is candid: ... *sed ego mallem ad illum scripsisses mihi illum satisfacere, non quo faceret, sed ut faceret* (... but I should prefer you to write to him that I'm terribly pleased with him, not about the way he is acting, but really to get him to act [in my favour], *Att.* 2.25.1). This observation bespeaks profound psychological insight. He is still confident of general support: *firmissima benevolentia hominum muniti sumus* ... (I'm fortified with the extreme goodwill of people, *ibid*. 2).

This confidence proved unfounded when Clodius' machinations came to fruition. After Clodius' bill *de capite civis Romani*, interdicting from fire and water those who had killed Roman citizens without popular trial, Cicero put off his brave front, trying to gain support as *supplex* (supplicant), but, when the mourning garb adopted by his family and friends (*Att.* 3.15) proved useless, he fled precipitately, in the middle of the night (Plut. *Cic.* 31). A second bill *de exsilio Ciceronis* turned apparently voluntary withdrawal into officially sanctioned exile.

The short notes to Atticus written on the first leg of the exile's journey are full of thoughts of suicide. These first informal notes reflect shock and misery, but very little factual detail. Cicero concentrates on means to reach Atticus himself, hoping for his friend's continued support and real aid. He upbraids his friend for having kept him from suicide, a consideration which is frequently repeated, but he is generous enough to admit that he may, at some later stage, be grateful for it.[11] From Brindisi more formal letters of appeal go to his immediate family (*Fam*. 14.4) and Atticus (*Att.* 3.7), both dated 29 April 58. The practical details of the plans outlined in the two letters are inconsistent. To Atticus he mentions Epirus as a stopover on a possible journey to Athens; to his family he proposes journeying to Cyzicus via Macedonia. Only his misery is consistent. He admits to yearning for death. To his family Cicero confesses to being routed by his tears, to Atticus that he hardly wants to see the light of day and flees from company.

The letter to 'his family' becomes, during its course, a personal address to his wife Terentia, and parts of its prose seem to pre-empt the formulaic woeful lover of later Roman elegy: *te quam primum, mea vita, cupio videre et in tuo complexu emori* (You, my life, I long to see and in your embrace I want to die, *Fam*. 14.4.1). Although the letter purports to be comforting his distressed wife, the focus is on Cicero's civic self. Its lachrymose and sentimental tone reflects the misery of a fugitive from Rome more than it expresses the longing of a husband bereft of the company of his wife. Consciousness of rectitude is no comfort, but an added affliction, as he explains with an alliterated rhetorical flourish: *non vitium nostrum, sed virtus nostra nos afflixit* (It wasn't a wen, but my very own virtue which wounded me, *ibid*. 5). His sin is none other than to have gone on living, but life away from Rome is not really living. His life is continued only vicariously, through Terentia: *si te habebo, non mihi plane videbor perisse* (If I'll still have you, I shan't seem to have died completely, *ibid*. 3). A later letter addresses his brother Quintus in vaguely similar terms, but the focus again is on self and what he has lost:

an ego possum aut non cogitare aliquando de te aut umquam sine lacrimis

107

cogitare? cum enim te desidero, fratrem solum desidero? ... quid mihi sine te
umquam aut tibi sine me iucundum fuit? (Q.Fr. 1.3.3).

Can I possibly not occasionally think about you, or ever do so without crying?
For, when I long for you, am I not longing for my only brother? ... what was
ever pleasant for me without sharing it with you, or for you without sharing
it with me?

Stress on Quintus as his 'only' brother is Marcus Cicero's stress on his total
isolation and alienation from all that he holds dear.[12]

The journey over the Adriatic is not recorded. Soon Cicero is settled in
Plancius' house at Dyrrachium. Appeals to Atticus follow in a constant
stream, a psychological outreach for comfort. An anxious fifteen months or
so were spent at the house of his patient friend. The distraught Cicero
could not so much as decide whether or when to leave Dyrrachium in order
to join Atticus in Epirus. Atticus appears as an indulgent, kind and
resourceful friend, albeit perhaps with less warmth of feeling for Cicero
than Cicero has for him.

Cicero's appeals are more often than not for spiritual rather than
material relief (as in *Att.* 3.7).[13] His correspondents seem to exist only as
sounding boards for this misery. Cicero's informal correspondence reflects
his physical and mental debilitation in exile and offers a paradigm for the
articulation of the day-to-day emotional vicissitudes of exile, displaying
those psychological aspects which ancient philosophical effort usually
aimed at dispelling. Philosophy is inadequate: 'no wisdom nor philosophy
has the power to bear such great pain ...' (Q.Fr. 1.3.5). Cicero considers
himself unique in his present suffering. Loss of his *patria* (homeland) is
poetically termed *aerumna* (total alienation of all possessions). Similarly,
his wife is designated *Terentiam, unam omnium aerumnossissimam* ...
(Terentia, a woman uniquely stripped of all that is worth having ..., *Att.*
3.23.8).[14]

Occasionally he escapes from his web of woe. The tatters of consolation
offered his wife on 29 April 58 remind Terentia that they had experienced
a full life together (*viximus, floruimus* – we had a good life, and we were
successful), and had been laid low by their virtues, not by vice. Here the
despondent spouse concedes that he is 'more moved by her misery than by
his own' (*Fam.* 14.4.5). To his brother, however, Cicero admits that he has
lost all hope (Q.Fr. 1.4.2).

Cicero may be seen as the creator of the epistolary topos 'complaints
from exile'.[15] Its characteristics are partly anti-consolatory, partly a reflection of the Roman social and political system of *amicitia* in which *obligatio*
played a large role. Appeals for aid, gratitude for such, and, quite frequently, ingratitude for apparently insufficient aid, reflect the realities of
Roman political life.

The exile is weighed down by a misery of mythical proportions; only full
restitution can remove it. Thoughts of suicide occurred initially, but Cicero

was no Stoic sage. Suicide might suit a Cato, but it was not for him. Later, in subsequent retellings of his epic banishment, avoidance of death was equated with 'keeping the State alive'. At first, however, Atticus is up-braided for having held him back, and death is a *desideratum* (a most desirable objective).[16] Consciousness of culpability, but only for having allowed himself to be eliminated as a political power, alternates with fears for affecting the safety of others.[17] He never admits that the irregular execution of the Catilinarian conspirators was a mistake, for he never sees it as such.[18] Like another Socrates, he is certain that he should have received great honours for having served the state.

Political aid is sought from others. Cicero again hopes for Varro's support (*Att.* 3.15.1 and 3.18.1). He trusts that Atticus will be able to suppress an unfortunately timed political speech against Curio.[19] If it is leaked, he hopes anxiously that it can be passed off as a forgery (*Att.* 3.12.2) and he continues to worry about it (*Att.* 3.15.3). In January 57 Cicero appeals to Metellus Nepos to keep his 'relatives' (Metellus Celer's wife Clodia and her brother, the original author of his banishment) from persecuting him (*Fam.* 5.4). After Cicero's return from banishment, a letter of gratitude from Nepos, thanking Cicero for services rendered, reflects the efficacy of the appeal in restoring mutual friendship (*Fam.* 5.3).[20]

On the occasion of Atticus' adoption by and inheritance from an uncle, he forces himself to pen a more cheerful letter, acknowledging his friend's assistance and his own petulance, but the general drift is morbid (*Att.* 3.20). The *me miserum* (woe is me!) of this letter (1) is repeated in a pleonastic phrase later *oro obtestorque te, ut Quintum fratrem ames, quem ego miserum misere perdidi* (I beg and plead with you, that you be kind to my brother Quintus, that poor fellow whom I most miserably have ruined, *Att.* 3.23.5).[21] The exile's letters to his brother and wife are even more lachrymose (*Q.Fr.* 1.3.2, 3); tears drop on letters from home and blot the words (*Fam.* 14.3.1); he lost all when he lost his family (*Fam.* 14.1.5).

In fine, Cicero in exile articulates severe inner misery. His cry is not for temporary relief of pain, but for an end to it (*Att.* 3.7.2). His plans change with every letter, but none comes to fruition.[22] He cannot face his brother (*Att.* 3.9.1), who is 'too cheerful' (*Att.* 3.18.1). Grief keeps him from writing (*Att.* 3.10.3 and 3.12.3) – this from a frequent correspondent to the patient recipient of letter upon letter. He reassures Atticus about the falsity of a rumour that his mind has become unhinged through grief (*Att.* 3.15.2).

While still in Italy, early in April 58, Cicero assured Atticus that his loss of prestige had not changed him: *ego enim idem sum. Inimici mei mea mihi, non me ipsum ademerunt* (I'm still the same man. My enemies merely took my things from me, not myself, *Att.* 3.5). This is philosophical equanimity indeed. After the *interdictio aquae et ignis* his family are 'dearer to him than life'; it is their loss that is unbearable (*Att.* 3.22.3). His cry, as exile, that loss of life means less than loss of his *patria* (*Att.* 3.26)[23] much later found echoes in his appeals to the exiled Marcellus to return to the capital, if only to die there.[24] Yet when there is talk of return, his material losses loom larger: return to Rome and restitution 'only' of citizenship and rank would not be enough (*Att.* 3.23).

For modern readers the puzzle in Cicero's presentation of self in these ingenuous letters lies in his apparent unawareness of a personal, private self separable from a civic self. Both are to him embodied in his material possessions, the support of his family, and the honours of which he has been stripped. In his appeals to friends his private and public *personae* are conflated. In this we can discern a stance later mirrored by the attitude evidenced by Seneca in his consolations to Helvia and Polybius, where presentations of an apparently private self, both as assured philosopher and debilitated exile, actually serve to portray a public and politically harmless self worthy of recall. When Cicero the politician is banished, Cicero the friend, brother and husband yearns over the powerful personage that he once was, and his 'second person outreach' to his correspondents in Rome comprises appeals from family and friends for succour and support of that public personage.

4.3 Ovid's poems as 'letters from exile'

Ovid in exile also exploits the letter as *sermo absentis* (conversation with an absent friend). Two fallacies frequently recur in the interpretation of Ovid's exilic works: the assumption that the exilic poems are all letters, and the interpretation of the poetic public letter as in every way the equivalent of a private prose letter, that is, confusion of secondary with primary epistle.

In any study of the differences between primary and secondary epistle, a complex spectrum of relationships between empirical author and 'model' author, model (or implied) reader and internal and external audiences comes into play. The creative artistry of Ovid (the poet who happened to have been exiled) is such that centuries of empirical readers were beguiled into thinking of these poems as true reflections of the emotions and appeals of the 'real exile'.

Admittedly Ovid's exilic 'letters' display the basic characteristics of the epistolary mode. Cicero's letters may have offered a model to the exiled poet, but Ovid's own *Heroides* offer the best paradigm.[25] Both sets of 'letters' are poetry, and hence partake of the characteristics of 'secondary' or 'literary' epistle. The concept of a letter as *sermo absentis* and the extent to which model and empirical readership are involved in the mind of the empirical and model writer enables the poet of the *Heroides* to depict a protagonist (a particular *persona*) as a character in isolation, but in outreach to, or imagined interaction with, another character (the second *persona* in the equation). The protagonist reaches out to this second *persona* with second person verbs, apostrophe and other forms of conversational address.

We have seen that the epistolary mode of each poem in the *Heroides* reflects the personality of a particular suffering heroine. Each poem focuses on an absent, sometimes perfidious lover or husband. This second person is as important a *persona* in the heroine's monologue as she is herself in the fabric of the poem. Finally, far more than in third person narrative, the literary letter 'crystallises' or 'freezes' time in a dimensionless *now*. This *now* exists for each heroine as ostensible writer of an individual letter at the ostensible moment of composition. Ovid's heroines start their appeal with reference to their present condition and work backward in time to narrate a happier past, but they also project into the future to predict what lies ahead.[26] The empirical reader, reading the poem in 'real time' (a time long after both the mythical protagonist's moment of writing and the moment of final denouement in her mythical history), and familiar with other works with which a particular poem is involved in intertextual discourse, is in the position of a 'privileged reader'. The privileged reader's greater knowledge and awareness of an outcome (which still lies in the projected future of the protagonist) turns every projection of a bleak (or happy) future for the writer into irony.[27] This observation held as true for Ovid's contemporary readership at Rome as it does for us today.

The *Heroides* are presented by Ovid as 'real letters' and not merely *suasoriae* in verse, so Jacobson (1974; *passim*).[28] He lists six points: these are formal letters, but fictitious, in verse form, each a free standing poem, all love letters, and all mythical. If we take this distinction as point of departure, we can similarly categorise Ovid's exilic letters, in particular those embodying some form of appeal. They have six complementary characteristics: they are formal letters, purportedly factual, in verse form, each a free-standing poem; most express affection but some express hatred; writer and addressee are from the 'real' Augustan world. Yet Ovid's exilic poetry is stylised, universalising the particular, and giving voice to all victims of exile. To the extent that these 'letters' were originally pitched at a wider readership than the ostensible addressee, we may categorise them as 'secondary epistle'.

Both Ovid's *Heroides* and his exilic letter poems are persuasive, involving the interaction between the writer as first person and the reader or listener as second person. In his poems from exile Ovid appears frequently to depict himself as a 'male Heroid', alone and alienated, but reaching out in appeal to his correspondents at Rome. Publication of the poems broadened the base of potential recipients, and we may guess at a considerable slippage between original addressee and ultimate audience.

For the sake of clarity we need here to review the concept of shifting *personae* in the exilic poems. Poet and exile are not necessarily or not always identical in all aspects, but the first person speaker in all but a few

111

cases[29] throughout Ovid's exilic *oeuvre* is an exile, a Roman poet, if not necessarily completely or exclusively Ovid-the-poet, the historic personage that was born at Sulmo in 42 BC. In the exilic works both 'exiled poet' and 'addressee' may be *personae* assumed or imagined by the creator-poet as manipulator of his material. From a scrutiny of the 'personages' assumed to be involved in the exilic poetry, we can deduce the dialectic levels of the poet's discourse.[30]

For the purpose of this discussion the terms 'empirical' and 'model', as relating to author and audience, will be expanded. I shall refer to the creative poet as 'Ovid' or 'the poet', to the implicit letter-writer as 'the exile' and to his explicit addressee as 'the addressee', 'ostensible addressee', or the 'internal audience'. For the wider range of potential readers, both contemporary and modern, I shall use the terms 'real' or 'external audience',[31] with recognition of the fact that such an audience is not static but always in a state of becoming, as long as the poems of exile are read.

Secondary epistle has many levels of appeal, each involving a different second person interlocutor or internal audience envisaged as recipient in the mind of the creator-poet. Appeal is conveyed through the normal dialectic means of assumed question and answer, apostrophe and direct address. Assumption by the exile as writer of more than emotional response by his distant interlocutors to such imagined conversation gives a further dialectic dimension to the exilic poetry. The identity of the absent interlocutor may differ from poem to poem. In our discussion of narrative we distinguished many shifting aspects of such internal audience. These distinctions apply even more urgently to ostensibly first person appeal, as we have seen in our discussion of comfort in exile. With the poems from Tomis we may distinguish Ovid-the-exile appealing to individual address-ees, but, through the publication of these works, we see him appealing to a wider readership, from whom an emotional response is elicited. Behind these creations we may distinguish Ovid the artist appealing to his external readers, both of his day and of future generations.[32] The response of his external audience, amusement or sympathy, is still part of the 'first person – second person interaction' implicit in all communication.

It has been noted that not all the exilic poems are letters, some even shifting internally from one mode to another, but all involve outreach to a second person. Discussion below will therefore consider different aspects of such first person – second person interaction. We shall concentrate in turn on Ovid's epistolary discourse, that is, the means whereby he creates the impression of conversation at remove, then the apparent objective of his discourse (evocation and affirmation of the ties of friendship and conjugal love), then on his transcendental outreach in hymns and prayers, to his Muse and to Augustus as god. Finally we shall consider the degree to which the interpersonal exchange between author and reader is still in a state of becoming, as adumbrated above.

Ovid in the *Heroides* consciously invokes the structural patterning and repetitiveness of myth. Various heroines write, their circumstances essentially the same. Each has lost all she holds dear, in the person of her addressee. Her letter is written at a moment of crisis. She does not know what lies ahead, nor does her addressee, whom she projects as reading the missive at some future moment when her 'now' will have become their common past. The privileged readers, in their quasi-Olympian knowledge of the outcome of the interaction of each individual pair, read more into the 'writer's' words than she herself is aware of. The empirical author, the poet himself, was himself in the same privileged position when he penned the poems, and conscious irony is an aspect of his style. With the hindsight of two thousand years we are in the position of a privileged reader with regard to our knowledge of the efficacy of the exile's pleas (they were not efficacious), but in the end we are baffled by the silence of centuries. Too much has been lost. We can only draw on our critical awareness of the creative author's style, and judge his contemporary appeal by the warmth of our own emotional responses.

The value of myth for subjective, psychological projection applies *mutatis mutandis* to the world of the exile, where only one person speaks in a structurally static, timeless situation. His outreach, to many individual addressees, is as unrewarded as that of all the women featured in the *Heroides* (with the exception of Penelope).[33] To his modern, privileged readership, at the remove of two millennia, the irony of his unrequited appeal is as obvious as the pathos of Medea's outreach to Jason in *Heroides* 12. Yet we as the modern readership are equally, perhaps more than the exile was himself, in the dark about the response of individual contemporary addressees to individual appeals. All we have to go on is the series of apparently thankless letters reaching out to a silent readership at Rome. It is this silence of non-response that contributes to the mythical dimension of the exile's appeals.

We have seen that whereas the 'writing' heroine knows only her past story, the creative poet of the *Heroides* can assume omniscience, and can also assume a privileged knowledge in his general readership, of the outcome of the myth. Narrative details can be condensed, shifted, or merely alluded to. The 'writing' exile knows his own past, but cannot know his future. The creative poet cannot presume any knowledge in his general readership of the exile's present or past circumstances. Cicero appears aware of this problem, giving very few details of the physical aspects of his exile. Mood rather than fact predominates. Like Cicero, the 'writers' in the *Heroides* and in the exilic poems also differ from narrators in epic or drama in that they convey metaphysical rather than physical information. Ovid in exile is, like Cicero, a single 'writer', reaching out to many addressees, but this 'writer' is largely a construct. Desolation and isolation are suggested by the repetitive offering of similar details to a wide circle. Their apparent lack of understanding of his circumstances, in spite of all his communications, emphasises this isolation. A constant unanswered call for response conveys the impression of a 'zone of silence' around the exile. Exilic time, although marked by frequent seasonal references, appears frozen in an ever-present winter.[34] Like Ovid's *Heroides*, the exile can play upon the contrasts of 'now' and 'then' to convey a picture of psychologically subjective, internalised suffering.

4.4 Ovid's use of literary epistolary devices

Ovid's exilic corpus does not appear to have been planned by the poet to form one grand scheme, with a clear-cut aim of completion over the course of eight to ten years. This is evident from the developing use of the letter form, which increases noticeably in the course of the *Tristia*, and reaches its peak in the unitary collection of 'Black Sea Letters', *Epistolae ex Ponto* 1-3.[35] The last poem in Book 4 of the Pontic Epistles is not a letter but a monologue, addressed to the exile's unspecified enemy. In this last book the poet is again moving away from the epistolary mode.[36]

A problem of literary epistolary composition is that the ostensible writer sometimes has to give the addressee information that he could have been expected to know, in order to establish a framework for the external audience's understanding. This the exiled poet largely manages to avoid. An exception is the hints of common knowledge shared only by the exile and Augustus, which he will not divulge to either his ostensible or his real readership, thereby retaining the reader's interest.

There is also the problem of credibility. The physical circumstance of the exile-as-hero may on occasion preclude writing or make writing difficult. The effect of immediacy is so great in the storm poems, *Tristia* 1.2 and 1.4 (prayers, not letters), that their despairing character has been interpreted by positivist critics as the direct result of sea-sickness and the difficulty of applying pen to paper in a violently tossing ship. So too, the *Botenbericht* of *Tristia* 1.3.91-100 (again not a letter, but reminiscing narrative) has occasioned conjecture as to 'how the exile could have known' about his wife's swoon. Willing suspension of disbelief in the external audience is needed to accept that *Ex Ponto* 4.14 is a written reply to criticism by the people of Tomis (suddenly fluent in Latin) that the poet had maligned them in his poetry.

Ovid uses various interlocutionary devices to turn the poems from exile into letters. Apostrophe and address of anonymous friends increase in frequency throughout the *Tristia*.[37] Friends are addressed by name in the *Epistolae ex Ponto*. The title of this work indicates the nature of the poems, but even in the *Tristia* a variety of 'conversational' epistolary devices, as with Horace's *Epistles*, create the feel of letters by strengthening the impression of *sermo absentis* (conversation at remove). These are: use of second person verbs, apostrophe, questions and answers to assumed questions (involvement of the absent interlocutor), and, epistolary greeting formulae at the beginnings and endings of individual poems.[38] Such epistolary outreach stretches through time as well as through space. 'Posterity' and the 'candid reader' seem often to be interchangeable.[39]

Most of the 'letters' from exile specifically indicate that they are letters, with variations of standard epistolary address, or use of the verb *mitto*, not *dico*, 'send', not 'say').[40] The first verses mostly characterise a poem as either 'letter' or 'not letter', but after that the epistolary stance is some-times undercut.[41] As 'second person' or absent interlocutor, the exile as speaker addresses his wife and anonymous friends in the *Tristia*, his wife and friends by name in the *Epistolae ex Ponto*.[42] Some letters are directed to public figures: *Tristia* 2 is addressed the emperor, also the implied recipient of at least some other poems.[43] Sometimes abstractions feature: the exiled poet's little book (*Tr.* 1.1), the exile's birthday (*Tr.* 3.13). *Tristia* 4.10 addresses posterity, a 'second person' yet to come into being.

Outreach to a second person, so one might expect, would involve fre-quent use of the personal pronoun *tu* in the vocative singular, but the form occurs only twice throughout Ovid's exilic corpus (*Tr.* 5.4.31 and 5.6.1). Writer and audience are involved in other ways, allowing for great subtlety of appeal. Vocatives are, however, frequent, as, for instance *posteritas* at *Tristia* 4.10.2. Not only the 'posterity' addressed here was the target of the exile's autobiography; his Roman reading public, perhaps even the em-peror himself, were meant to hear the poet's strong vindication of his art.

As in most non-narrative elegy, the second person or addressee as actor or interlocutor comes to the fore as a strongly-felt presence.[44] The pro-nouns *tu* and *vos* (in grammatical cases other than vocative) occur more than 500 times throughout the exilic oeuvre, so that there is a continuous feel of conversation. Modern discourse analysis has shown that semantic differentiation of grammatical 'persons' shows more combinations than has traditionally been thought. *Vos* implies either '*tu* plus *tu*', or '*tu* plus *ille*', or '*nos* minus *ego*'. Fugier (1976) suggests that *vos* as '*nos* minus *ego*' is the meaning most frequently implied by the exile. He considers himself a detached part of his Roman readership, private and public. Fugier's detailed study shows that, taking into consideration 'real' versus 'ostensi-ble' addressee and speaker, there are twenty-seven combinations and permutations of the persons *ego, tu, ille*. In the *Tristia* and *Epistolae ex Ponto* the most frequent *formulae* comprise conversations by *ego* (the exile) with *tu* (his addressee) about *ille* (the emperor) or about *ego* (himself and his situation).

The letters to the exile's wife[45] and to the young poetess Perilla, perhaps his stepdaughter (*Tr.* 3.7) often involve discussion by *ego* with *tu* about *tu* and *ego*. When the object of conversation is the *tu*, imperatives predomi-nate. When the object of conversation is *ego*,[46] verbs are in the present tense. When the poems refer to *ille* (very often Augustus), the most frequent tense is past, as in *Tristia* 1.2.93 *noluit hoc Caesar* (but Caesar did not want this to happen).

Strangely, very seldom do we have conversation by *ego* with *ego* about

115

ego. That is, the *Tristia* and Pontic epistles do not offer a series of soliloquies. Only once does the exile address himself by name. Ostensible impersonality and an Homeric echo in *Ex Ponto* 3.7.13 lends heroic stature to the exile: *hoc quoque, Naso, feres: etenim peiora tulisti* (This too, Naso, you will bear: for you have borne worse).[47]

Ostensible first person – second person involvement occasionally shades off from an ostensible addressee to another 'real' addressee or external audience, apostrophised in the vocative. Examples are the apostrophe of members of the imperial household, in poems not directly addressed to them. The ostensible 'digression' may be in fact the 'real' target, as, for instance, in *Ex Ponto* 4.8, to Suillius, Ovid's stepson-in-law, which digresses at verses 31 and 65 in apparent apostrophe of Germanicus. The poem is aimed at ingratiating the exile with a powerful potential patron. Similarly *Ex Ponto* 2.7, to Ovid's friend Atticus, digresses at verse 67 into an apostrophe of the emperor.[48]

Apostrophe often serves to point pathos, and to draw the external reader's sympathy. Significantly, *Ex Ponto* 4.16, the very last poem in the collection, ends on an apostrophe of *Livor* (personified carping Envy).[49] The concept of Envy as a vital, evil force that harms the purveyor of slighter genres such as lyric or elegy is a Hellenistic concept frequently exploited by Ovid. Its metrical or prosodic equivalence with both 'Caesar' and 'Livia' gives it a particular resonance in the exilic poems. A ruler that had no understanding of playful poetry, but exiled its chief proponent, is invoked in the minds of the external audience when Envy is reproached for inflicting countless blows on a lifeless corpse. The external reader, as second person-at-remove, is involved emotionally.

Apostrophe of the dead conveys a powerful effect of pathos. The consular Fabius Maximus, patronus the exile's wife, had been the object of appeal for intercession with Augustus (*Pont.* 2.10). As *amicus Caesaris* (member of Augustus' inner circle), he was a potentially powerful ally, and several poems are addressed to him, such as the playful narrative in *Ex Ponto* 3.3 telling Fabius about an epiphany of the god *Amor*, who had flown to Pontus to vindicate his devotee.[50] A later poem (*Pont.* 4.6) in pathetic apostrophe bewails the great man's having died before achieving the exile's recall, *Fabiae laus, Maxime, gentis* ... (Oh, pride of the Fabian family, dear Maximus ..., *Pont.* 4.6.9). The exile goes on darkly to blame himself for having been the cause of Fabius' death, leaving his readership with an impression of dangerous intrigue of which he had been a part, or perhaps only of the real danger of corresponding with the hapless outcast.[51]

Skilful use of questions adds to the epistolary 'feel' of the poems. In Cicero's correspondence, the convention of *sermo absentis* in primary epistle expects individual responses and thoughtful, not emotional, answers. Throughout the exilic poems Ovid appears acutely conscious of the conversational nature of his poetry, but his questions are pathetically coloured, aimed at eliciting sympathy from his readers.[52] Rhetorical questions may be of two kinds. In the first kind the speaker asks a question to which he expects an emotional response, in the second he pretends to reply to an assumed question. Only occasionally such questions are framed as *Selbstkorrektur* (the introspective corrective of soliloquy). Such questions convey pathos and involve both internal and external readers in the exile's plight, as in *Ex Pont.* 3.7.29-31, where the exile asks himself why he had ever thought that his lot could be relieved in any way. His readers are expected to reply with an upwelling of sympathy.[53]

Reciprocity is assumed as an emotional reaction on the part of the addressee to a question that distance and time prevents him from answering. Real reciprocity lies in the emotional response of the external audience to the writer's appeal, for instance to the anguished cry at *Tristia* 2.343-4:

> *Ei mihi, quid didici? cur me docuere parentes*
> *litteraque est oculos ulla morata meos?*

> Oh my, why did I study? Why did my parents educate me or why did any literature ever engage the attention of my eyes?

No rational reply is expected from the ostensible addressee, the emperor Augustus. This poem, the poet's *apologia pro vita sua* (justification of his life and deeds), purports to be addressed to Augustus. It is not a letter, but a 'speech for the defence'. Questions are therefore often casuistic rather than emotional or personal. In *Tristia* 2.31, for example, Augustus is offered the traditional argument for the justification of wrongdoing: 'if I had not sinned, how then would you have been able to forgive?'

Ostensible and real addressee may diverge widely. In this same poem, at vv. 313-14 the poet appears to be asking a question either of himself, or of the emperor. Alluding to the unfairness of Augustus' strictures on his amatory poetry, he asks why his Muse was 'too wanton' and why she taught people to love. Part of the joke of the *Ars Amatoria* was that it taught 'what everybody knows', and that promiscuity had been in existence long *before* anyone had read Ovid's book. Why, the poet asks, did he not rather sing of Troy or Thebes?

> *cur non Argolicis potius quae concidit armis*
> *vexata est iterum carmine Troia meo?*
> *cur tacui Thebas et vulnera mutua fratrum,*
> *et septem portas, sub duce quamque suo?*   (*Tr.* 2.317-20)

> Why didn't I rather harass Troy once more in my song, Troy that fell to Argive arms? Why did I keep mum about Thebes and the wounds that the two brothers inflicted on each other, and the Seven Gates, each under its own commander?

Key words that point to irony here are *vexata* (harassed), *iterum* (once more) and *tacui* (kept mum). The implication is that jaded, well-worn or outworn literary themes are *safer*. The poet is criticising Augustus' taste in literature and the emperor's outmoded literary conservatism. An apparently ingenuous rhetorical question conveys such criticism to an external audience.

The second type of question is assumed by the writer to have been addressed to him by an imaginary interlocutor. The basic difference between such assumptions and rhetorical questions, as discussed above, is that the poet supplies answers. Most often assumption of questioning represents an outreach to the poet's external audience. Communication from writer to reader lies at the heart of such questioning. Questions are only a means of focusing on the information, either factual or psychological, that the exile wants to convey.[54] Here his 'answers' are more important than the 'questions'. Apparently 'factual' answers often serve as a bid for sympathy.

Assumption of questioning is introduced by variant forms of *quaerere*, *requirere* or *rogare* (all meaning 'to question'). The absent interlocutor may be either an unspecified third person (*siquis*, 'someone', etc.) or an impersonal second person. The assumed question creates an impression of dialogue. It establishes movement within a poem, and, for the exile, communication with the outside world. The greeting formula *quid agis?*[55] is ostensibly taken at face value, and answered, as in *Tristia* 3.5.24:

> *si tamen interea, quid in his ego perditus oris*
> *(quod te credibile est quaerere) quaeris, agam:*
> *spe trahor exigua ...* [56]

And if perhaps in the mean time if you should ask what I'm doing, lost here on these shores (as well you might) – I'm dragged along by a slight hope ...

Frequently the answer to such an assumed question disarms criticism, as in: *cur igitur scribam, miraris: miror et ipse, /et tecum quaero saepe quid inde petam* (Why should I write, you wonder. I wonder myself, and along with you I question what I am looking for from my poetry, *Pont.* 1.5.29, 30). Such questions are often concerned with poetics, vindicating the exile's continued composition. In *Tristia* 5.1.35-80 a series of such questions offers the exiled poet an opportunity both to explain his motives, and to excuse the content of his verse. These questions are answered by counter-questions, e.g. *interea nostri quid agant nisi triste libelli?* (meantime, how should my books be doing if not sadly? v. 47). An objection that the poems are 'bad' (v. 69) is countered with: *fateor. quis te mala sumere cogit?* (I confess. But who drives you to read this drivel?).[57]

The pathos mounts. The final assumed question is 'why do I send these "bad" poems to Rome?' This offers a unique opportunity for self-explication, and for intense emotional appeal: *vobiscum cupio quolibet esse modo* (I long to be with you, in whatever way I can! v. 80). The answer also offers a strong vindication of the power of poetry to transcend time and distance, binding together the exile and his friends. The plural *you* here is the inclusive second person, involving internal and external readership, and even future generations.[58] The poet *is* 'with' his readers, in the most powerful way, through his poetry.

4.5 Ovid's poems as portrayal of the conventions of *amicitia*

Ovid's poems from exile are rooted (as are Cicero's letters) in the tradition of the Roman system of mutual obligation. Appeals to friends assume a conscious obligation which will be fulfilled by the correspondent. Public and private aspects of *amicitia* may be distinguished. *Amicitia*, as a political term for political alliance, often involved no more than a bond of mutual usefulness, to be discarded at will.[59] Both political alliance and private friendship involved mutual obligation. Ovid's exilic *oeuvre* involves both kinds of *amicitia*, but predominant is an almost Horatian celebration of personal affection above public politics. Gently sly self-irony and flippancy in expressions of affection indicates the health and durability of that friendship.

Syme (1978: chs V to IX), offers complete prosopographical details on Ovid's friends, which will not be repeated here.[60] Our concern here is not so much address of individual friends of the exile, as the manner in which the poet celebrates friendship. Disconcertingly, the exile protests over long intervals of time to different friends that 'this particular friend' was the exile's 'only true and real saviour and support'.[61] Such apparent insincerity serves to show the exile as shallow and self-seeking, even in his protestations of friendship. At the poetic level we find the observant artist depicting human nature and the conventions of friendly address for what they often are.[62] The exile often goes into transports of apology for breaking with initial anonymity (e.g. *Pont.* 1.2). This either works as reproach of the friend for cowardice, or it points to the arbitrary and cruel nature of the emperor, who is not to be offended.[63]

Ovid had at Rome been involved in the poetic coterie patronised by Messalla Corvinus. Familial *obligatio* in the case of the sons of Messalla Corvinus[64] or the 'testamentary request' of a deceased friend,[65] or the ties of *sodalitas*, with its religious connotation,[66] are used as the bases for appeal. The exile is indubitably lonely and misses his friends, but his focus is subjective. The exile imagines 'them' as missing 'me'. At *Ex Pont.* 3.5.39ff. the exile sadly wonders whether the *sodalitas* to whom Cotta reads aloud his most recent missives[67] ever miss the exiled poet from their number. It is Bacchus' feast day: the exile imagines his fellow-votaries around the festive board and the god looking around and missing *nescioquis ... cultor* (one or other of my adherents ... I'm not sure which, *Tr.* 5.3.34). Cotta was clearly a bosom friend of the love-poet when he was still

119

in Rome, and he was from a powerful family, but appeals for his aid diminish over time.[68]

Gratitude for aid, largely unspecified, and for fidelity, as contrasted with desertion by others, occurs most frequently in *Ex Ponto* 1-3, the collection which treats so largely of the duties of friendship. The very general terms of the poet's gratitude can frequently be explained as tactful eulogy leading up to more specific requests, mostly for intercession. Brutus is for instance requested to give aid to the poet's 'children', that is, to publish his books.[69]

In many of his appeals for aid the poet reciprocates with a favour, 'immortality by means of his song', diverting to a male friend a *topos* from elegy. Poetry has the power to immortalise friendship. Without it, the fame of the paragons of *amicitia* (Orestes and Pylades, Theseus and Pirithous) would never have reached posterity (*Pont.* 2.6.25). These mythical paragons, together with allusions to Vergil's Euryalus and Nisus, form part of a consistent web of imagery, often related to the poetic predilections of the correspondent.[70]

Address in letters from Pontus of certain friends who were also featured long before in the *Amores*, either attests to lasting affection or serves to rewrite the past. Ovid's friend Atticus, the recipient of *Ex Ponto* 2.4 and 7, featured in *Amores* 1.9, Ovid's jaunty poem on the similarities of 'love and war', '*militat omnis amans ...*' (every lover is a soldier ...). *Ex Ponto* 2.4 recalls the youthful, innocent fun they had when they exchanged poems and 'always went about together in Rome'. *Adynata*[71] (vv. 23-30) expressing the impossibility of Atticus' ever forgetting the exile, pathetically reflect the hardships that he endures. *Adynata* also feature in the second of these 'letters' to Atticus, *Ex Ponto* 2.7, a cry of despair about the exile's sufferings. The bounties of nature are more easily counted than are his woes (23-30). He is terrified of the savage Getae around him, and yet they pity him (31-42). If his woes were to be put into poetry, a new *Iliad* would emerge.

The poet is consciously creating an 'elegiac epic', using literary allusion to convey pathos. This is generic experimentation of the same order as the momentous innovation that produced his *Metamorphoses*.[72] The exile's statement, 'Three years of exile feel like ten' evokes the ten years of the Trojan siege, raising the exile's suffering to the dimension of myth (*Tr.* 5.10.1-4). His correspondents include Pomponius Macer, an epic poet, who was first addressed in *Amores* 2.18, a programmatic poem describing the poet's generic experimentation. Now Macer, the friend who is ever present in the exile's heart, is entreated to reciprocate with a similar vicarious hospitality (*Pont.* 2.10). This affectionately whimsical, rather pathetic poem nostalgically evokes the two poets' youthful and innocent travels outside Italy, in classic reference to the shortness of day and road.[73]

The collection *Ex Ponto* 1-3 may be seen as a celebration of friendship, an '*Ars Amicitiae*' offered to the poet's Roman readership as a surrogate for the offending *Ars Amatoria*. Towards the end of this collection, there is a profound change of tone, and the last book takes a new direction, also in the names of the persons celebrated in it. *Ex Ponto* 3.7 marks a change of approach. The exile expresses dull resignation to absolute loneliness and the vanity of his prayers (*Pont.* 3.7). This evokes a feeling of *déjà vu*, for his complaints are voiced in a network of literary allusion. The next poem accompanies a gift of poisoned arrows to Cotta Maximus (the 'only gift Pontus has to offer'), and then the collection closes with an explanation to Brutus, the poet's uncle by marriage, exonerating the 'poor quality' of the work with reference to the exile's desire to reach individual friends in turn (*Pont.* 3.9).

After this follows *Ex Ponto* 4 with new addressees, a new patron and a new tone. The first half of the book (*Pont.* 4.1 to 4.8) comprises ostensibly cheerful eulogies of public figures, increasingly undercut by pathos. The second half of the collection, its pathos notwithstanding, is often playful. For instance, *Ex Ponto* 4.10 and 4.12 joke on the metrical problems posed by Tuticanus' name. The two poems frame a consolation to Gallio on the death of his wife. This poem, the only attempt at the formal *consolatio*, appears to include a joking reference to the Augustan marriage laws compelling quick remarriage (*Pont.* 4.11.21-2).[74]

The topic of marriage is most frequent in relation to the exile's wife, who stayed in Rome to safeguard his affairs. The poet's depiction of marital affection in the exilic works is variously coloured. The exile's affection for his wife offers a new affirmation of the value of love within a marriage. This is contrary to every aspect of Roman erotic elegy, a conscious counter to the erstwhile love poet's earlier attitude.[75] In *Tristia* 1.3 we learn that his wife had wanted to accompany the exile.[76] Their conjugal closeness is given prominence in the central poem of the first book, *Tristia* 1.6. Mytho-logical *exempla* add a cosmic dimension, the first intimation of a web of mythical allusion, which recurs throughout, involving Andromache, Lao-damia and Penelope. These may be seen as the female equivalents of the paragon friends referred to above in our discussion of *amicitia*. The poet's use of both sets of names may have been prompted by his own treatment of their various myths in his *Heroides*, but there is an added piquancy in the fact that these sets occur just so in Parthenius' collection of 'characters famous for ...'. The creator-poet is showing his external readership the exile-as-poet grinding out cliché-ridden verse to impress his wife and friends with his dire need of their support.

Tristia 5, composed during the poet's second year of exile, has more poems addressed to his wife than any other part of the work.[77] Of these, 5.11.1-22, which explains the difference between 'exile' and 'relegation', should not be taken as evidence of the wife's lack of intelligence but shows the exile's use of an address to his wife as a means of making a public statement. *Tristia* 5.14.1-14 closes the book and the collection with the poet's statement that he has already conferred immortality upon her with his verse; she must not imitate Alcestis who died for Admetus, but live; she must appeal to Marcia, the wife of Fabius Maximus. Recourse to Tacitus' account of the death of Fabius (*Ann.* 1.5) shows us, as Ovid's latest external audience, the irony of this appeal. Marcia blamed herself for apparently unwittingly causing her husband's death when she reported to Livia that he had accompanied Augustus on a visit to his exiled grandson, Agrippa Postumus. Neither Agrippa nor Fabius long survived Augustus.

Often the exile's letters to his wife appear querulous and self-serving. *Tristia* 3.3 already displays a hint of doubt about his wife's attachment to the exile, which appears to grow. At *Tristia* 5.2.37-40 she is accused of 'also' deserting him, like his inconstant friends. *Ex Ponto* 3.1 shows some justification for past complaint when the exile waxes indignant (v. 30ff.) that his wife still does not appear to know 'what she should be doing'. He then spells out how to approach the emperor's wife.[78] At *Ex Ponto* 3.7.11, 12 the exile finally and sadly explains that he will burden his wife no longer with requests for aid, for she is as 'timid as she is good'. He does not explain why he still does not allow her to leave Rome and join him at Tomis. Perhaps she no longer wished to come. This would sadly undercut Ovid's picture of the unhappy couple as 'star-crossed lovers'. It would be better to think that perhaps the tone of *Ex Ponto* 4 is more cheerful because the exile's wife has joined him at last.[79]

The exile views every situation subjectively, whether the birthday of his wife, the triumph of a general, or the death of a friend's helpmeet. Life in exile seems to supersede all the normal limits between reality and irreality, between poet and product, between person and thing. The exile lives in isolation, space between him and Rome extending into infinity, time at Tomis freezing into ever-shifting moments of composition when his epistolary *now* appears to stand still, with reality at Rome fading into the paper on which the poet pins down a *persona*. In a world dominated by a consciousness of a uniquely lonely self, there is sometimes no limit between self and non-self, no limit between the poet who formerly wrote naughty poems and those poems themselves,[80] their banishment from the libraries of Rome, and the relegation of their creator to the ends of the earth.[81] The exile's constant aim seems to be to repudiate his former carefree self, while holding on to the creativity of that self as the only thing that still gives him a sense of identity. The creator-poet has fused the disgraced lover-poet and his banned love-poetry into a text that is a living palinode of all that went before: urbanity has given way to isolation, playfulness to apparent solemnity, love of the Muses has been ousted by ostensible repudiation, friendship takes the place of erotic games, and the former *lusor amorum* (player at love) is now a constant husband.

4.6 Appeal to a god: the exilic poems as prayer

Second person outreach can encompass communication between human and divine. Ovid's poems are not all epistolary, but often appear as literary hymns and prayers. Both hymns and prayers involve outreach to a 'second person', in this case, a god. Paradoxically, Ovid's 'outreach to a god' is mostly still to a human figure. Deification, or ostensible deification, of the emperor Augustus is a prominent feature of the poems from exile. Ovid adapts prayer and hymnic formulae, which bear a close affinity in literature, as in life. Ovidian penchant for inversion can turn either of these into cursing.[82] With Ovid, the possibility of parody should never be ignored.[83]

Our first example, of a hymn, cannot easily be interpreted as parodic, but rather as the appropriation of the language of religion to poetics. An address to the poet's Muse at *Tristia* 4.10.117-30, in Ovid's autobiographical sphragis, is a hymn in miniature, yet use of Callimachean terminology (*Helicon*, v. 120 and *livor*, v. 123) signals its relation to elegiac aesthetics.[84] His Muse removes the poet from his surroundings to a higher plane, where Envy cannot touch him. The hymn begins with thanks to the Muse, followed by an *aretelogia* (expression of praise) with anaphora of the pronoun *tu*.[85] Verses 117-20 involve a set of allusions closely interwoven with a sustained web of imagery that recurs throughout the *oeuvre*, also closely allied to the consolatory tradition: *solacia* (comfort in exile); *requies* (rest) and *medicina* (medicine – appropriate for imagery equating the exile's suffering with a wound); *dux* (military leader); *comes* (friend); removal from the Danube area (the scene of the poet's hardship); place on the Helicon (poetic escape). Emphatic vindication of poetic immortality and the poet's awareness of its rarity run counter to an image of exile-asdeath elsewhere almost consistently employed.[86]

Verses 123-4 challenge impersonal *livor*, which the privileged reader easily 'personalises' as the emperor Augustus himself. Verses 125-8 vigorously challenge literary censure by proclaiming the poet's pre-eminence among national poets. His Muse almost forgotten, the 'hymn' is turned into an avowal of personal power. Poet and Muse have become fused, and despite the modest phrasing of v. 129, the poet's use of *vates*,[87] 'singer of divine truth', indicates that exile and death no longer exist for him:

> siquid habent igitur vatum presagia veri,
> protinus ut moriar, non ero, terra, tuus.   (*Tr.* 4.10.129-30)

So if the presagings of prophets have any claim to truth, even if I were to die immediately, o earth, I shall not wholly be yours!

The hymn to his Muse becomes a hymn to the continued and sustaining power of his own creativity. In the coda the poet transcends both time and space, in his appeal to a 'second person', yet to come into being:

> sive favore tuli, sive hanc ego carmine famam,
> iure tibi grates, candide lector, ago.   (*Tr.* 4.10.131-2)

Whether at all I attained this fame by your favour or by my song, with justice I bring you thanks, dear reader.

Swoboda (1978) distinguishes the basic elements that comprised ancient prayer, some parts of which gain a life of their own and occur independently.[88] The formulaic elements of complete, formal prayer, are: apostrophe; a *verbum precandi* (praying verb) in the imperative or subjunctive-optative mood; *hypomnesis* – justification or the reason why the speaker may pray (occasionally also, in an epic digression, *aretalogia* – praise of the god); *vota*, counter-promises; often parenthetical *oro* (I ask), *precor* (I pray), or the 'delimiters' *dixi*, *dixit* (I/he said); formulae of salutation and honorific predicatives (adjectival or substantival); genealogical allusions; testimony of the god's powers.

Special occasions offer excuses for divine appeal. Prayers to the gods of Rome serve as springboards for appeal to human benefactors, that is, as *captatio benevolentiae*, poems aimed at gaining the sympathy of the exiled poet's reading public. *Tristia* 1.10, to the exile's tutelary deity, 'golden Minerva' is an elegant exercise in geographic versification. Identification of ship, exile and goddess in a common interest turns the exile into an Odysseus. Birthdays were traditionally celebrated with prayer. Two birthdays offer novel opportunities for pathetic appeal to the exile's readership as 'real' second person. At *Tristia* 3.13.19-26 he considers that funeral preparations would suit his birthday best but decides that his 'birthday wish' will be a prayer for release. Address of the natal spirit presiding over his wife's birthday (*Tr.* 5.5.13-26) offers a graceful birthday wish at remove.

Ovid's most frequent allusions to prayer comprise requests to the exile's friends to pray for him, usually a metaphor for intercession with the emperor on his behalf. Such requests mostly are for removal to a better place, not for absolute pardon. *Tristia* 1.5.35-44 is for aid unspecified, and is accompanied by a double justification: his friends may pray thus, for Caesar is fair and approves of fidelity in others, and because the exile was no rebel.[89] Counter-prayer, for the friend to be blessed, stresses reciprocity in such communication. Votive ritual following on *sic*, promising reciprocation, is frequent in prayer formulae. *Ex Ponto* 2.6.14-19 concludes a request for aid from Graecinus with a repeated votive *sic*, encompassing the friend's mother, wife, brothers and 'whole house' in a shower of goodwill. Caesar's approval is again the optimum. Then follows a negative justification, complete with mythological exempla (vv. 19-28) and an *aretalogia*, an encomium on Graecinus' piety as worthy of fame (vv. 29-34). This grandiloquent votive ritual, involving profound confusion between the votive object, Graecinus, and votive subject, 'the gods', is undercut by an apologetic, conversational postscript, complete with a grotesque mixed metaphor: no matter what aid his friend may bring, the exile, never trusting the wind alone, but always using oars as well, will ever be spurring him on to new efforts (vv. 35-8).[90]

The poet's style often deconstructs apparent religious solemnity. Reproach of Apollo and the Muses in *Tristia* 3.2 is undercut by jaunty alliteration of verses 3 and 4: *nec vos ... / docta sacerdoti turba tulistis opem* (and you learned lot didn't care a jot to lighten your poor priest's lot). Inconsistency of tone creates tension between words and message. It may equally deflect flippancy into an apparently serious mode. In this poem the exile's flight and suffering is evoked in concise, epic snatches, shifting at verse 19 into a querulous elegiac mode with a powerful image of the exile as *exclusus amator* (locked-out lover), knocking in vain at death's door (vv. 23, 24), culminating at verse 27 in an epic appeal to gods unspecified, cruel in their support of the anger of 'one god', to hasten on his dilatory fate and 'forbid the doors of death to remain closed' (vv. 29-30). Brevity heightens emotional appeal.

The exile is aware of the persuasive power of prayer,[91] often playfully alluding to its formal and ritualistic aspects; a wish for the ability to fly to Rome with mythical wings or chariots is followed by self-exhortation to pray to the god Augustus 'with suitable rites' for only he can 'grant the power to fly': *ille tibi pennasque potest currusque volucres / tradere. det reditum, protinus ales eris* (He can give you both wings and flying chariots. Should he grant your return, you immediately become a bird, *Tr.* 3.8.15, 16). Winged shadows seem to flicker over the page as we read, reminiscences of the metamorphoses of Scylla and her father, betrayer and betrayed, or Alcyone, heartbroken as her husband's dead body is washed up ashore, or Tereus, Procne and Philomela, saved by this change from the terrible consequences of a ghastly eternal triangle, or Daedalus, destroyer of his son and his nephew, and we wonder whether such a change is a boon.[92]

The poet appears to have culled his votive modes from different sources. *Tristia* 5.3.35-46, addressed to Bacchus, is reminiscent of an Orphic hymn.[93] The poem begins as a 'conversation' between the votary and his god. Verses 35-46 start with the imperative *fer ... opem* (bring aid!) and apostrophe *bone Liber* (Good Free One!), continuing with typical Orphic formulae introduced by anaphora of *sic* (37-42), and *hypomnesis*: *unum de numero me memor esse tuo* (remember that I am a member of your band, 44). A second *hypomnesis* underlies the explanation that 'gods have mutual commerce' (v. 45), with the implication that the god of wine (and drama) is on equal footing with the ruler of the exile's world, and the prayer that follows asks that Bacchus will use his divine power to change the equally divine Caesar's mind.[94]

With this we come to the most common object of prayerful address, the emperor himself. The scene is set with *Tristia* 1.2, a full-fledged and extended prayer. The apostrophe *Di maris et caeli* (gods of sea and sky), with parenthetical *hypomnesis* of a negative kind, *quid enim nisi vota supersunt?* (for what is left but prayers?, v. 1) introduces *preces* and a positive *hypomnesis, saepe premente deo fert deus alter opem* (often when one god oppresses, another brings aid, v. 4) followed by *exempla* from epic. Augustus is the most powerful god, to whose anger the lesser gods subscribe. The poem alternates vivid evocations of the exiled victim's emotions during a storm at sea with snatches of prayer,[95] combining effect and affect. A lessening of the storm is eagerly interpreted as a vindication of innocence, an answer *sub condicione* (showing that the condition of the prayer had been fulfilled, vv. 107-10). The condition was 'if I am innocent of crime, show me your favour'. By a trick of casuistry the poet shows that the answer to this votive condition has 'proved' the exile's innocence. By virtue of the divine commerce adumbrated in verse 4, Augustus has been manipulated into agreement.

A similar projected manipulation of the emperor lies behind the rhetorical virtuosity of an excursive multiple invocation in *Tristia* 2.155-78.[96] A series of twelve couplets maintains a periodic sentence of paratactic votive simplicity, with anaphora of *per* (by ...) and *sic* (so ...) alternating with adjectival clauses.[97] This ornate encapsulation of nationalistic and imperial fervour acts as the *hypomnesis* of a four-verse prayer. Glorious and hoped-for conditions (that Livia will complete her years with the emperor, Livia, the imperial lady 'without whom he would have been doomed to lonely celibacy', and that Tiberius will return triumphant from the German frontier) will come about, so the exile threatens, only when the 'father of his fatherland', true to this title, has put away his Jovian thunderbolts (vv. 179-82). A parenthetical explanation of the slightness of the exile's desires, although 'great gods have given greater things' (vv. 183-4) undercuts praise of Augustus' greatness. The votive argument, in combination with the alienating techniques of exuberant alliteration and hyperbaton[98] serve to signal that the adulation here displayed is more apparent than real. The reader is free to choose whether to be amazed or amused.

Ex Ponto 2.8, a 'letter' to Cotta Maximus, accompanied a gift of a Scythian quiver and arrows, reciprocation for a gift of 'silver portraits' of the imperial triad. This poem has given rise to much positivist acceptance that the exile had turned into a fervent devotee of the imperial cult, an assumption that I (arguably with complementary positivist assumptions) should most strenuously oppose.[99] This elaborate poem carries all the characteristic signals of slippage between overt and covert meaning to be read from any of Ovid's works. The first couplet sets the tone, with elaborate repetition, and intrusive alliteration:

> *Redditus est nobis Caesar cum Caesare nuper*
> *quos mihi misisti, Maxime Cotta, deos.*

Recently Caesar upon Caesar has been restored to me, those whom you mailed to me, my dear Maximus Cotta, the gods themselves!

From the first couplet onward these representative portraits are equated with 'the gods' themselves, and there is bland assumption of equivalence between 'Caesars' and 'gods'. The participle *redditus*, meaning 'given back', implies 'restored':[100] the angry gods that withdrew themselves from their votary are once more shining upon him. Allusive echoes from *Tristia* 1.2 of the angry storm gods becoming calm imply proof of the exile's innocence. His transports of joy at seeing once more the 'gods' he misses and, in their visages, Rome itself, lacking only the Palatine (vv. 5-20), are tempered at v. 21 by the creeping doubt, soon growing to certainty, that these visages are angry. At verse 23 the exile addresses Augustus himself, launching into a virtual votive frenzy, reversing the order of the 'prayer' in *Tristia* 2.155-82, and managing in tactless abandon to tread heavily on all the tenderest of the imperial corns. Suddenly the representation, although still a 'present deity', is also a representation of a man, not a god:

> *Parce, vir immenso maior virtutibus orbe*
> *iustaque vindictae supprime lora tuae.*

Spare me, o man greater in virtues than the great earth itself, and pull up the reins so appropriate to your vengeance!

The exile's grounds of appeal to 'the great man' follow in a series of *hypomneses*, introduced by *per* (by ..., 27-34). Verse 28 *numquam surdos in tua vota deos* ('gods never deaf to your prayers') would have reminded Augustus of his dynastic disappointments, the disgrace of his daughter and granddaughter and the Varian disaster. Allusion to Livia as *tori sociam, quae par tibi sola reperta est* ('the only one found suitable as companion in your bed', v. 29) ignores both Livia's previous marriage and Augustus' three marriages and other liaisons, and the following pentameter *et cui maiestas non onerosa tua est* (and for whom your majesty is not too heavy)[101] may equally be interpreted as sexual innuendo. Next, the emperor and his adoptive son Tiberius are reminded of the latter's (recent) adoption in apparently bland praise of Tiberius' heredity (v. 31). Then follows appeal for removal to a safer area (35-8).

Another series of votive conditions follows a prayer to Tiberius (37-42). Not least incongruous are conventional wishes for longevity for his imperial parents in terms of Nestor and the Cumaean Sibyl. Verse 42, *et possis filius esse dii* (and may you become the son of a god), may be construed as either a (dangerous) wish for Augustus' death and apotheosis, or a gibe at the imperial proclivity for god-making, as first exhibited by Augustus for his own adoptive father Julius. Similarly, the prayer to Livia ends in a flourish of good wishes for among others her *bonis nuribus* (good daughters-in-law), which calls to the reader's mind also those stepchildren that proved themselves not *bonae* (43-6).[102] Next Livia is reminded of the death of her son Drusus (47-50).

With such *hypomneses* as basis 'the gods' are then called upon to nod favourably to the exile's 'timid prayers', to show him the advantages of owning 'present deities' (51-2). The fact that the emperor's advent is always a sign of grace for gladiators (53-4) winds up this display of dubious adulation, serving as a signal of the incongruity between the exile's adoration and the poet's mockery of the wielders of absolute power at Rome.

Elaborate stylistic virtuosity, including alliteration, rhyme and hyperbaton in verses 23-36 support the conceptual daring of this provoking challenge to the Julian arrogation of deity. Its playful tone signals a double slippage between internal and external addressee; from 'letter' to Cotta, the poem has turned into a 'prayer' to the imperial family, and a provocative joke to all who wish to read it as such. In contrast to earlier flourishes of intricate word order, verses 57-62 are bare of hyperbaton, but have a strongly appealing alliterative pattern:

> *Felices illi, qui non simulacra, sed ipsos,*
> *quique deum coram corpora vera vident.*
> *quod quoniam nobis invidit inutile fatum*
> *quos dedit ars, vultus effigiumque colo.*
> *sic homines novere deos, quos arduus aether*
> *occulit, et colitur pro Iove forma Iovis.*

Happy are those who see not images but the gods themselves, and who see the bodies of the gods in front of their very faces, and, as useless fate has denied me that boon, I worship his face and his image, which art has given me. So people have known the gods, whom the high ether hides, and in the place of Jupiter the shape of Jupiter is worshipped.

Heavy syllabic alliteration here evokes archaic religious ritual. This may be taken as a profound statement on the nature of representation and reality in religion and art, but its obtrusive stylistic gymnastics offer a ribald counterpoint.[103] The passage, while ostensibly explaining the use of images as surrogate for true gods, emphasises the Caesars' arrogation of divinity.

Next the exile vows to fight against vast encircling Getic hordes, prepared to have his eyes torn out, rather than lose the precious images, his haven and his altar of safety (63-70). This vow suggests the threat that these divine figures in their earthly manifestation will share in his exile. Finally, the votary searches his own bosom, feeling that he asks too much, yet hoping that removal to a better place is at hand (71, 72). The faces of the portraits appear increasingly more benign, or rather, 'less sorrowful', *tristes* (not *irati*, angry), a term which connects the sad and sorry exiled poet and his kindly 'deities'. Their divine emotion is more akin to sorrow than to anger. A general prayer in the coda (75, 76), expresses the hope that these *timidae praesagia mentis* (prophecies of a timid mind) may prove true, and that the justified ire of the god (now in the singular) may grow less. The sober, apotropaic tone of the coda serves to point the playfulness of the rest of the poem. An impression of irreverently bold ridicule throughout the poem is not eclipsed by the apparent seriousness of its coda. The whole is clearly outreach, but its tone and presentation deconstruct the premises on which it is based. Among the series of 'second persons' with whom the poet-as-exile is potentially interacting we may postulate a serious diversity of interpretations and reactions to this poem, depending on where those persons stood in the spectrum of relationships we have considered as possibly operating between author and reader.

4.7 Non-reply by the second person: the rhetoric of silence

Next we turn to aspects of such interactive response, which may be summed up in a word: 'silence'. Silence, on many levels, is as important in Ovid's exilic poetry as speech: the silence enjoined upon the poet of love; the silence involving a discrepancy between archaeological facts and poetic depiction of the Dobroudja,[104] in a lack of detail about the exile's daily life, occasionally broken through by casual allusion to civic honours paid him by the Tomitans.[105] The greatest silence is the silence of non-reply.

Neither as *sermo absentis* nor as prayer do the exile's pleas receive any response. His outreach to the second person is essentially non-effective, and he remains surrounded by a virtual zone of silence.[106] All in Rome appear involved in a conspiracy of silence. The exile pours his heart out into a void, whence no echo of an answer returns. Questions are not answered, no reaction is evoked, not even from his wife who, we have seen, after four years is instructed as if new to his problems (*Pont.* 3.1.31ff.).

Non-response is elevated to a symbol for the hopelessness of exile, part of the many-faceted rhetoric of silence. The absent interlocutor bridges the gap of silence in the imagination of the poet.[107] Whether absent interlocutor and ostensible addressee are the same person, is seldom clear.[108] The versatile poet simultaneously conveys both the interaction of conversation and the pathos of monologue. The exile and his *alter ego* converse in the silence that surrounds them.[109] The exile's increasing recourse to mental travel (*Tr.* 3.5, 4.2, etc.) and surrogate appearances in Rome as his book (*Tr.* 3.1 and *Pont.* 4.5)[110] or with his 'mind's eye' (*Pont.* 3.4 and 4.4) bridge the gap.[111]

The exile too is silent about many things. He repeatedly refuses to 'reopen the emperor's wounds' by frequent, deliberate and elaborate *praeteritio* (emphasis by ostensible passing over) of what, he hints darkly, is the real reason for his exile, the *error* that was in some way tied up with the emperor personally (e.g. *Tr.* 3.6.12ff.). Of his contemporaries, we may imagine that those not in the know were made curious, the *cognoscenti* were amused, and the emperor was placed in a moral dilemma. Action cannot be taken against someone who refuses to hurt one, nor can 'the right version' be given if the 'wrong version' has not been published. The only recourse in such a position is to dignified silence, more eloquent than speech.

Central to the whole life of the exile is the profound and unmoving silence of Augustus and his refusal as head of state to pardon civil disobedience, and as angry god to be placated by prayers, tears or wishes.[112] So silent is this central figure that when the 'man' dies and 'becomes a god' the fact goes by almost unnoticed. *Ex Ponto* 4.5 speaks of Augustus as alive, the next poem speaks of him as dead.

Ovid manipulates silence as effectively as he uses words, to convey the pathos of the exile's position: the recurrent silence of non-reply and of non-effect, the suppression of the names of the exile's correspondents, implying that vengeance will be wreaked upon all who aided the victim of the emperor's wrath.[113] There is also the silence surrounding a foreigner who cannot understand those around him (*Tr.* 5.10.41ff.),[114] or the silence affecting an absent friend (*Pont.* 3.5.37-48).[115] There is the pathetic silence of an exile losing his mother tongue.[116] Finally, the silence of *Livor* is as venomous, profound and relentless as that of the emperor himself (*Pont.* 4.16.49ff.). These silences are as much constructs of the creator-poet as are any of the verbal virtuosities that we have considered above, and they tend towards the same effect: *the reader accepts the myth of exile as a poetic stylisation of an irrecoverable reality.*

Ovid has followed Cicero's lead, but has taken his myth-making further. Paul Veyne (1988: 154) in an important study proclaims that Roman erotic elegy is 'nothing more than an amusing paradox' (which, he notes, if all critics had accepted it as such, would have obviated the need for an explanatory book).[117] I similarly stand on the above sentence as central to my whole approach to Ovid's exilic poetry. The poetry of exile stylises an irrecoverable reality. It is a literary construct that represents a literary world clothed in the trappings of a new poetics, that is based on the redirected poetics of erotic elegy. No amount of research will produce the 'real reason' for Ovid's exile or the 'real circumstances' of his life – the poetry of exile represents not reality, but art sublimating that reality, whatever it may have been.[118]

Most of what Veyne postulates as central to erotic elegy (its vagueness of time and place, its artificiality and mannerisms, its irregularity and inconsistencies, its use of myth as a 'sign of authority', its lack of introspection in the *'ego'-persona*, its constant feel of engagement with an external reader and complete lack of introspection or soliloquy), I have found to be directly applicable to the nature of Ovid's exilic poetry. Yet Veyne falls into his own trap by historicising Ovid in exile, designating him (1988: 126) 'a person talking as a person and no longer as an author'. As I have read the poems, the underlying aesthetics of Ovid's exilic poetry are comparable to the whole of Veyne's thesis regarding erotic elegy as play, and Ovid is still an author talking as a *persona* in *sermo absentis* (conversation with an absent friend), where the absent one never replies.

4.8 Dialogue with posterity

So Ovid ostensibly reaches out, as a 'voice from beyond the grave' (a paradox we have seen as frequent in exilic literature), from the ultimate, existential silence which awaits all men, but the 'living' in Rome are mute. The interaction between the exile and posterity (*posteritas*, 'posterity', *Tr.* 4.10.2; *lector*, 'reader', *Tr.* 4.1.2; *candide lector*, 'dear reader', *Tr.* 1.11.35) started in silence, before 'posterity' had come into being. Here too Ovid's exilic poems sustain their dialectic level. Modern scholarship, as part of that posterity, shows by its reaction to the persuasiveness of the poet that the dialectic has developed in course of time.[119]

Thompson (1978: 196) points out that any poet requires the reassurance of an audience to test the validity of his art. To the Roman poet, accustomed to holding *recitationes* as a form of publication, the audience was essential, the reaction immediate. The exiled Ovid complains that writing what no one can read 'is like dancing in the dark' (*Pont.* 4.2.33, 34). A programmatic exposition of the poetics of exilic composition (*Pont.* 3.9) touches on his readers' complaints of 'monotony of tone and content'. The Roman reading public, receiving the poems consecutively over a period of years, may well have awaited each separate consignment with avidity and curiosity. Internal evidence for reaction by his Roman readership is clearly slight. External evidence, the fact of the preservation and tradition of the exilic corpus, implies some means of publication and circulation.

For modern readers to project their critical and emotional response back to the Roman readership of Ovid's time is potentially dangerous, yet an appraisal of Ovid's exilic poetry is incomplete without an evaluation of its impact on his contemporaries, and the degree to which the exile achieved his projected goal of outreach to posterity. We have noted that power was an essential element in ancient exile; the powerful exercised their power over the less powerful, or those aspiring to power, by means of decrees of exile. Ostensibly Ovid as poet did not quite fit into the pattern. Yet here too power was not unilaterally wielded. It is precisely through his dialogue with posterity that Ovid exploited the powerful potential of literary polemic. The reaction of his modern readership is witness to that fact. Ovid's exilic poetry, as a 'voice from the grave', transcends a contemporary conspiracy of silence, giving the loneliness of the exile a mythic dimension. The voice that speaks from both the silence of distance and the silence of centuries bridges the gap.[120]

We as modern readers are at a disadvantage at the historicist level: our ignorance of the true temper of the times.[121] We have the advantage, however, of hindsight. As privileged readers we know that, to the end, the 'angry god' remained silent. The poet has shown the inefficacy of praying to a man-god. Such a god does not answer prayer. As a man he is mighty, as a god he is silent and powerless, a victim of the power of poetry.[122]

From Me to You: Exilic Invective

5.1 Externalising blame

We have so far seen that interaction with a second person is central even to the most subjective aspects of exilic literature. The exile reaches out to those at Rome, and, particularly with missives that imply a wider circulation, such as Ovid's poems and Seneca's formal consolations (both apparently intended for publication), we have identified a series of potential readers other than the ostensible addressees.

A further factor we have distinguished is the exile's stylised depiction of both his past and his present relationship with a particular addressee. This also shades off into a stylised attitude towards the wider readership adumbrated in his levels of outreach. The exile's portrayal of self does not escape from a similar kaleidoscopic shifting of focuses. As will appear below, self-glorification and autobiographical self-mythicising is inherent to the second person literature of exile, but so too is subjectively coloured invective against the apparent initiator of the exile's misery.[1] Any portrayal of heroism, inevitably, needs a foil: the powers of darkness must bear a human face. Someone ordered the exile away from Rome, or otherwise contributed to his downfall. This personage is to blame, and it is the exile's right to blame him, whether during exile, with epistolary invective, or to his face, after glorious recall.

Of the exiled authors whose work we are reviewing in this study, Dio Chrysostomus is remarkable for not having resorted to this oblique method of self-justification: he scarcely refers to either the reason for his exile or the author of his woe.[2] Boethius' comments on the perfidy of his betrayers are relatively neutral (*Consol.* 1.pr.4) in the context of his general misery. Seneca appears to have gone to the opposite extreme, and his adulatory passages about the imperial family in the *Consolatio ad Polybium* (and, to a lesser degree, in the *Ad Helviam*) have laid him open to accusations of self-serving.

Cicero was very well aware of the active role of the powerful tribune Clodius in his ruin, but never appears to have had the courage to attack him directly, choosing rather to direct his ire against lesser role players. He was equally careful not to antagonise Caesar and Pompey (whose benign neglect had added to his miseries) and again chose to blame those who appeared as more vulnerable enemies. Invective against his enemies in various speeches after his return (parts of *Pro Sestio* and *De domo sua* and also the *In Pisonem*) illustrates Cicero's post-exilic ire. Although these speeches post-date Cicero's exile by months and even years, their focus (particularly the *In Pisonem*) is so much concentrated on the sufferings of the hero and the iniquities of his evil opponent, that I have chosen to consider these speeches as intrinsically 'exilic'.

The exiled Ovid's 'invective' is more subtle: polemic rather than true attack, with less focus on the second person, the object of the author's ire, than on the exile's woes. It may be argued that study of invective should have been included in our discussion of dialectic and the use of second person verbs: invective seems to focus on the offender. Invective is, however, intensely subjective. Its psychological focus is on the protagonist, not on his erstwhile antagonist. With Ovid the opponent is sketched in vague terms, even more elusively than the elegiac mistress and other minor *personae* of erotic elegy – focus is essentially on the suffering hero and outreach is toward his wider readership. Exilic invective functions as a transitional stage, between outreach to a second person and solipsistic concentration on the experiences, desires and fears of the first person. It functions as externalization of blame and helps the exile to see himself in an heroic light.

5.2 Ciceronian invective

After his return from exile, it was psychologically necessary for the vindicated Cicero to externalize the blame for his own political downfall. Clodius was too powerful; at first little public invective was aimed at him, and he merited only oblique references in the first months after Cicero's recall.[3] Two years later, in the *Pro Caelio* (5.11-13) Cicero redraws his formerly villainous picture of the Catilinarians, confesses to having himself nearly been taken in by Catiline when he was prosecuted by Clodius on a charge of corruption in 65, and casts Clodius as second villain in his portrayal of the corrupting influence of Clodia Metelli on Caelius. So in 56 Cicero could once more afford to attack his enemy openly.[4]

Other, less powerful enemies merited attack on a more extensive scale. Calpurnius Piso Caesoninus, consul in 58, proconsul of Macedonia in 57-55, was Julius Caesar's father-in-law. Together with his colleague Gabinius, he more than passively allowed Clodius to introduce the bill that precipitated Cicero's flight. Clodius' simultaneous second bill had assigned Macedonia to Piso and Cilicia (later changed to Syria) to Gabinius, thus ensuring their neutrality when he openly acted against Cicero. The two consuls were associated very strongly in fact and in Cicero's mind with his ignominious banishment. In January Piso, probably reading the temper of the times, had not allowed him the customary speaking turn in the Senate. Cicero, after his return, was eager to call Piso to account.

On Piso's return from his province in 55, the antagonists clashed in the Senate. The balance of influence between Piso and Cicero was at this stage such that it was safe for Cicero to publish their altercation. It is known that Piso had published a pamphlet of his own,[5] and the *In Pisonem* was probably its rebuttal.[6] Cicero was particularly affronted because Piso had ridiculed his ignominious flight and his tactless, self-glorifying poetry.[7] Fragment 20 of *In Pisonem*, quoted by Grillius (16 p. 72 Martin), may be from Piso's pamphlet: *Non me debes lacerare, quia non ego te in exilium misi, sed Caesar et Pompeius* (You shouldn't tear me to pieces, as I didn't send you into exile: it was Caesar and Pompey).[8]

Power was an important factor. Pompey and Caesar had, by default, been equally instrumental in Cicero's banishment, but were now increasingly influential, and Cicero clearly deemed it safer to avoid attacking them. They apparently ignored the publication of Cicero's pamphlet, but bided their time. Cicero was later ignominiously manoeuvred into defending Gabinius on a count of bribery.[9] The bitter pill had to be swallowed.

The *In Pisonem* is interesting for the view that it gives of the psychological make-up of the returned consular. Cicero's perception of his oppressor is mythologically coloured. His antagonist is a *monstrum* of heroic stature; his exile was an example of heroic suffering. The speech borrows heavily from the tradition of comic invective, and the picture that emerges, of a drunken sot of servile origin, unprepossessing appearance, and base habits, is sheer fiction, in the worst tradition of random caricature.[10] The pamphlet alternates allusions to the appearance, habits and deeds of the 'monster' with autobiographical passages portraying the heroic deeds of Cicero as *pater patriae*.[11] Piso and his associates, family and ancestry all share in the conventional abuse of comic invective.[12]

Cicero's invective focuses in turn on his opponent's antecedents, appearance, morals and personal habits, supposed avarice, pretentiousness, 'unroman' philhellenism and personal philosophy. Piso's known Epicureanism offered material for ridicule. These are undoubtedly stock themes, employed elsewhere by Cicero, and on occasion by others against the orator.[13] Focus on the supposed negative qualities of the antagonist alternates with exposition of the noble qualities of the heroic protagonist.

In the fragmentary first part of the pamphlet the focus is on Piso's ancestry, elaborated with a comic invention (rhetorical *mendaciunculum*, 'fibbing') about the consular's supposed embarrassment when all his relatives travelled to visit him on a farm cart (fr. 16). Innuendo and half-truth turn his 'swarthy appearance' into an indication of barbaric origins (fr. 8) and his North-Italian ancestry into Gaulish foreigners (fr. 9, 15). Inconsistency in attack is a characteristic of invective. The distantly connected family name of the Pisones Frugi (the 'frugal' Pisones) is contrasted by implication with the reputed profligacy of the Piso under attack.

The whole, whether speech or pamphlet, may be seen as a means of self-glorification devised by a man deeply hurt in his self-esteem, and still vividly reliving in his imagination the deep emotions elicited by his enforced removal from the hub of power, his feelings of alienation while so removed, and his supreme joy at his restoration. An added reason for bitterness is that his return from exile and physical re-admission to Rome did not entail a metaphysical return to power. Cicero's words reflect the self-absorption of the powerless. A look at his use of verbs is illuminating.

A first person verb (*viderem*) forms the psychological and syntactic climax to what is generally regarded as the introductory sentence of the oration:[14]

> *Pro di immortales! qui hic inluxit dies, mihi quidem, patres conscripti, peroptatus, ut hoc portentum huius loci, monstrum urbis, prodigium civitatis viderem!*

> By the immortal gods! The day which here gives its light was much awaited, at any rate by me, who hoped to see this ominous paradigm of depravity of this place, this monstrosity of the city, this *Wunderkind* of the state!

So, Cicero is glad to see his enemy back from his province. Now he may call him to account. The pamphlet seems to have started with a comical account of Cicero's expectations when he heard that Piso was returning. In fragment 18 repetition of key verbs in the first person serves for emphasis, illustrating Cicero's rhetorical second person involvement in the object of his ridicule. Focus is more on the attacker than on the attacked:

> *Putavi austerum hominem, putavi tristem, putavi gravem; sed video adulterum, video ganeonem, video parietum praesidio, video amicorum sordibus, video tenebris occultantem libidines suas.*

> I thought I'd see an austere man, I really thought I'd see him sad – even grave, I thought – but I see an adulterer, I see a glutton, I see a propper-up of walls, I see someone hiding his friends' lusts with filth, I see someone hiding his own in the shadows.

The pamphlet proper, as we have it, begins with second person verbs, switching abruptly to the third person at 2.6. These verbal forms alternate frequently, a rhetorical ploy commonly used for variety, but also denoting contempt, often serving the same function as a comic aside.[15] Yet in the end second and third person verbs are subservient to the solipsism that colours all Cicero's writings on his banishment. When Cicero blames Piso for tacitly allowing Clodius to have his way, formal, rhythmical clausulae and elaborate alliteration give the oration the tone of prophetic denunciation, as in 9.6: *Tacente te, a fatali portento prodigioque rei publicae Lex Aelia et Fufia eversa est ...* (While you kept mum, the Lex Aelia and Fufia was overturned by the fatal paradigm and monster of depravity ...)

Piso's public life draws unashamedly subjective focus, with emphasis on first person pronouns:

Is mihi gloriabatur se omnis magistratus sine repulsa adsecutum? Mihi ista licet de me vera cum gloria praedicare; omnis enim honores populus Romanus mihi ipsi non nomini detulit. Nam tu ... Piso est a populo Romano factus, non iste Piso ... (*Pis.* 2.6).

Does this fellow glory over me that he achieved every magistracy without ever being rejected [at the polls]? It is I who may rather speak roundly about myself, with true glory; for the Roman people accorded *me* all honours for my own sake and not because of a famous name. For you ... *a* Piso was made consul by the Roman people, not *that* Piso!

Cicero's own admirable participation in public life follows by contrast. *Selbstkorrektur* focuses on the heroic autobiographer: *miserum me! cum hac me nunc peste atque labe confero?* (Misery me! Do I now compare myself to that pernicious blot? *Pis.* 3.18).

The greater part of the pamphlet (2.6-63) contrasts in detail the actions of protagonist and antagonist. Sections 4-7 deal with the main achievements of Cicero's consulship, in appeal to his senatorial audience (or readership). The initial words of the sentences comprising sections 4, 5 and 6 are, in order: *ego*, nine times in succession, then *me*, *mihi* twice, *ego* again, *mihi* again. Concomitant verbs are in the first person. The personal pronoun *me* and first person possessive adjective recur throughout. Cicero is portrayed as the prime mover in every event.[16]

Analysis of Piso's consulship (8-11), starting with the events of early 58, before the main attack on Cicero had started, has subtly different emphasis. Events are drawn as *happening* by themselves, without apparent causality, nor with Piso as agent. Cicero spells this out: *nondum quae feceris, sed quae fieri passus sis dico* (I haven't yet started saying what you did, but what you allowed to happen! *Pis.* 10.15). This of course refers to Piso's inaction in allowing Clodius a free hand, but again the first person obtrudes. Again the protagonist's perception of events receives emphasis. This is not merely a rhetorical ploy, but should be seen as evidence of psychologically urgent personal involvement with the man whom the returned exile blames as the author of his misery.

The next section (12-21) deals with Piso's consulship and events at the time of Cicero's exile. All the subjective bitterness only hinted at in the desperate letters from Dyrrachium[17] now pours out in a self-centred attack on one who was in fact a neutral looker-on in the drama of Cicero's downfall. Piso has become a symbol. As symbol he is the focus of invective.[18] He is pictured as a muffled, furtive frequenter of drinking dens, offering the excuse of illness to explain excessive bibbing. Putrid teeth and halitosis complete the squalid picture. Apostrophe of Piso here reduces him to an unpleasant object, *caenum*, 'filth'.[19] The facts of Piso's consulate are difficult to extract from a wealth of comic invention. This overdrawn picture of monstrous vice was not meant to be believed, but to convey the speaker's emotional reactions to a perceived enemy.

If Piso is monstrous, filthy and debauched, his colleague Gabinius is an effeminate, shaven and shorn dancer, dripping with unguents. In his youth he was a companion in debauchery of Catiline, and he spent his consulship clicking castanets.[20] Clodius' henchman Cloelius is 'Clodius' own jackal'.[21] And Clodius is, conventionally, *sororius adulter* (debaucher of his sister, *Pis*. 28.5).[22]

Cicero's departure into banishment, always termed *discessus* by the returned exile, *fuga* by his enemies, is contrasted with Piso's departure for his province (sections 31-3).[23] For Cicero his departure brought pain, but also glory (*Pis*. 31.15ff.). Cicero next draws a series of contrasts where in every case he appears as more laudable. The whole of Italy stood transfixed with horror when he left; by contrast all were glad to see Piso go. Cicero's day of greatest misery was more laudable than Piso's day of greatest triumph (32-3).

History is rewritten in the glorious picture of the consensus in Italy which achieved Cicero's return from banishment. Piso's whole proconsulate was inferior to the signal honours accorded Cicero (*Pis*. 33-6). A garbled and imprecise discussion of Piso's term in Macedonia and Gabinius' term in Syria glosses over details (37-50). Then follow a dramatic comparison of Cicero's own triumphant return from exile with Piso's inglorious return from his province (51-63). Cicero's perception of the fickleness of the mob mentality was apparently never strong. His memory of the acclaim he received on his way to Rome has here become *a Brundisio usque Romam agmen perpetuum* (one long queue from Brindisi to Rome, 51-18). The description is vivid, the memory apparently more so. The letter of September 57 to Atticus (*Att*. 4.1) in which he recounted his welcome by the jubilant crowds, is redrawn and exaggerated. One sentence gives the key to Cicero's subjective perception of his own past:

> *Unus ille dies mihi quidem immortalitatis instar fuit quo in patriam redii, cum senatum egressum vidi populumque universum, cum mihi ipsa Roma prope convulsa sedibus suis ad complectendum conservatorem suum progredi visa est.* (*Pis*. 52.6)

> That one day on which I returned to the fatherland was to me just as good as immortality, when I saw the Senate come out, and the whole nation, when Rome herself seemed to me to have been almost uprooted from her foundations and issued forth to embrace her saviour.

This self-glorifying description rests solidly on a single fact, coloured by subjective interpretation: that the senate did cause Cicero's house to be rebuilt at state expense, *mihique, quod ante me nemini, pecunia publica aedificandam domum censuerunt* (They decreed that my house should be rebuilt for me with public money, something that had never been done for anybody before me, 52).[24]

Invective against Piso is therefore largely a springboard for self-justification. A scurrilous reference to the friendship between Piso and the Greek philosopher and poet Philodemus (68-72)[25] leads to an expurgated account of Cicero's relationship with Pompey (76-77) and Caesar (79-82). This picture of amicable friendship between the returned exile and the two most powerful men in the state differs from the fluctuations of anxiety depicted in the letters to Atticus, and from extant correspondence between Cicero and the triumvirs: *Me Cn. Pompeius, multis obsistentibus eius erga me studio atque amori, semper dilexit, semper sua coniunctione dignissimum iudicavit* ... (Gnaeus Pompeius always liked me, as he was always displaying tokens of his concern and love, and always considered me worthy of being associated with him ..., *Pis.* 76).[26] About Caesar he is more candid: *Ego C. Caesarem non eadem de re publica sensisse quae me scio* (Obviously I know that Gaius Caesar did not feel exactly the same as I did about the republic), but he goes on to reminisce about Caesar's favourable attitude to him in 59 BC (79).

So the powerful are mollified, but there may be a hidden reason for the attack on Caesar's father-in-law.[27] The bitterness of Cicero's onslaught on Piso reflects his inner attitude, also toward those enemies he dared not attack. Such passages cannot have strengthened Cicero's position with the triumvirs. The weakness of Cicero's public case against Piso is reflected in the fact that he refrained from any legal prosecution, content to resort to this kind of invective. Cicero's explanations as to why he was not prosecuting Piso are flaccid (83, 95).[28] He had no real case. Although he cited crimes such as *crudelitas* (83-5) *avaritia* (86-8), retention of war-booty and levying of warships beyond the legal number (90), his accusations against Piso are vague and unreasonable, compared with the precision of Cicero's accusations against Verres.

The object of the pamphlet is to vent spleen. The final paragraph (99) reflects this emphasis, beginning *numquam ego sanguinem expetivi tuum* (I never sought your blood!) and ending with ostensible threats *non moleste feram; ... fruar ... nec te minus libenter metuentem videbo ne reus fias quam reum, nec minus laetabor cum te semper sordidum, quam si paulisper sordidatum viderem* (I shall not take it ill; .... I shall enjoy ... and I shall see you cowering in fear that you will be arraigned no less gladly than if I saw you actually accused, and I shall be no less glad if I should see you in perpetual sackcloth and ashes than if I were to see you in mourning for a little while). These are not threats of active retribution.[29] One might enquire whether these are threats at all: would an antagonist really have been intimidated by the knowledge of future sensations in store for the speaker? Here again Cicero is identifying himself with the public weal. The invective of the *In Pisonem* is not the objective result of patriotic concern for the general welfare of the state, based on the proven or provable fact of corruption by the governor of a province, but a manifestation of the returned exile's subjective and embittered perception of a wrong done to himself as virtual personification of the state.

By this means Cicero could externalize his grievance against all who had contributed to his disempowerment. Piso precipitated his rage, but as antagonist he served as a mere foil for a focus on the returned exile himself. Although the pamphlet is composed as a rhetorical attack on a second person, the ostensible addressee fades into insignificance. The model addressee is the Roman public, whom Cicero wants to remind of his signal services to the state and the grave injustice done him when he was banished.

5.3 Ovid's exilic poems as invective

Cicero's imprecision of accusation appears explicit and specific when contrasted with Ovid's excursions into invective. Several poems in the *Tristia* and at least one in the *Epistolae ex Ponto* address an unknown enemy or enemies, in very vague terms. These may be seen as an exercise in anonymity, and their focus is, as with Cicero's outreach to a wider public, first on the exile himself and then very much on the poet's contemporary model readership at Rome and also – particularly – into the distant future. The villainous object of attack is vaguely designated and the nature of his transgression even more so. As with Cicero, the second person verbs of address very frequently shift toward first person emphasis on the writer as victim. At about the same time that he completed the fifth book of the *Tristia*, Ovid launched into a poem of invective on the Callimachean model. The general assumption is that the *Ibis* was composed during Ovid's third year of exile. Ovid's other poems to an enemy in the *Tristia* are shorter, experimental predecessors of the *Ibis*, which seem to have offered the poet an opportunity to exercise his ingenuity in a new direction.[30] In the *Epistolae ex Ponto* only 4.3 (and the last part of 4.16) refer to an enemy. Parallels between these poems and the *Ibis* will shed light on both. In what follows, a brief survey of these shorter poems will lead to a fuller discussion of the *Ibis*.

Ovid's poems of invective partake of the same unreal, dream-world quality that his other poems from exile exhibit. It is equally unwise to attempt any kind of historicist interpretation in the hope of identifying or pinning down the recognisable characteristics of the exile's enemy or enemies. Most of the poems of invective are extremely vague about what the antagonist was supposed to have done. Again we need to accept a shifting array of *personae* embodied in both the writer and the *tu* of his address. It is significant that the *Tristia* has four poems of invective, the *Epistolae ex Ponto* (the bulk of which most probably was composed after the *Ibis*) half that number. Once the longer poem of invective had been written, it would appear that the vein had been worked, and the poet turned away to other themes. This is, however, a literary critic's interpretation. An analysis of the exile's psychological make-up could lead to speculation that once his spleen had been vented, the exiled poet no longer felt the urge to vituperate. Such a reading may need to assume a closer identity between creator-poet and suffering exile than I have so far postulated, but it cannot be excluded. The *Ibis* works as a projection by the creator-poet of the suffering-exile-as-poetic-*persona*, setting to verse his raging anger at an unknown enemy. Gareth Williams in an important contribution (1996, the only extensive recent discussion of the work, except for the creatively free translation by Slavitt, 1990) argues that the *Ibis* represents the 'manic' phase of a manic-depressive's experience of hardship. That the *Tristia* has offered material for discussion of exilic depression as a psychological phenomenon has been noted by various researchers.[31]

Apart from the *Ibis*, much of Ovid's ostensible attack verges on the playful. 'Reproach' is often a better term. Much is conventional. In *Tristia* 1.8.37-46 the origins of a friend who ignored the exile's misery are designated in the standard form of reproach: 'born on rocks, with veins of flint and a tiger for a nurse.' Other instances are more specific, and Augustus is frequently the target. Ovid's first strong note of defiance, struck in the second year of exile, entails emphasis on the third person. It is an open challenge to the emperor. In a declaration of poetic independence, the exile informs the young poetess 'Perilla' that *Caesar in hoc potuit iuris habere nihil* (In this Caesar has no power, *Tr.* 3.7.48). Power is, as always, central in the consciousness of the exile, both the power wielded by the emperor, and his own empowerment by his Muse. Here the creative poet associates his exiled *persona* very strongly with Rome. As Augustus encouraged the celebration of *Roma et Augustus*,[32] so he celebrates his own poetic immortality in terms reminiscent of both Augustan power and Horatian poetic terminology:

> *dumque suis victrix omnem de montibus orbem*
> *prospiciet domitum Martia Roma, legar.* (*Tr.* 3.8.51-2)

And as long as martial Rome shall survey the whole vanquished world from its own high hills, I shall be read!

With the passive *legar* (I shall be read) in the triumphant final position in the couplet, the poet has drawn his human *persona* and his poetry as one.

Poetics and invective appear equally inextricably involved in the exile's consciousness. *Tristia* 4.9 apparently feebly threatens the addressee future 'world-wide' exposure through poetry (vv. 21, 22). If a consistent enemy is to be assumed, one may conjecture that this is a 'promise' perhaps realised later by the *Ibis*.[33] The emphasis is strongly subjective. Again the poem focuses only vaguely on the antagonist, clearly on the suffering hero as protagonist. The exile as poet is portrayed as a reluctant Philoctetes, desperately seeking healing from the instrument of his pain, his practice of poetry. The poem exhibits typically Ovidian word-play. The *coda* offers a pun on *canere*, resting on the confusion of military formula and the concept of a 'singing' Muse: *cane, Musa, receptus, / dum licet huic nomen dissimulare suum* (Sound the retreat, oh Muse of mine, while this fellow still may keep his name a secret! vv. 31-2). The reader expects an object such as 'song' or 'poem', after the imperative and apostrophe of the Muse, so that the next word, *receptus*, comes as a surprise, turning a musical trope into a military metaphor. The Muse must retreat lest it proclaim the identity of the secret offender.

These are the last words the poet and his Muse together produce before they burst forth in *Tristia* 4.10, a triumphant exposition of the exile's identity and antecedents and a vindication of the tenor of his life's work. Green's translation (1994: 79) of the first couplet captures Ovid's conscious creation of a poetic 'I', itself heavily allusive of poetic predecessors. The poet pretends that his 'poetic I' is a spent force, but during the course of the poem the reader discovers that this is not so. Yet Green's metrics, by ignoring the implications of *qui fuerim* (that I formerly was) and empha-sising 'you read', loses some of the subtlety:

> *Ille ego qui fuerim, tenerorum lusor amorum*
> *quem legis, ut noris, accipe posteritas.*   (*Tr.* 4.10.1-2)

> Who was this 'I' you read, this trifler in tender passions?
> You want to know, posterity? Then attend: ...

Emphasis on the identity of the poet contrasts with the anonymity of the antagonist that was emphasised in the last line of the previous poem, as we saw above. Here the poet has created a dialogue not only between writer and unknown addressee, but between two poems, in point and counterpoint. With the contrast between invective and self-justification Ovid shows his readership exilic *consolatio* in action, attention to the delights and endlessly playful possibilities of poetic composition, thereby drawing the exile in another guise, as a self-consoler, whiling away his dreary time.

The themes of a traditional *consolatio ad exulem* are reversed in *Tristia* 5.8 to berate another secret foe. Here the accent initially concentrates on the enemy, the external and malevolent second person, but, as so often, the focus gets blurred and then sharpens, and ostensible second person out-reach once more shifts through the three grammatical persons, from the addressee, via the emperor, to the writer. The exile enquires whether his enemy does not fear either the turning wheel of Fortune (5-10), or some form of punishment (11-14). A disquisition on the fickleness of Fortune (15-20) is followed by praise of the amiability of the emperor who will relieve the exile's lot (21-36). The gentle reprobation of this poem exploits the possibilities of reversal within the range of human experiences, even the reversal of the writer's exile. The implication of such fluidity in the human condition is that nothing is fixed, not even the identities of persecutor and victim. Their roles may still be reversed, and the victim will once more be seen in Rome, and will then watch his enemy's downfall. A curse in the coda prays that this enemy may be exiled on a 'more serious charge' (37-8) than was the poet. *Polyptoton* of the verb **vide-*, changing from second person *videas* (you may see) to first, *videam* (may I see) underscores this suggestion of permutability. A poem that plays with contrast and shift renders it not impossible to equate 'this enemy' with the emperor himself, even when it ostensibly extols his benevolence.

Ovid's *Ibis* is a single long elegiac poem of invective, aimed at an unnamed enemy. The poem, deriving from the Callimachean heritage, is unique in Latin literature. The original Greek *Ibis* is wholly lost. Its form and format can only be guessed at. Its content was stringent invective, directed at one of the Hellenistic poet's literary enemies, perhaps a plagiarist, formerly conjectured to have been Apollonius Rhodius, his erstwhile pupil, the composer of the epic *Argonautica*. This has recently been questioned.[34] The name 'Ibis' refers to the Egyptian scavenger bird which 'lives off filth and pollutes whatever it touches, including what it takes from others'.[35] The Roman poet borrowed title, topic and theme, perhaps only to apply his elegiac skills in a new direction, perhaps to attack a real enemy, who tried to take something from the living poet, his good name, his possessions, or his poetry, either by plagiarism, or by extreme censorship.

The identity of Ovid's 'Ibis' in his Callimachean imitation, and the enemy or series of enemies berated in these poems, and perhaps of the person behind apostrophised *Livor* ('mordant Envy') in *Ex Ponto* 4.16, remains a contentious issue. More than one enemy (or none at all) may have been involved. Guesses range from Hyginus, keeper of the Palatine library, to M. Ateius Capito, to the poet's correspondent Messalinus Corvinus, who perhaps disappointed the exile's expectations, and finally, to Augustus himself, the fount and origin of the exiled poet's woes.[36] The invective could have been aimed at whosoever chose to apply it to himself, or to multiple enemies, or to a personal enemy *and* to the emperor. Williams (1996: 4-22), following Housman, argues for the hostile *persona* as fiction, and offers (p. 23) as *raison d'être* of the *Ibis* the portrayal of 'a perverse obsessiveness which can never fully satisfy the sadistic relish on which it feeds' and suggests that the poem is 'a contrived display of an irrational psychology erupting in violence'. The 'speaker' in this poem has a 'deranged *persona*' that has lost control, but the creative poet is still fully in command of the process of portrayal (pp. 126-8).

The *Ibis* offers a bridge between the anonymous letters of the *Tristia* and the addressed letters of the second exilic collection. Frequent self-referential allusion between this poem and the two collections works in two ways. The poem echoes and adapts verses from the *Tristia*, thereby giving these phrases a new twist.[37] Echoes of phrases from the *Ibis* in the *Epistolae ex Ponto* carry with them the atmosphere of their predecessor, giving a sinister colouring to ostensibly innocent phrases. For example, in *Ibis* 141 the writer threatens to continue haunting the enemy after his own death, *cum fuero vacuas dilapsus in auras* (when I shall have vanished into empty air). A variation *ille est tenues dilapsus in auras* (he vanished into thin air, *Pont.* 3.3.94, of the apparition of *Amor*), works by allusion to turn the god into a ghost, a fitting end for the deity whose self-designated major devotee has come to an unfortunate end. A claim that the exiled poet is 'dangling the Julian names in his poetry, much as devotees dangle a sistrum of the Magna Mater' (*Pont.* 1.1.45-6), and an allusion to a votary of the goddess as a 'blinded penitent' (*privatus lumine*, vv. 51-4) echoes *Ibis* 453-6, where the allusion was, however, to the self-castration of Attis, the devotee of Cybele, the Magna Mater. This Ovidian self-reference turns an ostensibly innocent metaphor into an insinuation that the bearer of the Julian name politically emasculates his opponents.[38]

The *Ibis* consists of 644 verses of imprecation in the Roman tradition of scurrilous invective, couched in abstruse, Alexandrian mythological terminology. Its title appears as a typically Ovidian pun: the word is the name for an Egyptian bird, but is also the Latin for 'You shall go forth!' a reflection of the writer's lot, rather than the lot of his addressee.[39] As with Ciceronian invective, focus throughout is less on the second person than on the subjective perception of the harm done to the 'writer' by the unknown enemy and the frantic tirade of repetition of curses that never satisfies while it feeds the exile's lurid imagination. Catullan political imprecation (e.g. 37, 40, 108 etc.) and Tibullus' elegiac curses of the *lena* (procuress, Tib. 1.5.49-56) offer a pale foreshadowing of the multiplications of doom threatened against the antagonist in this strange work. *Selbstironie* combined with apparently bitterly vicious attack underlies the poet's black comedy, showing the influence of Graeco-Roman New Comedy.

The reader is led to believe that the addressee in some way harmed the poet's work and attacked his victim's wife (vv. 13-14), thereby forcing him for the 'first time' to write words harmful to 'any other beside himself' (v. 5). Very few of the imprecations heaped in such abandon can be understood without a profound knowledge of Greek (and Roman) literary history. The poem carries with it as it were a vast subtext of commentary; in the words of Williams (1996: 95), '[any] running commentary *becomes* part of the text ... which only privileged readers share (but not his Ibis)'.[40] The enemy is destined to be baffled and confused by the learned web of allusions, and a wider readership is invited to try to distinguish the literary sources, while simultaneously admiring the controlled obscurantism of the learned creative poet and sympathising with the growing megalomania of the virtually deranged exile.

The enemy is presented with an excursive biography of himself, from before his birth to a series of gruesome deaths. All the stars in the firmament were unfavourable at his birth and the Fates prophesied endless dire ends for him. This poem leans heavily on the idea of address and apostrophe, but the second person is frequently superseded by the first, as in the exile's promise to be the final harbinger of the dread fate only half-predicted for the ill-starred infant at its birth. The litany of misfortunes was so long that Clotho had promised that a prophet would arise to complete her arduous task:

> *et, ne longa suo praesagia diceret ore,*
>   *'fata canet vates qui tua' dixit 'erit'.*
> *ille ego sum vates: ex me tua vulnera disces,*
>   *dent modo di vires in mea verba suas;*
> *carminibusque meis accedunt pondera rerum,*
>   *quae rata per luctus experiare tuos.*   (*Ibis* 245-50)

And, so that she didn't have to recite her lengthy prophecies in her own voice, she said, 'There will be a soothsayer who will sing your doom'. That soothsayer am I: from me you will learn your wounds, if only the gods will give their own power to my words; and in my songs the weight will increase of those woes which she thought up for you to experience through your suffering.

Focus is firmly on the exile as prophet. The familiar declaration of identity is given a new twist with the addition of *vates*, turning pronominal *ille* (he) into adjectival 'that', with concomitant switch of stressed subject and unstressed predicative after the copulative *sum* ('I am'). This subtlety is rendered in my translation by inversion of word-order, 'That soothsayer am I!' As soothsayer the exile is confident of one thing: his ability, with the aid of the gods, to bring about the ruin of his enemy through his song.

The pattern of imprecation is illogical.[41] Ovid's *Ibis* is gloriously incon-sistent. Emasculation is wished upon the enemy twice over (vv. 273-4, 453-6), alternating with the generation of unnatural progeny (355-4) and a diet of his own children (427-8). The exile vows, as we have seen, to haunt his enemy after death, (141-8), but also to prevent both the enemy's escape through death (123-4) and his very funeral (163-72). The crowning incon-sistency is a promise to shed tears of pity over the enemy's lot, with the rider that these tears will bring the exile his highest joy (207-8).

The most vicious final curse, after the unhappy enemy has concentrated upon himself the whole gamut of standard mythical punishments (vv. 191-4; 591-2; 633-4) and a series of unnatural deaths undergone by poetic predecessors,[42] is for the enemy to be doomed to spend his days among the Getae and Sarmatians, and to die there (637-8). From this imprecation as the culmination of catastrophes we may deduce the exile's sense of the enormity of his punishment at the hands of Augustus. No mischance can be worse than the one he has experienced. After this preliminary, 'real' curses, in a different metre (iambics, the usual metre for invective) will follow and expose the enemy's name (641-4):

5. From Me to You: Exilic Invective

denique Sarmaticas inter Geticasque sagittas
  his precor ut vivas et moriare locis.
haec tibi tantisper subito sint missa libello,
  immemores ne nos esse querare tui:
pauca quidem, fateor; sed di dent plura rogatis
  multiplicentque suo vota favore mea.
postmodo plura leges et nomen habentis verum*,
  et pede quo debent acria bella geri.   (*Ibis* 637-44)

*Owen (OUP 1915): *versus*

Finally, I pray that you may live among Sarmatian and Getic arrows and die in these places. These curses have in the meantime been sent to you in this little book, just so that you won't complain that I have forgotten you: they're really too few, I admit; but may the gods add more to what have been prayed for, and multiply my wishes as a favour. In a little while you'll read more (verses), ones that bear your (true) name, and in the metre that sharper battles should be fought.

Slavitt's inventively free rendition of the poem offers six lines for Ovid's eight, but captures the spirit of the original (1990: 243-4):

> Or maybe you die out here from one of the poisoned Getan
>   arrows I worry about! It's hardly complete,
> a short and hasty list, for the gods are inventive: their
>   talents for pain being much greater than mine.
> Adieu then, Ibis: next time, your name will appear *en clair*,
>   as it already does on so many privy walls.

This is as good an example as any to quote from the poem to indicate the self-absorption of the ranting exile. As with Cicero's attack on a known enemy, its real focus is the *persona* of the suffering hero, a hero that enjoys the favour of the gods, but in the case of our creative poet we again discern a literary distance between the controlling author and the uncontrolled, manic 'speaker' of endless curses, of which exile is the culmination. It is the uncontrolled speaker that threatens to expose his enemy in his next exercise of poetic penmanship.[43]

But we know what did follow this attack on an anonymous enemy: the Black Sea Letters, of which most are addressed to friends by name. In this collection *Ex Ponto* 4.3 addresses a new enemy.[44] Again the poet has a new and playful reason to be silent about the name of 'the enemy'. He does not want this person to enjoy or share his own fame (vv. 3, 4). The most obvious persecutor who has been immortalised in the exilic poems is Augustus himself, but the enemy is designated in terms clearly indicating an erstwhile friend, who is reproached for deserting the exile. Again subjective focus is strongly upon the protagonist, with no fewer than four couplets (11-18) repeating the personal and vindicatory *ille ego* of *Tristia* 4.10.1.

145

Invective directed at the addressee is restricted to epithets: *perfide* (untrustworthy cad, 17), *demens* (madman, 30), *improbe* (villain, 34).

The consolatory *topos* of the fickleness of Fortune is again a theme. That this inconstancy is closely related to the inconstancy of the addressee is pointed by repetition of *Fortuna* in the penultimate position in lines 7 and 29, followed by polyptoton of the verb **reced-* (*quia contraxit vultum, Fortuna, recedis*, 'because Fortune turned her face away, you draw back', and *cur, si Fortuna recedit ...*, 'why, if Fortune withdraws, do you ...'). The association of unfavourable Fortune and an unkind friend seems to invite both speculation as to the personal identity of the faithless friend and identification of this friend with the powerful controller of the exile's lot, but it is better to avoid fruitless historicist speculation and to concentrate upon what the poetry conveys.

The exile quotes examples from history to underscore the lability of Fortune. These all may be connected in some way with the emperor himself or with past victims of the Julian family (Croesus and Dionysius as monarchs coming to a bad end, Marius with his multiple consulships, and Pompey the great, victim of Julius Caesar's monarchical aspirations).[45] Again speculation seems to be invited about the possible danger inherent in drawing such explicit attention to dangerous themes. Such a poem, if the model readership at Rome included the emperor himself, would serve to underscore his victim's stress on the dangers inherent in crossing him, while itself teetering on the brink.

There is a lacuna at verse 44, conjectured by Green (1994: 354) as referring to Pompey's known end, decapitation on the Egyptian shore. Its natural corollary, banishment to the opposite ends of the earth, is shown as the fate of the protagonist. It is drawn in terms of the realisation of the ultimate *adynaton*. If someone had said to the poet that he would have to go to the Euxinus and live in fear of being transfixed by Getic arrows, he would have told his interlocutor to go and take an emetic.[46] The last word of line 51, *ibis* (you will go forth!) invites connection with the curse poem. It may be seen as one of those transient felicities of expression which should not be pressed too hard for levels of interpretation, but do offer a subtle counterpoint to what is said.

Sum tamen haec passus (Yet I suffered this, v. 55), says the exile. The impossible came to pass. He explains that he might have evaded the arrows of the mortal Getae, but not those of the high god, a clear allusion to Augustus himself. The implication is clearly that his antagonist may suffer a similar fate. This threat again vaguely involves the *topos* of the mutability of the human condition. The adjective *tristia* connects enemy and exile, both in danger from the fickle representative of Fate, the imperial 'god' himself.

> *tu quoque fac timeas, et quae tibi laeta videntur,*
> *dum loqueris, fieri tristia posse puta.*   (*Pont.* 4.3.57-8)

You had also better look out and consider that what now looks good to you may turn dismal while you're still speaking!

In the final poem of the exilic corpus, personified Envy is addressed. In the context of a discourse on living exponents of literature (*Pont.* 4.16.3-46) the literary importance of *Livor* as a detractor of generic mode, not a would-be thief, assassin or even *delator* (secret informant), must be stressed. The term comes from the Callimachean tradition of the carping detractor of the 'slender Muse' (as in the *Hymn to Apollo* 105-9). It is normally seen as an abstraction rather than a personification, but here the enemy is addressed in personal terms as *invide* (you, jealous person!) in the first line of the poem. This turns what follows into personal address. *Livor*, an unknown enemy, the personification of negative literary criticism, in Callimachean terminology is the *Ibis*, a proponent of large-scale epic, the carping critic of lyric, elegy and the 'slender Muse'. In Roman terms, *Livor* is embodied in a ruler who demanded national epic from his poets, who did not appreciate the light-hearted, parodic art of the last of the elegists. By extension, *Livor* is the censor who punished the composer of an irreverent 'Art of Love'. As the *Ibis* was threatened with various cycles of life and death leading to the ultimate curse, living death among Danubian savages, so *Ex Ponto* 4.16 may still, even after his death, be addressed to Augustus and what he stood for.[47]

The poet's vindication of his art against detracting Envy shows that Ovidian invective is subjective. Focus is on the immortality of his poetry, not the harm done by his detractor. The poet who died in exile did not have the opportunity, enjoyed by Cicero after his return, of vituperating against enemies whose power proved to be less enduring than his own. Ovid's persuasive literary power is illustrated by the fact that critics continue to attempt the impossible by trying to identify those enemies immortalised by his invective. Ovid, a poet who created his art for art's sake, needed only the possibility of experimenting with Callimachean recrimination as incentive to produce such a poem without necessarily having, at the time of composition, a single, specific, human enemy. His megalomaniacal 'speaker' in the *Ibis* works more to round out the picture of the varieties of emotional response to oppression than to punish a certain enemy. The creative poet could show his protagonist as losing all sense of proportion and control, brandishing a literary bludgeon to macabre effect. Below we shall consider how he also could show the same protagonist in subtle attack, his pen a rapier, even a scalpel, in contentious polemic against his chief persecutor.

5.4 Defence as attack: Ovid's *controversia* against Augustus

The anonymity of Ovid's unnamed enemies is balanced by the certainty that his exile was decreed by the powerful figure of the emperor. Augustus could have expected that Ovid would, in a defence of his poetry and morals,

147

touch on the real circumstances, perhaps political, of the debacle of AD 8, but he apparently never did. Instead, *Tristia* 2 is a single, long, autobio-graphically-coloured poem, comprising an extensive defence of the poet's art and life. While ostensibly concerned with the exile as protagonist, its polemical thrust involves criticism of, even attack on, the emperor as second person. Although the poem has the persuasive thrust of all rhetoric, with the second person strongly designated as object of appeal, the poet weaves ostensibly autobiographical allusions, protestations of gratitude and discussion of poetics into a network of accusation. Elaborate self-justification against clearly lightweight accusations show these accusa-tions up as trifling and the accuser as arbitrary. Elaborate *praeteritio* of the unnamed fault on the part of the exile that had wounded the emperor serves to highlight the exile's *error*, and to whet the curiosity of all other readers, a process that has continued over the centuries.[48]

Few have paused to reflect on why, if Ovid was relegated because of his subversive elegiacs, he chose for his major medium, while apparently clamouring for forgiveness and return, the very elegiacs in which he had first offended. *Tristia* 2.255-300 and 359-467 together offer a reprise of almost the whole corpus of ancient literature, Greek and Roman, as one long celebration of *amor*. But ostensibly *Tristia* 2 it is a 'speech in his defence'. It hardly seems like an apology, or a true attempt to sing of *Roma et Augustus*. Chapter 4 showed that other parts of the poem are equally dubious as prayer.

Throughout the exilic corpus his readers appear to be invited to inter-pret the poet's recourse to poetry in his own defence as a Philoctetes-like concession to inevitability. The exiled poet at *Tristia* 4.10.23-6 tells poster-ity about his youthful experiences as *declamator* after his father had tried to dissuade him from writing poetry:

> motus eram dictis totoque Helicone relicto
>   scribere temptabam verba soluta modis:
> sponte sua carmen numeros veniebat ad aptos,
>   et quod temptabam dicere* versus erat.

* Luck: *scribere*

I was moved by his words and abandoned Helicon entirely, and started trying to write words free from metre: but all by itself a song kept coming to suitable measures and what I tried to say (write), really was verse.[49]

So in exile Ovid resorted to his poetry as a means of clearing himself. In antiquity a close relationship was seen between erotics and rhetoric. *Peitho* (Persuasion) was a follower of Aphrodite.[50] This was the only type of oratory with which the young Ovid had felt comfortable. According to Seneca, Ovid rarely declaimed *controversiae*, as he disliked argumentation, normally preferring persuasive *suasoriae* (*Contr.* 2.2.12), yet *Tristia* 2 may be designated as a poetical exercise in an imaginary *controversia*:

> *A poet is privately accused by a despot of corrupting public morals by precept and precedent and is sent into exile. He knows that this is merely a political pretext, but may not divulge the real reason and has no legal basis of defence. He appeals to his persecutor for a better place of exile.*

The pattern of argument of *Tristia* 2 falls into two parts, of which the second, from 207ff. (in Owen's 1924 division, the *refutatio*) comprises the defensive use of an '*Ars Poetica*'.[51] Open defence works as hidden attack. The exile's tone is at first ostensibly meek and repentant. The poem ostensibly addresses Augustus, but one may postulate a whole range of potential model readers. Often address of the emperor as second person acts as a springboard for wider outreach. The poet explains why he is again seeking what harmed him (1-12) with reference to Augustus' poetic commissioning of grand epic (13-26). Precedents for mercy follow (29-52), with reference to the exile's past loyalty and former glorification of the ruler through song (53-66), which the discerning reader may remember with amusement as not always as innocent as it seemed.[52] This leads to the contrast of other poets' praise of the emperor with the songs that ruined the poet (67-88).

Another appeal based on the exile's past civic virtues (89-102) is followed by the first hint that some misdemeanour other than his poetry was involved, hastily glossed over with elaborate *praeteritio* (103-8). A second appeal refers to the exile's antecedents and his fame as poet (109-20). Verses 121-39 offer a counter-accusation, while ingenuously praising Augustus for allowing the condemned man as *relegatus* (banished with retention of property rights) to retain his property. Verse 127 gratefully acknowledges *vita data est, citraque necem tua constitit ira* (my life was granted me, and your anger stopped short of the death penalty). Ostensible gratitude for a life spared amounts to an accusation of despotism. In Roman law no citizen could have been executed without the sanction of a popular hearing, as Cicero had found to his cost.

The exile next expresses gratitude to Augustus for an *in camera* trial and condemnation, and for having privately enjoined him to go to his place of relegation (131-5). In legal terms, this apparent boon was a great disadvantage. The problem with condemnation without a legal and public trial is that it grants the victim no public platform upon which to argue his defence. These verses concentrate on Augustus' arrogation of judiciary power:

> nec mea decreto damnasti facta senatus,
>   nec mea selecto iudice iussa fuga est.
> tristibus invectus verbis (ita principe dignum)
>   ultus es offensas, ut decet, ipse tuas.

And you did not condemn my deeds by decree of the Senate, nor was my flight commanded by a select judiciary. You inveighed against me with sorrowful words (such is a deed worthy of the first man in the state) and you yourself, as you should, avenged your own wrongs.

These couplets illustrate the classic generic characteristic of elegy: statement in the hexameter and restatement in the pentameter. Repetition of praise, however, deconstructs by over-emphasis what it appears to admire. Clues are to be found in variations on normal legal procedure (*nec decreto damnasti senatus/ nec selecto iudice iussa*), personal retribution by the emperor (*invectus/ ultus ... offensas*) and the bland acceptance that this was as it should be (*dignum/ decet*). This 'praise' itself does not hold up to scrutiny. The actions of the emperor clearly are not admirable in his fictive 'restored Republic', but show it for what it is, the domain of a despot.

Verses 140-54 proclaim in elegant phrases the exile's hopes for mitigation of sentence. Then follow the prayers for the imperial household, and for Augustan military victories, discussed above, in Chapter 4.[53] These form the basis for a final appeal that wraps up the first half of the poem. The appeal for clemency that follows echoes one of the few set *controversiae* recorded by Seneca the Elder as actually spoken in the poet's youth: *parce, pater ...* (O father, spare ..., 181).[54] This youthful exercise had been based on a typically involved hypothetical case study involving the exercise of the *patria potestas* (father's right over life and death) for the condemnation to death of a young girl by her own father. Here the phrase is completed with *... patriae* (... of the fatherland). This bland appeal for clemency the exile bases on Augustus' reputation for kindness (179-82).[55] The 'father of the state' was in fact extremely harsh to his own progeny.[56] An appeal couched in these terms by a poet banished simultaneously with the emperor's own granddaughter (whose mother, the emperor's own daughter, was also languishing in exile) is clearly saying more than it appears to, but in a terminology that, on the surface, could not be faulted.

Finally, the exile's appeal is not so much for forgiveness and recall, as for 'a better place of exile' (183-206). The exile is relegated to the 'seven-mouthed Ister', oppressed beneath the cold pole of Callisto, reminiscent of Jupiter's prime victim in *Metamorphoses* 1. *Parrhasiae gelido virginis axe premor* (I am hard-pressed beneath the cold axis of the Parrhasian maiden, *Tr.* 2.190).[57] In the context of Suetonius' statement (*Aug.* 80) that Augustus had a constellation of seven birth-marks, corresponding exactly with the Great Bear, and Ovid's own consistent association of Augustus with Jupiter, the allusion suggests oppression by Augustus himself. That Augustus can be *both* a 'Callisto' *and* a 'Jupiter' is the kind of inconsistency that probably would not have troubled our poet much.[58] An 'informed reader' could be left to recontextualise such an allusive (and elusive) signal.

The second half of this long poem is more openly offensive. Much of it is taken up with a vigorous defence of the poet's art, amounting to use of poetics as attack on a cultural barbarian. Verses 207-12 specify the two counts against the poet, *carmen et error* (a song and a mistake, 207). Every allusion to the exile's *error* is a form of *praeteritio*, evoking curiosity and renewing the emperor's 'wound'. Denial of moral corruption is preceded (213-50) by a virtual accusation of neglect of the affairs of state while the emperor 'wasted his time' in reprehensible *otium* (pursuit of leisure), and a second, mutually exclusive charge, that the emperor either did not read Ovid's offensive poems or could not have read them properly. If he had, he would have found them harmless.

Ovid's arguments are specious where they are not insulting. An ingenious exposition of the most honoured elements of Roman life as potential moral corrupters (251-300) touches not only on poetry, but also on some of the emperor's public benefactions, proudly listed in his *Res Gestae* (e.g. 295-6 the temple of Mars Ultor, *RG* 21). The argument that perverse minds can be corrupted by anything, while the chaste are never corrupted by what they see (301-11) attacks the imperial prudery inherent in the accusation that Ovid's *carmen* had worked to corrupt Roman minds. Ostensible self-recrimination for not having kept to stock epic themes offers negative comment on Augustus' literary taste. An apparent *recusatio* exposes the limitations of Augustus' appeal for the composition of 'national poetry' (313-38) to glorify his own deeds. From 339 onwards the poet expounds the separation between his life and his art, here too, perhaps, an attack on the exile's powerful persecutor.[59]

The central statement of this section is concise: *nec liber est indicium animi, sed honesta voluntas* (nor is a book an indication of my attitude, but rather [look at my] innocuous intention, 357). The poem then shifts into the didactic mode, reviewing virtually the whole corpus of Greek and Roman literature, arguing for its largely erotic nature. At v. 471 the exile launches into an excursus on the kind of didactic poetry that was often written on trivial subjects. The main thrust of argument is that poetry does not *teach*, but only *displays*, (presumably aberrant) behaviour. A subtle shift in argument shows that poetry on occasion teaches reprehensible *skills*, without necessarily inculcating reprehensible *morals*.

Shifts in argument are subtly casuistic. A discussion of Augustus' moral and fiscal support of the mimic stage is blandly approving (495-520) of the emperor's *comis maiestas* (courteous majesty, 512). Verses 495-6 ask 'what if I had composed mimes?' and 519-20 remind the emperor that he had himself watched musical stagings of the poet's works. Finally 521-8 discuss the common Roman predilection for pornographic art, an aberration present even in the emperor's home.

A second *recusatio* follows (529-38). The poet's talent is 'too small' adequately to sing the emperor's praises. This leads to the thought that even the greatest national poet's *magnum opus* is really 'only a love-story', and in a famously bathetic pentameter line that echoes both Vergil's words and his cadences, Ovid thrusts Aeneas into both a Phoenician liaison and into Roman elegy: *tuae Aeneidos auctor / contulit in Tyrios arma virumque toros* (the author of your favourite *Aeneid* hurled both arms and the man into a Tyrian marriage-bed, 533-4). The introduction of the second person possessive adjective *tuae* denoting Augustus encapsulates a wealth of literary-critical assumptions, while deconstructing the Augustan programme of literary propaganda.

From verses 539 to 578 the exile runs through a final virtuoso display of arguments: he is being punished in his old age for the sins of his youth, his best works are redolent of the emperor's name, he never harmed anybody with his wit, and, in a pathetic finale, of all the many 'lascivious' authors he listed, he was the only one ever harmed by his verse.

With this we return to another poet that suffered at the hands of Augustus, but not for his poetry. Gallus, an ingenious and talented lieutenant of the young Octavian, one of the first to feel the effects of the loss of the later emperor's *amicitia*, committed suicide rather mysteriously, at some time between the years 29 and 26 BC.[60] The young Ovid started his poetic career soon after. An effective *damnatio memoriae* of Gallus has left little of his oeuvre from which to make a balanced judgement of its influence, particularly on Ovidian style, but Ovid clearly considered him as an important model.[61] He is generally accepted to have been one of the most important formulators of the Roman erotic elegy as a separate genre. Ovid was consistently loyal to the first poet to fall foul of Augustus. Fleeting allusions to him occur throughout the Ovidian oeuvre.[62] Gallus features in two other passages in the exilic works in which Ovid discusses poets and poetry.[63] It may be argued that memories of youthful hero-worship caused the ageing poet more than thirty years after his predecessor's death to celebrate him in such a variety of ways.

An ostensibly harmless allusion, at *Tristia* 2.446, to the older poet's death as resulting from *nimio mero* (too much wine)[64] offers the most direct but subtle challenge to Augustus in the whole poem. According to Suetonius, Gallus incurred Octavian's displeasure by 'showing ingratitude and an envious nature'. Dio Cassius speaks of 'disrespectful gossip', but Ovid says he was drunk, with the implication that he spoke out of turn. The most notorious instance of an 'inebriated friend who spoke out of turn' was the Macedonian Cleitus, killed in a sudden rage by Alexander the Great.[65] The philosopher Anaxarchus consoled the grieving and penitent prince with the thought that Alexander as ruler of the world was placed by Zeus above the normal control of justice and law. Ovid's oblique allusion to the death of a friend at the hands of the ruler who was often perceived by Augustus as a role model, implies recondite but clear criticism of Augustus as supralegal dispenser of injustice. If he had not already been sent into exile, such a challenge of the authority of the princeps could have offered enough material for another *in camera* trial and condemnation. Yet we do not know whether Augustus actually ever read (or was meant to read) this poem.

We have already postulated the existence of a range of potential audiences. Both in his outreach through publication to a contemporary reading public and through his dialogue with posterity, Ovid exploited the powerful potential of literary polemic, thereby proclaiming himself to have been the victim of a despotic god, an unreasonable man and a treacherous friend. The whole poem is a clever *controversia* set in verse, aimed at impressing its readership with its wit, audacity, ornamentation and versatility. Its tactlessness (at best) and strong criticism of the emperor (at worst) are subtly combined. The exiled poet has succeeded in employing, in an ostensibly deprecatory framework, a wide-ranging rhetorical defence as a weapon of attack.

We have agreed that it is almost impossible to weigh what the reactions and possible response of his contemporaries may have been to Ovid's second person address of the emperor. Of Augustus' own reaction we can judge even less. We can only consider the effect of Ovid's defence on our view of Augustus' achievements and of the construct of himself and his era that Augustus sought by various means to create. The voice that speaks over distance in space and time bridges the gap.

As with the ruined monuments of Augustan Rome, that still convey an impression of greatness, enough potential subversion is discernible in Ovid's exilic poetry to serve as a voice that transcends a contemporary conspiracy of silence, giving the outlines of a picture to be filled in by the modern reader's own creative imagination. In Ovid's defence of his life and works he has given the loneliness of the exile and the arbitrariness of his powerful oppressor a mythic dimension. Behind the abject exile an irreverent ghost of the former *lusor amorum* still stands: 'So, Augustus, you wanted me to celebrate you in my verse; here is your celebration – with a vengeance!' The negative picture that emerges of Augustus and his attitude to literature has made a lasting impression on posterity – this seems to show the efficacy of Ovid's defence as a means of attack.

In the success of his subtle polemic we may contrast Ovid (who never returned from his place of banishment) with Cicero, the returned exile, whose overt attack on Piso and covert rage at Clodius, Caesar and Pompey, has left us with little more than a picture of his own hurt pride and helpless rage at his loss of power. That this loss weighed heavily with the consular while he was still in exile will be the point of departure for our next chapter.

THE THIRD STAGE

THE FIRST PERSON: EXILIC SUBJECTIVITY

Preamble: Of Times and Places

It is in the nature of autobiography that individual focus colours the most dispassionate account. This is particularly true of poetical autobiography, and of attempts to justify the protagonist in the eyes of his opponents. We have seen that, in the case of both Cicero and Ovid, ostensible efforts at outreach to or even attack on a second person often reflect no more than solipsism at one remove, with frequent allusion to the writer as protagonist, and use of the first person. The true 'first person literature of exile', to which we now turn, has an even greater predominance of verbs in the first person. Its spatial focus is predominantly on the place of exile. Temporal focus is, however, more subtle and emanates from a number of different vantage points. An author in exile may reflect on his past (on his former life in Rome), on the present, with emphasis on both place and circumstance of exile, or on the future, either imagining himself in continued exile, or safe at last after a projected glorious recall and vindication. Conversely, after his return, the restored exile may resort to self-justification and further self-exculpation relating to events that originally led to his exile, or he may choose to recount his experiences and emotions during exile, perhaps also giving a description of the place of exile.[1] Preterite verbs predominate in retrospection, present verbs in introspection or description.

The returned exile has an opportunity to comment on what he has experienced; his comment can be on the exile itself, that is, autobiographical reportage of what he felt and suffered. Such reportage need not be 'factual' but may comprise an attempt to rewrite history, giving a new and possibly more heroic colouring to the erstwhile exile's deeds and reactions. On the other hand, the returned exile can produce an *apologia pro vita sua*, offering comment on the reasons for his exile. What he writes is, in all instances, in no way objective; subjective recolouring of recent history is aimed at eliciting, from contemporaries and posterity, a favourable judgement of the exile's past actions.

155

Cicero shows himself as consistently aware of the value of autobiography to colour a view of the author's deeds for both his contemporaries and posterity. His schematic *commentarii* in Greek and Latin on his consulship were completed before his exile (*Att.* 1.19). That these were meant to glorify, but also to justify, the great deeds of 63 BC, there can be no doubt. These *commentarii* were intended as working documents for a more florid approach by his contemporaries, the historiographer Lucceius and the polymath Posidonius, both of whom apparently declined to oblige.[2] Cicero has been much censured for his request that Lucceius colour his biography more brightly than life, *plusculum etiam, quam concedat veritas* (even a spot more than truth would allow, *Fam.* 5.12.4), *epistula enim non erubescit* (for a letter doesn't blush, *ibid.* 1). His explanation for his need to record his own deeds, whether pleasant or unpleasant, offers a psychological key to the practice of historical hindsight: *Habet enim praeteriti doloris secura recordatio delectationem* (For remembering past pain in present safety has a certain enjoyable flavour, *ibid.* 5).[3] Its inverse also holds good: remembrance in an unhappy present of a happier past often sharpens the pain, unless the sufferer has true control over his emotions and attitudes, the kind of control ostensibly offered by the tenets of philosophy. Examination of the first person depiction of exile will need to reflect both these aspects.

In discussion of the first person we remain aware of a spectrum of *personae*, each with a different voice. The internal monologue of true introspection is seldom prominent. The 'I'-writer demonstrates consistent awareness of an audience, to whom he is conveying a report about the 'I'-exile. Behind these two *personae* stands the creative author who selects and transforms his material, translating it into a chosen generic mode, adapted to the model audience that he envisages. The assumption that the 'model audience' may also exhibit a range of identities underlies all our previous discussion and will here also be assumed.

Chapter 6 will discuss retrospection by various of our protagonists. The thrust of its argument will offer in mirrored order the temporal vantage points of these different authors, starting with the returned Cicero (6.1), reflecting on his past exile and glorious return, and then moving on to the two philosophers, Dio Chrysostomus (6.2) and Boethius (6.3), of whom the former dispassionately reports, after the end of his banishment, on the characteristics of such an altered state, and on his reactions to these circumstances. With Boethius we come to an exiled prisoner, still incarcerated, and likely to remain so, whose apparently equally dispassionate account of his own reactions reports on an alteration in his mental state during exile. The chapter ends with discussion of the exiled Ovid's reminiscences of the distant, happy days at Rome (6.4) before the imperial decree irrevocably altered his state of being into the hopeless, unchanging present of irredeemable exile.

Chapter 7 will discuss the exile's depiction of his present state, concentrating on Ovid (7.3 to 5), but with some discussion of aspects of our other protagonists' appraisal of their surroundings (7.1, 7.2). It will show that apparently 'factual' description is seldom realistic, and that the psychological alienation of an exile is often made concrete by allusive use of opposing depictions of time and space. Time is frozen into an endless 'now', and space stretches out infinitely, Rome becoming an unattainable 'there'. Both these aspects gain their significance relative to the vantage point of the writer, experiencing the full horror of isolation as the heroically innocent victim of either divine ire or human malevolence.

6

Retrospection

6.1 Cicero: rewriting history

When Cicero had been at Dyrrachium for more than a year, the political climate changed, and it suited the triumvirs, particularly Pompey, and also the Senate (who probably saw in Clodius' demagoguery an increasing threat to their power) to have Cicero restored. Consequently he was recalled, more by default than by the universal acclaim he later so fondly extolled, and returned to Rome from banishment early in September 57 BC. Within the first weeks he publicly, in two separate speeches, thanked the Senate and the people for his restitution.

The returned exile had a unique opportunity to comment on his experience; in various speeches after his return, hurriedly composed in the first flush of ebullient victory, Cicero rewrote history, giving an heroic colouring to his deeds and reactions, and offering an *apologia pro vita sua*, recasting the reasons for his withdrawal in a favourable light.[4] Cicero's speeches of thanks differ hugely from the despairing *cris de coeur* penned during exile.[5] A noble and heroic philosophical sage,[6] who bravely bore all vicissitudes, sacrificing his all for the fatherland, emerges from the speeches. That his journey from Brundisium to Rome resembled a triumphal march (*Att.* 4.1) need not be doubted, but this should rather be ascribed to the notorious fickleness of mob mentality than to a conscious popular vindication of Ciceronian rectitude.

Cicero's attitude to his own exile was not static, but changed considerably over time. We have already (Chapter 5) seen one version of his revisionism in his attack on Piso as defence of his own policies. In what follows we shall trace Cicero's gradual rewriting of his own past in more and more glorious terms.

In the speeches that touch on his exile Cicero creates an almost formulaic referential web. Certain narrative allusions are appropriated and established as virtual metaphors for his own heroism. The *exemplum* of the voluntary exile in 100 BC by Q. Metellus Numidicus (who left Rome to pre-empt civil war) is frequently repeated.[7] Cicero's famous *apologia* for his change of political front, written to P. Lentulus in December 54, also refers to Metellus, who, Cicero says, some aver was *fracto animo et demisso* (exhibited a broken and dismal attitude). His enemies imagined the same about him: *abiectiore animo futurum, cum respublica maiorem etiam mihi animum, quam umquam habuissem, daret* ([they thought] ... that I would be downcast in my mind, although the republic gave me greater courage than I had ever had, *Fam.* 1.9.16). His 'greater courage', he adds, was 'because the whole state wanted his return'.[8]

Like his Catilinarian orations, Cicero's speeches before Senate, commons and pontiffs, spoken in the first flush of his return, are adapted to the susceptibilities of their respective audiences.[9] Allusions to exilic *exempla* (Opimius, Q. Metellus Numidicus and Gaius Marius) vary in their presentation, as do references to contemporaries. To the Senate Cicero emphasises the respective roles in his recall of the consuls Publius Lentulus Spinther and Quintus Metellus Nepos, and the influential Pompey (*Red. in Sen.* 6). The people, again, are assured that their soft-hearted yielding to the tearful pleas of Cicero's brother and his son-in-law Gaius Dolabella achieved the restoration of the exile (*Red. Pop.* 7, 8). He assures the citizens that it had formerly been impossible for them to succumb before the tears of his wife and children, because these were kept from them *aut itineribus necessariis aut magnam partem tectis ac tenebris* ... (either by necessary journeys or in a large part by [the fact that they were hidden] behind walls [literally under roofs] and in shadows, *Red. Pop.* 10). A pathetic tone sets the key.

Marius, like Cicero a *novus homo* (first senatorial member of a particular family) from Arpinum, serves as particular *exemplum* to the people. He was an autocratic revolutionary who *exercitu se armisque revocavit* (who called himself back from exile by resorting to an armed struggle, *Red. Pop.* 7), in comparison with whom Cicero's peaceful and popularly acclaimed return stands in noble contrast (*ibid.* 7-11). This *exemplum* cannot, however, be wholly negative: Gaius Marius was, after all, a popular hero, and so he is portrayed as a Ciceronian prototype, also doomed to do battle against a power larger than both:

> *Vidi ego fortissimum virum, municipem meum, C. Marium – quoniam nobis quasi aliqua fatali necessitate non solum cum his, qui haec delere voluissent, sed etiam cum fortuna belligerandum fuit.* (*Red. Pop.* 7)[10]

> I looked to that very brave man, my fellow-Arpinite, Gaius Marius, because both of us were forced by an almost fatal necessity not only to fight against these men who wanted to destroy this state of ours, but also with Fortune herself.

This paragon, Cicero says, was, like the orator himself, never bowed down by his misfortune, remaining courageous until his circumstances changed. Cicero himself, however, was the better man, for he refrained from wreaking vengeance upon his enemies; his return occurred *in pace atque otio* (in peace and tranquillity, 21). As sagacious statesman, Cicero promises that his sole revenge upon each of several classes of enemies will be 'wise administration of the state, cautious wariness in dealing with erstwhile friends, devotion to glory and virtue, and prosecution of *mercatores provinciarum*' (those that sold out their provinces)[11] – that is, his power restored, the hero promises to wield it justly (22).

In Cicero's speech to the Senate Marius is dismissed in a sentence 'as a consular who all but abolished the Senate after his return' (*Red. in Sen.* 38). Here the magnanimity of the consuls of 57, who had worked for Cicero's return, is compared with the villainy of those who had allowed him to be exiled. *Topoi* from the consolatory genre are adapted to the situation. If exile is death, then return is rebirth: the noble Lentulus, so the Senate is assured, established Cicero's 'day of birth' when he restored him to the bosom of his family (*ibid.* 27). Gratitude to individual members of the nobility is spelled out, and the returned consular gives thanks to his former host in Macedonia, Gnaeus Plancius, who, 'had I been a general, would (as *quaestor*) have been my "son", but now he is my "father"...' (*ibid.* 34). Cicero's brother and son-in-law receive their dues of praise, in much the same terms as in the speech before the people (*ibid.* 37, 38). Ties of blood and alliance merit identical treatment before Senate and people.

At the end of September Cicero spoke before the College of Pontiffs (*Oratio de domo sua* – Speech about his house), appealing for the deconsecration of the site of his house, which had been razed by Clodius, demanding that the 'impious' temple to Libertas that Clodius had caused to be erected on the site should be removed. The appeal was ultimately successful and the Senate ordered compensation for the destruction of this house as well as other of his properties.

In this speech, for which Cicero presumably had some three weeks to prepare, he thoroughly rewrites the subjective history of his banishment. The psychological process of sublimation is clearly at work. The argument depends largely on the question of the legality of Clodius' enactments: Cicero begins by declaring Clodius' adoption into the plebeian order as illegal (*Dom.* 32-42). So all his tribunician enactments may be ruled out of order. Cicero now puts a new construction on the enactments that related directly to him, arguing that he never was a 'real' exile, for he had done nothing to forfeit citizenship (72-92).[12] It is clear that the term *exsul*, although technically never applicable to him, rankled, and he expends much effort in dispelling all allusion to it. His 'exile' was a form of proscription, the result of Clodius' lusting after his property, which ended in expulsion rather than death (51). On the other hand, the younger Cato's honourable expedition to Cyprus is construed as 'exile' (52).[13]

Legal issues are exploited in every possible direction: Lucius Cotta had shown that no new law establishing Cicero's reinstatement was needed, as his 'banishment' had been illegal (*Dom.* 68); the 'law' promulgated by Clodius, forbidding discussion of Cicero's case in the Senate, had been void, and Lentulus had subsequently ignored it (68-70); all at Rome had continued to name Cicero in civic and legal documents, thereby confirming his full civic status; Lucius Cotta, the ex-Censor, swore that, if in that time a census had taken place, he would have included Cicero's name on the senatorial roll (84).

Discussion of the nature of exile takes place on two levels. Philosophically, Cicero reverts to the consolatory *topos* that exile bears a *nomen calamitatis, non turpitudinis* (the name of a calamity, but not its disgrace, *Dom.* 72). Legally, he emphasises, a citizen who has left Rome voluntarily can lose citizenship only by an effort of his own will, by accepting the citizenship of a Latin colony, so Clodius' ruling had never amounted to Cicero's loss of citizenship, but merely to *tecti et aquae et ignis interdictio* (an interdiction from shelter, water and fire, 78). Publius Popilius and Quintus Metellus are cited as historical precedents. Clodius' own father had lost his command, and, by implication, his status, during the eighties, but *nemo umquam sanus exsulem appellavit* (no one in his right mind ever called him an exile) – for it had occurred in turbulent times (83-6).

So the *apologia* continues. The illegality of Cicero's banishment was matched only by his innocence and renown. His flight is presented as voluntary withdrawal to save the state from turmoil (*Dom.* 87-96). This speech, delivered so soon after his return, candidly acknowledges Cicero's own grief during exile, his lack of philosophical resignation, and the insinuation by others that the orator had been totally broken in spirit. Justification follows these admissions, and the returned exile's sufferings are raised to the heroic level. If he had not felt thus, he says, at leaving family, hearth and home, *patriae denique causa patriam ipsam amittere* (in sum, losing his fatherland itself for the sake of the fatherland), his sacrifice for the welfare of the state would not have been so great. Had he been wholly in control of his emotions, philosophically immutable, his withdrawal would not have been so sublime. He had been willing to suffer in body and spirit to save his country from suffering. His grief served only to point to the greatness of his sacrifice (97-8).[14]

So, less than a month after his return, we may already discern the workings of selective memory: past pain is romanticised. That his memory of past misery was conveniently dispelled by the happiness and triumph of his recall, is as much part of the statesman's psychological make-up as the misery itself. He was equally despairing after another personal tragedy, the death of Tullia in 45. The next step in the psychological process of dealing with the past is expurgation. Cicero's peroration conveniently forgets the exile's anguished cry, 'If I lose all I hold dear, what am I?' (*Att.* 3.15). Cicero, as true philosopher, here contends that man's property is transient. Its loss offers the sage a chance to be steadfast. The loss of Cicero's house is an external evil and harmful only insofar as it symbolises the disgrace and ignominy inflicted upon the state. The restoration of his house will, while restoring his physical comforts to Cicero, restore the honour of the Roman state (*Dom.* 147). And so it came to pass. The house was rebuilt at state expense. Cicero was vindicated, in his own eyes, if not in the eyes of others.

In the following years, in speeches defending those who had aided Cicero, notably Sestius, charged with violence and bribery, in March 56, and Gnaeus Plancius, arraigned for bribery in 54,[15] we have essentially the same themes, illuminated by dramatic overdrawing. The process of sublimation is at work. As in the *In Pisonem*, in Cicero's invective against his enemies in parts of *Pro Sestio* and *De domo sua*, history is rewritten.

In the speech for Sestius, after some months, we may trace a further development in Cicero's view of the past. His banishment now is depicted as a time of heroic fortitude, when a gallant noble had willingly sacrificed all, including his personal comfort, to the preservation of the state from unnecessary bloodshed. This hero was cheerful and resourceful in exile, until his recall by all the best elements of Roman society. He never feared death for himself, but knew that his death would mean the death of the Republic. He promises to hold on to the power which was restored to him. Thanks to the integrity of his spirit, he was beaten, but never despairing (*Sest.* 36ff., *passim*). The Cicero depicted in this speech is by no means the Cicero of the despairing letters of 58.

The defence of Sestius is important for its general discussion of exile as a political tool, its view of the conventions of *amicitia*, and of the political use and abuse of augury. The view of Cicero's heroic, self-sacrificial withdrawal to save the state from bloodshed is by now firmly established (*Sest.* 49). The orator declares his willingness to return into exile with any other of his former defenders, should they be similarly condemned (*Sest.* 144-7).[16] His own precipitate flight from Rome, after Clodius' first bill, is now construed as 'giving way to save the state from civil war' (*Sest.* 43-9).[17] The implication is that all Italy, except a handful of persecutors, would have risen up in Cicero's defence, precipitating widespread bloodshed, if the noble hero, another Metellus, had not withdrawn, taking, as it were, the focal point of potential unrest with him. We need not doubt that Cicero by now fervently believes his own expurgated version, but here he has difficulty to justify his former eagerness to resort to arms to secure his return, which stands in unfavourable contrast with the willing continuation of his own exile by the heroic Regulus (*Sest.* 127-8).[18]

By 54, in the speech defending Plancius, Cicero indignantly refutes a consistent innuendo by the prosecution that he had fled in 58 because he had feared death. Hindsight has by now construed Clodius' bill *de civis capite Romani* (about the capital punishment of a Roman citizen) as an indubitable and bloody threat of arms; had the hero stayed, and had he (inevitably) fallen by armed violence, he would have gained immortality through the sacrifice of his life in the interests of the state. Such a noble death would, however, have robbed the state of *id exemplum, qualis futurus in me restituendo fuisset senatus populusque Romanus* (that example which the Senate and people of Rome would have been [to the world] in restoring me, *Planc.* 90).

The defence of Cicero's former host offers his advocate a further opportunity for rewriting the past in virtually epic terms. The hero has once again grown in stature. By now he claims that a total holocaust of cosmic proportions had threatened all Italy (*Planc.* 95). Cicero's heroism is equalled only by what he portrays as the heroic fortitude of the governor of Sicily, Gaius Vergilius, who had realised that his powers were too puny alone to assail the powers of darkness ranged against them (*Planc.* 96). Gnaeus Plancius' heroic efforts on behalf of the exiled Cicero are melodramatically portrayed. Both heroes are raised to a mythical level, with tears, groans and laments, vigils and superhuman watches: but it was Plancius, prostrate with sympathetic grief, who required encouragement from Cicero, *vana quaedam miser atque inania falso spe inductus* (miserable as he was from the vain and empty hope that he had falsely been induced to cherish, *Planc.* 101). The exile had promised his sympathetic friend that, if ever he were restored, he would devote his life to grateful recompense for services rendered. At Plancius' trial this promise is being fulfilled. Now, for the first time, the moment has come that Cicero can resort to tears and laments, but these are vicarious, since Cicero's tears are for Plancius, now also threatened with exile. Cicero's final appeal is that the jury should devote some tears to Plancius, as they had before shed them for him (*Planc.* 104). Gone is all memory of letters from home awash with his tears (*Fam.* 14.3.1). Throughout exile Cicero had remained dry-eyed. Others had wept for him; the implication is that he had remained steadfast.

The exile's heroic stature was now firmly established in his own perceptions. It just needed a poetic pen to do it full justice. In the eyes of Cicero, then, his second person accounts could never do full justice to the greatness of his sufferings and the glory of his vindication. Both needed the impersonal approach of heroic narrative. When no one else could be found to do so, the hero himself resorted to epic. That will be the introductory topic of Chapter 8.

6.2 Dio Chrysostomus: dispassionate appraisal of exile

So our highly emotional philosopher-politician considerably rethought his own past. His comments may be seen as the outward evidence of intense, emotional brooding over months and years about the injustice and ingratitude of those who had failed him, and intense personal reworking of his own memories of the events that led up to his banishment. With our next philosopher, Dio Chrysostomus, exiled towards the end of the first century AD, we seem to have found a truly impersonal and judicious narrator of events 'just as they were'. That such impartiality is unattainable is a given in the criticism of historiography. Discussion below of Dio's reportage will reveal a similar truism about his self-presentation in the context of various orations.

Dio Chrysostomus was one of a number of philosophers who suffered exile under Domitian, while serving as the focal point of Stoic opposition to imperial rule.[19] The details of Dio's banishment (possibly AD 82)[20] are not wholly clear, and there are problems relating to the dating of his speeches referring to exile. The 13th Oration of Dio Chrysostomus ('on his exile'), which gives the clearest account of his banishment, offers some autobiographical details, tantalisingly meagre to an historiographer, but sufficient for a literary analysis of Dio's depiction of the psychological reactions to exile of a 'true philosopher'. Allusions to his exile in certain other orations can be consulted to fill in the outline.

There is little reason to doubt the fact of the exile's wanderings, yet this is by no means straight autobiographical narrative.[21] Dio's apparently 'true story' of exile offers a stylisation of details. Some 'autobiographical' incidents reminiscent of famous predecessors are suspiciously literary, for instance, he tells of landing in the 'Hollows of Euboea'. He assumes in different orations the role of a Timotheus or an Aristotle, and in *Oratio* 57 he plays 'Nestor'. His depiction of his stay in the hut of his rescuer shows influence of the Homeric Odysseus-Eumaios episode (*Or.* 7.2).[22]

Dio also travelled as far as Scythia, and is reputed by Philostratos *VS* 1.7.488 to have written an ethnographic treatise on the Getae. It is unclear whether his travels to Scythia were undertaken during his exile or after he had heard of his recall by Trajan in AD 96, or whether these took place earlier, under Vespasian.[23] Philostratos does not construe Dio's visit to the Getae as true 'exile', for, in his version, Dio had not been ordered by the ruler to go into exile. Philostratos' account of Dio's travels to Scythia betrays a mythicising colouring similar to Dio's own account of his exilic philosophising.[24] For instance, his biographer avers that Dio, already back in Rome at the time of the death of Domitian, quelled a riotous military mob. Like a true Odysseus, the philosopher stripped off his mendicant's rags, leapt to the tribunal, and, after delivering an indictment of Domitian's despotism, showed himself as a sage by calming the soldiers by the sheer force of his intellect.[25]

Dio's ethnographic work on the Getae, reported by Philostratos, is unfortunately lost. The autobiographical details of his visit to the Getae occur in *Oratio* 12.17, 18, delivered at Olympia in 97, about a year after his restitution to favour by Trajan. From Dio's narrative it appears as if sheer intellectual curiosity drove him to tour Scythia 'to see things as they are'. The philosopher was not doing research on the exactness of, for instance, Ovid's portrayal of Scythia. The area was the typical *terra incognita* of Greek and Roman prejudice and there was a long tradition of half-known 'facts' which he could have wished to verify.[26] His purpose was 'to see strong men contending for control and power, and their opponents fighting for freedom and their fatherland' (*Or.* 12.19, 20). Dio's account of these Scythian opponents comprises largely impersonal ethnographic observations. These are, according to his own testimony, the result of autopsy, but he does not record personal encounters with members of tribes from this legendary area. There is no indication that Dio was familiar with Ovid's exile. He gives no hint of such in any of his allusions either to the Scythians, or to exile, but the connections seems to cry out to be made. More of this below.

Dio's Oration 13 is composed in the style of a Stoic-Cynic confession, depicting a man who has made his peace with God and man, yet Dio's heroic self-portrait is not cast into the exact mould of one of his *exempla*. In various orations Dio draws a picture of the truly philosophical sage, an heroic figure in philosopher's dress. There has been much controversy on Dio's status as philosopher, and whether exile had caused in Dio a 'conversion', from sophist to philosopher. The difference between 'sophist' and 'philosopher' often hinges on whether the protagonist had a formal 'school' or merely a 'following'. Dio Chrysostomus in exile apparently had neither.[27] He attests to unattached wandering, addressing groups of people wherever he met them.[28] Yet this ostensible autobiographical reportage appears, on closer examination, as ingeniously crafted from various strains.

The mythicised protagonist, a composite Odysseus-Socrates (fleshed out with fleeting glimpses of Diogenes and Zeno), gives few details on the material changes in his circumstances, but rather shows how he found happiness in serving the cause of truth as he saw it. The hero's philosophical research was of a practical nature. He shows himself as going to question the Delphic oracle, but not to ask the traditional 'Is exile an evil?', but rather, 'I have been exiled, what should I do now?' Dio's depiction of his decision to consult the god at Delphi draws heavily on the Socrates of Plato's *Apology* 20 (6-9).[29] Possibly both the Apolline 'prophecy' (*Or.* 13.9) and the meeting with an old prophetess near Olympia (*Or.* 1.52-6) were retrospective fiction,[30] consistent with the mythicising or heroising nature of exilic or post-exilic autobiography, and with Dio's style elsewhere.

The answer of the oracle was that Dio should continue with what he was engaged upon 'until he came to the uttermost ends of the earth' (*Or.* 13.9). The philosopher reports feeling surprised, but that he remembered that Odysseus had continued to wander afar, at the behest of the seer Teiresias, 'until he came to a place where navigation was unknown'[31] and concluded that there was no reason why the orator should not also do so. So Dio set off on his journey, and, as portrayed by Philostratos, for him 'the uttermost ends of the earth' were Scythia and the homes of the Getae.[32] In this he appears to follow Ovid.

The picture of the hero's travels is as stylised as ever were Cicero's constant redrawings of his own past, and it would be easy to draw a line through to Ovid's portrayal of Scythia. Dio's ethnographical references to the area cannot be connected in any concrete way with the poet, but it is hard to resist making a connection between Scythia and exile without drawing the poet into the equation, given the possible similarity of the circumstances of their banishment as being the result of imperial disfavour.

Von Arnim's monumental work, dating from 1898, is still the standard commentary on Dio, but its critical attitude to the philosopher's writings is no longer fashionable. He takes much of the philosopher's self-portrayal as a reflection of the historical figure, without due recognition of the stylisation of such a depiction. His bland discussion (234ff.) of alternatives that lay within the exiled philosopher's sphere of choice offers us a foil for a more nuanced interpretation of the author's self-presentation. Von Arnim points out that, had Dio taken up residence and citizenship elsewhere in the Roman world, he would have lost the title to his properties in Bithynia. By wandering, Dio held open the possibility of return. So far, so good. Von Arnim suggests that Dio's manner of practising philosophy had of necessity to change to the ethico-political after his exile, for he had lost his sphere of influence as a sophist both at Rome and at Prusa. His immune tax-status as a wealthy sophist could also have been better protected if he did not settle in any other city, so Nutton (1971), who shows that Dio's broad view and stress on the 'community of the Roman empire' made of him a 'world citizen' during his wanderings.[33]

Von Arnim's remarks call for modification. That Dio's apparently guileless second person narrative is not quite as ingenuous as it appears, has become a major thread in its interpretation. Putting aside any attempt either at revisionism or extensive research on the 'historical' aspects of Dio's reports on exile, let us try to distinguish what it is that the orator chooses to convey both to his immediate (empirical) audience, and, through publication of his orations, to a wider readership.

First, Dio, although showing himself as perfectly conscious of his own innocence and rectitude, presents his readers with a man who exhibits no acrimonious feelings towards the anonymous abuser of power who exiled him from Rome. This is a philosophical *topos*, also ascribed to Epictetus.[34] If Dio made no attempt at extensive polemic against the emperor who had deprived him of his former position of honour, neither did he try to curry favour. Neither of these options suited Dio's personality; he claims proudly (*Or.* 50.8) that he had too much self-respect to demean himself by flattery to regain Domitian's favour. Dio could have found temporary refuge in any one of a number of eastern cities, if not his home town, but his presence might have endangered its civic status.[35] He then draws a remarkable picture of an Odyssean sage, doomed to wander, willingly exploiting his lot for the benefit of mankind, by bringing others to an 'understanding of true happiness'.[36]

Dio's first person narrative follows the conventional style of philosophical dialectic, personalised in his own particular way, an internal discussion between two aspects of the interlocutionary 'I', questioner and questioned.

6. Retrospection

Taking the fact of his exile for granted, Dio commences with apparently guileless candour,[37] 'When it fell to my lot to be exiled ... I began to consider whether this matter of banishment was really a grievous thing and a misfortune, as it is in the view of the majority ...' (*Or.* 13.1, 2, trans. I.W. Cahoon).[38] We are back with the problem of exile as a moral phenomenon, in Dio's case couched in the form of a first person report of past impersonal deliberation.

The oration is not pure reportage. As autobiographical evidence of exile, only its first third (sections 1-13) is of importance. This introductory section involves a succinct account of the exile's initial train of argument, drawing details from the consolatory tradition (1-13), which is then followed by a paraphrase (via the pseudo-Platonic *Cleitophon*)[39] of Socratic dialectic on the phenomenon of exile, recast as a diatribe addressed to a variety of audiences (14-28). These ruminations do not, however, so much address the problem of exile as a moral phenomenon, than offer general 'Socratic' discourse on the nature of happiness and of the desirable. The peroration was apparently lost, and the oration ends rather suddenly with a brief resumé of Dio's own philosophical discourses during exile (29-37). Again, this last extant passage does not touch directly on exile. The 29th and 30th sections place Dio back in Rome, delivering, presumably, philosophical discourses after his recall, 'speaking,' as he puts it, 'in the words of Socrates'.

Apothegms, dialectic and wit combine to convey a subtly favourable picture. The reason for his exile Dio dismisses in a jocular reference to the practice of enforced quasi-*suttee* among the Scythians – as they bury 'cupbearers and cooks and concubines' with their kings, so 'despots throw in several others for no reason whatever with those who are being executed' – or, in Dio's case, 'exiled' (*Or.* 13.1). So Dio describes his exile as following upon that of another, more powerful figure. From this we may deduce that his association with a patron at Rome who fell foul of the emperor Domitian led to Dio's banishment, that is, guilt by association.[40]

Dio's conclusions about the intrinsic nature of exile follow the familiar consolatory pattern. It is perception, not reality, that makes potential ills like exile, poverty, old age or sickness weigh either heavy or light. Perception is guided by Providence to suit the personal strength and sagacity of the one afflicted (*Or.* 13.3).[41] Dio's choice of Odysseus and Orestes as *exempla* (*Or.* 13.4, 5), while apparently echoing Ovid, is typical of the exilic deliberations we have considered elsewhere.[42] *Exempla* based on contemporary history reflect the ubiquity of exile. Dio tells his audience at Athens that he recalls many 'wars waged by those exiles seeking restoration'. The importance of achieving death on their own soil drove many of these to continuing battle (*Or.* 13.6). Such reflections, he says, forced him initially to think that he was the victim of a terrible affliction. Careful consideration of the voluntary exile which Apollo exhorted Croesus to pursue,[43] brought him to the realisation that exile is not necessarily shameful, nor unprofitable (*Or.* 13.6-8).

So Dio shows us a hero whose emotional reaction to exile was slight, and, as befitted a philosopher, it was kept well in hand. J.W. Cahoon, Loeb editor of Dio, (1932: 397), suggests that the philosopher's allusion, in his oration on Charidemus, to a 'sorely distressed soul that has in its life drunk deeply of misfortune and grief' (*Or.* 30.25) reflects his own state of mind when in exile. Cahoon suggests (398) that the three views of life put forth in the consolation of his 'father' by 'Charidemus' in his thirtieth oration represent three stages in Dio's own philosophical belief: first, that the world is a prison to which men are sent as punishment, next, that the world is a colony of the gods where men are first protected, and then, as they develop philosophical resilience, are expected to fend for themselves, and lastly, that the world is a beautiful palace where men banquet until they are summoned by God to live with Him. By implication Dio has come to this truth through his purging experience of exile. Such historicist speculation is highly problematic. At most we can conclude that Dio chooses to portray himself in his thirteenth oration as an exiled philosopher who during exile progressed towards psychological self-sufficiency.

6.3 Boethius: calm after the storm

Coming as it does after a long sequence of historical and literary precedents, Boethius' exilic work deals in an essentially familiar philosophical content. Problems are mostly related to the structure and form of the *Consolatio Philosophiae*, and to the philosophical thrust and pagan colouring given to it by an author known for his Christian persuasion.[44] The pagan antecedents for the philosopher's mélange of arguments are for the most part identifiable.[45] Its most remarkable feature is its tripled *personae* ('I' as both narrator and object of narrative, but also as interlocutor). This is a step further than Ovid's Medea in *Heroides* 12, who is drawn as the disillusioned wife of the perfidious Jason, looking back on the innocent self she had been when first she succumbed to his wiles.

Although we may accept that the *Consolatio Philosophiae* sprang from the author's intensely personal experience of imprisonment and exile,[46] its philosophical colouring and the persuasive thrust of its dialectic preclude much of the content from being interpreted as strictly autobiographical. Nor do first person verbs predominate. More of this below. In the first two books the dialogue is shaped in such a way that the first person, the imprisoned exile himself and his philosophical failure, appear as focal point. Personified *Philosophia* questions the downcast exile, and gradually a picture appears of both his misery and the injustice he suffered. The answers and remonstrances of *Philosophia* receive a proportionally larger treatment, but the focus is personal. The author achieves both the immediacy of the autobiographical stance and the dialectic feel of persuasive rhetoric.

Here the critical method that we have so far consistently employed will help to clarify the literary issue. The work is strongly didactic, but it is a reportage of auto-didacticism, cast as dialogue. The empirical author has chosen to set his dialogue in the autobiographical mode. We can again distinguish a shifting series of *personae*. Behind both the downcast prisoner and the knowledgeable embodiment of wisdom stands the creative author who has chosen to offer autobiographical reminiscence as interchange between two *personae*, first person 'I' and second person *Philosophia*. About this second person the first person 'I' as narrator reports in the third person, and her interrogation of himself as 'exiled I' is couched as second person outreach. We are back with the complicated structure of narrative reportage discussed by Eco (1995: 15-17).

In his monograph Lerer (1985) stresses the dialogic aspects of the *Consolatio Philosophiae* while discussing its literary method. He draws a distinction (p. 6) between dialectic and true philosophical dialogue. The interlocutor draws from the protagonist first information and then affirmations of the truths that she sets forth. By the third book only the prisoner has regained enough philosophic momentum to enable him to sustain true argumentative dialogue, and by the fifth book he has gained enough understanding to keep him silent enough to listen to a philosophical monologue.[47] In what follows, we shall concentrate on aspects of the narrator 'I' as 'exiled I'.

This disjunction of personalities acts as an effective means of conveying information that the creative author does not at this stage wish to portray the imprisoned exile as possessing. The device creates the effect of 'dramatic irony', placing the reader in the position of 'interested and informed audience' that can watch a gradual unfolding of understanding in the protagonist. For example, in the second book *Philosophia* offers facts from the exile's past life as a means to comfort him. The imprisoned 'I' is shown as having forgotten certain facts about his own past. By using this second *persona*, *Philosophia*, as a mouthpiece to remind the consular of his past achievements, happy family life, and the fulfilment he experienced as a father when his two sons simultaneously achieved the consulship (2.pr.3.5-8), the creative author conveys to his readership knowledge essential for the imprisoned exile's comfort, which is at his disposal, but which he cannot yet, for lack of philosophical fortitude, make his own.

Philosophia begins with *praeteritio* of the exile's blessings, his education at the hands of upright men, 'the guardians of his youth', and the heights of honour he attained in his early years. The fact of his sons' early preferment is offered in an elaborate periodic sentence. Here the pointed contrast between first and second person (both representations of different aspects of the 'narrating I') is a device that illustrates the degree progress that still needs to be made before the prisoner's problem can be solved.

Distance is lent by the second person verb forms, showing that this information has in no way yet been internalised by the sufferer. Comforting thoughts are potentially available to the protagonist, but he cannot yet make them his own. Second person narration creates self-consolation at remove:

> *Si quis rerum mortalium fructus ullum beatitudinis pondus habet, poteritne illius memoria lucis quantalibet ingruentium malorum mole deleri, cum duos pariter consules liberos tuos domo provehi sub frequentia patrum, sub plebis vidisti, cum eisdem in curia curules insidentibus tu regiae laudis orator ingenii gloriam facundiaeque meruisti, cum in circo duorum medius consulum circumfusae multitudinis expectationem triumphali largitione satiasti?* (2.pr.3.8)

If the fruits of human endeavour have any weight, could a certain memory of that light be extinguished by the burden of growing ills, when you have actually seen your two sons simultaneously being conveyed from home as consuls in a crowd of Senators and surrounded by the general populace, when you as speaker of imperial laudations have earned praise for your talent and eloquence, while the two of them were presiding on the consular seats in the Senate, and when you, standing in the middle between the two consuls, have satisfied the expectation of the surrounding multitude with triumphal largesse?[48]

Before the imprisoned exile can derive comfort from the memory of past happiness, *Philosophia* herself redraws the picture in sharper lines: *Dedisti ut opinor verba Fortunae, dum te illa demulcet, dum te ut delicias suas fovet* (You hoodwinked Fortune, as I see it, then while she soothed you, while she cherished you as her darling, 2.pr.3.9). So Fortune smiled on him often – will the prisoner now rail at her for her first defection? So the prisoner's own past happiness is told him by his interlocutor as if it had befallen another; it is not part of his own immediate emotional history. What he tells in the first person is a far sadder tale.

As was shown in Chapter 1, the *Consolatio* consists of alternating verse and prose sections. The first line of the first poem introduces the protagonist, anonymously but in autobiographical mode, and suggests his altered state by ending on a first person preterite, *Carmina qui quondam studio florente peregi* (I who finished off happy songs long ago when my scholarship was still flourishing ...). The effects of this altered state are spelled out in the next line, *flebilis heu maestos cogor inire modos* (I am now forced to take up a mournful metre).[49] All the essential elements of his changed circumstances are spelled out; the writer tells his readers that he is a poet of formerly cheerful poetry and that he is at the mercy of external circumstances over which he has no control. This has not extinguished his poetic talent, but has sent it in a new, unhappy direction.

The first lines of the first prose section stress the autobiographical nature of the work even more pointedly: *Haec dum mecum tacitus ipse*

reputarem queremoniamque lacrimabilem stili tacito officio signarem.
astitisse mihi supra verticem visa est mulier reverendi admodum vultus …
(While I was silently thinking over these things and was about to set my
tearful complaint forth in writing [literally: with the silent aid of a pen] it
seemed to me that a women with an aspect certainly worthy of adoration
had come to stand over me, … 1.pr.1.1a). The personal adverb *mecum* and
personal verb phrase *ipse reputarem* signal what is to come, the duality of
personae and the internal, cerebral nature of the mental exercise in which
the writer is engaged, also emphasised by polyptoton of *tacitus* – writer
and pen share the same characteristic, for they are essentially one.

The exiled prisoner's internal struggle is externalised by the venerable
figure which he next notices (significantly indicated by a perfect infinitive
astitisse, 'had stood by', with the implication that his comforter had been
available to him long before he deigned to notice her). His narrative
thereafter moves to the third person, until *Philosophia* speaks, at first not
directly addressing the 'poor victim' from whom she drives away the 'false
Muses' (1.pr.1.11). Boethius' autobiographical narrative continues reporting on his own silence, *At ego … obstupui visuque in terra defixo …*
expectare tacitus coepi (but I remained dumb, and with my eyes cast down
to the ground, I silently began to wait expectantly, 1.pr.1.13). The exiled
persona is silent and attentive, and personified Philosophy holds centre
stage.

So the introductory sections of Book 1, both verse and prose, serve to set
the scene. Personified *Philosophia* appears to the afflicted singer of the
opening elegy (1.m.1), drives away the Muses that inspired it and counters
it with a suitable dirge (1.m.2). She claims that she alone can heal him,
citing as *exempla* philosophers whom she had formerly aided (1.pr.3). In
the course of the fourth prose section, the victim at last sets forth his
plight. We need to resort to secondary sources to gain a complete factual
picture of the perfidy and ingratitude of former friends and underlings
which led to the senatorial decree of exile.[50] The imprisoned exile's own
outpourings of pent-up woe convey the depth of his emotion, not a lucid
exposition of the facts leading to his exile.

Exclamations, rhetorical questions and a self-exculpatory catalogue of
the imprisoned exile's services to individuals jostle with accusations and
hints of the ingratitude of both the Senate and these individuals (1.pr.4.25-
85).[51] The exile's rhetoric is elegant, with paranomastic wordplay, balance
and contrast, alliteration and other literary devices, yet it conveys passionate urgency. A single example will suffice:

Quotiens ego Conigastum in inbecilli cuiusque fortunas impetum facientem
obvius excepi … Numquam me ab iure ad iniuriam quisquam (quicquam, P)
detraxit. Provincialium fortunas tum privatis rapinis tum publicis vectigali-
bus pessumdari non aliter quam qui patiebantur indolui.   (1.pr.4.10-11)

How many times didn't I face up to Conigastus when he tried to make

171

inroads on the fortunes of every poor fellow around ... Never did anybody
(anything) manage to draw me away from just action toward inflicting injury.
I mourned about the estates of the provincials, which sometimes were ruined
by private rapine and sometimes by excessive taxation, just as much as did
the people who suffered these wrongs.

During the course of Book 3 the focus shifts to *Philosophia* in a largely
impersonal discussion of the relative nature of happiness and pain. At the
ninth prose section of this book, *Philosophia* announces that she will show
that no man can achieve all parts of a single *summum bonum*. A hymn of
praise to the Creator-God (in epic metre) follows, marking a transition.[52]
The focus is now on God, the epitome of all good. At the twelfth prose
section of book 3, the imprisoned exile emerges in a new role, questioning
Philosophia on existential problems which she must solve or refute. It is
clear that her earlier efforts at consolation have been effective, and that
the reconverted exile now is freed from his burden of woe to the extent that
he can explore a wider scope of human problems and divine solutions.
Socratic dialectic has become Academic dialogue. The topic is discussion of
exile in general terms, with questions about the nature of Providence and
the response of humanity to the claims of choice.

The last 'personal' allusion to Boethius' problem, the exile that gave rise
to his *Consolatio*, appears in the fifth prose section of Book 4. The prisoner
accepts *Philosophia*'s thesis that wickedness is a disease of the mind, more
harmful to its perpetrator than to its victim, but he counters that the
human condition can still lead to the personal perception of the ascendancy
of happiness over misery: *neque enim sapientium quisquam exul inops
ignominiosusque esse malit* ... (for neither does any of the philosophers
choose to be an exile, without resources and disgraced ..., 4.pr.5.2). The
tone here is dispassionate. It clearly shows that the imprisoned exile has
passed from the stormy rebellion or deep depression of the earlier books to
a philosophical judgement of exile as merely a non-*desideratum*.

Whether the work is truly autobiographical, or whether its Menippean
form and largely traditional content are literary and conventional, this
passage shows that the disgraced consular had, during the course of his
imprisonment, long before he sat down to pen the dialogue, achieved a
state of tranquil acceptance of his lot. The first person reportage of misery
and rebellion in the first two books is, therefore, like Dio's thirteenth
oration, a dispassionate account of past woe. Its dialogue form gives it the
immediacy of true conversation. Medical imagery, common to the consolatory genre, combines with a shift of tone in the third book to show that the
healing power of Philosophia has prevailed. The crisis is past and the
patient has recovered.

It takes an effort of will in the reader to realise that the protagonist, the
exiled Boethius (as pupil of Philosophy) and his antagonist or mentor,
Philosophy herself, are one. Both are *personae* used by the creative author

172

to convey his fluctuations of emotion and thought. The ability of the historical personage Boethius, in the last months of his life, to produce this rhetorical, philosophical and poetic *tour de force* is proof of his control over these emotions. The *Consolatio Philosophiae* functions as a retrospective report of an existential problem that the imprisoned exile has satisfactorily solved.[53] It serves as self-revealing evidence of the empirical author's attitude to life, rather than as autobiographical fact.

6.4 Ovid: the self before exile

We have so far discussed our various creative authors' different means of stylisation of their retrospective reportages on their own exile. In the case of Ovid retrospection involves outreach, from the perspective of his exilic 'now', backwards in time to the happy days before he was exiled. Again we need to distinguish between the exile, who happens to be a poet, and the creative poet, who happens to have been exiled. We have consistently noted that Ovid's exilic poems are, in spite of intense research by numerous scholars, of little value as biographical and historical source material, offering meagre details on the poet's life, past or present, as it related to the fact of his exile. Even his autobiographical poem, *Tristia* 4.10, is reticent about the reasons for the poet's exile. Of more interest than the exile's revelations about his past life, is the poet's way of framing this information. *What* the poet tells about the exile's past must be interpreted in the light of *how* it is told.

Discussion below will be less concerned with first person verb forms and preterite tenses than in the earlier part of this chapter. Focus will be on the manner in which a stylised self is portrayed while at the same time a past stylised self is rewritten. The term 'autobiography' is of particular importance in Ovidian context, for his poems from exile, while ostensibly autobiographical, in fact appear to have as one of their chief polemical aims to disprove a belief ascribed by the exile to the emperor Augustus, that his previous erotic poetry had been highly autobiographical. Carried to its logical conclusion, this brings about the paradox that readerly belief in the veracity of the exile's presentation of self and representation of his own past involves mutually exclusive epistemologies. The model readership (which in Ovid's exilic context purports to include Augustus himself) is invited simultaneously to believe and disbelieve the poet's vatic voice. The paradox cannot be resolved, and must be accepted as one of the central aspects of the Ovidian myth of exile.[54] Our discussion will therefore first cover aspects of his past life that emerge in passing throughout the exilic oeuvre, and will end with a consideration of what the poet's ostensible first person treatment of his own life and works conveys about Augustus' attitude to both.

No poet's literary autobiography can be absolutely separated from the ordinary details of his life, but is coloured by it, and *vice versa*. Taking

Tristia 1.3, the description of the exile's last night in Rome, to mark the point of separation between 'past' and 'present,' we can distinguish two phases in the poet's life. The poet supplies certain information about his past life, his relation to fellow poets, to his family and friends, and to Augustus. Most often this information emerges by chance in poems meant to evoke pathos, and involves shifts of emotion.

Tristia 1.3 depicts graphically, but selectively, the break between 'present' and 'past'. The picture is impressionistic, a 'flashback' framed in tears, the 'living dead' recalling his moment of death, and mourning over the loss of himself:

> *Cum subit illius tristissima noctis imago,*
> *qua mihi supremum tempus in urbe fuit,*
> *cum repeto noctem qua tot mihi cara reliqui*
> *labitur ex oculis nunc quoque gutta meis*   (*Tr.* 1.3.1-4)

When the very sad image of that last night, which was the last time I was in the city, occurs to me, when I think again about the night on which I left so many things that were dear to me, even now a tear drips from my eyes.

He depicts the progression of the fatal last night, the victim's unpreparedness of body and spirit, his mental stupor and the wailing of his household, a pathetic appeal to the gods of the Capitol, and a tragic farewell as the exile tore himself from a beloved wife. Factual details, names, equipage, means of travel, food for the journey, or, more important, the reason for the exile's departure – none of these is given.[55] Depiction of the exile's state is psychological, rather than literal. We have as facts: Caesar ordered his departure (5); his wife wanted to go along, but did not (17, 18); his daughter was in Libya (19), and did not know of his fate; his friends mourned his departure (15, 21-6, 77-8, etc.); he was going to Scythia (61); he left at dawn.[56] The poem is strikingly pathetic, but the heroic dimensions of the protagonist's grief point to self-irony and a conscious parody of both epic and elegiac farewell-scenes. The exile's wife could have accompanied him, had he allowed her to do so. She remained behind to look after his interests in Rome. The *Botenbericht* describing her reaction after his departure (91-100) is coloured with pathos, bordering on bathos in its stereotyped evocation of the tragic stage.

The lonely and ailing exile often depicts himself as already dead, conjuring up an epitaph at *Tristia* 3.3.73-6, which proudly vindicates himself as *lusor tenerorum amorum* (player of tender love-games). He ignores all his other poetic achievements, or perhaps interprets them all (as in his exposition in *Tr.* 2 of Greek and Roman literature) as depictions of love in its varied facets: [57]

> HIC · EGO · QUI · IACEO · TENERORUM · LUSOR · AMORUM
> INGENIO · PERII · NASO · POETA · MEO

6. Retrospection

AT · TIBI · QUI · TRANSIS · NE · SIT · GRAVE · QUISQUIS · AMASTI
DICERE · NASONIS · MOLLITER · OSSA · CUBENT   (*Tr.* 3.3.73-6)

I WHO LIE HERE, THE PLAYER OF TENDER LOVE-POEMS, NASO THE POET, DIED FROM
AN OVERDOSE OF MY OWN TALENT. BUT FOR YOU WHO PASS OVER MY GRAVE,
WHOEVER HAS ALSO LOVED, HOPEFULLY IT SHOULDN'T BE HARD TO PRAY THAT THE
BONES OF NASO MAY REST EASY!

Ovid's literary autobiography is coloured by what he suppresses, as for instance what he 'saw' that aroused Augustus' anger (*Tr.* 2.103, 104).[58] The little information about his banishment that the poet offers an individual correspondent sometimes appears gratuitous, and is clearly aimed at informing a wider readership. A detailed explanation in *Tristia* 5.11.9-22 of the difference between *exsilium* and *relegatio*, with which his wife could (after three years) reasonably have been expected to be familiar, offers an excuse to offer covert criticism of their common persecutor. At the same time it is a public restatement of his position, whether for Augustus' own consumption, or merely to reiterate the unreasonableness of the punishment inflicted on the poet.

Some 'facts' are conveyed, without proof, as the opinions that he asserts that Augustus held about him which he attempts to refute, e.g. *Tristia* 2.345-6, *ob Artes / quas ratus es vetitos sollicitare toros* (because of the *Ars*, which you thought was soliciting access to unlawful liaisons). In *Tristia* 2.519-20 the emperor is reminded (and posterity informed) that the poet's songs were danced to at mimes 'which the emperor enjoyed'. In all cases, the poet himself is our source of Augustus' supposed opinion of his past life, and his judgements are filtered through Ovid's interpretation of them. The interpretative process involved is reminiscent of Cicero's subjective perception of his exile and the historical events that led to it. More on this below.

Tristia 4.10 offers a 'complete autobiography', with careful selection of facts.[59] The poem is consciously coloured by evocation of literary antecedents, and by its tone of artistic independence. Manipulation and suppression of certain details considered important in modern biography (names and dates of his marriages and details of his divorces) follow ancient biographical convention. Yet we are given more details of his life between birth and manhood and about his three marriages than ancient convention dictated. The artistically innovative poem powerfully portrays Ovid's position as a man of letters. The concluding hymn to the poet's Muse (117ff.) contrasts with the negative judgement of the young poet's father (21, 22) and is a public restatement of the artist's appreciation of the value of his art:

> *Gratia, Musa, tibi: nam tu solacia praebes,*
> *tu curae requies, tu medicina venis.*
> *tu dux et comes es, tu nos abducis ab Histro,*

Displaced Persons

in medioque mihi das Helicone locum
tu mihi, quod rarum est, vivo sublime dedisti
nomen, ab exsequiis quod dare fama solet.   (*Tr.* 4.10.117-22)[60]

Thank you, Muse: for you offer me solace, you come as rest from care, as balm, you are my leader and companion, you take me away from the Ister and give me a place in the midst of Helicon. And you gave me while still alive something which is very rare, a name which fame usually bestows only after someone has been buried.

Strong personal feeling is paramount, and literal details merely provide the frame upon which the poetry is hung. Details of the death of the poet's brother (31-2) his marriages, two divorces and final, happy third marriage (69-74) stress the importance of personal relationships in the poet's life. The poem in its entirety conveys more about the exile's present awareness of his value as a poet than it does about his civic life. His attitude to his poetry fluctuates over time, but in the end creates a finally positive picture.[61]

Ovid's fame as love poet was apparently in no way diminished by his relegation. Initially the exile implies that, with his relegation, the poet's entire oeuvre was banned from public libraries. The works continued to circulate privately, and *Tristia* 1.1.105-20 seems to imply that Augustus would himself have kept them in his library. By *Tristia* 3.14 the exile rewrites his earlier claim that his poetry was also banished: *est fuga dicta mihi, non est fuga dicta libellis* (flight was enjoined me, no flight was dictated to my books, v. 9).[62] The theme of literary innocence continues throughout. *Ex Ponto* 1.1, addressed to his friend Brutus, the potential publisher of the exilic works, again discusses the former banning of Ovid's books (3-12), reaffirming the exile's innocence (21-30). The writings of the regicides Brutus and Antony are freely read at Rome (23, 24). The exile hastens to add, *nec me nominibus furiosus confero tantis* (but I don't like a madman compare myself with such great names 25), for he did not take up savage arms 'against the god' (26). This is pure polemic. Augustus is equated with the gods in terms which could have caused offence. Moreover, the word '*furiosus*' dangerously insinuates that the imperial family is vindictive, and *tantis* implies that the regicides had heroic stature.[63] Pertinent use of their names contrasts with for instance the anonymity of Augustus' *Res Gestae* 1 (Antony as a 'faction') and 2 (Brutus as 'murderer of my father').[64]

Only fleeting glimpses of his early life emerge. Two passages, *Ex Ponto* 2.4.19-22 and 2.10.21-46, together offer a 'complete view', in revised form, of the poet's youth. With his friend Atticus he enjoyed the kind of social life as young-men-about-Rome also portrayed in the Catullan friendship poems, sharing and exchanging poetry. With his fellow-poet Macer the young poet undertook the conventional grand tour of affluent young Romans, travelling to Asia Minor and Sicily. The road was shortened, and the day condensed, by pleasant converse, in the usual Callimachean mode.[65] A poet is in a unique position to adapt allusion to his own works to alter earlier impressions.[66] Nostalgia for the innocence of his youth therefore offers an artful corrective for a view of the poet's erotic works as autobiographical. His past attitudes may be strengthened by his present conscious reiteration of his credo: that *ingenium* is more important than *ars*, but that his art is absolutely independent, 'art for art's sake', and that personal relationships take precedence above public and civic duties.

The exile rewrites his conjugal history. His attitude to his wife in the exilic poems serves to change an impression of flagrant personal immorality in his erotic works. His present fidelity, projected back to the poet's youth, will strengthen the exile's claim of a vast distinction between the poet's art and his life. The tenderness of the poet's farewell to his wife (*Tr.* 1.3), and the intimate and loving relationship that speaks from his gratitude to her (*Tr.* 1.6.5-15), sharing of intimate jokes (*Tr.* 3.3.15-24), pride in her present fidelity and consciousness of her past pride in him (*Tr.* 4.3.11-20), combine to create a picture of conjugal bliss, late-blossoming but real, which must act as corrective to the picture of youthful profligacy, if not rank immorality, postulated by Augustus. The poet's third wife, as connection of an intimate of the empress Livia, would have brought him within the imperial circle. Ovid's wife and Marcia, wife of Fabius Maximus, were connected in some way (*Pont.* 1.2.136-50).[67] The 'political' marriage blossoms into a 'great love' the moment the exile leaves Rome.[68] Eulogies of his wife are not totally disinterested. She must put his case to Livia. In exchange, he offers her immortality, as the *lusor amorum* formerly promised it to his mistress Corinna.

In *Ex Ponto* 1.4 the exiled poet colours the past by means of a projection of the future. The tone is playful and loving, depicting the exile as an 'older man' (an idea borrowed from Propertius, clothed in the words of Tibullus) returning to an 'older wife' in a sentimentally pathetic imaginary homecoming scene, a Nestor and Odysseus in one. The picture is, so Benedum (1967: 22), *nicht ohne Selbstironie*, but clearly intended to depict lasting conjugal affection[69] as a counter to portrayals of the exiled husband as an erstwhile *desultor amorum* (love's acrobat), leaping from bed to bed.

At *Ex Ponto* 2.11.13-20 the 'goodness' of the exile's wife is eulogised. In this context, the harshly recriminatory tone of the next poem, 3.1, is startling. The picture of star-crossed lovers separated by cruel fate has worn thin, and the poem, while purporting to teach his wife 'how to pray to Livia', shows her up as totally ineffectual against the power of a cruel and arbitrary witch.[70] This picture of less than conjugal rapport is softened by Ovid's final allusion to a wife who is as 'diffident as she is chaste' (*Pont.* 3.7.11, 12), whom he no longer wishes to burden. The picture fades on this dubious note, and we meet the exile's nameless wife no more. The following four years have no allusions to her, no poems addressed to her. Yet the one-sided correspondence has served its purpose. The portrait of the jaunty philanderer of the *Amores* or the cynical *praeceptor amoris* of the *Ars Amatoria* has been softened. The new picture of middle-aged affection, projected into the past, alters the portrait of the artist as a young man.

So Ovid's exilic poems do not offer a chronological, factual autobiography. Where he does provide information, the focus is subjective.[71] Ovid's conception of time appears very elastic. The poet's 'objectionable poetry' was a product of his 'extreme youth' (*Tr.* 2.539). The *Ars Amatoria* was published only about eight years before his banishment, and was banned even later, after his fortieth birthday. The artist's hand is reshaping the past, placing it in a better light.

Ovid's treatment of space is equally impressionistic. Vast distances stretch between him and Rome, but he can reach both Rome and his distant friends in his imagination. Pathos and longing speak from *Tristia* 3.4.55-9, the poet's first explicit allusion to his powers of mental travel, conveying an impression of vivid and familiar memories of Roman topography.[72] This memory grows as time passes.

Throughout, Ovid's portrayal of details of past friendship concentrates on feeling rather than fact, emphasising the priority of personal emotion before imperial power. The last book of Pontic epistles shifts to a new set of addressees. The poet's tact overcomes awkwardness stemming from apparent neglect of old friends. Friends' past kindnesses are still remembered.[73] In this phase the exile's personal past appears to have partly faded in his mind, but his imagination has retained and enlarged public memories, of the grandeur of Augustan Rome, and of those trappings of Republican civil life which Augustus had retained. Yet information about the poet's civic past is often more emotional than 'factual'. In *Ex Ponto* 4.4 and 4.9 the exile dwells lovingly on the imagined civic pomp of a consular inauguration, projecting himself as citizen into an active civic life. This is not evidence of new-found active Republicanism (nor of Augustan loyalty), but a subtle restatement and shift of the interests of his former life into a more innocuous sphere. History is being rewritten.

In the first three books of Pontic epistles the exile's past relationships with various friends often feature. Nostalgic memories of people and places merge and coalesce. Details emerge in passing.[74] Old ties of *amicitia* existed between the poet and Messalla Corvinus, the father of Messalinus and Cotta Maximus (*Pont.* 1.7.27-36).[75] Poems to the two brothers (*Pont.* 1.7 and 9) frame a poem that mourns the loss of Ovid's Paelignian estates and the gardens overlooking the junction of the Via Flaminia and Via Clodia, in terms reminiscent of the dispossessed from Vergil's *Eclogues* 1 and 9. Evocation of pastoral brings with it the Vergilian suggestion that rural Italy paid a high price for the *pax Augusta*. *Ex Ponto* 1.8.45-8 should not be interpreted as a 'true' picture of our poet in former days, a gentleman farmer, standing perspiring over irrigation furrows or planting young apple trees. The exiled poet owned estates, but was not a husbandman. As always, Ovid's approach is literary. Detail is subservient to mood. He is depicting the pathos of an unusual circumstance in terms that will be familiar to his Roman readership. He is a new Meliboeius, a displaced person doomed to wander and never to enjoy the fruits of his own labours.

> *quos ego nesciocui colui, quibus ipse solebam*
> *ad sata fontanas, nec pudet, addere aquas:*
> *sunt ubi, si vivunt, nostra quoque consita quaedam,*
> *sed non et nostra poma legenda manu?* (*Pont.* 1.8.45-8)

... [my gardens] that I cultivated for somebody else, where I used to irrigate the crops (I'm not ashamed to admit it): where are they – if they are still alive – those apple trees also planted by my hand, but not to be plucked by the same hand?

Memories of the city are equally strong. *Tristia* 3.1.19-44, portraying the author's book as a weary traveller arriving in Rome, reflects the exile's former familiarity with Augustan Rome. The topography of Rome as experienced by the little book as traveller at 3.1 is recognisably that of the 'marbled forum' of the Augustan building programme.[76] The poem features the fora of the Caesars, the temple of Vesta, the temple of Apollo Palatinus and the Portico Octavia, the last two with their libraries, the theatre of Marcellus 'with the temples near it', the temple of Jupiter Libertas. The atrium of Liberty and the library of Asinius Pollio, which were commissioned by Julius Caesar (*Tr.* 3.1.72), are particularly important for their twin implications of physical freedom and intellectual independence. Punning play on *libertas* emphasises that the book enjoys more freedom than does its author.[77]

This is, however, no mere remembrance of things past. Intrinsic in the poetry of exile is the tension of polemical dialogue with his unseen oppressor. His evocation of the sights of Rome is couched not in subjective first person *memini*, 'I remember', but is drawn, as in Boethius' dialogue, as first person narrative about an *alter ego*, visiting for the first time those scenes strongly remembered by the exile. The ploy works to place the writer in Rome in the person of his book, while simultaneously situating him as exile at the ends of the earth.[78]

> *inde petens dextram 'porta est' ait 'ista Palati:*
> *hic Stator, hoc primum condita Roma loco est'.*
> *singula dum miror, uideo fulgentibus armis*
> *conspicuos postes tectaque digna deo.*
> *'et Iovis haec' dixi 'domus est?' quod ut esse putarem,*
> *augurium menti querna corona dabat.*
> *cuius ut accepi dominum, 'non fallimur,' inquam,*
> *'et magni uerum est hanc Iovis esse domum.*
> *cur tamen opposita uelatur ianua lauro,*
> *cingit et augustas arbor opaca comas?*
> *num quia perpetuos meruit domus ista triumphos?*
> *an quia Leucadio semper amata deo est?'* (*Tr.* 3.1.31-42)[79]

Displaced Persons

And then, turning to the right, he said, 'That is the entrance to the Palace; here is Jupiter the Stayer, on this place Rome was first built.' While I'm admiring these different places, I see ostentatious doorposts and roofs worthy of the dwelling of a god. 'And this is Jove's house', says I, and the civic crown gave credence to this idea so that I thought it really was so. And when I understood whose house it was, I said, 'So I'm not wrong, and this really is the house of the great Jupiter! Why else is the door wreathed in laurel and does a shady tree encircle its august panels? Wasn't it because this house earned perpetual triumphs and because it has always been loved by the Leucadian god?'

This apparently guileless presentation of Augustan Rome veils a polemical attack on Augustus' association of himself with deity.[80] This leads to the final question we need to address, namely, what were the opinions held by Augustus which the exiled poet is seeking to alter? The poet is our only source. An explicit statement at *Tristia* 2.207 gives *carmen* and *error* as the two reasons for the poet's relegation, which we have noted were both inadequate reasons for civic expulsion or exile. A chronological survey will reveal a meagre crop of facts. Ovid's first touches on his *error* at *Tristia* 1.2.99; details are kept tantalisingly vague. Expressions of gratitude for friends' support frequently shift into explanations, in veiled terms, of what the exile's *error* had entailed, reflecting a dreadful memory of the moment of shock, of sadness and a desire to expiate guilt by redrawing it as excusable, short-sighted innocence: 'I was silly' (*Tr.* 1.5.42, *Pont.* 1.7.44), 'It was a mistake' (*Tr.* 3.5.52), and finally, to Cotta Maximus, 'You were angry at first, but when you understood, you were kind' (*Pont.* 2.3.61-5).

Expressions of strong remorse about the past, addressed to the emperor himself, may imply criticism of some sort.[81] Frequent *praeteritio* keeps the reader's interest focused on the 'wrong suffered by the emperor' and on the accidental witness, a latter-day Actaeon.[82] From *Tristia* 1.2.59-70 we learn only that Augustus considered that the storm-tossed exile deserved what he was getting. From *Tristia* 2.29 onwards we begin to discover what Augustus thought, or rather, what the poet chooses to depict him as thinking.[83] At first the discussion is general. The exile admits culpability, but reminds the emperor of his former approval of the poet (89) and of the veniality of the supposed misdemeanour. At *Tristia* 2.212 the accusation is at last put into words: *arguor obsceni doctor adulterii* (I am accused of being the teacher of vile adultery). The poet refutes the charge; his intended readership were the worldly-wise. The second charge, adduced from the first, is personal moral turpitude (*Tr.* 2.348ff.). These form the two complementary aspects of the *carmen*-half of the accusation against the exile.[84] Throughout the exilic oeuvre allusions to the poet's past life serve to counter this charge.[85]

The notion ascribed to the emperor, of a basic conflation of Ovid's art and life, that is, of the erotic poems as 'autobiography', is first refuted at *Tristia* 2.353, *crede mihi, distant mores a carmine nostro* (believe me, my morals are far different from my poetry). This is the central paradox of the exilic poems: in exile the fusion of the poet's life and art is complete. The autobiographical letter form graphically fuses life and art,[86] portraying what the exiled poet has set out to deny. The poet's exile is his final metamorphosis, equating past art with present life, illustrating the factual reality of 'impossible', literary changes. The living poet is the heroic victim of an angry god. Life and art are one. Ovid's denials of 'autobiography' in his past works are coloured by the very 'autobiographical' nature of his present poetry. The very persuasiveness of his depiction of present conjugal affection recolours his past, but serves to cast a reflection backwards, not of marital fidelity, but of 'truth' in his former portrayal of extramarital relationships.

It appears futile to attempt a rational reconciliation of this paradox with the counter-paradox expressed at *Tristia* 1.7.11, 12, *carmina maior imago / sunt mea* (my songs are a greater representation of me). The poet's simultaneous combination and contradiction of art and life leads the critic into problems of 'belief'. Some critics solve the paradox by doubting not only Ovid's portrayal of Augustus' opinion, but by doubting the fact of exile itself.[87] According to this model, the poet associated himself to such a degree with his works, that when these were banished from the public libraries at Rome, he pretended to have been banished himself and spent ten years composing the exilic poems as a 'literary frolic' whereby he carried on a polemic against Augustus. The contemporary silence of other sources (including early historiographers such as Tacitus) seems to support this thesis, as does the observable literary fact that their polemical nature makes these poems unsuitable as vehicles for pleas for recall. Against the theory we may offer the argument that the 'game' appears to have been extended for too long a time to have been purely fictitious, and that the emotional consistency of the oeuvre is higher than in the erotic poems (which our poet himself designates as fiction). There is also the problem of the weakness of the motives ascribed to the poet by the various theorists.[88]

The problem is, however, literary, and it can, as suggested above, be solved by accepting the inconsistencies in Ovidian poetics as part of the myth of exile. The literary myth of exile is not Ovid's creation. It is the perfection of a literary form established by the exiled Cicero, whose subjective depiction of his exile and return served to elevate the orator (in his own eyes at least) to a similar, mythic plane. It serves as an heroic model for subsequent exilic self-portraiture, which we have seen imitated by our exiled philosophers, whether consciously or unconsciously.

The Horror of Isolation

7.1 The inner life

Analysis of outreach to an audience or readership (most often removed in time and place) and interaction with a 'second person' in various guises have informed a major part of our study so far. Yet the literature of exile has the protagonist as its main concern. The exile's reaction to the external aspects of exile and his presentation of self within the place of exile could be expected to form part of the solipsistic focus of his writings. Portrayal of 'place' involves both 'space' and 'time' in the perception of the suffering exile. The exile moves through space and time towards his place of exile, or remains in a fixed place while reaching out though space to his readers at Rome, with recognition of the usual restrictions imposed by multi-faceted epistolary time.

In all cases we find the exile more concerned with his inner life than with externals. Of our various exiles, only Ovid gives his readers some details about his immediate surroundings. This chapter will concentrate on Ovid's portrayal of his exile. As will become clear below, very little of what he chooses to convey to his readership about his place of exile appears to hold any relationship with reality, as verifiable by archaeology.

Discussion of Ovid's treatment of time and space will be preceded by a brief review of our other exiles and a slightly more detailed analysis of Cicero's emotional profile as reflected in his letters from Dyrrachium. Cicero's informal correspondence reflects his physical and mental debilitation and offers a paradigm for the articulation of the day-to-day emotional vicissitudes of exile. Ovid universalises these vicissitudes by means of his exilic poetry. Ovid's depiction of the physical aspects of his exile is subjectively coloured and reflects the exile's inner state.[1] Other exiles show greater mental resilience, but display an equal paucity of factual detail about their physical circumstances. Seneca's few scant references to Corsica show an Ovidian colouring[2] and Dio Chrysostomus provides some ethnographic details about the Scyths, but we have noted the difficulty of certainly relating Dio's Scythian journey to his exile.

The concern of both Seneca and Boethius is to draw a psychological portrait, the former of continuing fortitude, the latter of his achievement of such fortitude. Boethius offers the most extreme example of exilic

concentration on inner life. While mapping his progression toward psychological and mental fortitude, he does not at all refer to the externals of his
place of imprisonment and exile. In the first two books of the *Consolatio
Philosophiae* the protagonist is bowed down by his woeful circumstances.
We have seen his psychological progress graphically portrayed by means
of dialectic, which allows the reader to travel with the protagonist on the
road toward sublimation, while observing every fluctuation of the prisoner's emotion. For the reader the *persona* of *Philosophia* with her probing
questions acts as a guide to the course of the patient's disease and
recovery.[3] By the ninth verse section of Book 3[4] the erstwhile philosopher's
reconversion has been completed, and the protagonist is eager to leave
behind the trammels of his exilic woe and to pursue truth, with *Philosophia* firmly established as his guide. His inner life has triumphed over
outer circumstances.

7.2 Cicero's exilic myth

Boethius' exiled consular predecessor, Cicero, never achieved this type of
fortitude. Cicero's consistent reluctance to leave the capital is well attested. For him, to be in Rome was to be at the hub of the universe, and
every journey was *obscura et sordida* (grubby and squalid).[5] Writing from
Formiae in April 59 BC, he explains: *Narro tibi, plane **relegatus** mihi
videor, posteaquam in Formiano sum* (I tell you, I really seem to have been
relegated since I came here to Formiae, *Att.* 2.11). This reluctance lay
behind his refusal of the proconsulate in the year after the Catilinarian
conspiracy, and it breathes from every letter written from Cilicia when
finally, long after his ignominious exile and triumphant recall, Cicero
undertook the delayed proconsulate, on occasion admitting to Caelius
Rufus, *vidisti quam abhorrerem ab urbe relinquenda* (You saw how I really
was horrified by the prospect of having to leave the city, *Fam.* 2.16.2).[6]

   This horror is the prominent emotion of Cicero's months in Greece after
his banishment by senatorial decree. As we have seen, speeches after his
return recolour his reactions to exile, without attempting to redraw the
physical aspects of his exile as either squalid or dangerous. Although the
'other half' of such conversations at remove is lost, the letters of Cicero's
exilic period attest to a continued exchange of information, news, some
practical details of the exile's travelling arrangements and intentions,
attempts by family and friends to console and offer practical advice, and
the exile's continued psychological reaction to it all. Continued political
manoeuvring by friends and foes alike, in Rome and elsewhere, are
documented in twenty-seven letters to Atticus,[7] and a handful of letters to
his family and brother. The collection offers valuable historical documen-
tation of the exile of a Roman consular,[8] but its chief interest lies in its
psychological fabric as self-revelation. The letters give no details about his
daily life, not even about incidents on his journey into exile.

What sets Cicero apart from our other exiles is the fact that his correspondence is informal, aimed to reach not a notional 'model readership', but very real persons in his immediate circle, who can be of aid to him, if only psychologically. Cicero's early letters from exile may therefore be considered as evidence of genuine outreach to a second person, and genuine portrayal of the circumstances of the writer as person (not *persona*) without the type of rhetorical or philosophical stylisation apparent in the formal documents that make out other texts. Yet here, too, the creative author is at work, selecting and giving emphasis, filling in details that will persuade his correspondents of the writer's misery and the horror of his circumstances.[9] A description of a comfortable stay in a friend's country house in Greece would therefore not be called for.

Cicero in exile appears unconscious of the philosophical ideal of the soul's creation of its own happiness by the practice of virtue. His self-revelatory letters from exile, particularly those to Atticus, give a view of the historical course of his exile that reflects the vacillations of a sensitive nature subjected to largely self-inflicted misery.[10] The focus is on the author: important verbs are in the first person, possessive adjectives *meus* and *noster* abound: the exile is wrapped in a self-imposed cocoon of misery.[11] Plans for safeguarding himself are couched in military idiom, as in *Ad Atticum* 3.7, on the need to take refuge in a *castellum* (fort), and on occasion he appears almost pugnacious.[12] Cicero is, however, still a scholar, conscious of the philosophical tradition of consolation, and, as was shown in Chapter 3, various letters follow the pattern of the philosophical discussion of exile, albeit negatively. He mourns, refusing all comfort; only restitution will bring him happiness: *sin omnia sunt obstructa, id ipsum fac ut sciamus et nos aliquando aut obiurgare aut communiter consolari desine* (But if all roads to aid are blocked, see to it that you tell me, and stop either telling me off or comforting me with consolatory commonplaces, *Att.* 3.15.7).

We have noted (Chapter 4) that Cicero's formal letters to his immediate family (*Fam.* 14.4) and to Atticus (*Att.* 3.7), dated 29 April 58, together offer a paradigm for what could be considered an 'anti-consolationary' yearning for death. Very little practical details emerge, and what is offered, is inconsistent. The letter to his family addresses the exile's wife in an upwelling of sentimental grief in stylised, almost elegiac phraseology. Throughout his months in Greece letters show as few signs of fortitude; the emphasis is on what the exile has been, what he has lost, and what he is now; the possessions of which he was stripped are 'dearer to him than life' (*Att.* 3.22). He has no sense of guilt about the irregular nature of the execution of the conspirators; like another Socrates, he expects a reward from the state. He is a hero of mythical proportions; no other has ever suffered greater loss. Of objectivity there is no question, of the physical facts of his place of exile nothing. *Cicero exsul* has entered the world of myth.

7.3 Exilic self-sufficiency: time encapsulated and space transcended

It requires a poet to take this subjective focus and with it create a universalised portrayal of the timeless desolation of exile. Ovid's poems from exile make manifest the *myth of exile*, first established by Cicero, with this difference: Ovid creates a complete picture of his surroundings, but this picture is verifiably fantastic.[13] In what follows we shall consider in turn the manner in which Ovid portrays exilic time and space, with particular attention to how he presents the geography and ethnography of his place of exile, and, finally, his portrait of the poet-as-exile.

Ovid incorporates awareness of time and space as the centrally organising factors of the life of an exile. In his *Heroides* Ovid as 'articulate poet' uses the device of a 'present' moment, frozen in time, interpreted by the perceptions of his 'suffering heroines', alone and at far removal from their distant addressees, whose minds range backwards and forwards in time and simultaneously transcend space.[14] In considering the poet's own exile, we have consistently distinguished the levels 'suffering man' and 'articulate poet'. Ovid's articulation of the exile's inner suffering gives a complete view of the psychology of exile as both objective and subjective reality.[15] On occasion the distance between 'articulator' and 'sufferer' is enlarged by a quizzically humorous stance.[16]

The 'timeless now' of exile is most intimately involved with the 'terrible here' of the place of exile. The storm poems (*Tr.* 1.2, 1.4 and 1.11) externalise the traveller's own inner turmoil, and are physical manifestations of the emperor's anger,[17] an ultimate exercise in the pathetic fallacy. The immediacy of 'present tense' depiction and the conceit of composition or speech within the hurricane show the exile within the 'here and now' of the emperor's anger. This 'here' shifts with the exile to Tomis, and the terrible features of the place and its inhabitants are a continued externalisation of a psychological perception of menace.

The encapsulation of time by means of the normal epistolary remove involved in true letter-writing reflects a basic aspect of exilic psychology. The poet, writing in an exilic 'now and here', projects his readers' reception of a poem in a future 'then' and distant 'there'. A further time shift occurs when he pleads (as in *Tristia* 1.11) that his readers should, at the time when they read it, remember the circumstances, already past, within which the letter-poem was written. The device conflates present, future and past. A variation on this pattern involves double shifts in time. For instance, at *Tristia* 3.6 the letter-poem is enjoined in the poet's 'here and now' to go to find the young poetess Perilla in a future 'there and then'. The poet remembers his own life as Perilla's mentor in a past 'there and then long ago', and predicts future, more distant, fame for her 'there'.

Ovid's exilic poems, although produced in the course of about eight years, encapsulate time in the sense that the oeuvre consists of an ever-shifting series of 'nows'.[18] Each 'now', with few if any exceptions, carries with it a perception of outer reality interpreted as inner reality, but also involves both past and future. It looks backwards with longing and remorse to what the exile has lost, and forward with fear of imminent danger, but also with desire and longing for imminent release. Emotion is conveyed in a completely isolated, one-directional outward reach in a perpetual present, of which the main characteristic is a baffling silence of non-communication.[19] The poems, even those cast as 'letters', reflect non-communication, for there is no real response.[20]

From poem to poem the articulate poet wrestles with the problem of communicating pathos 'now' without reference to any response to a previous 'now' situation. Every year passed in exile forms part of an agglutinated 'now', with very little perception of progression within it. The only progression discernible is in the Geticising and consequent barbarising of the poet-as-exile, frequently announced in consistently elegant verse, and an increase in pessimism in the exile-as-poet, as he becomes increasingly aware of the uselessness of outreach and the hopelessness of his situation. Yet the outreach continues, and poetic composition is a form of therapy.

In the exiled poet's depictions of his own physical debilitation and rapid ageing, pathos speaks from externals. This portrayal works cumulatively. At first the exile's inner suffering must be deduced from the poet's explicit statements about untoward external circumstances of exile.[21] A reader might reasonably have expected progression in accuracy of placement of the place of exile and in physical details, as time passed and the unfamiliar became all too familiar, but in this aspect too, there is no progress. In time some personal details emerge. By the second year the exile is old and feeble, oppressed by the North Star (*Tr.* 4.8.1, 2, 41). By the next year we learn without surprise that the three years that have passed, feel like ten (5.10.1-8). For the exile all is frozen in timeless 'now'. Time has ceased: *stare putes, adeo procedunt tempora tarde* (you'd think it's standing still, so slowly does time pass, 5.10.5).

The complaint that three years 'feel like ten' not only places Tomis in the world of myth, but it also sets the scene for anti-pastoral, where shepherds wear helmets and sheep fear war, where pastoral 'timelessness' is not suggested by the pleasant noonday hum of bees, but by an endless Polar night. In his sixth year of exile, the poet complains that, whereas time wears away all things, it has simply passed him by, and his death has been vanquished:

> *tempus edax igitur praetor nos omnia perdit,*
> *cessat duritia mors quoque victa mea.*   (*Pont.* 4.10.7, 8)

Mordant time, then, destroys everything except me; my death stops, also vanquished by my hard lot.

That all this is essentially a repetition of what he has said before, emphasises the monotonous timelessness of the exile's perpetual 'now'. This complaint is frequent. In *Tristia* 4.6 the exile complains that time, which wears away all things, has not changed his ills. His perception of time as non-progressive influences his perception of place, and encapsulation encompasses both.[22] This colours the exile's perceptions of shifting 'now', lost 'past' and imminent 'future' in a series of contrasts, where 'here' is bad, and 'there' is good. The exiled poet becomes ever more conscious of his powers of mental transposition,[23] first spelled out in Ovid's hymn to his Muse, *tu nos abducis ad Histro* ... (you draw me away from the Ister ..., *Tr.* 4.10.117ff.).

Space in its turn also influences time. The distance by sea of Tomis from Rome is of course greater than the north-south difference between their respective latitudes, but Ovid portrays a vast gulf between the two worlds. He claims that letters are rare, that a year is needed for a single exchange. Yet in another poem the exile imagines that a letter would reach Rome in 'less than ten days'. His readers are not expected to look for consistency, but give their sympathy. Once the exile is in the Black Sea area, space expands to a vast nothingness:

> *Nos freta sideribus totis distantia mensos*
> *sors tulit in Geticos Sarmaticos sinus.*   (*Tr.* 1.5.62-3)

Fate carried me, who had crossed seas whole constellations apart, into the bays (or 'bosoms') of the Getae and Sarmatians.

What may be termed 'vicarious travel in time' may feature as either past or future, as viewed from the 'timeless now' of inner misery. Although the exile's appeals for restitution imply a future when he will have returned, this golden future is seldom made explicit. Only in the complexities of epistolary time shifts between writer and recipient (as discussed in the Preamble to the Second Stage) does the exile at all feature future projection. For him virtually everything else is seen in the light of a bleak 'now' and a colourful 'then'. Yet the hymn to the poet's Muse shows a present not wholly desolate, and demonstrates the exile's ability to transcend space and time through his poetry (as in *Tr.* 4.10.117ff.).

Projection of the future is 'factual' in a description of the itinerary of the ship on which the exile is travelling to Pontus (*Tr.* 1.10). On occasion it involves complimentary prophecy, often of a triumph.[24] Psychological projection in future time may involve fears and desires, reflecting the exile's perception of imminent danger offered by physical reality.[25] A perceptive expression of emotion speaks from the playful fear of being, after death, 'the only Roman spirit among fierce Sarmatian ghosts' (*Tr.* 3.3.63, 64). *Tristia* 1.2.107-10 portrays progress of time within the 'now' of the storm. From an initial expression of his hopes and fears the traveller moves to the calm at the end of the storm. The answer to his prayer has come, and it is a portent for future answers of a more extensive kind. Here the 'now' of his suffering has allowed a small shift to a better 'now', to foreshadow an even better, future 'then'.

We have seen that the exile's departure from Rome (*Tr.* 1.3, discussed in Chapter 6) is the point of separation between past and present. Pride in his own past speaks from the exile's memories of the time before the blow fell.[26] Everything that happened after that night is coloured by the horror of isolation on the Getic shore. Yet information is dealt out sparingly to his readership at Rome. More on this below.

Later another minor break, less absolute, is marked by *Ex Ponto* 3.7, in which the poet expresses his resolve to cease disturbing his wife. The strongly pathetic renunciation of all further appeals is essentially an acceptance of the arrest of time. The exile's happy past stopped when he reached Tomis. There is no happy future. He is caught up in an endless 'now' which is simply another dimension of 'here', until, at some unspecified moment, the Fates take over:

> *venimus in Geticos fines: moriamur in illis,*
>   *Parcaque ad extremum qua mea coepit eat.*   (*Pont.* 3.7.19, 20)

I have come to the Getic area: let me die within its confines, and let my bitter fate reach the end from where it began.

After this the 'now' encompasses ever less of the exile's immediate surroundings and ever more of an inner fantasy in which he experiences at remove the sights and sounds of Rome. 'Here' gives way to 'there' in the exile's inner life.

In *Tristia* 1.3 'the last night in Rome' offers the first instance of a backward movement in time, which is relative to the 'now' of thinking about it.[27] The poem starts *Cum subit illa tristissima noctis imago ...* (When that very sad picture of the night arises suddenly ..., 1). Loss and longing for the time before the exile's departure is frequently expressed in similar terms, comparing 'what I was then' with 'what I am now', and also 'where I was then' with 'where I am now'.[28] This memory is expressed in terms of an apparition in the following:

> *Roma domusque subit desideriumque locorum,*
>   *quicquid et amissa restat in urbe mei.*   (*Tr.* 3.2.21, 22)

Rome and my home suddenly arise in my thoughts, and a longing for those places and for whatever else of mine that I lost which is still in the city.

This moment of separation is invoked frequently, often in relation to gratitude for the aid and sympathy offered by friends.[29]

In the last book, *Ex Ponto* 4.11 (also discussed in the introductory chapter as an illustration of the consolatory tradition), exhibits shifts of space between Tomis and Rome that are less subtle, shifts of time that are more so. The exile, speaking in his 'now' at Tomis, apologises for having neglected his friend Gallio since he arrived 'here', that is, in the timeless present of his exile at the ends of the earth. He remembers Gallio's sympathetic mourning, 'then', when the blow fell, when the poet was still 'there' at Rome. Since that moment, Gallio's wife has died 'there' at Rome, but the poet does not wish to send words of consolation from his place of exile, for the news had taken some time to reach him 'here', and time (which works 'normally' in Rome) may already have healed the wound. Gallio may, by means of remarriage, already have moved into a new plane of 'future' happiness 'there' at Rome, not yet communicated to the exile still bound by the 'now' of continued sympathetic association with the correspondent's possibly long past unhappiness.

Vicarious transposition in space by means of personification of the exile's poems involves similar shifts in time. The tone is set by *Tristia* 1.1 where the exile, as 'speaker' in his 'now', instructs his book on where to go and what to do 'then' in its projected movement to the 'there', which is Rome. At *Tristia* 3.1.1ff. the personified poem itself 'speaks' in its own 'now' which has a 'past' (of arrival at Rome) already behind it. This ingenuous monologue is produced by the exiled poet, writing in his own 'now', in which the monologue is a projection, both in time and space.

In *Tristia* 3.8 the exile expresses the wish for mythical wings, or a chariot with which to transcend space. Tacit acceptance of myth as 'truth' is undercut by the exile's admonition to himself to 'stop believing in puerile impossibilities' (v. 11) and to turn to the 'divine reality' of *Augusti numen* (the godship of Augustus, 13). The poem offers a graphic depiction of the psychosomatic miseries of exile, which are delimited with reference to both time and space: *ut tetigi Pontum ... ossa tegit macies* (then when I reached Pontus ... I became skeleton-thin, 27). Time and space will also mark the final limits of both the emperor's anger and the exile's suffering:

> *at quoniam semel est odio civiliter usus,*
> *mutato levior sit fuga nostra loco.* (*Tr.* 3.8.41, 42)

But as he once tempered his anger in a civilised way, may my exile then be made lighter by a change of place.

Ex Ponto 1.1 reminds the exile's friend Brutus that the poems come to Rome as a projection of himself. An inversion of this vicarious travel in space occurs at 2.8, where Cotta's gift of silver portraits[30] 'represents' the imperial family, who have been 'restored to the exile', and are addressed as *praesentes dei* ('present deities'). The deities have entered the world of the exile, and may share his dangers.

More often a whole poem is couched in terms of the completely 'timeless

189

now', reflecting a subjective perception of the psychological contrast between 'they (or you) there', and 'I, here'. In *Tristia* 1.7 the poet reaches out
to friends who have his portrait 'there', as a surrogate for himself, reminding them that his poetry (including his *Metamorphoses*) is a better portrait
of himself, and showing exile as the final metamorphosis. In *Tristia* 3.12
'they, there' enjoy the beauties of an Italian spring, whereas 'I, here'
experience only a sad 'non-winter'.[31]

This contrast between the miseries of exile and the joys of Italy and
Rome enhances the portrayal of his miseries. The information at *Tristia*
5.7.25, 26 that 'they there' dance to the poet's songs, serves to deepen the
exile's inner misery, externalised as fear of the fierce and wild savages
around him. In an extended example, *Ex Ponto* 1.8 (to Severus) starts with
a depiction of the warlike place of exile, made more concrete by a concise
allusion to the taking of the citadel of Aegisos (1-19). Passage of time has
changed nothing (vv. 25-8). Then follows a loving evocation of Rome and
the poet's country estates near Sulmo (41-6). From nostalgic longing for a
real but unattainable 'there', the exile shifts to a futuristic fantasy about
an unreal and equally unattainable 'here', conjuring up a Tibullan fantasy
about himself in a timeless Getic pastoral landscape, without war and
without danger (51-60). The poem ends with a picture of a busy Severus
enjoying shifts of 'real time' and 'real place' in Italy, moving from the
Campus Martius to the porticoes of the city, or from Umbria to his Alban
estates, along the Via Appia (63-8).[32]

Pastoral can be subverted in other ways to extend the reader's awareness of the horrors of the place. The effect is sometimes consciously
comical. In a ridiculous anti-pastoral scene the poet pretends to see a
shepherd plying his pipe, helmet on head: *sub galea pastor iunctis pice
cantat avenis, / proque lupos pavidae bella verentur oves* (under a helmet
the shepherd plies his pan-pipes, and in stead of the wolf, the shaking
sheep fear war, *Tr.* 5.10.25, 26).[33] Such bathos illustrates the inner resilience of an exile who can still afford to laugh at himself and his readers.[34]

7.4 Ovid's depiction of his place of exile

So we see that the bulk of Ovid's exilic poetry deals with the present
circumstances of the exile, his 'endless now' in a terrible 'here at the ends
of the earth'. The major part of the physical details Ovid gives about his
place of exile cannot be taken as exaggeration which merely needs toning
down in order to be acceptable as geographical or ethnographic information. These details are purposely fantastic and have little if any relation to
physical reality. They represent the externalisation of internal misery, and
are not the causes of that misery.

A desire to evoke sympathy from his readership 'there at Rome, where
time passes normally', tempered with humour, colours his portrayal of
the-exile-as-lonely-hero and his battle to survive the epic onslaughts of

malevolent external forces. We may conclude that the poet's portrayal of what the exile sees and experiences, is literary.[35] In what follows below a brief survey of what the poet presents will show that his geographical depiction of the Pontic area depends heavily on literary sources, and shows little progression throughout the oeuvre, either in accuracy of placement or in greater familiarity with local circumstances. The chapter will end with a consideration of what the poet conveys about the exile's outer circumstances and inner life.

Ovid uses Homer, particularly the *Odyssey*, but also Vergil's *Georgics* and *Aeneid*, as well as frequent intertextual allusion to his own works, to portray his surroundings. At *Ex Ponto* 4.14.9-14 the Pontic area is depicted as a lifeless, cold and unhappy wasteland in intertextual terms reminiscent of the underworld in *Aeneid* 6, or of Ovid's own 'home of Famine' in *Metamorphoses* 8.788-91:

> *est locus extremis Scythiae in oris,*
> *triste solum, sterilis, sine fruge, sine arbore tellus:*
> *Frigus iners illic habitant Pallorque Tremorque*
> *et ieiuna Fames ....*

There is a frozen place on the furthest shores of Scythia: the soil is barren, sterile, without produce, and the earth is treeless: there dwell sluggish Cold, and Pallor, and Ague, and hungry Famine ...

Ovid exploits the general confusion in ancient literature between the northern area, *Scythia Maior* (or Scythia proper), situated in Ukraine or Belorus, north of the Sea of Azov (Lake Maeotis), and *Scythia Minor*, or Moesia, today's Bosnia and Croatia and parts of Roumania. In Roman literature, the savage inhabitants of Moesia were usually called *Daci*. Ovid always uses the poetic (Greek) term *Getae* (as in Vergil and Horace). Augustus in his *Res Gestae* 30.2-31.2 writes of 'suppressing a *Dacorum exercitus*' (Dacian army) and 'achieving the friendship of Scyths, Sarmatians and Bastarnae'.[36] Ovid pretends that he meets every one of these tribes, and they are not friendly, as Augustus claims.

The first book of the *Tristia* is an 'elegiac epic' in miniature, complete with flashbacks, and narration of a heartrending parting, another 'fall of Troy'. The exile is an epic hero, a combined Odysseus-Aeneas hounded by the supreme god Augustus-Jupiter, who towers over all other gods, those gods whose temples and cults Augustus had worked to restore. An impression of eye-witness immediacy in the storm poems (*Tr.* 1.2, 1.4, 1.11) is strengthened by the use of present tense verbs, imperatives and apostrophe, and by progression in the gods' response to the victim's prayers. Literary influence is discernibly stronger than personal impressions.[37] The winds conspire with the stars against the traveller (*Tr.* 1.11.16, 19), but after the storm has settled, a strange calm pervades the rest of Ovid's exilic oeuvre. There is no graphic depiction of howling storms in the Pontic area, only occasional passing allusions to the winds as one of the horrors of exile.[38]

Letters or greetings come to his friends from the place, 'here on the Getic shore' and its variants.[39] Verifiably fantastic details have little relationship to reality, but together they form a picture of sterile loneliness, of the exile as the only cultured man among hosts of savages.[40] The city of Tomis reflects a confusion of barbarian stereotype and mythical malevolence. Details of the city are vague, with an allusion to gates (*Tr.* 3.14.41), and bad defence by the city's bastion, or *tumulus*, which archaeology has been unable to trace (*Tr.* 5.10.17). There is a city wall, which marauders on horse-back encircle as they surge over the frozen Ister (*Pont.* 1.2.17-20).

In *Tristia* 3.9 the etymology of Tomis shows the 'now' of the place as luridly coloured by its remote mythical past. The Medea-myth tinges Ovid's geographical depiction of the place with a suitable tone of horror, as in his fanciful and aptly cruel etymology for Tomis. Its name comes from the Greek word for 'cut', *temnô*, he says, because, '... this place was called "Tomis", for there, they say, the sister cut up her own brother's limbs' (*Tr.* 3.9.1-4). The city is Greek, he concedes, but its state of 'civilisation' is immediately undercut by its connection with this myth.[41]

The ghastliness and isolation of the place dawns on the exile only gradually, and the reader is equally gradually primed with details that grow in horror as he travels on his reluctant way. At *Tristia* 1.2.82 the reader is informed that the traveller is heading for the *Sarmatis tellus* (Sarmatian soil). In Tristia 1.3 we learn that the poet's daughter is in Lybia (v. 19) when her father departs for its traditional antipodes, Scythia (v. 61). Only by the fifth poem of the first book does the poet reveal that he is headed for the land of the Getae and Sarmatians, fierce barbarians. The exile's destination Tomis lies south of the mouth of the Ister, on roughly the same latitude as Bologna in Italy, i.e., about 240 km further north than Rome, but it is consistently placed 'directly under' the Pole star, or even more graphically presented as 'oppressed by' the North Pole, a *topos* familiar from Apollodorus, which functions to stress the distance and desolation of the place of exile. This constellation soon becomes the most consistent symbol for the place of exile.[42]

The cosmic scene is set at the farewell from Rome, where time is measured by the revolution of Ursa Maior or Callisto, The Great Bear. In the mythical Pontic world of Ovid's exile the city groans beneath its weight. Poor Callisto, so Ovid tells us in the *Metamorphoses*, was seduced by the supreme god Jupiter. Her mistress Diana punished her severely for becoming pregnant, and she first became a bear, and then a constellation. We have noted before that oppression by the Bear constellation may be a metaphor for oppression by Augustus, who, so Suetonius notes (*Aug.* 80), had a birthmark resembling Ursa Major.[43]

Similarly, punning allusions to the left-hand shore of Euxine Pontus as *sinister* have cosmic and metaphorical significance. Strabo alludes to the west coast of Pontus as *ta aristera tou Pontou* (the right-hand side of Pontus), but he is offering a *periplous* (travelogue) as it would be experienced by a southward-bound traveller. Ovid's ship is travelling northwards, and so the coast is on its left. His 'left-hand' metaphor extends the literal designation for the coast in *periplous* of this kind with conscious allusion to the inhospitality of the area. In common speech, Neo-Pythagorean influence had interpreted the left hand as unfavourable. In Roman augural language the left was favourable only when the augur faced *south*. Sometimes such 'scientific' information is spelled out more exactly. In *Tristia* 4.3 the poet transmits messages by the stars, appealing to them to watch over his wife. The idea of timeless stars set against the temporal troubles of humanity is a traditional *topos*. Our poet hastens to refer to Greek and Phoenician use of stars in navigation, thereby adding an 'objective, scientific' touch: these stars are guides that truly help humanity. Therefore the exile has a 'scientific' basis for his appeal.[44]

Such deliberate conflation of poetry and science becomes clear in a poem (*Pont.* 4.10) attempting an explanation for the verifiable phenomenon of the occasionally frozen sea. The poet places his scientific excursion into a mythological framework by starting with an allusion to his 'sixth year on the Cimmerian shore' (v. 1). This conflates an Homeric mythical north with the Cimmerian Bosphorus, the strait, at least 850 km distant from Tomis, that connects Lake Maeotis with the Pontus Euxinus.

Ovid's scientific explanation starts with an echo of Lucretius: *crede tamen: nec te causas nescire sinemus* ... (and believe me: for I shall not allow you to remain ignorant of the reasons for this ..., *Pont.* 4.10.37) The poet offers to explain why the 'Sarmatian sea' freezes: the area is closest to the 'Wagon' constellation and all the coldest stars, and the north winds arise there (39-42). He knows that this is dull material, unsuitable for poetry, but writing relieves his pain and makes him forget his surroundings (65-8). What he tells applies well to the area of the Sea of Azov (Maeotis) which would feel the cold winds from the Russian Steppes. Fantasy gives way to reality when he offers scientific (and correct) geographical information. Pontus is the 'Black Sea', 'scarcely blue', because so many rivers flow into it and make its surface water almost fresh. Calm stretches of fresh water are generally darker than the brilliant blue of the salty Mediterranean. This dark blue fresh water freezes over, and traps the heavier salty water beneath:

> *Copia tot laticum, quas auget, adulterat undas,*
> *nec patitur vires aequor habere suas.*
> *quin etiam, stagno similis pigraeque paludi,*
> *caeruleus vix est diluiturque color.*
> *innatat unda freto dulcis, leviorque marina est,*
> *quae proprium mixto de sale pondus habet ...*   (*Pont.* 4.10.59-62)

Such a flood of fresh water tempers the sea into which it runs, and does not allow it to retain its salinity. Indeed, just like the water of a lake or a sluggish swamp, it is almost black, and its colour is livid. The fresh water lies on top of the current, being lighter than the sea water, which is heavy from its admixture of salt ...

Ovid's catalogue of rivers (*Pont.* 47-58) is reminiscent of typically epic word music: Lycus, Sagaris, Penius, Hypanis, Cales, Halys, Parthenius, Cynapses, Tyras, Thermodon, Phasis, Borysthenius, Dryapses, Melanthus, Tanais and the Danube (not Ister, but *Danuvius*). The names in Ovid's catalogue of rivers that feed this fresh water lake occur in early Black Sea *periplous* (descriptions of coastal journeys) used by the geographers Strabo, Arrian and Ptolemy, but also in the poets. Of these names, the Tanais occurs *inter alia* in Vergil *Geor.* 4, Aratus, and Ovid himself, the Phasis and the Parthenius in Callimachos'*Aetia*. Ovid claims that the area is the 'birthplace of the winds': *hinc oritur Boreas* (Here rises the North Wind, v. 41). In an early *periplous* a mouth of the Ister is called the *Boreum stoma*.[45] Ovid's catalogue is not geographical, but poetic, a sound-painting which charms the ear and impresses by its length.

An assertion that perpetual snows lie on the ground from year to year (starting at *Tr.* 3.2.8, at a time when one could assume familiarity with the area) is repeated throughout[46] until finally an independent witness to this 'fact' is solemnly invoked (*Pont.* 4.7.7). Such playful invocation is however not factual testimony. Ovid's source is Vergil, whose Scythia (*Geor.* 3.349-83) draws the Danube 'with its golden sands' northwards past Lake Maeotis (the Sea of Azov). Ovid draws Vergil's snowbound Scythia south and west into the realm of Moesian reality, but his description of life in Tomis in *Tristia* 3.10 depends largely on Vergil's picture of a mythical frozen Scythia:

> ... *qua Scythiae gentes Maeotiaque unda,*
> *turbidus et torquens flaventis Hister harenas,*
> *quaque redit medium Rhodope porrecta sub axem ...*   (*Geor.* 3.349-51)

(at the place where) are to be found the Scythian tribes and Lake Maeotis, and the turbulent Ister churns up its golden sands, and where Rhodope bends back, stretching as far as the central pole.

Let us briefly consider Vergil's geography. *Georgics* 3.349-83 appears to confuse traditional material with an accurate picture of Moesia. Vergil's Scyths live simultaneously next to both the Sea of Azov (lake Maeotis) and the Danube, which Vergil shows as wandering through the South Russian Steppes before mouthing into Maeotis, surrounded by the Rhodope mountains (of Thrace). This area actually does have the characteristics of mythical Scythia: great cold, freezing winds sweeping over the flat plains, and perhaps permanent snow on the mountains. But the picture is not geographically exact. It is a literary *topos*. Vergil's literary depiction of

7. The Horror of Isolation

Scythia is confused with Homer's Cimmeria. Where Vergil has drawn the Danube 'with its golden sands' northwards past the Sea of Azov, Ovid brings Vergil's snowbound poetic Scythia south and west into Moesia, a real place. Ovid improves the geography of the older poet. His Ister (Danube) follows its right course, accurate by about sixty kilometres, but the exile's world is still imaginary, a suitable place of punishment for the mythical hero, an *Ovidius multipatiens* (longsuffering Ovid).

So Ovid's geography is taken from books, and details are selected that will impress his readers with the horrors that face the exile daily. Closer contact with the area does not improve the exile's initial impression of isolation and desolation. The treeless plain offers no grapevines, no fruit trees, not even green leaves. The landscape is bare and sterile:

> *non hic pampinea dulcis latet uva sub umbra,*
> *nec cumulant altos fervida musta lacus*
> *poma negat regio ...*
> ...
> *aspiceres nudos sine fronde, sine arbore, campos.*
> *heu loca felici non adeunda viro!*   (*Tr.* 3.10.71-3, 75-6)

The sweet grape doesn't nestle here under the trailing shade, and they don't fill deep containers with foaming must. The area won't yield apples .... You would see only bare, leafless, treeless plains: alas, these are places not to be approached by a happy man.

The water is not fit for drinking. The only plant the exile sees growing on the vast and bare plain is, suitably, wormwood, *absinthia*.[47] This offers a negative echo of Lucretius' use of poetry to sweeten his lesson in atomism.[48] Here is nothing to sweeten the bitter scene. The Pontic earth shares in the bitterness of its crop (*Pont.* 3.1.25). So we can deduce that the 'perpetual snows' do sometimes melt. Glorious inconsistency prevails.

The frozen Danube allows the local inhabitants to draw their ox carts over the ice. The exile swears that the sea itself freezes over and that he has walked on sea ice, where dolphins cannot jump, and ships and living fish are frozen fast. This must be fantasy. Black Sea winters can sometimes be harsh, but summers are very hot. Allusions to the frozen Ister allowing incursions of marauders start at *Tristia* 2.196 and continue throughout.[49]

The picture is one of horror and desolation. In contrast with the balmy summer days of gentle carousing in Italy, a perpetual winter is spent sucking at frozen wine (*Tr.* 3.10.23-4), and local hospitality, such as it is, is frigid. Like Vergil, Ovid depicts perpetual snow, sharpened by sudden frosts, so cold that frozen wine keeps the shape of its jar. The hospitable savages chop off pieces of wine to offer their guest:

> *nudaque consistunt, formam servantia testae,*
> *vina, nec hausta meri, sed data frusta bibunt.*   (*Tr.* 3.10.24-5)

The wine stands bare, maintaining the shape of the jar, and they don't get draughts of strong drink, but are served chunks of it.

Ovid's picture amplifies and partially inverts *Georgics* 3.379-80 where Vergil's Scyths 'chop' their wine, but have a fermented brew with which to shorten a long polar night in carousing. Ovid's Getae (with the Sauromatae and Bessi – on whom more below) have a harder life, and do not seem to enjoy the same pleasures that compensate Vergil's Scyths for life in perpetual snow, sudden frosts and *inhabitabile frigor* (uninhabitable cold). Ovid's Getae have a hyperbolical nothing. We have seen that Ovid's Tomitan landscape does not cultivate vineyards, or any other trees. The wine which freezes, it seems, is not local, for no *musta* can be brewed. Even the water is scarcely fit for drinking.[50]

Ovid's ethnography, like his geography, is firmly based in literature. Our poet uses tribal and national names from Black Sea areas far beyond Tomis. His Roman readership would have been impressed by the variety of these barbarian names, wild savages living among half-wild Greeks. Tomis was formerly a Milesian colony. But this Greek city has decadent inhabitants, who speak Greek of a sort, highly influenced by local barbarism (*Tr.* 5.7.51). They wear the same clothing made from skins and terrible Persian trousers as the 'Getae and Sarmatians'. These are warlike, the 'very image of Mars',[51] barbarian bowman riding on horseback, horrible savages, with long hair, beards tinkling with icicles, bearing quiverfuls of poisoned arrows.[52]

This is the Ovidian version of traditional *topoi*. Archaeology has shown us a high degree of Hellenisation and Romanisation of the Dacians around Tomis, between the Danube and the Black Sea, and even of the free Dacians from beyond the Danube. Tomitan archaeological finds show a fine indigenous culture, use of Roman artefacts, even coins, also locally made fine Thracian metalwork, and inscriptions in Greek and Latin.[53] Ovid shows us none of this. Beards, barbarity and belligerence feature to the end, with little variation. The savages continue tough and bearded, shooting, like all Thracians and Scyths throughout literature, poisoned arrows from their horses as they gallop past.[54] They never read, nor vote, but settle civic affairs by means of duels in the market place. Danger threatens on every hand.

Sometimes the shaking of quivers signifies war, but finally these quivers become symbolic of the Orphic power of poetry to tame their savage breasts. We have noted before that, at a magnificent *recitatio* which the exile holds in the Tomitan marketplace, he sings in Getic about the catasterisation of the 'god Augustus'. The savages listen attentively, and at the end a murmur rises from the group, and they growl, shake their quivers, and clash their arms in savage approval. When the poet, now thoroughly Geticised, had sung a 'Getic song' about the apotheosis of Augustus, a murmur of wonder went through their serried ranks and *et*

196

caput et plenas omnes movere pharetras (They shook their heads and their full quivers, *Pont.* 4.13.35), a sign of the taming, Orphic power of poetry, or of the power of the new god. Ovid's little joke contrasts the power of his Getic Muse on the savages with the stolid resistance met by Julius Caesar from the illiterate pirates who had captured him, when he tried to read them his own poems and declaimed speeches at them.[55]

In *Tristia* 2 local inhabitants are depicted as victims of transdanuvian marauders, shot down by poisoned arrows or carried away northwards into slavery, where:

> *longius hac nihil est, nisis tantum frigus et hostes*
> *et maris adstricto quae coit unda gelu*   (*Tr.* 2.195-6)

further than this there is nothing but the cold and the foe, and the waves of the sea which stiffen into hard ice.

The pathetic victims seem at other times to be the same inhuman Getae whom the exile hates and fears, and about whom graphic reports are sent back to a horrified Rome. When the local inhabitants fall victim to the northern hordes (*Tr.* 3.10.50-70),[56] they are pathetic fellow-victims of the dangerous area. These are the very *inhumanae Getae* whom the exile usually hates and fears (cf. *Tr.* 5.10.31-2).[57] The poet does not distinguish between marauders and victims. Here both are unnamed, whereas elsewhere the various tribal names jostle one another indiscriminately. In the *Epistolae ex Ponto* tribal names are a frequent means of placing the exile.[58]

The inhabitants are not always inhuman. The Tomitans are on occasion kind to the miserable exile (*Pont.* 4.9.95 and 4.14.23), and the feeling is on occasion reciprocated. At last, however, the Getae appear to have learnt, by reciprocation, to understand Latin, and they become justifiably wrathful at the exile's depiction of their savagery. Their anger offers one more opportunity for ingenious reversal. He loves them, the exile says; it is only the Getic land which he hates with every fibre of his being. This landscape is worthy of hatred, threatening by its very appearance, with no safe harbour to which to flee, for the land has even more horrors to offer than the sea. 'Wherever I look, there is nothing but the image of death!' he cries.[59]

So the exiled poet is a world-citizen of a poetic place – a literary fantasy woven into myth. We do not need to make concessions for 'understandable exaggeration'. Better to accept Ovid's portrayal of the horrors of the place as imaginary, as myth, a myth that externalises the internal horror of isolation and carries with it a higher-order truth: that Augustus brought great misery to a Roman citizen, who sustained himself by exercising his persuasive, poetic creativity.

7.5 The exiled poet in his surroundings

It is a commonplace of criticism that an epic hero is defined by his own words, his deeds and by what others say about him. In a lesser degree the epic poet occasionally adds his own authorial comment. The reader is ostensibly expected to 'sit back and enjoy it'. The epic frame lends a certain distance to both author and reader. In Roman erotic elegy, on the other hand, the authorial *persona* is often more precisely defined than is the object of the lover's ardour, and the reader as 'non-speaking figure' is clearly discernible as the object of authorial address.

These different degrees of relation and remove all come into play in Ovid's exilic poetry. The creator-poet works with a series of *personae*, as we have seen. To the degree that the poet is drawing an epic portrait of a larger-than-life, *'Ovidius heros'*, a lonely, long-suffering survivor in a malevolent, mythical world, there is a certain epic distancing between the author and the personage about whom he reports. Yet the poems from exile are also offered as 'the hero's own words', from which readers may derive an opinion of his character. The poems simultaneously represent the hero's deeds; the heroic exiled poet is still plying his trade, and his exilic poetry is the tangible result. Lastly, the discernible distance between creative poet and suffering exile allows the creator-poet as narrator to become the 'epic other' as commentator, while simultaneously offering occasional authorial comment. Yet to the degree that the exile is also drawn as elegiac lover, sad and *exclusus* from Rome, who woos a coy 'mistress' in the person of the capricious emperor, the 'poet-as-suffering-lover' speaks, and both Rome and Augustus as the objects of his ardour are mute. As readers of elegy, the poet's audience is actively involved (by his solicitation of their creative response) in recreating in their minds the three-dimensional 'holograph' of the poet-as-exile that is suggested by this multiplicity of projections.

These projections relate more fully to the exile's inner suffering than to externals. The holograph shows a shadowy, toga-clad Roman Orpheus, golden-voiced, pinned down on the extreme shores of Pontus, beset by the bellicose onslaughts of howling savages, whom he quells by his song and who follow his example in humble adoration of the great new ruler of his and their world. But it is a mirage. Shimmering through it comes the powerful image of the versatile inner life of a Roman poet, sure in his craft, burdened by an unfair oppressor, but able, through the strength of his vatic impulse, to travel at will and to insinuate himself into the minds and hearts of his audience. What he leaves there is a paradoxical view of a frail body housing an indomitable spirit that can turn the horrors of isolation into poetic inspiration. Part of the paradox is an apparently consistent inability in the exiled poet to realise to what degree he has actually broken through his own isolation into the warmth of his readers' perceptive appreciation of the creative poet's art.[60]

198

7. The Horror of Isolation

At *Tristia* 5.12.53 the horror of isolation is fully spelled out in the exile's cry that he has no books to read, nor any audience for his poetry.[61] Yet we have seen that the poems from exile show evidence of much book-learning. The poet either had a prodigious memory or he is dealing in fiction. As we have seen, the hospitality offered by the barbarous and inclement place of exile could have given full scope to the poet's powers of description, but it is sparsely depicted. The poet's fantastic depiction of impossible cold and inhumanely fierce enemies, contrasted with his sympathetic and vicarious participation in the suffering of the Getic victims of attack, gives a concrete vividness to the exile's longings to be elsewhere.[62] Impossibilities such as frozen wine and perpetual snows offer a poetic means of externalising the exile's inner suffering. He is aware of his own subjective fear, but is mostly unable to define its causes in more than general terms. He even fears his friends:

> non igitur verear quod te rear esse verendum,
>   cuius amor nobis pignora mille dedit,
> sed quia res timida est omnis miser ...   (Pont. 2.7.35-7)

I'm not scared because I think you should be feared, you whose love has given me a thousand proofs, but because any unfortunate is a fearful creature anyway ...

We are given few details. The exile experiences dangerous hospitality in this barbarous place. His house is inadequate, food is bad, there is no doctor when he is ill. On one occasion he dictates to a secretary, who then disappears, and he never has anyone even to speak to in Latin. He meets the occasional sailor and eagerly invites him 'home' for questioning, to a house he shares with savages. These living quarters are appropriately squalid, his house offering no *discrimen* between the exile and his savage neighbour.[63] A nocturnal visitor, the dishevelled Amor that has come to vindicate the exile's innocence, clutches at a solid wooden bedstead, the only article of domestic furniture deemed worthy of mention in the whole exilic corpus, but this is an apparition and not reality.[64]

We never see the exile moving about the rooms of his house, humble or otherwise, or in the market place of Tomis, or visiting local inhabitants. We simply have him at last speaking full-fledged Getic. Only once we see him walking on the beach, but here too the realistic decor sets the stage for another fantastic apparition. A tame and incorporeal *Fama* brings news of Rome. This is the pleasant opposite of the Vergilian monster that went roaring through the streets of Carthage in *Aeneid* 4.

> ... mihi, cum fulva solus spatiarer harena,
>   visa est a tergo pinna dedisse sonum.
> respicio, nec erat corpus, quod cernere possem,
>   verba tamen sunt haec aure recepta mea ...   (Pont. 4.4.11-14)

I seemed to have heard a wing rustle while I was walking alone along the golden sand. I looked back, and there was no physical body for me to see, but these words were heard ringing in my ears ...

Just as when the poet sang in Getic, so these visitors to the Getic shore have only one topic: distant Rome and its illustrious inhabitants. *Amor* predicts Tiberius' triumph, *Fama* brings news of the triumph of Sextus Pompeius, a lately-acquired patron with whom the poet has an intriguing relationship, unique in his works, as between chattel and owner.[65]

Unlike Ovid's other works, the exilic poems feature few religious practices, and these are barbaric. Of local religion we hear nothing, although there is archaeological evidence for lively Greek culture. There were local cults of a Zeus Ombrinus (the rain-bringer), the Nymphs, Demeter and Apollo, together with the cult of the Thracian horseman. Ovid depicts a world bare of all religion except the cult of the bloodthirsty Tauric Artemis, to the north-east on the Crimean Peninsula. Ovid's Roman readers could not have known that the Crimea is about 800 km from Tomis. In mythic space, this sanguinary cult also stains its neighbour Tomis, as we saw in Chapter 2: 'and not far from us is the place where the dreadful Tauric altar of the quiver-bearing goddess is sprinkled with blood'. Ovid's Roman readership was presented with a world in which no gods held sway except this monstrous goddess, and his angry persecutor, Augustus-Jupiter.

In time, and with glorious inconsistency, a magnificently elaborate shrine to the Imperial triad, forming part of the exile's humble hut, is conjured up for Graecinus' edification (*Pont.* 4.9.105-12). It apparently houses the silver images of the imperial triad sent to him by Cotta Maximus, perhaps a coin or medallion, or something similar, also featuring Augustus' two grandsons – Drusus II, son of Tiberius, and Germanicus. The whole Pontic world daily sees the humble exile worshipping these kind beings, whose cult he propagates with missionary zeal. We saw in *Ex Ponto* 2.8 that their softened faces give him hope of recall. As *praesentes dei* they share in the dangers that face the outcast, and their preservation paradoxically depends upon his.

'Incorporeal' we can almost imagine the exile to be, for his agonies appear to be largely those of the spirit. Yet some physical details are given. The book at *Tristia* 1.1.3-14, as the exile's *alter ego*, looks suitably dishevelled. While still on his journey, the traveller now fears corporeal death and then fears tortured life, as a storm-tossed mariner should (*Tr.* 1.2.40, 51). *Tristia* 4.1.71-6 has the 'aged exile', sword and shield in hand, defending life and limb, another Priam, forced to do battle in his old age.

The exile's first contact with the Pontic area causes physical ills, reflections of his tortured spirit, so graphically conveyed that they have merited modern medical and psychiatric attention.[66] Modern diagnoses of Ovid's poems from exile as evidence of 'extreme depression', attest to the poetic power of a skilful poet, whose *summa ars celavit artem* (art has concealed his art).[67] His physical symptoms are languor, insomnia and, at *Tristia* 5.13.3-6, racking pains 'in the side' suggesting pleurisy, but also the discomfort of enforced celibacy, equally painful to either a *lusor amorum* (player at love) or an affectionate husband.

At *Ex Ponto* 1.10 the exile's misery is conveyed in terms of a different set of physical symptoms: no pain or fever (vv. 5, 6) but loss of *taste* (7) and *smell* (13). The poet-exile's inner experience of loneliness extends his sensory metaphor to a claim to *feel* the cold, *see* savages all around him, and *hear* no reply to all his bootless cries. His other symptoms, insomnia (21-4) and paleness, are often characteristic of the over-eager lover of elegy.[68] Not only the place of his relegation harms the exile, and he knows it: *unda locusque nocent et causa valentior istis, / anxietas animi, quae mihi semper adest* ('the sea and the place harm me, and another matter stronger than either, anxiety of the mind, which perpetually haunts me', vv. 35, 36). This is his central woe. *Anxietas animi* (mental anxiety) colours the exile's perception of external reality. This poem gives a clinically correct portrayal of acute depression.

The pathos of exile has been universalised.[69] In the *anxietas animi* of the articulate exile can be read a reflection of a similar *anxietas* experienced by all victims of exile everywhere. For Ovid's readership in Rome it could not have been difficult to imagine a similar mental agony in Augustus' exiled grandson Agrippa Postumus, even more so in Agrippa's intelligent and sensitive mother and lively sister. Even Tiberius, while in his self-chosen retreat on the island of Rhodes, may have felt a similar frustrated anxiety when Augustus forced him to remain there after he expressed the desire to return.

In the *Epistolae ex Ponto* the exile's suffering is expressed more fully in terms of internal feelings, as is shown by an increase of words of affect.[70] *Ex Ponto* 1.2 refers to bad dreams, showing the depression and helpless misery of one who cannot be 'metamorphosed':

> *ille ego sum, lignum qui non admittar in ullum:*
> *ille ego sum, frustra qui lapis esse velim.* (*Pont.* 1.2.33, 34)

I am that he, who will by no means be allowed to turn into wood; I am that he, who in vain wish I could become stone.

Intertextual allusion in this couplet is dense. The personal phrase *ille ego* evokes the opening lines of Vergil's *Aeneid*, the poet's own previous use of the phrase in his triumphant autobiographical statement (*Tr.* 4.10.1), and its reuse as a threat of revenge at *Ibis* 247. The reader is invited to interpret the present passage in the light of its predecessors. A rounded personality emerges. He is depressed, yes, but capable of both manic delusions of revenge and deeply felt pride in his real achievements as a poet worthy of comparison with the best.

From enjoying life as a 'young' forty-nine-year-old, the exile shifts within a year to being an 'old and grey' quinquegenarian (*Tr.* 4.6.41). That same year sees him white-haired, singing a final 'swan-song' (*Tr.* 4.8.1-4), full of years, *anni fragiles et inertior aetas* (frail years and too slow old age), feeling the full weight of oppression beneath the North Star (v. 41). He is an 'old and grey' Odysseus-figure, longing for his supposedly equally ancient wife (*Pont.* 1.4.1, 2). This realistic touch, while contrasting the 'normal passage of time' at Rome and timeless, mythical thraldom on the Getic shores, moves the *cara coniunx* (beloved wife) out of the sphere of myth where perpetual youth holds a Penelope forever alluring.[71]

The *lusor amorum* has, however, been so thoroughly defeated that the poet never hints at a liaison with a local female. Such a menage would undercut the picture of tender conjugal ties and rigidly ascetic fidelity created by the lonely exile's letters to his distant wife. His erotic fantasies are now only about her, sometimes jokingly in delicate *double entendre*. Fidelity is not difficult, for the Getic women are ugly, dumb child-bearers, with no Ovidian *cultus*, unprepossessing, hardy and unfamiliar even with the art of weaving.[72] They grind their meal with large pestles and mortars, and carry water on their heads like the strong peasant women praised by Varro (*De re rustica* 2.10.6-9).

Language, as depicted by the exile, initially offers a problem in communication, but it also represents the silence enjoined the poet by the despot who exiled him. The problem is twofold: inability to understand, and loss of his native speech. There is strong pathos in the depiction of the lonely exile who has forgotten his Latin through 'long disuse' (*Tr.* 5.7.57, 58) and 'talks to himself' (v. 63).[73] The plea of 'long disuse' (in roughly the third year of exile) bears no relation to the tremendous poetic output of a prolific writer. The exiled poet is indulging in the enjoyment of a self-pity unrelated to reality.[74]

At first he can understand nothing. *Barbarus hic ego sum* (Here I am the barbarian, *Tr.* 5.10.37) he complains. In this place of horror all his assumptions about Roman *cultus* have been turned onto their heads. Exile displaces everything, including established values. To be a Roman is to be a foreigner, an uninitiated stranger. Even his gestures are misunderstood. This claim is made toward the end of the second year of exile, some time after his declaration that he is a 'Roman poet' no longer, but is considered a genius amongst the Sarmatians (*Tr.* 5.1.73, 74). In time the savages have started to talk to him in Getic, which the exile conveniently now understands, together with Sarmatian. The distance of Sarmatia from Tomis suggests that this is poetic fantasy, or, in a Greek city, strange fact.[75] We have seen that in the end the savages, too, have learnt, in their turn, to understand Latin, and they are angry that he has depicted them as savages. He hurries to placate them.

Twice he announces his transformation into a Getic and Sarmatian poet in evocative onomatopoeic verses, evoking in consecutive couplets both the

guttural Germanic growl of the northern hordes and the 'iotacised' sounds
of the decadent Greek dialect of the area:

> *Omnia barbariae loca sunt vocis ferinae,*
> *omniaque hostilis plena timore soni.*
> *ipse mihi videor iam dedidicisse Latine*
> *nam didici Getice Sarmatice loqui.*   (*Tr.* 5.12.55-8)

The whole place is full of a barbarous growling, filled with the terror of
enemy sounds. I seem to myself to have unlearnt my Latin, for I have learnt
to chatter in Getic and Sarmatic.

The distance of Sarmatia from Tomis casts doubt on the statement *nam
didici Sarmatice Getice loqui* (repeated at *Pont.* 3.2.40). This is poetic
fiction clothed in onomatopoeic word-music.

Suddenly, in the last book from exile, the solitary and pain-racked
near-wraith appears, sporadically, as a Sarmatian genius, as the honoured
'elder poet of the Tomitan area'. The inhuman Getae have seemingly
realised his worth and have desisted – not from using him as a target for
their arrows, but – from *taxing* him. At *Ex Ponto* 4.9.101-2 the exile
informs his readers that by public decree he has been made *immunis* ('tax
exempt'), not only at Tomis, but the in the *proxima ... oppida* (next towns)
too (103-4). This boon was granted, he says, out of pity, and appreciation
for the piety with which he cherished his household shrine, replete with
imperial images (105-14). The stock stupid slave of Roman Comedy is
always named *Geta*, for good reason. The Pontic world was not aware that
Ovid, as *relegatus* and not *exsul* (with retention of his Roman citizenship),
would not have been liable for local taxation.[76] That the tax system of one
village would extend its jurisdiction over the inhabitants of the next is
equally unlikely. The poet's subtle sense of humour is at play.

In all, Ovid's details are verifiably fantastic, with little or no relationship to reality, but together they form a picture of sterile loneliness, of the
exile as the only cultured man among hosts of savages or quasi-savages.
Ovidius exsul is not a disgraced Roman living in a Greek city on the edge
of empire. His world is distorted. *Ovidius heros* is a mythical hero, living
in a poetic world, a Tityon or Prometheus pinned down in a vast triangle
marked by the Bosporus in the south, the Tanais in the north, and Maeotis
in the east:

> *Proxima sideribus tellus Erymanthidos Vrsae*
> *me tenet, adsticta terra perusta gelu.*
> *Bosporos et Tanais superant Scythiaeque paludes.*   (*Tr.* 3.4b.47-9)

A land close to the Great Bear holds me fast, a country frozen by solid ice.
Bosporos and Tanais and the Scythian swamps are too much for me ...

Ovidius poeta has with his geography universalised exile. Isolation transcendent is its chief feature, but there is one power, abundantly his, that can defeat its horror: the power of the imagination. An essentially healthy mind finds its own means of sublimation. From a 'now' frozen in time, and from a 'here', which he chooses to depict as literally 'frozen', the exile has two means of mental escape. Projection in time is reflected in the assurance of his immortality; projection is space is reflected in an increasing awareness of his ability to engage in mental travel.[77] Both these forms of sublimation are effected by means of his poetry. Immortality is assured, not only for the poet himself, but as the gift that lies within his power to confer on others.[78] Transcendence in space is achieved not only when the exile conjures up the sights and sounds of Rome, but also by his mentally drawing his friends into his sphere and there holding imaginary conversations with them.[79]

The exile's ability to achieve mental escape is specifically articulated in *Ex Ponto* 4.9. This poem falls within the last book of Pontic epistles, in which mental travel is both explicitly evoked and tacitly practised. This is the sublimation which only a very talented and creative poet can achieve: *mente tamen, quae sola loco non exulat, utar* (I shall use my mind, which alone is not an exile in this place, v. 41). The exiled poet's escape in time is finally articulated in the last poem of the collection, *Ex Ponto* 4.16.3: *famaque post cineres maior venit* (and our fame grows greater after we have been reduced to ashes). Clearly, then, we need now to consider the poetry whereby such escape and sublimation is achieved.

THE FOURTH STAGE

THE POETRY OF EXILE

Preamble: Universalising the Particular

Discussion to date has concentrated on the most prolific writers of exilic literature, and particularly on Ovid. In our progression from consideration of third person narrative to first person introspection, we have increasingly concentrated on Ovid as the prime example of the 'first person' portrayer of exile and of the mental vicissitudes of a displaced person. Ovid has loomed larger and larger in our discussion of the stylisation of exile, and this trend will continue in the Fourth Stage (8.2 below). As poet he reveals his own emotion, while universalising suffering. In Chapter 8 the generic range of the poetry of exile will be considered, which, while starting with Cicero's forays into historicising epic (8.1), will mean concentration on Ovid's generic experimentation. With Ovid, elegy returns to its roots as *flebile carmen* (8.3), but it also shares in the characteristics of other 'lesser genres', that stand in opposition to epic. With vigorous *recusatio* (8.4) it proceeds to show what has been Ovid's final answer to the Augustan challenge: the power of the ruler over the spirit of the poet is strongly repudiated (8.5).

Ovid was, however, not the only exile that resorted to poetry, that is, to metrical formalising of his feelings. Traditionally the elegiac metre was the medium of lament, what moderns would consider the most subjective manner of uttering emotion. Section 8.1 shows that, if we take the poet's manner and degree of subjectivity as criteria, the hexameter poetry composed by Cicero on his consulship (of which some fragments remain)[1] and on his exile (which has been wholly lost) fall under the same rubric as Cicero's subjective rewriting of the past in various speeches after his return.

Conversely, the lyric poems which alternate with prose in Boethius' *Consolatio Philosophiae* (9.6) appear at first reading as celebrations of cosmic themes or of the mutability of Fortuna, not meriting inclusion as subjective reflections on exile. However, Boethius' poetry forms an integral part of his portrayal of the prisoner's progress back to the life-giving rule of Philosophy, and will be discussed as such. Seneca (9.5) has been plausibly linked to a collection of lyric poems in the *Anthologia Latina*,[2] which show a clear affinity with Ovidian themes and what we know of Seneca's own circumstances. These poets each show Ovidian influence, and hence will merit attention in Chapter 9, when Ovid's influence in forming the conventions of exilic poetry are considered (9.1 to 4). To the degree to which each of our authors succeeds in distancing his creative self from his suffering self, he succeeds in universalising some aspect of the particular in his own experience. The work ends with an Epilogue in which Ovid's influence within the twentieth century is briefly surveyed.

8

Generic Range in the Poetry
of Exile

8.1 Ciceronian epic

There is a clear dichotomy between Cicero's subjective perception of his banishment and the historical events that led to it. This cleft shows clearly in the fragments that remain of his attempts at personalised epic. Cicero was aware of the possibility inherent in poetry for heroising persons and deeds. He also was aware that he was consciously embarking on self-propaganda (*Att.* 1.19 and 20, 2.1.1, *Arch.* 12.30).[3] When he could not persuade his friend the poet Archias (*Att.* 1.16.15)[4] to 'write up' the great deeds of his consulate, Cicero determined to do so himself, starting with schematic *commentarii* (brief narrative outlines) in Greek and Latin, and then turning to poetry (*Att.* 1.20). That such propaganda would have been expedient in the dark days before his banishment, is clear.

Cicero probably completed the *commentarii* on his consulship before his banishment. As we saw in Chapter 6, these were meant as the data to be fleshed out into 'history' by his friends Lucceius and Posidonius, both of whom refused to oblige. *Ad Atticum* 2.1 reports on Posidonius' reaction to his Greek *commentarius*; its thoroughness, Cicero writes, has left Posidonius *deterritum* (scared off).[5] One may judge that all three authors found the task beyond their powers of straining veracity.[6]

The quality of Cicero's epic poem *De consulatu suo* has been much criticised, not least by Cicero's contemporaries. The extant fragment, comprising some eighty verses, probably from its second book, seems largely to bear out this criticism, which was canonised in Juvenal's famous verses:

> *O fortunatam natam me consule Romam!*
> *Antoni gladios potuit contemnere si sic*
> *omnia dixisset!*   (*Sat.* 10.122f.[7])

'Oh, happy Rome new-born, borne high with me as consul! He could have despised Antony's sword if all his rhetoric had been so bombastic!'

207

Cicero's reputation as poet could perhaps have stood higher with modern critics if more of his poetry on other topics had survived. His Latin version of Aratus' *Phaenomena* is well-known for the direction it gave later imitators, including the patron that Ovid tried in vain to conciliate, Germanicus Caesar.[8] The fragment from the *De consulatu suo* appears to draw upon Cicero's own earlier interest in cosmology and celestial portents (1-41), Etruscan lore (42-54) and cult observance (55-70a). The 'speaker' is the Muse Urania, but the focus is on Cicero as epic hero. Predictably, much of the fragment is autobiographical. Due respect is accorded the type of liberal education the consular poet himself had enjoyed (70b-76) and the fragment ends with emphasis on his early inclination towards poetry and statecraft (77-8). The State and the Muses each deserved well of the hero:

> *Tu tamen anxiferas curas requiete relaxans,*
> *quod patriae vacat, id studiis nobisque sacrasti.* (*De consulatu suo* 77-8)

You, however, when you laid aside anxious care in rest, devoted to us and to your studies what leisure moments remained after due devotion to the fatherland.

To the facts of the eventful closing weeks of 63 BC we have scant reference here. A single verse, alluding to the hero's 'fearful apprehension of what the night might bring' may refer either to the consul's consciousness of physical danger or to his awaiting the outcome of the Allobroges affair. Other insignificant fragments of uncertain provenance survive, including the despised *O fortunatam* ... and *Cedant arma togae, concedat laurea laudi* (armour gives way to civilian attire, and the laurel is less important than public acclaim), which Cicero indignantly defends at *In Pisonem* 73, 74. Three verses from the third book survive, comprising apostrophe, presumably of the hero, by the Muse Calliope (cf. *Att.* 2.3.4). The hero is incited to strive for still greater renown. The last of the surviving fragments offers a charming instance of zeugma epitomising the objects of presumably Ciceronian patriotism: *in montes patrios et ad incunabula nostra* (towards the mountains of our fatherland and for the sake of our children's cradles).[9]

After Cicero's return from banishment, the complete story of his consulate, banishment and restitution merited similar treatment, also undertaken by the protagonist himself, for lack of an independent author. The *De temporibus suis*, relating the story of his banishment and return in epic verse, was not, as has sometimes been suggested, an alternate name for a reworking and updating of the *De consolatu suo*, which had been published long before the second poem was completed.[10] Unfortunately nothing of the exilic poem has survived, and we can only attempt a reconstruction from allusions in letters[11] and by means of comparison with the tone and thrust of the prose works we have considered above, and the style of the extant fragments of Cicero's other poems.

The poem would have been as redolent of heroising epic and cosmic apparatus and as bombastic as the extant fragments of the *De consulatu suo*. Similarly, its object would have been the rewriting of history in mythological and heroic terms. Its *raison d'être* would have been self-justification, in similar vein to the various speeches after exile. The psychological impetus that produced such a work would have been the same: the once powerful, now stripped of his power, needed to restore himself in the eyes of the public, perhaps also in his own eyes. Allusions in various letters reflect, in turn, the projected scope of the lost poem (*Fam.* 5.12.8), the poet's own supreme satisfaction with his composition and his brother's concurrence of opinion (*Q.Fr.* 2.7.1), his early circulation of some parts of it (Quintus was asked to give it to Caesar to read for comment, *Q.Fr.* 2.13.2, 2.15.5), some of its divine and mythological apparatus – Apollo speaks in the council of the gods about Piso's and Gabienus' respective 'sale' and 'loss' of their armies (*Q.Fr.* 3.1.24), motifs familiar from Ciceronian invective – and, finally, that the poem comprised three books (a modestly epic length), and that Cicero wanted Lentulus to publish it (*Fam.* 1.9.23).

Büchner (1939: 1250-2), referring to *Ad Familiares* 1.6.2 and 1.9.23, and *Pro Sestio* 58, conjectures that the content of the three books would have been: (1) witness to Cicero's merit, the names of friends and enemies, perhaps also the Bona Dea affair;[12] (2) roughly the content of *Q.Fr.* 2.7.1 and 3.1.24, ending with a *concilium deorum* where Jupiter and Apollo discuss his enemies; (3) Cicero's return. That his career was drawn in glorious mythological colour is clear from a fragment from Pseudo-Sallust, *In Cic.* 4.7, quoted by the anonymous author as an example of Cicero's *'insolentia'* (arrogance). It claims that 'Minerva taught him all the arts' and *Juppiter Optimus Maximus in concilium deorum admisit, Italia exulem umeris suis reportavit* (Jupiter the Best and Greatest admitted him to the council of the gods, and Italy carried him back on her shoulders).[13]

That Cicero was probably very sensitive about criticism of his poetry is suggested by Seneca, *Dial.* 5.37.5: *Cicero, si derideres carmina eius, inimicus esset* (If you laughed at Cicero's poetry, he became your enemy). At least part of Cicero's vituperative ire was raised against Piso's apparent gibe that it had not been envy of Cicero, but 'his bad poem on his consulship' that had led to his banishment. Cicero's initial reaction was to pretend to take the outrageous statement at face value, refuting it with reference to the minuting of the Clodian bill which had enjoined his interdiction from fire and water (*Pis.* 72). Yet the gibe must have rankled. Cicero was never comfortable under criticism. His sensitivity about the verse *cedant arma* … is attested by the fact that he defended it on more than one subsequent occasion.[14]

Cicero's poems appear as an attempt to create 'the second person poetry of power' through which his readers would gain a true impression of his greatness and the malignity of the powers of darkness ranged against him.

As with his post-return rhetoric, the poems offer a subjective reflection of a myopic removal from Cicero's own consciousness of what *was*, in favour of what *could or should have been*. The failure of Cicero's verse to impress lies mostly in the fact that he did not achieve universality. His epic is bathetic because it is subjective. We need to consider whether and in what respects Ovid's poetry succeeded where Cicero failed.

8.2 Ovid and power

With Ovid we do have a poet banished 'because of his (morally) bad poetry'. With him, however, the psychological issue is different. Ovid never did have political power, in fact, he tells us that he deliberately eschewed a public career (*Tr.* 4.10.35-38). Yet what literary influence Ovid had, was 'power' of a different sort. Augustus was aware of the propagandistic power of literature. Poets that did not conform felt his ire. Ovid's exile, on the possibly trumped-up charge that the *Ars Amatoria* was corrupting Roman morals (*Tr.* 2.207, 239ff.), was ostensibly an attempt on the part of Augustus to reduce Ovid's literary power, his influence on his contemporary readers.[15]

Ovid's poems from exile purport to offer a defence of his life and art, but often appear as strongly rhetorical attack, as we have seen. Yet we have no clear idea of the effect of his missives from Tomis on a contemporary Roman readership. Of all the mysteries that surround Ovid's exile, not least is the question of publication, namely, whether the nine books of elegiacs, which he produced in about eight to ten years of exile, were circulated privately, published openly, or merely sent to individual addressees. If the books were openly circulated, they must have produced some greater effect on their readership than mere amusement. In this effect lay Ovid's lasting power: by means of the poetry of exile he was giving literary voice to the many victims of exile in the Roman world, as well as colouring Augustus' much-vaunted *pax Augusta* in a strange new light.[16] In this he was perhaps more successful than Cicero, whose wildest protestations against the injustice he had experienced seem to evoke more pity for the exile than belief in the justness of his cause.

Much of the success of Ovid's colouring of our view of Augustus through his exilic poetry lies in his ostensible submission to the emperor's criticism, which often seems to invite negative reinterpretation. A view that art should be functional, particularly in the national or moral sphere, underlies much totalitarian thought.[17] In this view, poetry can vindicate the exercise of power. Augustus' call for the celebration of *Roma et Augustus* had been met by Ovid in a host of different ways, none of them particularly acceptable within the Augustan ideological framework. His elegiac *Amores* and *Ars Amatoria* sang of a world where making love, not war, was supreme, and where *Amor,* not Roma, held absolute sway, where violence was restricted to protestations of undying troth, and warfare was limited

210

to lovers' quarrels and passionate reconciliations – not so much a sexual revolution as a witty acknowledgement of the moral *status quo*.[18]

When Ovid resorted to the epic metre, it was to a vastly different effect. Opinions are still very much divided on the Augustanism of the *Metamorphoses*, seen by some as Ovid's answer to Augustus' call, by others as another irreverent travesty of the canons of both genre and taste. Galinsky (1997) puts these speculations firmly in their place in an important paper on Ovid's own view of his craft in the *Metamorphoses*. He stresses that ancient authors were more concerned with *models* than *genres*.[19] Ulrich Schmitzer (1990) has collected a formidable array of *loci* in which he reads irreverence, irony, criticism or even a heavily negative portrayal of the emperor's person, family life and political aims.[20] One may criticise Schmitzer on individual aspects, but his general argument is cogent. Whether the *Fasti* (again in elegiacs) was Ovid's somewhat late attempt at serious national poetry is equally debated.[21] More on this below.

It needs to be explained why, if Ovid was relegated because of his subversive elegiacs, he chose for his major medium (while apparently clamouring for forgiveness and return) the very elegiacs in which he had first offended. We have seen that Ovidian poetic 'apology' for the two things which he claims Augustus has accused him of doing (*writing* some things he should not have, and *seeing* something forbidden, thereby wounding the emperor personally), is couched in *Tristia* 2 in the vigorous terms of a rhetorical *controversia*. Where the exile does not plead innocence, he makes veiled but strong counter-accusations. Augustus appears as that worst of monsters, a curtailer of free speech and a literary iconoclast.

In what follows we shall first briefly consider Ovid's exilic poetry as elegy, that is, lament, and then discuss how Ovid uses the conventions of *recusatio* to show up Augustus' call for the celebration of *Roma et Augustus* as unwarranted interference in his poetic freedom. Next certain intertextual strands will be traced in an attempt to relate the exilic poetry to a number of different works (and diverse genres) that either serve to colour what he says in exile, or against which the author seems to be pitching his material. The chapter ends with a consideration of the extent to which Ovid's exilic poetry works to repudiate political power through the power of his Muse.

8.3 *Flebile carmen*: Ovid's exilic poetry as elegy

The most basic common characteristic of all ancient elegy, if considered according to its contemporary criteria, was metre. Ovid chose this form as the consistent medium for his exilic writings. We need to consider why and how he did this. The poet's various earlier works in this metre all appear to exercise an influence on his exilic oeuvre. Before Ovid's earlier mythological, didactic and national excursions into the genre, Roman elegy had come to have a very specialised meaning relating to its essentially erotic content. Ovid's humorous inversion of erotic elegy in the *Amores* and his adaptation of its conventions and metre to didactic poetry in the *Ars Amatoria* had apparently prompted him to adapt the convention even further. We have seen that the *Heroides* and *Fasti* gave new direction to the elegiac tradition. Exile gave impetus to the poet's creative ingenuity in once again adapting his elegy to new circumstances.

In this section, after brief discussion of its origins, we shall consider Ovid's innovative adaptation in exile of the various conventions of the genre. Formally, the *Tristia* and *Epistolae ex Ponto* conform to the Roman elegiac tradition. The principle of *variatio* orders these collections of disparate poems written in the elegiac metre. Each collection, whether comprising a single book (*Tr.* 5) or a closely allied group (*Pont.* 1-3), has its programmatic *prooemium*[22] and epilogue.[23] Pairing of poems, where either tone or stance is varied, occurs.[24] Yet the tone is vastly different. In exile, Roman elegy returns to its origins as a *flebile carmen* (sad song).[25] The sadness is perhaps not new, but its cause most definitely is; from lament at the harshness of a mistress, the poet turns to lament at the harshness of the emperor, of Fate, and of his physical surroundings.

The origins of Roman elegy are fairly obscure. Different theories about its development from Greek prototypes are, however, consistent in ascribing a central role to Cornelius Gallus, the politician-poet who fell foul of Augustus.[26] Quintilian's canon of four elegiac poets, Tibullus, Propertius, Ovid, Gallus, appears based on order of preference (10.1.93). Ovid places himself chronologically fourth in the series, Gallus, Tibullus, Propertius (*Tr.* 4.10.53, 54).[27] Gallus' innovation may have been formal, imitating Catullus' expansion of epigram into longer poems, while reducing the Greek elegiac (which, like epic, was conventionally a single connected poem, encompassing a whole book) to a collection of shorter, discrete and subjective poems with no formal linkages. Catullus had already incorporated myth into subjective elegy. Gallus may have developed this concept by placing himself 'within a myth' (possibly the myth of Acontius).[28] Subjective 'entering into myth' of the suffering *persona* (whether lover or exile) appears as a characteristic of earlier elegy, to which our poet returns.[29] In exile, Ovid creates the myth of an heroic exile persecuted by an angry god.[30]

Roman erotic elegy is never 'narrative', depicting the chronology of an *affaire* from first joy to final disenchantment. This applies *mutatis mutandis* equally to Ovid's exilic oeuvre.[31] Presentation of psychological 'facts' does not create a psychological 'narrative'. The composite picture of the exile's psychological relationship with Augustus, with Tomis and its inhabitants and with his Muse, is impressionistic and diffuse, showing an interesting protagonist in an interesting situation where he experiences a series of interesting emotions, sparked off by the actions of an interesting antagonist. In exile, the antagonist is in turn Augustus, Scythia, and the poet's Muse.

8. Generic Range in the Poetry of Exile

Traditionally, elegy is a *flebile carmen* (sad song).[32] Roman erotic elegy largely involved a suffering, unsuccessful lover, who does not aim at marriage. The so-called 'myth of erotic elegy', a complete, perhaps largely unreal world in which the protagonist experiences hardships at the hands of a cruel mistress, may be either an inversion of Roman social practices of the Augustan era, or a reflection of its less salubrious side. This is the world also portrayed in the *Ars Amatoria*.[33] That Ovid's *Amores* are essentially a burlesque of the elegiac tradition is generally accepted. The poet playfully inverts what is already an inversion of the normal moral code (canonised by Augustus by means of his marriage laws), also inverting the elegists' veneration of *simplicitas* to praise of *cultus* as the highest virtue. The jaunty lover of *Amores* 1 exhibits all the symptoms of love, such as pallor and emaciation, before he finds the girl. His Muse, not the girl, inspires his poetry. The girl, 'Corinna', is his *domina* (mistress), but he reduces the conventional elegiac plea, that she remain faithful, to the cynical request that he should be kept in the dark as to her infidelities. Ovid's *Amores* often show an awareness of reality, a redrawal of the erotic myth into the 'real world', where cause and effect do count. Similarly, Ovid's awareness of the realities of Roman social life and the inefficacy of laws to influence moral conduct, lies behind much of his argument in *Tristia* 2.[34]

In the *Tristia* and *Epistolae ex Ponto* the *topos* of the 'hardships of love' has been inverted to 'the hardships of exile'. Physical debilitation and emaciation are equally features of the standard elegiac lover and the unhappy exile, as depicted in *Tristia* 3.8 and *Ex Ponto* 1.10. The poet's ability to confer immortality on his mistress is transferred to the exile's wife, but the *topos* is also inverted to include the immortality offered to the poet by his Muse. The concept of 'dying of love' and even the specialised erotic value attached to *perire* have been turned into the central image of exile.[35] Since Gallus, Roman erotic elegy evidenced a strong association between love, departure and death.[36] Ovid's exilic poems, in their consistent exploitation of the metaphor of exile as death, with his usual ingenuity reverse the traditional *propemptikon* (lament at the departure of the beloved). The subjective protagonist is the one that leaves, but also the one to 'die', a ploy later used by Seneca in his adaptation of the consolatory *suasoria*.[37]

In Ovid's exilic *propemptikon*, *Tristia* 3.1, the 'beloved' that is departing, is the exile himself.[38] The exilic storm poems, *Tristia* 1.2, 1.4 and 1.11, offer the logical conclusion of a tradition that presents navigation as dangerous and impious, usually advanced as an argument to persuade the beloved to remain with the lover. The exile can never celebrate his home-coming, but frequently imagines himself doing so. In a touching inversion of elegiac 'home-coming' the exile imagines himself embracing his wife and feeling how aged and thin she has become through vicarious suffering (*Pont.* 1.4.47-56).[39]

213

Other specialised subgenres of elegy, [40] such as the *paraklausithyron* or *komos* (lament before the lover's closed door), and *genethliakon* (birthday poem), received burlesque treatment in the *Amores*.[41] *Tristia* 3.2.24ff. offers a new version of a *paraklausithyron*. This time it is not a sad lover before his mistress' door, but an even sadder exile knocking and receiving no admittance at death's door. *Tristia* 3.13, addressing the exile's own birthday, inverts the *topos* of a *genethliakon* into its diametric opposite, with an effect that Cairns (1972: 128f.) calls 'almost blasphemous'. A poem celebrating his wife's birthday (*Tr.* 5.5) subverts usually joyful celebration into a subjective narration of the distant husband's vicarious and lonely birthday ritual, comprising just another aspect of his sadness.[42]

The poet stresses frequently, by playful punning allusion,[43] that the poetry of exile does not have 'love' as its topic. The whole oeuvre is ostensibly aimed at negating the poet's earlier amorous creativity. An inversion of the central elegiac theme of the 'lover as soldier' (*Am.* 3.9) could therefore be expected. The poet does not, however, offer as substitute a celebration of the glories of Augustan imperial warfare. He redraws the picture of the erstwhile lover, as a new but reluctant soldier, battling, first, with an unholy conspiracy by the dire powers of nature and an insufficiently established *pax Augusta*, and, second, with his own lot as the unhappy victim of supreme and unrelenting divine ire (*Pont.* 1.2.27, 28).[44] While the exile 'makes war and not love', the poet again creates something new from a tradition that he himself formerly sent into new directions.

8.4 Exilic *recusatio*: Ovid's *apologia pro vita arteque sua*[45]

It was conventional for non-epic poets to speak of their poetry as negligible, as in Catullus' reference to his poems as *nugae* (nothings) in *Carm.* 1.4. Ostensible modesty in the Catullan *quidquid hoc libelli / qualecumque* (this little book, whatever it's like, *ibid.* 8, 9) is undercut by the fierce pride of the conclusion of the poem.[46] Similarly, Ovid's ostensibly negative view of his exilic verse is frequently undercut by positive vindication, as in *Tristia* 4.10.117ff., the poet's hymn to his Muse. This mix of denigration of his ability and pride in its power starts at *Tristia* 1.6.29-36, with an explanation to his wife that his 'slight' poetic powers will be devoted to ensuring her immortality.[47]

Such poetic denigration was traditionally offered in a *recusatio*, an explanation by the poet of a minor genre of his reasons for avoiding epic.[48] Wimmel (1960) usefully notes the following elements in *recusatio* in its fullest form: a noble patron's request to sing of kings and heroes, an apology based on the weakness and inferiority of the poet's talent as opposed to the redoubtable grandeur of the topic proposed, an attempt to comply, which is foiled by the apparition of a divine warning figure, frustration of an attempt by Envy to harm the poet, and finally, vindication of the poet's work, slender though it be, on the authority of a higher god.[49]

In Ovid's exilic oeuvre this 'authority' is the poet's Muse, [50] who is occasionally, particularly in the earlier books, portrayed as a kind of blind necessity, an *Ananke*, driving the poet to his doom.

Throughout his oeuvre, Ovid exploits the possibilities of the genre in various guises,[51] particularly in his vindication, in the Callimachean tradition, of the power of his lesser poetry to withstand the onslaughts of *Livor edax* ('mordant Envy', as in *Am.* 1.15.1, *Rem.* 389). The *topoi* recur in the exilic works. Ovid's consistent use of elements of *recusatio* was in the past the single most misunderstood aspect of his exilic poetry. Continued protests of debilitated powers, inability to meet the requirements of the Augustan demand for national epic, and pleas of helplessness, weakening verbal facility, even loss of his mother tongue, should not be taken at face value.[52] They are the poet's adaptations of the recusatory technique to his apologetic purpose.[53]

We have seen that Ovid's longest elegy, *Tristia* 2, offers a virtuoso reprise of the whole corpus of ancient literature, Greek and Roman, as one long celebration of *amor*, in which the poet sees himself as the only exponent to suffer for it.[54] Parts of *Tristia* 2 are clearly recusatory. Verses 321-38 exhibit the characteristics distinguished by Wimmel: the call to write national poetry (321-2), by the ruler, whose own deeds merit renown (323-4); the poet's initial willingness (325-6); his inability couched in agricultural (327-8) and nautical (329-30) terms; denigration even of an ability to master smaller genres (331-2); the impossibility of attempting standard mythological epic (333-4); the greater challenge of singing of the deeds of the great patron (335-6); attempt and failure (337-8);[55] return to a lesser genre (339-40). Innovation lies in the identity of the 'warning god': not Apollo or the Muses, *sed me mea fata trahebant* (but my fate dragged me thence, 341).

From verse 548 onward the poet revokes all he has said with gay abandon, again employing nautical imagery: *saepe dedi nostrae grandia vela rati* (I often hoisted grand sails on my ship), alluding to his (lost) tragedy, the *Medea*, to the *Metamorphoses*, which he designates as 'an epic combining Lucretian origins of things with Vergilian celebration of the present era' (549-60), and to the *Fasti* (touted here as his own 'national poetry'), suitably dedicated to the noble patron. This is counter-*recusatio*, as playful as its prototype, offering a vigorous defence of so-called 'lesser genres' while it insists that his tales of rape and changing forms (which readers would remember included the metamorphosis of Julius Caesar into a god) were his honest attempt to come to grips with epic themes.[56]

In *Tristia* 4.10 an apologia for the poet's life is couched in recusatory terms, adapted and partly reversed. The young poet's father, who tried to deflect his attention from poetry (21), represents the influential patron; public life, which the young poet attempted, represents the 'great deeds of heroes'. The poet's 'lesser powers' are expressed in terms of physical weakness:

curia restabat: clavi mensura coacta est;
  maius erat nostris viribus illud opus.
nec patiens corpus, nec mens fuit apta labori,
  sollicitaeque fugax ambitionis eram.   (*Tr.* 4.10.35-8)

> The senate was all I hadn't yet reached; the wide stripe of my youthful garb
> was narrowed to formal dimensions; but that job was too great for my feeble
> powers. My body couldn't take the strain, my mind couldn't concentrate, and
> I became a refugee from political candidacy and the worries it brings.

The 'warning god' is represented by the Muses themselves, who called
the poet to their service. He has since devoted himself to poetry, admiring
and honouring other poets as *praesentes divi* (present gods). Here Ovid
depicts himself solely as elegist, ignoring his excursions into epic and
tragedy.[57] After further autobiographical details, including persecution by
malignant fate, Ovid phrases the vindication of his Muse against *livor
iniquo/ ... dente ...* (jealousy with its mean teeth, *ibid.* 123, 124) in a
combination of Hesiodic and Horatian terms, affirming his power as *vates*,
singer of divine truth (v. 129).[58]

Ovidian *recusatio* is discernibly programmatic, consistently appearing
in the first and last poems of each book, except in *Ex Ponto* 4, where it
occurs in the second poem.[59] Our poet does not frame all his recusatory
attempts in the full-blown pattern distinguished by Wimmel. *Topoi* most
frequently omitted are the explicit reference to a noble patron's expectations, and the 'warning god' that deflects the poet from his attempt. The
most consistently occurring *topos* is 'paucity of poetic skill'. In what follows
we shall consider variations on the pattern, which recur as a constant
element of the poet's rebuttals of the censure he imputes to Augustus.

A Callimachean *recusatio* appears in *Ex Ponto* 3 in serial form. Its third
poem announces a forthcoming triumph. The epiphany of the sad and
sorry *Amor*, solemnly vindicating the poet's purity of intention in a parody
of formulary Roman legal rhetoric (*Pont.* 3.3.67-80), calls him away from
previous, less weighty themes.[60] The 'warning god-figure' here speaks for
the noble patron, by implication calling for the poetic celebration of a
triumph. In the next poem the mooted triumph poem (now either lost or
never attempted) is excused for its 'poor quality' in new terms. The poet
was sad (*Pont.* 3.4.1-6, 45-50) and he had to write at second-hand, depending on his 'mind's eye' (16-36) and on hearsay (37-44). The theme is no
longer fresh in people's minds (51-62) and a tepid topic is not worthy of the
great general Tiberius (63-4). His Muse has apologised for herself (65-6).

Predictably, a counter-*recusatio* intervenes, with a vindication of the
poet's position in the sacred college of poets (67-72). Equally predictably,
the power of *livor* with its carping tooth (73-4) is discounted, for the poet,
being virtually dead, is beyond the power of envy (75-6). In a return to the
recusatory mode, the poet illustrates the superiority of his will to celebrate
the prince over the feebleness of his deed, the triumph-poem itself (79-82).

The subject would have been too great even for Vergil (83-4). The unsuitability of elegy for epic themes is illustrated with the playful adaptation (from *Am.* 1.1.1) of chariot-imagery, to a ludicrous cart with wheels of disparate size (85-8). The poem finally shifts into a triumphant vindication of the prophetic power of poetry (93-4), turning 'triumph' into 'prophecy', and giving in miniature what the poet has before pretended to have been unequal to presenting (95-114). This is a subtle poetic adaptation of *praeteritio* as rhetorical device.[61]

Poetics, that is, discussion of the poet's craft, is a frequent theme in ancient poetry. The conventions of *recusatio* inform much of the poetics of Ovid's exilic works, colouring what he says of his own manner of composition by relating it to the externals of his place of exile ('my poetry is bad because I live in a bad place').[62] Here we need to distinguish between the person of the creative poet, in control of his material, and a *persona*, the debilitated poet-exile, object of his discourse. Conventional denigration of the exilic poetry is justified in terms of the place of exile:

> *siqua videbuntur casu non dicta Latine,*
> *in qua scribebat, barbara terra fuit.*   (*Tr.* 3.1.17, 18)

If [the poems] perhaps will seem to have been said in an un-Latin way, it was a barbarous country in which [their author] was writing.[63]

The elegance of Ovid's Latin is not the issue; it continues unaltered. The real point is the fact that the poet is exiled to a barbarous land. These poems no longer are 'sung' (*canta*) but are 'said' (*dicta*). Exile has made the formerly inspired singer descend into prose, and in broken Latin, at that.

As always with Ovid, the disgraced exile manages to have every argument both ways. *Ex Ponto* 1.5 explains to Cotta Maximus that the poet's talent has rusted away (3-8), that he composes without correction, a *topos* familiar since Horace (9-20),[64] but that his Muse, 'does not need polish to make him famous among the Getae' (57-70). This is in itself a negative factor; it is no cause for joy to the debilitated poet-exile that the barbarians among whom he composes are happy with any old stuff. The poem manages to exploit the pathetic appeal of both fame and non-fame, of being celebrated at Rome while not being there to enjoy it (75-82), and the pathos inherent in doubt whether the poet's fame has survived his living death (83-6). Similarly *Tristia* 5.7 recalls his former work with pride, denying that the poet, living among the Sarmatians, has 'forgotten love poetry' (21-5), and commenting that his works are being 'danced to' in Rome. He is gratified to have heard this, and explains that he is still composing, albeit in 'broken Latin' (57-8), for poetry offers oblivion from his woes. The barbarity of his poetry and the barbarity of his surroundings are equally open to question.

Often unfavourable place and unkind emperor seem conjoined in their persecution of poet and poetry. Both serve to reduce the quality of the exile-poet's work, but he goes on writing, in the hope of placating his persecutor, who is drawn in negative terms. *Tristia* 1.11 concludes the first volume with a plea for the 'candid reader's' indulgence (1, 2), for the storm at sea had frightened the poet-exile so much that the quality of his work was affected (33-42). The picture of the fearful poet holding body, soul, paper and pen together in the face of a howling storm, is a charming fantasy concluding an interesting book. The last two couplets may be read as a metaphor for the emperor's persecution of the poet for daring to continue composition in the face of his censure:

> improba pugnat hiemps indignaturque, quod ausim
>   scribere se rigidas incutiente minas.
> vincat hiemps hominem; sed eodem tempore, quaeso,
>   ipse modum statuam carminis, illa sui.   (*Tr.* 1.11.41-4)

Unkind winter batters me, indignant that I should dare to go on scribbling while he battles on with his unbending threats. Let the storm beat the man; but at the same time, I pray, let me put an end to my poem, just as winter puts an end to her storm.

We must take as incredible a claim that the exiled poet's talent has 'waned through disuse' (*Tr.* 5.12.21-32). This poem dates from about AD 11, when the poet's output was steady, frequent, and prolific. It is a reply to a friend's consolatory exhortation to cheer himself by writing. Protestations of sterility are framed by the outrageous but solemn plea that such circumstances would have kept Socrates from writing, and the equally outrageous assertion that the poet is now following the *lathê biosas*-principle, preferring to remain unknown.[65] Similarly the richness of his literary allusion throughout has created an atmosphere within which the reader must either admire the poet's phenomenally prodigious memory, or laugh heartily at the exile's claim (51-8) that he has no books in exile, is speaking Getic and Sarmatian, seems to have forgotten his Latin, and consigns to the fire whatever he writes (59-68).[66]

Throughout counter-*recusatio* accompanies nearly every claim by the exile-poet of waning powers. The introductory poem of the second book of Pontic epistles strikes a new counter-recusatory note. First *recusatio* is proffered at second-hand. The poet tells Salanus, Germanicus' friend and tutor of oratory, that his talent failed him in an attempt to portray Germanicus' triumph (27-32). Salanus is thanked for approbation of the poet's 'small talents' (17-26). Thereafter the exile gratuitously offers Germanicus future celebration in his poetry, in exchange for aid (49-66). The exile is again having it both ways, but his reliance on the efficacy of his kind of poetry to confer lasting fame has gained in prominence against earlier claims of poetic weakness.[67]

Finally, *Ex Ponto* 4.16 offers a unique approach to Callimachean *recu-*

satio. After reviling an enemy, the personification of *Livor* (1, 2), the exiled poet justifies his own position by placing himself 'last but not least' in a long catalogue of poets, ranging from exponents of epic, through pastoral, Pindaric odes, tragedy, comedy and lyric, to elegiac poetry (*Pont*. 4.16.3-46). He does not excuse himself for not attempting the 'greater' forms, merely shows himself as great in his chosen field. A final pathetic repudiation of *Livor* (47-52) depicts a poetic voice that lives on, after all things, even life itself, have been lost. *Livor* may continue to carp, but its very attack is proof of the immortality of the exile's poetry. Here it is difficult to distinguish separate *personae*. Creator-poet and exile together have survived the onslaughts of a powerful opponent, co-operating in a final rebuttal of his power to destroy.

8.5 Ovid's answer to the Augustan challenge: the poetry of power repudiated

So Ovid creatively repudiates, by pretending subservience, the wielder of political power who sought to still his poetic voice. His answer to Augustus' call for 'national poetry' was equally ambivalent. The challenge of 'national usefulness' that Augustus offered the poets of his time was met differently by different poets. It is a topic that still receives much critical attention, but this debate cannot be re-argued here. Suffice it to say that each poet coped in his own way with a basic uneasiness. Vergil's answer was perhaps the exposition of the personal travails of a public figure. Horace offered his readers the chance to interpret at least some of his national and political poetry as ironic. Tibullus by and large ignored the plea. Propertius' fourth book has been variously interpreted.[68]

We have seen that Ovid rose to the Augustan challenge in a host of different ways, none of them particularly acceptable within the Augustan ideological framework. Sometimes the poet appears to counter the challenge directly, as in his frequent intertextual allusions to Cornelius Gallus, who appears to play a role in the anti-Augustan texture of the poetry, as well as in its elegiac origins, as we have seen above.[69] Ovid's close association with Gallus may have been more than mere admiration of a predecessor. Gallus' loss of imperial *amicitia* was exile of a sort, as it deprived the politician of all further access to power, and to the political community within which he functioned. Gallus sought refuge in death. Ovid, no politician, experienced 'living death', while exploring new ways to retain his literary power. *Recusatio* is only one of these ways.

In this section we shall consider how Ovid combines intertextual allusion to a variety of works, including his own, with an apparently bland but often ironic acceptance of Augustus' own prescriptive moral and literary parameters, thereby repudiating the emperor's claim to power over the private lives of Roman citizens. Not the least of his weapons is the allusive use of Augustus' own autobiography. In addition, reminiscences of people and things that Augustus would best have forgotten range from the disgraced Gallus to Augustus' own wayward daughter and aspects of the poet's own earlier works.

We start with Gallus. A sentiment in Vergil's *Eclogues* 10.69, often echoed in elegy, and generally accepted as originating with Gallus, *Omnia vincit Amor; et nos cedamus Amori* (Love conquers everything; let us also give way to love), is adapted by our poet to offer an apparent palinode to the disgraced erotic elegy of the exile's former life. Ovid vindicates his belief in his own intellectual power, by reworking the formula to read: *animus tamen omnia vincit* (still, my intellect conquers everything, *Pont.* 2.7.75). This is as suitable a monument to Gallus as it is to Ovid.

The last four of the Gallan verses found at Quasr Ibrîm are fragmentary, but seem to refer to the divine inspiration required by any poetic composition that would be worthy of the poet's mistress. The phrase *carmina ... digna*[70] clearly belongs to the corpus of formulary elegiac diction. Ovid's use of the term, as pathetic fallacy, to point to the condition of the exile, inverts the Gallan concept of divine inspiration.[71] As we have noted in the section above, the exiled poet shows his poems as suitable to his condition and the place of exile:

> *carmina nulla sunt scripta, aut qualia cernis,*
> *digna sui domini tempore, digna loco.* (*Tr.* 5.12.35)

No songs have been written except the kind that you see, worthy of the straits of their owner, and worthy of the place.

These examples illustrate not only the poetic convenience of available Gallan *topoi* and precedents, but Ovid's apparently deliberate employment of literary allusions as weapons of polemic. These he combines with echoes of Augustus' autobiography to form a network of innuendo. Ironic allusions to what appears as Augustus' own view of his achievements are frequent. Ovid's source would have been the thirteen books of Augustus' lost autobiography, the *Commentarii de vita sua*, covering the emperor's life up to about 25 BC. This document, probably literary in style but propagandistic in thrust,[72] was far more detailed than Augustus' extant *Res Gestae*.[73] Ovid would, by AD 9, have been aware of the thrust of Augustus' autobiographical statements, perhaps with the text of either or both documents.

Ovid's own autobiography, *Tristia* 4.10.3-108, appears to allude to contrasting aspects in the careers of poet and emperor. At nineteen, the emperor chose the way to public achievement, the poet turned to the privacy of personal *otium*. The emperor's adoptive ancestry, although bolstered by the myth of the divinity of the Julian line, contrasts with the poet's reliance on 'real nobility from a long line'. Critics read other parallels, such as number of marriages and progeniture of a single daughter by each, but the analogy should not be pushed.[74]

8. Generic Range in the Poetry of Exile

Amores 2.7.17f., *resque domi gestas et mea bella cano* (both my achievements in my bedroom and my sort of battles I sing) employs a formula reminiscent of the opening words of the introduction to the *Res Gestae*: *Rerum gestarum divi Augusti ... exemplar subiectum* (a copy is set out below of the achievements of the divine Augustus)[75] The phrase is an autobiographical cliché. Whether the similarity is coincidental or deliberate, the supremacy of private emotion over public involvement underlies Ovidian celebration of the palindromic *Amor*, when celebration of Roma was called for. Passages in the exilic poems seem to celebrate *Roma et Augustus* in terms reminiscent of the *Res Gestae* itself. In exile the poet appears at last to have repudiated erotic *amor* as he celebrates *Roma* and his friends at home, but the Rome he longs for is still the Rome of private affection.[76] In its martial aspects, Rome's powerlessness to pacify the savages of its own distant provinces receives most emphasis. His 'Augustus' is an unjust despot.[77]

Ovid's treatment of *Roma et Augustus* cannot be neatly separated and treated *seriatim*. The twin concepts are as inextricably intertwined here, as ever in the imagination of the emperor's subjects, or in his own intentions.[78] Augustus' claim to have established the 'Augustan Peace' (*RG* 12 and 13, Suet. *Aug.* 22.1) seems to be willfully countered by much of Ovid's depiction of life at Tomis. Roman generals occasionally triumph, Augustus simultaneously rules at home and abroad through the mediation of his adopted son Tiberius (*Tr.* 2.225-32), but in the Pontic area there is no hope of peace.[79] The *pax Romana* (Roman Peace) is never termed such. Its absence is spelled out at *Ex Ponto* 2.5.18 *quae minus Augusta pace fruatur humus* (a soil that enjoys too little of the Augustan Peace).

Augustus' claim that through the agency of his stepson, Tiberius, he defeated and pacified the peoples from across the Danube is echoed in *Tristia* 2.173 ff. (*per quem bella geri ...* etc., 'through whose agency you wage your wars'), but it is countered and refuted by the exile's every statement about the unpacified state of Tomis. Throughout the nine years or so of Ovid's exile, campaigns on the Rhine wax and wane, Roman armies subjugate all Europe, but the town is in a perpetual state of siege. Since the *Georgics* and before, Roman readers have known that marauders cross the frozen river; from Ovid they get no more factual detail, but learn of the fears of a Roman exile living in a sham state of peace. In *Tristia* 3.10 the poet echoes a Vergilian, stylised depiction of war-torn Scythia,[80] affording contrast with most of Augustus' claims to 'suppression of a Dacian army' (*RG* 30.2, Suet. *Aug.* 21.1).

The poet strongly associates the exile as *persona* with the powerful patron whom he has offended. In a 'swan-song' (which does not prove to be such), *Tristia* 5.1.69-78 appears as a disarming acknowledgement of the poor quality of the poetry, yet he goes on to claim *inter Sauromatas ingeniosus eram* (among the Sauromati I was becoming a genius, 74). The Sarmatians (and Bastarnae, as at *Tr.* 2.198) in so far as they can be geographically placed, inhabited far-flung stretches of southern Russia to the north, distant from Tomis. Ovid's frequent portrayal of their ferocity (as in *Tr.* 4.8.16) counters Augustus' claim: *Nostram amicitiam appetiverunt per legatos Bastarnae Scythaeque et Sarmatarum qui sunt citra flumen Tanaim et ultra reges, Albanorumque rex et Hiberorum et Medorum* (The Bastarnae, Scythians and the kings of the Sarmatians on either side of the river Don, and the kings of the Albanians and the Iberians and the Medes sent embassies to seek our friendship, *RG* 31.2).[81] As in Augustus' designation of his wreath of friendly nations, the actual distance between Tomis and the far-northern 'Sarmatian land' is ignored by Ovid. Both authors impress upon the civilised world the distance they have traversed: Augustus as eager empire-builder, Ovid as reluctant exile. Both are appreciated by the savage world they describe.

During his 'speech for his defence', the exiled poet ironically refers to Augustan moral reform, and the Augustan marriage laws:

> *urbs quoque te et legum lassat tutela tuarum*
> *et morum, similis quos cupis esse tuis.*   (*Tr.* 2.233-4)

The city, too, tires you, and also the guardianship of your laws and their morals, which you want to be like yours.

The phrasing appears to echo and conflate statements in *RG* 6, referring to Augustus' appointment by the Senate and people as *curator legum et morum* (guardian of laws and morals), and *RG* 8.5, which commemorates rather ambiguously phrased 'new laws' which revived the obsolescent customs of the Roman ancestors, and Augustus' example in practising them: *Legibus novis me auctore latis multa exempla maiorum exolescentia iam ex nostro saeculo reduxi et ipse multarum rerum exempla imitanda posteris tradidi* (By new laws passed on my proposal I brought back into use many exemplary practices of our ancestors which were disappearing in our time, and in many ways I myself transmitted exemplary practices to posterity for their imitation (trans. Brunt and Moore)). The verbal echo is faint. The conceptual echo is strong. Ovid leaves it to his reader to remember tales of Augustus' various extra-marital excursions and blandly echoes the pious wish that Roman citizens will follow his example.

In this poem Ovid concludes that Augustus' many duties have left him no *otium*, no time to read the poet's early work, particularly the offending erotic works. As O'Gorman (1997: n. 34) notes, the poet figures the emperor as 'model reader' and ascribes to him a reinscription of censorship into poetic discourse. The allusion here gains in piquancy when one recognises Vergil's *tantae molis erat* ... (so great was the burden ...) *in hoc tantarum pondere rerum* (in this burden of such great matters, *Tr.* 2.237). This may not so much be parody of Vergil's national poetry, as completion, addition of another facet. Vergil was perhaps not wholly uncritical of Augustan imperial achievement. Ovid is more certainly critical of Augustan regulation of private morality by means of civil laws, and the Augustan national ethic.

The unprecedented intrusion of the state into private morality was perhaps the most startling innovation of the imperial regime. Yet the exiled poet's attitude to his wife appears, in contrast with the amorality of his erotic elegies, to support the ideal of the sanctity of marriage propagated in *leges Iuliae* and the *lex Papia Poppaea*. These laws as embodiment of traditional Roman ethics had turned previously private codes into public ones. Here, by appropriating the Augustan ideal of *pietas*, the poet is at least paying lip service to Roman traditional views, but he still shows that morality stems from private choice and not from public coercion.[82]

Last we turn to the poet's use of self-referential allusion as one of the ways whereby he could counter Augustus' control over his creativity. Ovid's response to the national ideal in the exilic poems gains in piquancy when it is read in conjunction with his other 'national' work. The *Fasti*, the work on which the poet was engaged when the blow of relegation fell, is often designated Ovid's most 'sincere' answer to Augustan demands for ideologically useful and nationalistically ornamental poetry, but this interpretation is coming into increasing question.[83] The *Fasti*, chronologically closest in time of composition to the exilic works, form an important link with the poet's earlier models, acting as a filter, verbally and conceptually. Their influence is important at the verbal level, particularly in the poet's manner of indicating time, in certain cosmic concepts, in the treatment of aspects of the Roman national myth, in depictions of Rome, and in interpretation of the endeavours and achievements of the *Pax Augusta*.[84] The general trends of thought and tone in the two works often coincide.[85]

Of the 'twelve books' of the *Fasti* (*sex ... totidemque libellos*, 'six books, and as many again', *Tr.* 2.549), July to December may have been lost, or may never have been written.[86] Critics have read ironical and anti-nationalistic burlesque into the *Fasti*: only in praising Augustus could a poet succeed in opposing him. Celebration of the calendar was one way of pointing to Augustus' appropriation even of the designators of time in service of his imperial image, such as the Horologium Augusti. Both by what the poet includes and what he omits his ostensible homage can work as subversion.

Ovid's celebration of Augustus' achievement of the title *pater patriae*[87] at *Fasti* 2.133-44 is nonchalantly disrespectful. In a naively glib series of odious comparisons between Augustus and Romulus, not the least suggestive is verse 139 *tu rapis, hic castas duce se iubet esse maritas* (you, Romulus, grab – more properly, *rape* – wives, he commands wives to be chaste, while following your lead). Contrast of Romulus' divine descent with Augustus' deification of his own father offers subtle comment on imperial arrogation of divinity. In a similar fashion, the exile freely uses the terms *pater patriae* and *parens* (*Tr.* 2.157, 181 and 574) in address to the emperor, subverting its referential range by such appropriation.

Augustus' proud boast that he restored eighty-two temples (*RG* 20.4, Suet. *Aug.* 30.2) appears to have prompted Ovid virtually to negate the whole of the Roman pantheon in the exilic poems. Apart from Augustus as Jupiter, the Roman gods hardly feature. However, a formerly 'foreign' cult, now well established and under imperial patronage, the cult of the Magna Mater, receives particular attention in *Ex Ponto* 1.1.37-54. Syncretism had long since conflated the Egyptian Isis, the Phrygian Cybele and the Roman Mater Matuta into a singly conceptualised deity. The Pontic epistles start with a curious address to Brutus, demanding his services as publisher (*Pont.* 1.1), admitting to the sad contents of his poems (15-16) and depicting the exile-poet as a votive of Cybele (45-6), propitiating a powerful antagonist, as a blinded votary of the dire goddess, who still continues to shout her praise. He explicitly denies all wrong-doing, comparing himself favourably (and dangerously) with Brutus and Antony (23-6).

Ovid's discursive treatment of the Attis myth, the story of the chaste Claudia Quintia and the inauguration of the cult at Rome in *Fasti* 4.179-372 offered the poet an opportunity of ostensibly placating various members of the imperial family, including Livia as a human 'Magna Mater'. With her connections to the Claudian line, Livia would in a sense offer opposition to the Julian Venus. The narrative there is irreverent and fraught with dubious innuendo.[88] Now in *Ex Ponto* 1.1 the poet in a fanciful and bold metaphor explains that the exile is a mendicant before the temple of this revered goddess (whose temple, the reader will remember, Augustus elaborately restored, so *RG* 19.2):

> *en ego pro sistro Phrygique foramine buxi*
> *gentis Iuliae nomina sancta fero.* (*Pont.* 1.1.45-6)

Look, I'm not carrying a sistrum or pipe of Phrygian boxwood; I dangle the hallowed names of the Julian family.

The Julian names are irreverently likened to castanets. Augustus, and not Livia, is being celebrated with the rites of the Magna Mater. Next (47-54) the poet alludes to penitents, who have 'put out their eyes', sitting before the temple of Isis, the scene of their sacrilege. Verbal self-echoes are subtle, *meruisse* (53) for *merui* (*Fast.* 4.239), just enough alliteration with *p*, to evoke memories of the thrust of the *Fasti* passage: the self-inflicted castration of Attis. The intertextual echo virtually compels the reader to interpret the so-called 'blinding of a penitent' as a euphemism.[89] The whole passage, with its graphic picture of bizarre cult practices, is evocative of the cosmopolitan Rome of Augustus. Its implication points to a virtual literary emasculation of the poet at the behest of a cruel and despotic (male) 'goddess'.

8. Generic Range in the Poetry of Exile

In Ovid's works the Augustan building programme and his moral reforms are sometimes conflated and mocked together. His treatment of the stock idea of Romulus as the founder of Roman greatness at *Ars Amatoria* 1.89ff. is obvious burlesque, also in its deliberate switch of the venue of the rape of the Sabines from a religious festival to the theatre. The same irreverent burlesque of puritanical Roman views of circus and theatre lies behind Ovid's casuistic arguments in *Tristia* 2.279-84, that these are the places for assignations and pickups, of *amor* at its most casual. Roman porticoes serve the same purpose.[90] At *Tristia* 2.285 the exile asks the emperor:

> *cum quaedam spatientur in hoc, ut amator eodem*
> *conveniat, quare porticus ulla patet?*

While one woman can cruise an arcade so that a lover can meet her there, why on earth is any arcade allowed to stay open?

The place for pick-ups is the *porticus Liviae*, housing the shrine to *Concordia*, dedicated by Livia and Tiberius in 7 BC, possibly to celebrate 'the concord of married love' between Augustus and Livia.[91] So it's their fault that Roman lovers transgress. The same irreverence that made fun of Augustus' appropriation of traditional religion in Ovid's *Fasti* here shines from the exilic poem. Several passages in the *Fasti* feature *Concordia* (e.g. 1.637ff.). *Fasti* 6 opens with a quarrel between three goddesses, Juno (queen of heaven, and patroness of Livia) Juventus (to whom Augustus had built a temple, *RG* 19), and the goddess 'Concordia'. Each claims to be the eponymous goddess of the month of June. The poet-narrator, a wiser 'second Paris', refuses to be caught, and does not give his final judgement (6.97-100).[92] The clash between their patron deities and the personification of concord may insinuate its opposite in the relationship of Livia and Augustus.

The theme of triumph and imperial panegyric is frequently ironised.[93] Various triumph poems appear 'national' in intention. These reverse the poet's stance in the *Amores*, where the 'ascendancy of *AMOR*' appears as the direct palinode of the nationalistic concept of *ROMA*. Yet we have seen that '*Amor triumphans*' receives a sad echo at *Ex Ponto* 3.3, where a bedraggled personified 'Amor', after his long flight to the ends of the earth, has just enough strength left to be able to first to vindicate the exile and then to announce Tiberius' impending triumph. A debilitated *AMOR* implies a powerless *ROMA*.

The exile twice claims (to Salanus *Pont.* 2.5.27ff., Rufinus *Pont.* 3.4.3ff.) that he had composed a triumph poem, but there is no trace of such a poem. A 'prophecy' of a future triumph (3.4.93-6) claiming divine inspiration, appears to vindicate the poet's Muse. The preceding couplet, ironically placing the exile 'beside the Ister, whose water is drunk by *non bene*

225

pacatis ... Getis' (badly-tamed Getae), undercuts this vision of triumph. The poem is an exercise in *praeteritio*; the poet is explaining that his 'debilitated powers' (vv. 4-22) and lack of eye-witness accounts, have rendered him unable to do justice to Tiberius' triumph. He lists as 'beyond his powers of description' all the usual elements of such a triumph (23-70). Yet this most literary poet in his other works seldom relied on physical observation. We have noted before that the whole elegant exercise, complete with conventional recusatory preamble, may be the very 'triumph poem' that he promises. *Praeteritio* works as a travesty of convention. As we noted above, the playful adaptation of a typically Ovidian *topos*, the disparity in size of the wheels of his 'poetic chariot' (85, 6), being a typical recusatory metaphor, is a strong pointer to irony. The poem is a joke.

As in the *Fasti*, allusions to Augustus' family life are problematic. References to Tiberius appear as near-gibes, underlining the younger man's late adoption into the imperial family.[94] Free use of the terms *pater patriae* and *parens* (*Tr.* 2.157, 181 and 574) are adapted to Augustus' 'fathering' of Tiberius, who favours his *pater* in face and fortune. A poem celebrating Tiberius' projected triumph of the year 12 describes a monument, the *Ara iustitiae Augusti*, inaugurated on 8 January, AD 13.[95] The exile writes of it by hearsay. The monument is an outward and visible sign of Tiberius' inward and spiritual grace. His bosom is a temple dedicated to his *pater*, at which, so the exile has heard, the divine son:

> *tura prius sanctis imposuisse focis*
> *iustitiamque sui caste placasse parentis*
> *illo quae templum pectore semper habet.*   (*Pont.* 2.1.32-4)

... had first offered incense on the sacred hearth, and had with chaste zeal placated the figure of his own true father's Justice, which he holds eternally enshrined in that great heart of his.

The concept of an imperial heart as a 'temple' and prototype of the marble edifice recurs; now Justice is ensconced in Augustus' own bosom. Interpretation of irony is left to the reader's own judgement:

> *Iustitia vires temperat ille suas.*
> *nuper eam Caesar facto de marmore templo*
> *iampridem posuit mentis in aede suo.*   (*Pont.* 3.6.24-6)

With Justice he tempers his strength. Recently Caesar placed her in a temple made of marble, that goddess whom he long before had placed in the shrine of his thought.

This conceit features in a poem that suggests, by over-vigorous denial, that Augustus is a fearful despot, a very Phalaris or Busiris. Green (1994: 345) puts it well: '[readers may] judge (7) "the magnitude of Caesar's clemency" ... from the public panic and grovelling appeals that Ovid's poem so graphically evokes'. Panegyric is undercut by its own terminology. The cult of Justice must be served by mitigating the 'cruel and unusual punishment' meted out to the exile. Publication of the poem, by definition after the event it celebrates, offers further proof of its empty hope. There was no recall, and therefore no justice.

Wide-ranging intertextual allusion plays a role in Ovid's depiction of Augustus as god. The poet's attitude to Augustus throughout his exile is a reduction to its logical conclusion of the careful and conditional prophecies of apotheosis as offered by Vergil (*Ecl.* 1.7: *erit ille mihi semper deus,* 'he will always be a god to me') and Horace (*Carm.* 3.3 and 3.5). It is also a development, beyond logic, of a divine concept that supersedes the cults that the emperor strove to restore, in part a recognition of Hellenistic practice.[96] In the East inscriptions equating the emperor with Jupiter-Zeus were at all times more common than in the West, but the nature and strength of the imperial cult in the West is gaining greater attention in recent studies.[97] The *ara numinis Augusti* (altar of Augustan divine power) of around AD 6 and the Narbonne inscriptions of AD 11 and 12 (*CIL* 12.4333) regulate the adoration of the *genius* (protective spirit) of the *numen* (divine power) of Augustus, and imply factual acceptance of the divinity of the emperor.[98] Ovid frequently uses the term *numen* as a synonym for Augustus.[99]

For the exile *ira Iovis* is indistinguishable from *ira Caesaris* (*Tr.* 3.11.17 etc.).[100] There is a great deal of material on Ovid's treatment of Augustus as divine.[101] Of these the most important recent work is that of Barchiesi (1997), who emphasises that Ovid's 'Anti-Augustanism' should be read not in terms of power, but in terms of discourse and language. Ovid 'picks out the weak points in Augustan discourse and shows himself as someone who sees the connection between political persuasion and the remodelling of Roman identity' (1997: 256). Suffice it to close this chapter with the observation that aspects of the exile's apotheosis of the emperor – as a Jupiter whose thunderclap left him *attonitus* (dumb-struck), as a Poseidon-Juno that persecuted him, a *fato profugus*, an Odysseus-Aeneas, driven forth by Fate – leave an impression of dubious adulation and futile worship. Augustus has, from *Tristia* 1.1.81-84 onwards, alternately been portrayed as Jupiter, and honoured with prayers for (or threats of) his apotheosis.[102]

Near the end of his life (*Pont.* 4.13.25, 26) Ovid depicts the re-apotheosis of a divinity that he has intermittently acknowledged throughout the first years of exile. A final, incongruous reversal alludes to the *novitas* of his godship, when apotheosis has finally been achieved (4.13.24). It comes as no surprise that this celebration was announced in the perhaps fictitious framework of the grotesque *recitatio* in the Tomitan market-place, and that this wonderful new god touched the savage hearts of the Getic savages, who clashed their arms and growled their guttural approval.

So even at the ends of the earth and in a foreign tongue, the exile-poet cannot escape from the demands of imperial panegyric. The last generic experiment that the exile undertakes subscribes to a greater *novitas*; never before has a persecuted Roman poet sung in barbarous tones of the greatest of the gods. In Getan Tomis the emperor bestrides Olympus as sole god, eclipsing the religion Augustus sought to restore among his Roman subjects. The exile may be the victim of this god's anger, but the 'god' is the victim of the poet's allusively mocking pen. The range of Ovid's generic experimentation still has a centrality of focus: poet and persecutor. In the words of the Cartesian paraphrase by Fantham (1996: 121), Ovid's existential salvation in exile was *'Cano, ergo sum'* – 'I sing, therefore I am!'

9

Exile Universalised: Ovid's Contribution to the Exilic Genre

9.1 Ovid's use of convention in his exilic poetry

Ovid was clearly creating something new in his poetry from exile. We need now to examine his methods and the poetic effect of this new genre, before proceeding to an examination of his influence on later exilic literature. We have so far carefully distinguished between the creative author as a person who was exiled, the suffering exile as *persona* who undergoes travails of heroic proportions and the poet-exile as another *persona*, the ostensible author, who shows himself aware of his own creative processes. In the end these must needs coalesce into Ovid-the-poet, a creative exile who used his literary voice as a powerful polemical tool, who gained comfort from his acts of creation and who fictionalised his autobiographical portrayal by entering the world of myth.

The creative exiled poet shows through self-revelation (of his creative hand, rather than of his daily routine) in his first person exilic epistles a unity of life and art that continuously undercuts the poet-exile's arguments that the two are distinct (*Tr.* 2.339-356).[1] This paradox lies central to the nature of Ovid's exilic experimentation. As the Pontic region scarcely shows a difference in bleakness between land, sea and sky (*Pont.* 2.2.93, 94; 3.1.20), so the outer circumstances and inner life of the exile are displayed before his distant readers in a variety of apparently minute shifts in monotony, demonstrating another unity, of poetry and poet, of art and life.[2] Ovid's poems from exile offer the supreme example of that creativity in exile that relieves the exile's lot, as advocated in formal *consolationes*.

Two questions remain to be asked: by what means does Ovid create this new functional unity between poet, exile and work, and how does he turn it into myth? Ovid, being Ovid, as always makes use of literary convention, but in unconventional ways. We have seen that generic experimentation is fundamental to this unconventionality.[3]

Cairns (1972) differentiates between *genre* or 'kind', and *topos* or 'aspect' of literature. Cairns' idiosyncratic use of the term genre (which may be loosely designated as 'specialised type') has been much challenged, but remains useful, as does his emphasis on the centrality of convention in the ancients' approach to literary kinds. According to the principles expounded by Cairns, a generic convention can become a *topos*, or subdivision, of another and different genre. There has been much discussion of his thesis in the intervening years, but its general principles still offer a useful taxonomy. Galinsky (1997) assembles the arguments, including current emphasis on reception: that a work only becomes part of a particular generic tradition after its readers have perceived it to be such. In Chapter 1 we assessed all literature about exile as essentially a single genre, using Aristotle's definition of focus on man-within-a-specific-situation. Our reception of the psychological unity of the disparate works considered in this study, turns these works (according to the definitions of both Aristotle and Galinsky) into a single genre. Ovid formalised its *topoi*.

Topoi may be simple, such as the fear of sheep for wolves to illustrate helplessness, or they may involve a complex set of ideas, such as the interrelationship of love and war. Ovid, in his creation of the poetic exilic genre, employed conventional *topoi* in unconventional ways, both as stylised units of thought, or *loci communes*,[4] and as units of diction. The poet's originality lay in his intertextual application of these commonplaces. Throughout his creative life, Ovid frequently reworked the same theme or re-used the same phrases, that is, self-reference is part of his style. A single phrase, transported to a new literary environment, would bring with it a conceptual background of considerable complexity. In his exilic poetry the *topoi* of exile are partly adaptations of conventional themes and partly striking new creations. For example, his sometimes incredible picture of the savage denizens of Pontus (e.g. *Tr.* 5.10.27-34) offers a stylised presentation of Roman cultural and racial prejudice which the exiled poet exploits to elicit sympathy.[5]

Echo and allusion work as a poetic short-hand, bringing the conceptual framework of an earlier work to bear as a counterpoint to the framework of a new poem, which gains a double or stronger set of meanings. This intertextual counterpoint either supports the thrust of the poem, or carries a cross-current of meaning, to create irony. The influence of echo and allusion may be retroactive. Re-use of a *topos* places an earlier work in a new perspective.[6]

Intertextuality may occur at the verbal, stylistic or conceptual levels. A single example of such multiplicity in imitation will suffice. Tibullan elegiac pastoral proclaims the value of *simplicitas*, while striving to draw an urban *domina* ('mistress') into a rustic ambience which brings no true relief to the lover's suffering. In Tibullan reverie the lover imagines himself bringing both his patron (Messalla Corvinus) and his current mistress to his simple home (e.g. Tib. 1.5). This is undercut by reality: a return to the demands of both venial urban eroticism and military or political life. Lenz (1997) discusses Tibullan influence in the *Tristia*. At *Ex Ponto* 1.8.33-60 Ovid essays into the pastoral mode, in a characteristic blend of distant past and distant future, recalling happy days in the

Paelignian countryside of Italy, and imagining a charming picture of himself as ploughman, urging on his oxen in Getic, and finding relief from his woes in pastoral plenty. But in true Tibullan fashion, the vignette is undercut by a return to the harsh reality of his timeless present (61-2).[131] This 'reality' is furthermore a literary version of prevalent Roman prejudice about unknown foreign shores. The ploy recurs elsewhere. Sheep fearing war and not the wolf (a bizarre example of the pathetic fallacy) and the herdsman piping his lay, not beneath a spreading oak or beech, but beneath his military helmet (*Tr.* 5.10.25, 26), offer a playful travesty of the pastoral mode.

Ovid's referential use of myth is one of the most important aspects of his exilic poetry.[7] When, for instance, he terms his poetry an 'Oedipus' or a 'Telegonus' in *Tristia* 1.6, he is emphasising its innocence and lack of purposeful malignity.[8] We have noted as particularly important his re-use of mythical characters from the *Heroides* or *Metamorphoses*, such as the paragons of wifely virtue or Callisto as one of the first of Jupiter's victims.

This chapter will briefly examine some of the devices whereby Ovid creates the conventions of exilic literature, and then trace aspects of its influence in the poetry of two of our other exiles, Seneca and Boethius. After a retrospective review of the *personae* and personalities in exile as we have followed their progress through our consideration of grammatical persons, it will end with a final consideration of the generic issues raised in Chapter 1.

9.2 The *adynata* of exile

Ovid with increasing frequency exploits, as poetic device, the *adynaton*, a psycho-linguistic characteristic of all speech,[9] whereby the impossibility of a contingency is illustrated by analogy with an obvious impossibility from the sphere of nature. Ovid's use of the various types of *adynata* increases through the years of exile. One could say that the exile's perception of reality has shifted from a quasi-Aristotelian to a fully Platonic mode; potential has become the true reality.

Not technically *adynata*, but equally 'impossible', are the related devices which Ovid frequently exploits of the personified surrogate, mental travel and wishful thinking. The exile lives within his own fantasy, 'seeing' with the 'mind's eye' those scenes of Roman civic life from which he has been excluded. This lies close to Cicero's conception of the letter as surrogate for the second person, as *sermo absentis*. Cicero's grammatical genitive reflects an objective focus; the first person speaks to the second person, who is absent, that is, 'conversation *with* the absent'. We have seen as central to Ovid's adaptation of epistolary convention to the circumstances of exile his development of a virtually new concept, the hopelessness of non-reply, the poetic letter as *sermo surdi mutique* (conversation with the deaf and mute). The exile reaches out in vain to a second person, who never replies, and in the end he turns within himself for inner communion. Ovid's inner communion becomes a new, subjective *sermo absentis*, for the exile, as first person, *is* the absent communicator. But as absent communicator he deals in the impossible, for in his inner eye he sees his poems arriving in Rome as surrogates for himself, and he imagines himself in conversation, through these poems, with his distant friends. His poems become surrogate subjective 'conversation *by* the absent'.

Ovid in his lengthiest work dealt consistently in the impossible. The whole of the *Metamorphoses* consistently demands suspension of disbelief. Exile as the poet's metamorphosis is the ultimate *adynaton* that has come true, and from that follows that all other impossibilities of nature can actually take place. In *Tristia* 1.5.47ff. the exile claims to have suffered 'more and in greater measure than anyone could ever have believed'. As the impossible has happened, from this point onwards *anything* can happen.[10] This sets the tone for Ovid's whole exilic oeuvre. The exile's perception and the poet's depiction of reality involve a shift in the limits between the possible and the impossible, most fully expressed in a powerful passage from the last book:

> *'litus ad Euxinum' si quis mihi diceret 'ibis,*
> *et metues, arcu ne feriare Getae':*
> *'i, bibe' dixissem 'purgantes pectora sucos,*
> *quicquid et in tota nascitur Anticyra'.*
> *sum tamen haec passus ...* (*Pont*. 4.3.51-5)

If someone should have said to me, 'You will go to the Euxine shore, and there you will fear to be struck by Getic archery', I'd have said, 'Rubbish! Go and drink an emetic and clear your brain, and take whatever else grows in the whole of Anticyra'.[11] Yet I *have* suffered this fate ...

Formerly the exile would have considered as mad anyone who suggested that he would end up at Tomis, but now he has been relegated to the Pontic shore. Because this existential convulsion is real, nothing else in life is fixed, and all other convulsions of nature are possible.

The *adynata* of Ovid's exile become progressively more closely related to aspects of his condition. For example, a common *topos* denoting 'impossibility', 'reversal of the course of an (unnamed) river', informs an *adynaton* at *Ex Ponto* 4.5.41-4. In the next poem, which is of almost the same length, at an almost parallel position in its structure (4.6.45-6), this 'impossible' phenomenon is applied to the Hister. Local colour heightens the pathos of exile, serving to strengthen the impression of a fantastic, mythical world where the normal borders between reality and unreality are totally blurred.

A special form of *adynaton*, the 'impossible count', shows a similar topical progression from general to particularly exilic. The exile's ills are as innumerable 'as particles of dust', or 'as the stars' in the well-worn simile of *Tristia* 1.5.47, repeated at 4.10.107-8. After this, exilic colouring increases, contrasting nostalgic allusions to the sweetness of Italy, sand on the seashore, spring flowers, ears of grain and apples in autumn, with the harshness of the Danubian area (*Tr.* 4.1.55-9). Italian allusions become progressively more specific; *Tristia* 5.1.31-3 compares the exile's woes with the number of grains of sand in the Tiber or blades of grass on the Campus Martius. Although a reversal of the conventional praise of Italy, it is urgently pathetic:

> *quot frutices silvae, quot flavas Thybris harenas*
> *mollia quot Martis gramina campus habet,*
> *tot mala pertulimus, ...*

As many berries as the woods produce or golden sands that the Tiber has on its banks, as many soft blades of grass as the Campus Martius has, so many ills have I borne to the end, ...

Hereafter emphasis shifts to the unpleasant aspects of the Pontic area while simultaneously stressing the beauties he misses; in *Tristia* 5.2.23-7 dangerous beasts in the forests of Scythia are 'as many as' the fishes (of Pontus), sea shells (neutral), flowers in a rose garden (pleasant), poppy seeds (which would bring forgetfulness to the lonely exile) and 'feathers on the back of a bird', again an evocation of the Italian spring, in strong contrast to the exile's ills.[12] Ovid portrays the despair of an exile in terms of an inversion of all that Rome offered.

9.3 Ovidian humour in exile

Not all Ovidian inversion involves despair. It is generally accepted that Ovid's major contribution to the tradition of Roman erotic elegy was his humour.[13] Even in exile the poet's sense of fun is sometimes discernible. A problem inherent in the appreciation of Ovidian humour, also in his exilic literature, is that it is virtually impossible finally to establish the poet's subjective intention.[14] The fact that the exile's longing can be couched in a literary, elegiac form has been so unobtrusively established as convention that we do not query the validity of the mode of expression. Readers accept poetry as a medium and the poem as a work of art. Yet when the writer of a poetic letter from exile humorously undercuts pathos, readers are at a loss. Is the exile laughing at himself, or are two *personae* here at loggerheads? Is the poet laughing at his creation, the literary *persona*? As noted above, we have so far in this study consistently assumed such duality as a deliberate aspect of the creative author's self-conscious style. Yet in this chapter we are, paradoxically, attempting to trace a new fusion of poet and product, which would include the assumption

233

that at some level, at least, the poetry of exile reflects the subjective emotions of an exiled poet.

The solution to our paradox would perhaps lie in our acceptance of the distancing effect of humour. Humour involves the audience by evoking a certain response, but it also lends distance and a certain objectivity, so that the reader's involvement can be manipulated or limited. It can be used to tone down tragedy. The exiled Ovid reveals mental suffering of a mythical immensity which he undercuts with bathos, thereby revealing a new reality, the resilient strength of the human spirit. Inconsistencies of approach and variations in tone together create a psychologically consistent portrait.[15] At the same time humour can also serve as another layer of protection, insulating the suffering but creative artist from too close a scrutiny of his emotions by the distant readership whose ultimate reactions he can only imagine.

A further problem is that distance in time and diversity in social, political and cultural outlook from the ancients causes the modern reader to react differently to the devices by which the poet reaches out to his readership. We do not really know how to read Ovidian (or Horatian) humour in any particular genre, even less do we know how their contemporaries took it. Ovid repeatedly tells Augustus that he, the emperor, did not know how to read the poet's earlier works, but even this is Ovid reading the emperor's readings. The problem gains in complexity over the centuries.

Even this is not insurmountable. The manner of reading of a work of literature by any one reader in any one generation or area reflects the sum of readerly reactions of which that particular reader is aware. At the turn of the second millennium general disillusionment with the power brokers of this world has awakened a new awareness of potential subversion in poets formerly considered whole-hearted supporters of the imperial regime.[16] Readers are at present far more willing to accept that ostensibly straightforward panegyric may be at least ambivalent, at most highly ironic. It is with such eyes that I tend to read Ovid's attitude to Augustus.[17]

At a simpler level, humour is one of the ways in which humanity manages to survive the misfortunes that beset it. In poetry self-irony works as *captatio benevolentiae*.[18] The playful personification of the exiled poet's book as his ambassador at *Tristia* 1.1 is supported by a disarming appeal to his readers to 'place the poet's fortunes, as a last reversal of nature, amongst his *Metamorphoses*' (*Tr.* 1.1.119, 120). Throughout the storm poems topical literary allusions, deliberately inflated to comically epic proportions, illustrate the exile's fears and wishes. *Tristia* 1.11.24 epitomises the all-too-human reaction to a stormy passage: 'first I was afraid I should die, and then I was afraid I should not die'. Whimsy rather than pathos speaks from the picture of sea and land competing to extinguish the unfortunate victim, a hero of Homeric stature (*ibid.* 24 to 30). *Tristia* 1.11 continues the playful depiction of a persecuted hero, [19] supporting a larger-than-life and over-elaborate comparison in *Tristia* 1.5.57-84 of the exile's lot with that of Odysseus.

Whimsy and pathos are not mutually exclusive. In the exile's *propemptikon* ('poem celebrating the departure of the beloved'), *Tristia* 1.3, the pathos of Ovid's portrayal of the banished poet's last night at Rome is not diminished by its sometimes mock-epic tones. Its component parts are largely conventional, and yet Goethe considered it the most moving poem in the collection. The greater part of the poem (5-100) is dramatic in form, with dialogue, shift of scenes, non-speaking characters, unity but progression in time, alternation of speech with choral lament (reported at 21-6 and 77, 78) and finally, a *Botenbericht* (91-100), 'attested' only by *narratur* ('it is reported', 91), which has prompted speculation about 'how the exile could have known' about his wife's swooning after he had gone. The whole passage is literary, and not necessarily literal. That the poet is serious about the agony suffered by a departing exile does not mean that some playful self-irony is not also involved. Depiction of his departure as 'a second fall of Troy' (*ibid.* 25, 26) is playful exaggeration.

Ovidian humour frequently serves to undercut pathos, as in the exile's graceful but extremely tactless appeal to Cotys, King of Thrace, in *Ex Ponto* 2.9. This poem was published at Rome, and had a Roman readership. Apart from the name of the addressee, we have no proof that it ever was literally meant for, sent to, or reached, the Thracian king. A long passage lauding the prince's noble descent and good qualities (vv. 1-20), is followed by the *exemplum* of divine aid to a sufferer persecuted by another god (21-36). This appears as typically Hellenistic adulation of a ruler. It is followed by an elaborate appeal based on the prince's state of education and the degree to which the liberal arts have deflected his congenital impulse towards bloodshed and his training in aggressive archery (47-65). Either Ovid's chief *error* was want of tact, or this poem is meant to be funny. Tactless compliments are offered the king: 'If one removed the author's name from the king's poetry, no one would guess from its style that a *barbarian* had composed it' (51, 52). The poet draws a ludicrously incongruous picture of the prince shooting his arrows backward in true Thracian fashion before picking up his pen to compose poetry (57-62). The concluding lines offer clumsy *praeteritio*, in apparently deliberately heavy-handed 'refusal to discuss' Ovid's *culpa* towards Augustus. Pointed reference to the *Ars* as sole reason for his banishment strengthens the impression of either tactlessness or deliberate irony.[20]

Within the context of the exilic corpus it is reasonable to assume that this poem is essentially humorous and its gaucherie a deliberate ploy to evoke an amused reaction in its Roman readership. I offer this against Green (1994: 328) *ad loc.*: 'The patronising quality of these lines disconcerts precisely because of its complete unconsciousness'. If Green is right, I would argue that this is the 'unconsciousness' of the exile-poet as *persona*, just as the master-lover in the *Ars* often is presented by his creator as a stupid and unbearably chauvinistic male. Here, then, I again assume a distance between exile and creative poet, who is gently mocking current Roman preconceptions.

Ovid's depiction of life at Tomis and the appearance and customs of its inhabitants is tinged alternately with humour and pathos. Details are humorously exaggerated, for instance we have seen the Getae depicted in *Tristia* 3.10 as breached savages with hairy locks tinkling with icicles, serving chunks of frozen wine to their guests (vv. 21-4) in the rare intervals when they are not preparing poisoned arrows with which to transfix these same guests. We have noted before that the famous poem recounting the exiled poet's Getic *recitatio* in the Tomitan market place offers a comical adaptation of the pathetic fallacy: the new Orpheus soothes the savage breasts of the 'inhuman Getae', moving them to a dumb display of wonder, shown by their animal-like growls of approbation, nodding and clashing of weapons:

> *Haec ubi non patria perlegi scripta Camena,*
> *venit et ad digitos ultima charta meos,*
> *et caput et plenas omnes movere pharetras,*
> *et longum Getico murmur in ore fuit*   (*Pont*. 4.13.33-6)

When I finished reading this poem written by the aid of a foreign Muse, and the last page was unrolled under my fingers, they shook both their heads and their full quivers, and a long-drawn-out murmur arose from each Getic mouth.

The joke has some subtle verbal and acoustic touches. The syllepsis involved in *caput et ...pharetras* exhibits a comic incongruity. Prevalence of *o* and *u* in verse 36 offers an onomatopoeic reprise of the sounds of wonder emitted by the savages. For the usual (Greek) *Musa* as petrified metaphor for 'poetic production', the Roman equivalent concept *Camena* is applied, which in its turn is negated by *non* and the adjective *patria* as circumlocution for 'Latin'. The Getae are the very antithesis of all that is Roman, as the poet-exile ponderously explains.

Scott (1930) comments on the 'Getic *recitatio*': 'he wrote for the Getae a poem explaining the apotheosis of Augustus in exactly the same way that he had years before unfolded to his Latin readers the deification of Julius Caesar'. The critic took both these instances at face value. Manner of and focus in critical reading have changed considerably over nearly seventy years. The irony and potential irreverence of the treatment of the subject of Caesar's apotheosis in *Metamorphoses* 15 has received considerable attention.[21] We have noted as equally irreverent Ovid's depiction, near the end of his life (*Pont*. 4.13.25, 26), of a re-apotheosis of a divinity that he has intermittently acknowledged throughout the first years of exile. Augustus has, from *Tristia* 1.1.81-4 onwards, alternately been portrayed as Jupiter, and honoured with prayers for (or threats of) his apotheosis.[22]

Some of Ovid's allusions to Augustus' foreign policy involves virtual mockery of his propensity to conduct wars through the agency of others, including Tiberius, his late-adopted stepson. Here adulatory overkill works as a pointer to irony.[23] Similarly, some allusions to the imperial kin appear less than kind. Each evocation of the 'pious' members of the imperial household implies reference to the 'impious' Juliae (e.g. *Tr.* 1.2.104, *Pont.* 2.2.73, 74). These allusions do not appear to be fortuitous, or merely tactless. 'Malice' is perhaps too strong a word, and 'humour' is too mild. Bland and apparently guileless allusions to the empress Livia as the only woman worthy of the Augustan *pulvinar* ('divine divan', not *torus* 'marriage bed') without whose existence the 'god' would have had to remain celibate (*Tr.* 2.161-5), appear irreverent at best, and cruelly funny in the light of the fact that both had been married before, and that the imperial couple's only two 'children' were those of Livia's first husband.[24] Equation of Augustus with Jupiter serves to remind the reader of the extra-marital propensities of both personages. This parallel is, for instance, irreverently pointed by the near juxtaposition of *Tristia* 2.161-5 (praise of Livia) and 289-92. In the second passage the emperor (and the general reader) are reminded of Jupiter's excursions into mortal paternity, and the grief of Juno over so many *paelices* (rival lovers).

We have noted before that the humour involved in Ovid's description of his 'Getic *recitatio*' gains its final punch through inversion in the next poem (*Pont.* 4.14). The exile explains that the Tomitans consider him to have maligned them in his poetry (vv. 15, 16). Once more the poet-exile suffers because of what he has written. Ovid does not attempt to explain how these barbarians now can understand Latin, merely citing this as another instance of the harm poetry has done him. His comments are suitably hyperbolic (17-30); he hates the neighbouring Getae and the countryside, but Tomis itself was a haven of refuge to him, and he, like another Latona at Delos, found sanctuary there. He wholeheartedly loves the Tomitans.[25] Beside the accusation of disingenuousness to which the poet lays himself open, the picture of the exile as pregnant female victim of divine rape and relentless persecution is not without its lighter side.[26]

The most clearly comical poem in the exilic collection is *Ex Ponto* 28 (discussed in detail in Chapter 4), in which the exile goes into transports of joy at the gift of silver portraits (whether medals, statuettes or coins) of the imperial triad. This poem is rich in elaborate poetic devices, with Ovid often an indication of irony. The poem may represent playful thanks for a gift of money, coins bearing the likenesses of the emperor, his wife and his destined heir.[27] Extravagant protestations of joy and promises to set up a private shrine appear as part of an elaborate joke, concluded with a whimsical plea that *now* the emperor *must* move the exile, lest these 'never-to-be-separated-from-him' precious portraits should fall a prey to Getic marauders.[28] As in the gift-poem, *Amores* 2.15, human attributes reflecting changing emotions are ascribed to inanimate objects: the imperial portraits are shown displaying anger and mollification (vv. 21, 22 and 73, 74), in terms reminiscent of similar emotions in the storm gods of *Tristia* 1.2.107-10.

Such a playful approach is an important aspect of Ovidian *variatio*. Gentle *Selbstironie* in communication with a friend has here been extended to a third person, the emperor and his family. The poet seems to expect the third person to reciprocate with self-ironic acknowledgement. The emperor did not reflect the poet's attitude, and his consistent misunderstanding of Ovidian humour underlies the exile's tragedy. Ovid appears here, as elsewhere, to be the victim of his own sometimes over-exuberant sense of the ridiculous.[29] When the exile is the object of gentle raillery, the poet is on safer ground. In *Tristia* 3.3 an imaginary deathbed scene calls for sympathy from the exile's wife and also from the absent wider readership. There is a certain discernible distance between poet and exile; the poet 'watches' the 'dying' exile, and turns the imaginary scene into a joke. An irreverent sexual innuendo in verses 23, 24 undercuts the pathos: if he were at his last gasp, and his wife should arrive, *...resurgam / spesque tui nobis causa vigoris erit* (I should rise up, and hope of you would cause new vigour in me).

So Ovidian humour works on a variety of levels, from the whimsical to the sharply ironical. Its existence in exile was one of the ways in which a comforting Muse preserved the sanity of her votary. Another was her inspiration of a creative adaptation of myth to the circumstances of the poet's exile, and *vice versa*.

9.4 Imagery: the creation of the metaphors of exile

Multiple levels of meaning characterise all aspects of our poet's art. In the later books of exilic poetry increasing use of themes adapted to the exilic situation (or based on certain topics woven into a consistent pattern) creates an exilic convention. Ovidian metaphor is functional at all times, its objective framework of recurrent figures of thought allowing the poet to move simultaneously within two semantic dimensions.[30] An outstanding example is consistent allusion to a frozen landscape, eternal winter, and the freezing of the Black Sea (e.g. *Tr.* 3.10.37).[31] By depicting a fictional frozen world Ovid creates a set of metaphors for exile. The sterile landscape becomes a symbol for inner sterility. In this section the occurrence of certain of these topics will be traced chronologically in order to show their thematic pervasiveness.

The poet uses the concept of travel and distance, involving both time and space, as an objective framework for portrayal of pathos.[32] *Tristia* 1.1 presents the 'book as a weary traveller', 1.2 has the first person narrator experiencing a storm, 1.3 shows the exile's sad departure from Rome. Here, of particular interest is the apparently conventional employment of celestial signs to denote progression of time. At verse 28 peaceful night is ruled by *Luna* shining over the Capitol, symbol of Rome. The movement of the Great Bear over the night sky (vv. 47, 48) heralds dawn and departure. This introduces the theme of the place of exile as dominated by the northern constellation.[33] At last full day comes with the rising of Lucifer, the morning star (v. 72), designated as *stella gravis nobis* ('a star that bears down heavily on me'). Conventional depiction of time has been transformed into a *topos* of exile, emphasising the hardship of a lot where even the heavenly bodies conspire against the departing exile.

The cosmic scene having been set, *Tristia* 1.4 depicts another storm, and only by 1.5 do we learn who the storm-tossed traveller is. 'Storm', 'sea' and 'shipwreck' have been established as physical threats, as externalisations of the inner turmoil of the exiled poet, and as the physical manifestation of the wrath of the 'angry god'. The sea, storms and ships remain the most consistently recurrent image in the *Tristia* and are carried through into the *Epistolae ex Ponto*.[34]

Alternating with, sometimes supporting, shipwreck imagery, is the concept of exile as death, which first appears at *Tristia* 1.2.65, 66 and recurs throughout the oeuvre, culminating in no fewer than six allusions in *Ex Ponto* 4.16 (vv. 1, 3, 4, 47, 48, 51), on which more below. Play on *perire* evokes echoes of erotic punning on verbs of dying.[35] On occasion the poet knocks at death's door (*Tr.* 3.2.23), sometimes he wishes that death would come to end his exile (*Tr.* 3.3.35, 36; 3.8.39, 40), he thinks of his wife as a widow (*Tr.* 5.5.48) or he wishes that he had never been born. Occasionally the exile faces death 'bravely' (*Pont.* 3.7.40). Like a dying Vergil he has burnt his great epic (*Tr.* 4.10.63, 64). He speaks 'from beyond the grave' (*Tr.* 3.10.1-4). He writes his own epitaph (*Tr.* 3.3.73-6), or his own obituary (*Tr.* 4.10).[36] He is a *simulacrum* ('ghost') of his former self (*Tr.* 3.11.31), or even *cineres* ('ashes', *Tr.* 3.11.26).

From depicting his departure as 'similar to' a funeral in *Tristia* 1.3.89, the exile progresses to absolute use of the metaphor (*Tr.* 3.14.20 and 5.1.14). His songs become dirges at his own funeral. But then again he vindicates his poetry; it has granted him immortality (*Pont.* 3.2.27-30). Death is his theme from first to last[37] but at the end he twice speaks of an anastasis, at *Ex Ponto* 4.8.47, 48, and again in 4.9. This last combines the two predominant sets of images, seafaring and death:

> *et si quem dabit aura sinum, iactate rudentes,*[38]
> *exeat e Stygiis ut mea navis aquis.*   (*Pont.* 4.9.73, 74)

And if the breeze should produce some little billow in the sail, throw off the ropes, so that my ship may set sail away from the Stygian waters!

Cicero exploited the metaphor of exile as civil death; loss of *salus* meant both loss of health and loss of civic rights.[39] Ovid is inconsistent in his play between exile as death, and death as either the final threat or the final release. These mutually exclusive concepts alternate, an indication that the poet is dealing in fiction. A rider at *Tristia* 1.4.28 *si modo, qui periit ille perire potest* (at least, if anyone who is dead really can die), points the metaphorical quality of the image.[40]

Illness is allied to death. Ovid's third consistent figure, familiar from the consolatory genre, is 'wounding and illness'. Allusions to 'wounds' fall into two categories: those inflicted unwittingly on the emperor by the unfortunate poet, his unexplained *error*, and those inflicted consciously by Augustus, in retaliation. The exile cryptically refuses to 'lacerate the emperor's wounds again'.[41] *Praeteritio* achieves what the poet pretends to avoid.

His own miseries or 'wounds', usually of the mind or spirit, first occur at *Tristia* 1.1.99, and are repeated with increasing frequency. From 'wounding' as metaphor for the exile's misery, comes 'healing' as term for aid from family or friends.[42] His Muse is medicine for his sick soul (*Tr.* 4.10.118). By *Ex Ponto* 4.14.4, 5 all that the exile has left, is his life, and even health (*salus*) is hateful (*invisa*) because his miseries do not end.

From the poet's first depiction of physical debilitation as a concomitant to mental suffering, to the exile's last despairingly defiant outburst against Envy, he develops an increasing awareness of the primacy of mental affliction over physical suffering. In *Tristia* 3.8 physical and mental suffering go together. The cry is familiar to readers of Cicero's exilic correspondence:

> *ut tetigi Pontum, vexant insomnia vixque*
> *ossa tegit macies nec iuvat ora cibus:*
> ...
> *nec melius valeo quam corpore mente, sed aegra est*
> *utraque pars aeque, binaque damna fero.* (*Tr.* 3.8.27-8; 33-4)

From the moment I reached Pontus, insomnia haunts me and my meagre flesh scarcely covers my bones, and food doesn't taste like anything at all ... Nor am I any better in my mind than in my body, but both parts of me are equally unwell, and I bear a double doom.

The terminology of navigation, medicine, warfare and death gives pathetic colour to the exilic poems. Inconsistent use of the imagery of exile as death, threatened life, and illness emphasises pathos. With these come a consistently greater reliance on the powers of mental travel to transcend both space and time. Juxtaposition of concepts seldom undercuts pathos, for the imagery within a single poem is usually consistent. When occasionally an apparently injudicious mixture of metaphors appears to do so, a perhaps deliberate gaucherie achieves objectivity. The poet can still laugh a little at the exile. A certain insulation saves the poet from disturbing or embarrassing subjectivity.[43]

The pathos of the exile's final cry is so striking that the mixed metaphor does not obtrude. The exile has been cremated (48). He has lost all except his life (49). He can still feel pain (50). His limbs are dead (51). There is no more place for Envy's blows (52). Analysed thus, the imagery appears inconsistent, even incongruous. Yet as an outburst of non-literal speech, portraying the extremes of mental suffering, the picture is consistent and convincing:

> *ergo summotum patria proscindere, Livor,*
> *desine neu cineres sparge, cruente, meos.*
> *omnia perdidimus: tantummodo vita relicta est*
> *praebeat ut sensum materiamque mali.*
> *quid iuvat extinctos ferrum demittere in artus?*
> *non habet in nobis iam nova plaga locum.*   (*Pont.* 4.16.47-52)

> So, Malice,[44] sheathe your bloody claws, spare this poor exile,
> don't scatter my ashes after death!
> I have lost all: only bare life remains to quicken
> the awareness and substance of my pain.
> What pleasure do you get from stabbing this dead body?
> There is no space in me now for another wound.

9.5 Poetry ascribed to Seneca

So the last word we hear of our exiled poet is a cry of utter despair, but retrospect brings reminiscences of endless nuances of hope and humour, submission and defiance, creativity and consolation. These together form the fabric of Ovid's poetry of exile, setting a pattern for others to follow. Yet in his creation of the literary genre of exilic poetry, Ovid had a perhaps surprisingly small following. One of these may have been the younger Seneca, whose public reaction to exile is recorded in his two *consolationes*. There is, however, an apparently anonymous corpus of seventy-two epigrams and a few lyrical poems in the *Anthologia Latina*, which has, with very good reason, been attributed to Seneca.[45] Of these, poems 2 and 3 refer to the island Corsica, depicting it in very unfavourable terms, 18 is an epitaph of a sort, and 19 and 25 address an enemy (or *Livor* in the abstract) in Ovidian terms. Poems 26 and 27 similarly affirm the immortality of the author's poetry.[46] Various other poems reflect a Stoic philosophy akin to that of the known Senecan corpus. Cumulative evidence favours the interpretation of the whole as a random collection of Senecan *'nugae'* (trifles).[47]

Seneca's Danish biographer, Villy Sørenson (trans. 1984: 121) considers that the body of poems as we have them may all be allocated to the period of Seneca's exile. This is very likely.[48] As with Ovid, mythicising of exile forms part of the fabric of Seneca's poetry of exile. Sørenson (1984: 114-15), accepts as factual the poet's depiction of Corsica as barren and stony (*Epigr.* 2 and 3). I would disagree. The depiction of the place as treeless and without harvests appears stylised, apparently based on Ovid's (largely

241

mythical) depiction of Tomis.[49] In *Epigr.* 18, addressed to the poet's native city, which now must mourn his 'death,' Seneca depicts himself as latter-day Prometheus: *infigor scopulo* ('I am fixed to a crag', v. 14) he claims.[50]

There are other examples of mythical stylisation of the place of exile. *Epigr.* 3.1-3 bears comparison with Ovid's *Ex Ponto* 1.3.5ff.:

> Seneca:
> *barbara praeruptis inclusa est Corsica saxis*
>   *horrida, desertis undique vasta locis.*
> *non* poma *autumnus, segetes non* educat *aestas* ... etc.

Barbarous Corsica is bound about by looming cliffs; it rises up vast with desert places. The autumn produces no fruit and the summer no corn ... etc.

> Ovid:
> *non ager hic* pomum, *non dulces* educat *uvas,*
>   *non salices ripa, robora monte vigent* ... etc.

No field here produces any fruit, no sweet grapes at all, the riverbank has no reeds, nor do oaks grow strong on the mountain ... etc.

Imitation is both verbal and conceptual. Seneca clearly admired Ovid, whom he both quoted and imitated, not only in these epigrams, but also in his many allusions to the poet in his prose works.[51] However, the depiction of his place of exile as uninhabitable may be traced back to the consolatory *topos* prevalent long before Ovid, as we identified it in Chapter 3: choice of a place of exile, giving preference to the solitude and safe intellectual retreat offered by even the most inhospitable of rocky islands.

There is an interesting dichotomy in the corpus. Seneca's approach to immortality differs from epigram to epigram. Only the last (*Epigr.* 71), Seneca's so-called 'epitaph', expresses the Stoic sentiments of his prose works; it reaffirms the immortality of these prose works, and of his soul, which is being called to heaven by God, leaving his bones to the stony earth. Other poems that refer to immortality, bespeak the immortality conferred by poetry, as for instance:

> *carmina sola carent fato mortem repellunt;*
>   *carminibus vives semper, Homere, tuis.*   (*Epigr.* 26.9, 10)

Songs alone cheat fate and repel death; in your lays, Homer, you will ever live.

In his defiance of Fate Seneca here evinces an attitude totally different from the consistent tenor of his prose works.[52] The thought of the poem is Ovidian, although its major metaphor, the impermanence even of the Egyptian pyramids, is a conflation of strains from the tradition of the immortalising power of poetry, familiar also from Horace. Poem 27, with its emphatic placement of an Ovidian echo at the end of the first verse, is clearly indicative of Seneca's debt to Ovid:

> *nullum opus exsurgit, quod non annosa vetustas*
> *expugnet, quod non vertat iniqua dies*[53]   (*Epigr.* 27.1, 2)

No work arises that an age filled with years may not destroy, that some unkind day will not overthrow.

These opening lines repeat the thought of *Epigr.* 26, that poetry is indestructible, here (as in *Met.* 15.868ff.) by time, not the 'Fate' of 26. An Ovidian echo, *magnos ad sidera montes* (high mountains that reach the stars)[54] at the end of verse 3 serves to underline the intertextual connection. The last couplet rephrases Ovid's emphatic vindication of his *ingenium*. The verbal echoes are clear:

> Seneca:
> Ingenio *mors nulla iacet, vacat undique tutum;*
>   *Inlaesum semper* carmina nomen *habent.*   (*Epigr.* 27.5, 6)

No death looms over *genius*, it is safely free on all counts; my *songs* have a *name* that is never harmed.

> Ovid:
> *Invide, quid laceras Nasonis* carmina *rapti?*
>   *Non solet* ingeniis *summa nocere dies*
> *famaque post cineres maior venit. et mihi* nomen
>   *tum quoque, cum vivis adnumerarer, erat.*   (*Pont.* 4.16.1-4)

Envy, why do you tear down the *songs* of Naso, who was snatched away from Rome? No final day ever harms *genius*, and fame grows greater after all has been reduced to ashes. Yet I then already had a *name*, then while I still was counted among the living.

In these poems, as in Ovid's, the relationship between exile, death, poetry and immortality is clearly affirmed. It may be argued that here the anonymous poet deviates so strongly from the attitude to life evidenced in the bulk of Seneca's philosophical oeuvre, that these pseudo-Ovidian *nugae* are not his, or, if they are, should best be ignored. Yet various studies (particularly those of Degl' Innocenti Pierini) have shown that there is such a close verbal affinity in these poems with aspects of Seneca's philosophical and dramatic works that they may with confidence be ascribed to the philosopher. If these are indeed Seneca's 'poems from exile', as they seem emphatically to be, we may interpret their content as a counterthrust to Seneca's prose works from exile. These poems carry the message that all attempts by the politically powerful to neutralise such little power as their opponents possess, can be defeated by poetry. With Seneca, as with

Ovid, poetry has power to immortalise, and to defeat both *'tempus edax'* (*Epigr.* 1.1) and carping *Livor* (*Epigr.* 19.7).[55]

9.6 Boethius' elegiacs

Boethius in prison experiences inner exile. He claims to be working without recourse to books (*Consol.* 1.pr.4.7). It has been suggested that he composed parts of his great philosophical work, perhaps some of the poetic interludes, before his exile, but Courcelle (1967: 333) refutes this idea with specific reference to the unity between the sections of prose and verse of his 'Menippean satura'. Like Ovid in exile, Boethius appears to be striking a consciously 'derelict pose'. Lack of books would symbolise the forlornness of the exile. It is essential to remember that the narrative of first two books of the *Consolatio Philosophiae*, although disguised as autobiography, is essentially a literary fiction. Like Ovid, Boethius is exploiting the possibilities of literature to universalise his own plight, raising it to a stylised portrait of the exile-as-hero in a mythical milieu. Boethius' myth is created by the apparition in turn of the female figures *Philosophia* and *Fortuna*. The latter is defeated, and the former vindicates her power over the exile.

The *Consolatio* has a Menippean form but does not share its satirical spirit. Between each two rhetorical sections is interspersed a poem, in any one of a variety of metres.[56] The poetry is heavily influenced by a vast classical tradition,[57] including Senecan choral lyric[58] but for the purposes of this study we shall concentrate on Ovidian undertones only. The poetry is Roman in spirit, not Neoplatonic, yet O'Daly (1991: 68) hears in it the voice of another *persona*: that of 'Boethius-the-poet-with-a-philosopher's-voice'.[59] He considers the poems to be a 'vigorous and sophisticated sequence ... reflecting and elaborating the Latin poetic tradition from Lucretius to Seneca's tragedies' (p. vii). We should remember that for the prisoner, as for Ovid, the creation of this work in its entirety represented that literary creativity to which the consolatory tradition had always enjoined exiles to turn. The poetry is an essential part of that creativity. In the words of Glei (1985), Boethius saw *poesis* (poetry) as *poiêsis* (creativity).

Only the opening poem of the *Consolatio Philosophiae* is in the elegiac metre. A reader picking up the work for the first time, and knowing no more than that its author too, was exiled, will recognise Ovidian turns of phrase and Ovidian concepts. Such a reader may assume that here is a conscious continuation of the tradition of exilic elegy as created by Ovid, but within the first few paragraphs of the first prose section personified *Philosophia* banishes the disabled philosopher-poet's own elegiac Muses in no uncertain terms, as *scenicas meretriculas* (play-acting little prostitutes), unworthy and unable to heal the sick man, liable consciously to poison him with *dulcibus ... venenis* (sweet poisons, *Consol.* 1.pr.1.26-32).

She proposes to hand the patient over to her true 'Muses', who will presumably inspire the subsequent poetic sections of the work.

After the first poem (consisting of eleven elegiac couplets) the imprisoned exile therefore turns to other forms. These comprise thirty-eight poems, in a variety of metres: hexameter, hendecasyllables, and a number of lyrical forms.[60] The majority of these are sung by Dame Philosophy herself, while the prisoner becomes increasingly mute.[61] The centrally important 3.m.9, which marks the crisis in the patient's condition and his return to mental health, clothes largely Platonic thought in 'classical' hexameter verse.[62] Close to this poem is 3.m.12, written in glyconics, which gives a reprise of the story of Orpheus in the Underworld, shortening and simplifying the tale as taken from Vergil and Ovid.[63] Its ostensible message is contained in the last line *perdit, dum videt inferos* (he lost out, while he looked at what was below, 3.m.12.58), with the implication that the prisoner should learn from Orpheus' sad tale and fix his mind on higher things. Its more complex message seems to be that in the end poetry fails to win through; Orpheus lost (even actively *killed*) his wife (*vidit, perdidit, occidit*, 'he saw, he lost, he killed', *ibid.* 51). Poetry is in the end at best ineffectual, at worst, destructive.[64] This is put into the mouth of Dame Philosophy; behind her we still can discern the creative author using both poetry and prose as *Selbsttrost* in a vast network of literary allusion.

His Muse is the final purveyor of solace to Ovid in exile. The poetic sections of Boethius' *Consolatio Philosophiae* are so clearly integrated into the texture of his work, that one might assume that the sustaining and comforting power of the Muses would also receive recognition in the later exile's work.[65] Yet this is not wholly so. The author progressively shifts his emphasis away from the verse sections. By subtle distancing the creative poet can both show his protagonist being weaned from a 'lower form' of literature and enjoy the solace that poetic creativity still brings him. Only in the first book his verses precede the prose passages, apparently offering only temporary support to the anguished spirit of the prisoner.[66]

The poems are shown to work as a crutch to hold up the errant philosopher's wavering spirit long enough for the medicine of philosophy to complete its healing process. This is reminiscent of the prose passages of invocation to God that are interspersed between narrative passages in the autobiographical *Confessiones* of Augustine, which appears as an intertextual presence in the work.[67] There is a close topical connection between each prose-verse pair. In the first book the lyrical passages precede prose exhortations; in subsequent books they serve to sum up or epitomise what has gone before. As the pupil becomes stronger in his willing return to dependence on his mentor, the philosophical passages grow longer and the poetry seems to play a less prominent role. Boethius progressively shifts his emphasis away from the verse sections. Apparently arbitrarily longer or shorter episodic prose passages carry the weight of argument in Books 2 to 5, with the poetry in the end merely serving as gnomic comment.[68]

In this Boethius appears to be aware of both Christian and pagan precedents. The influence of Augustine, his Christian predecessor in auto-biographical poetic prose, is prominent, but so is a wide range of ancient philosophers and the pagan poets.[69] In his choice of the Menippean form and in his adept versification, Boethius appears to take a conscious stand against Augustine, but also against the spirit that moved Plato to banish poets and poetry from his ideal state, while he retains the Platonic concept of *anamnesis*.[70] For Boethius, the highest truth is not to be clothed in poetic form, yet for him poetry still has a role to play. Poetry is subservient to prose, but, as a serviceable tool in the hand of Philosophy, it is worthy of inclusion in a serious work.[71] As was Lucretius' Epicurean intention, to sweeten the rim of the cup of philosophy by means of the honey of poetry, so Boethius' poetic interludes seem merely to sweeten the teachings of his apparition.[72]

Boethius' poetry cannot be read divorced from his prose. It has been noticed throughout this study that the literature of exile is seldom free from the politics that caused that exile. Boethius gives very little contemporary comment, apart from naming the ingrates who turned on him (1.pr.4.7-46). His outburst is followed by one of the few songs laid in the mouth of the prisoner (1.m.5), a prayer bewailing his lot and questioning the justice of the Almighty. This serves as an indication to Dame Philosophy of how far her former pupil has fallen from grace and she gives his complaints short shrift (1.pr.5), after which she comforts him with a counter-song showing God as in control (1.m.6). Yet the poems perform an important political function. The theme of tyranny runs through several of the poems, indirectly pointing to the injustice of his persecutors, but as it would involve considerable allegorising in order to relate them directly to the politics of his day, I shall not pursue this line further.[73] More important is the fact that the poems, while showing affinities with a wide range of classical predecessors, tend, in their general tone and thrust, to celebrate the divine in celestial terms. This accords well with Philosophy's aim to raise the prisoner's attention from the mundane to the heavenly.

The work starts with the prisoner's own words. The introductory elegy, as programmatic poem, merits close attention. He is downcast and weak and, predictably, resorts to *flebile carmen*. The first poem, first prose section, and second poem together constitute what may be termed an 'anti-*recusatio*'; the imprisoned exile descends to the 'lowest type of composition' (that is, elegy), is warned away from it, and progresses to contemplation of greater things. Crabbe (1981a: 247) emphasises the witty playfulness that prompted an author *in extremis* to choose the Ovidian exilic medium for his prologue, if only to reject it for the body of his work in favour of his own unique adaptation of the consolatory tradition. In the prologue he manages to weld together the two traditions.

> *Carmina qui quondam studio florente peregi*
> *Flebilis heu maestos cogor inire modos.*
> *Ecce mihi lacerae dictant scribenda Camenae*
> *Et ueris elegi fletibus ora rigant.*
> *Has saltem nullus potuit peruincere terror,*
> *Ne nostrum comites prosequerentur iter.*
> *Gloria felicis olim uiridisque iuuentae*
> *Solantur maesti nunc mea fata senis.*
> *Venit enim properata malis inopsina senectus*
> *Et dolor aetatem iussit inesse suam.*
> *Intempestiui funduntur uertice cani*
> *Et tremit effeto corpore laxa cutis.*
> *Mors hominum felix quae se nec dulcibus annis*
> *Inserit et maestis saepe uocata uenit.*
> *Eheu quam surda miseros auertitur aure*
> *Et flentes oculos claudere saeua negat.*
> *Dum leuibus male fida bonis fortuna faueret,*
> *Paene caput tristis merserat hora meum.*
> *Nunc quia fallacem mutauit nubila uultum,*
> *Protrahit ingratas impia uita moras.*
> *Quid me felicem totiens iactastis amici?*
> *Qui cecidit, stabili non erat ille gradu.*[74]

I that with youthful heart did verses write,
Must now my woes in doleful tunes indite.
My work is framed by Muses torn and rude,
And my sad cheeks are with true tears bedewed:
For these alone no terror could affray
From being partners of my weary way.
The art that was my young life's joy and glory
Becomes my solace now I'm old and sorry;
Sorrow has filched my youth from me, the thief!
My days are numbered not by time, but Grief.[75]
Untimely hoary hairs cover my head,
And my loose skin quakes on my flesh half-dead.
O happy death, that spareth sweetest years,
And comes in sorrow often called with tears.
Alas, how deaf is he to wretch's cries;
And loath he is to close up weeping eyes;
While trustless chance me with vain favours crowned,
That saddest hour my life had almost drowned;
Now she hath clouded her deceitful face,
My spiteful days prolong their weary race.
My friends, why did you count me fortunate?
He that is fallen, ne'er stood in settled state.[76]

Although the poem employs *topoi* familiar from Ovid, and even echoes individual Ovidian expressions, Boethius' elegy, as versification, is a far cry from Ovid's. The texture of this short poem is much denser than any one of Ovid's longer effusions. The interlocking structural pattern of its topics is consequently more clearly discernible.

The poet has borrowed four basic Ovidian themes: (a) Contrast of a former happy state with a present state of misery; (b) consequent change in the type of poetry in which the exile indulges; (c) the equation of unwelcome life with tardy and hard-hearted death, and (d) the fickleness and mutability of Fortune.

Of these *topoi*, the first and last are also recognisable as elements of the consolatory genre, whereas the second (poetics and the discussion of literary resources) features in the consolatory tradition as a means of overcoming the hardships of both exile and bereavement. With Cicero and Ovid we have seen life as an exile equated with death, and in Seneca's consolation to his mother we have seen an inverted conflation of these concepts: the exile as 'deceased' consoles the living in her 'bereavement'. Boethius' treatment of this theme lies closer to Cicero and Ovid than to Seneca; for him, in this poem, death is hateful because it is tardy and because it is deaf to his pleas to come and end his misery.

In the course of eleven couplets the poet interweaves the four topics in the pattern: a (+b +d); b; a (+b); b; a; a; c; c (+a); d, c, d (+a). This oversimplified scheme does less than justice to the denseness of the verse. The first couplet picks up three of the topics, and may be assumed to imply the fourth. In emphatic first position in the hexameter *Carmina* introduces poetics as topic, although the thrust of the couplet contrasts the poet's former state and preoccupations with his present woes and elegiac composition *qui quondam studio florente peregi* (I who once when my studies flourished wrote [poetry]).[77] The pentameter turns to the passive voice: *cogor*, (I am forced ...) but again the second theme obtrudes in the emphatic positioning of *maestos ... modos* (sad ... measures). Alliteration contrasts *florente* (flourishing, 1) with *flebilis* (tearful, 2). What caused this change of state is not explained. The reader awaits a revelation of the agent of change, who will ultimately prove to be *male fida ... Fortuna* (untrustworthy Fortune, 17), although in v. 3 apparent blame is laid on the poet's *lacerae ... Camenae* (tattered Muses), themselves mutilated, like mourners at a Roman funeral, but still dictating to their votary what he should write.

Other Ovidian themes (also familiar from Cicero's exile) are interwoven with the four main topics. Verses 4-6 involve 'the true tears of elegy'[78] as 'companions to a journey'. The main thrust of the third couplet (5, 6) is by implication the change in the exile's state; he is deserted by all, only his tears are not prevented by the general terror from accompanying him. The next couplet shows, in Ovidian terms, a sad old man being comforted by the poetry that was his pride in his happy youth. Again topics (a) and (b) are skilfully intermingled:

9. Exile Universalised: Ovid's Contribution to the Exilic Genre

Gloria felicis olim viridisque inventae
Solantur maesti nunc mea fata senis.

The former glory of my flourishing youth now comforts the lot of a sad old man.

The term *mea fata*, frequent in Ovid, has undergone a subtle shift: Ovid's *fatum* was often equated with his persecutor as an objective reality that hurled him to his doom. Boethius' *fatum* is subjective: it is his suffering lot, the lot that is comforted by means of poetry.[79]

The central four couplets of the poem take up the themes of the exile's age and debilitation and his desire for death. In the first two, Boethius is, like Ovid, prematurely old; troubles and grief, not time, have added to his years. Here verbal echoes are fainter, but conceptually the couplets reflect frequent Ovidian sentiments. The exile is grey and his body emaciated and ill. A single dactylic pentameter (12) gives a concise but tellingly acoustic version of trembling and wrinkled eld:

> *Et tremit effeto corpore laxa cutis*[80]

And all a-tremble my loose skin on a dead body shakes.[81]

The second set of two couplets in the centre of the poem deals with longed-for death and its cruelty in refusing to visit the miserable victim. Again the thought closely parallels Ovidian despair at the refusal of death to open its door to him (*Tr.* 3.2). Boethius' objective physical metaphor, involving the 'deaf ear' of Death (15), is carried over into a subjective physical appeal in the next verse for Death to come and close the sufferer's weeping eyes, *flentes oculos*. This is reminiscent of *flebilis* in the opening couplet.

The alliterative significance of the sound *f* is picked up in the next couplet (17, 18), which introduces the idea of the fickleness of fortune. Here at last the poet firmly connects himself with the exiled Ovid, both verbally (*tristis*, 'sad') and conceptually (*merserat*, 'drowned', alluding to the shipwreck metaphor frequent in the older poet):

> *Dum levibus male fida bonis fortuna faveret,*
> *Paene caput tristis merserat hora meum*

While fickle Fortune favoured me with insignificant favours, now this sad hour nearly submerged my head.

In the penultimate couplet this theme gives way to the thematic complement of the tardiness of death: hated life protracts its sway. In the hexameter (19) alliteration of *f* in *fallacem* (deceitful) refers back to *fortuna* in verse 17, understood here as qualified by the unusual epithet *nubila* 'clouded'. The pentameter (20) has *impia vita* (spiteful life) as new subject.

The poem ends with apostrophe of those short-sighted friends who formerly called the poet 'happy'. By a paranomastic trick (also a favourite device with Ovid) the negative *fallacem* (deceitful) of verse 1 is echoed in the positive *felicem* (desired) of verse 21, adversely influencing the tone of the verse. Both words fill the second foot and emphatic first half of the third foot in their respective verses. *Fallacem* is preceded by a dactyl /*Nunc quia*/ ('now because', patterned as / – ∪ ∪ /), whereas the potentially optimistic word *felicem* is toned down by the slow emphasis of monosyllables in the spondaic first foot, /*Quid me*/ (/ – – /).

The pentameter of this last couplet opens with *qui*, echoing the *quid me* of its preceding hexameter. Here another fully dactylic verse with its uneven rhythm underlines the instability of the human condition: a man's fall underscores the fact that he formerly stood on a slippery step. The concept is new to the poetry of exile, and can be seen as Boethius' contribution to the genre, culled from philosophy. It rephrases the idea of the mutability of *fortuna*. It is essentially harking back to Solon's 'Count no man happy until you have seen his end'.

Such then, is Boethius' attempt at continuing the elegiacs of exile, from which Philosophia soon weans him. It is remarkable, however, that a six verse epigram (discovered by Barth and published in 1624),[82] ascribed to one Symmachus (either Boethius' son or his father-in-law), celebrates the exiled consular in the same despised metre that had informed the Ovidian exilic corpus.

SUMMACHI VERSUS
Fortunae et uirtutus opus, Seuerine Boethi,
  E patria pulsus non tua per scelera,
Tandem ignotus habes qui te colat, ut tua uirtus
  Vt tua fortuna promeruitque sophôs
Post obitum dant fata locum, post fata superstes
  Vxoris propriae te quoque fama colit.

EPIGRAM BY SYMMACHUS
Boethius! model of all weal and worth,[83]
Unjustly from thy country driven forth,
Thy fame, unfamed at last, yet one shall praise,
One voice the cry of approbation raise;
What life denied, through death kind heaven giveth;
Thine honour in thy wife's for ever liveth.

The epigram covers exilic themes complementing those of Boethius' introductory poem: that the consular was unjustly exiled (1, 2) that his fortune (a positive equivalent of his virtue) and his virtue will still be praised (3, 4) and that Fate will give him, after his death, what was denied before (5,

6). In punning play *fata* occurs twice in the fifth verse, first in positive terms, as 'kind Fate', and then as the equivalent of 'death'.

Two recognisably Ovidian echoes complete the fifth verse *post fata* (after your death) and *superstes* (relic). It would appear to be poetic justice of a unique kind that the imprisoned and martyred exile is here assured of immortality in terms of his wife's fame.[84] Centuries before, the exiled Ovid, in a reversal of Roman elegiac convention, had raised his absent wife to a position of honour in his exilic poetry and had promised to confer immortality upon her by means of his elegiacs.[85] Such is the final paradox of the literature of exile. The fame of Boethius (here emphatically designated an 'exile') has, so posterity is informed, been preserved by means of the lasting fame of his faithful wife.

Epilogue

In our progress through the grammatical persons of exilic literature we have met many personalities. Of these, in the end those authors who present us with a series of alternating *personae* have proved the most complex and challenging. Common to all has been a conscious distancing between creative author and autobiographical 'I', who, in each case, but perhaps in varying degrees, has been given heroic, mythical stature. In the world of the exile we have seen the hero standing alone. There is always at least one other presence, the imagined reader, who also may seem to shimmer into a series of separate *personae*, of which some seem more sympathetic than others, and among whom one may often distinguish the malevolent power whose influence placed the exile in his invidious position. These readers as *personae* comprise the composite 'second person-as-addressee'.

Central to the horror of exile is the horror of isolation, often portrayed as loss of speech,[1] but, because we are dealing in *verbalised* thought, this 'loss' is as stylised as the mythic dimensions of the hero's woe which it strives to portray. Exile both remains a topic of third person narrative and gains importance as the springboard of ancient first person autobiographical outreach to a second person. Tales of exile abound. Our literate and literary exiles continue to write, and they write to be read. In commonality of intention (an autobiographical urge 'to portray their own exile') they are united as producers of what we have increasingly seen as a single genre, in the Aristotelian sense of 'writings about humanity-within-a-given-situation'.

Opposed to the 'imagined' or 'ostensible' readers are the 'real' readers of exilic literature, in the continuum of the literary tradition. These often become the next purveyors of the same tradition. Ovid's myth of exile has gripped the imagination of many authors, some who were actually banned to the same regions, such as Pushkin, who himself suffered exile to the Crimea.

Normally the *Metamorphoses* are considered the chief Ovidian source from which later ages drew, but the exilic poetry also has a poetic *Nachleben*. The most exhaustive discussion of exilic typology is a monograph by Froesch (1976). The book consists of short comments, mostly of a literary-critical nature, and long prose translations from the exilic works illustrating the critic's various points. It has a very extensive and useful bibliography. I should not weary my reader with a complete excursus on those many works either quoted or otherwise referred to throughout the course of this study, which would include not only Ovid's imitators, but also translators, but I end with a rapid review of some of the most bizarre, ingenious or important, starting with the *Carmina Burana*. Viarre (1980) quotes *Bibit pauper / Bibit exsul et ignotus* (The poor man drinks, so drinks too the exiled unknown) as an example of Ovidian 'inspiration' of a poem.

In all ages poets would turn to Ovid if they felt their circumstances resembled his. The youthful John Milton was 'sent down from Cambridge' to his father's house in London at the age of 17. His *Elegia Prima* is an amusing reversal of the Ovidian example: London as 'place of exile' offers all that Rome would have offered an otiose resident, and Cambridge as the 'house' he has left, is as unpleasant as Tomis. Open flouting of the homophobic *mores* of his time made of Oscar Wilde another Ovid; for him, too, poetry was life, and life poetry. His offence was against the accepted morality of his time, as much as Ovid's ever was against the morals Augustus wanted to propagate. His 'exile' was imprisonment, for him a living grave whence he, too, expressed his inner thoughts: 'All trials are trials for one's life, just as all sentences are sentences of death, and three times have I been tried ...' (from Wilde's *De Profundis*, quoted by 'Stuart Mason' = Millard 1912: 203-4). Mason also quotes from a letter by R. Buchanan in *The Star*, 23 April 1895: 'Two-thirds of all Mr. Wilde has written is purely ironical, and it is only because they are now told that the writer is a wicked man that people begin to consider his writings wicked'. One could imagine, *mutatis mutandis*, one of Ovid's contemporaries, perhaps Cotta or Macer, saying much the same

Sometimes the story of Ovid's banishment served as direct inspiration for fictionalisation of his life. From the thirties we have John Masefield's long narrative poem linking Ovid with Julia the Younger and a production of his *Medea* (1936). Its typifying of Augustus is worth quoting:

> ... a white head
> which swayed the world a thousand miles away,
> turn where you would: a little cold white voice
> spoke to me without passion, finally!

Green (1982b) quotes from an unpublished poem by Dr Caroline Callway Preston of Ottawa. It is a *cri de coeur* of the general reader who cannot find the 'real Ovid' in the varied and fragmented approaches of so many critics. She finally finds him in his works. The poem is sensitive and shows an awareness, not only of the puzzling aspects of the Ovidian oeuvre, but also of its beauty.

Before the fall of the various totalitarian regimes of the Communist world, Ovid often seemed to work as a rallying-point for protest literature.

Smolak (1980) gives a startling view of the legends that arose around the view of Ovid as a 'rebel author', for instance, 'the poet refused to write the *Carmen Saeculare* and was exiled'. Smolak gives a balanced discussion of the type of generic over-simplification and type-casting which gives rise to erroneous self-identifications with the poet, as, for instance, by an East German poet who felt trammeled by both DDR authoritarianism and the West German capitalistic literary market. A Roumanian poet in Italy, A.L. Gregorian (1958) celebrates Ovid at the Black Sea, bewails the modern poet's 'reversed exile' to Rome and the 'Getae in chains' (presumably under Communist rule).

A Russian poet, J. Borovski (1959), writing from Leningrad, celebrates the bimillennium of the poet (a year after his Western counterparts). I quote the closing couplets of the rather pedestrian poem:

> *rite igitur tibi natales bis mille peractos*
> *grato prosequitur pectore posteritas.*
> *vive vale aeternum, crescat tibi gloria pollens*
> *neu desunt umquam qui tua verba legant.*

Therefore as your birthday has been duly celebrated for twice a thousand years, posterity follows you with grateful heart. Live on eternally, and fare you well! May your all-powerful glory grow and may there never be a lack of those who would read your words.

So much for poetry. This century has seen at least three novelists who found their inspiration in the amazing power and beauty with which Ovid imbued his fictional world. A Roumanian exile in Paris composed a remarkable compendium of facts, fictions, legends and theories (even unto the 'Christian' aspects of Fränkel's 1945 criticism of Ovid as 'a poet between two worlds'). Vintila Horia wrote the novel *Dieu est né en exil* in the late 1950s. It was translated by A. Lytten Sells and published in English in 1961. It is very ingenious in some of its decorative flourishes: the exile has a dog called Augustus, he writes Getic love poems to help a friend's courtship, he journeys inland. His acceptance of a monotheistic 'pre-Christian' god, the Thracian Zamolxis, is however patently absurd. The work is very firmly bedded in Horia's own perception of his own exile as a fugitive from Communism and the depth of his personal faith. Katz (1992) gives interesting background on Horia's involvement in Hitlerian anti-Semitism and its subsequent influence on readings of his novel.[2]

The next excursion into novelistic fantasy virtually takes the poet's name in vain. Malouf (*c.* 1970), sets his novel in Tomis where his 'exiled poet' has 'visions' of 'the Child' that inspired his poetry, but which ultimately turns out to be a proverbial 'wild child' whom the hero tames. To the extent that this 'wild child' may be associated with *Amor* as the wayward pupil of the erstwhile *lusor amorum* (as in *Pont.* 3.3), the fantasy works, but in the end we must surmise that it was Ovid's portrayal of the fantastic externals of his place of banishment that prompted the author to set his tale in Tomis. Malouf may have chosen Ovid as his protagonist simply to fit the poet and his place of relegation into a fantasy plot because the wildness of the place as described by Ovid gripped his imagination.

The third and most impressive of the novels based on the outlines of Ovid's story is the Austrian author Ransmayr's post-modern excursion into 'magic realism'. Published in Germany as *Die Letzte Welt* (Frankfort-am-Main, Eichborn) and translated into English by John Woods (1990), it is a blend of 'facts' culled from Ovid's exilic poems with the fantasies of Ovid's own *Metamorphoses*. This work, in its emphasis on the dangers inherent in the kind of politics that seeks to tame literature, shows, as few others do, the timelessness of Ovidian subversive creativity. Christensen (1992: 140) comments that the work makes Ovid 'more politically radical, thematically apocalyptic and aesthetically post-modern than [he is] usually pictured'. Its theme is the search for the poet by a friend, Cotta (simultaneously like and unlike the poet's correspondent of that name) in the arid, mountainous country that is Ransmayr's Tomis, in an era that is simultaneously redolent of Augustus, of Mussolini and of every other dictator that ever threatened the integrity of spirit of any author, anywhere. Cotta never finds the poet, but he meets with personages that re-enact the metamorphic details of characters from Ovid's compendium of myths, while mysteriously reminiscing about the poet who had dwelt among them.

In the end the searcher finds the lost poet's message in the 'tattered banners' woven by the deaf-mute weaver 'Arachne'. She has in this way preserved the stories told her by the poet. This is no place to initiate a discussion of the semiotic significance critics see in Ovid's narrative in *Metamorphoses* 6 of Arachne's weaving of a complex tapestry showing the deeds of the gods. Its is enough to say that Ransmayr has succeeded in capturing the richness of layered thought that makes all of Ovid's poetry an inexhaustible source of new discoveries for every new generation of readers, also those with an own political (or literary) programme. A critic like Nethersole (1992), for instance relates the work to what he terms the 'crisis of the novel'.[3]

I close with an interesting double example that may be traced back to Ovid as establisher both of the conventions of exilic literature and of protest against public interference into private morality. When the Afrikaans poet N.P. Van Wyk Louw was teaching in Amsterdam in the 1950s, he produced a volume of 'sad songs' entitled *Tristia*. Longing for South Africa, his *patria* and his spiritual Rome, is a central theme, but so too is criticism of the country. South Africa was then in the first years of the formal establishment of racism as a political principle (*apartheid*) and as a means of ordering the state, a system that later turned the eyes of the world upon the country as the place where the state interfered with the basic fabric of human existence. As with his predecessors, Louw's work reflects the political issues of his era, but also his own cultural preferences. He would like to remake Africa in a European, Mediterranean image:[4]

> *My land, my dor, verlate land:*
> *iets wens olywe groei in jou:*
> *dat alles klein, Latyns, gaan word*
> *en kalk-wit kerkies bou.* ('H. Petrus', *Tristia*)

> My land, my drab, deserted land:
> oh, that olives grew in you,
> that all could shrink to Latin size
> and sprout small chalk-white churches too. ('St. Peter', *Tristia*)

Strongly influenced by Louw, in the seventies came Breyten Breytenbach, the *enfant terrible* of the Afrikaans literary scene. No Latinist, he had a stronger and more direct affinity with Ovid; he transgressed the grotesque, race-besotted South African marriage laws by wedding a 'brown' Vietnamese.[5] The ideology of *apartheid* had become firmly established as the ruling principle of South African society, and central to it was a rigid set of embargoes on interracial marriage, far more stringent than Augustus' attempts to regulate Roman domestic morality by means of legislation. These embargoes turned that most private and moral of human customs, marriage (if contracted between 'unsuitable' partners), into the most immoral of South African public 'crimes'. Breytenbach spent many years, with his wife, in self-imposed exile in Paris, writing in his beloved and hated Afrikaans, but publishing in his home country. He, too, wanted to remake his lost home into a spiritual haven, an ideal state, an *alma Roma* where *amor* is replaced by a universal *caritas*:

> *My broer, my dor, verlate broer:*
> *iets wens dat mens weer in jou groei*
> *dat alles groots, Afrikaans gaan word*
> *en jy ook in mensbruin mense bloei.* ('Bruin reisbrief', *Oorblyfsels*)

> My brother, my drab, deserted brother,
> oh that your human heart would come alive
> that greatness Afrikaans could be
> and you too as brown humanity could thrive
> ('Brown travelogue', *Remains*)

This poem consciously imitates Louw, but Ovid looms large in it as an unconscious intertext. Ovid would have understood its political thrust and the love of his mother-tongue which the poet exhibits while rejecting its authoritarian abuse in the kind of oppressive and censorious legislation that strove to direct private lives by public decree. And when Breytenbach, inept political intriguer that he was, secretly slipped back into the country and was caught red-handed in a vain political plot, his love-hate writings from prison, also those in English, reflect the psychological resilience that we have seen enhanced in our Roman exiles by the solace offered by their literary exertions.

Breytenbach in prison exhibits an inner exile, an alienation from the religion that was subverted for political ends, a questioning of the values of the wielders of political and judicial power, a concern for literary and cultural issues voiced in ingenious, punning play, and an ostensible self-denigration, that point for point agree with the intellectual resistance voiced by Ovid in his own love-hate relationship with *Roma aeterna*:

> There may be silences. There will certainly be silences. The moon outside the bars will be curled like a cold white caterpillar, but the cold white light will be copious nevertheless, and white and cold the inundated world. Don Espejuelo's eyes will be closed to slits against the acrid smoke of the cheap snout he used to roll his pills [cigarettes]. 'Homesick?' he would ask. Crack a joint. 'Home? What home? Where ...? What a debilitating concept. Fool! Fool!'

INSERT

It is certainly true that the whole process of punishment, the inordinate insistence upon punishment, the proliferation of prisons, the amplification of the concept and its applications until you have a prison universe, an alternative world, a culture of darkness – it is certainly true that all this ties in with the Protestant ethic. I don't know off-hand of any culture where you are, as in No Man's Land, born guilty to die guilty except (very rarely: Heaven is a tight joint) when you are, provisionally and arbitrarily, saved by the Investerrogator. With luck (or if the Law does not cover enough ground) the Greyshits, His soldiers on earth, will desist for the time being from punishing or terrorising you. The dichotomy is 'guilt'/freedom. Where freedom does not exist, except as a subversive idea.

It is not only the cadre within which you evolve. The dichotomy has its objective existence also inside you. You are guilty even when you do not yet know of what. You are the mirroring of your environment with all its broken monkeys. Where freedom does not exist except as a subversive idea.

It can be said that we have to do here with real democracy. You are a consciousness-generating, surroundings-expanding force, the way the termite is. You are a twinge of Conscience. And the Conscience, the great Justification, is the *State*. The State *is* in reality the earthly shape and the terrestrial abode of Him, the Interstigator. And Minister Kruger[6] said, 'The highest good is the security of the State'. (Can we allow the killing of God? Let us all unite to combat evil ... which dwells within us .... To suicide, citizens!)

The State lives inside you. You are its condition. Except that the State is pure though jealous. Thou shalt have no other idols or urinations or blots. There will be no dissidence. You will not prostrate yourself before any other idea. Who else will be able to punish you? What other security can compare with the foot and the neck? There is no freedom (*that* is a fart of the heart) – there can only be guilt in its million convolutions and revelations. There can only be the twitching of many moustaches.

But the celebration of guilt can only take place in secret places. That too is part of the ethic: the need to hide, the need to pretend. It could be that other cultures, at other times, made a public display of their intimate rites – that they broke and burned their heretics on the market place. We, in our twisted ways, have to be subtle. We are not to be known, we are only to be raped.

The true confessions of an albino terrorist (1984: 214-15)

Breytenbach's wordplay and soundplay in Afrikaans are almost impossible to render into another language. His ingenious distortions here of the English words 'investigator' and 'instigator', with the underlying echo of 'interrogation' and 'terrorism' is worthy of an Ovid, but takes the process of *paranomasia* a step further than ever discerned in his Roman counterpart in the investigations of Ahl (1986). Breytenbach is as defiant of the state as Ovid was, but coarser and less subtle. It is a reflection of the profound political change in the modern poet's home country (and mine) that he is now seen as the honoured elder poet of the Afrikaans literary scene. The exiled Ovid could only boast that he had become a *poeta Getes*. He remained in exile. Only his spirit was free to roam, but no amount of paranomastic play ever turned this word into 'Rome'.

Today still, the literature of exile frees the displaced writer from his burden of loneliness and provides him with a versatile tool for significant interaction with others. The exiled 'I' tells a distant 'you' about the 'him' upon whom his words will exert revenge. By this means the displaced person creates his own place in history.

Notes

1. Exiled Persons

1. Boethius merits inclusion in this study, both in his own right and in his position as virtually the 'last Classical author'. This Christian scholar assured his own lasting memorial by adapting pagan literary tradition to pagan philosophy. At the same time Boethius appears as the precursor of modern 'Western' man, whose particular religious persuasion may be a fact of his life, but does not necessarily explicitly inform what he writes. The individual colouring that he imparts to his work stems from literary preference, not from crusading religious conviction. Boethius' *Consolatio Philosophiae* does not pretend to give a new, Christian answer to the existential problems and profound alienation involved in the imprisonment and exile of a Roman politician, but refines the pagan thought that had sustained (or failed to sustain) a vast procession of his pagan predecessors.

2. On Ovid's creation of the myth of exile Claassen (1988: 158-69); Ehlers (1988: 144-57); Doblhofer (1987: 261-73).

3. Ulpian *D* XXXXVIII.19.2 pr (1207); Levy (1963: 325-78).

4. Cic. *Balb*. 11.27; 12.29-30.

5. Cic. *Dom*. 30, 78.

6. Plin. Min. *Ep*. 4.11. Bonjour (1985) argues for Ovid's poetry as conscious transgression of his interdiction.

7. J. 331/2-29; 654; Appian 6.c.1.31; Gaius 1.128, Ulpian 11.12, 32, 1.2. Cf. Mommsen (1887: 6, 47, 51, 53, 140 and 141 n. 1).

8. Polyb. *Hist*. 6.14.7. Livy 1.1.50; 3.58.10; 25.4.9; 29.21.1.

9. Grasmück (1978: 62-102).

10. Recent studies: Williams (1996), Doblhofer (1987), Grasmück (1978) and the introduction to Caballero and Viansino (1995: 16-20).

11. On Cicero's letters as 'a good substitute for the history Cicero never wrote', Nepos *Att*. 16.3-4 and Fr. 58. Cf. Fleck (1993) on Cicero's historiographical sources.

12. Cicero *Q.Fr*. 1.1.45 *ego, quia cum tua lego, te audire, et quia cum ad te scribo, tecum loqui videor* ... (I seem to hear your voice when I read your letter, and when I write to you I feel as if I'm speaking to you).

13. E.g. Quintilian's reading list for orators, 10.1.20-31.

14. The term 'intertextual' refers not so much to direct quotation of a previous work (frequent in ancient literary convention) but the 'presence' of an older work, that must be recognised by a reader to impart additional meaning the text at hand (Vincent 1994). Du Plooy (1986) offers a readable journey through this minefield.

15. Recent critics that touch on this: Redmond (1997), Buchan (1995), Desmond (1993), Farrell (1992).

16. Related by Redmond (1997), as the 'theory whereby we use structure to create meaning out of disorder', to Ovidian penchant for 'disorder' in the *Metamor-*

phoses. Ovid shows himself in *Tr.* 2.255-466 keenly aware of the role of the reader in constructing meaning, so Buchan (1995).

17. Eco in his Norton lectures (Eco 1994: 15-16 and 144 nn. 14, 15), compares it with Iser's concepts of the 'Implied Reader' and 'Implied' or 'Virtual Author'. Cf. Downing (1993): 'The author makes a self, while the self makes a book of the self.'

18. Rawson (1985: 280-1).

19. Aristotle's *Poetics* are descriptive rather than normative. In *Poetics* 1.1447a18-b29, reacting against Plato's tripartite division of literature (*mimesis* – 'imitation' – narration and a combined mode, *Republic* 3.394B and C), he takes *mimesis* in literature as given, but offers three further criteria: medium, object and manner of presentation. He distributes the various *media* of literature, rhythm, words, and melody variously in the different genres he distinguishes, as summarised by Celliers (1986).

20. Aristotle next focuses on the *object*, man-in-action, distinguishing between 'heroic' and 'common' man as the protagonists in, respectively, tragedy and comedy (*Poetics* 2.1448a1-18). In *Poetics* 3.1448a19-28, ignoring the Platonic 'mixed' genre, he distinguishes between only two *manners* of presentation, narrative and dramatic, a generic division that considers use of either third person or first person verbs. Continuous prose and lyric poetry are excluded from all the above approaches; Celliers (1986).

21. The Peripatetics confined their interpretation to a bipartite system: whatever was not dramatic (even epic, elegy, iambic and lyrical poetry) was considered to be narrative. Quintilian's analysis (*Inst.* 10) was empiric, largely concentrating on style, where *metre* was the poetic criterion, and *manner* (high, middle or low style) the criterion of prose. His concentration on *imitatio* (*Inst.* 1.11.3 and 10.2.1) emphasised the importance of tradition and its fluid, creative adaptation in Roman literature.

22. As in Cicero, *Orator* 61-8.

23. This view has been adapted by Cairns (1972), reapplying Menander Rhetor's use of taxonomic rhetorical terminology to poetry. Beside the 'large concepts' of epic and elegy, tragedy and comedy, oratory and philosophy, he distinguishes as subgenres or classes of literature, also in respect of poetry, the divisions of ancient rhetoric, and advocates analysis of individual poems into subgenres or *topoi*, subsuming an essential 'generic mix' in ancient poetry, or 'generic experimentation'. His approach has generally been acclaimed, but has also been criticised for exhibiting a paradoxical combination of rigidity and fluidity in its taxonomy, e.g. by Griffin (1981). Yet topical sub-classification within broader metrical classification, will, for instance, distinguish pastoral from heroic epic.

24. Modern reception theory is addressed in understandable terms by Glücklich (1988), Du Plooy (1986) and Eco (1994).

25. The concept 'empirical reader' may be further categorised into 'empirical' or 'ostensible' *addressee*, the person who is the first recipient of a particular work (of greater importance in the limited form that publication of ancient texts took), and 'empirical' or 'real-life' *reader*, of whom there have been thousands over the intervening centuries, and of whom the present critic and her readership comprise some of the latest instances.

26. For example, exile was decreed as punishment for capital crime; Paul. D. 48.1.2 (260): *per has poenas eximitur caput de civitate* (by this punishment his person – lit. *head* – is cut off from the state).

27. Cf. Cugusi (1983: 252).

28. Plut. *ad loc.* On Caeso, Servilius Ahala and Camillus, also see Cic. *Dom.* 32.86, Plut. *Mor.* 605E.

29. Cf. Cic. *Fin.* 2.65, etc. For further references, see discussion in Chapter 2 and Mix (1970: 35ff.). Mix postulates that the 'heroic Regulus' was a creation of Cicero's, on which he thereafter sustained himself, but offers a cautionary rider (38 n. 59) that such a patriotic version was perhaps already current.

30. Val. Max. 3.8.5 and 1.5.5.9; Cic. *Red. Pop.* 3.6; *Planc.* 36.88; *Red. in Sen.* 15.37-8. Fragments survive of Cicero's epic poem on Marius. See Ewbank (1933); also Soubirac (1972: 42-51).

31. Negative: *Red. in Sen.* 15.37-8, *Planc.* 36.88; positive: *Red. Pop.* 3.6.

32. Cf. Hor. *Carmina* 1.7.1; See Wilson (1965: 129, 162-70).

33. Sall. *Jug.* 16.2ff.; Plut. *C. Gracch.* 18.2.

34. Cic. *Brut.* 224ff.; *Planc.* 36, etc.; Appian *B.Civ.* 1.28-33; Plut. *Mar.* 28-30. Grün (1965: 576-80).

35. Peter (1914: CCLIV-CCLXI) references and (187-190) *testimonia* and fragments; Kallet-Marx (1990). See Rawson (1985: 64, 109) on the claim by Theophanes of Mytilene, rejected by Plutarch and criticised by Strabo 11.C 528, that Rutilius had urged Mithridates to massacre Roman citizens. Kroll (1939: 1179) comments that Cicero exhibits no sign of philosophy when he needs it most, and that he cannot follow the example of Rutilius.

36. So Petersson (1920: 253), Gelzer *RE* 7.A.1.878. Critics differ on Cicero's intentions. Stockton (1971: 118) reckons Cicero hoped that Catiline would already have left before the Senate meeting. See Stroh (1982).

37. Cic. *Dom.* 32.86, Plut. *Mor.* 605E.

38. *Fam.* 15.1-4. Cf. Williams (1958: 225-7).

39. See the new edition by Degl' Innocenti Pierini (1996). This important critic has received less attention in the Anglo-Saxon world than her meticulous scholarship warrants. Cf. Claassen (1992) and (1996a), Gottlieb (1982). Froesch (1976: 80-83) discusses Cicero's letters as source for Ovid. Cf. Leopold (1904).

40. On shifts in Cicero's perception of his exile, Grasmück (1978: 110-26), Claassen (1992a), Narducci (1997).

41. Lossmann (1962) sees the year 54 as pivotal in this relationship. This study concentrates on the earlier letters.

42. Sall. *Cat.* 52; Vell. Pat., 2.35.3. See Cartwright (1984: 34-7) and Dorey (1965 *passim*).

43. Cf. Plut. *Mor.* 605E. Waters (1970), supported by Seager (1973) and countered by Phillips (1976), argues that Cicero blew the affair out of proportion to suit his own purposes. Rundell (1979: 301-28) argues plausibly for a view of Clodius as less of a populist and demagogue than of a political force with continued influence in the Senate, whose attitude to Cicero remained consistent, belying Cicero's view of his banishment as a 'freak occurrence'. Cf. Mandell (1983-4) on the nature of Roman political rivalry in the last years of the Republic.

44. *Att.* 2.5.1, 2.16.2.

45. Cic. *Pis.* 9 designates these as *ex servitiorum faece constituta* (made up from the dregs of servility).

46. Plut. *Pomp.* 45.4.

47. Cic. *Sest.* 55, *Prov. Cons.* 46 and *Pis.* 9 presents this as 'abolition' of the office. Mitchell (1986: 172-6) questions this. Cf. Rundell (1979: 309-13).

48. According to Cicero, *Sest.* 39, *tribunum popularem a se alienare nolebant* (they did not wish to alienate a popular tribune from their cause). Cf. *Red. in Sen.* 32, *Har. Resp.* 47, *Prov. Cons.* 42, *Pis.* 79.

49. Cicero later (*Dom.* 72) denied that it ever was exile. Technically, Clodius' action against him was later construed as *privilegium* (a private law enacted against a single person) and therefore the enactment was invalid, so Gelzer (1939: 920).

50. The dating of these early missives and Cicero's route are problematical. Cf. Shackleton Bailey (1965: 227-35), App. I.

51. His defence of Gabinius (54) was unsuccessful. On Cicero's varying attitudes, Grasmück (1978: 115-24).

52. See the end of this chapter.

53. Also in another fragment quoted by the scholiast on Juvenal *Sat.* 5.109.

54. Plut. *Mor.* 607C quotes Empedocles on the more traditional, diametrically opposite philosophical assumption equating life on earth with 'exile from heaven'.

55. Van Stekelenburg (1971: 21f).

56. Kassel (1958: 13 and 46) cites Gorgias' composition of fictional consolations to historical figures.

57. Macmullen (1967: 66 and 310 n. 22), Manning (1981: 12-20).

58. With Bion he was influential in the development of the *diatribe*. His fragments *peri phugês* date from *c.* 242-229 BC, so Dörrie (1979: 5.570). Manning (1981: 67) fixes the *datum ante quam* at 227.

59. Fr. Hense p. 50ff. Cf. Jagu (1979) and Lutz (1947), also Macmullen (1967: 310).

60. De Lacy and Einarson (Plut. *Mor.* vol. 7, 1949: 515 n. a) quote Gieseke (1891) and Hässler (1935); cf. Macmullen (1967: 65-6), Bowersock (1969: 36-88).

61. Von Arnim (1898: 234-43).

62. Cic. *Parad.* 1.8: *omnia mecum porto* (I carry everything with me); Seneca *Ep.* 9.18, *Const. Sap.* 5.6.

63. Döring (1972: 141) lists *testimonia*, and variant sources.

64. On exile as a disease, Doblhofer (1987: 59).

65. Shackleton Bailey *ad loc.* assigns it to 46, ascribing its concerns to political disquiet rather than bereavement.

66. *Fam.* 5.16. Cf. Williams (1958: 390 n. a.)

67. Van Wageningen (1916), following the nineteenth-century critic Buresch, cites Cicero's probable sources: the Academic Crantor's *consolatio* to Hippocles on the death of his children, Panaetius, Plato, Diogenes, Clitomachus, Carneades and Posidonius, probably others also, possibly sources for Jerome's catalogue in the *Epistola ad Heliodorum de morte Nepotiani* (*Ep.* 60.5.2.); see Scourfield (1993) *ad loc.*, Cic. *Div.* 2.1.3, Plezia (1989) and Doignon (1993).

68. Discussed in a sympathetic introduction by Ian Kidd (1992).

69. See the scathing review by Phillipson (1918), upheld by David Scourfield in a personal communication, Sept. 1993.

70. Cf. Degl' Innocenti Pierini (1990b: 213-50); Savon (1979), Grimal (1984), Grasmück (1978: 138).

71. Recently edited, with introduction, by Caballero and Viansino (1995), who trace the tradition back to Bion.

72. De Lacy and Einarson (1949: 513), Mommsen (1887: 47, 51).

73. The so-called *Consolatio ad Liviam* on the death of Drusus, an elegy of 237 couplets, which is part lament, part mythicising celebration of her dead son, may date from about 13 but is almost certainly not by Ovid, so Fuhrmann (1979: 1.1282). Degl' Innocenti Pierini (1990b: 234) dates it *post* Seneca, and traces the influence of his *Consolatio ad Polybium* in its attitude to the imperial household.

74. De Lacy (1947) sees in *Tr.* 3.7 an almost Stoic defiance and triumphant 'elevation of the goods of the mind above country, home and life' but 'the effect, not the philosophy, ... is primary for Ovid'.

75. See Claassen (1989: 252-66) and De Lacy (1947: 153-61).

76. Doblhofer (1987: 102-9, 261-73).

77. This poem has been given an unusual interpretation by Paoletta (1993) who assumes that Gallio's new wife ('Annaea Seneca') was Ovid's (ex-) first wife, thereby ingeniously linking Ovid with the Seneca family (we know that Gallio adopted one of the sons of Seneca the Elder). She identifies Ovid's fictional heroine of the *Amores* with the empress Livia, thereby offering an ingenious new explanation for the emperor's ire, by assuming that Annaea and Livia conspired to 'frame' the poet in the eyes of Augustus. All this is based on an allegorical interpretation of a cryptogram by the painter Isaicus, to be found in the Naples Archaeological Museum, the original provenance of which the author assumes to have been the house of Germanicus and Agrippina at Oplontis. She dates the painting to AD 24. There is no proof, except for the name 'Livia' labelling a picture of a spider.

78. See the recent edition by Costa (1994).

79. Degl' Innocenti Pierini (1990b: 213) puts the problem into perspective with reference to moderns' 'idealisation' of Seneca, and shows (213-50) that the whole works as conformist panegyric that is completely in accord with the author's 'understandable debilitation in exile'.

80. It also romanticises the protagonist, showing him as an Homeric hero, overcoming great odds. Cf. Von Arnim (1898: 223-308) and Jones (1978: 45-55). See Chapter 6 for more extensive references.

81. The most recent commentary available is that of O'Donnell (1984).

82. Milanese (1995) argues for Boethius' initial admiration of Cicero as a paradigm of political martyrdom, but his gradual shift towards showing the vanity of *gloria* against the lasting value of the contemplative life.

83. See Chapters 3 and 9 for extensive references. Fuhrmann (1984), Gibson (1981), Masi (1981) and Obertello (1981) combine in four volumes wide-ranging scholarship on his oeuvre with discussion and indices of the tradition of his influence. Courcelle (1967), still the standard work on the *Consolatio Philosophiae*, combines discussion with extensive illustration. Cf. Buresch (1886: 121-42).

84. See Kaylor (1992) for a thorough bibliography, also his comment (p. 14) that mediaeval readers would not have distinguished prisoner and author.

85. See Watts (1969: 7, 8) and Courcelle (1967: 340 *et passim*) on views of Boethius as last Roman or first mediaeval philosopher.

86. Uhlfelder (1981) argues for his conscious use of established literary traditions, including Lucretius, Seneca and Roman comedy. Gruber (1978: 16-19) adds others.

87. See extensive discussion in Chapter 9. Crabbe (1981a: 260ff.) compares the poetic interludes with Augustine's prose addresses to God in the *Confessiones*. Curley (1987) shows that Boethius uses the poetic interludes to place his philosophy in literary perspective, the verse carrying the universals of the philosophy.

88. Boethius' philosophical sources merit study. See Milanese (1995); cf. Courcelle (1967: 114-27, 203ff., 333-40), Gruber (1978: 27-40), Kirkby (1981: 61), Crabbe (1981a: 239 and 1981b).

89. On Boethius as translator of Greek philosophy, Chapter 3; also Kirkby (1981: 56); his Christian background, Crabbe (1981a: 261), Starnes (1981), Mohrmann (1976), against these, De Vogel (1981).

90. Gruber (1978: 24-42), Gegenschatz (1958).

91. Claassen (1992a), Narducci (1997).

92. See Chapter 2 for a fuller discussion of the sequence of events.

93. *Att.* 3.1-3.12, 3.19, 3.25, 3.27, 4.1. See Chapter 4.

94. See the chronological listing in Degl' Innocenti Pierini (1996: 165-6); Gottlieb (1982: 281-96).

95. Designated 'Heimwehkrankheit' by Ernst Doblhofer (1987: 99-178). Cf. Trisoglio (1984: 125). As will be seen below, Cicero was not *exiled*, but 'relegated', that is, *banished with retention of his property*, but the terms are used indiscriminately by modern authors.

96. Narducci (1996) shows that Cicero never draws himself as a Stoic, as he is far more aware of what he gave up for the sake of his fatherland than a true Stoic would, who would have despised attachment to worldly possessions.

97. His house had been razed by Clodius, its grounds consecrated to Libertas. See Narducci (1996) on Cicero's philosophical stance, and Claassen (1992a: 19-47) for his reactions to exile.

98. Cf. Grasmück (1978: 110).

99. Rawson (1975: 117) labels these 'highly rhetorical apologias'. On Cicero's varying attitudes, Grasmück (1978: 115-24).

100. Usefully listed by Verdière (1992); cf. Claassen (1994).

101. Claassen (1990a) and Chapter 7.

102. Schmitzer (1990) argues for subversive attacks on the emperor Augustus and his regime on almost every page.

103. Newlands (1995), against whom a more cautious Fantham (1997), who writes of Ovid's 'ambidexterity' in working with two very different kinds of poetry at once.

104. Dating and chronology, Claassen (1986) Section 4.1.

105. See Chapters 4, 5 and 9; Ehlers (1988), Claassen (1987).

106. E.g. *Pont.* 2.5.18 *quae minus Augusta pace fruatur humus* (the soil that enjoys too little of Augustus' peace); cf. *Tr.* 3.10.67 and 5.2.31, 32.

107. On the literary character of the genre, Froesch (1969) ch. 4.

108. Barsby (1978), Block (1982).

109. 'Verbal schizophrenia', Doblhofer (1986).

110. Chapters 4, 8 and 9; Doblhofer (1987: 277-81). Earlier: Heinze (1919: 1-130); De Saint Denis (*c.* 1954 *passim*); Vulpe (1959: 39-62); Lechi (1978: 1-22).

111. See Chapter 4 for discussion of *candide lector*, *Tr.* 1.11.35, *lector*, 4.1.2; *posteritas*, 4.10.2 ('dear reader', 'posterity').

112. Winkler (1985) largely follows Rudd (1964) in arguing for the author as actor, a variation on Allen's (1950) rejection of the earlier biographical approach in favour of stylistic suitability. Recent criticism connects style and personality, Quinn (1979: 194ff.) and Griffin (1981) and (1985). On the Ovidian 'I'-*persona* as deliberate construct, see Downing (1993, relating Ovid to Kierkegaard and Mann), Feichlinger (1993, on the *Amores*) and Miller (1994, *Ars Amatoria*).

113. See Desmond (1993) on Ovid's 'hypothesis of the female reader' in *Her.* 7, Smith (1994) on first person reinterpretation in the *Heroides* of Vergilian third person narrative, and Chelte (1994) on women's voices in general.

114. Chwalek (1996) flatteringly bases his 1994 Frankfurt Dissertation largely on aspects of my work, against which he appears to argue for Ovid's essential unity, a 'direct identification' (p. 205) between poet and elegiac 'I'. His chief objection is against my postulated 'Verwirrung' of terms (p. 23), while conceding that I do in the end see a coalescence of the various *personae*. For me, as will become clear below, the essential paradox of Ovid's exile is precisely that shifting coalescence; see similar concerns in Lenz (1993). Eco (1994: 18-23) engagingly maps a similar analysis of Edgar Allen Poe's *The narrative of Arthur Gordon Pym*.

115. With Ovid, readers who want to take his descriptions literally need to 'suspend belief', the opposite of the process required of readers of acknowledged fiction, while bearing in mind the words of Eco (1994: 116): 'With fictional universes, we know without a doubt that they do have a message and that an authorial entity stands behind them as creator, as well as within them as a set of reading instructions.' The author-creator behind the text leaves it to the model reader to discover within the text an implicit set of reading instructions that helps to make sense of the exile's wildest exaggerations. Ovid's exilic universe is fictional as far as externals go; I hope to show that internally he is consistent and exact in his depiction of the psychology of exile. Ahl (1984a) offers pointers in the reading of ambiguous texts as criticism of the powerful.

116. Return to a traditional generic division implies return to the ancient conceptualisation of the nature of a genre and what it entails; cf. Redmond (1997), Labate (1991), Von Albrecht (1976).

117. So Lee (1958-9).

118. Considered such by Nagle (1980). See Chapter 8.

119. Zingerle (1869, reprinted 1967), Ganzenmüller (1911), Döpp (1969).

120. Cf. Bews (1984), Claassen (1990b).

121. On Catullan, Vergilian and Ovidian 'all-inclusive multiple reference and conflation', Thomas (1982a).

122. Green (1981) indicates the ambiguity of *Am.* 3.3.19 *sine pondere testes* (which Green translates as 'a puffball witness', neatly rendering the ambiguity of *testis* as both 'witness' and 'testicle'). An almost similar expression at *Pont.* 4.9.49, 50 clearly carries no second meaning: *Musa mea est index nimium quoque vera malorum / atque incorrupti pondera testis habet* (My Muse is an indubitable indication of my miseries, and it has the weight of an incorruptible witness). The Muse is his 'honest witness', and so a pun would be inappropriate. Here an ambiguous phrase has been firmly redirected – a ploy that will serve to underscore its innocence in its previous context. See Claassen (forthcoming in *Classical Bulletin*, 1998).

123. Jacobson (1974: 331-2) terms the epistle a 'catch-all genre'.

124. Cornelia was Augustus' stepdaughter. Her son Paullus became the husband of Julia Minor, and was later executed for treason.

125. Fitton Brown (1985), refuted by Helzle (1988a), Ehlers (1988), most recently dismissed by Green (1994: xvii).

126. See Miller (1994) for an analysis of the comic manipulation of the *persona* as teacher; also Downing (1993: 15-18).

127. Both of these are seen by recent critics as subversive, and, by virtue of their revision after the poet left Rome, as comprising part of his 'exilic oeuvre' – Redmond (1997), Barchiesi (1997), Newlands (1995), Schmitzer (1990) and Boyle (1997).

128. I argue against this in Claassen (1989b).

129. See Chapter 8; cf. Claassen (1986) Sections 9.4.8 and 9.

130. See Barchiesi (1997 *passim*) and Galinsky (1997). On simultaneous multiple levels of meaning, Williams (1980: xii and 189). Ovidian ingenuity can apparently focus on defence (as in *Tr.* 2) as a mode of attack. The subgenre of elegiac *recusatio* ('apology for non-participation in expected epic versification') can shade into rhetorical *accusatio* ('indictment').

2. The Third Person: Exilic Narrative

1. In the wide array of handbooks reviewing modern literary theory available to the lay scholar I have chosen to be informed by two works written in Afrikaans, Du Plooy (1986) and the guide to literary studies edited by Cloete, Botha and

Malan (1985). Beside these, Eco (1994) is articulate and readable on theory of narrative and semiotics, and Conte (1994) discusses genres and readers in relation to the Classics, giving what in other fields would be called an overview of reception theory. The hermeneutics of reception are put into further perspective by Martindale (1993), who stresses the importance of the history of reception to be read from translation and imitation. Awareness of the role of reception in the judgement of literature is not new to this century. Ovid, *Tr.* 2.280ff., shows himself keenly aware of the reader's role in determining what constitutes objectionable literature; cf. Buchan (1995).

2. Du Plooy (1986: 320-67) gives an ordered account, which she applies to a particular text as case study. Recent work by post-structuralists gives a more nuanced view of hermeneutic possibilities, stressing the interpretative role of readers to read meaning into a text as a set of signs which gain resonance through the specific decoding strategies of a particular reader in a particular context. See Martindale (1993) and the collection of essays edited by Benjamin (1988).

3. For example, Ovid apparently consciously confused the stories of the two Scyllae (*Met.* 8.6-161, 13.730-14.74, *Her.* 8.119), so Casali (1994), Degl' Innocenti Pierini (1995d).

4. Walters (1984) in Segal (1996) gives a good overview of Lévi-Strauss' theory and Classicists' reactions *pro* and *contra*, while vigorously defending the theory on philological grounds.

5. Seidel (1986).

6. Aesch. *Suppl.* 214, quoted by Plut. *Mor.* 417E and 607C.

7. Fragment quoted in Plut. *Mor.* 600F (identified by Einarson & De Lacey *ad loc.* as Nauck. Trag. Graec., Adespota 392 (Crates Fr. 15. Diels, *Poetarum Phil.* Fr. p. 222)). 'Universality' as *topos* is often applied to Socrates. Cf. Cic. *Tusc.* 5.108.

8. Plut. *Mor.* 602E, Thuc. 2.102, Pausanias 8.24.8-9.

9. Plut. *Mor.* 607, Teles p. 2.28.4, ed. Hense.

10. Eur. *Elec.* 233-6. Cf. Dio Chrys. *Or.* 13.5, Musonius Fr. IX (Lutz 1947: 80f.), Sen. *Polun. exul*; cf. Doblhofer (1986).

11. Eur. *Phoen.* 388ff., countered by Plut. *Mor.* 605F to 606F, Musonius, p. 48. 6ff., p. 50. 15ff. (ed. Hense).

12. *Phoen.* 344ff.

13. E.g. Dio Chrys. *Or.* 13.4, Ovid *Pont.* 1.3.33; 4.14.35, and the famous passage (*Tr.* 1.5.57-84) in which he compares his lot with that of Odysseus.

14. Cf. Dio Chrys *Or.* 7.81ff. on his treatment by the poor people of the Hollows of Euboea.

15. On 'epic glorification of exile', Doblhofer (1987: 196).

16. Various words point to the fact of exile and connect opposing parties in a common fate. Vergil employs the word *profugus* in different contexts, to the Trojans (7.300 and 10.158) and to the Greek Acron (10.720). *Pulsus* ('driven out') is an even stronger word, and is used of Aeneas twice (1.385 and 7.217), but also of the Greek Idomeneus (3.121-2), Mezentius (10.852), Metabus (11.539), Evander (8.333).

17. Bruwer (1974: 7-41), who also argues for the interpretation of the neutral word *missus*, when used of Antores in 10.779, as 'exiled' – sent away from Argos.

18. On creativity versus sterility in exile, Bruwer (1974): kings, 65-135; Helenus and Andromache, 136-64, Dido, 165-98, Aeneas, 199-221.

19. That allusion is also reminiscent of Gallus, the emperor Augustus' first poet-victim, is discussed in Chapter 8.

20. Admittedly this is one line longer than Vergil's own oblique narrative in *Geo.* 4.481-4 of the same phenomenon.

21. Umberto Eco (1994: 71) explains this frequent phenomenon in ancient texts by saying that modern film makers borrow techniques from literature, not *vice versa*.

22. In contrast, Boethius' lyric version, some five centuries on, reduces the process to three verbs, *vidit, perdidit, occidit* (he saw her, he lost her, he killed her, *Cons. Phil.* 3.m.12.51), reminiscent of Julius Caesar's famous *veni, vidi, vici*. See Chapter 9, and O'Daly (1991: 52-8).

23. Critics like Vincent (1994) and Spahlinger (1996: 131-51) read an allegory for the vatic power (or powerlessness) of the artist into Ovid's portrayal of Orpheus, Pygmalion and Arachne. Boethius' treatment of the theme appears to subscribe to a similar interpretation.

24. Dramas by Euripides and Seneca; Apollonius Rhodius' *Argonautica*. Galis (1992) argues for the Euripidean Medea as essentially non-feminine, 'fashioned in the model of the Homeric hero'. Hinds (1993) discussing three of Ovid's versions, refers to the myth's 'own vigorous intertextual life' in Euripides, Apollonius, Ennius and Ovid. To these we may add Accius, commented on by Degl' Innocenti Pierini (1980 and 1995e) and Manilius, designated by Baldini Moscadi (1993) an 'interpreter' of Ovid. Van Zyl Smit (1988) identifies over sixty literary versions.

25. Discussed by Rosati (1989). Baldini Moscadi (1996), on v. 276, notes that Medea is her own *dos* (dowry).

26. For further discussion of intertextual allusion, particularly manipulation of tenses in *Her.* 12, see Barchiesi (1993); Bessone (1995, on Catullan echoes); in other poems, Casali (1995).

27. On the *Medea* of Ovid and Seneca as the prototype exile: Doblhofer (1987: 96, 285-9).

28. Apollodorus 1.9.24, Cicero, *ND* 3.67, and Apollonius Rhodius 4.305.

29. These include the phrase *inter inhumanae nomina barbariae* (among the names of inhuman barbarity, v. 2) and the functional, central placement of *Graias* in v. 4: *inque Getis Graias constituere domos* (and built their Greek homes among the Getae).

30. Podossinov (1987: 150-61 *et passim*), Pippidi (1977), Popescu (1956), also discussion in Chapter 7.

31. Absyrtus' name was traditionally connected with an island in the Danube, Hyginus 133. For sources and variants, Della Corte (1973: 278-9).

32. A device taken from Accius' version of the myth, so Degl' Innocenti Pierini (1980 and 1995e).

33. Green (1994: 55) renders the pun with 'Hence the name Tomis, because (they say) the sister / *anatomised* her brother's body here.'

34. Fabius was also the hero to whom *Amor* was bidden by Horace to go, when he sang 'Love, leave me alone', *Carm.* 4.1.

35. That the locality is removed from Tomis by several hundred kilometres as the crow would fly over the sea, is an irrelevance that would not have troubled a Roman readership, with its less than perfect grasp of geography, but does help us to put the fictional nature of the situation into perspective (Claassen 1990a: 84).

36. See Green (1994: 33) for verbal echoes.

37. Doblhofer (1987: 76-9).

38. Plut. *Mor.* 602A, Teles p. 22.14f. (ed. Hense); Aristeides *Or.* 20.9, vol. 2 p. 19 (ed. Keil).

39. Cleomenes the Spartan forced 'Cleisthenes and the accursed' into 'voluntary exile'; some 700 Athenian families accompanied him, Herodotus 5.70-2.

40. Her. 1.29-34. Diog. Laert. 1.46-66

41. Her. 1.59-64, 5.62-3.

42. Thuc. 6.54-9.

43. Diog. Laert. 1.94; Her. I.50-3.

44. Thuc. 1.135-9.

45. Thuc. 6.53-8.108; Xenoph *Hell*. 1 and 2; Plut. *Vit. Nic.* and *Alc.*

46. Thuc. 104-6. See Procter (1980: 40).

47. Plut. *Mor*. 603B, Paus. 5.6.5. Diog. Laert. 2.48-51 ascribes it to collusion with Sparta.

48. Cf. Diog. Laert. 2.18-47, Plut. *Mor*. 601A. This ideological view was given factual reality in the practice of the later Roman empire. Nutton (1971) shows that wealthy citizens from the provinces, if they travelled to Rome to escape local liturgies (*ad hoc* taxation for specific projects), were denied tax immunity there on the grounds that they were citizens of the 'community of the Roman empire' and therefore as *incolae* (husbandmen) of Rome were liable for tax at Rome; cf. *Dig*. 50.1.29.1

49. Plut. *Mor*. 602A; Diog. Laert. 6.36-8, 74.

50. Perhaps from poison, Diog. Laert. 5.1-11.

51. Diog. Laert. 5.36.

52. See Dougan and Henry (1934) *Tusc.* vol. II, n. *ad loc.*

53. Crantor's *On grief* influenced Cicero. Burial on native soil was to Crantor the ultimate boon (Diog. Laert. 4.24-7). Cf. Ac. Pr. 2.44. Aristippus of Cyrene wrote *To the exiles*, quoted in Diog. Laert. 2.84. On Cicero and Greek philosophers, Colish (1985: 71-9).

54. *Mor*. 605B-D.

55. Cf. Grasmück (1978: 15-32).

56. E.g. Cic. *Fin*. 2.65. Kornhardt (1954: 121) quotes Polybius and the pro-Punic Philinos.

57. Metrical considerations probably gave rise to the *hendiadys*, coupling of nominatives with *atque* where in prose we might expect a descriptive genitive.

58. So Colish (1985: 287).

59. Livy 30.37; 33.48ff.; Nepos, *Vit. Han.*7-10; Plut. *Mor*. 606.

60. Cf. Hor. *Carm*. 1.7.1; See Wilson (1965: 129, 162-70).

61. Sall. *Jug*. 16.2ff.; Plut. *G Gracch*. 18.2.

62. Cic. *Brut*. 224ff.; *Planc*. 36, etc.; Appian *B.C.* 1.28-33; Plut. *Mar*. 28-30.

63. Val. Max. 3.8.5 and 1.5.5.9; Cic. *Red in Sen*. 15.37-8. Cf. Carney (1961).

64. Ewbank (1933) and Monditori (1963), Cic. *Red in Sen*. 15.37-8; *Red. Pop*. 3.6; *Planc*. 36.88.

65. Peter (1914) vol. I pp. CCLIV-CCLXI, references, and pp. 187-90 *testimonia* and fragments; see above (p. 261 n. 35) for claim by Theophanes of Mytilene, rejected by Plutarch and criticised by Strabo 11.C 528, that Rutilius had urged Mithridates to massacre Roman citizens. Cf. Cic. *Fam*. 1, 9, 26, *Planc*. 13.33, *Balb*. 11, 28, Macr. *Sat*. 1.16.34; Liv. 39.50.11; Gell. 6.14.8; Plut. *Marius* 28; Plut. *Pomp*. 37; Athen. 12, 16 p. 543A.

66. See Wilson (1965: 164-70).

67. Miriam Griffin (1989: 16) ascribes his aversion from politics to adherence to the Epicurean doctrine.

68. *Fam*. 13.1. Cicero's careful disavowal of Epicureanism casts an interesting light on Memmius' attitude to Lucretius, who had dedicated his poem to him. Lucretius' comment on the way certain exiles wallow in their misery (*De rer. nat.* 3.40-54), perhaps, by contrast, reflects Memmius' fortitude in exile. See M. Griffin (1989: 16-17).

69. *Flacc*. 70ff.

70. Sen. *Helv*. 8.1, 9.4-6 quotes Brutus' *De Virtute* on Marcellus' fortitude.

71. *Fam*. 4.12.

72. Robinson (1994) stresses that Cicero himself never used the word *exilium*, preferring *discessus, fuga, digressus, profectio, exitus*. Mandel (1983-4) fairly adequately covers the ideological positioning of rival groups of the era. For Cicero's role see Cicero's various modern biographers as listed and discussed in Claassen (1992a); cf. Callies (1982).

73. Roller (1997) ascribes to such 'colouring' discrepancies in these accounts, as well as in: Livy, *Per.* 120; Sen. *Contr.* 7.2, *Suas.* 6-7; Val. Max. 5.3.4; Vell. Pat. 2.66; App. *B.C.* 4.19-20.

74. Häsler (1935: 58) postulates an infusion of Dio's own *Ergänzungen*. Millar (1964: 32-8) is cautious about Dio's sources: Dio could have had recourse to 'non-historiographical material' such as the letters. See H. Dörrie, *Der Kleine Pauly* (1: 1979: 950). Cf. Büdinger (1881: 233) on Asinius Pollio as source.

75. As I have shown elsewhere in relation to the circumstances relating to Cicero's divorce of his wife Terentia. Claassen (1996b: 208-32).

76. Most recently collected and annotated by Degl' Innocenti Pierini (1996); cf. Claassen (1992a).

77. Thoroughly discussed by Rundell (1979); cf. Mandel (1983-4) on Caesar's enactments.

78. Syme adds L. Domitius Ahenobarbus (*consul* 16 BC), and L. Aemilius Paullus (*consul* AD 1), husband of the younger Julia. Both escaped in 2 BC, but Paullus also fell when his wife was banished in AD 8.

79. See Mackie (1992) for the semantic range of the word as exploited by Ovid.

80. 'A collision of might and right', so Grasmück (1978: 130).

81. For a political evaluation of the exile of both Juliae, Syme (1974). For the younger Julia, Levick (1976). Barnes (1981) implausibly suggests that Paullus was condemned for conspiracy in AD 6 and that Julia's pregnancy (by Silanus) in 8 caused her downfall. For Ovid, see Green (1994: xviii-xix) for a summary of recent speculation.

82. Green (1982a) draws Ovid as pawn, even scapegoat.

83. For conjectural dating, Viarre (1976).

84. Redmond (1997) sees in Ovid's creation the ancient equivalent of 'postmodern fluidity' which works as a coherent semiotic system to signal his structuring of the limits of identity.

85. The extant books of the *Fasti* were reworked after AD 9. Barchiesi (1997), Newlands (1995) firmly connect them with Ovid's exile, as do Porte (1984) and Marin (1958). Newlands (1995) and Boyle (in a personal communication) consider that Books 1 to 6 form an artistic unit and that the 'missing months' were never written.

86. See Griffin (1984) on literary coercion and (1985: 1-29) on poetry as a reflection of Roman life.

87. Thibault (1964: 125-9) lists hypotheses chronologically. Verdière (1992) lists theories since 1964.

88. Trapp (1973: 74-6) lists other sites. Though well designated by Strabo, Pomponius Mela and Pliny the Elder, Tomis was 'lost' in vague mediaeval geography.

89. Fitton Brown (1985). The *Halieutica* is now considered non-Ovidian. Statius, *Silvae* 1.2. 254-5, celebrating a friend's marriage, is explicit: *ambissent laudare diem, nec tristis in ipsis/Naso Tomis* (they'd have gone around praising the day, and Naso would not even have been sad at Tomis).

90. Thibault (1964: 22-3). Fitton Brown (1984) and Janssen (1951), and now Hoffmann and Schmidt (unpublished) discuss the poet's exile as literary fiction. See Chapter 1.

91. From Eusebius' tradition of the (lost) *De poetis* of Suetonius, Thibault 1964: 22 and n. 58.

92. Plutarch, *Mor.* 602E, concludes that Tiberius' exile could not have been 'very restful'.

93. Tac. *Ann.* 6.6 and Suet. *Tib.* 67 record a 'confession' in a letter after the fall of Seianus. Tacitus' comment is coloured by his prejudice.

94. Ascribed by Dreyer, *Der Kleine Pauly*, quoted by Abel (1985: 665), to Seneca's illness – possibly tuberculosis.

95. Accused in the senate during Claudius' reign, condemned to exile in Corsica, *Polyb.* 2.1; 13.2; 18.9, where he was not unhappy, *Helv.* 4.1-3; 20.1-2, although personally discomfited, *Polyb.* 13.3; 18.9. Cf. Motto (1970), *passim*, for further exile-related references and Degl' Innocenti Pierini (1990: 103-61, 211-48) for discussion.

96. Dio Cass. 60-1; the Scholiast on Juvenal 5.109: *sub Claudio quasi conscius adulterium Juliae Germanici filiae in Corsicam relegatus est* (he was banished to Corsica under Claudius on the pretext that he was party to the adultery of Julia, the daughter of Germanicus).

97. Abel (1985: 665-8).

98. Seneca consciously used Plato's *Apology of Socrates* and the apology of Rutilius Rufus, both of whom claimed justice, not mercy, from their judges, Abel (1985: 669 n. 148, 695-703); cf. Kallet-Marx (1990); Griffin (1976: 5) suggests that his attitude in *Cons. Helv.* presupposes innocence, in *Polyb.* allows for possible guilt.

99. Meinel (1972: 1-3 and nn. 3-7), Sørenson (1984: 11-113).

100. Hugo, in the *viva voce* defence of his dissertation (Utrecht 1957) proposes (Apothegm 10): 'The reason why Tacitus says so little about Seneca as an historic figure is that he was unsure how to treat him, not because he was not wicked enough to serve as an *exemplum*, but because there were too many discrepancies in Seneca's life and character.' Bruwer (1964: 20-2) argues for a literary interpretation. See Edwards (1997).

101. So Bruwer (1964: 39-40); cf. Tac. *Ann.* 13.2, 3.

102. E.g. *Polyb.* 3.5; 7.1-4; 8.1-2; 12.3-5; 13.1-4; 14.1-2; 16.6. Degl' Innocenti Pierini (1990b: 213-47) plausibly argues for consistency in an exile desperate to conciliate his oppressor..

103. Quintilian (10.1.129) criticises Seneca's 'inability to curb excess' in style, not his moral turpitude. Suetonius reports Caligula's comment on Seneca's style (*harena sine calce*, 'sand without lime', *Cal.* 53.2), offering nothing profound on his character. Cf. Bruwer (1964: 89-106).

104. We have seen that these problems also occur in Dio's depiction of Cicero; cf. Fergus Millar (1964: 28-55, 73-82).

105. Degl' Innocenti Pierini (1995a and b), Abel (1985: 667-8); on the poetry, Chapter 9.

106. Scafuro (1989) discusses Livy's narrative of the event as deliberately comical.

107. Griffin (1989: 19) discusses the fear and suspicion with which even philosophy was regarded, and regards the expulsion of philosophers from Rome in 161 BC as evidence for suspicion of novelty in education as a threat to tradition. Cf. Sen. *Helv.* 10.8.

108. On mobility in the late Republic, Wilson (1965) *passim*.

109. Plin. Min. *Ep.* 3.11, on the death or exile of many of his friends: Senecio Rusticus and Helvidius killed; Mauricus Gratilla, Arria and Fannius exiled. Stoicism served to sharpen the critical impulse, providing the courage to revolt, so Macmullen (1967: 44-64).

110. Macmullen (1967: 70-82, and 311, nn. 27-9), Jerphagnon (1984).

111. Dio Cass. 66.13.2, Them. 173c, Tac. *Hist.* 3.81, *Ann.* 15.71. Jones (1978: 48 and 175 n. 32) quotes the probably erroneous tradition (Diog. Laert. 7.168, Philostr. *VA* 5.19), queried by Hense (1905: xxxi), that Musonius worked in a chain gang near Corinth. Cf. Colish (1985: 41), Lutz (1947) and Jagu (1979).

112. *Diss.* 2.12.17-25; Xenakakis (1969: 5) discusses the tradition and Epictetus' comments on exile and suicide (11.16.16-23).

113. Cf. Macmullen (1967: 42-3), Brancacci (1985) and Puiggali (1980 and 1982) on the relation between the various philosophers.

114. Demetrius' history as narrated by Philostratus is fraught with inconsistencies and is dubiously verifiable, so Bowie (1978: 1685-99); cf. Flinterman (1993: 74-98, 148).

115. Sidebottom (1996), queries much of the tradition that shows Dio as a 'friend' of Vespasian. Jones (1990) suggests M. Arrecinus Clemens. Moles (1983) reassesses Von Arnim (1898: 223-4) on the divergent evidence of various traditions.

116. On the power of sophistic families to enhance the circumstances of their native cities, Bowersock (1969) chs II and III.

117. Methy (1994) shows that Dio's disassociation from the idea of Rome allowed him to retain his Hellenism while accepting and justifying Roman domination; cf. Jones (1978: 54, 55 and chs 11 and 12). Like Pliny, Dio is expressing the ideology of his time.

118. See Koolmeister and Tallmeister (1981) *passim*, Moles (1978).

119. Mensching (1963), Introd. and fragments.

120. Philos. *VS* 489, Ps-Dio of Prusa (=Fav.?) 37. Swain (1989) interprets aspects of Favorinus' *Peri phugês* as implying no more than an unfavourable judgement by Hadrian of Favorinus' delivery of an oration.

121. Diog. Laert. 6.23, 8.53, and Lucian *Eunuch* 7. Standard editions are: Barigazzi (1966) and Norsa & Vitelli (1931). Cf. Häsler (1885), *passim*. Bowersock (1969: 36), considers the tenuous evidence from the few extent fragments, and warns against the pat assumption of Favorinus' exile, suggesting (90-109) that in Rome the 'play-wars' of rival sophists from the Greek East offered a harmless emotional outlet for city rivalries.

122. Bowie (1978) considers the evidence for individual incidents in the *Life*, and concludes (p. 1699) that the weight of evidence is against literal veracity. It should be taken as a 'tribute to the literary skills of Philostratus'. Anderson (1976: 89-94) argues for the work as comic fiction in the style of Lucian.

123. Flinterman (1993: 145-80) discusses the histories of these emperors as a background to his discussion of Apollonian Pythagorism. He considers (p. 153) the tradition that Vespasian went to Egypt to meet Apollonius as typical of encomiastic distortion. Bowersock's introduction to Jones' translation (1970: 13) stresses parallelism with Christ as the reason for Philostratus' portrayal of persecution under Domitian, whom the philosopher designates as 'worse than Nero and on a par with Tiberius' (7.4-8.3).

124. Sidebottom (1996) queries the inclusion of Nerva, suggesting his relative L Salvius Otho Cocceianus as more likely; cf. Schmitz (1996) on Apollonius and Trajan.

125. An example is the woman who gave birth to a three-headed monster, interpreted by the hero as signifying the three emperors Galba, Vitellius and Otho, who succeeded each other rapidly in 69 (5.13). Cf. Jones (1970: 13) and Flinterman (1993: 153-63).

126. Phil. *VA* 8.29. This rapid survey was taken from Mead (1901, repr. 1980: 73-80). Jones (1970: 10) suggests that Philostratos' source 'Damis' may be fictitious.

127. Patch (1947). For other sources, e.g. *Excerpta Valensiana* II.85-7, Morton (1981), Matthews (1981: 38-43) nn. 1, 3-45, 57, 61-3, Obertello (1981b).

128. His popularity is attested by a vast array of mediaeval imitators; see bibliography by Kaylor (1992), also Tester (1989) Relihan (1990), Atkinson (1996), Hoenen and Nauta (1997).

129. See Atzalos (1993) on his introduction to and translation of Aristotle's *Categories*, Tester (1989) on mediaeval philosophy and Shanzer (1983) on his eclectic use of Hermetic writings.

130. For an analysis of possible reasons for Theodoric's treatment of the scholar-statesman, Watts (1969) 9-18.

131. Grasmück (1978: 135-8), Häsler (1932: 28ff.).

132. Podossinov (1987: 163-4), perhaps rightly, interprets this as factual evidence of Roman involvement in the area.

133. So Green 1984 *ad loc.*

134. Green (1994: 342) notes that hereafter Ovid steers clear of references to Germanicus when attempting to mollify Tiberius.

135. Wimmel (1960) offers an important clue to the interpretation of Ovid's often ostensibly negative judgement of the exilic works. In the Callimachean tradition *recusatio* has as its more salient elements: the request of a dignitary for patriotic poetry, the refusal by the poet on the grounds of the smallness of his talent and the greatness of the task, a warning god that calls him away, vindicating his choice of the humbler mode, and a defiant challenge to personified Envy to do its worst. Imagery is consistently related to water, sailing, or travel on land, as here.

136. The body of *Pont.* 3.4 is more concerned with poetics and the power of poetry against mordacious Envy, than with Tiberian glory. The exile claims to be drawing from memory and his 'mind's eye', whereas other poets could rely on autopsy.

137. Livia as mother of Tiberius, *Pont.* 3.3.87, 3.4.95-100, Tiberius as father of Germanicus and Drusus, and – by means of a rather clumsy zeugma – of the 'Fatherland', 3.3.87-8.

138. Cf. Claassen (1988); Doblhofer (1987: 277-81); earlier: Heinze (1919), De Saint Denis, Vulpe (1959), Rahn (1958), Lechi (1978).

139. The Latin word *focus* literally means a hearth.

140. Hom. *Il.* 2.564, 4.403, 5.319, Paus. 2.18.5, 8.46.2, 9.8.7, Apollod. 3.63, 68, 73, 75, 121. For Evadne also Eur. *Suppl.* 980ff., Apollod. 3.79, Verg. *Aen.* 6.447.

141. Hom. *Il.* 2.700f. Eust. 325, Ov. *Her.* 13.9. His life, marriage and the prophecy regarding his death are frequent in ancient literature. For a full set of references, see G. Radke, *Der Kleine Pauly* (1979: 4.1195).

142. Isbell (1990: 11) points out that Ovid clearly here evokes the scene between Hector and Andromache, *Iliad* 6.390-502, for Laodamia the 'nameless wife' of the Trojan Hector who may kill her husband.

143. Cf. *Pont.* 1.10.25, 26.

144. See Claassen (1989a) for a fuller discussion. Christoph Ransmayr's remarkable post-modern novel (1988, trans. Woods 1990) transforms the poet into one of his own characters from the *Metamorphoses*, carrying the mythological transformation process one step further. See Christensen (1992).

3. Comfort in Exile

1. Peter (1901) remains the standard work, to which Thräde's (1970) analysis of epistolary topics provides a valuable extension.

2. It would be safe to surmise that Cicero did not write his most intimate missives with an eye to publication; with the younger Pliny we can be less sure.

3. Downing (1993: 2-13) speaks of a 'conscious interplay between the author's own project of book-making and his character's project of self-making'. I chose to distinguish three Ovidian *personae* in my doctoral dissertation (1986) *poeta, exul,* and *vates,* or 'poet', 'exile' and 'prophet' (or, better, 'speaker of truth'). This may also appear as a *persona,* another creation by the creator-poet as separate personage. See Claassen (1990b). The multiplication of speaking *personae* ('voices') in the *Heroides* is receiving increasing attention, especially among feminist critics, e.g. Lindheim (1995) discusses the degree to which Ovid as 'male author' 'ventriloquises' his female heroines, thereby giving their utterances a masculine perspective. I have not had access to the paper delivered by Pamela Gordon at the Washington APA meeting, December 1993, entitled 'Sappho double-crossed: the mannish Muse of *Heroides* 15', but its title seems to suggest a similar approach.

4. Termed the 'privileged reader' by Williams (1992), following Kennedy.

5. Davis (1995) discusses Ovid's adaptation in *Her.* 4 of Euripides' Phaedra from the *Hippolytus* in much the same terms, also stressing other aspects of Ovidian foreshadowing of the future, such as use of epithets that encode references to future events, and apparently guileless stress by the 'writer' on aspects which to the privileged reader convey irony (e.g. Phaedra's reference to Hippolytus' skill as a charioteer). Cf. Casali (1990) on Ovid's doubling of epistolary strategies in *Her.* 4 – the 'letter' refers to another letter. These allusions would convey little to a reader unfamiliar with Euripides.

6. Galis (1992) problematically construes Euripides' depiction as showing Medea to be an 'Homeric hero' who commits infanticide as last stage in her metamorphosis. Even if this were true for the Euripidean text, it cannot apply to any of Ovid's versions, where Medea's feminine nature receives considerable emphasis.

7. I summarise its major lines in Claassen (1996b: 208-32).

8. *Fam.* 2.4.1. Cf. *Fam.* 4.13, 6.10, 15.19, *Att.* 5.5, 7.5, 8.14, 9.10, 12.53, *Q.Fr.* 1.1.45; Thräde (1970: 28-47).

9. Shackleton Bailey *ad loc.* gives the date as 56; the Loeb editor Williams (1958) tentatively dates it four years later. The earlier date is preferable in the light of Sittius' subsequent reconciliation with Caesar. Lossmann (1962: 3) considers the year 54 as crucial in highlighting the relationship between Caesar and Cicero.

10. Narducci (1997) quotes Publilius Syrus 5.33 *ubi innocens damnatur, pars patriae exulat* (Where an innocent man is condemned, a part of the fatherland is exiled).

11. Strassburger (1931: 59-70) sees Cicero's *consensus omnium bonorum* (agreement of all good men) as wider that the *concordia ordinum* (agreement of the orders).

12. Fadius had been Cicero's quaestor in 63 and was now living in exile outside Rome, having probably been charged (in Pompey's new law courts) with bribery connected with his election to the praetorship.

13. See Claassen (1996b: 208-32) for a detailed exposition.

14. Narducci (1997) argues that these letters show a profound ideological change in Cicero, also indicated in his *Tusculan disputations,* away from his earlier stance about exile as an evil (as evidenced in his speech *De domo sua*), to the concept of exile as a positive good. Narducci (p. 72) sees this as 'a symptom of the degree of desperation in the political controversy which underlies *Tusculanae disputationes*'. It may also indicate Cicero's all too human ability to hold two opposite views simultaneously, and to be more philosophical about the ills of others than about his own. See discussion below on the differences in attitude evinced by Seneca in the two consolations he wrote from exile.

15. E.g. To Manlius Torquatus (*Fam.* 6.1), Trebianus (6.10A) and Q. Ligarius (6.13).

16. *Fam.* 6.22. Ahenobarbus was the nephew of Cato, who took his own life after Thapsus. Williams (1958: vol. 1: 518), n. 'a', citing Tyrrell and Purser, suggests that Ahenobarbus may have planned to join the Pompeians in Spain. In the event he stayed somewhat uneasily in Italy. The dating of this letter is problematic. See Shackleton Bailey (1977: vol. 2: 387).

17. *Fam.* 5.21. See Williams (1958: vol. 1: 422 n. 'a').

18. On Cicero's use of philosophy in support of divergent arguments, see Griffin (1989: 30). Plezia (1989) reckons that the (lost) *Hortensius* may have been a philosophical consolation to his friends for the loss of republican freedom that exhorted them toward duty to their faction; cf. Doignon (1993).

19. Touched on by Rawson (1989: 239 n. 33), quoting Plut. *Mor.* 797D.

20. To Q. Ligarius, *Fam.* 6.13 and 14; to Trebianus *Fam.* 6.10A and B, and to Servius Sulpicius, not exiled, but away from Rome, representing Caesar as governor of Achaea (4.3). Of other consolatory letters, one to C. Toranius (*Fam.* 6.20), distinguishes between earlier consolation and present admonition, and the next (21) reflects on their common interest in the welfare of the state, promising practical aid.

21. Cf. Ovid's various disclaimers, similarly worded.

22. Shackleton Bailey *ad* 6.6 infers this from Suetonius' statement that Caesar took the offensive document in good spirit, for, at the time when it appeared, Caecina had still been serving under Pompey.

23. Seneca, *Helv.* 9.4 quotes Brutus *De Virt.* (lost, but mentioned in Cic. *Fin.* 1.8) who reports visiting Marcellus there, and being so impressed with his fortitude that, on leaving him, he felt as if it were he that was going into exile. This is exploited by Seneca, who further stresses that Caesar had avoided touching at the island, out of shame at having disgraced so great a man.

24. *Fam.* 6.6 explains Cicero's apparent spineless acquiescence in Caesar's overthrow of legal government: *Vel iniquissimam pacem iustissimo bello anteferrem* (I should prefer the most iniquitous peace above war). The pardon of Marcellus was reported by Cicero to Servius Sulpicius in September or October 46 (*Fam.* 4.4).

25. Annas (1989: 171) shows Cicero, also in his philosophical disquisitions, as 'very much on the side of the institution of private property'; cf. Strassburger (1931: 61) on Cicero's emphasis on the right of each order to safeguard personal property.

26. See Fiocchi (1990) for variant dating and order of the letters, and a detailed commentary on the arguments put forth by Cicero. She discusses Marcellus' stance as a 'dignified silence', which, in the end, his death helped him to maintain.

27. Cf. *Att.* 13.10, 13.22.2, Liv. *Per.* 115, Val. Max. 9.11.14.

28. The school established in 385 BC by Plato. Its tenets influenced Cicero's thought.

29. Claassen (1992a) and (1996a), Narducci (1997).

30. *si ... fortuna fecerit* can be either fut. perf. ind., showing confidence ('when Fortune will have caused...'), or perf. subj., denoting unreality ('if Fortune would only have caused ...'), but fut. simp. '*exsequar, ut putes* ('I shall follow, as you think

...') indicates the former. Shackleton Bailey (1965) vol. 2 *ad loc.* comments on 'lack of taste' here.

31. Doblhofer (1986: 166ff.), Grasmück (1978: 115).

32. Van Stekelenburg (1971: 23) conjectures that '*Philiskos tis aner*' is a Sophist philosopher, a contemporary of Dio Cassius, and not a contemporary of Cicero. See Claassen (1996a).

33. See Berrigan (1966) for a summary of its contents. Plutarch, *Cic.* 41.8, reports 'philosophers came together from all sides to offer Cicero consolation' (trans. Moles) after Tullia's death. Moles (1988: 38) regards this statement as outright invention, but it may well be a generalisation based on letters such as Servius Sulpicius Rufus' famous consolation on her death (*Fam.* 4.5), and Plutarch's awareness of the general prevalence of the consolatory tradition.

34. Berrigan (1966) sees Dio, too, 'like all great historians ... (as) a moral instructor.' Cf. Millar (1964: 73-9), Van Stekelenburg (1971: 14).

35. Plutarch's consolations of various persons were briefly considered in Chapter 1.

36. See Kassel (1958: 13).

37. Plut. *Mor.* 599A-607F is a formal *consolatio* to an exile from Sardis, probably living in Athens, perhaps Menemachus of Sardis, roughly contemporaneous with Dio Chrysostomus, Epictetus, Musonius and Favorinus. See De Lacy and Einarson (1959) vol. vii, 575-9, and Caballero and Viansino (1995: 16-19).

38. Fechner (1986: 247) and Reinhold (1986) show that Dio consistently sees parallels between the fall of the Republic and his own era. This observation may cautiously be applied as argument for Philiscus as a Greek contemporary. Cf. the paper by Alain Gowing delivered at the Leeds International Latin Seminar, May 1993.

39. Millar (1966: 34) advocates care in postulating historiographical influence. What he says can be applied *mutatis mutandis* to use of consolatory topics.

40. Parallels in Dio are noted by Millar (1966: 50), n. 3. Cf. Mensching (1963) and Savon (1979).

41. Cf. fragments of Teles, Musonius Rufus and Favorinus, Buresch (1886: 37-8 and 93), Lutz (1947).

42. Cf. Epictetus *Diss.* I.11.33, II.16.16-23 (Xenakakis 1979), Musonius fr.. IX (Lutz 1947: 68).

43. Cf. Plut. 600A.

44. Musonius fr. XLIII (Lutz 1947: 138).

45. Dio on more than one occasion emphasises Cicero's own role in alienating potential support by his manner in his speeches, e.g. 38.12.5, 38.29.1 (referring to the orator's '*káthodon spoudásês*'). Plut. *Cic.* 5.6 similarly refers to Cicero's '*kakoêtheías*', and lists instances of his malicious wit in *Cic.* 24-7.

46. Kallet-Marx (1990): *Fortuna* compensated Rutilius Rufus with glorious exile on Lesbos.

47. Grasmück (1978: 129): 'a second, spiritual banishment.' Doblhofer (1987: 221, quoting Herescu 1959): 'interior exile.' McKendrick (1989: 113) quotes Augustine on Cicero's conversion from 'Romanness' to a higher reality, but this was during his seclusion after Tullia's death.

48. One of these arduous duties is 'to go on an embassy to Rome', a Greek dilemma in the Roman world (602C).

49. Millar (1966: 51) and more recently Gowing suggest that the author is thinking of his own Campanian villa, and his use of it. Soubirac (1972: 48) n. 1 conjectures that the close of Cicero's *de temporibus suis* entailed a question by Jupiter on his preferences: study of politics, or of philosophy.

50. Sen. *Marc.* 23. See De Lacy and Einarson (1959: 569), *ad loc.*, n. 'd'.

51. Clodius has undergone some revision and rehabilitation, from the careful views expressed by critics like Pocock (1924) and Loposzko and Kowalski (1993) to Utcenko (1975: 151-7, who rewrites his biography in Marxist terms), to Rundell (1979) who rightly emphasises that Cicero is our only, and very biased, source.

52. Cf. Cic. *Tusc.* 5.107, Sen. *Helv.* 6.4.5 and Favorinus *Peri phugês* 8.41.

53. For a full list of ancient sources, Gelzer (1939) *RE Cicero* 7.A.1 (1087-8).

54. A long passage (605F-607A) analyses and refutes Euripides' depiction of the evils of exile, *Phoenissae* 388ff.

55. Swain (1990: 192-203) stresses Plutarch's portrayal of Cicero as lacking philosophical fortitude.

56. Divergent opinions of Dio's portrayal of Cicero are summarised by Fechner (1986: 53-7), who would consider the overall picture to be consistent.

57. Sen. *Marc.* 23. See De Lacy and Einarson (1959: 569), *ad loc.*, n. 'd'.

58. So Costa (1997: xiii), following Griffin (1976: 414) reads Quint. 4.2.31ff. Cicero, *Fam.* 9.8 reminds Varro of the *mos dialogorum* (the custom of dialogue-writing) that ascribes words to 'speakers'.

59. Tac. *Ann.* 4.34ff. Cf. Macmullen (1967: 41-6). See Kierdorf (1987) for recent textual criticism.

60. Arguments vary from 39, under Gaius (Abel 1985: 703 and Griffin 1976: 23 on various dating) to 34-37, soon after the fall of Seianus, when Tiberius was still alive (Bellemore 1992).

61. Griffin (1976: 397-8) argues that 'ten months', referred to by the exile in relation to the time the state allowed women for mourning (*Helv.* 16) need not be taken absolutely, as an argument that she still was in mourning when he wrote. That it was in his interest, as a general *captatio benevolentiae*, to have the document published as soon after the child died (and he was exiled) may be taken as a given.

62. So Abel (1985: 712), Atkinson (1985: 867-8). Against these, Borgo (1978). See Timothy (1973: 111ff.) for a collection of Seneca's own arguments for the use of ideas borrowed from other philosophical schools, particularly Epicureanism.

63. Plut. *Cons ad uxorem* (*Mor.* 612A, B): the death of a child is good.

64. Yet some of the most useful recent work on Seneca's exile has been Degl' Innocenti Pierini's various careful textual comparisons and analyses that trace Senecan self-referential use of words and concepts from his various dramas in his consolations and exilic poems, e.g. 1990d, 1993-4, 1995a and b.

65. Which here would amount to analysis of the effects of Seneca's use of consolatory *topoi* as signifiers of meaning in a context divorced from their original potential as utterances, given the Derridean distinction between iterability and imitability; cf. discussion by Ferrari in Benjamin (1988: 59-71).

66. Manning (1981: 9-20).

67. Cf. Moreschini (1977), Cicero as source for Seneca; Manning (1974) and Borgo (1978), Seneca's philosophical melange in his *consolationes*; Kerasidi (1983).

68. So Rosati (1981). Shelton (1995) discusses persuasive devices in the *Ad Marciam*.

69. As Stoic Seneca has frequently ridiculed Fortuna (Gummere 1947: viii); here his approach is Peripatetic (Manning 1974 and Atkinson 1985), perhaps influenced by Posidonius via Cicero, Abel (1985: 712).

70. For the antecedents of this argument, Manning (1981: 67).

71. The four main distinguishable sections of consolatory argument are represented by (1) an exhortation to contain mourning, (2) the externality of Fortune's gifts, (3) the universality of the human condition and (4) refutation of the concept of death 'as an evil'. This pattern recurs three times in the passage: first in the general precepts, then in the precepts relating to Marcia, and finally in the peroration of Cremutius Cordus, so Manning (1981: 8-11).

72. Bellemore (1992: 233) bases her early dating on the argument that the *exempla* are aimed at conciliating Tiberius. She argues that Seneca 'manipulated his philosophy and his friends to gain imperial recognition' under Tiberius. Griffin (1976: 23) quotes the theory of Z. Stewart that Seneca, who was related to Seianus, needed to show that he had friends who had suffered under Seianus when Gaius inveighed against his supporters in 39.

73. Atkinson (1985). Degl' Innocenti Pierini (1990b: 213-47) more charitably explains its tone as understandable if its author wished to conciliate a powerful member of the newly emerging bureaucratic class. She shows (pp. 223-4) its influence as setting the precedent for later literary panegyric.

74. Composed in the first months of exile, it predates the *Ad Polybium* by a year, Abel (1985: 717).

75. In relation to the Lucilian letters Edwards (1997: 33) speaks of 'fissures and slippages in the picture of the auctorial self', with shifts of voice that render problematic all his apparently confessional statements. Similarly, about Apuleius' self-presentation Winkler (1985) differentiates between *auctor* and *actor*.

76. Detailed analysis, Meinel (1972: 30-6).

77. Hor. *Carmina* 3.30, Ovid *Met.* 15.870-92. Cf. discussion of similar concepts in the poetry ascribed to him, Chapter 9.

78. Edwards (1987) quotes Seneca himself as consciously taking a stance in his attitude to letter-writing in direct opposition to Cicero's unconscious self-revelation. This I should ascribe to the differences between primary and secondary epistle, 'real' versus 'literary' letters.

79. Major dialectic differences between the *Ad Marciam* and the *Ad Helviam*: *Ad Marciam* is more clearly 'psychagogic', moving from the familiar to the unfamiliar; *Ad Helviam* reflects the psychological strength of the addressee, and Seneca's own consciousness of rectitude, Abel (1985: 712 and 715). Cf. Degl' Innocenti Pierini (1990b: 229). There seem to be some reminiscences of Plato's *Apology of Socrates* in the *Ad Helviam*.

80. Cicero advised Ampius Balbus (*Fam.* 6.12) to take up historiography. Cf. Thomas (1982b) and Claassen (1990a: 65-94).

81. Bruwer (1964: 39, 40) postulates deliberate ironic intention on the part of the author.

82. Griffin (1976: 5-6) suggests that the *Ad Helviam* presumes his innocence, the *Ad Polybium* seems to allow for his possible, even probable, guilt.

83. Degl' Innocenti Pierini (1981b) and (1990b: 241) postulates an admonitory intention. Insofar as it can be dated to about 42 or 43, we must assume that it was not efficacious, for Seneca spent at least five years more on Corsica, before his recall by Claudius' next wife, Agrippina.

84. The suggestion (8) that Polybius should attempt animal fables in Latin presents a problem. Seneca appears unaware of Phaedrus' fables which date from before AD 41. Familiarity with all aspects of contemporary literature should not be demanded of a Stoic philosopher. Cf. Sørenson (1984: 119).

85. Degl' Innocenti Pierini (1990b) reads in this prostration similarities with Seneca's presentation of Thyestes' attitude in the *Thyestes*, whereas his 'Oedipus' in *Phoen.* 104 represents the positive view of the *Ad Helviam*.

86. The intertextual allusion to *Tr.* 3.14.47ff. is clear, with the following key terms or concepts picked up here: *circumsoner ...,* / *videor Geticis scribere posse modis* / ... *timeo ne sint inmixta Latinis* / ... *scriptis Pontica verba legas* (I am surrounded by sounds. I seem to be able to write in Getic measures. ... I fear that mixed up with my Latin ... you would read words written in Pontic).

87. See Watts (1969: 7, 8) and Courcelle (1967: 340 *et passim*) on views of Boethius as last Roman or first mediaeval philosopher.

88. Its content is not satirical, as in Seneca's *Apocolocyntosis* or the *Satyricon* of Petronius.

89. On Boethius' literary method, Lerer (1985) *passim*, reviewed by Gruber (1988). Lerer stresses the differences in relationship between author and reader from the time of Cicero to the time of Boethius. Cicero could use the dialogue form in his philosophical treatises as a notional continuation of a lively Greek tradition of actual didactic conversation. By Boethius' time the tradition has been stultified and limited to the world of books. Boethius makes a distinction between dialectic, dialogue in didactic mode, and true dialogue. His Dame Philosophy moves from the first to the second mode and finally to monologue. Boethius' hermeneutics (his reception and mediation of a vast textual tradition) is important for understanding his authorial role. He creates himself as reader living only for his books and his network of allusion reads like a syllabus of study. The prisoner's silence as he listens to Philosophy's monologue is the silence of a reader engaging fully with literary texts; cf. Fuhrmann (1994: 153) and Milanese (1995).

90. Against this, problematically, Relihan (1990: 129 n. 31) reads Philosophy's 'ultimate failure to answer the prisoner's existential questions' from his silence and from the proffering of poetry as a substitute. Relihan fails to convince.

91. Courcelle (1967: 338) distinguishes 'the literary fiction' of Books I and 2 from an established but eclectic *Weltanschauung* in Books 3 to 5. For Boethius' sources, *id*. 115, 125, 333-7 *et passim*. Kaylor (1992: 16) quotes H.M. Barrett, *Boethius, some aspects of his times and work* (1940), for sources.

92. On exile as a disease, Doblhofer (1987: 59).

93. Discussed by Lerer (1985: *passim*); Sharples (1991), reviewed by Samuels (1993), associates the work with Cicero's *De Fato*.

94. I do not intend to discuss in detail the philosophical strains discernible in this work, which shows a healthy eclecticism in using aspects from the major schools of Greek thought, with the Platonic concept of *anamnesis* (remembering truths lost at birth), the Stoic idea of self-sufficiency and Cynic didactic diatribe as literary models, as well as Cicero's brand of Academic thought taking pride of place; cf. Atzalos (1993), Crabbe (1981b). Mohrmann (196) speaks of its ethos as 'vaguely Christian'. Tester (1989: 22f.) points out that the Platonic distinction between 'eternity' and 'endless duration of time' gained resonance with Christian philosophers to solve a problem that did not exist for pagan philosophers with no concept of an omnipotent, omniscient God, the problem of creation by God versus free will in humanity. Boethius was concerned with reconciling contradictory dogmas and his answer is based on the distinction between Providence and Fate, and eternity and time.

95. Curley (1987: 346) shows that the metre used here (dactylic trimeter catalectic & adonic) is reminiscent of the elegiac verse just dismissed by the apparition, but consciously different from it. The topic of versification will be pursued below, in Chapter 9.

96. See e.g. Curley (1987: 283).

97. Boeth. *Consol*. 2.pr.7, and book 5; cf. Tester (1989: 22), Relihan (1990). On relativity of time and eternity, Plut. *Mor*. 111C, D, Sen. *Marc*. 19.4. On place and the universe, Plut. *Mor*. 601C, Cic. *Tusc*. 1.7.40, Sen. *Marc*. 21.2.

4. From You to Me: Exilic Appeal

1. We have seen that posterity castigates Seneca for doing exactly that in his appeal to Polybius.

2. As discussed in Chapter 3, also Cicero *Fam.* 4.13.1, to Nigidius Figulus on kinds of letters to exiles.

3. Marquos Casquero (1983: 388-9) and Cugusi (1983: 23).

4. Claassen (1988).

5. Cf. Oros. 5.17.12. The philosopher Aurelius Opilius accompanied him to Smyrna (Suet. *Gram.* 6.2).

6. Cic *Brut.* 30.113. Rutilius disputed on cosmology with Scipio during their investiture of Numantia, Cic *Rep.* 1.11.17.

7. *Testimonia* from Macrobius, Livy, Plutarch and Athenaeus suggest antiquities rather than exculpatory autobiography.

8. Peter (1914: 187-90 and CCLIV-CCLXI).

9. Another fragment indicates his exile as involuntary: *Publius Rutilius de vita sua: 'quod si inuitum abire siuissent ...'* (P.R. about his autobiography: 'Although they allowed me to leave unwillingly...' Diomed. I p. 374 K). Peter (1914: 190) has variants *siuissent, seuissent, siuisset.*

10. Cugusi (1983: 105-29), Kassies (1981: 272).

11. *Desire for death: Att.* 3.3, 3.4, 3.6, 3.7, 3.9, 3.15, 3.23, 4.1, *Fam:* 14.3, 14.4, 15.4, *Q.Fr.* 1. 3.1-2, 7, 10, *Q.Fr.* 1.4. Return is rebirth: *Att.* 3.20. Later, after Thapsus, death as escape from ruin: *Fam.* 4.13.2.

12. In an article on the relationship between Cicero and his wife (Claassen 1996b: 208-32) I discuss the prominence at all times of his affection for his brother, whose defection to the Caesarean cause seemed for a time to lead to a total breakdown of Cicero's sense of self.

13. *General need of a friend: Att.* 3.1-12, 3.19, 3.25, 3.27, 4.1. *Gratitude for friendship: Att.* 3.14, 3.15 (only in part), *Q.Fr.* 1.3.2 and 7, 1.4.5. *Aid for family: Att.* 3.22, 3.23, 3.27, *Fam.* 14.1-3, and later, in 49: *Fam.* 14.7. *Friendship displayed toward others: Fam.* 4.13, 5.10A and B, 6.5, 6.6.

14. *No one else has suffered such before: Att.* 3.7, 3.8.4, 3.10, 3.12, 3.13, 3.15.2.

15. Thoroughly analysed by Degl' Innocenti Pierini (1997, forthcoming).

16. *Att.* 3.3, 3.4, 3.6, 3.7, 3.9, 3.15, 3.20, 3.23, 4.1, *Fam.* 14.3.3, 14.4.1, *Q.Fr.* 1.3.1-2, 7, 10, *Q.Fr.* 1.4. Cf. *Off.* 1.112.

17. *Own fault: Att.* 3.12, 3.13, 3.14, 3.15 (*in me ipsum peccavi ... caeci, caeci [eramus] ... meam amentiam accuso,* 'I sinned against my very self ... I was blind, blind ... I accuse my own mindlessness') 3.19, 4.1, *Fam.* 14.1, 14.2, 14.3, *Q.Fr.* 1.3.1, 7 (*ironical self-exculpation*); *perhaps not own fault: Fam.* 14.4, *Q.Fr.* 1.4; *fear for the safety of others, particularly Quintus: Att.* 3.4, 3.7, 3.8, 3.9, 3.17, 3.19, 3.23.8, *Fam.* 14.1.1, 14.2.2, 14.3.1, 14.4.3, *Q.Fr.* 1.3.1-2.

18. J.P.V.D. Balsdon (1964: 191-2).

19. Probably his *In Clodium et Curionem* of 61; Crawford (1984: 9-10 and 107-8) suggests it was suppressed from respect for Curio, not fear of Clodius.

20. Earlier letters from 62, *Fam.* 5.1, 5.2, between Q. Metellus Celer and Cicero, reflect shifts in loyalties, Shackleton Bailey *Fam.* vol. 1, 273ff. and 291. Cf. Richards (1935: 87).

21. The defence of his host Plancius recasts Cicero's past emotions: *non dicam miser nam hoc quidem abhorret a virtute verbum* (I should not say 'miserable' for the word itself draws back in horror from virtue, *Planc.* 77).

22. Possible destinations: *Cyzicus: Fam.* 14.4, *Att.* 3.6, 3.13, 3.15; *Athens*: 3.7; *through Thessalonica to Epirus*: 3.7, 3.8, 3.19.

23. *Sense of loss*: *Att.* 3.10.2, 3.15.2, 3.19.3, 3.20.2, 4.1, *Fam.* 14.1.5, 14.2.3, 14.4.3, *Q.Fr.* 1.3.3, 6, 1.4.5.

24. *Fam.* 4.7 to 12; see above, Chapter 3.

25. Parallels between Cicero and Ovid are listed by Degl' Innocenti Pierini (1997). On innovation in the *Heroides*, see e..g. Smith (1994), Desmond (1993), Spoth (1992 and 1993) Sabot (1981), Seeck (1975), Baca (1969).

26. In the Penelope-poem (*Her.* 1), the heroine appears conscious of the passage of time, imagining Ulysses' homecoming, when she will have grown old. A similar projection, inverted to apply to the exiled Ovid's wife, occurs at *Pont.* 1.4.52. See Barchiesi (1993) on Ovid's allusive use of tense.

27. So formulated by Williams (1992).

28. This means that, although couched in persuasive language, they would not be able to function without the epistolary framing device of salutation and greet-ing, so Kirfel (1969), reviewed by Viarre (1970). Luck (1961b) differentiates between *Brief* (private letter) and *Epistel* (open letter). Cf. Rahn (1958) on *sermo absentis*. There is now an increasing awareness of the dramatic background to the poems, Hinds (1993), Casali (1995a and b), Davis (1995), Bessone (1995).

29. Exceptions: *Tr.* 3.1 the book itself; *Pont.* 4.5 the poet's elegiacs; *Pont.* 3.2 an old Getic man; *Pont.* 3.3 dialogue between the exile and *Amor*.

30. These 'personages' are sometimes multiplied by the presence of *personae* or 'masks' on occasion assumed by the creator-poet himself.

31. I am aware of the danger of postulating a 'real' audience, as this implies an understanding of the poet's intentions, with all the concomitant nuancing of understanding, but the term is used so by Fugier (1976), whose work I find particularly illuminating.

32. Reception has implications for textual criticism, Von Albrecht (1981); cf. Davisson (1983), Winkler (1985 *passim*).

33. Murray (1994) reviews Felson-Rubin's presentation of Ovid's Penelope as poetic construct, stressing the polytopism of the character as symbol for the 'undecideability' of Ovidian semiotics.

34. Lenz (1993) associates Ovid's portrayal of winter in *Tr.* 3.10 with his stylisation of the elegiac 'I'; Chwalek (1996: 23-4, 31-43, 111, 203-5) closely associ-ates the poet and the poetic 'I' in exile; cf. Feichlinger (1993) on 'I' in the *Amores*, Miller (1984) in the *Ars Amatoria*.

35. In the first book of the *Tristia* there are three, possibly four, letters out of eleven poems, while *Tr.* 2 is a declamation in verse. In the second year of exile, *Tr.* 3 has five, possibly six letters out of fourteen poems, and *Tr.* 4 has three out of ten that are clearly letters; fewer than half the poems are epistolary. During the next year the increase is noticeable: seven are letters, and one (*Tr.* 5.4) 'speaks' as a 'personified letter'. *Tr.* 5.11 and 5.12 purport to answer letters from the exile's wife, involving true *sermo absentis*. Of the *Epistolae ex Ponto,* 1.4 has no address or apostrophe, but appears as a Heroid-type monologue addressed to the exile's wife. *Pont.* 1.5 is clearly an answer to a letter. *Pont.* 3.1 and 3.7 reach out to 'all the exile's friends' as more obviously 'open letters'. In the last part of the collection, *Pont.* 4.3 (to an enemy) is anonymous, 4.4 is a descriptive poem and 4.5 is a monologue addressed to the book of poems.

36. On arrangement by addressee, Della Corte (1974: 7-25), on individual addressees, Syme (1978) chs V, VII, VIII and IX, and Froesch (1968) ch. 3.

37. Honorific forms of address occur at *Tr.* 3.6.19, 3.14.1, 4.4.1, 2, *Pont.* 2.4.2, 2.11.28, 3.5.7, 37, 4.6.22, 4.8.1, 4.12.20 and 22. Anonymous terms for friends include *optime* (best of friends, *Tr.* 1.7.5), *amici* or *amice* ([dear] friend or friends, *Tr.* 3.4.63, 3.6.14), *care* and *carissime* (dear and dearest [friend], *Tr.* 3.5.17 and 3.6.1

respectively). The exile's most frequent form of address to his wife is *coniunx* ([dear] wife, yoke-mate, *Tr.* 3.3.15) with variations, *optima coniunx* (best of wives, *ibid.* 55) *fidissima coniunx* (most faithful wife, *Pont.* 1.4.45). *Tr.* 5.14.2 has the honorific address *o mihi me coniunx carior* (o wife, dearer to me than I am myself). At *Tr.* 1.6.3 she is simply *uxor* (wife), but at *Tr.* 3.3.27 and 52 the language of erotic elegy is echoed in *carissima* (dearest) and *lux mea* (light of my [life]); cf. Miller (1994) on use of address.

38. These will not be treated in detail, as they have received considerable attention from Davisson (1981) and (1985).

39. The reader: *Tr.* 3.1.1, 4.1.2, 104, 5.1.1, 65, 66, *Pont.* 3.4.13. *Posteritas*: *Tr.* 4.10.2, 91, 92.

40. Davisson (1981). Letter salutations occur in: *Tr.* 5.13, *Pont.* 1.3, 1.7, 1.8, 1.10, 2.2, 2.5, 3.2, 3.4, 3.5, 4.9. *Pont.* 2.10 refers to a seal. Allusion to omission of addressee's name: *Tr.* 4.9, 5.9, *Pont.* 3.6, 4.3.

41. Kirfel (1969: 29ff.), Della Corte (1974: 11).

42. *Tr.* 1.5.35ff., 3.4.47ff. and *Pont.* 3.7 are addressed to his whole circle of friends; *Tr.* 3.11, 4.9, 5.8, *Pont.* 4.3 and 4.16, to an enemy or individual enemies.

43. Stabryla (1994) considers the poem more successful as a defence of poetry than of himself as citizen. Other poems apparently directed at the emperor as secondary addressee are *Tr.* 3.8, 4.2, *Pont.* 1.1. *Pont.* 2.1 addresses Germanicus. *Pont.* 2.9 is addressed to Cotys, king of Thrace.

44. Abel (1930).

45. E.g. *Tr.* 1.6, 3.3, 4.3, 5.2, 5.5, 5.11, 5.14, *Pont.* 1.4, 3.1.

46. E.g. *Tr.* 3.8.25, 5.2.7, *Pont.* 1.3.17, 3.1.69.

47. Address of his books or poems or his Muse closely involves poet and *oeuvre* to the point of internal identification: *Tr.* 1.1.1, 2.1, 3.7.1-10, 4.9.31, 4.10.117ff., 5.7.55, 5.12.45, *Pont.* 4.5.1.

48. Address of an unknown enemy, or enemies, appears to shade off into apostrophe of the originator of the exile's ills, the emperor himself: *Tr.* 1.8.11, 3.11.1, 56, 5.8.3 and *Pont.* 4.3.17, 34. See Chapter 5.

49. *Livor*: Claassen (1996c: 571-90); in *recusatio*: Claassen (1986a) Section 9.4.9.

50. This poem gains in piquancy with the memory that an ageing Horace in *Carm.* 4.1 had sung 'Love, leave me alone, go to plague Fabius Maximus!' On its implications, Kenney (1965).

51. Tac. *Ann.* 1.5. On the death of Fabius Maximus, Agrippa Postumus and the involvement of Fabius' wife Marcia, Syme (1978) ch. VIII. In *Tr.* 4.10.87 the exile invokes the shades of his parents, and in *Pont.* 1.9.44 the deceased Celsus in a poem mourning his death.

52. Questions with the verb in the subjunctive are either generic or gnomic, are critical in tone, and expect a critical response from the reader. Gnomic questions, which may be rephrased as statements, express general truths. At *Pont.* 4.10.82: *quis labor est puram non temerasse fidem?* the answer expected would be an emotional exclamation, 'No, no, it is no hardship not to betray trust!' Generic questions require no answer except an emotional appreciation of pathos, as in *Tr.* 1.2.12 *quis vetat* ... (Who would forbid ...); *Tr.* 2.442 *quis dubitet* ... (Who would doubt ...); *Pont.* 3.1.37 *quis enim mihi tam sit iniquus, / optet ut exsilium pace carere meum?* (Who would be so unfair to me that he would hope that my exile would lack all peace?). Deliberative questions reflect inner argument, and do not convey a second person outreach, but rather point the exile's solitude: *Tr.* 4.1.29, and 91, *Pont.* 1.2.7 *quid* ... *faciam?*, *Tr.* 5.2.39 *quid agam?* (both 'What should I do?'), *Tr.* 5.2.41: *quo ferar? unde petam?* (Where should I turn, where seek comfort?). Direct and personal questions offer another means of criticising either enemies (*Tr.* 5.8.3, 4, *Pont.* 4.3.29, 30) or reluctant friends (*Tr.* 5.2.37, *Pont.* 3.6.5, 15, 44).

53. Pathetic questions in *Pont.* 1-3: 1.3.37, 38, 1.5.79-82, 1.7.3-6, 2.6.11, 12, 3.1.3-6, 3.4.41, 42 and also 63, 64, 3.9.19, 37, 38.

54. Details of his physical state are given to the exile's wife after he has assumed (*Tr.* 3.3.5, 6) that she wonders about the state of his spirit. At *Tr.* 4.10.92 the assumed inquiry of the *studiosa ... pectora* (keen hearts) of those interested in the exile, works as a springboard for the pathetic depiction of an 'old, grey-haired poet' being driven from home.

55. Literally 'What are you doing?', but normally the equivalent of English 'How are you?' or the American 'How're ya doin'?', e.g. *neve roga quid agam* (don't ask how I'm doing! *Pont.* 1.8.3).

56. *Forsitan/forsan* (perhaps) with an interrogative verb indicate an assumed question: *Pont.* 1.2.5, 4.1.27 and 4.5.29; Also *cur ... rogas?* (why do you ask?): 3.6.5, 6, 3.9.13, 14; subjunctives: *quaeras* (should you ask) 1.10.26 and *licet* (maybe) 4.9.113. Occasionally the exile answers apparently real questions asked him in letters, 3.1.33. Request: 1.5.2 *ut sua verba legas, Maxime, Naso rogat* (Naso asks that you should read his words). Enquiry of a third person: 4.9.82ff. and 88ff. Often the exile forestalls questions with *rogare/desine* (stop asking! 1.6.23, 24); *neve roga* (and don't ask! 1.8.3); *neve roges* (nor should you ask 2.9.73).

57. Often the form of the answer belies its apparent content. At *Pont.* 3.9.12-24 an imaginary question as to why the exile does not correct what he writes, is answered in an extended medical simile. The artistry and sure control of the verse belies the assumption of careless, uncorrected, metrical babbling. For the labour of correction as a *topos* with Catullus and Horace, see Luck (1961b: 243 and 261).

58. There are numerous other examples, often using humour to disarm criticism. Playful pathos speaks from assumed questions in *Pont.* 1.1.11-14. If Brutus wants to know what to do with these new books, he can put them in the place left vacant by the *Ars Amatoria*. And if he asks why they have come, he must accept them, for whatever reason, as long as that reason is not *Amor*. The joke elicits sympathetic amusement as response.

59. Hellegouarc'h (1963) *passim*, Lechi (1978), Syme (1978: 152-54, 172-7), Lyne (1980: 1-41, 190-234). On Augustan *amicitiam renuntiare* (renunciation of friendship) see Rogers (1959 and 1966).

60. These friends' names appear at various stages during the *Epistolae ex Ponto*, eight appear in 1, five more in 2. *Pont.* 3 has no new names. Fabius Maximus is the chief patron of the first three Pontic books. Two other 'great men' are the sons of Messalla Corvinus. In 4, the last phase of the poet's life, almost all his earlier addressees are discarded. His new patron is Sextus Pompeius. Other public figures such as Vestalis and other literary colleagues appear. *Pont.* 4 has eight new names, with only Brutus (4.6), possibly the publisher of *Pont.* 1-3, and Graecinus (4.9) reappearing from the earlier collection. This Graecinus is familiar from *Am.* 2.10 where he was blamed by the lover-poet for 'guiding him into two love affairs at once'. *Pont.* 1.6 praises this friend in general terms, 2.6 promises him immortality through verse. The poem reaffirms friendship, but, more importantly, it eschews *amor* in favour of civic celebration. *Pont.* 4.9 has a very different tone, reminiscent of Ciceronian correspondence before and after exile. It celebrates the impending consulship of Graecinus (*cos. suff.* AD 16) and that of his brother Flaccus, both *novi homines* (first in their family to achieve senatorial status). Relatives of the poet's wife feature among the public correspondents: Rufus, her uncle, is thanked for his aid (2.11). Suillius, her son-in-law, perhaps married to the young Perilla of *Tristia* 3.7, is formally approached in 4.8 for the sake of his connection with Germanicus.

61. *Tr.* 5.9.1ff., clearly to Cotta Maximus; *Pont.* 1.9, on Celsus' aid; *Pont.* 1.6.41, 42, he was 'kept from suicide', as in *Att.* 3.3; *Pont.* 4.5.35, 34, Sextus Pompeius helped to safeguard his journey.

62. Ostensibly disarming address to a friend often leads to attack or reproach, for desertion (*Tr.* 1.8 and 5.6) or for not writing (4.7 and 5.13). A friend who expects the poet to write cheerfully is accused of being unfeeling (5.12.1-10).

63. At *Pont.* 1.7.1-36 the exile with manipulative *praeteritio* declares himself willing to disavow friendship for Messalinus 'if it should cause affront'. *Pont.* 3.6, addressed to a friend who is still afraid to be named, is a public letter, equally open to personal acceptance by whichever of the exile's erstwhile friends had hitherto neglected him.

64. *Tr.* 4.4.23-34 clearly to Messalinus; *Tr.* 4.5.1, 2, *Pont.* 2.3.69ff. to Cotta.

65. *Pont.* 1.9 to Cotta on the death of Celsus.

66. 'Confraternity', most often in a religious or quasi-religious connection, as in an inscription (*CIL* 8.91109) commemorating a *sodalitas* of Liber; cf. *Tr.* 5.9.1ff., to Cotta, on service to the Muses, also *Pont.* 3.5.

67. This is tantamount to informal publication.

68. The last three letters to Cotta (*Pont.* 3.2, 3.5, 3.8) do not ask him to intercede with Augustus. On the obsequiousness of the Messallae to the imperial family, Syme (1978: 128ff.). This may explain why no appeals for aid prevailed.

69. This request opens the first book of the collection *Pont.* 1-3, and is implied again at its close, 3.9, also addressed to Brutus and offering a brief statement of poetics, with the apparently ingenuous assertions of 'poor quality' and 'collection in no order', typical of the conventions of poetic closure.

70. Albinovanus, author of a *Theseid*, is urged to emulate his epic hero in the fidelity of his friendship (*Pont.* 4.10.71, 72).

71. 'Impossible conditions' which imply that their fruition will make all things possible. See Davisson (1980), Claassen (1986a) Section 8, 2.

72. Farrell (1992) discusses alternatives in generic interpretation of the *Metamorphoses* and suggests as critical model the concept of deliberate 'dialogue' between genres, which he terms (p. 240) 'a refracted array of broken images, [reflecting] ... the divided imagery of a world dominated by flux'. He postulates an underlying voice in dialogue with itself, exploiting incongruity and representing the confrontation of poetry with the authoritative climate of the late Augustan principate.

73. Not to be confused with (Aemilius) Macer from whom Ovid culled a pastiche, 'against bad poets', Quint. 4.3.96; or with the Macer who wrote poems on natural history, *Tr.* 4.10.44; see White (1992), and also Williams (1991). Poetics remain a common bond, as attested in *Pont.* 4.16.6.

74. See discussion of this poem in Chapter 1.

75. The exile's affectionate addresses to his wife give credence to his patently absurd statement at *Tr.* 2.347-54 that in the past he could not write about adultery 'as he hardly knew what it was'. A playfully affectionate address in *Tr.* 3.3 combines loving conjugal apostrophe, *coniunx* (wife, v. 15), *carissima* (darling, v. 27), *optima coniunx* (best wife of all, v. 55) with endearments and terms from erotic elegy, *domina* (mistress, vv. 23 and 41) and *mea lux* (my light, v. 53), and sexual punning. The poem charms with its varied appeal and depiction of genuine affection, offering a final reassessment of the poet's view of himself as *lusor amorum*. O'Gorman (1997) shows that such assimilation of his wife and the elegiac *puella* amounts to appropriation of the Augustan ideal of *pietas* (obligation to family and to the gods) into his elegiac discourse, a discourse which Gibson (1993) shows also appropriated the conventions of *amicitia*. Yet this 'letter' also appears to echo the tone of the four extant letters from Cicero to his wife from Thessaly, particularly *Fam.* 14.4.

76. Doblhofer (1980a), Kenney (1965).

77. *Tr.* 5.2, 5.5 on her birthday, 5.11, 5.14. Luck (1977: 277).

78. The fluctuating moods of *Tr.* 4.3.31-47 evidence a self-centred appeal similar to those addressed to friends. Mythical allusions, to the three paragon wives of myth (vv. 29-30, 63-4, 75) and also to victims of thunderbolts (vv. 66, 67) turn this poem finally into a public statement of the cosmic dimensions of the exile's suffering. Johnson (1997) discusses the degree to which Livia as imperial wife is presented negatively in this and other poems.

79. As conjectured by Green (1994: xxvii), and strongly argued for by Helzle (1989a).

80. Stabryla (1994), Chwalek (1996: 205) postulates a final bridging of the distance between the two worlds by the identification of the poet with the elegiac 'I'.

81. I show elsewhere (Claassen 1990b) that by the reverse of the process of personification, the poet increasingly shows himself as depersonalised.

82. *Ibis* 67-126.

83. In *Tr.* 1.2, 1.4 and *Pont.* 2.8 elaborate prayer formulae, apparent bids for divine sympathy, verge closely on the bathetic.

84. *Anth. Pal.* 7.42; Fairweather (1987), Wimmel (1960), Claassen (1986a) Section 15, and (1988) *passim*.

85. A distinguishing features of hymnic formulae, Abel (1930).

86. Unique to Ovid, Doblhofer (1980b); paralleled by Boethius' use of *Philosophia* as *persona*; cf. Claassen (1996c: 571-90).

87. Newman (1967) assumes that Ovid merely equates *vates* and *poeta*, countered by me (Claassen 1986a: 318-20, and 1988 *passim*).

88. He quotes hymns from the *Fasti*, also *Am.* 2.13.1-25, 3.2.43-4, *Her.* 18.61-74, *Rem.* 704-6.

89. Prayers for leniency: *Tr.* 3.5.23-53, *Pont.* 1.6.41-8; thanks for attempting prayer: *Pont.* 4.8.1-6.

90. Prayers are often fraught with ambiguity. *Pont.* 1.1.77-80 humbly expresses the hope that the gods *quorum sumus omnia* (translated by Green 1994 as 'whose pawn I am') will believe that the exile is miserable, penitent and worthy of aid, and will remove him to a place 'free from Scythian bows'. To pray for more than that, would be too bold. Grating alliteration and elegantly balanced arrangement of rhyme and hyperbaton contrasts with the ostensible humility of the concept: *plus isto, duri, si precer, oris ero* (were I to pray for more, bone-hard of jaw I'd be). A poem to Germanicus' tutor of rhetoric, Salanus, ends with the suitable prayer that Germanicus will succeed to the imperial rule, well controlled by the 'reins' held by Salanus (*Pont.* 2.5.73-6). This appeal, if it was read by either Germanicus or Tiberius, could have caused further offence. It is up to the reader to decide whether the exile is flogging a dead horse.

91. *Pont.* 2.9.16-36, on *utilitas* as reason for human prayer and divine answer.

92. *Met.* 6.412-674 Tereus, Procne and Philomela; 8.1-151 Scylla; 8.152-259 Daedalus; 11.345-748 Alcyone.

93. Swoboda (1978), also on *Tr.* 1.2.1-13, 1.3.31-40, 1.4.25-8, 4.3.1-10, 4.10.115-28. *Tr.* 2.55-74 is *hypomnesis*, piety as a basis for clemency. See Luck (1977: 110) on *Tr.* 2.155-82.

94. *flectere tempta / Caesareum numen numine, Bacche, tuo* (try to change the mind of Caesar by your power, o Bacchus! 45-6). Polyptoton of *numen*, 'power' and 'mind' shows the falsity of attributing godlike power to Augustus.

95. Vv. 59-70, 71-4, 87-90, and 105, 106.

96. Focardi (1975) on *Tr.* 2 as rhetoric and prayer, shows that Augustus is addressed throughout as *god* and not as *judge* or *father*; see Ford (1977) and Claassen (1986a) *passim*, as against Evans (1983) Introd.

97. As an exception, one parenthetical explanation is attached to a previous clause (vv. 175, 176).

98. Elaborate split phrasing with Ovid often signals layers of meaning, Claassen (1989b).

99. My construction of this passage is that these were coins (probably with Augustus on the obverse, Livia and Tiberius on the reverse, as were current from the mint of Lyon at the time, as illustrated in Fishwick 1993, plates XIII-XVI), and that his friend had sent the exile a gift of money. Price (1984: *passim*) in his thorough exposition of imperial cult in the Greek East discusses the interpretative problem implied by modern critics' questioning of the relationship between ancient 'belief in' and 'worship of' the Roman emperors. Beside the obvious point of humanity's ability simultaneously to hold opposite views, he suggests (p. 247) that the key lies in the fact that both politics and religion are ways of systematically constructing power. Fishwick (1990) argues that the imperial policy set by Augustus may be read as *post eventum* 'prophecy' in Dio Cassius' fictitious debate between Maecenas and Agrippa on kingship (Dio 35). He stresses that gold or silver likenesses (although considered permissible if representing ordinary citizens) were explicitly restricted, as also attested by Augustus' *Res Gestae* 24.2, where Augustus claimed to have melted down eighty silver statues. Ovid, by his apparently bland acceptance of the absolute divinity of the emperor, shows up its discrepancies and thereby systematically deconstructs it, in his turn wielding his own kind of literary power; cf. Feeney (1991: 222) on Ovid's 'remorseless' pursuit of the implications of the claimed identification.

100. The first meaning of this word is technical, 'restore', in the context of 'return of hostages or captives', but also as a synonym for *restituo*, meaning reinstate, as in the restoration of civic rights to a returned exile. Irony may be read from the presentation of the images of the emperor and family as 'returned' to the Dobroudja.

101. Claassen (1998); cf. Mackie (1992) on *maiestas* in the *Fasti*.

102. O'Gorman (1997) argues that Ovid appropriates Augustus' own terms for portraying family relationships, thereby ironising the concepts; cf. Claassen (1987).

102. The effects include *s-s-s* in v. 57, *cor-cor-v-v-v* 58, *invidit inutile* 59, then two non-alliterative verses, and then *occulit et colitur pro Iove forma Iovis* 62.

104. See Claassen (1990a) and Podossinov (1987) *passim*.

105. He is exempt from tax, *Pont.* 4.9.101-4; a honorific wreath was offered him publicly, *Pont.* 4.14.55, 56.

106. Fugier (1976) postulates a 'zone of speech', the poems, *around* Augustus' silence, and beyond that, a further zone of silence, non-response or absence.

107. The important *tu* figure need only exist in the mind of the poet, Abel (1930).

108. *Ille* is frequent for *tu Caesar*, Fugier (1976).

109. 'Conversation' not 'soliloquy' is carried on by means of contrast or tension between first person and imagined second person; cf. Chwalek (1996: 32-4).

110. In *Tr.* 3.1 the book's fears reflect the poet's (real or assumed) fear of Augustus. It has a different, independent personality. See Claassen (1989b).

111. Skelton (1978: 58) on the relativity and conflation of space and time in the poet's perception.

112. Hart Nibbrig (1981: 226ff.) on 'rhetoric of silence': *'Ins Schweigen der Antwort'* (In silence [lies] the answer, ch. XV).

113. Vehement denial of the possibility of such in *Pont.* 3.6 emphasises the emperor's despotism and the danger in crossing him.

114. Hart Nibbrig (1981: ch. III, 87), on 'the silence of being a foreigner'.

115. *Id.* ch. X, 168, on the 'language of absence'.

116. *Id.* ch. IV, 101 on *'Ichverlust und Sprachverlust'*; Doblhofer (1987).

117. Kennedy (1993: 91) offers an interesting two-pronged analysis of Veyne's rejection of the historicising of elegy, which he does by splitting the identity of the lover-poet, much as I have separated poet and exile. Kennedy first (pp. 91-6) gives a positive account of Veyne's thesis, which postulates aesthetics as the key to interpretation of the poets' depiction of Roman society in elegy, separating socio-logy firmly from semiotics, after which he proceeds (pp. 97-100) to deconstruct this thesis with reference to Veyne's acceptance of aesthetics as an absolute, instead of as a variable.

118. This is much the approach of Chwalek (1996), the title of whose work conveys my central thesis very well: *Die verwandlung des Exils in die elegische Welt* (The metamorphosis of exile in the elegiac world). Nagle (1982) adumbrates this approach but stops short in her analyses. Cf. recent scholarship on Ovid's other elegiac poetry noted above.

119. More interesting than scholarly analyses are the various novels based on Ovid's story, such as Horia (1961), Malouf (*c.* 1970), and most recently, Ransmayr (1990) whose post-modern tour-de-force is considered by Nethersole (1992) as representative of 'history as one of the last enabling conditions for the bourgeois novel'. See Epilogue.

120. Herescu (1958a) interprets the poet's 'epitaph' *Tr.* 3.3.73-6 as deliberate accusation before posterity, *dedecus Augusto* (a source of shame to Augustus), to Ovid's own greater glory, as with Cremutius Cordus, who at his death indicted Augustus before the senate (Tac. *Ann.* 4.34-5, Suet. *Tib.* 61, Dio Cassius 57.24).

121. Also of the time and circumstances of the exile's death; cf. Claassen (1986b).

122. Ahl (1984b) stresses that Roman poetry has a 'political soul', which our romantic notions distort when we expect other things of it. We must remain aware of its deliberate persuasiveness.

5. From Me to You: Exilic Invective

1. Doblhofer (1987: 215-20).

2. Much about his exile is uncertain, but it is generally associated with the fall of Titus Flavius Sabinus, so Sidebottom (1996). It should be noted that Dio's self-dramatisation of himself as wanderer borrows heavily from the *Odyssey* (Kindstrand 1973: 31, 130-4) and also from Plato's portrayal of Socrates. Moles (1978: 99) speaks of his 'plagiarising Socrates' biography'.

3. E.g. *Dom.* 2 and 3. Fragments from the Ciceronian invective *In Clodium et Curionem* probably date from about 61, before his banishment, Crawford (1984: 106-10). Cf. Geffcken (1973: 56-89).

4. *Pis.* 28.5. Cf. *Cael.* 13.32ff. and 15.36ff.

5. The scurrilous so-called *In Ciceronem* of Pseudo-Sallust is sometimes as-cribed to Piso. Becker (1973: 744) quotes this cogent theory as emanating from

Reitzenstein and Schwartz (1898); Zielinski (1912: 280) guesses as author Asinius Pollio; Koster (1980: 177) does not venture an opinion.

6. Koster (1980: 210) and Nisbet (1961: xiv).

7. See Nisbet (1961), *Introduction*, for further analysis of the events and relationships of 59-7, with references.

8. Nisbet (1961: 57), Koster (1980: 223).

9. Gabinius returned from his province in 54, was prosecuted and acquitted on a charge of *maiestas*, then arraigned for bribery. Cicero's enforced defence was unsuccessful. He was exiled, Nisbet (1961: 191-2); Crawford (1984: 188-97).

10. On the tradition: Koster (1980: *passim*); Opelt (1965); Nisbet (1961: 192-7), App. VI; cf. Cic. *Red. in Sen.* 5.15, 6.13, 16; *Sest.* 1-8, 19-24.

11. Koster (1980: 228), citing Graff (1963: 205), considers that paragraphs 4-31 comprise the epitome of Cicero's view of self.

12. Fr. 16, 8, 9, 15; *Pis.* 1, 13, 22, 37, 41, 42, 66, 67, 92. Cf. *Red. in Sen.* 12, 13, 16; *Sest.* 18, Nisbet (1961: 85-6 n. 6, 194-6).

13. E.g. Ps.-Sallust *In Cic.* 2, 5; see Nisbet (1961) App. VI, Rundell (1979: 301-2), Jerphagnon (1984).

14. Fr. 1 (from the *florilegium C*) may have been the opening words, so Quintilian and Diomedes. Nisbet (1961: 51) suggests that between 130 and 170 lines are missing from the introduction.

15. Cf. parr. 16, 22, 31, 78, and Nisbet (1961: 59).

16. Koster (1980: 228), notes this phenomenon, and, 243, discusses a similar emphasis on self in *Pis.* 34: '*me*', '*me*', '*me*', '*ad meam*', '*mei*', '*de mea*'; 35: '*de me*' thrice.

17. *Att.* 3.7, 3.8, 3.12, 3.13, 3.15, 3.20, 3.23, 3.26, 4.1; *Fam* 14.1, 14.3; *Q.Fr.* 1.3.1, 4; 1.4.1, 5.

18. For circumstantially detailed comic invention, Opelt (1965: 153-9), Nisbet (1961: 196), Achard (1981: 226, 288).

19. For the abusive terms in the speech, Nisbet (1961: 196).

20. *Pis.* 18.19, 20.25, 41; *Red. in Sen.* 12, 13, 16; *Sest.* 18, Nisbet (1961: 194-6).

21. Nisbet (1961: 85-6 n. 6).

22. Cf. *Cael.* 13.32ff. and 15.36ff.

23 Cicero increasingly saw it as an honourable withdrawal to save the state from civil war (*Sest.* 36.5, *Vat.* 3); see Robinson (1994).

24. Asconius 12 (on *Pis.* 52) quotes two cases (M. Val. Maximus and P Val. Volesus) to whom houses were granted as reward for service to the state.

25. Nisbet (1961: 183-6), App. III.

26. *Att.* 9.52, 9.13.3, 9.19.2, 10.4.3. App. *B.C.* 2.16. Nisbet (1961: 144-5, n. 19): 'Cicero ... cannot state the truth, that Pompey had betrayed him.'

27. So Nisbet (1961: xvi).

28. Cf. Nisbet (1961: 175-6).

29. Verbs in the last sentence denote the speaker's subjective sensation: *non moleste feram*, 'I shall happily bear'; *fruar*, 'I shall enjoy'; *videbo*, 'I shall perceive'; *laetabor*, 'I shall be overjoyed'; *si ... viderem*, 'if I were to have perceived'.

30. *Tr.* 1.8, 3.11, 4.9, 5.8 and *Pont.* 4.3, also the last lines of 4.16. Whether one enemy is consistently addressed is unclear. An unknown enemy is addressed as *improbe* at *Tr.* 3.11.1, 5.8.3, *Ibis* 40, and *Pont.* 4.3.34. This personage is equated in *Tr.* 3.11 (as in *Ibis* 439) with monstrous tyrants from mythical history. This poem ends on a curse, wishing the enemy the worst fate that can befall humankind: *ipse velim poenas experiare meas* (I wish that you would yourself experience my pains v. 74). The thrust of the line is subjective, its second person verb being offset by the first person adjective *meas* standing in the final, emphatic position. See Green (1994: 248).

31. Williams (1996: 112-13) refers to 'melancholy as precursor to mania in bipolar affective disorder'; cf. Di Iorio (1981) reviewing Carrer (1976), Pigeaud (1981 and 1984).

32. Price (1984: 247-8), Fishwick (1990) and (1993: 53-91).

33. Perhaps an allusion to the persecution of Cornelius Gallus, so Marshall (1976), cf. Luck (1977: 264).

34. For up to date discussion, Watson (1991), reviewed by Pulleyn (1993), more briefly, Williams (1996: 3-4), Lefkowitz (1981: 128). Ovid's poem has poetics and literary history as binding theme, Williams (1992); cf. Rosen (1988) and Morgan (1990).

35. Strabo 17.823, Ovid *Ibis* 449-50 (Postgate's Housman edition 1905).

36. Janssens (1981) guesses Ateius Capito. From the ornithological identity of '*corvinus*' and '*ibis*' he offers Messalinus as alternative. From the fact that different rulers, historical and mythological, feature in the *Ibis*, 295f Philip of Macedon, 297f Alexander the Great, etc., he postulates Augustus as the 'real' enemy. Other conjectures are Thrasyllus, Luccaeus, Cassius Severus and the professional delator Labienus, author of an epigram on the joys of seeing others' pain (Sen. *Contr.* 10.4.2-25), echo *Met.* 12.607-8, *Ibis* 207-8.

37. *Adynata* from *Tr.* 5.13.21-2 are picked up at *Ibis* 199, subsequently colouring numerical similes at *Pont.* 2.7.26 and 4.15.10.

38. Johnson (1997) demonstrates how self-reference in poems as widely separated in time of composition as two years can turn ostensibly innocent allusions to the empress Livia into mordant criticism. She postulates as single 'highly informed reader' the creator-poet's own wife. We may postulate a shorter break between the time of composition of the *Ibis* and *Pont.* 1.1, but not necessarily contemporaneity, as the introductory poem of a collection was (together with the concluding poem) often the last to be written.

39. This occurs in the first verse of the first poem from exile (whether it is chronologically first is immaterial), *Tr.* 1.1.1, *Parve (nec invideo) sine me, liber, ibis in urbem* (dear little book – I'm not jealous – you will go forth to the city). Heyworth (1993) comments on its greater ambiguity as the first word of Horace *Epode* 1, a position that would have entailed its use as short title to the work. Ovid may in the fifth and sixth feet of his line consciously be imitating the cadence of the first Horatian hemistich with his echoing of *i* and *b* and *u* (*ibis in urbem* for *ibis Liburnis*, contrasting his (strictly speaking) inanimate and powerless addressee with Horace's address of Maecenas, thereby drawing attention to his lack of a powerful patron. The matter cannot be pressed.

40. Williams (1996: 3-5) does not attempt to add another version to the series of commentaries he reviews in the first pages of his Introduction, to my mind rightly deeming an understanding of why the poem was produced as more important than the deciphering of puzzles deliberately created by our poet to baffle his readership. This present work will adhere to the same principle.

41. The enemy goes through at least three life cycles. Housman's (1918) proposed transpositions cannot achieve consistency. Williams (1996) has now definitively shown that consistency should not be sought. Verse references here are to Postgate's 1905 edition of Housman's earlier emendations.

42. Rosen (1988), Morgan (1990), Williams (1996: 102-3).

43. It may be doubted that this was ever attempted by the poet; cf. Williams (1992) and (1996: 15-17) on the generic innovation of the *Ibis*.

44. Green (1994: 353) suggests Macer, the friend from the poet's youth with whom he went on a Grand Tour, but stresses the fruitlessness of such conjecture. He does, however, suggest that this 'enemy' is a different personage from the person castigated in *Tr.* 4.9 and in the *Ibis*. See White (1992).

45. Croesus (37-8), Dionysius II of Syracuse (39-40), Pompeius Magnus (40-4), Marius (45-8). Cf. Wimmel (1960) *passim*.

46. Seen by the ancients as efficacious in clearing the brain as well as the belly, so Green (1994: 354).

47. The paranomastic play, Caesar-*Livor*-Livia, is prosodically and acoustically equivalent.

48. Vide the proliferation of theories that have given rise to books such as those of Thibault (1964) and Verdière (1992), reviewed by Claassen (1994) as well as articles *pro* and *con* a host of other theories.

49. That his use here of the *topos* of 'effortless composition' is not wholly conventional is corroborated by Seneca the Elder, *Contr.* 2.2.8: *Habebat ille comptum et decens et amabile ingenium. Oratio eius iam tum nihil aliud poterat videri quam solutum carmen* (He had a neat, appropriate and attractive talent for speaking. His oratory already then didn't sound so much like anything else than an unmetrical song).

50. Stroh (1979).

51. The first half may be divided as follows: Introduction, 1-28; admission of guilt, 29-154; the first epilogue, 155-206; refutation, 207-end, so Owen (1924).

52. Barchiesi (1997), Hall (1997), Redmond (1997), O'Gorman (1997), Newlands (1995), Powell (1992) with Kennedy (1992) and (1993); against the tone of most of these stands Fantham (1995). The most recent trend is to consider the Ovidian approach as open-ended: subversion may be read into poems, or not, depending upon the reader's attitude. This is probably closer to Ovid's own approach; cf. Ahl (1984a).

53. The prayer for *adsueta ... Victoria* (Victory, as she is wont to do) to fly around Augustus' representative, Tiberius, is particularly dangerous in AD 9, just after the Varian disaster.

54. Sen. Maior *Contr.* 2.2.9. The formula of v. 181 follows a previous *parce precor* (spare me, I pray, v. 179) repeated from *Met.* 2.361 and 362; 4.921; *Her.* 7.163, 15.11, 17.45, 19.117. Cf. *Tr.* 3.11.32, 5.2.53, *Pont.* 2.8.25 and Tib. 1.4.83 *parce, puer* (hold back, boy).

55. Cf. Aug. *RG* 34.2, on his own clemency, virtue, piety and justice.

56. The two Julias and Agrippa Postumus were alluded to by Augustus as his 'boils', Suet. *Aug.* 65.

57. The constellation of the Great Bear revolves around the Pole star.

58. Johnson (1996) reviews discussion by Amy Richlin of the Callisto myth in *Met.* 2.409-530 and *Fasti* 2.153-92, agreeing that Jupiter's treatment of Callisto may be seen as a sign of the power of patriarchy, but denying its 'entertainment-value' in either of Ovid's versions, where a 'rotten reality' is given a 'deconstructive punch: rape is not love' (p. 21).

59. These topics will be treated in greater detail below, in Chapter 8, in discussion of Ovid's answer to the Augustan challenge and his repudiation of the poetry of power. Cf. Barchiesi (1997) and Ehlers (1988).

60. Cass. Dio 53.23, Suet *Aug.* 66. The 'real reason' for Gallus' suicide is as obscure as the 'real reason' for Ovid's relegation. Boucher (1966: 49-56) postulates a political misstep at Rome, perhaps criticism of Augustus' new title, after Gallus' return from Egypt. A former friend, Valerius Largus, was his chief accuser, the prototype delator of later time. Cf. Rogers (1959 and 1966), Schmitzer (1997).

61. The Quasr Ibrîm fragments ascribed to Gallus have opened up new and

interesting trains of thought. Of the four legible words of verse 1, TRISTIA ·
NEQVIT[IA …]A · LYCORI · TVA (sad … Lycoris, through your wantonness …), the first
two have obvious Ovidian parallels, and of these *tristia* occupies a very special
place in his exilic oeuvre. A likely conjecture for the *lacuna* is *fata*, as in *Tr*. 3.3.38
et fient ipso tristia fata loco (and my lot will become as sad as this place). *Fata*
reappears as the first word of a four-verse epigram (plausibly conjectured by
Fairweather 1984 to represent a segment of an amoebaean song-contest) (vv. 2-5,
of which I here quote the first couplet): FATA · MIHI · CAESAR · TVM · ERVNT · MEA ·
DVLCIA · QVOM · TV / MAXIMA · ROMANAE · PARS · ERI<S>· HISTORIAE. (My lot, O Caesar,
will then become truly sweet when you will be the greatest part of Roman history).
The lapse by a scribe in verse 3: *erit* for *eris*, may indicate a 'luxury edition' – the
opposite of Ovid's cheap editions in *Tr*. 1.1.5-12 and 3.1.13, 14. For facsimiles, see
Parsons (1981). Allusions in Vergil's *Eclogues* 6 and 10, dating from before Gallus'
death, are non-political, Boucher (1966: 59ff.) This topic will be further pursued in
Chapter 8.

62. His name occurs seven times. Of these, a passage from Rem (579ff.),
apparently an imitation of the notion of Gallus 'looking for solitude' (as in Verg. *Ecl*
10.52) is significant for the vocabulary and concepts that recur in the exilic works:
tristis … solus … ante oculos facies stabit (sad … alone … the vision will stand
before your eyes). In Ovid's exilic poetry the concept of the 'mind's eye' grows in
importance. See Winniczuc (1959 and 1960) for references, and parallels from
Vergil *Ecl*. 10 (Gallus dying of love), and Prop. 1.8, 1.18 and 2.19.

63. *Tr*. 4.10.41ff. and 5.1.15ff. At 4.10.53 he is 'the first of the elegists'. The
implication of 5.1.19 *atque utinam numero non nos essemus in isto* (and I wish that
I was not one of their number!) is not a wish that Ovid had not written love poetry
(which he frequently vindicates) but that he, too, 'were not dead'.

64. Repeated at *Tr*. 3.5.48, as a denial of having 'spoken out of turn after too
much wine'.

65. Curt. 8.1.9, Plut. *Alex.* 50-2.

6. Retrospection

1. On exilic literature as therapy, Doblhofer (1987: 179ff.)

2. Cf. *Att*. 1.19, Plut. *Caes*. 100.8; Muller (1883: vol. 3: 297), Grasmück (1978:
110-34).

3. After this follows his famous observation on the history of Themistocles as a
drama with acts and scenes (*idem*). See Wiseman (1979) chs 1, 3 *et passim*.

4. See Büchner (1964: 193) for chronological order.

5. Discussed in Chapter 4; cf. Trisoglio (1984: 125-6).

6. Narducci (1997) discusses the major strands of Ciceronian philosophy, insofar
as it influenced Cicero's view of his own exile. He moved over time from viewing
exile as an evil to the view of exile as a positive good, a sign, so Narducci, of his
political desperation while writing the *Tusculan Disputations*.

7. *Planc*. 69, *Red. Pop.* 6, 10, 11, *Pis.* 20, *Red. in Sen.* 25, 37, 38, *Sest.* 37.

8. Lossmann (1962) sees the year 54 as crucial in Cicero's changing attitude to
Caesar and notes (p. 142) that Caesar's ascendance enforced Cicero's acquiescence
when he was required to defend Vatinius.

9. Achard (1981: 207). For detailed analysis, see Mack (1967: 18-47, 83-112 and
120). To the people the personal is emphasised, the style is emotional; in the Senate
focus is less subjective. This is in accord with Cicero's own rules of rhetoric, *De Or*.
2.333.

10. Cf. Mack (1967: 106-7). Sest. 37 labels Marius *conservator patriae* (saviour of the fatherland). Cf. *Pis*. 43, and comment by Nisbet (1961: 104); also Richards (1935: 88), and Rawson (1975: 117), on the normally sceptic Cicero's treatment of his dream about Marius (*Div.* 1.59).

11. This was one of the accusations Cicero trumped up against Piso.

12. Cf. *Q. Fr.* 3.2.2, 'Gabinius called me an exile', Robinson (1994).

13. This was coloured by Cicero's need to denigrate all Clodius' enactments while conciliating the potentially powerful Cato by rewriting Cato's involvement with Clodius, so Rundell (1984: 315-16). Cf. Strabo 14.6.84.

14. Narducci (1997) shows that Cicero's stress on his sacrifice indicates a repudiation of the Stoic ideal of virtue as the only good; cf. *Fin.* 4 and Annas (1989) on his attitude to private property.

15. The arraignment was by P Tullius Albinovanus and T Claudius, probably acting for Clodius. Sestius had, with Milo, formerly worked for Cicero's return.

16. Thierfelder (1965: 392) argues that Cicero was either aware that he had won the case before he said this, and so his 'bluff' could not be called, or that he added it only to the published version.

17. Cf. *Vat.* 6, 7, *Red. in Sen.* 6: *Ego meam salutem deserui, ne propter me civium vulneribus res publica cruarentur* (I gave up my own safety, lest the state should bleed from the wounds of citizens on my behalf).

18. Cicero needed to stress Clodius' violence in order to justify his own retreat, and the inertia of the *boni*, so Rundell (1979: 318); Lintott (1968: 189).

19. See Sidebottom (1996), Methy (1994), Xenatakis (1969). The second Sophistic has more importance in Roman history than in Greek literature, so Bowersock (1979: 58).

20. Jones (1990) argues for a later date, perhaps 92.

21. Von Arnim (1898) ch. 3, Moles (1978), Brancacci (1985: 98-103). On Dio's idealisation of himself, the Getae, and the emperor Trajan, Sidebottom (1996), Jones (1978: 46, 50, 118 *et passim*).

22. As Anderson (1976: 95) points out, the tell-tale signifier of fiction, an authorial claim to 'autopsy, not hearsay', is present in this narrative.

23. Sidebottom (1996) summarises the tradition of Dio's amicable relationship with the 'good' Flavians, and shows how most of the orthodoxies disintegrate under the cold scrutiny of reason. Cf. Jones (1958: 51-2), Von Arnim (1898: 303ff.). Moles (1983) argues against recent theories of dating.

24. Brancacci (1985: 97-9); Bowie (1978: 1685-99), in the context of discussion of the literary nature of Philostratus' life of Apollonius, points out that past critics' acceptance of the veracity of his various narratives is a tribute to Philostratus' literary skills, not evidence of fact.

25. Possibly Dio's self-mythicising in his lost *Getica* and *Borysthenica* was Philostratos' source, so Von Arnim (1898: 224ff.).

26. The following autobiographical details emerge. The philosopher, although visiting a military camp, went as a private citizen, unarmed and unmilitary. He pointedly compares the non-military nature of his personal and ethical equipment with the bustle and noise of military preparation. On the extent of Dio's travels, Von Arnim (1898: 301ff.); on their nature, Moles (1978); on dating, C.P. Jones (1978: 50), against whom B.W. Jones (1990).

27. The term 'sophist' frequently was used as the Greek equivalent for both the Roman 'rhetor' or teacher of rhetoric, and 'orator', public speaker. Von Arnim (1898) ch. 3 sees Dio before his exile as 'not yet' a philosopher, deducing that he 'must have been banished on another count.' Dio had been a pupil of Musonius, but suppresses the fact in what Moles (1978: 96) terms a 'wholly disingenuous account of his career'. Moles considers Dio's 'conversion' from one state to another as wholly fictitious, invented by the orator to modify his earlier attacks on philosophy under Trajan, and to gratify a personal taste for self-dramatisation. Cf. Hense (1905: xxii-xxvii), Bowersock (1969: 11-15), Puiggiali (1982). See Quet (1978).

28. Dio Chrys. *Orr.* 1.50, 19.1-2, 36 and 45.1-2. Von Arnim (1898: 260-75) considers that many of Dio's best works date from his exilic period, e.g. the four Diogenes-speeches (*Orr.* 6, 8-10). As these are, however, largely narrative or ethical, they fall outside our consideration of Dio's autobiographical revelation of the feelings of an exile. Cf. Jones (1978) ch. 6, Bowersock (1969: 110ff.).

29. Moles (1978: 98-9) discusses Dio's creation of the composite *persona* Socrates-Diogenes-Zeno and its relationship to his own 'model audience', and considers that it is unclear whether the audience was meant by the creative author to recognise this *persona* as fictive; cf. Kindstrand (1973: 130) on myth as a pedagogical tool in the Second Sophistic.

30. Jones (1978: 50), Puiggiali (1982).

31. *Od.* 11.119ff.

32. Philostr. *VS* I.7 (488), also reported by Dio in *Or.* 36.

33. We saw in Chapter 2 that this idea is a commonplace of exilic consolation. Cf. Cic. *Leg.* 2.2.5 on membership of two states, by birth, and by citizenship. The concept became a fact of law only in the age of the *Constitutio Antoniana*.

34. 'I must go into exile: does anyone, then, keep me from going with a smile and cheerful and serene?' (Epictetus 1.1.22, trans. Oldfather); cf. Xenatakis (1969: 4, 5).

35. Methy (1994) and Sidebottom (1996) discuss the manner in which Greek thinkers of the first century both accepted the realities of Roman imperial power and redrew these as aspects of Greek thought, virtually creating a picture of Italian dominance as executive power emanating from Greek policy-making; cf. Schmitz (1996).

36. Cf. Epic. 1.29.6, 7.

37. On the general simplicity and directness of Dio's style, Philostr. *VS* 487, Von Arnim (1898: 252-5).

38. Cf. Stilpo, Stob. 2.7 (103 Hense): 'they say that all exile is terrible in respect of the requirements of law and civilisation, and the manner of travel involved.'

39. Von Arnim (1898: 256-60), Doblhofer (1987: 241-50). Cf. Musonius fr. IX (Lutz 1947: 72ff.) and Epictetus 11.16.16-23 (on exile and suicide), quoted by Xenatakis (1969: 5).

40. Sidebottom (1996) summarises the tradition of speculation about the identity of this powerful figure, and reaffirms Von Arnim's suggestion of T. Flavius Sabinus. Jones (1990) suggests M. Arrecinus Clemens. For the purpose of our literary discussion no final identification is needed.

41. Cf. Epictetus 1.11.33.

42. Musonius fr. IX (Lutz 1947: 42). Puiggiali (1982).

43. *Her.* 1.55.

44. Boethius as translator of Greek philosophy Milanese (1995), Glei (1985), Kirkby (1981: 56); his Christian background, Relihan (1990), Shanzer (1983), Crabbe (1981a: 261), Starnes (1981), Mohrmann (1976), against these, De Vogel (1981).

45. Boethius' greatness as philosopher lay not so much in his originality, but in his faculty of synthesis, Asztalos (1993), Reitz (1990), Courcelle (1967: 114-27, 203ff., 333-40), Gruber (1978: 27-40), Kirkby (1981: 61), Crabbe (1981a: 239 and 1981b).

46. The reader will remember that he was in prison at Pavia, north of Rome, what O'Daly (1991: 23) terms a 'philosophically displaced person'.

47. Against Lerer Relihan (1990) argues that the prisoner is silent at the end because Philosophy cannot give him all the answers and that the work essentially shows up the failure of philosophy to answer the most important existential problems of humanity.

48. Translation of the preterite verbs by perfect brings out the idea that the result of past glories should stay with him in his present misery.

49. *Consol.* 1.m.1.11-12. The poem will be discussed at greater length in Chapter 9.

50. Procopius *History of the wars* 5.1.32-4; Excerpta Valensiana 85-7. Matthews (1981: 38-43) n. 1 *et passim*, Kirkby (1981: 61-2).

51. Boethius as aristocratic Roman intellectual was charged with defending, *ultra vires*, the autonomy of the Senate, Kirkby (1981: 62), O'Daly (1991: 1-5).

52. Influenced by Plato's *Timaeus*, Crabbe (1981b). It sets the idea of determinism against the concept of free will and is central to understanding the thrust of Boethian argument. It shows poetry as a suitable vehicle for philosophy, so O'Daly (1991: 49-54). See Tester (1989: 22).

53. See Fuhrmann (1994: 153) on the author's strength of mind in using such an elaborate form while in dire straits and Crabbe (1981a: 256) on Boethius' autobiographical mode as deliberate challenge to Augustine's *Confessiones*.

54. See Claassen (1988) for a thorough discussion. More scholars now subscribe to a similar stance regarding Ovidian ambivalence, e.g. Barchiesi (1997), Galinsky (1997), Newlands (1995), Kennedy (1993). See Ahl (1984a).

55. Cf. Cicero's notes from April 58.

56. Doblhofer (1980a). The antipodal 'Lybia' may be as fictitious as Ovid's 'Scythia'.

57. Perhaps an echo and inversion of Aeschylus' famous epitaph. Cf. Herescu (1958a).

58. Also who 'Corinna' was (*Tr.* 4.10.59, 60).

59. Paratore (1958), D'Agostino (1969), Fredericks (Nagle) (1976). For its literary antecedents: Fairweather (1985), perhaps Augustus' *Commentarium de vita sua* (Summary of his life) or even his *Res Gestae* (Deeds); see O'Gorman (1997) on Ovid's subversion of Augustan themes.

60. On poetry as friend and enemy, Claassen (1989a).

61. Claassen (1989a and b).

62. The scene is set for a whimsical conceit. Ovid's books are children who do not share the banishment of their father (*Tr.* 3.14.9-12). Like the goddess Pallas Athena, they sprang whole from their creator's head (vv. 13.14). The *Metamorphoses* was 'unfinished', for the exile is another 'deceased Vergil' (vv. 21-4).The exile draws himself as a composite of favourite Roman poets. The recusatory phrases *hoc ... nescioquid* and *quicumque* (vv. 25, 26) echo Catullus 1 (this little book, whatever it's like ...).

63. Doblhofer (1987: 201-14), Ehlers (1988).

64. Early versions of the *RG* would have been in circulation for several years before the emperor's death, Syme (1974). Augustus does not refer to the Battle of Perugia in his official autobiography, and depicts Actium as a war against foreign aggression. Ovid's occasional equation of Augustus' various campaigns with a Gigantomachia is deliberate *reductio ad absurdum* of the arrogation of divine status to the imperial dynasty, and of Augustus' own interpretation of the civil wars.

65. Callim. *Epigr.* 2, Verg. *Ecl.* 9.51-2. See Williams (1991); on Macer, White (1992).

66. Words formerly used in erotic double entendre may be restored to a single level of meaning, in retrospect altering their earlier context, Claassen (1998).

67. Marcia was a descendant of Claudia Quintia (*Fast.* 6.797-812), Littlewood (1981), and also related to Macer, Green (1994: xvii). Cf. *Pont.* 3.1.78.

68. Analysed by Casazza (1979); questioned by Boissier (1867). Green (1982b) ascribes the poet's greater productivity to his new-found domestic stability and tentatively suggests (1994: xvii) that she ultimately joined him at Tomis.

69. On *Tr.* 4.3, Nisbet (1982). Cf. *Tr.* 5.4.41-7, 5.14.21-8, and the positive evocation of his happy third marriage in 4.10. Cazzaniga (1967) argues from inscriptionary evidence that Philetas of Cos celebrated his wife (Bittis); so Ovid follows ancient convention in *Tr.* 1.6.2, 3 and *Pont.* 3.1.58-60 (Bittis = *uxor* – 'wife').

70. In all cases, Green (1994 *ad locc.*), here also O'Gorman (1997), Staffhorst (1965: 6); Davisson (1983).

71. From *Tr.* 1.9.17-22, 3.13.9, 10 and *Pont.* 3.2.15-24 we learn that all the poet's friends left him after the blow fell, and, at *Tr.* 2.88, that 'all followed the angry expression of Caesar'. From *Tr.* 2.109-18 we learn that his family name was without stain, until his condemnation, which stopped short *citra necem* (v. 127) again pointing the irregularity of Augustus' procedure.

72. Doblhofer (1987: 143-62), Bonjour (1985). At *Tr.* 3.12.1-24, an evocation of the Italian spring focuses not so much on description as on pathos. Throughout the contrast is between what the exile experiences 'now' and what he has lost. *Tr.* 3.7.11-30 shows the exiled poet as erstwhile elder artist, a fatherly guide to a studious young poetess; cf. Della Corte (1975-76).

73. *Pont.* 4.1.1, 4.5.29, and 4.15.3 assert vaguely that Sextus Pompeius 'saved the poet's life'. No details are given. *Pont.* 4.6.25-6 recalls Brutus' sympathetic tears, and 4.11.3, 4 those of Gallio. As in the poem to Atticus, 4.12.19-22 commemorates joyful sharing of poetic interests with Tuticanus. For prosopography, Syme (1979) chs V and IX, also Green (1994 *ad locc.*). Evocations of friendship: *Tr.* 1.5.1-14, 1.8.27-36, 2.563, 3.5.1-4 (cf. *Pont.* 2.5.7-10), *Tr.* 3.6.1-10, 5.9, 5.13.25-32 echoing Callim. *Epigr.* 2 (cf. Luck 1961b), *Pont.* 1.5.1, 2, 3.2, 3.3.105.

74. The poet's friend Graecinus was away from Rome when the blow of relegation fell. Hope kept the exile from suicide (*Pont.* 1.6.1-2, 41ff.).

75. Poems to the two brothers often occur in pairs. From details in *Pont.* 2.2 and 2.3 we can interpret the anonymous *Tr.* 4.4 and 4.5 as a similar pair. Cotta was the closer in degree of friendship. The death of their common friend Celsus is the springboard for appeal to Cotta. Celsus had mourned over the exile's departure as if a brother had died (*Pont.* 1.9.17, 18).

76. *RG* 19-21, Suet. *Aug.* 29, 30. Identification of the buildings in *Tr.* 3.1, Green (1994: 234-5), Lugli (1958-9 and 1959).

77. Hinds (1985: 14).

78. Claassen (1990b).

79. Buildings erected to commemorate Julius Caesar, the temple of Divus Julius, the Basilica Julia, and the temple of Mars Ultor (*RG* 21, Suet. *Aug.* 30.1) do not feature in the poem; cf. *Tr.* 2.295. An allusion to the Regia (*Tr.* 3.1.30) appears to contrast the humble dwelling of pristine Roman rulers with the ostentation of the Augustan dwelling.

80. Allusion to the divine status of the emperor elevates his 'house' (the Domus Livia on the Palatine) to a 'temple'. Ovid's allusion to the *corona civica* on the door and his description of the mansion (*Tr.* 3.1.33-42) bear a close affinity with Augustus' extant version of the honours accorded him after the ostentatious 'restitution of the Republic' in the years 28-7 BC ('... I was named Augustus by decree of the senate, and the door-posts of my house were publicly wreathed with bay leaves and a civic crown was fixed over my door and a golden shield was set in the Curia Julia, which, as attested by the inscription thereon, was given me by the senate and people of Rome on account of my courage, clemency, justice and piety', *Res Gestae* 34.2, trans. Brunt and Moore 1967). Verbal and conceptual parallels may be summarised as follows, with Augustus' words from the *RG* in parentheses: (*Augustus*) – *augustas* ...*comas* (v. 40): (*laureis*) – *lauro* (v. 39) and *arbor opaca* (v. 40); (*postes*) – *postes* (v. 34); (*coronaque civica*) – *querna corona* (v. 36); (*super ianuam meam fixa*, 'fixed above my door') – *opposita velatur ianua*; (*clupeus aureus*, 'golden shield') – *fulgentibus armis* (v. 33).

81. *Tr.* 2.13-139 and 207-470, 5.9, 5.11. Cf. Ehlers (1988).

82. Claassen (1987) and (1989b), Doblhofer (1987: 282-3).

83. 'Augustus as the angry god' is a creation of the poet. Cf. Claassen (1987), Redmond (1997), Lieberg (1982), Ginsberg (1983) and Bonjour (1985).

84. Most of *Tr.* 2 offers 'facts' to disprove the emperor's opinion, Dickenson (1973). *Tr.* 4.4.24 depicts Messalla Corvinus as approving the poet's 'blameless life'.

85. The charge, frequently reiterated in the first years of exile, is never elaborated. At *Pont.* 3.3.65-75 an apparition of 'Amor' finally delivers a formal rebuttal, Claassen (1991).

86. Luck (1961b) on Ovid's epistolary mediation between life and art.

87 Adumbrated early in the century by J.J. Hoffman, repeated by Janssen (1951), Fitton Brown (1985) and Hofmann and Schmidt (unpublished, 1989), refuted by Ehlers (1988), Green (1994: xvii, quoting Little 1990).

88. The argument of Janssen and Fitton Brown, that the 'fiction' was invented to excuse the poet's 'failing powers', is patently absurd, and may be refuted by analysis of any one of the poems in question, which scintillate with Ovidian ingenuity. See Claassen (1989a). Helzle (1988) offers a rather weak argument against Fitton Brown, based on the assumption that Brown's quotation from the weather charts provided by the Roumanian Bureau of Information 'must be' wrong. That the Dobroudja is subject to inclement weather was recently attested to me by a member of the British High Commission in Cape Town, who was formerly stationed in Roumania. He recalls organising a picnic for two hundred British sailors on a small island on the so-called 'Lake of Ovid' near Constanza, where a freezing wind whipped up such choppy waves that most of the sailors were sea-sick. On the other hand, Ovid's 'Tomis' is bleak but virtually windless, only once showing chimneys blown down, and thereafter the area is strangely calm (*Tr.* 3.10.17-18; Claassen 1990a).

7. The Horror of Isolation

1. Thoroughly assessed by Franga (1970).

2. Degl' Innocenti Pierini (1981a, 1990b: 161-6) Gahan (1985), Grasmück (1978: 139).

3. In 1.pr.6 *Philosophia* spells out the nature of this illness: it is *amnesia*, loss of memory of the divine purpose with mankind. The patient is not immediately convinced. By 2.pr.4 he, however, accepts that it is wrong to consider that 'the greatest misery lies in the memory of past happiness'. Both Plato and Augustine play a role in the author's choice of the metaphor of *anamnesis*. Where Augustine's *Confessiones* show the pilgrim's progress from ignorance to full knowledge of Good, Boethius' tale involves three stages: original attainment of true knowledge, his subsequent loss of this knowledge, and his reconversion to an even more sublime state. On Platonic influence in Boethius, see Crabbe (1981b), Gruber (1978: 36-41), and on his philosophy in general Tester (1989).

4. Crabbe (1981a: 258-9, 1981b).

5. Cf. his advice to Caelius: *Urbem, urbem, mi Rufe, cole, et in ista luce vive!* (The city, my dear Rufus, enjoy the city, and live in that light! *Fam.* 2.12.2).

6. Cf. *Fam.* 3.2.2.

7. A conjectured chronological ordering transposes letters 2 and 3, Shackleton Bailey (1965) vol. II. Concordance: vol. VII (1970: 104).

8. Chronology of details:

The journey: From Rome to Brindisi, March-April 58: *Att.* 3.1-7, *Fam.* 14.4; Thessaly, May-Oct. 58: *Att.* 3.8-21, *Q.Fr.* 1.3.1-4.4, *Fam.* 14.1-3; Dyrrachium, Nov. 58 – Feb. 57: *Att.* 3.22-7; then probably with Atticus, Epirus, until September 57.

Political manoeuvres at Rome: *Att.* 3.4-27; *Q.Fr.* 1.3, 1.4; *Fam.* 14.1, 14.2.

Cicero's plans for the future: *Att.* 3.7, 3.8, 3.13, 3.14-17, 19-22; *Fam.* 14.4 and (chronologically later) 14.2.

Cicero's possessions at Rome: *Att.* 3.5, 3.9, 3.19, 3.20, 3.23, 3.24, 3.27, 4.2; *Fam.* 14.4, 14.1; *Q.Fr.*1.3.

The return journey: *Att.* 4.1.

9. Cf. Shackleton Bailey (1965) vol. II (App. I), 227-35.

10. Cf. Grasmück (1978: 110-22).

11. *Heimwehkrankheit*, Doblhofer (1987: 99-1178). Cf. Trisoglio (1984: 125).

12. Cf. *Att.* 3.23.8: *des operam ut uno impetu perfringatur* (you should see to it that he is crushed by one sudden attack).

13. For parallels, comprising 'exilic *topoi*', Froesch (1976: 80-1). Cf. Fuhrmann (1994), quoting Barthes on myth as symbol, documenting contemporary society.

14. Bolton (1994) discusses the adjective *sola* (alone) as it defines Ariadne in *Her.* 10. *Solus* is frequent in Ovid, but more often in its related meaning of 'only (one to ...)'. The word designates the exile's isolation only at *Tr.* 2.189, 5.6.15, 5.12.10, *Pont.* 4.2.39, 4.4.11.

15. Cf. Ginsberg (1983). Barsby (1978: 42) interprets the *ego*-figure here as essentially the historic Ovid, countered by Hoffmann and Schmidt at a Liverpool Conference, April 1989. Cf. Ehlers (1990).

16. See Chapter 9, also Claassen (1998) and (1986a) Sections 8.4 and 9.1; Frécaut (1972: 345) emphasises that humour pervades the exilic poetry, to the exclusion of tragedy.

17. Kröner (1970a and 1970b), Posch (1972), compared with Friedrich (1956) and De Saint Denis (undated: 352). *Tr.* 1.2 echoes Ovid's own storms in the *Metamorphoses*, so Hinds (1985). González Vázquez (1993) predictably finds Ovid's storm poem, *Tr.* 1.2, more 'baroque' than its prototype *Aen.* 1.81-123.

18. Boethius' reportage of dialogue gives a shifting focus to a similar series of 'nows'.

19. Cf. Fugier (1976) and Claassen (1986a) Section 7.1.

20. Acknowledgements of communications of various kinds (*Pont.* 1.9, 4.8), a gift (2.8), a complaint (3.9), prose letters (4.4), never answers to requests by the exile.

21. *Tr.* 5.1, 5.7, 5.10.

22. At *Tr.* 3.13 a complaint that the exile's birthday should also have 'remained behind in Rome' and not followed him to the place of exile, expresses a desire for the arrest of time.

23. On the vocabulary of the imagination, Bouynot (1958-59), Claassen (1986a), Section 5.2.1.

24. *Tr.* 4.2, *Pont.* 2.1, 3.3, 4.4, 4.8.

25. *Tr.* 1.2 death at sea, 2.179 the Getae.

26. *Tr.* 2.356ff., 3.3.73-6.

27. Doblhofer (1987: 81-96).

28. Memories of past happiness: *Pont.* 2.4, 4.3, 4.12.

29. *Tr.* 1.5, 3.5, 4.4, 4.5, 5.9, *Pont.* 1.6, 1.7, 2.3.

30. I have suggested earlier (Chapter 4) that Cotta sent him some money, coins with Augustus on the obverse, and Livia and Tiberius on the reverse, a quite common mint of the time. See discussion in Claassen (1987).

31. There are many examples. In *Tr.* 4.3 the stars transcend space, for they can be 'there' and 'here' simultaneously. The festival of Bacchus gives the exile an opportunity to wonder whether 'they', the circle of his *sodales* (boon companions), miss him 'there'. The triumph poem *Pont.* 4.4 shifts from 'there' to 'here'. The address to Cotys (*Pont.* 2.9) and rapport with locals in *Pont.* 4 indicate a psychological shift from 'you, there', to 'you, here', so Fugier (1976). Other subtleties of time and space: *Tr.* 4.1, 4.8, 5.1, 5.2, 5.4, *Pont.* 1.1, 2.5, 3.1, 3.6, 4.13.

32. Vicarious transition: *Pont.* 2.2, 3.8, 4.4, 4.5, 4.15.

33. The standard critical connotation of *avena* with lyric poetry should not be overstressed here, but the poet may also be conveying a paradoxical picture of himself as 'poet under arms'.

34. To undercut pathos by means of humour or by excessive adoption of certain stylistic devices is a consistent Ovidian ploy, Ahl (1986).

35. Balkan studies offer factual information on the prehistory, linguistic history and cultural history of the Danube area, differing from Ovid's portrayal in every detail: *Actes du congresses international des etudes Balkaniques et Sud-Est Europeennes*, Sofia (1969) and Athens (1972); Mihailov, *Actes* (1972) ascribes the popularity of the Balkan with Greek and Roman authors to the Graeco-Thracian origin of many myths. Cf. Micu (1981 and 1983), Podossinov (1987), Claassen (1990a).

36. Ovid followed many sources. Herodotus (5th cent. BC) frequently refers to Scythians, but these lived west of lake Maeotis, in today's Moldavia, which Ptolemy (2nd cent. AD) calls *Sarmatia Europaea*. Arrian (3rd cent. BC) and Ptolemy show Scythians living north-east of Lake Maeotis, due north of the Caspian Sea, today's Kazakstan. Callimachus (*Aetia* 1.1.15) has Massagetae as archers living east of the Caspian Sea, today's Uzbekistan. See Chapter 8 for further discussion of his intertextual allusions to the *Res Gestae*.

37. De Saint Denis (undated: 377), Griffin (1985).

38. *Tr.* 3.11.8, 3.10.11 and 17, 4.1.22, 4.8.41, *Pont.* 1.5.72, 4.12.35, 4.10.41.

39. *Pont.* 1.1.2, 1.9.45, 2.2.3, 4, 3.7.19.

40. On the linguistic and educational level of the Dobroudja, Popescu (1956), Pippidi (1977); Greek connections, Busolt (1920) and Lambrino (1934).

41. The *Actes*, noted above, create a totally different picture, showing archaeological evidence of early Hellenisation and rapid Romanisation, advanced urban development, and cultural connections with, among others, Miletus. Cf. Coliu (1934), Bucovala (1968, 1969a & b, 1983), Claassen (1986a) *passim*. Ovid refers to other myths, such as the story of Iphigeneia at Taurus, stressing the custom of human sacrifice (*Tr.* 4.4.63, 64 and *Pont.* 3.2.57, 58). He locates the Crimean peninsula close to Tomis, for better effect.

42. *Tr.* 1.4.1, 1.5.61, 3.4.47, 3.10.3 and 12, 4.3.1-10, 5.2.64, 5.3.7, 5.5.39, 40, *Pont.* 2.7.58, 4.7.2, 4.15.36. Micu (1981).

43. Cf. *Met.* 2.401-510, the tale of Callisto's catasterisation as the Bear constellation, discussed by Johnson (1996).

44. Claassen (1998), Martin (1966), Evans (1974) Gahan (1978).

45. A Greek Milesian tribal name to be found in the area is *'Boreis'*. Vergil *Geor.* 3 refers to 'Hyperborean coasts' as a synonym for 'frozen Scythia with its sweeping winds' and in *Aen.* 12. 'Hyperborean' is a synonym for 'northern'. The Phasis (east),

Hypanis and Borysthenes (north-west) occur in the second-century *periplous* of both Ptolemy and Arrian, who used earlier geographical catalogues. Of Ovid's list, Ptolemy has (working clockwise from the Ister): *Kalon stoma*, Tyras, Lycus and Tanais, (flowing into lake Maeotis), Halys and Parthenius. Arrian has the same or another Lycus, flowing along the southern Black Sea shore, and Thermedon.

46. E.g. at *Tr.* 5.2.65, *Pont.* 1.3.50.

47. *Artemisia Pontica*, Luck (1977: 324).

48. Lucr. *De rer. nat.* 1.936-42, *Tr.* 3.9.71-6 and 3.12.11-16; *Tr.* 5.13.21 and *Pont.* 3.1.24; cf. Columella *De re rust.* 12.35.

49. *Tr.* 2.203, 3.10.31-54, 5.10.1, 2, *Pont.* 1.2.79, 2.4.1, 3.3.26, 4.9.85, 86. See Lenz (1993).

50. *Tr.* 4.8.26, *Pont.* 2.7.74, and *Tr.* 5.7.1, 2.

51. On Milesian cults, Bilabel (1920: 97ff.). Ares was the chief god of Tomis (Her. 1). An inscription commemorates games in honour of Ares, so Tocilescu (1900: 224), quoted by Bilabel.

52. *Tr.* 3.10.19-22, 4.10.110, 5.7.17, 18, *Pont.* 1.2.80, 1.5.62, 66, 74, *Tr.* 5.1.46 and *Pont.* 1.2.81-6. The physical appearance of the people and their 'inhumanity' are *topoi* from Apollodorus, Ephorus and Strabo 7.3.6 and 9, even Cic. *Fam.* 9.15.

53. An exhibition showing Thracian archaeology and history in the context of its importance for major Greek myths and belief systems, such as Orphism and Pythagorism, was mounted in the Italian city of Florence, October – December 1997. It fully bears out my observations on the fictional nature of Ovid's depiction of the area.

54. The 'Scythian' poison-tipped arrow, a Greek literary *topos*, is the major threat to the exile's safety (*Tr.* 3.10.64, 65, 4.10.110 onwards). Arrows fly over the city walls so thick and fast that they stand on the roofs like thatch (*Pont.* 1.2.21, 22). At *Pont.* 1.8.6 the shaking of quivers signifies war, at 3.8 a quiver full of arrows is the only gift the harsh land can produce.

55. Plut. *Caes.* II.2. The poet's gradual 'development into a *Poeta Getes*', judged by Doblhofer (1986) to symbolise his personal tragedy, is thoroughly refuted by Podossinov (1987: 55ff.). A poetic fantasy requires a literary response: suspension of disbelief in the reader.

56. Xenoph. *Anab.* 7.4.15-17.

57. Cf. *formulae* 'inhumanos ...Getas' consistently used up to *Pont.* 4.13, 22, and *feros* ...Getas (4.15.40); Gandeva (1976) and (1969a), Podossinov (1987).

58. *Bastarnae, Sauromatae, Sidones, Coli, Tibarenae, Getae* (*Tr.* 2.197, 198 and 191, 192, Owen 1905: varied in other editions), *Scythicus* (3.4.46); *Threicius* (3.14.47); *Bessi* (4.1.67), *Bistoniae* (*Pont.* 1.3.59), 'golden-haired *Coralli* (4.2.37, 4.8, 83, 84), *Iazyxes* (4.7.9). On their geographical distribution, Piru (1981), Podossinov (1987).

59. *Tr.* 1.11.23-6. This again is poetic fancy. The Tomitan harbour was used in the Augustan era for the export of Thracian agricultural products, Danor, *Actes* (1969) vol. II.

60. This is discussed more fully in Claassen (1990b: 102-16).

61. Criticism no longer accepts the poet's typically recusatory denigration of his work, or claims to a lack of books. Andre (1968) Introduction, suggests Ovid had Callimachus' *Aetia* and his own works at Tomis, probably some servants. Boethius' claims to have no books at Pavia, 1.pr.4.3, may be an exilic *topos*. Crabbe (1981a: 239-41 and nn. 38, 39) argues that he worked from 'a store of accumulated learning'.

62. *Tr.* 3.10.9-26, 55-66.

63. *Tr.* 5.10.29. See Degl' Innocenti Pierini (1980a) and Gahan (1985).

64. *Pont.* 3.3.14. See discussion of the whole passage in Chapter 2, and in Claassen (1991: 27-41).

65. *Pont.* 4.1.28-36; 4.4, 5 and 15 are also dedicated to him. See Green (1994: xlv-vi, 350-1), also Claassen (1990b).

66. *Tr.* 3.3.1-4, 3.8.24-34 and 4.6.41-4; cf. Williams (1996 *passim*).

67. Gelma (1933), Nicolai (1973) and the review of Carrer by Di Iorio (1981). Cf. Pigeaud (1984), Doblhofer (1987: 59-72, 99-101).

68. This may be read into a possible erotic double entendre: *parvus ...sucus* (a little juice) combined with *membraque sunt cera pallidiora nova* (and my members are paler than new wax, vv. 27-8), which is then specifically negated, *nec vires adimit Veneris damnosa voluptas* (but my powers don't admit of dangerous enjoyment of Love's play, v. 33). Such a reading would depend on taking plural for singular, not uncommon in poetry. As always with Ovid, readers are left to make what they will of his text.

69. On universality, Besslich (1972). On the depiction of pathos in the exilic oeuvre as characteristic of the poet's creativity, Freundt (1973: 63).

70. Cf. Claassen (1986a) Section 5.2.1.

71. Such realism tempers the artificiality of, for instance, a comparison of the exile's 'cold heart' with the 'frigid place of exile' (*Pont.* 3.4.34).

72. *Pont.* 3.8.9-12. Cf. Varro *De agricultura* 2.10.6-9, about Illyricum.

73. Cic. *Tusc.* 5.116: 'non-understanding of a foreign language is a kind of deafness.' On loss of use of one's native tongue as loss of personality, Doblhofer (1980b and 1986), Hart Nibbrig (1981) *passim*.

74. Cf. *Tr.* 4.3.37 *est quaedam flere voluptas* (there is a certain pleasure in crying) with Cicero *Fam.* 5.12.4: *Habet enim praeteriti doloris secura recordatio delectationem* (recalling past pain in safety offers a certain delight).

75. *Pont.* 3.2. Syme (1978: 16ff.) shows that Sarmatian would have been useless in local communication.

76. Nutton (1971) shows that certain sophists of the first century were made exempt at Rome but would still have been liable for tax in their home towns. *Pont.* 4.9.101 *nec mihi credideris* (and you wouldn't have believed me) requires disbelief as response. Extreme examples of misinterpretation may be found in Lozovan (1961) and Duell (*Studi Grosso* undated), as discussed by Claassen (1986a) Section 11, n. 29.

77. Cicero *Fam.* 15.16, *Tusc.* 5.114, 115 may be Ovid's source for 'mind's eye,' vicarious travel, or superior vision. Bonjour (1985) argues for Ovid's consciousness of transcendental evasion of his civic interdiction.

78. To his wife: *Tr.* 1.6, 4.3, 5.14; Perilla will achieve it by her own poetry, 3.6; to an enemy, 4.9; to Graecinus, *Pont.* 2.6.

79. At *Pont.* 2.10.47-52 the exiled poet expects his friend Macer to reciprocate: as he holds Macer dear in his own heart, so Macer must make room for the exile, for his friend's heart is a happier place to be in. See above, Chapter 4, and Claassen (1986a) Section 7.4.

8. Generic Range in the Poetry of Exile

1. Editions by Soubirac (1972), Ewbank (1933) and Traglia (1963).

2. Edition as 'Senecan', Prato (1964). See Degl' Innocenti Pierini (1990b: 103-66).

3. 'History must report truth, poetry must be entertaining', Cic. *Leg.* 1.1.1. Cf. *Arch.* 5.12-6.14.

4. Archias did start on one, but did not complete it, *Arch.* 11.28, 12.31.

5. See Büchner *RE* 7.A.1 (1939) 1245 on the theory of Häfner and Drumann that the Latin prose version was never written.

6. It should perhaps not have been such a great problem. Wiseman (1979: ch. 2), offers a useful discussion of historical distortion as an accepted and *discounted* tool of rhetoric in ancient historiography. He also argues (ch. 3) for the ancient view of the essential unity of history and poetry.

7. Seneca *Contr. 3 praef.* 8, p. 243K, Tac. *Dial.* 21, 6, Quint. 9.4.41 and 11.1.24, Seneca *Dial.* 5.37.5, Mart. 2.89.3-4, Plut. *Cic.* 2.4, 40.2, Schol. Cic. Bob. p. 101 Hild., *id.* p. 144, Ewbank (1933: 27-32).

8. Clausen (1986: 159-70). Kubiak (1981: 12-22, esp. 19, 20), Traglia (1963: 8-11 and 190-1), Ewbank (1933: 23-4 and 36-8), Soubirac, *ad loc.*

9. Cf. *Att.* 2.15.3.

10. Harrison (1990) and Hose (1995) review the scanty evidence, cf. Büchner (1939: 1250), Ewbank (1933: 18, 19).

11. For *testimonia*, Traglia (1963: 50-4, 59-61).

12. Büchner disagrees with Ewbank's hypothesis that the consulate and a council of gods comprised Book 1.

13. If this is from the *De temporibus suis*, as is likely, it indicates Piso as possible author of the pseudo-Sallustian *in Cic.*, for from *Pis.* 72 we know that Piso had, at least once, criticised Cicero's poetry, Nisbet (1961: 197-8) App. VII.

14. Cic. *Off.* 1.22.77, *Phil.* 2.8.20.

15. Its ambiguities are discussed by Barchiesi (1997, esp. 1-9, 40-2), Fantham (1996: 102-23), Feeney (1992), Kennedy (1992).

16. Fantham (1996: 121) considers that apart from Ovid's, there was 'no other voice on intellectual freedom and suppression'. Hinds (1988: 21) refers to 'passively acquiescent panegyric' as an 'effective rhetoric of subversion'.

17. Cf. Stanford (1980) ch. 5, for a detailed evaluation in general contexts.

18. Thoroughly treated by Veyne (1988) and Kennedy (1993). O'Gorman (1997) discusses Ovid's subversion of Augustan themes. Ahl (1984b: 49) discusses the verbal equivalence of the name of the city and the Greek word for 'power'.

19. Labate (1991) terms Ovid's subversion of his models 'post-generic experimentation'.

20. Schmitzer's Table of Contents lists nineteen passages in which he discerns criticism of the emperor and of his treatment of others, including his daughter.

21. Barchiesi (1997: 19) sees the *Fasti* as a conscious denial of the Augustan world of *arma*. Newlands (1995 *passim*) reads criticism of Augustus into the work, against whom Fantham (1995 and 1997) sounds a note of caution. Feeney (1992) and Kennedy (1992) give a more nuanced view of Ovid's use of Augustan terms of reference.

22. Korzeniewski (1964) discusses Ovid's playful adaptation of the elegiac *prooemium*, involving whimsical dialogue, at *Tr.* 1.1 and 3.1, with the book as the poet's ambassador, and at *Pont.* 1.1 and 4.1, with the poet's dedicatee.

23. Except perhaps in the case of the last collection (*Pont.* 4), which does, however, exhibit some signs of conscious arrangement, with contrasts of topics and symmetry of addressees as interlacing principles of variation. See Helzle (1989b).

24. Books as ambassadors: *Tr.* 1.1 and 3.1; storm poetry: 1.2 and 1.4, with a 'triplication' in 1.11. Triplication in shifts of the exile's attitude towards the Getae: *Pont.* 4.13, 4.14 and 4.15. See Morgan (1977) ch. 5.

25. Estève-Forriol (1962) usefully collects basic elements of the Roman poetry of mourning and consolation, extrapolating from a wide range which includes Hor. *Carm.* 1.24, Ov. *Am.* 2.6, 3.9 and Prop. 4.11. See Read (1997) on Ovid's use of

Tibullan imitation in his lament for Tibullus, and Lenz (1997) on the Tibullan presence in the *Tristia*.

26. The origins of Latin elegy have been ascribed by some critics to adaptation of the Neoteric tradition to the epigrams of Catullus. Cornelius Gallus, who is known to have written only in the elegiac metre, is seen as the greatest innovator. Recent speculation by Fabre-Serris (1995a: 28-9), and Fantham (1996: 59-60) emphasises the importance attached by his contemporaries to his innovations, whatever these comprised. Some critics admit of no earlier Greek tradition, so Jacoby (1905), Day (1938) and Maltby (1980). Others ascribe the development of Roman erotic elegy to a more diverse Greek elegiac tradition, involving Philetas, Minermus, Antimachos, Hermesianax, Alexander of Aetolia and Phanocles, Callimachus and Parthenius, Callinus, Archilochus and Theognis, also mime and new comedy. The genre is distinguished by the length of its poems and their inclusion in a thematic collection, with as its binding factor, a single (or at most two) object of amatory address, whether mistress or boy, and as subjective topic the poet-lover's feelings: hopes and fears, joys and disappointments. This subjectivity is the only truly innovative aspect of Roman erotic elegy, clothing 'fiction' as 'fact'. In this view, the diversity of Ovid's exilic elegies would indicate a partial return to the topical diversity of the Greek elegiacs, so Day (1938: 127-37) and McKeown (1979). For a concise review, see Cairns (1979b: 214ff.). In both these views, Cornelius Gallus features as the pivotal figure. An assumption of the essentially non-political, if not anti-political, nature of early Roman elegy, based on observation of Tibullus and Lygdamus (Tib. 3), Propertius' apparently reluctant move into national poetry in his fourth book, and Vergil's portrait of 'Gallus the lover' in his Eclogues, was upset by the discovery that vv. 2-5 of the Qasr Ibrîm fragments draw a 'Caesar' into Gallus' elegiac world. The dating of the fragments is uncertain (cf. Whitaker 1983). Whether Julius or Augustus Caesar is meant, is unclear. This intrusion is not wholly surprising. Vergil's pastoral world is also peopled with politicians, including Gallus himself. Gallus stands at the beginning of the Roman elegiac tradition, which shares some of the characteristics of Catullan political epigram (e.g. Cat. *Carm.* 93).

27. Schmitzer (1997) ingeniously (and persuasively) argues for Gallus, a victim of Augustus' caprice, as the 'parrot' mourned in Ovid's famous elegy on the death of Corinna's parrot, usually seen as a travesty of Catullus' sparrow-poems. Ovid's view of the primacy of Gallus is perhaps not chronological, but may indicate preference, so Boucher (1966: 99).

28. Fabre-Serris (1995b) considers that Vergil in *Ecl.* 2 and 10 criticises Gallus for his imitation of Greek elegy.

29. Fabre-Serris (1995a: 392-2); Claassen (1988).

30. Barchiesi (1997: 42-8) discusses the phenomenon in relation to the *Fasti*.

31. The eight or nine years of Ovid's exile may be divided into five chronological phases: Phase 1: *Tr.* 1, 2, Phase 2: *Tr.* 3, 4, Phase 3: *Tr.* 5, Phase 4: *Pont.* 1-3, Phase 5: *Pont.* 4; Claassen (1986a) Section 4.1. Phase one depicts the exile's emotions during the early part of exile, some aspects of the journey there and his initial indignation against the emperor. The second phase, representing the first year of exile, presents the reader with no factual details about the exile's settling into a new environment. The third and fourth phases, representing the next two years of exile, appear to have been the most prolific, and also indicate a gradual decline into hopelessness. The last phase dates from about the death of Augustus in AD 14 to the poet's possible own demise in about 17. *Pont.* 4 features new dedicatees and an increased reliance on the power of the poet's mind to transcend physical circumstances. See Green (1994: xliv-v) on its particular problems.

301

32. *Tr.* 5.1.5, repeated from *Ep Sappho* (*Her.* 15).

33. So Lilja (1965), Holleman (1971 and 1976) and Syme (1978: 200ff.). Griffin (1985: ch. 1), argues for the reflection of a 'real' world. More recent critics, such as O'Gorman (1997), Barchiesi (1997: 40), Green (1996) Veyne (1988) Kennedy (1992 and 1993) tend rather to emphasise the interrelation of politics and elegiac poetics, and the slide between the two, particularly in Ovid.

34. Elegies addressed to the exiled poet's wife perhaps reflect a return to an earlier tradition that predated the tradition of using metrically equivalent names for the beloved, as practised by Roman poets from Lucilius onwards.

35. O'Gorman (1997: 121) sees the poems as a 'poetically self-conscious reflection of the issues of earlier works'. Cf. Claassen (1986) Section 6.1

36. As established by Antimachos' elegy for *Lyde*. This was adapted by Gallus in a *propemptikon* (departure poem) for his mistress *Lycoris*, setting the tone for *propemptika* at the departure of the beloved for a distant shore, rather than at her death. Cairns' (1979) useful adaptation of rhetorical terminology to poetics is followed here.

37. Degl' Innocenti Pierini (1990b: 162-3). She also (1990a) discusses an 'elegy on the death of Ovid' by the humanist Polizano (1493); cf. Claassen (1996c).

38. *Tr.* 3.1 resembles an Euripidean drama complete with *Botenbericht* (vv. 91-100). Janssen (1951) sees it as a burlesque of all departure scenes.

39. The same argument is applied in *Her.* 1.116 by Ovid's Penelope: *protinus ut venias, facta videbor anus* (as soon as you arrive, you will see me as an old woman).

40. Minor aspects of elegiac art such as 'gift poems' are reflected in *Pont.* 2.8 and 3.8. The first acknowledges a 'gift received', the silver portraits of the imperial family, sent by Cotta Maximus (Syme 1978 identifies the 'Maximus' of *Pont.* 3.8 as Cotta and not Fabius Maximus). The second poem apparently accompanies the return gift of a 'Scythian quiver.' The gift poems occupy similar positions in the second and third books, and may also be seen as a complementary pair.

41. Labate (1991), Veyne (1988 *passim*), Feeney (1992), Kennedy (1992), Dickson (1964), Yardley (1978) and Cairns (1972: 38f., 110f., 127f. and 220).

42. In *Tr.* 3.13 the poet plays with the idea of death, in 5.5 with the idea of return, Luck (1977: 298). Inversion turns the two poems into a pair.

43. *Tr.* 1.1.67, 5.1.22, 5.7.21, *Pont.* 1.1.14.

44. See Hinds (1988: 27) and Barchiesi (1997: 22-4) on the centrality of Ovidian aversion to warfare, also in the *Fasti*. *Pont.* 3.8 inverts the elegiac *topos* of the relative value of poetry and war.

45. 'Apology for his life and art.'

46. *Tr.* 1.1.3-12 subtly echoes, by playful inversion, an aspect of the Catullan introductory poem. The little book is unkempt and hirsute, in mourning, as behoved an exile's child. It is also the exact opposite of Catullus' *lepidum ... libellum / arida modo pumice expolitum* (dear little book, all nicely polished with dry pumice, Cat. 1.1, 2). *Incultus* (dishevelled, *Tr.* 1.1.3) alludes by inversion to Catullus' *expolitum* (polished). *Pumice* (Cat 1.2) is picked up in verse 11, also negatively. The same ploy occurs at the beginning of the third book (*Tr.* 3.1). The book itself refers to its unkempt state (vv. 8-18) again picking up *pumice* (3.1.13), negating the idea of polish with *erubui domino cultior esse meo* (I blushed to be smarter than my boss, *ibid.* 14). This is also denial of the poet's earlier preference in his erotic works for *cultus*. A second reason for the book's unkempt appearance and 'lapses into barbarous verbal solecisms', is that it hails from a barbarous country. An allusion to the 'limping' form of the couplet echoes and adapts *Am.* 1.1.1 (a laughing Cupid stole a foot). The whole is a playful conceit, to be taken as little seriously as Catullus' ostensibly deprecatory phrases. Cf. Hinds (1985: 14).

47. At *Tr.* 1.7 Ovid confesses to having tried to burn the *Metamorphoses* (vv. 15-22) claiming that it lacks a final finish, which he begs his readers to excuse (vv. 23-32). The six-verse superscription he offers for the *magnum opus* exploits the theme of a 'dying Vergil' for pathetic emphasis. Cf. O'Hara (1995). He is vindicating his poetic power and claiming restoration and return, so Hinds (1985: 21-7).

48. Traceable from Callimachus' *Aetia*, Prologue 1.1-35, onwards.

49. Wimmel discusses *recusatio* in Propertius, Horace, Vergil, Catullus and Ovid: *Rem.* 394ff., *AA* 2.493ff., *Am.* 1.1.1ff., 1.15.35, 36, 2.1, 3.1 (where *Elegia* and *Tragoedia* together represent Apollo as 'warning god'), *Tr.* 2.315-42. The consistent imagery in *recusatio* involves water (fountains, rivers, seas, sailing, drinking or votive use), travel (by road or at sea, ships, carts and chariots), dreams and dream sequences, and agriculture (termed 'Hesiodic' by Wimmel).

50. Claassen (1989a); Wimmel (1960), *passim*.

51. E.g. when a laughing Cupid 'steals a foot from epic hexameter,' creating an elegiac couplet (*Am.* 1.1), or in his attitude to Augustan panegyric (*Am.* 2.1.18), also noted by critics quoted above. See Schmitzer (1994) on *Am.* 3.15 as consciously opposing Horatian attitudes in *Carm.* 3.30.10-14 and 1.6.5-12.

52. Janssen (1951) undercuts a well-argued thesis arguing the 'fiction of Ovid's exile' by attributing consciousness of 'weakened ability' to the poet.

53. Also as an argument for recall, Helzle (1988a).

54. On this complex poem Barchiesi (1997: 27) is worth quoting; it invites, he says, 'a non-univocal reading of itself'.

55. *Recusatio* underlines the 'tiredness' of the *topos* held before him by the ruler, so Wimmel (1960). Other recusatory elements: 'mixture of art and life' (*Tr.* 2.11, 12); Augustus as thundering Jupiter (vv. 33-4); the gigantomachia as imagery (vv. 69-70); 'smallness' of the poet's genre (vv. 75-6); water and boat imagery (vv. 99-100); poetic predecessors (361ff.); a greater poet (529ff.), *invida ... natura* as *Livor* (grudging nature as Envy, vv. 531-2); the *Aeneid* as combination of great and small genres (vv. 533-4).

56. A similar plea of innocence and defence of his Muse speaks from the poet's *apologia pro vita sua* in *Tr.* 4.10. Here the poet first vindicates his life in terms of his art, and finally vindicates his art in terms of its lasting value as guide and as monument (v. 117ff.). See Claassen (1989a).

57. Similarly, Ovid's imagined epitaph in *Tr.* 3.3 denotes him solely as *lusor tenerorum amorum* (player of tender love-games).

58. Cf. *Pont.* 4.8.67-8. Newman (1967: 188ff. and 397-425) denies Ovid any serious understanding of the *vates*-concept. I should prefer to say Ovid is re-establishing the independence of the term, consciously freeing it from Augustan overtones. Barchiesi (1997: 48) speaks of the 'double image of an illusionist who plays with form, and a *vates* who proclaims an official truth' – at which point the 'illusionist vanishes'.

59. *Pont.* 4.2 offers a good example of recusatory agricultural imagery. The poet compares the 'barren field' of his poetic endeavour unfavourably with the fertile productivity of his friend Severus. Poems with recusatory aspects: *Tr.* 1.1, 1.6, 1.7, 1.9, 1.11, 2.317-56 and 529-78, 3.1, 3.14, 4.1, 4.10, 5.1, 5.7, 5.8, 5.12, *Pont.* 1.1, 1.5, 2.1, 2.5, 3.4, 3.9, 4.2, 4.8, 4.13.

60. See discussion of narrative in Chapter 2, Claassen (1991).

61. The recusatory pattern of *Pont.* 4 is rather similar. A poem to Severus, 4.2, starts with conventional agricultural imagery (15-26) commenting that it is hard to write when there is no one to recite to (27-41). *Pont.* 4.13, to Ovid's friend and fellow poet Carus, begins as a discussion on the recognisability of style, shifting into comparison of the 'power' of Carus' poetry with the 'weakness' of Ovid's own

(11-16). The poem then turns into a counter-*recusatio* of a curious kind. These 'weak powers' have been employed to treat of the great topic of the Caesars in the Getic language (17-32), which moved the locals to demand that such a Caesar should restore the poet. A flat and desperate statement, that poetry achieves nothing (41-2) offers subtle *recusatio*, which is curiously undercut by a final appeal to Carus' 'superior power as poet' to celebrate the deeds of his patron Germanicus, thereby achieving the exile's remission of sentence (4.13.49-50).

62. For instance, in *Pont.* 3.9.17-20 the poet disclaims any sort of order in the arrangement of the collection that comprises the first three books of Pontic epistles. On the coherence and careful arrangement of the collection, see Froesch (1968 and 1976). Cf. Claassen (1986a) Sections 9.4.10 and 13.

63. Similarly *Tr.* 3.1 shows the work as barbarous, appropriate to a barbarous place. The book ends at 3.14.25-52 with a similar plea, offering, as reasons for its supposed decadence, the locality, the poet's circumstances and suffering, the destruction of his talent by hardship, isolation, and contamination by local languages. *Tr.* 4 is introduced with a similar plea (4.1.1-4), but continues with a playful vindication of the utility of the poet's Muse; it relieves his suffering and beguiles his time. This book is concluded by the famous *sphragis* (4.10.117ff.), which supports, in strongly positive Callimachean terms, the earlier negative defence of his Muse of the opening poem.

64. The *topos* of the *labor limae* (the 'convention of careless composition') is a frequent concomitant of *recusatio*, as in *Tr.* 1.7.23-32, 5.1.69, 72, *Pont.* 1.5.15-20.

65. Degl' Innocenti Pierini (1992b) traces the theme from Horace through Ovid to Seneca, whose use of the concept she discusses further in an article on the chorus as authorial comment in Senecan drama (1993-4).

66. Implicitly countered by recent examinations of intertextuality in the exilic works by Labate (1991), Degl'Innocenti Pierini (1992), Schmitzer (1994), Barchiesi (1995), O'Hara (1995), O'Gorman (1997).

67. Occasionally the reader is led to deduce by implication that the exile still has retained his persuasive poetic power. A complaint of libel by the Tomitans (*Pont.* 4.14.15-22) comically reverses the recusatory *topos* of the inefficacy of poetry. His poetry has been only too effective. The Tomitans are incensed after discovering that the poet has portrayed them adversely to his Roman readership. He hastens to explain that it is their surroundings, not the people themselves, that he finds so uncongenial.

68. See Fantham (1996: 56-122), and Powell's collection of papers, *Roman poetry and propaganda in the time of Augustus* (1992a), from which I have quoted Feeney and Kennedy, above.

69. Gallus and the other elegists obviously are not listed among living poets at *Pont.* 4.16.5ff. Verses 4 and 5 of the Qasr Ibrîm fragments of Gallus' lost *corpus* seem to stand closer to the type of Vergilian or Horatian 'public poetry' than do the other elegists. Gallus 4 and 5 echo the call to 'old-fashioned piety' as found in Hor. *Carm.* 3.6. Ovidian treatment of the Augustan building programme sheds an ironic light on the patriotic stance of these verses. Augustus' new Rome as depicted in *Tr.* 3.1.27ff., and allusions to temples as places of assignation in 2.287 together offer an irreverent counterpoint to the Gallan sentiment.

70. Hinds (1983) quotes echoes or parallels of *carmina ...digna*: Lucretius (3, 420; 5, 1), Vergil (*Ecl.* 8.9 and four instances from the *Culex, Ciris* and *Catalepton*), Horace (*AP* 90f.), Propertius (4.7.83f.), Ovid (*Am.* 1.3.19f., *Met.* 5.344f., *Tr.* 5.12.35, *Pont.* 1.2.132) and *Priapeia* 2.2. Conceptual parallels: three instances in the *Eclogues* (4.3; 9.35f.; 10.2f.), *Tr.* 2.241f. and *Pont.* 4.12.27.

71. He applies the phrase to Tuticanus' poem on the wanderings of Odysseus, which he deems 'worthy of Homer', inverting the Gallan objective usage (good enough to praise his mistress) to a subjective mode (good enough to have been composed by Homer): *dignam Maeoniis Phaeacida condere chartis/ cum te Pieriae perdocuere deae* (as the Muses taught you to put down on paper a song about the son of Phaeacus that was worthy of a Homer, *Pont.* 4.12.27, 28).

72. Malcovati (1928). Suet. *Aug.* 85. Cf. *id.* 101.4. Fairweather (1987: 193-5) notes parallels between *Tr.* 4.10 and aspects of the *Res Gestae*, but argues for Ovid's use of the *Commentarii*. Dr Fairweather offered helpful comment on an earlier version of this section.

73. Cf. Brunt and Moore (1967), Introduction, Syme (1974), Heuss (1975) and various articles in *Wege der Forschung – Augustus* (Schmitthener 1969).

74. Fairweather (1985: 193-5) notes parallels with Augustus' life: both were from equestrian stock (*Tr.* 4.10.7, 8, Suet. *Aug.* 2.3), both were for a time *tresviri* (*RG* 1.4, *Tr.* 4.10.34), both achieved most happiness from a third, childless marriage (*Tr.* 4.10.69-71, Suet. *Aug.* 61-5). Both had daughters by their second marriages, both were grandfathers.

75. *Am.* 2.7.17 also appears to echo *Aen.* 1.1 *arma virumque cano* ...The *Amores* almost certainly predate the first draft of the *RG*, dated by Syme (1972) to 2 BC. Brunt and Moore assume its existence as early as 23 BC.

76. Barchiesi (1997: 48) lists possibilities for verbal play: *ROMA* vs. *AMORes*, vs. Met*AMOR*phoses; the postponement of Augustan celebration is *MORA*; all reminiscences of the author of *arma virumque* (arms and the man – Vergilius *MARO*). Ahl (1984b) adds *mores* to these: Augustus' attempt at moral control. Labate (1991) refers to 'intentional polemic' against Ovid's predecessors. O'Gorman (1997) refers to 'realignment' of the Augustan ideals, even Augustus as 'rival lover' and Rome as the 'beloved'.

77. Interpreted as such in Ransmayr's post-modern work of fiction (1990), which goes further in this direction, so Christensen (1992) shows, than Ovid does himself.

78. Cf. Duncan Fishwick (1990), and his more extensive monograph on the imperial cult in the Latin West (1993), especially its Introduction (pp. 33-92); cf. Barchiesi (1997: 9).

79. *Tr.* 3.10.67 and 5.2.31, 32. Cf. Augustus' claims to pacification of the Northeast, *RG* 29-33, Suet. *Aug.* 21.1.

80. Vergil's Scythia (*Geor.* 3.349-83) contrasts with its traditional antipodes Libya (*Geor.* 3.339ff.). Ovid's 'last night in Rome' tosses off (*Tr.* 1.3.19, 20) a passing allusion to his daughter as being then 'in Libya', pointing ahead to 'Scythia' (v. 61).

81. Ovid consistently uses the poetic (Greek) *Getae* for *Daci* (as in Hor. *Carm* 4.15.21f.), but they are the same people. On the tribes, Podossinov (1987) *passim*, Syme (1978: 166-8); for Tiberius' campaigns (*RG* 30), *idem* 48-71.

82. Yet depiction of the local Getic matrons as unfamiliar with weaving (*Pont.* 3.8.11) illustrates continued Ovidian concern with the superiority of *cultus*. These Getic women represent the same level of rusticity that other poets extolled in the pristine Sabines, but they cannot meet the Augustan ideal of womanhood, the *lanifica* and *prolegera* (wool-worker and child-bearer) of which Livia was usually displayed as the paragon. The 'national ideal' is treated ironically. Cf. O'Gorman (1997: 114-17).

83. Generic typification is difficult. The *Fasti* are a mélange of imitations of Hellenistic models, from Callimachus' *Aetia* and Aratus' *Phaenomena* (perhaps with Cicero as mediator) to the poeticising of non-literary material such as Hellenistic *periplous*. The metre is elegiac, the framework chronological, the content Roman national myth in a calendar of festive days, clothed in sometimes fanciful, even ludicrous, aetiological explanation. See Barchiesi (1997, a translation into English of his 1994 work in Italian on the poet's treatment of the prince in the *Fasti*), with Newlands (1995), which attempts to show the unity of the work and its 'ludic' qualities, and which Fantham (1997) designates as 'complementary' to Barchiesi's earlier work; also Hinds (1988), Feeney (1992), Mackie (1992) and Fantham's more cautious 1995 review article on recent scholarship. Older critics: Sidari (1977-78), Janssen (1951: 80).

84. Note the significance of the title of Newland's work, *Playing with time* (1995). She emphasises (p. 23) that Augustus through his monuments 'emblematised his control over time', thereby showing his power. Time in *Tr.* 1.3 is demarcated in cosmic terms, so Doblhofer (1980a); Ovid depicts time in various ways relating to the seasons: *Tr.* 4.6.19 two harvesting seasons; 4.7.1 twice spring after cold winter; 5.10.1 Ister frozen thrice; *Pont.* 1.2.25 a fourth winter finds him fighting; 1.8.28 the Pleiades have passed four times; 4.6.5 an 'Olympiad' of five years has passed, and a *lustrum* (five-year period); 4.10.1 the twice third summer has come; 4.13.39 the sixth winter has come, so Wartenburg (1884).

85. The *Fasti* were clearly reworked after exile, rededicated (to Germanicus), and the first dedication (to Augustus) was removed to the beginning of Book 2.

86. Newlands (1995 *passim*) argues for its completeness. By 'half-finishing' a poem on the Roman calendar as symbolic of Augustan control over time, Ovid was reproaching the leaders who exiled him from the city he commemorated, and thereby regaining control.

87. *RG* 35, Suet. *Aug.* 58.1, 2. O'Gorman (1997) points out that Augustus is shown as exercising his *patria potestas* (power of life and death) at *Tr.* 3.1.50, just as did the father of the Danaids (*ibid.* 61). Cf. Bonjour (1985).

88. E.g. the Muses are the 'granddaughters of Cybele', *Fasti* 4.191.

89. See the implications of 'blinding' as discussed in Chapter 5.

90. On the Romulus passage, O'Gorman (1997), on Ovid's recommendation of Augustus' public buildings as safe for cruising, Barchiesi (1997: 32).

91. Tiberius brought a statue of Hestia-Vesta from Rhodes for the shrine (Dio Cass. 55.9.6). Ovid also features the *porticus Octavia* at *Tr.* 3.1.69, 70, listed by Augustus in *RG* 19.1.

92. O'Hara (1995) distinguishes the poet as being more learned than his narrator as *persona* in the poem. See discussion of persons and *personae* in Chapter 1. Cf. Newlands (1995 *passim* and 1996).

93. Cf. Mader (1991) on Ovidian panegyric in his other works.

94. Cf. *Met.* 15.751-61 with *Pont.* 2.8.31, 4.13.27.

95. Syme (1978: 41).

96. Theocr. *Idd.* 14, 15, 16, 17, and *fragm. Berenice.* Griffiths (1979: 3-8) on its dangers, and (9 to 106) on Theocritus' solution.

97. Particularly in Fishwick (1993: 92-122 and plate XIIIb), to a lesser degree, Price (1984 *passim*). Representative documents are to be found in Ehrenberg and Jones (1949: 74-89), Chisholm and Ferguson (1981: 164-8). Cf. Ward (1933), Scott (1930).

98. Well documented by Fishwick (1993: 86-9, 97-106, 117-26); cf. Pippidi (1931).

99. The postulated date of composition of *Tr.* 5 would coincide roughly with that of the inscription. A high frequency of occurrences of the word *numen* in this book would not reflect knowledge of this inscription, but rather an awareness of or emphasis on the *Zeitgeist*. The exile's claim at *Pont.* 4.9.105-16 to daily prayer to the imperial gods in his domestic shrine was accepted by Syme (1978: 167), whereas Fantham (1996: 123) assumes some irony, but also sees the beginnings of imperial courtliness. Celebration, in a private shrine, of silver statuettes of himself, expressly forbidden by Augustus (so Price 1982: 178-80), if it were not a poetic fiction, might rather have annoyed than pleased the emperor. Calling the 'Pontic land' to witness is not proof.

100. Scott (1930) lists in the same semantic set: *ira ... dei/ Iovis/ Caesaris/ numinis/ laesi dei* etc., also occasionally *...viri* (anger of ...Jupiter/ Caesar/ a god/ a deity that has been injured/ a man).

101. Earlier critics such as Little (1982) and Littlewood (1981), Marg (1958-9) and Marin (1958), Claassen (1987) and the authors quoted above in connection with the *Fasti*. Price (1984) is important for his emphasis on the regulation of religion as a visible manifestation of power.

102. *Tr.* 5.2.52, 5.5.61-4, 5.8.29, 5.11.25-7.

9. Exile Universalised

1. Chwalek (1996 *passim*) argues for their essential unity. On alternate fusion and distinction of life and art, Froesch (1976) and Nicolai (1973).

2. Videau-Delibes (1991: 331) considers that the originality of the *Tristia* lies in the way it describes Ovid's physical metamorphosis by portraying change in the landscape and climate that he experiences. Cf. Claassen (1990b).

3. For example, Farrell (1992) postulates an 'internal dialogue' in *Met.* 13.719-897 which goes beyond generic tensions to exploit incongruity as a critique on the authoritarianism of the late Augustan principate. Redmond (1997) speaks of his 'violation of multiple canons' by means of a mix of 'contradictory genres'.

4. Assembled in collections (Parthenius' tales, Hyginus' *Fabulae*), catalogues of mountains, rivers or cities (*periplous*). On catalogues and repertoires, Gassner (1972), Lascu (1972).

5. Barchiesi (1997: 35) notes the paradox inherent in the fact that the hirsute armed Getae become the subject of the kind of poetry (elegy) that has always rejected them. Franga (1990) sees in his comparison between barbarity and *romanitas* a 'spiritual message in material terms'. Degl' Innocenti Pierini (1990b: 129-32) shows that Ovid's depiction of Tomis is an inversion of the traditional *laudes Italiae* (praise of Italy).

6. See my forthcoming paper on Ovidian punning, *Classical Bulletin*, 1998.

7. Most of Ovid's poetry (e.g. myth in *Tr.* 1.6) cannot be understood without a grasp of ancient literary convention, Kenney (1965).

8. Hinds (1985).

9. Cauter (1930) identifies 156 *adynata* in all Latin poetry: 82 in all lyric, 37 in Ovid: 27 in the exilic poems and *Ibis*.

10. It is spelt out again at *Tr.* 3.2.1-12.

11. Anticyra was famous for 'hellebore', a plant, perhaps the hydrangea, supposed to cure madness.

12. On interplay between simile and theme, Pearson (1980). On 'almost obsessional use of pseudo-symbolic images', Viarre (1974).

13. Nuances of Ovidian comedic writing may in turn involve 'whimsy', 'fun', 'play', 'humour', 'wit', 'irony' or 'deliberate bathos'. 'Humour' in some sense or the other covers all these.

14. Galinsky (1997) puts into perspective the current avoidance of the concept in favour of reception with the remark that 'intentionalism is ascribed [to] an author in choice of genre but nothing else', and postulates that with Ovid the critic may assume the intention to evoke a certain response. Barchiesi (1997: 31) usefully emphasises that such response can be ambiguous: 'all can be read with double vision'.

15. On Ovid's representation of character through multiple perspectives, Ginsberg (1983: 48ff.).

16. This was made very clear by speaker after speaker at the Pacific Rim Latin Literature Conference, held at Durban, South Africa, in June 1997. Publications arising from this conference will shift perspectives on Roman authors ranging from Horace and Ovid to Lucan, Martial and Curtius Rufus.

17. This is the attitude evidenced by most recent critics quoted in Chapter 8; cf. Ahl (1984a).

18. A frequent ploy in Horace, whose self-deprecation in, for instance, *Sat.* 1.5 and 1.9 has frequently been noted.

19. On the playful coda of *Tr.* 1.11, Ellsworth (1980).

20. This 'tactless exile', like the heartless *praeceptor amoris* in the *Ars Amatoria*, may be deliberate fiction, (without implying that the poet was not banished).

21. Segal (1969b), Galinsky (1975) *ad loc.*; cf. Newlands (1996).

22. *Tr.* 5.2.52, 5.5.61-4, 5.8.29, 5.11.25-7.

23. *Tr.* 2.51, 52 appears to allude to recent civil wars, not only those of Julius Caesar's time. Allusions to a *Gigantomachia* may imply the struggles with Brutus and Antony, explicitly named at *Pont.* 1.1.23-6, 1.2.121ff., Scott (1930).

24. Fishwick (1993: 90) shows that the cult of the emperor was fostered at Rome by indirect means, e.g. by attribution of a *pulvinar* to him, for watching the games. Cf. *Fasti* 1.649, 650, *Pont.* 2.2.69, 3.1.114-18 and 145-50 for instances of apparent adulation.

25. 'Getae' in *Pont.* 4.13, Greek-speaking 'Tomitans' in 14, are seldom clearly differentiated, Claassen (1990a), Podossinov (1987: 117f., 126-46).

26. A final retraction in the coda (vv. 61, 62) hedges the poet against accusations of lying. His prayer that the place be made *safer* and *warmer* inverts his earlier pleas for removal to a 'safer place in which to be miserable' (e.g. *Tr.* 5.2.77, 78). Hinds (1989) ascribed these diminished aspirations to the possibility that his wife had by now joined him at Tomis.

27. Perhaps coined at Lyon. Cf. Reece (1970) *passim*, also Plates XIII-XV in Fishwick (1993: 121-4).

28. Similarly, the exile's sacrifices at a household shrine, sacred to the Caesars, appears, in Ovidian context, suspiciously fictional (*Pont.* 4.9.105-12).

29. Recent works on the strained relationship between Augustus and Ovid, Barchiesi (1997) and Newlands (1995) *passim*, O'Gorman (1997), Claassen (1987), against whom Fantham (1995).

30. Williams (1980: i-xii, and 189ff.).

31. Thoroughly refuted by Podossinov (1987) *passim*. See Chapter 7 for discussion, also Feichtinger (1993). For ancient sources of conventional misconceptions about Pontus, Lozovan (1958-9).

32. *Oculi* and *imago* ('eyes', 'picture, image'), as metaphors adapted to exile, convey the poet's power to transcend time, space and circumstance, Claassen (1990b) Viarre (1974).

33. The North Star is part of the Lesser Bear constellation.

34. Navigation and horse racing consistently symbolise poetic composition in the *Ars Amatoria*. Both these *topoi* inform the tradition of *recusatio*, discussed in Chapter 8; cf. Murgatroyd (1982). Transference colours the navigatory imagery in the exilic poems. Composition of poetry has become a risky, storm-tossed affair.

35. On punning on *perire* in the *Amores*, Adams (1982: 224-6), Davis (1980) and Thomas (1964). See Claassen (1996c). Cf. the English metaphysical poets.

36. Veremans (1981) interprets *Tr.* 4.10.132 as the words of a 'dying man'.

37. Death, dying or funerals: *Tr.* 1.2.65, 66; 1.3.86, 98, 99; 1.5.41; 1.6.11; 1.11.20; 3.2.23, 25; 3.3.35, 36, 53, 54, 66; 3.5.6, 11-16; 3.8.39, 40; 3.10.11 (cf. Luck 1977 p. 211); 3.11.25, 26, 31, 32; 3.14.20, 21; 4.1.23; 4.2.73; 4.3.40, 41; 4.4.75; 4.4.40; 4.10.63, 122; 5.1.14, 17, 18, 48; 5.4.32; 5.5.48; 5.7.23, 24; 5.11.12; 5.14.12; *Pont.* 1.2.150; 1.3.9, 10; 1.5.85, 86; 1.6.31-9; 1.7.10, 54; 1.9.17, 18, 56; 2.2.45; 2.3.3; 2.3.42; 2.11.7; 3.1.6, 67; 3.1.71, 105, 109, 112; 3.2.27-30; 3.4.73, 75, 76, 91; 3.5.33, 34, 45; 3.7.19, 20, 24, 40; 3.9.28; 4.1.17; 4.8.47, 48; 4.15.6; 4.16.1, 3, 4, 47, 48, 51.

38. Owen (1915) has *laxate*, 'loosen', but the essential thrust is the same.

39. *Salus* can mean 'health', 'safety' or 'sound civic status' as well as the noun from the commonly used imperative greeting, '*Salve!*' *Tr.* 1.1.19, 27, 3.10.1, 4.10.79. On puns on *salus*, Claassen (1986a) Section 5.2.3. On loss of the mother tongue as symptomatic of loss of civic life, Doblhofer (1980b). Cf. the etymology and application of the word *infans*, 'not-(yet)-speaking' (child), from *fari*, 'to utter'.

40. Perhaps substitute punning on civic death for erotic punning elsewhere.

41. *Tr.* 2.209, 4.4.41, 42 and *Pont.* 2.2.57

42. Wounds: *Tr.* 1.1.99; 1.3.35; 2.20; 3.6.29; 3.11.19, 64; 4.1.36, 97; 5.1.52; 5.2.10, 18; 5.5.15 (his wife's); 5.7.34; *Pont.* 1.3.6, 7, 16, 22, 88; 1.5.23; 1.6.22; 2.3.94; 2.7.13; 4.11.3, 4, 19. Illness: *Tr.* 3.8.23-40; 5.1.33; 5.6.11; *Pont.* 1.3.1-8, 12, 90, 92; 2.3.46; 3.1.69; 3.4.7, 8, 31; 4.14.5, 6. *Pont.* 2.3.46 equates *culpa* with *furor*.

43. Williams (1980: 190).

44. This translation is from Green 1994: 200.

45. Degl' Innocenti Pierini (1980a, 1981a) bases her arguments for Senecan authorship on unity of expression and the 'Ovidian presence' in both *consolationes* and epigrams. To this she adds intertextual evidence adduced from verbal and conceptual similarities between the poems and some of Seneca's dramas (1990b: 134-66, 1995a and b). Cf. Jacobi (1988), reviewed by her (1990c).

46. For references here and below I use the numbering system of the edition by Prato (1964). Shackleton Bailey has recently revised Riese's edition of the *Anthologia*, but I have not seen either.

47. Prato (1964: 1-9) on the background to the poems, and 9-15 on Ovidian influence. Cf. Sørenson (1984: 113-20).

48. Frequent echoes of his exilic poetry are an oblique argument for the authenticity of Ovid's exile as an historical fact.

49. I accept the extensive arguments of Degl' Innocenti Pierini (1981a) and (1990b: 164), also treated Gahan (1985); cf. Grasmück (1978: 139).

50. See discussion by Degl' Innocenti Pierini (1990b: 135-42).

51. Motto (1970: 27) cites: *Testimonia*: *QN* 3.27.13, *Ep.* 79.5, *De Cons. Sap.* 17.1. Quotations: *Ep.* 33.4; 90.20; 110, 1; 115.12; *De Ira* 1.3.5; 2.9.2; *Vit. Beat.* 20.5; *Ben.* 4.14.1; 5.15.3; 7.23.1; *QN* 1.3.4; 2.44.1; 3.1.1; 3.20.3, 5-6; 3.26.4; 3.27.13-14; 3.28.2; 4 *prol.* 19; 4.3.4; 5.14.1; 5.16.1; 7.10.1. See Degl' Innocenti Pierini (1990b *passim*, 1995a and b).

52. With Seneca, *Chance, Fate, Fortune, Necessity, Providence* and *God* are sometimes equated and sometimes differentiated; *Fate* is inexorable (*Polyb.* 1.4; 3.3; *Helv.* 15.3; 18.6), Motto (1970: 45ff.). On similar inconsistencies in Livy and Ovid, Kajanto (1957 and 1961). Degl' Innocenti Pierini (1992c) traces the development of the Epicurean sentiment of 'living quietly' from Horace, to Ovid, to Seneca and in her book (1990b: 219-41) she discusses Seneca's ambivalent attitude to the contemplative life.

53. Cf. *Tr.* 5.2.11.

54. Reminiscent of the cadence of *Tr.* 1.11.21: *tollens ad sidera palmas* (lifting his palms to the heavens).

55. Ovidian echoes are particularly strong in *Epigr.* 19; conceptually the equivalent of *Pont.* 4.16; verbally: 1: *Quisquis es* (whoever you are), *Tr.* 3.11.56, 4.1.104; 2: *nostrum cinerem* (my ashes), cf.. *Pont.* 4.16.48; 4: *stringis in extinctum tela cruenta caput* (you tend your bloody arrows toward an extinct life), *Tr.* 2.529, 5.7.34; 7: *Livor, Tr.* 4.10.123, *Pont.* 3.4.74, 4.16.47; 9: *mea ...fata, Tr.* 2.341, 3.4.34, 3.6.15, 5.2.30, 5.3.5, 5.8.10, *Pont.* 1.2.63, 1.2.94, 1.9.22; 10: *bustis* (funeral pyre), *Tr.* 3.11.26, *Pont.* 3.2.31. Degl' Innocenti Pierini (1995b) sees in the poetics of epigram 37 the seeds of Martial's recusatory stance, elevating the contemplative life where *humanitas* is the central doctrine.

56. Thoroughly treated by O'Daly (1991). For metrical analyses, see O'Donnell (1984) *ad locc.* and Büchner (1977).

57. Beside intertextual allusion, O'Daly (1991: 69) identifies quotations from Homer, Euripides, Juvenal, Catullus, Horace, Lucan, Parmenides, Vergil. The poems can only be understood against the background of Boethius' work as literary critic (*id.* p. vii); cf. Shanzer (1983). Uhlfelder (1981) argues for Boethius' conscious use of established literary traditions, including Lucretius, Seneca and Roman comedy. Gruber (1978: 16-19) and Courcelle (1967: 115) add others, including Cicero *Somnium Scipionis*, Macrobius and Seneca's *Ad Marciam*.

58. Degl' Innocenti Pierini (1993-4) hears in Seneca's choral odes an authorial and autobiographical voice that on occasion refers to his own exile.

59. Glei (1985), discussing Boethian poetics, stresses that by including poetry within a philosophical work, Boethius is consciously posing as anti-Platonic; for him poet as *poiêtês* and philosopher are one; cf. Plato *Pol.* 473D and O'Daly (1991: 53-4).

60. Book 1: prologue and six other poems, Book 2: eight; Book 3: twelve; Book 4: seven; Book 5: five. For analysis of *metra*, Büchner (1977); of content, Alfonsi (1954).

61. Relihan (1990) postulates that in the end Dame Philosophy cannot adequately explain the central paradox, the coexistence of divine foreknowledge and human free will; hence no 'last poem', and hence the collection of poems as a 'bouquet of roses laid at the feet of a beloved mistress' with which the prisoner 'consoles his consoler'. Relihan's argument does not fully convince.

62. Uhlfelder (1981), Crabbe (1981b), Gruber (1978: 36ff.). Tränkle (1977) speculates that a sixth book, either lost or not written, would have placed 3.m.9 more centrally. O'Daly (1991: 28), rejecting Tränkle's arguments, favours Gruber's argument for its completeness.

63. O'Donnell (1984: 213, *ad loc.*) considers this poem as heavily indebted to Seneca, *Hercules furens*, 569-89.

64. O'Daly (1991: 52-8) sees in it an object lesson; Orpheus was overcome by passion; *amor* is to be avoided.

65. Crabbe (1981b), Chadwick (1981), Chamberlain (1970), Uhlfelder (1981).

66. One of the oldest surviving musical annotations (AD *c.* 1000), MS AUCT F.1.15, in the Bodleian library, Oxford, has ten of these poems marked in staffless nuemes, Page (1980: 306f.).

67. So Crabbe (1981a: 251-60); cf. O'Daly (1991: 23-5).

68. Uhlfelder (1981), Watts (1969: 20-1).

69. As noted by Shanzer (1983), O'Daly (1991) and O'Donnell (1984) *passim.* Boethius is, unlike Augustine, not 'a Christian writer', but rather 'a Christian who wrote'. Crabbe (1981a) argues that Augustine's influence works in two ways: first to affirm that poetry is a specious medium, unworthy to carry the full burden of philosophical argument, and second, as a standard, set in Augustine's *Dialogus de ordine*, against which Boethius pits his ingenuity. In his way Boethius, at the dawn of the mediaeval era, was both the last of the Classical authors and the first of the humanists; he was, as learned secular Christian, preparing the way for a world where erudition would not be the sole domain of the Church. Boethius' unashamed use of pagan tradition was his greatest innovation as Christian author.

70. Boethius' use of his Platonic models is complex, involving, at different stages, acceptance, adaptation and rejection. See discussion in Chapter 3. Cf. Crabbe (1981b), Uhlfelder (1981).

71. Boethius' sometimes ambivalent attitude to poetry is construed as wholly positive by Chamberlain (1970) with reference to his *De musica*.

72. Cf. Lucr. *De Rer. Nat.* I.936-50. For O'Daly (1991) the poetry does not represent a Lucretian attempt to 'sweeten bitter philosophy', but is rather a 'milder form' of that philosophy (p. 35), which he relates to the ancient tradition of philosophising in verse (p. 15). The contrast may be less stark than he indicates.

73. See for instance 1.m.4 (on tyranny), 2.m.6 and 3.m.4 (on Nero, the archtypical Roman tyrant), 4.m.2 (tyrants as slaves of their own passions); Courcelle (1967) App., Crabbe (1981b: 321).

74. From the Loeb translation by H.F. Stewart and E.K.Rand (1926: 128-31), with the English translation of 'I.T.'

75. Literally 'For old Age, unlooked for, sped by evils, has come, and Grief has bidden her years lie on me'.

76. Translation by 'I.T.' (1609) in Stewart and Rand (Loeb 1926).

77. Beside Ovidian echoes, Boethius' debt to Vergil and Horace is also clear, Crabbe (1981a: 247).

78. Presumably in opposition to the feckless tears of the elegiac lover.

79. On contrast of *fatum* and *providentia*, Gegenschatz (1958).

80. On Ovid's similarly functional use of dactylics, Claassen (1989b).

81. This translation attempts to imitate the dactylic stress-pattern, as follows:

$$- \cup \cup / - \cup \cup / - // - \cup \cup / - \cup \cup / -$$

82. On its authenticity, Stewart and Rand (1926: 412, n. 'a').

83. Anon. trans. from Stewart and Rand (1926: 412).

84. O'Daly (1991: 2) relates that Boethius' wife Rusticiana demolished the statues of her husband's persecutor, Theodoric, at some after Justinian's invasion of Gothic Italy in 535. It is to be surmised that the poem refers to this deed.

85. Helzle (1989a) argues that Ovid's wife is not treated as an elegiac *domina*, but as a friend and patroness, and that the style of her praise is taken from the Greek tradition of panegyric, which had been subverted by Propertius and Tibullus. This would then, to my mind, be another example of Ovid's conscious return of elegy to a more innocuous sphere.

Epilogue

1. Modern exilic literature continues to display the same characteristics, as demonstrated by Ash (1982) in her discussion of the dispossession of Jewish lyric poets as 'the most subversive' of intellectuals under Nazism. These include loss of authority, problems in finding a publisher, contextual estrangement from both their mother tongue and the host language (resulting in either reduction or contamination of diction), obsession with spiritual and physical change, petrification of verse forms, self-consciousness about the nature of their poetry, and parody of older poets as the ultimate 'weapon against those who would corrupt all tradition at home'. The editors of this collection (Spalek and Bell 1982: xiii) note that the most salient characteristic of exilic literature is its involvement in some manner with the political situation that caused it. Cheauré (1994) lists common feelings between Ovid and modern-day exiles; helplessness against the powerful, a desire to survive, exile as 'living death', general alienation and a desire for a 'safer place of exile'.

2. The author was awarded a major literary prize, which was subsequently rescinded, even though the author later abjured his former sentiments.

3. As with Ovid's exilic poetry, one of the topics of the work is poetics. Nethersole (1992) sees in the novel's thematisation of history and its self-reflective narrative process a relation to contemporary theoretical concerns about the direction that story-telling should take.

4. This and the following poem are quoted in Olivier (1972).

5. Katz (1992) reads another work from the South African apartheid era, J.M. Coetzee's *Age of iron* (1990), as more directly Ovidian. It traces the 'inner exile' of a Latin teacher, dying of cancer (a symbol of outer decay), and her experience of political alienation. Katz quotes John Glad, editor of a modern work *The literature of exile* (1990) on Victor Hugo's claim that 'exile is life'. Banished writers prefer the Ovidian 'exile is death'.

6. Notorious for his cool reaction to the death in detention of the freedom fighter Steve Biko.

Bibliography

Abbreviations are those employed by *L'Année Philologique*. For classical authors, unless otherwise specified, recourse was had to the Loeb editions. Only those whose editors' comments are quoted, are listed below.

A. General and theoretical

Ahl, F., 'The art of safe criticism in Greece and Rome', *AJPh* 105 (1984a) pp. 74-208.

Anderson, G., *Studies in Lucian's comic fiction* (Brill, Leiden, 1976).

Ash, A., 'Lyric poetry in exile', in J.M. Spalek & R.F. Bell (edd.), *Exile, the writer's experience* (Univ. of North Carolina Press, Chapel Hill, 1982).

Becker, C., 'Sallust', *ANRW* 1.3 (1973) pp. 720-54.

Bekker, I. (ed.), *Apollodorus: Bibliotheca* (Teubner, Leipzig, 1865).

Benjamin, A. (ed.), *Post-structuralist classics* (Routledge, London, 1988).

Breytenbach, B., *The true confessions of an albino terrorist* (Faber & Faber, London, 1984).

Brunt, P.A. & Moore, J.M. (edd.), *Res Gestae Divi Augusti* (OUP, Oxford, 1967).

Buresch, C., *Consolationum a Graecis Romanisque scriptarum historia critica* (Leipzig, 1886).

Caballero, R. & Giovanni Viansino, *Plutarcho L'Esilio* (M. D'Auria, Naples, 1995).

Cairns, F., *Generic composition in Greek and Roman poetry* (EUP, Edinburgh, 1972).

Cairns, F., *Tibullus: a Hellenistic poet at Rome* (CUP, Cambridge, 1979).

Cauter, H.V., 'The figure *adynaton* in Greek and Latin poetry', *AJP* 51 (1930) pp. 32-41.

Celliers, L., *Genresisteme in die klassieke letterkunde en die nawerking daarvan in die Westerse letterkunde* (Inaugural diss. University of Orange Free State, Bloemfontein, 1986).

Cloete, T.T., Botha, E. & Malan, C. (edd.), *Gids by die literatuurstudie* (HAUM, Pretoria, 1985).

Colish, M.L., *The Stoic tradition from Antiquity to the Early Middle Ages*; Vol. 1: *Stoicism in Classical Latin literature* (Leiden, Brill, 1985).

Conte, G.B., *Genres and readers*, trans. Glen W. Most (Johns Hopkins UP, Baltimore, 1994).

Cotton, H.M., 'Greek and Latin epistolary formulae. Some light on Cicero's letter writing', *AJPh* 105 (1984) pp. 409-25.

Cugusi, P., *Evoluzione e forme dell' epistolografia latina nella tarda repubblica e nei primi due secoli dell'impero, con cenni sull' epistolografia preciceroniana* (Herder, Rome, 1983).

De Lacy, P.H. & Einarson, B., *Plutarch's Moralia* in fifteen volumes (Loeb Classical Library, 1949).

Deroux, C., 'La lettre poétique de Catulle à Horace', *Didactica class. Gandensia* 20 (1980) pp. 149-66.

Dihle, A., *Die Goldene Rege. Eine Einführung in die Geschichte der antiken und frühchristlichen Vulgärethik* (Göttingen, 1962).

Dircksen, M.R., *'n Narratologiese analise van Tacitus, Historiae (1.1-49)* (Diss. D.Litt. et Phil., Rand Afrikaans University, 1996).

Doblhofer, E., *Exil und Emigration: Zum Erlebnis der Heimatferne in der römischen Literatur* (Darmstadt, Wissenschaftliche Buchgesellschaft, 1987).

Dunkle, J.R., 'The Greek tyrant and Roman political invective of the late republic', *TAPhA* 98 (1967) pp. 151-71.

Dunkle, J.R., 'The rhetorical tyrant in Roman historiography: Sallust, Livy and Tacitus', *CW* 65 (1971) pp. 12-20.

Du Plooy, H., *Verhaalteorie in die twintigste eeu* (Butterworths, Durban, 1986).

Eco, U., *Six walks in the fictional woods* (HUP, Cambridge, 1994).

Elliot, R.C., *The literary persona* (UCP, Chicago, 1982).

Estève-Forriol, J., *Die Trauer und Trostgedichte in der römischen Literatür* (Diss. Ludwig-Maximilians Universität, München, 1962).

Evrard, E., 'Aux origines de l'élégie roumaine: quelques distiques de Gallus récemment découverts', *LEC* 52 (1984) pp. 25-38

Fantham, E., *Roman literary culture from Cicero to Apuleius* (Johns Hopkins UP, Baltimore, 1996).

Feeney, D.C., *The Gods in epic* (Clarendon, Oxford, 1991).

Fishwick, D., 'Dio and Maecenas: The emperor and the ruler cult', *Phoenix* 44.3 (1990) pp. 267-75.

Fishwick, D., *The imperial cult in the Latin West* vol. 1.1 (Brill, Leiden, 1993 2nd ed.).

Giangrande, L., *The use of* spoudaiogeloion *in Greek and Roman literature* (Mouton, The Hague & Paris, 1972).

Gieseke, A., *De philosophorum veterum quae ad exilium spectant sententiis* (Leipzig, 1891).

Ginsberg, W., *The cast of character: the representation of personality in ancient and mediaeval literature* (UTP, Toronto, 1983).

Glücklich, H.J., 'Interpretation Lateinunterricht', *Der Altsprachliche Unterricht* 6 (1988) pp. 43-59.

Grasmück, E.L., *Exilium. Untersuchungen zur Verbannung in der Antike* (Ferdinand Schöningh, Paderborn, 1978).

Griffin, J., 'Genre and real life in Latin poetry', *JRS* 71 (1981) pp. 39-49.

Griffin, J., 'Augustus and the poets: *Caesar qui cogere posset*', in F. Millar & E. Segal (edd.), *Caesar Augustus, seven aspects* (Clarendon, Oxford 1984) pp. 189-219.

Griffin, J., *Latin poets and Roman life* (Duckworth, London, 1985).

Griffin, M. & Barnes, J. (edd.), *Philosophia Togata: essays on philosophy and Roman society* (Clarendon, Oxford, 1989).

Griffiths, F.T., *Theocritus at Court. Mnemosyne Suppl* 55 (Brill, Leiden, 1979).

Helzle, M., review of Ernst Doblhofer *Exil und Emigration: zum Erlebnis der Heimatferne in der römischen Literatur* in *LCM* 12 (1988b).

Heuss, A., 'Zeitgeschichte als Ideologie: Komposition und Gedankenführung der *Res Gestae Divi Augusti*', *Monumentum Chiloniense: studien zur Augusteischen zeit* (1975) pp. 55-94.

Jerphagnon, L., 'Que le tyran est contre nature. Sur quelques clichés de l'historiographie latine', *CPhPJ* 6 (1984) pp. 39-50.

Johann, H.T., *Trauer und Trost* (München, 1968).

Kassel, R., *Untersuchungen zur Griechischen und römischen Konsolationsliteratur* (Beck, München, 1958).

Kidd, I. & Waterfield, R., *Plutarch: Essays* (Harmondsworth, Penguin, 1992).

Klassen, W., 'A child of peace: Luke X.6 in first century context', *NTS* 27 (1981) pp. 488-506.

Koster, S., *Die Invektive in der griechischen und römischen Literatur* (Meisenheim, Hain, 1980).

Kovel'man, A.B., 'The private letter in Graeco-Roman Egypt as a literary genre', in Russian with English resumé, *VDI* 174 (1985) pp. 134-54.

Lefkowitz, M.R., *The lives of the Greek poets* (Duckworth, London, 1981).

Levy, E., 'Die römische Kapitalstrafe', *Sitzungsberichte d. Heidelberger Akad. d. Wiss., phil.-hist. Klasse* 5 (1930) in *Levy Gesammelte Schriften* II (Gras, Cologne, 1963) pp. 325-78.

Luck, G., review of H. Beckby (ed.), *Anthologia Graeca 2, Buch 7-8 griechisch-deutsch* (Heinemann, München, 1957) in *Gnomon* 34 (1959a) pp. 51-5.

Malcovati, H. (ed.), *Caesaris Augusti imperatoris operum fragmenta* (Torino, 1928).

Marcos Casquero, M.A., 'Epistolografía Romana', *Helmantica* 34 (1983) pp. 377-406.

Martindale, C., *Redeeming the text: Latin poetry and the hermeneutics of reception* (CUP, Cambridge, 1993).

Mommsen, T., *Römisches Staatsrecht* III.I (Hirzel, Leipzig, 1887).

Bibliography: General & Theoretical

Most, G.W., Petersmann, H. & Ritter, A.M., *Philanthropia kai eusebeia. Festschrift für Albrecht Dihle zum 70 Geburtstag* (Vandenhoeck & Ruprecht, Göttingen, 1993).

Nakhov, I.M., 'La catharsis tragique et le genre de la consolation (à propos de l'essence de la catharsis)', in Russian, *Dzetemata = VKF* 8 (Moscow University, 1984).

Neumeister, C. (ed.), *Antike Texte in Forschung und Schule. Festschrift für Willibald Heilmann zum 65. Geburtstag* (Frankfurt am Main, 1993).

Olivier, S.P., *Aspekte van ballingskap en vaderland in die poësie van Breyten Breytenbach* (MA Diss., Stellenbosch, 1972).

Opelt, I., *Die lateinischen Schimpfwörter und verwandte sprachliche Erscheinungen* (Heidelberg, Winter, 1965).

Peter, H., *Der Brief in der römische Literatur* (Leipzig, 1901; repr. Hildesheim, 1965).

Pippidi, D.M., 'Le *numen Augusti*: observations sur une forme occidentale du culte impérial', *REL* (1931) pp. 83-111.

Powell, A. (ed.), *Roman poetry and propaganda in the age of Augustus* (BCP, Bristol, 1992a)

Price, S.R.F., *Rituals and power in the Roman imperial cult in Asia Minor* (CUP, Cambridge, 1984).

Rawson, E., *Intellectual life in the late Roman republic* (Duckworth, London, 1985).

Reece, R., *Roman coins* (Benn, London, 1970).

Rudd, N., 'The style and the man', *Phoenix* 18 (1964) pp. 216-31.

Rudd, N., *Lines of enquiry: studies in Latin poetry* (CUP, Cambridge, 1976) pp. 1-31, 146-80.

Schmitthenner, W. (ed.), *Augustus. Wege der Forschung* (Darmstadt, 1969).

Scourfield, J.H.D., *Consoling Heliodorus: a commentary on Jerome 60* (Clarendon, Oxford, 1993).

Segal, R.A. (ed.), *Structuralism in myth: Lévi-Strauss, Barthes, Dumézil, and Propp* (Garland, New York, 1996).

Seidel, M., *Exile and the narrative imagination* (London, Yale University Press, 1986).

Skelton, R., *Poetic truth* (Heinemann Educational, London, 1978).

Spalek, J.M., & Bell, R.F. (edd.), *Exile, the writer's experience* (Univ. of North Carolina Press, Chapel Hill, 1982).

Stanford, W.B., *Enemies of poetry* (Routledge & Kegan Paul, London, 1980).

Taylor, L.R., *The divinity of the Roman emperor. APA Monograph* I (1931).

Thomas, R.F., 'Catullus and the polemics of poetic reference (Poem 6 1-18)', *AJPh* 103 (1982a) pp. 144-64.

Thomas, R.F., *Lands and peoples in Roman poetry: the Roman ethnographical tradition* (CUP, Cambridge, 1982b).

Thompson, D., *The uses of poetry* (CUP, Cambridge, 1978).

Thräde, K., *Grundzüge der griechisch-römischer Brieftopik* (Beck, München, 1970).

Trilling, L., *Sincerity and authenticity* (OUP, Oxford, 1972).

Trypanis, C.A. (ed.), *Callimachus fragments* (Loeb Classical Library, London, 1958).

Van Stekelenburg, A.V., *Redevoeringen bij Cassius Dio* (Diss. Leiden, 1971).

Van Wageningen, J., *De Ciceronis libro Consolationis* (Noordhof, Groningen, 1916).

Van Wyk Louw, N.P., *Tristia en ander verse* (Human & Rousseau, Cape Town, 1962).

Van Zyl Smit, B., *Contemporary Witch* (Diss. Stellenbosch, 1988).

Walters, K.R., 'Another showdown at the cleft way: an inquiry into classicists' criticism of Lévi-Strauss' myth analysis', *CW* 77.6 (1984) pp. 337-51 (= 1996) in R.A. Segal (ed.), *Structuralism in myth: Lévi-Strauss, Barthes, Dumézil, and Propp* (Garland, New York, 1996).

Ward, M.M., 'The association of Augustus with Jupiter', *Stud. e Mat. di Stor. della relig.* 9 (1933) pp. 203-24.

Winkler, J.J., *Auctor and actor* (UCP, Berkeley, 1985).

Winterbottom, M. (ed.), *The elder Seneca* (Loeb Classical Library, 1974).

Wiseman, T.P., *Clio's cosmetics* (LUP, Leicester, 1979).

Woodman, A.J., *Rhetoric in classical historiography* (Croom Helm, London, 1988).

Woodman, T. & Powell, J., *Author and audience in Latin literature* (CUP, Cambridge, 1992).

Bibliography: Exilic Narratives / Cicero

B. Exilic narratives

Bowersock, G.W., review of F. Millar: *A study of Cassius Dio, Gnomon* 37 (1965) pp. 469-74.

Bruwer, S.M., *The theme of exile in Virgil's Aeneid* (Diss. Stellenbosch, 1974).

Döring, K., *Die Megariker: Kommentierte sammlung der Testimonien* (Grüner, Amsterdam, 1972).

Fechner, D., *Untersuchengen zu Cassius Dios Sicht der Römischen Republik* (Olms, Hildesheim, 1986).

Godolphin, F.R., *The Greek historians* vol. I (Random House, New York 1942).

Grün E.S., 'The exile of Metellus Numidicus', *Latomus* 25 (1965) pp. 576-80.

Hicks, R.D., *Diogenes Laertius* (Loeb Classical Library, 1925).

Kallet-Marx, R., 'The trial of Rutilius Rufus', *Phoenix* 44.2 (1990) pp. 122-39.

Kornhardt, H., 'Regulus und die Cannaegefangenen', *Hermes* 82 (1954) pp. 85-123.

Leopold, H.M.R., *Exulum trias, sive de Cicerone, Ovidio, Seneca exulibus* (Diss. Utrecht, published Gouda, 1904).

Millar, F., *A study of Cassius Dio* (OUP, Oxford, 1964).

Mix, E.R., *Marcus Atilius Regulus: Exemplum historicum* (The Hague, Mouton, 1970).

Moles, J.L., *Plutarch: The life of Cicero* (Aris & Phillips, Warminster, 1988).

Muller, C., *Fragmenta historicorum Graecorum* (Firmin-Didot, Paris, 1883).

Peter, H., *Historicorum Romanorum reliquiae* vol. I (Teubner, Leipzig, 1914).

Procter, D., *The experience of Thucydides* (Aris & Phillips, Warminster, 1980).

Reinhold, M., 'In praise of Cassius Dio', *AC* 55 (1986) pp. 213-22.

Scafuro, A., 'Livy's comic narrative of the Bacchanalia', *Helios* 16 (1989) pp. 119-42.

Schmitthener, W., review of F. Millar, *A study of Cassius Dio, Gymnasium* 73 (1966) pp. 307-8.

Wilson, A.J.N., *Emigration from Italy in the Republican age of Rome* (Manchester UP, New York, 1965).

C. Cicero

Achard, G., *Pratique rhétorique et idéologie politique dans le discours 'optimates' de Cicéron* (Brill, Leiden, 1981).

Annas, J., 'Cicero on Stoic moral philosophy and private property', in M. Griffin & J. Barnes (edd.), *Philosophia Togata: essays on philosophy and Roman society* (Clarendon, Oxford, 1989) pp. 151-73.

Balsdon, J.P.V.D., 'Cicero the man', in T.A. Dorey (ed.), *Cicero* (Routledge & Kegan Paul, London, 1964) pp. 171-214.

Berrigan, J.R., '*Consolatio Philosophiae* in Dio Cassius', *CB* 42 (1966) pp. 59-61.

Buchheit, V., 'Plutarch, Cicero und Livius über die Humanisierung Roms durch König Numa', *Symbolae Osloenses* 46 (1991) pp. 71-96.

Büchner, K., 'Cicero: Briefe, Fragmenten', *RE* 7.A.1 (1939) 1193-1274.

Callies, H., 'Cicero und die Krise seiner Zeit. Auffassungsmöglichkeit, Analyse, Verstehen', in L. Hieber & R.W. Mueller (edd.), *Gegenwart der Antike. Zur Kritik bürgerlicher Auffassungen von Natur und Gesellschaft* (Campus Verlag, Frankfurt, 1982) pp. 105-19.

Carcopino, J., *Cicero: the secrets of his correspondence*, trans. E.O. Lorimer (Routledge & Kegan Paul, London, 1951).

Carney, T.F., 'The flight and exile of Marius', *G&R* NS 8.2 (1961) pp. 98-121.

Carp, I., 'Two matrons of the late republic', *Women's studies* 8 (Gordon R. Breath, London, 1981) pp. 189-200.

Cartwright, D., 'Cicero and Catiline', *Classicum* 10 (1984) pp. 34-7.

Claassen, J.M., 'Cicero's banishment: *Tempora et Mores*', *AClass* 35 (1992a) pp. 19-47.

Claassen, J.M., 'Dio's Cicero and the consolatory tradition', *PLILS* 9 (1996a) pp. 29-45.

Claassen, J.M., 'Documents of a crumbling marriage: the case of Cicero and Terentia', *Phoenix* 50 (1996b) pp. 208-32.

Clausen, W., 'Cicero and the new poetry', *HSPh* 90 (1986) pp. 159-70.

Cotton, H.M., '*Mirificum genus commendationis*: Cicero and the Latin letter of recommendation', *AJPh* 106 (1985) pp. 328-34.

Bibliography: Cicero

Craig, C.P., 'Cicero's strategy of embarrassment in the speech for Plancius', *AJPh* 111 (1990) pp. 75-81.

Crawford, J.W., *M. Tullius Cicero: the lost and unpublished orations* (Vandenhoeck & Ruprecht, Göttingen, 1984).

Degl' Innocenti Pierini, R., 'Il Foscolo e la letteratura classica sull'esilio: appunti di lettura', *Maia* 44.2 (1992a) pp. 147-55.

Degl' Innocenti Pierini, R., ed., *Marco Tullio Cicerone: lettere dall'esilio* (Firenze, Casa Editrice le Lettere, 1996).

Dixon, S., 'Family finances: Tullia and Terentia', *Antichthon* 18 (1984) pp. 78-101.

Doignon, J., 'Souvenirs ciceroniens (*Hortensius, Consolation*) et virgiliens dans l'exposé d'Augustin sur l'état humain d'ignorance et de difficulté', *VChr* 47.2 (1993) pp. 131-9.

Dorey, T.A. (ed.), *Cicero* (Routledge & Kegan Paul, London, 1964).

Dougan, T.W. (ed.), *M Tulli Ciceronis Tusculanarum disputationum libri quinque* (Cambridge, 1905).

Dougan, T.W. & Henry, R.M. (edd.), *Ciceronis Tusculanae disputationes* vol II. (Cambridge, 1934).

Ewbank, W.W. (ed.), *The poems of Cicero* (LUP, London, 1933).

Ferrarino P., 'Cicerone poeta e critico. La sua prima produzione poetica', in *Scritti Scelti Opuscoli Accad.* XV (Firenze, Olschki, 1986) pp. 46-50.

Fiocchi, L., 'Cicerone e la riabilitazione di Marcello', *RFIC* 148 (1990) pp. 179-99.

Fleck, M., *Cicero als Historiker* (Teubner, Stuttgart, 1993).

Fuhrmann, M. (ed.), 'Über Macht und Ohnmacht eines Intellektuellen in der Politik', in E. Olshausen, *Humanismus und Politik. Humanist Bildung* 7 (Hist Inst. der Univ. Stuttgart 1983).

Gardner, M.C., *Cicero the speeches: Pro Sestio and In Vatinium* (Loeb Classical Library, 1958).

Geffcken, F.C. *Comedy in the Pro Caelio* (Leiden, 1973).

Gelzer, M. (ed.), *M. Tullius Cicero* (Alfred Druckenmüller, Stuttgart, 1939 = *RE* 7.A.1).

Gigon, O., 'Cicero und die griechische Philosophie', *ANRW* I.4 (1973) pp. 226-61.

Glucker, J., 'As has been rightly said ... by me', *LCM* 13 (1988) pp. 6-9.

Gottlieb, G., 'Politische Theorie und politische Wirklichkeit dargestelt am Beispiel Ciceros', *Polit Stud.* 33 (München, 1982) pp. 281-96.

Griffin, M., 'Philosophy, politics and politicians at Rome', in M. Griffin & J. Barnes (edd.), *Philosophia Togata: essays on philosophy and Roman society* (Clarendon, Oxford, 1989) pp. 1-37.

Harrison, S.J., 'Cicero's *De temporibus suis*: the evidence reconsidered', *Hermes* 118.1 (1990) pp. 455-63.

Hieber, L. & Mueller, R.W. (ed.), *Gegenwart der Antike. Zur Kritik bürgerlicher Auffassungen von Natur und Gesellschaft* (Campus Verlag, Frankfurt, 1982).

Jocelyn, H.D., 'Urania's discourse in Cicero's poem on his consulship. Some problems', *Ciceroniana* 5 (1984) pp. 39-54.

Kassies, W., *'Dic, Marce Tulli!* The relation Cicero-Caesar as reflected in some letters', *Lampas* 14 (1981) pp. 262-74.

Kroll, W., 'Cicero: Rhetorische Schriften' *RE* 7.A.1 (1939) 1179-1103.

Kubiak, D.P., 'The Orion episode of Cicero's *Aratea*', *CJ* 77 (1981) pp. 12-22.

Leach, E.W., 'Absence and desire in Cicero's *De Amicitia*', *Classical World* 87 (1993) pp. 3-20.

Lintott, A.W., *Violence in Republican Rome* (Oxford, 1968).

Lossmann, F., 'Cicero und Caesar in Jahre 54: Studien zur Theorie und Praxis der römischen Freundschaft', *Hermes Einzelschr.* 17.13 (1962).

Loposzko, T. & Kowalski, H., 'Catalina und Clodius – Analogien und Differenzen', *Klio* 72 (1993) 199-215.

Mandel, J., 'The nature of the struggle between the rival camps in the last days of the Republic', *RSA* (1983-84) pp. 255-311.

Milanese, Di Guido, 'Tra Cicerone e Boezio. Linee di ricerca', *A Classica Univ. Scient. Debrecen.* (1995).

Mitchell, T.N., *Cicero, the ascending years* (Yale UP, New Haven, 1979).

Mitchell, T.N., *Cicero, the senior statesman* (Yale UP, New Haven, 1991).

Mitchell, T.N., 'The *leges Clodiae* and *obnuntiatio*', *CQ* 36 (1986) pp. 172-6.

Munzer, F., *Philiscus* 3 *RE* 19.2 (1938), 2379.

Narducci, E., 'Perceptions of exile in Cicero: the philosophical interpretation of a real experience', *AJPh* 118 (1997) pp. 55-73.

Nisbet, R.G.M. (ed.), *M Tulli Ciceronis In L Calpurnium Pisonem oratio* (CUP, Cambridge, 1961).

Opelt, I., *Die lateinischen Schimpfwörter und verwandte sprachliche Erscheinungen* (Heidelberg, Winter, 1965).

Petersson, T., *Cicero: a biography* (Univ. California Press, Berkeley, 1920).

Phillips, E.J., 'Catiline's conspiracy', *Historia* 25 (1976) pp. 441-8.

Phillipson, R., 'Cicero: Philosophische Schriften', *RE* 7.A.1 (1939) 1104-1192.

Phillipson, R., 'Philiscus 8', *RE* 19.2 (1938) 2384.

Plezia, M., 'De Ciceronis Hortensio dialogo sive de consolatione philosophiae' (in Polish, resumé in Latin), *Meander* 44 (1989) pp. 311-22.

Rawson, E., 'The interpretation of Cicero's *De legibus*', *ANRW* 1.4 (1973) pp. 334-56.

Rawson, E., *Cicero, a portrait*, (Allen Lane, London, 1975).

Richards, G.C., *Cicero, a study* (Chatto & Windus, 1935).

Ridley, R.T., '*Falsi triumphi, plures consulatus*', *Latomus* 42 (1983) pp. 372-82.

Robinson, A., 'Cicero's references to his banishment', *CW* 87 (1994) pp. 475-80.

Roller, M.B., '*Color*-blindness: Cicero's death, declamation, and the production of history', *CPh* 92.2 (1997) pp. 109-30.

Rundell, W.M.F., 'Cicero and Clodius: the question of credibility', *Historia* 28 (1979) pp. 301-28.

Scullard, H.H., 'The political career of a *Novus Homo*', in T.A. Dorey (ed.), *Cicero* (Routledge & Kegan Paul, London, 1964) pp. 1-25.

Seager, R., 'Iusta Catilinae', *Historia* 22 (1973) pp. 240-8.

Shackleton Bailey, D.R. (ed.), *Cicero's letters to Atticus* vols I-VII (Cambridge, 1965-70).

Shackleton Bailey, D.R. (ed.), *Cicero Epistulae ad familiares* vols I & II (Cambridge, 1976).

Shackleton Bailey, D.R. (ed.), *Cicero Epistulae ad Quintum fratrem et M Brutum* (Cambridge, 1980).

Shackleton Bailey, D.R., *Cicero: Back from exile: six speeches upon his return* (American Philological Association, New Baskerville, 1991).

Shackleton Bailey, D.R. (transl.) *Cicero's letters to his friends*, vols. 1 & 2 (Penguin, Harmondsworth, 1978)

Skinner, M.B., 'Clodia Metelli', *TAPhA* 113 (1983) pp. 273-87.

Soubirac, J. (ed.), *Cicéron, Aratea – fragments poétiques* (Paris, 1972).

Stockton, D., *Cicero: a political biography* (OUP, Oxford, 1971).

Strasburger, H., *Concordia ordinum, eine Untersuchung zur Politik Caesars* (Diss. Frankfurt, 1931).

Strasburger, H., *Ciceros philosophisches spätwerk als Aufruf gegen die Herrschaft Caesars* (Spudasmata, Olms, Hildesheim, 1982).

Stroh, W., 'Über Absicht und Verlauf Ciceros ersten Catilinarian', *AU* 29.1 (1982) 7-15.

Thierfelder, A., 'Über den Wert der Bemerkungen zur eigenen Person is Ciceros Prozessreden,' *Gymnasium* 72 (1965) 392-410.

Townend, G.B., 'The poems', in T.A. Dorey (ed.), *Cicero* (Routledge & Kegan Paul, London, 1964) pp. 109-34.

Traglia, A. (ed.), *M Tulli Ciceronis poetica fragmenta* (Arnold Mondatori, Pisa, 1963).

Trisoglio, F., 'La quotidianità rapporti sociali in Cicerone epistolografo', *CCC* 5 (1984) pp. 95-143.

Van Den Bruwaene, 'Influence d'Aratus et de Rhodes sur l'oeuvre philosophique de Cicéron', *ANRW* I.4 (1973) pp. 428-37.

Waters, K.H., 'Cicero, Sallust and Catiline', *Historia* 19 (1970) pp. 195-215.

Watts, N.H., *Cicero, the speeches: Pro Archia poeta, Post reditum in senatu, Post reditum ad Quirites, De domo sua, De Haruspicum responsis, Pro Plancio* (Loeb Classical Library, 1945).

Williams, W.G. (ed.), *Cicero, the letters to his friends* vols I-III (Loeb Classical Library, 1958).

Winterbottom, M., 'Cicero and the silver age', in W. Ludwig (ed.), 'Eloquence et rhétorique

Bibliography: Ovid

chez Cicéro. Sept exposés suivis de discussions', *Entretiens sur l'antiquité class.* 28 (Vandoeuvres – Genève, Fond-Hardt, 1982) pp. 237-74.

Wiseman, T.P., 'I Clodia', *PCA* 78 (1981) p. 21.

Zielinski, T., *Cicero in Wandel der Jahrhunderte* (Teubner, Leipzig, 1912).

D. Ovid

Abel, W., *Die Anredeformen bei den römischen Elegiekern: Untersuchungen zur elegische Form* (Diss. Berlin 1930).

Actes du Ier Congres International des Etudes Balkaniques et Sud-Est Europeennes vols II & VI (Acad. des Sciences, Sofia, 1969).

Actes du IIe Congres International des Etudes Balkaniques et Sud-Est Europeennes vols I, II & V (Athens, 1972).

Adamesteanu, D., 'Sopra il Geticum libellum (Pont IV 13, 19)', *Ovidiana* (1958) pp. 391-5.

Adams, J.N., *The Latin sexual vocabulary* (Duckworth, London, 1982).

Ahl, F. & Garthwaite, J., 'The rider and the horse: politics and power in Roman poetry', *ANRW* 32.1 (1984b) pp. 40-124.

Ahl, F., *Metaformations: soundplay and wordplay in Ovid and other classical poets* (Cornell Univ. Press, Ithaca, 1986).

Akrigg, M., 'An intrusive gloss in Ovid *Ex Ponto* 4.13', *Phoenix* 40 (1986) p. 322.

Allen, A.W., ' "Sincerity" and the Roman elegists', *CPh* (1950) pp. 145-60.

André, J. (ed.), *Ovide: Tristes* (Budé, Paris, 1968).

André, J. (ed.), *Ovide: Pontiques* (Budé, Paris, 1977).

Antony, H., *Humor in der Augusteischen Dichtung* (Gerstenberg, Hildesheim, 1976).

Aricescu, A., 'Le mur d'enceinte de Tomi à l'époque d'Ovide', *Ovidianum* (1966) pp. 85-90.

Aricescu, A., 'Despre zidul de aparare al Tomisului in vremea lui Ovidius', *Pontica* 5 (1972) pp. 439-46.

Atti del Convegno Internazionale Ovidiana (Sulmona & Rome, 1958-9).

Baca, A.R., 'Ovid's claim to originality and *Heroides* I', *PAPhA* 100 (1969) pp. 1-10.

Bakker, J.T.H., *Publii Ovidii Nasonis Tristium Liber V* (Diss. Groningen, 1946).

Baldini Moscadi, L., 'La Medea Maniliana: Manilio interprete di Ovidio', *Prometheus* 19.2-3 (1993) pp. 225-9.

Baldini Moscadi, L., 'Il dono di Medea (a proposito di Ovidio *Met.* 7.276)', *Prometheus* 22.3 (1996) pp. 231-8.

Barchiesi, A., 'Future reflexive: two modes of allusion and Ovid's *Heroides*', *HSPh* 95 (1993) pp. 333-65.

Barchiesi, A., review of C. Hintermeier *Die Briefpaare in Ovids* Heroides. *Tradition und Innovation* (Steiner, Stuttgart, 1993) in *JRS* 85 (1995) pp. 325-27.

Barchiesi, A., *The poet and the prince: Ovid and Augustan discourse* (Univ. California Press, Berkeley, 1997).

Barsby, J.A., 'Ovid', *G&R NS in Classics* 12 (Oxford, 1978).

Barbour, K.M., 'The geographical knowledge of the Greeks and Romans', *MusAfr* 3 (1974) pp. 57-76.

Barbu, N.I., 'Ovid und sein Verbannungsort Tomis', *Das Altertum* 21 (1975) pp. 22-6.

Barbu, N.I., Dobriu, E. & Nasta, M., *Ovidianum Acta conventus omnium gentium Ovidianis studiis fovendis* (Bucharest, 1976).

Barnes, T.D., 'Julia's child', *Phoenix* 35 (1981) pp. 362-63.

Batty, R.M., 'On Getic and Sarmatian shores: Ovid's account of the Danube lands', *Historia* 43.1 (1994) pp. 88-111.

Beck, R., 'Ovid, Augustus and a nut tree', *Phoenix* 19 (1965) pp. 146-52.

Benedum, J., *Studien zur Dichtkunst des späten Ovids* (Diss. Giessen, 1967).

Bernhardt, U., *Die Funktion der Kataloge in Ovids Exilpoesie* (Hildesheim, Olms-Weidemann, 1986).

Besslich, S., 'Ovid's Winter in Tomis, zu *Trist*.III.10', *Gymnasium* 79 (1972) pp. 177-91.

Bessone, F., 'Medea's response to Catullus: Ovid, *Heroides* 12.33-4 and Catullus 76.1-6', *CQ* 45.2 (1995) pp. 575-8.

Bews, J.P., 'The metamorphosis of Virgil in the *Tristia* of Ovid', *BICS* 31 (1984) pp. 51-60.

Bibliography: Ovid

Bilabel, F., 'Die Ionische Kolonisation', *Philologus Suppl.* 14-I (1920) pp. 123-4.

Binns, J.W. (ed.), *Ovid* (Routledge & Kegan Paul, London, 1973).

Block, E., 'Poetics in exile. An analysis of *Epistolae ex Ponto* 3.9', *ClAnt* I (1982) pp. 18-27.

Boillat, M., *'Mutatas dicere formas.* Intentions et réalité', *Coll. Latomus* 189 (1985) pp. 43-56.

Boissier, G., 'L'exil d'Ovide', *RDM* 69 (1867) pp. 580-612.

Boissier, G., *L'opposition sous les Césars* (Librairie Hachette, Paris, 2nd ed. 1913).

Bolton, M.C., 'The isolating effect of *sola* in *Heroides* 10', *Phoenix* 48 (1994) pp. 42-50.

Bonjour, M., *'Roma interdicta*: transgression de l'interdit dans les Tristes et les Pontiques d'Ovide', *Coll. Latomus* 189 (1985) pp. 9-23.

Boucher, J-P., *Gaius Cornelius Gallus* (Société d'édition 'Les belles lettres', Paris, 1966).

Bouynot, Y., 'Misère et grandeur de l'exil', *Atti del Conv.* I (1958-9) pp. 249-68.

Bouynot, Y., 'Ovide, *Tristes* III.3. Etude rythmique et stylistique', *Acta Philologica* 3 (p.m. Herescu) (1964) pp. 39-51.

Boyle, A., *The imperial muse* (Aureal Publishers, Victoria, 1988).

Brisson, J-P., *Rome et l'âge d'or* (Paris, Ed. la Découverte, 1992).

Broeze, V., 'Ovid's autobiographical use of mythology in the *Tristia* and *Epistolae ex Ponto*', *EMC* 16 (1972) pp. 37-42.

Buchan, M., *'Ovidius Imperamator*: beginnings and endings of love poems and empire in the *Amores*', *Arethusa* 28.1 (1995) pp. 53-83.

Bucovala, M., 'Noi morminte de epoca Romana timpurie la Tomis' (Roumanian with French summary), *Pontice* (1968) pp. 269-306.

Bucovala, M., 'Traditii elenistice in materialele funerare de epoca Romana timpurie la Tomis', *Pontica* 2 (1969a) pp. 297-332.

Bucovala, M., 'Über Grabbeigaben frührömischer Zeit in Tomis', *Pontica* 2 (1969b) p. 338.

Bucovala, M., 'Vase si obiecte de bronz Romane timpurie din Tomis', *Pontica* 15 (1983) pp. 235-48.

Busolt, G., *Griechische Staatskunde* Erster Hauptteil (Beck, München, 1920).

Butrica, J.L., 'Taking enemies for chains. Ovid *Ex Ponto* 4.13.15 again', *Phoenix* 43 (1989) pp. 258-9.

Cameron, A., 'Ancient anagrams', *AJPh* 116.3 (1995) pp. 477-84.

Casali, S., 'Ancora su Medea e Scilla (Ovidio, *Heroides* 12.124)', *MD* 32 (1994) pp. 173-4.

Casali, S., 'Strategies of tension (Ovid, *Heroides* 4)', *PCPhS* 41 (1995a) pp. 1-15.

Casali, S., 'Tragic irony in Ovid, *Heroides* 9 and 11', *CQ* 45.2 (1995b) pp. 505-11.

Cazzaniga, I., 'Bittis Coa', *PP* 22 (1967) p. 294.

Casazza, J.A., *Corinna and the tradition of love elegy* (MA Diss. Austin, Texas, 1979).

Cheauré, C., *'Cum patriam amisi, tunc me perisse putato!* Publius Ovidius Naso teilte das Schicksal der Flüchtlinge unserer Zeit', *AU* 37.1 (1994) pp. 4-7.

Chelte, J.S., *Philomela's tapestry: empowering voice through text, texture, and silence* (Diss. University of Massachussetts, 1994), summarised in S. Redmond, *Recent Ovidian Bibliography*, Internet http://www.nyu.edu/classics/latin2/ovidbib.htm.

Chisholm, K. & Ferguson, J., *Rome: the Augustan age: a source book* (OUP, Oxford, 1981).

Christensen, P.J., 'The metamorphosis of Ovid in Christoph Ransmayr's *The last world*', *Classical and Modern Literature* 12.2 (1992) pp. 139-51.

Chwalek, B., *Die Verwandlung des Exils in die elegische Welt. Studien zu den 'Tristia' und 'Ex Ponto' Ovids* (Frankfurt am Main, 1996).

Claassen, J.M., *Poeta, exsul, vates: a stylistic and literary analysis of Ovid's Tristia and Epistulae ex Ponto* (Diss. Stellenbosch, 1986).

Claassen, J.M., 'International interest in Ovid's exile and the search for Ovid's tomb', *Akroterion* 31.4 (1986b).

Claassen, J.M., 'Error and the imperial household: an angry god and the exiled Ovid's fate', *AClass* 34 (1987) pp. 31-47.

Claassen, J.M., 'Ovid's poems from exile: the creation of a myth and the triumph of poetry', *A&A* 34 (1988) pp. 158-69.

Claassen, J.M., 'Carmen and Poetics', *Coll. Latomus, Studies in Roman history and Latin literature* 5 (1989a) pp. 252-66.

Claassen, J.M., 'Metre and emotion in Ovid's exilic poetry', *CW* 82 (1989b) pp. 351-65.

Bibliography: Ovid

Claassen, J.M., 'Ovid's poetic Pontus', *Papers of the Leeds International Latin Seminar* 6 (1990a) pp. 29-45.

Claassen, J.M., 'Ovid's wavering identity: personification and depersonalisation in the exilic poems', *Latomus* 49.1 (1990b) pp. 102-16.

Claassen, J.M., 'Une analyse stylistique et littéraire d'Ovide (*Epistulae ex Ponto* 3, 3). *Praeceptor amoris* ou *praeceptor Amoris?*', *Les Études Classiques* 59 (1991) pp. 27-41.

Claassen, J.M., 'Structure, chronology, tone and undertone: an examination of tonal variation in Ovid's exilic poetry', *Akroterion* 37.3-4 (1992b) pp. 98-113.

Claassen, J.M., 'Ovid's exile: is the secret out yet?' review of R.Verdière, *Le secret du voltigeur d'amour, ou, Le mystère de la relégation d'Ovide* (*Latomus*, Bruxelles, 1992) in *Scholia* 3 (1994) pp. 107-11.

Claassen, J.M., 'Exile, death and immortality: voices from the grave', *Latomus* 55.3 (1996b) pp. 571-90.

Coliu, E., 'Un sarcophage à symboles à Tomis', *Istros* I (1934) pp. 81-116.

Corciu, N., 'L'attitude humaine d'Ovide envers les Tomitans', *Ovidianum* (1976) pp. 203-7.

Courtney, E., 'Emendations in Ovid', *Symbolae Osloensis* 64 (1989).

D'Agostino, V., 'L'elegia autobiografica di Ovidio (*Tristia* IV.10)', in *Hommages a Marcel Ronard, Coll. Latomus* (1969) pp. 292-302.

D'Agostino, V., review of Romano *Poesia e scienza. Nasonis poetae lacrimae Tomitanae* (Saggio VI Loffredo, Napoli, 1978) in *RSC* 27 (1979) pp. 147-8.

Dant, R., '*Imago*: Untersuchungen zum Bildbegriff der Römer', *Bibl. der Klass. Alt. Wiss.* NF ser. 2.56 (Heidelberg, 1975).

Davis, J.T., '*Exempla* and anti-*exempla* in the *Amores* of Ovid', *Latomus* 39 (1980) pp. 412-17.

Davis, J.T., '*Risit Amor*: aspects of literary burlesque in Ovid's *Amores*', *ANRW* II 31.3 (1981) pp. 2460-2506.

Davis, P.J., 'Rewriting Euripides: Ovid, *Heroides* 4', *Scholia* 4 (1995) pp. 41-55.

Davisson, M.H., (Thomson) '*Omnia naturae praepostera legibus ibunt*. ADYNATA in Ovid's exile poems' (*sic*), *CJ* 76 (1980) pp. 124-8.

Davisson, M.H. (Thomson), 'The function of openings in Ovid's exile epistles' (*sic*), *CB* 58 (1981) pp. 17-22.

Davisson, M.H. (Thomson), '*Duritia* and creativity in exile. *Epistolae ex Ponto* 4.10', *ClAnt* I (1982) pp. 28-42.

Davisson, M.H. (Thomson), '*Magna tibi imposita est nostris persona libellis:* playwright and actor in Ovid's *Epistolae ex Ponto* 3.1', *CJ* 79 (1983) pp. 17-22.

Davisson, M.H. (Thomson), '*Tristia* 5.13 and Ovid's use of epistolary form and content', *CJ* 81 (1985) pp. 238-46.

Davisson, M.H.T., 'The observers of Daedalus and Icarus in Ovid', *CW* 90.4 (1997) pp. 263-78.

Day, A.A., *The origins of Latin love-elegy* (OUP, Oxford, 1938).

Deferrari, R.J., Inviolata, M., Barry, M., McGuire, R.P., *A concordance of Ovid*, 2 vols (1939; repr. Georg Olms, Hildesheim, 1969).

Degl' Innocenti Pierini, R., 'Studi su Accio' (*Quaderni dell'Instituto di Filologia classica G. Pascali di Firenze* 1) (CLUFS, Firenze, 1980).

Degl' Innocenti Pierini, R., 'Seneca emulo di Ovidio nella rappresentazione del diluvio universale. *Nat. quaest* 3, 27, 13 sgg', *A&R* 29 (1984) pp. 143-61.

Degl' Innocenti Pierini, R., 'Il Poliziano e Ovidio esule. Per l'esegesi dell'elegia *De Ovidii exilio et morte*', *Res Publica Litterarum* 13 (1990a) pp. 215-27.

Degl' Innocenti Pierini, R., *Tra Ovidio e Seneca* (Patron Editore, Bologna 1990b).

Degl' Innocenti Pierini, R., '*Numerosus Horatius*. Aspetti della presenza oraziana in Ovidio', in *Atti del Convegno Orazio. Umanità, politica, cultura – Gubbio, 20-22 ottobre 1992* (Perugia, 1995c) pp. 101-16.

Degl' Innocenti Pierini, R., 'Due note sul mito di Scilla in Ovidio e nella Ciris', *A&R* 40.2-3 (1995d) pp. 72-7.

Degl' Innocenti Pierini, R., 'L'apparizione di Argo nella Medea di Accio. Storia e fortuna di una scena mitica', in *Atti V Seminario sulla tragedia romana*, Palermo, 1994, *Quaderni di Cultura e di tradizione classica* 11 (1995e) pp. 45-60.

Degl' Innocenti Pierini, R., 'Ovidio esule e le epistola Ciceroniane dell'esilio', in *Atti del*

Bibliography: Ovid

Colloquium Tullianum, Monte S. Angelo, 24-27 Aprile 1997, forthcoming in *Ciceroniana* 18 (1997).

De Jonge, T.H.J., *Publii Ovidii Nasonis Tristium liber IV, Commentaria exegetico instructus* (Diss. Groningen, 1951).

De Lacy, P., 'Philosophical doctrine and poetic technique in Ovid', *CJ* 43 (1947) pp. 153-61.

Della Corte, F., *I Tristia*, trans. & comm. 2 vols (Tilgher, Genova, 1973).

Della Corte, F., 'L'elegia della lontenanza (Ovid *Am.* 2.16)', *AFLNice* 50 (1985) pp. 367-71.

Della Corte, F., 'Le tre moglie di Ovidio', in G. Papponetti (ed.), *Ovidio, poeta della memoria. Atti del Convegno Internazionale di Studi, Sulmona, 19-21 Ottobre 1989. Comitato, Celebrazione Ovidiane* (Herder, Roma, 1991) pp. 247-58.

De Saint Denis, *Le rôle de la mer dans la poésie latine* (publisher unknown, n.d., c. 1954).

Des Bourne, S., 'Augustus' legislation on morals – which morals and what aims?', *Symbolae Osloensis* 59 (1984) pp. 93-113.

Desmond, M., 'When Dido reads Virgil: gender and intertextuality in Ovid's *Heroides* 7', *Helios* 20.1 (1993) p. 56.

Dickenson, R.J., 'The *Tristia*: poetry in exile', in J.W. Binns (ed.), *Ovid* (Routledge & Kegan Paul, London, 1973) pp. 154-90.

Dickson, T.W., 'Borrowed themes in Ovid's *Amores*', *CJ* 59 (1964) pp. 175-80.

Di Iorio, review of P. Carrer, *La dépression d'Ovide* (Laboratoires Ciba-Geigy, Rueil-Malmaison, 1976) in *Maia* 33 (1981) pp. 98-9.

Diggle, J., 'Notes on Ovid's *Tristia*, Books I-II', *CQ* 30 (1980) pp. 401-19.

Doblhofer, E., 'Ovids Spiel mit Zweifel und Verzweiflung: Stilistische und litteratur-typologische Betrachtungen zur *Tristia* und *ex Ponto*', *WJA* NF 4 (1978) pp. 121-41.

Doblhofer, E., 'Ovids Abschied von Rom: Versuch einer Modelinterpretation', *AV* 23 (1980a) pp. 81-97.

Doblhofer, E., 'Ovids Exilpoesie: Mittel, Frucht und Denkmal dichterischer Selbsbehauptung', *AU* 23 (1980b) pp. 59-80.

Doblhofer, E., 'Die Sprachnot des Verbannten am Beispiel Ovids', in *Festschrift Munari* (Hildesheim, Weidmann, 1986) pp. 100-16.

Döpp, S., *Vergilischer Einfluss im Werk Ovids* (Verlag UNI-Druck, München, 1969).

Dörrie, H., *Der heroische Brief. Bestandsaufnahme, Geschichte, Kritik einer humanistisch-barocken Literaturgattung* (De Gruyter, Berlin, 1968).

Downing, E., *Artificial I's: the self as artwork in Ovid, Kierkegaard and Thomas Mann* (Niemeyer, Tübingen, 1993).

Drucker, M., *Der verbannte Dichter und der Kaisar-Gott: Studien zu Ovids späten Elegien* (Diss. Heidelberg, 1975-77).

Ebersbach, V., *Der Verbannte von Tomi* (Berlin, Buchverlag der Morgen, 1984).

Ehlers, W.W., 'Poet und Exil: Zum Verständnis der Exildichtung Ovids', *A&A* 34.2 (1988) pp. 144-57.

Ehrenberg, V. & Jones, A.H.M., *Documents illustrating the reigns of Augustus and Tiberius* (Clarendon, Oxford, 1949).

Elliot, A.G., 'Ovid and the critics: Seneca, Quintilian and "seriousness"', *Helios* 12 (1985) pp. 9-20.

Ellsworth, J.D., 'Ovid's *Iliad*', *Prudentia* 12 (1980) pp. 23-9.

Enzinger, C., *LEO's Palindrome Collection: Latin palindromes.* (1998) Internet: http://www.cosy.sbg.ac.at/~leo/palindrome/latin.htm.

Evans, H.B., 'Winter and warfare in Ovid's Tomis (T3.10)', *CJ* 70 (1974) pp. 1-9.

Evans, H.B., *Publica carmina: Ovid's books from exile* (Univ. Nebraska Press, Lincoln & London, 1983).

Fabre-Serris, J., 'Jeux de modèles dans l'alexandrinisme romain: les hommages à Gallus dans la Bucolique X et l'élégie 1, 20 de Properce et ses échos ovidiens', *REL* 73 (1995a) pp. 124-37.

Fabre-Serris, J., *Mythe et poesie dans les Metamorphoses d'Ovide: fonctions et significations de la mythologie dans la Rome augustéenne* (Klinsieck, Paris, 1995b).

Fairweather J., 'Ovid's autobiographical poem *Tristia* 4.10', *CQ* 37 (1987) pp. 181-96.

Fantham, E., 'Rewriting and rereading the *Fasti*: Augustus, Ovid and recent classical scholarship', *Antichthon* 29 (1995) pp. 42-59.

322

Fantham, E., review of C.E. Newlands, *Playing with time: Ovid and the Fasti* (1995), in *CR* 47.1 (1997) pp. 46-8.

Farrell, J., 'Dialogue of genres in Ovid's "Lovesong of Polyphemus" (*Metamorphoses* 13.719-897)', *AJPh* 113.2 (1992) pp. 235-68.

Favez, C., 'Les Gètes et leur pays vus par Ovide', *Latomus* 10 (1951) pp. 425-32.

Feeney, D.C., '*Si licet et fas est*: Ovid's *Fasti* and the problem of free speech under the Principate', in A. Powell (ed.), *Roman poetry and propaganda in the age of Augustus* (1992) pp. 1-25.

Feichlinger, B., review of B.M. Gauly, *Liebeserfahrungen: zur Rolle des elegischen Ich in Ovids 'Amores'* (1991) in *Grazer Beiträge* 19 (1993) pp. 268-70.

Fitton Brown, A.D., 'The unreality of Ovid's Tomitan exile', *LCM* 10.2 (1985) pp. 19-22.

Flory, M.B., '*Sic exempla parantur*: Livia's shrine to Concordia and the porticus Liviae', *Historia* 33 (1984) pp. 309-30.

Focardi, G., 'Difesa, preghiera, ironia nel II libro dei *Tristia* di Ovidio', *SIFC* 47 (1975) pp. 86-129.

Ford, B.B., *Tristia II: Ovid's opposition to Augustus* (Diss. Rutgers, 1977).

Franga, L., 'Ovidius si spatiul danubiano-pontic', *Thraco-Dacica* 11.1, 2 (1990) pp. 225-38.

Fränkel, H., *Ovid: a poet between two worlds* (Sather Class. lectures, Berkeley 1945; 3rd repr. 1969).

Frécaut, J.M., *L'Esprit et l'humeur chez Ovide* (Presses Universitaires, Grenoble, 1972).

Frécaut, J.M., & Porte, D. (edd.), *Journées ovidiennes de Parménie. Actes du Colloque sur Ovide (24-26 juin 1983)*, Coll. *Latomus* 189 (1985a).

Frécaut, J.M., 'Un thème particulier dans les *Metamorphoses* d'Ovide. Le personnage métamorphose gardant la conscience de soi (*mens antiqua manet* 11.485)' (1985b) in Frécaut & Porte (edd.), *Journées ovidiennes de Parménie*, pp. 115-43.

Fredericks, B.R. (Nagle), '*Tristia* 4.10, Poet's autobiography and poetic biography', *TAPA* 106 (1976) pp. 139-54.

Friedrich, W-H., 'Epische Unwetter', in *Festschrift für Bruno Snell* (München, 1956) pp. 77-87.

Froesch, H., 'Ovid als Dichter des Exils', *Abh zur Kunst, Musik und Literaturwiss.* 218 (Bouvier, Bonn, 1976).

Froesch, H., *Ovids Epistolae ex Ponto 1-3 als Gedichtsammlung* (Diss. Bonn, 1968).

Fugier, H., 'Communication et structures textuelles dans les Tristes d'Ovide', *Revue Romane* (Copenhagen) 11 (1976) pp. 74-98.

Fuhrmann, M., 'Mythos und Herrschaft in Christa Wolfs *Kassandra* und Christoph Ransmayrs *Die Letzte Welt*', *AU* 37.2 (1994) pp. 11-24.

Gahan, J.J., 'Ovid, The poet in winter', *CJ* 73 (1978) pp. 198-202.

Galinsky, G.K., 'The triumph theme in Augustan elegy', *WS* 82 NF 3 (1969) pp. 75-107.

Galinsky, G.K., 'Hercules Ovidianus (*Metamorphoses* 9.1-272)', *WS* NF 6 (1972a) pp. 93-116.

Galinsky, G.K., 'Ovid's Metamorphosis of myth', in G.K. Galinsky (ed.), *Perspectives on Roman poetry* (1972b) pp. 105-27.

Galinsky, G.K., *Ovid's Metamorphoses, an introduction to the basic aspects* (Univ. California Press, Berkeley, 1975).

Galinsky, G.K., 'Augustus' legislation on morals and marriage', *Philologus* 125 (1981) pp. 126-44.

Galinsky, G.K., 'Ovid's poetology in the Metamorphoses', in W. Schubert (ed.), *Festschrift für Michael von Albrecht* (pre-publication on Internet, 1997).

Galis, L., 'Medea's metamorphosis', *Eranos* 90.2 (1992) pp. 65-81.

Gamel, M-K., 'Introduction to *Contemporary interpretations of Ovid*, and works cited', *Helios* 12 (1985) pp. 3-8, 81-8.

Gandeva, R., 'Moralische und soziale Charakteristik der West und Nord Balkanbevölkerung bei Ovid', in *Actes Ier Congr. internat. des Et. Balk. & Sud. Est. Eur.* vol. II (Sofia, 1969) pp. 127-39.

Gandeva, R., 'Socia lingua in der Griechischen Polis zur Zeit Ovids', in Jurewicz & Kuch (edd.), *Die Krise der griechischen Polis* (Berlin, 1969) pp. 77-80.

Gandeva, R., 'De Ovidio exsule misericordia turbae Tomitanae regionis commoto', *Ovidianum* (1976) pp. 295-9.

Bibliography: Ovid

Gandeva, R., 'Thrakische Motive in der römischen Dichtung (Ov. *Pont.* 2.9)', in *Spravitelno Literaturosmane, Et. de litt. Compareé* 3 (Sofia, 1983) pp. 73-86.

Gantar, K., '*Tristia* II als eine Quelle zur Erschliessung der ovidischen Poetik', *ZAnt* 35 (1975) pp. 94-102.

Ganzenmüller, W., 'Aus Ovids Werkstatt', *Philologus* 70 (1911) pp. 274-311.

Gariepy, R.J., 'Recent scholarship on Ovid (1958-1968)', *CW* 64 (1970) pp. 37-56.

Gassner, J., *Kataloge in römischen Epos: Vergil-Ovid-Lucan* (Diss. Augsburg, 1972).

Gelma, E., 'La dépression mélancholique du poète Ovide pendant son exil', *Le médium d'Alsace et de Lorraine* 11.15.1 (1933) pp. 28-44.

Gibson, R.K., 'How to win girlfriends and influence them: *amicitia* in Roman love elegy', *PCPhS* 41 (1995) pp. 62-82.

González Vázquez, J., 'En Torno a la retractatio de un pasaje Virgiliano en *Tristia* 1, 2', *Latomus* 52 (1993) pp. 75-83.

Gordon, P., 'Sappho double-crossed: the mannish muse of *Heroides* 15', paper delivered at the Annual Meeting of the American Philological Association, Washington, DC, December 27-30 (1993).

Gosling, A., review of C.E. Newlands, *Playing with time: Ovid and the Fasti* (Cornell, 1995), in *Scholia Reviews* NS 5 (1996) 125-30.

Graeber, G., *Quaestionum Ovidianum pars prior* (Sam. Lucas, Eberfeld, 1881).

Green, C.M.C., 'Terms of venery: *Ars Amatoria* I', *TAPA* 126 (1996) pp. 221-63.

Green, P., '*Carmen et error. Prophasis* and *aitia* in the matter of Ovid's exile', *ClAnt* I (1982a) pp. 202-20.

Green, P., *Ovid, the erotic poems* (Penguin Books, Harmondsworth, 1982b).

Green, P., 'Ovid in Tomis', *Grand Street* 2 (1982c) pp. 116-30.

Green, P., *Ovid, the poems of exile* (Penguin, Harmondsworth, 1994).

Griffin, A.H.F., 'Ovid, *Tristia* 1.2 and the tradition of literary sea storms', *Pegasus* 28 (1985) pp. 28-34.

Gross, N.P., 'Rhetorical wit and amatory persuasion in Ovid', *CJ* 74 (1979) pp. 305-18.

Gross, N.P., 'Ovid, *Amores* 1, 8: whose amatory rhetoric?', *CW* 89 (1996) pp. 197-206.

Hall, J.B., 'Conjectures in Ovid's *Ex Ponto*', *RivFil* 121 (1993) pp. 289-96.

Hall, J.B., review of A. Barchiesi, *Il poeta e il principe. Ovidio e il discorso Augusteo* (1994) in *CR* 47.1 (1997) pp. 43-6.

Hart Nibrigg, C.L., *Rhetorik des Schweigens: Versuch über den Schatten literarischer Rede* (Suhrkamp, Frankfort-am-Main, 1981).

Heinze, R., 'Ovids elegische Erzählung', *Berichte über die Verh. der sächsischen Akad. der Wiss.* 71 (Teubner, Leipzig, 1919) pp. 1-130.

Hellegouarc'h, J., *Le vocabulaire latin des relations et des partis politiques sous la République* (Les Belles Lettres, Paris, 1963).

Hellegouarc'h, J., 'Aspects stylistiques de l'expression de la tristesse et de la douleur dans les poèmes ovidiens de l'exil', *Ovidianum* (1976) pp. 325-40.

Helzle, M., 'Ovid's poetics of exile', *Illinois Classical Studies* 13 (1988a) pp. 73-83.

Helzle, M., 'Mr. and Mrs. Ovid', *G&R* 36 (1989a) pp. 183-93.

Helzle, M., *Publii Ovidii Nasonis epistularum ex Ponto liber IV. A commentary on poems 1-7, 16* (Spudasmata, Hildesheim, Olms, 1989b).

Helzle, M., review of *Publio Ovidio Nason, Cartas desde el Ponto. Libro II*, Introd. ed. crit. trad. y comm. de Ana Pérez Vega, Sevilla (1989) in *Gnomon* 65 (1993) pp. 34-6.

Herescu, N.I., 'Le sens de l'épitaphe ovidienne', *Ovidiana* (1958a) pp. 420-42.

Herescu, N.I. (ed.), *Ovidiana: Recherches sur Ovide publiées a l'occasion du bimillénaire de la naissance du poète* (Les Belles Lettres, Paris, 1958b).

Hexter, R.J., *Ovid and medieval schooling. Studies in medieval school commentaries on Ovid's Ars Amatoria, Epistulae ex Ponto and Epistulae Heroidum* (München, Arbeo-Gesellschaft, 1986).

Heyworth, S.J., 'Ars Moratoria (Ovid, *AA* 1.681-704)', *LCM* 17.4 (1992) pp. 59-61.

Heyworth, S.J., 'Horace's *Ibis*: on the titles, unity, and contents of the *Epodes*', *PLILS* 7 (ARCA 32, 1993) pp. 85-96.

Heyworth, S.J., 'Notes on Ovid's *Tristia*', *PCPhS* 41 (1995) pp 138-52.

Bibliography: Ovid

Hinds, S., 'An allusion in the literary tradition of the Proserpina myth', *CQ* 32 (1982) pp. 476-8.

Hinds, S., '*Carmina digna*: Gallus P Qasr Ibrîm 6-7 metamorphosed', *PLILS* 4, (1983) pp. 43-54.

Hinds, S., 'Booking the return trip: Ovid and *Tristia* 1', *PCPhS* 31 (1985) pp. 21-32.

Hinds, S., 'Generalising about Ovid', in A. Boyle, *The imperial muse* (Aureal Publishers, Victoria, 1988) pp. 4-31.

Hinds, S., 'Medea in Ovid: scenes from the life of an intertextual heroine', *Materiali e Discussioni* 30 (1993) pp. 9-47.

Holleman, A.W.J., 'Ovid and politics', *Historia* 20 (1971) pp. 458-66.

Holleman, A.W.J., '*Feminae virtus*: some new thoughts on the conflict between Augustus and Ovid', *Ovidianum* (1976) pp. 341-55.

Hopkinson, N., 'Juxtaposed prosodic variants in Greek and Latin poetry', *Glotta* 60 (1982) pp. 162-77.

Horia, V., *God was born in exile*, trans. from the French by A. Lytton Sells (St Martin's Press, New York, 1961).

Horsfall, N., 'Epic and burlesque in Ovid, *Met.* VIII 260ff.', *CJ* 74 (1979) pp. 319-32.

Housman, A.E., 'Transpositions in the *Ibis* of Ovid' (*J Phil* 1918) in J. Diggle & F.R.D. Goodyear (edd.), *The classical papers of A.E. Housman* (vol. III, 1972) 969-81.

Jacobson, H., *Ovid's Heroides* (Princeton Univ. Press, Princeton, 1974).

Jacoby, 'Zur Entstehung der römische Elegie', *RhM* 60 (1905) pp. 38-105.

Janssen, Dr Otger, OFM 1951: 'De Verbanning van Ovidius, waarheid of fiktie?', in *Uit de Romeinse Keizertijd, Collectanea Franciscana Neerlandica* VI-3, pp. 77-105.

Janssens, L., 'Deux complexes d'acrostiches délateurs d' "Ibis", alias C Ateius Capito. Le mysticisme du culte d' "Abrasax" ', *RPh* 55 (1981) pp. 57-71.

Johnson, P.J., 'Ovid's Livia in exile', *CW* 90.6 (1997) pp. 403-20.

Johnson W.R., 'Ringing down the curtain on love', *Helios* 12 (1985) pp. 21-8.

Johnson W.R., 'The rapes of Callisto', *CJ* 92.1 (1996) pp. 9-24.

Kajanto, I., *God and fate in Livy* (Turun Yliopisto, Turku, 1957).

Kajanto, I., *Ovid's conception of fate* (Turun Yliopisto, Turku, 1961).

Katz, P.B., 'Ovid's last world: an age of iron', *Classical and Modern Literature* 12.2 (1992) pp. 127-37.

Kennedy, D.F., 'The epistolary mode and the first of Ovid's *Heroides*', *CQ* 34 (1984) pp. 413-22.

Kennedy, D.F., ' "Augustan" and "anti-Augustan": reflections on terms of reference', in A. Powell (ed.), *Roman poetry and propaganda in the age of Augustus* (1992) pp. 29-47.

Kennedy, D., *The arts of love: five studies in the discourse of Roman love elegy* (CUP, Cambridge, 1993).

Kenney, E.J., '*Nequitiae poeta*', *Ovidiana* (1958) pp. 201-9.

Kenney, E.J., 'The poetry of Ovid's exile', *PCPhS* 191 (1965) pp. 37-49.

Kenney, E.J., 'Ovid and the law', *YCIS* 21 (1969) pp. 241-63.

Kenney, E.J., '*Ovidius prooemians*', *PCPhS* (1976) pp. 202, 43-53.

Kirfel, E.A., *Untersuchungen zur Briefform der Heroides Ovids* (Verlag Paul Haupt, Bern & Stuttgart, 1969).

Knox P.E., 'The old Gallus', *Hermes* 113 (1985) pp. 497-510.

Korzeniewski, D., 'Ovids elegisches Proömium', *Hermes* 92 (1964) pp. 182-213.

Koster, S., 'Ovid und die Elegie', in P. Neukam (ed.), *Klassische Antike und Gegenwart, Dialog Schule-Wiss. Klass. Spr. & Lit.* 19 (Bayer, München, 1985) pp. 7-26.

Kraus, W., 'Der Forschungsbericht, Ovid, I Bericht, I Teil', *Anzeiger für die Altertumswissenschaft* 11 (1958) pp. 129-46.

Kraus, W., 'Ovid', in Von Albrecht & Zinn (edd.), *Ovid* (Wege der Forschung, Darmstadt, 1966) pp. 67ff. (= *RE* 1942/66).

Kröner, H.O., 'Aufbau und Ziel der Elegie Ovids, *Tristia* 1.2', *Emerita* 38 (1970a) pp. 163-97.

Kröner, H.O., 'Elegisches Unwetter', *Poetica* 3 (1970b) pp. 388-408.

Labate, M., 'Poetica Ovidiana dell'elegia: la retorica della città', *MD* 3 (1979) pp. 9-67.

Labate, M., 'La memoria impertinente e altra intertestualità Ovidiana', in I. Gallo & L. Nicastri, *Cultura poesia ideologia nell' opera di Ovidio* (Edizioni Scientifiche Italiane, Napoli, 1991) pp. 41-59.

Lamacchia, R., 'Sull'evoluzione semantica di *poena* (son sens chez Ovide)', *Studia Florentina A Ronconi oblata* (1969) pp. 135-54.

Lambrino, S., 'Les tribus Ioniennes d'Histria', *Istros* I (1934) pp. 117-28.

Lambrino, S., 'Tomis, cité gréco-gète, chez Ovide', *Ovidiana* (1958) pp. 379-90.

Lascu, N., 'L'epitaffio di Ovidio (Epigrafia e poesia)', in *Studi classici in onore di Q. Cataudella* vol. III (Fac. di Lett e. Filos., Catania, 1972) pp. 331-8.

Lechi, F., 'La palinodia del poeta elegiaco. I carmi Ovidiani dell'esilio', *A&R* 22 (1978) pp. 1-22.

Lee, A.G., 'An appreciation of *Tristia* III.viii', *G&R* 18, first series (1949) pp. 113-20.

Lee, A.G., 'The originality of Ovid', *Atti del Conv* II (1958-9) pp. 405-12.

Lenz, F.W., 'Ovid *Tristia* 1.3.75f.', *Maia* 14 (1962) pp. 109-16.

Lenz, F.W., 'Ovids dichterisches Ingenium (zu *Amores* 1.5)', *Das Altertum* 13 (1967) pp. 164-75.

Lenz, L., 'Eis und Exil (zu Tristien III 10)', in C. Neumeister (ed.), *Antike Texte in Forschung und Schule. Festschrift für Willibald Heilmann zum 65. Geburtstag* (Frankfurt am Main, 1993) pp. 147-66.

Lenz, L., 'Tibull in den Tristien', *Gymnasium* 104 (1997) pp. 301-17.

Levick, B., 'The fall of Julia the Younger', *Latomus* 35 (1976) pp. 301-39.

Lieberg, G., 'Ovide et les Muses', *LEC* 48 (1980) pp. 3-22.

Lieberg, G., *Poeta creator: Studien zu einer Figur der antiken Dichtung* (Verlag Gieben, Amsterdam, 1982).

Lilja, S., *The Roman elegists' attitude to women* (Diss. Helsinki, 1965).

Lindheim, S.H., *Voices of desire: the ventriloquized letters of Ovid's* Heroides (Diss. Brown University, 1995) summarised in *DA* (Internet: http://www.nyu.edu/cgi-bin/cgiwrap/~redmonds/ovidsearch.p/).

Linse, E., *De Ovidio Nasone vocabulorum inventore* (Tremona = Dortmund, 1891).

Little, D.A., 'Politics in Augustan poetry', *ANRW* II.30.1 (1982) pp. 254-370.

Littlewood, R.J., 'Poetic artistry and dynastic politics. Ovid at the Ludi Megalensis, *Fasti* IV.179-372', *CQ* 31 (1981) pp. 381-95.

Lozovan, E., 'Ovide et le bilinguisme', *Ovidiana* (1958) pp. 396-403.

Lozovan, E., 'Réalités pontiques et nécessités littéraires chez Ovide', *Atti del Conv.* II (1958-59) pp. 355-70.

Lozovan, E., 'Ovide, agonothète de Tomes', *REL* 39 (1961) pp. 172-81.

Lucente, G., L., *The narrative of realism and myth* (Johns Hopkins UP, Baltimore, 1979).

Luck, G., 'Textproblemen der Tristien', *Philologus* 103 (1959b) pp. 100-13.

Luck, G., 'Brief und Epistel in der Antike', *Das Altertum* 7 (1961a) pp. 77-84.

Luck, G., 'Notes on the language and text of Ovid's *Tristia*', *HSCP* 65 (1961b) pp. 241-61.

Luck, G. (ed.), *P Ovidius Naso*: Tristia, *Band I: Text und Übersetzung* (Winter, Heidelberg, 1967).

Luck, G., *P Ovidius Naso*: Tristia, *Band II: Kommentar* (Winter, Heidelberg, 1977).

Luck, G., 'Vermutungen zu Ovids *Epistulae ex Ponto*', *Festschrift Munari* (Hildesheim, Weidmann, 1986) pp. 117-33.

Lugli, G., 'Commento topografico all'elegia I del III libro dei Tristia', *Atti del Conv* II (1958-9) pp. 397-403.

Lugli, G., 'Commento topografico all'elegia I del III libro dei Tristia', *Studi Ovidiani* (1959) pp. 29-37.

Lyne, R.O.A.M., *The Latin love poets from Catullus to Horace* (Clarendon, Oxford, 1980).

MacKenzie, M.F., review of D.R. Slavitt, *Ovid's poetry of exile* (Lincoln, Nebr., UNP 1986) in *Library Journal* 115 (1990) p. 96.

Mackie, N., 'Ovid and the birth of *Maiestas*', in A. Powell (ed.), *Roman poetry and propaganda in the age of Augustus* (1992) pp. 83-97.

Mader, G., 'Panegyric and persuasion in Ovid', *Latomus* 50 (1991) pp. 139-49.

Malouf, D., *An imaginary life* (George Braziller, New York, *c.* 1970).

Maltby, R., *Latin love elegy* (Bristol Classical Press, Bristol, 1980).

Marache, R., 'La révolte d'Ovide exilé contre Auguste', *Ovidiana* (1958) pp. 412-19.

Marcovitch, M., 'Tanta moles', *PP* 25 (1970) pp. 429-30.

Marg, W., 'Zur Behandlung des Augustus in den Tristien', *Atti del Conventu* II (1958-9) pp. 345-54.

Marin, D., 'Ovidio fu relegato per la sua opposizione al regime Augusteo?' *Acta Philologica* I (1958) pp. 99-252.

Marshall, A.J., 'Library resources and creative writing at Rome', *Phoenix* 30 (1976) pp. 252-64.

Martin, R., 'Virgile et la "Scythie" (Georgiques III 349-82)', *REL* 144 (1966) pp. 286-304.

Martin, P.M., 'A propos de l'exile d'Ovide ... et de la succession d'Auguste', *Latomus* 45 (1986) pp. 609-11.

Martz, L.R., *Milton: poet of exile* (Yale UP, New Haven, 1986).

Masefield, J., *A letter from Pontus and other poems* (Macmillan, New York, 1936).

McGann, M.J., review of M. Steudel, *Die Literaturparodie in Ovids Ars Amatoria*, Alt. Wiss. *Texte & Stud.* 25 (Hildesheim, Olms, 1992) in *Gnomon* 69.2 (1997) pp. 119-23.

McKeown, J.C., 'Augustan elegy and mime', *PCPhS* (1979) pp. 71-84.

Melville, A.D., *Sorrows of an exile*, trans. with intr. & notes by E.J. Kenney (Clarendon, Oxford, 1992).

Micu, J., 'Pontus Euxinus in opercle Ovidiene din exil', *Pontica* 14 (1981) pp. 317-27.

Miller, J.F., 'Apostrophe, aside and the didactic addressee. Poetic strategies in *Ars Amatoria* III', *Materiali e discussioni per l'analisi dei testi classici* 31 (1994) pp. 231-42.

Morgan, J.D., 'The death of Cinna the poet', *CQ* 40 (1990) pp. 558-9.

Morgan, K., *Ovid's art of imitation (Propertian echoes in the Amores)*, Mnemosyne Suppl. 47 (1977).

Müller, U., 'Lügende Dichter', in Kreizer (ed.), *Gestaltungsgeschichte und Gesellschaftsgeschichte, Lit., Kunst und Musikwiss. Studien* (Stuttgart, 1965) pp. 32-50.

Munteanu, M., 'Les divinités du Panthéon Gréco-Romain dans les villages de la Dobroudja Romaine', *Pontica* 6 (1973) pp. 73-86.

Murgatroyd, P., *From Ovid with love: Selections from* Ars Amatoria *I and II* (Bolchazy-Carducci, Chicago, 1982).

Murgia, C.E., 'Imitation and authenticity in Ovid. *Metamorphoses* 1.477 and *Heroides* 15', *AJPh* 106 (1985) pp. 456-74.

Murray, P., review of N. Felson-Rubin, *Paragon in flirtation: regarding Penelope: from character to poetics* in *Times Literary Supplement* (1994) p. 26.

Musgrave, M.W., 'Change of perspective in Ovid, *Metamorphoses* 12.11-23', *AJPh* 118.2 (1997) pp. 267-83.

Nagle, B.R. (Fredericks), *The poetics of exile: program and polemic in the* Tristia *and* Epistulae ex Ponto *of Ovid.* Coll. Latomus 170 (1980 = Diss. Indiana 1975).

Nagle, B.R., 'Ovid: a poet between two novelists', *Helios* 12 (1985) pp. 65-74.

Németh, B., 'Caelestia sacra. Zur Frage des Ovidischen Selbstbewusstseins', *Acta Class. Univ. Scient. Debreceniensis* (Hungaria) 19 (1980) pp. 67ff.

Nemethy, G., *Commentarius Exegeticus ad Ovidii Tristia* (Sumptibus Academiae Litterarum Hungaricae, Budapest, 1973).

Nethersole, R., 'Vom Ende der Geschichte und dem Anfang von Geschichten: Christoph Ransmayrs *Die letzte Welt*', *Acta Germanica* 21 (1992) pp. 229-45.

Newlands, C.E., *Playing with time: Ovid and the Fasti* (Cornell UP, Ithaca, 1995).

Newlands, C.E., 'Transgressive acts: Ovid's treatment of the Ides of March', *CPh* 91.4 (1996) pp. 320-38.

Newman, J.K., *Augustus and the new poetry.* Coll. Latomus 88 (1967).

Nicolai, W., 'Phantasie und Wirklichkeit bei Ovid', *A&A* 19 (1973) pp. 107-16.

Nisbet, R.G.M., 'Great and lesser bear (Ovid *Tristia* 4.3)', *JRS* 72 (1982) pp. 49-56.

Norwood, F., 'The riddle of Ovid's *relegatio*', *CPh* 58 (1963) pp. 150-63.

O'Gorman, E., 'Love and the family: Augustus and Ovidian elegy', *Arethusa* 30.1 (1997) pp. 103-24.

O'Hara, J., 'Vergil's best reader? Ovidian commentary on Vergilian etymological wordplay', *CJ* 91.3 (1995) pp. 255-75.

Owen, S.G. (ed.), *P Ovidii Nasonis Tristium Liber Secundus* (OUP, Oxford, 1924).

Owen, S.G., 'Ovid's use of the simile', *CR* 45 (1931) pp. 97-106.

Owen, S.G. (ed.), *P Ovidii Nasonis Tristium libri quinque, Ibis, ex Ponto libri quattuor, Halieutica fragmenta* (OUP, Oxford, 1915/63).

Paoletta, H., 'De Ovidii relegati causis ex eius temporum picta cryptographia micropan-archaeologico modo nuperrime perspectis', *Latinitas* 42 (1993) pp. 88-108.

Papadopoulou, T., 'The presentation of inner self: Euripides' *Medea* 1021-55 and Apollonius Rhodius' *Argonautica* 3, 772-801', *Mnemosyne* 50.6 (1997) pp. 641-63.

Papponetti, G. (ed.), *Ovidio, poeta della memoria. Atti del Convegno Internazionale di Studi Sulmona 19-21 Ottobre 1989. Comitato, Celebrazione Ovidiane* (Herder, Roma, 1991).

Paratore, E., 'L'elegia autobiografica di Ovidio (*Tristia* 4.10)', *Ovidiana* (1958) pp. 353-78.

Parker, D., 'The Ovidian coda', *Arion* 8 (1969) pp. 80-97.

Parsons, P., 'The oldest Roman book ever found', *Omnibus* I (1981) pp. 1-4.

Pearson, C.S., 'Simile and imagery in Ovid *Heroides* 4 & 5', *ICS* 5 (1980) pp. 110-29.

Perkill, C.G., 'The "dying Gallus" and the design of *Eclogue* 10', *CPh* 91.2 (1996) pp. 128-40.

Pichon, R., *De sermone amatoria apud Latinos elegiarum scriptores: Index verborum amato-rium* (Paris, 1902) pp. 75-303.

Pigeaud, J., *La maladie de l'âme: étude sur la relation de l'âme et du corps dans la tradition médico-philosophique antique* (Paris, 1981).

Pigeaud, J., 'Prolégomènes à une histoire de la mélancolie', in G. Giannantoni & M. Vegetti (edd.), *La scienza ellenistica. Atti delle tre giornale di studio kenatesi a Pavia dal 14 al 16 April 1982, Collana Elenchos* 9 (Naples, 1984).

Pippidi, D.M., 'Tomis, cité géto-grèque à l'époque d'Ovide?', *Athenaeum* 55 (1977) pp. 250-6.

Piru, A., 'Ovid in the city of Tomi', *Mosaic* 12 (1981) pp. 54-6.

Podossinov, A.V., 'Ovid as a source for the history of West Pontus' (in Russian with English summary), *VDI* 156 (1981) pp. 174-94.

Podossinov, A.V., *Ovids Dichtung als Quelle für die Geschichte des Schwartzmeergebiets. Xenia* 19 (Schuller, Konstanz, 1987).

Popescu, D., 'Considerati asupra educatiei teneretului la Histria in legatura cutrei inscripti inedite', *Studii si Cercetari de Istorie Veche* 7 (1956) pp. 343-65.

Porte, D., 'Un épisode satirique des Fastes et l'exil d'Ovide', *Latomus* 43 (1984) pp. 284-306.

Posch, S., 'Zu Ovid *Trist.* 1.2 und 1.4: zu zwei Beispielen neoterischer Poesie', *Serta philol. Aenipontana* 2 (1972) pp. 83-105.

Posch, S., *P Ovidius Naso: Tristia I Interpretationen. Band I: Die Elegien 1-4. Commentatio-nes Aenipontanae* 28 (Wagner, Innsbruck, 1983).

Postgate, J.P., *Corpus poetarum Latinorum* (Bell, London, 1905).

Powell, A., 'The Aeneid and the embarrassments of Augustus', in A. Powell (ed.), *Roman poetry and propaganda in the age of Augustus* (1992b) pp. 141-74.

Poznanski, L., 'A propos de la droite et la gauche chez Ovide', *SCI* 4 (1978) pp. 50-62.

Pulleyn, S., review of L. Watson, *Arae: the curse poetry of Antiquity* (Class. & Med. Papers & Monographs, Cairns, Leeds, 1991) in *CR* 43 (1993) pp. 72-3.

Purnelle-Sinart, A. & Purnelle, G., *Ovide: Ars Amatoria, Remedia Amoris, De medicamine: Index verborum, listes de fréquence, Relevés grammaticaux* (Liege, Centre Informatique de Philosophie et Lettres, 1987).

Radulescu, A., 'L'exil d'Ovide: légendes et réalités archéologiques', *Ovidianum* (1976) pp. 521-6.

Rahn, H., 'Ovids elegische Epistel', *A&A* 7 (1958) pp. 105-20.

Ransmayr, C., *The last world*, trans. J. Woods (Paladin Grafton, London, 1990).

Redmond, S., 'Ars Anarchic: Ovid's semiotic invention in the *Metamorphoses*', in *Sean Redmond's Homepage* (1997, Internet: http://www.nyu.edu/cgi-bin/cgiwrap/~red-monds/ovidsearch.p/).

Reed, J.D., 'Ovid's elegy on Tibullus and its models', *CPh* 92.3 (1997) pp. 260-9.

Ricci, J.L., 'Il topos della poesia consolatrice (in riferimento ad Ov *Trist* 4.1.3 sqq; 4.10.117 sqq; 5.1.33 sqq)', *Inv. Luc.* I (1979) pp. 143-70.

Richmond, J.A., 'The authorship of the *Halieutica* ascribed to Ovid', *Philologus* 120 (1976) pp. 92-106.

Richmond, J.A., 'The latter days of a love poet: Ovid in exile', *Classics Ireland* 2 (1995) pp. 97-120.

Ritchie, A.L., 'Notes on Ovid's *Tristia*', *CQ* 43 (1995) pp. 512-16.

Rogers, R.S., 'The emperor's displeasure – *amicitiam renuntiare'*, *TAPA* 90 (1959) pp. 224-37.
Rogers, R.S., 'The emperor's displeasure and Ovid', *TAPA* 97 (1966) pp. 373-8.
Rosati, G., 'L'esistenza letteraria. Ovidio e l'autoscienza della poesia', *MD* 2 (1979) pp. 101-36.
Rosati, G., 'Medea esule: Ovidio *Her*. 12.110', *RFIC* 117 (1989) pp. 181-5
Rosen, R.M., 'Hipponax and his enemies in Ovid's *Ibis'*, *CQ* 38.2 (1988) pp. 291-6.
Sabot, A.F., 'Les Héroïdes d'Ovide: préciosité, rhétorique et poésie', *ANRW* II.31.3 (1981) pp. 2552-2636.
Salceanu, G., 'De la Metamorfoze la Triste si Pontice', *Pontica* 4 (1971) pp. 221-33.
Schilling, R., 'Ovide et sa Muse où les leçons d'un exil', *REL* 50 (1972) pp. 205-11.
Schilling, R., 'De Nasonis interiore religione', *Ovidianum* (1976) pp. 549-54.
Schmitzer, U., *Zeitgeschichte in Ovids Metamorphosen: Mythologische Dichtung unter politischem Anspruch. Beiträge zur Altertumkunde* 4 (B.G. Teubner, Stuttgart, 1990).
Schmitzer, U., 'Non modo militiae turbine factus eques: Ovids Selbstbewusstsein und die Polemik gegen Horaz in der Elegie *am*. 3.15', *Philologus* 138.1 (1994) pp. 101-17.
Schmitzer, U., 'Gallus im Elysium. Ein Versuch über Ovids Trauerelegie auf den toten Papagei Corinnas (*am*. 2, 6)', *Gymnasium* 104 (1997) pp. 245-70.
Scott, K., 'Emperor-worship in Ovid', *TAPA* 61 (1930) pp. 43-69.
Scott, K., 'Another of Ovid's errors?', *CJ* 26 (1931) pp. 293-6.
Seeck, G.A., 'Ich-Erzähler und Erzähler-Ich in Ovids *Heroides*. Zur Entstehung des neuzeitlichen literarischen Menschen', in *Monumentum Chiloniense: Studien zur augusteischen zeit. Kieler Festschrift für Erich Burck* (Hakkert, Amsterdam, 1975) pp. 436-70.
Segal, C.P., *Landscape in Ovid's* Metamorphoses. *A study in the transformations of a literary symbol, Hermes Einzelschr*. 23 (1969a).
Segal, C.P., 'Myth and philosophy in the *Metamorphoses*: Ovid's Augustanism and the Augustan conclusion to Book XV', *AJP* 90 (1969b) pp. 257-92.
Segal, C.P., 'Ovid's *Metamorphoses*: Greek myth in Augustan Rome', *SPh* 68 (1971) pp. 371-94.
Segal, C.P., 'Ovid's Orpheus and Augustan ideology', *TAPA* 103 (1972) pp. 473-94.
Shackleton Bailey, D.R., 'Notes on Ovid's poems from exile', *CQ* 32 (1982) pp. 390-8.
Sidari, D., 'Il problema partico nella poesia Ovidiana', *AIV* 136 (1977-8) pp. 35-54.
Slavitt, D.R., *The* Tristia *of Ovid* (Univ. of Nebraska Press, Lincoln, 1986).
Slavitt, D.R., *Ovid's poetry of exile* (Johns Hopkins UP, Baltimore, 1990).
Smith, R..A., 'Fantasy, myth, and love letters: text in Ovid's *Heroides'*, *Arethusa* 27.2 (1994) pp. 247-73.
Smolak, K., 'Der verbannte Dichter. Identifizierungen mit Ovid in Mittelalter und Neuzeit', *WS* NF 14 (1980) pp. 158-91.
Soraci, G., 'Il lessico della lontananza in Ovidio', *Atti III Convegno naz. di Pedag. Francavilla*, L'Aquila Ist. di Lingue e Lett. Class. (1980) pp. 3-12.
Spahlinger, L., *Ars latet arte sua: Untersuchungen zur Poetologie in den Metamorphosen Ovids* (Stuttgart/Leipzig, 1996).
Spoth, F., *Ovids Heroides als Elegien. Zetemata* 89 (München, C.H. Beck, 1992).
Spoth, F., 'Ovids Ariadne-Brief (*Her*. 10) und die römische Liebeselegie', *Würzburger Jahrbücher für die Altertumswissenschaft* NF 19 (1993) pp. 239-60.
Stabryla, S., 'In defence of the anatomy of the poetic world (some remarks on Ovid's *Tristia* II)', *Hermes* 122 (1994) pp. 469-78.
Staffhorst, U., *P Ovidius Naso, Pont. III 1-3: Kommentar* (Diss. Würzburg, 1965).
Steudel, M., *Die Literaturparodie in Ovids Ars Amatoria, Alt. Wiss. Texte & Stud.* 25 (Hildesheim, Olms, 1992).
Stirrup, B.E., 'Ovid: poet of imagined reality', *Latomus* 40 (1981) pp. 88-104.
Stroh, W., 'Rhetorik und Erotik. Eine Studie zu Ovids liebesdidaktischen Gedichten', *WJA* NF 5 (1979) pp. 117-32.
Stroh, W., 'Tröstende Musen. Zur literarhistorischen Stellung und Bedeutung von Ovids Exilgedichten', *ANRW* II.31.3 (1981) pp. 2638-2684.
Stroh, W., 'Die Ursprünge der römische Liebeselegie: ein altes Problem im Licht eines neuen Fundes', *Poetica* 15 (1983) pp. 205-46.

Swoboda, M., 'De Ovidii carminum elegiacorum fragmentis hymnico-precatoriis', *Eos* 66 (1978) pp. 73-90.

Syme, R., *Danubian papers* (Bibliothèque d'études du sud-est Européen, Bucharest, 1971).

Syme, R., 'The crisis of 2 BC', *Sitz. Bayerische Akad. der Wiss. Phil-Hist. Klasse* 7 (1974).

Syme, R., *History in Ovid* (Clarendon, Oxford, 1978).

Thibault, J.C., *The mystery of Ovid's exile* (UCP, Berkeley, 1964).

Thomas, E., 'Variations on a military theme in Ovid's *Amores*', *G&R* (1964) pp. 151-64.

Thomas, R.F., 'Ovid's attempt at tragedy', *AJPh* 99 (1978) pp. 447-50.

Thomson, M.H. (= Davisson), *Detachment and manipulation in the exile poems [sic] of Ovid* (Diss. Berkeley, 1979, summarised in *DA* 40, 1980).

Tracey, V.A., 'Ovid and Corinna', *EMC* 21 (1977) pp. 86-91.

Trapp, J.B., 'Ovid's tomb', *JWI* 36 (1973) pp. 35-76.

Treu, M., 'Ovid und Sappho', *PP* 8 (1953) pp. 356-64.

Valafridus (Wilfried Stroh), 'Heroides Ovidianae cur Epistolas scribant', in G. Papponetti (ed.), *Ovidio, poeta della memoria. Atti del Convegno Internazionale di Studi Sulmona 19-21 Ottobre 1989. Comitato, Celebrazione Ovidiane* (Herder, Roma, 1991) pp. 201-44.

Verdière, R., *Le secret du voltigeur d'amour, ou, Le mystère de la relégation d'Ovide, Coll. Latomus* (Bruxelles, 1992).

Veremans, J., 'The autobiography of Ovid', *Mosaic* 12 (1981) pp. 26-58.

Vessey, D.W.T., 'Humor and humanity in Ovid's *Heroides*', *Arethusa* 9 (1976) pp. 91-110.

Veyne, P., *Roman erotic elegy: love, poetry and the West* (Univ. Chicago Press, Chicago, 1988).

Viarre, S., 'L'image et le symbole dans la poésie d'Ovide. Recherches sur l'imaginaire', *REL* 52 (1974) pp. 263-80.

Viarre, S., *Ovide, essai de lecture poétique* (Les Belles Lettres, Paris, 1976).

Viarre, S., 'Exil Ovidien exil medieval', in R. Chevallier (ed.), *Colloque présence d'Ovide, Coll. Caesarodunum* 17 (1980).

Viarre S., 'Les Muses de l'exil ou les *Metamorphoses* de la memorie', in G. Papponetti (ed.), *Ovidio, poeta della memoria. Atti del Convegno Internazionale di Studi Sulmona 19-21 Ottobre 1989. Comitato, Celebrazione Ovidiane* (Herder, Roma, 1991) pp. 117-41.

Videau-Delibes, A., *Les Tristes d'Ovide et l'élégie romaine* (Klincksieck, Paris, 1991).

Vincent, M., 'Between Ovid and Barthes: ekphrasis, orality, textuality in Ovid's Arachne', *Arethusa* 27 (1994) pp. 361-86.

Von Albrecht, M., 'Ovids Humor, ein Schlüssel zur Interpretation der *Metamorphosen*', *AV* 6 (1963) pp. 47-72.

Von Albrecht, M., 'Dichter und Leser, am Beispiel Ovids', *Gymnasium* 88 (1981) pp. 222-35.

Vulpe, R., 'Ovidio nella città dell' esilio', *Studi Ovidiani* (1959) pp. 39-62.

Vulpe, R., 'Notes d'histoire tomitaine', *Pontice* 2 (1969) pp. 166-7.

Wallner, G., 'Quomodo mediae aetatis poetae Ovidium secuti sint', *Latinitas* 42 (1994) pp. 83-104.

Wartenburg, G., *Quaestiones ovidianae: quibus agitur de* Tristium, Ibidis, Epistolarumque, *quae Ex Ponto inscribuntur, temporibus* (Diss. Berlin, 1884).

Watson, L.C., 'Ovid *Amores* 1.6: a parody of a hymn?', *Mnemosyne* 35 (1982) pp. 92-102.

Watson, L.C., 'Arae: the curse poetry of antiquity', *Classical and Medieval Papers and Monographs* 26 (Cairns, Leeds, 1991).

Watt, W.S., 'Notes on Ovid's poems from exile', *ICS* 13 (1988) pp. 85-93.

Wheeler, A.L., 'Erotic teaching in Roman elegy and the Greek sources', *CPh* 5 (1910) pp. 440-50; *CPh* 6 (1911) pp. 56-77.

Wheeler, A.L. (ed.), *Tristia. Ex Ponto* (Loeb Classical Library, London, 1924).

Whitaker, R., 'Gallus and the "Classical" Augustans (Virgil and Horace)', in F. Cairns (ed.), *Papers of the Liverpool Latin Seminar* 4 (1983) pp. 55-60.

White, P., 'Pompeius Macer and Ovid', *CQ* 42.1 (1992) pp. 210-18.

Wiedemann, T., 'The political background to Ovid's *Tristia* II', *CQ* 25 (1975) pp. 264-71.

Wilkens, E.G., 'A classification of the similes of Ovid', *CW* 25 (1932) pp. 73-8, 81-6.

Williams, Gordon, 'Poetry in the moral climate of Augustan Rome', *JRS* 52 (1962) pp. 28-46.

Williams, G., *Change and decline: Roman literature in the early empire* (UCP, Berkeley, 1978).

Williams, G., *Figures of thought in Roman poetry* (YUP, New Haven, Conn, 1980).

Bibliography: Seneca

Williams, Gareth D., 'Conversing after sunset: A Callimachean echo in Ovid's exile (*sic*) poetry', *CQ* 41 (1991) pp. 169-77.

Williams, G.D., 'On Ovid's *Ibis*: a poem in context', *PCPhS* 38 (1992a) pp. 171-89.

Williams, G.D., 'Ovid's Canace. Dramatic irony in *Heroides* 11', *CQ* (1992b) pp. 201-9.

Williams, G.D., *Banished voices* (CUP, Cambridge, 1994).

Williams, G.D., *The Curse of Exile: a study of Ovid's 'Ibis' (CPhS Suppl.* 19, Cambridge, 1996).

Williams, G.D., 'Representations of the book roll in Latin poetry. Ovid *Tr.* 1.1.3-14 and related texts', *Mnemosyne* series IV, 45 (1992) pp. 178-89.

Willige W., *Publius Ovidius Naso, Briefe aus der Verbannung. Tristia. Epistulae ex Ponto*, trans. Willige, comm. Niklas Holzberg (Fischer, Frankfurt-am-Main, 1993).

Wimmel, W., *Kallimachos in Rom: Die Nachfolge seines apologetischen Dichtens in der Augusteerzeit*, *Hermes Einzelschr.* 16 (1960).

Winniczuk, L., 'Ovids elegy in epistolographic theory' (= De Ovidii carminibus in Ponto scriptis observationes aliquot) in Polish, with Latin summary, *Meander* 12 (1957) pp. 319-70.

Winniczuk, L., 'Korneliusz Gallus i Publiusz Owidiusz Nazo', *Meander* 14 (1959) pp. 223-32.

Winniczuk, L., 'Cornelius Gallus und Ovid', in *Röm. Lit. der Augusteischen Zeit* (Berlin, 1960) pp. 26-35.

Winniczuk, L., 'Humour and wit in Ovid's *Fasti*', *Eos* 62 (1974) pp. 93-104.

Wise, V., 'Ovid's *Medea* and the magic of language', *Ramus* II (1982) pp. 16-25.

Yardley, J.C., 'The elegiac paraclausithyron', *Eranos* 76 (1978) pp. 19-34.

Zingerle, A., *Ovidius und sein Verhältnis zu den Vorgängern und gleichzeitigen römischen Dichtern* (Olms, Hildesheim, 1869; repr. 1967).

Zinn, E., 'Elemente des Humors in Augusteischer Dichtung', *Gymnasium* 67 (1960) pp. 41-56.

E. Seneca

Abel, K., 'Seneca: Leben und Leistung', *ANRW* II. 32.2 (1985) pp. 653-775.

Atkinson, J.E., 'Seneca's *Consolatio ad Polybium*', *ANRW* II.32.2 (1985) pp. 860-84.

Basore, J.W., *Seneca: moral essays* vol. II (Loeb Classical Library, 1935).

Bellemore, J., 'The dating of Seneca's *ad Marciam de Consolatione*', *CQ* 42.1 (1992) pp. 219-33.

Borgo, A., 'Considerazioni sul valore pratico e la funzione sociale delle consolationes di Seneca', *Vichiana* 7 (1978) pp. 66-109.

Bruwer, S.M., *Tacitus se Seneca* (MA Diss., Stellenbosch, 1964).

Costa, C.D.N., *Seneca: dialogues and letters* (Penguin, Harmondsworth, 1997).

Currie, H.M., *The younger Seneca: selected prose* (Bristol Classical Press, 1977).

Degl' Innocenti Pierini, R., 'Echi delle elegie ovidiane dall' esilio nelle consolationes *ad Helviam* e *ad Polybium* di Seneca', *SIFC* 52 (1980) pp. 109-43.

Degl' Innocenti Pierini, R., '*In angulo defixus*: Seneca e l'emarginazione dell' esilio', *SIFC* 53 (1981a) pp. 225-32.

Degl' Innocenti Pierini, R., 'Motivi consolatori e ideologia imperiale nella *Consolatio ad Polybium* di Seneca', *QFL* I (1981b) pp. 115-47.

Degl' Innocenti Pierini, R., review of R. Jacobi, *Der Einfluss Ovids auf den Tragiker Seneca* (De Gruyter, Berlin, 1988) in *A&R* (1990c) pp. 117-20.

Degl' Innocenti Pierini, R., 'Il tema dell'esilio nelle tragedie di Seneca: Autobiografia, meditazione filosofica, modelli letterari nel *Thyestes* e nell' *Oedipus*', *Quaderni di Cultura e di Tradizione Classica* 8 – 1990 (Università degli Studi di Palermo, Istituto di Filologia Latina, 1992b) pp. 71-83.

Degl' Innocenti Pierini, R., '*Vivi nascosto*: Riflessi di un tema epicureo in Orazio, Ovidio e Seneca', *Prometheus* 18 (1992c) pp. 150-72.

Degl' Innocenti Pierini, R., 'Lo spazio dell'autore: I cori delle tragedie senecane tra filosofia ed autobiografia', *La Fortezza* IV.2-V.1 (1993-94) pp. 37-48.

Degl' Innocenti Pierini, R., 'Studi sugli epigrammi attribuiti a Seneca I: Il padrone del tempo', *Prometheus* 21.2 (1995a) pp. 161-86.

Degl' Innocenti Pierini, R., 'Studi sugli epigrammi attribuiti a Seneca II: Tra elegia ed epigramma: tracce di una poetica', *Prometheus* 21.3 (1995b) pp. 193-227.

331

Degl' Innocenti Pierini, R., 'L'apparizione di Argo nella Medea di Accio. Storia e fortuna di una scena mitica', in *Atti V Seminario sulla tragedia romana, Palermo, 1994, Quaderni di Cultura e di tradizione classica* 11 (1995e) pp. 45-60.

Dingel J., '*Corsica terribilis*: Über zwei Epigramme Senecas', *RhM* 137.3-4 (1994) pp. 346-51.

Dunn, F.M., 'A prose hexameter in Seneca? (*Consolatio ad Marciam* 26, 7)', *AJPh* 110 (1989) pp. 488-91.

Edwards, C., 'Self-scrutiny and self-transformation in Seneca's letters', *G&R* 44.1 (1997) pp. 23-38.

Gahan, J.J., 'Seneca, Ovid and exile', *CW* 78 (1985) pp. 145-7.

Griffin, M., *A philosopher in politics* (OUP, Oxford, 1976).

Grimal, P., 'Sénèque juge de Cicéron', *MEFRA* 96 (1984) pp. 655-70.

Gummere, R., *Seneca: ad Lucilium, epistulae morales* vol. I (Loeb Classical Library, 1947).

Hermes, E. (ed.), *L Annaei Senecae libros XII* (Teubner, Leipzig, 1923).

Hijmans, B.L. Jr., *Inlaboratus et facilis. Aspects of structure in some letters of Seneca, Mnemosyne Suppl.* 83 (1976).

Hugo, A.M., *Calvijn en Seneca* (Diss. Utrecht, 1957).

Jacobi, R., *Der Einfluss Ovids auf der Tragiker Seneca* (De Gruyter, Berlin, 1988).

Kerasidi, N.K.H., 'Quelques particularités de l'argumentation consolatrice de Sénèque' (in Russian, with German resumé), *InFil* 70 = *PK Fil* 29 (1983) pp. 101-8.

Kierdorf, W., 'Kritische und exegetische Bemerkungen zu Senecas Trostschrift an Marcia (Dial. 6)', *Hermes* (1987) pp. 202-11.

Manning, C.E., 'The consolatory tradition and Seneca's attitude to the emotions', *G&R* NS 21 (1974) pp. 71-81.

Manning, C.E., *On Seneca's Ad Marciam* (Brill, Leiden, 1981).

Meinel, P., *Seneca über seine Verbannung* (Habelt, Bonn, 1972).

Moreschini, C., 'Cicerone filosofo fonte di Seneca', *RCCM* 19 (1977) pp. 527-34.

Motto, A.L., *Seneca sourcebook: guide to the thought of Lucius Annaeus Seneca in the extant prose works* (Hakkert, Amsterdam, 1970).

Nutton, V., 'Two notes on immunities: *Digest* 27.1.6.10&11', *JRS* 61 (1971) pp. 52-63.

Prato, C., *Gli epigrammi attribuiti a L. Anneo Seneca* (Edizioni dell' Ateneo, Rome, 1964).

Rosati, G., 'Seneca sulla lettera filosofica: un genere letterario nel cammino verso la sagezza', *Maia* 33 (1981) pp. 3-15.

Savon, H., 'Une consolation imitée de Sénèque et de Saint Cyprian (Pseudo-Jérôme, *epistula* 5, *ad amicum aegrotum*)', *RecAug* 14 (1979) pp. 153-90.

Smiley, C.N., 'Seneca and the Stoic theory of literary style', in E.A. Birge (ed.), *Classical studies in honor of Charles Forster Smith* (Madison, 1919).

Sørenson, V., *Seneca the humanist at the court of Nero*, trans. W.G. Jones (Canongate, Edinburgh, 1984).

Timothy, H.B., *The tenets of Stoicism, assembled and systematized from the works of L. Annaeus Seneca* (Hakkert, Amsterdam, 1973).

Zwierlein, O., 'Unterdrückte Klagen beim Tod des Pompeius (Lucan 7, 43) und des Cremutius Cordus (Sen. *consol. Marc.* 1, 2)', *Hermes* 118.2 (1990) pp. 184-91

F. Exile During Empire: The First-Century Philosophers

Annas, J. & Barnes, J., *The modes of scepticism: ancient texts and modern interpretations* (CUP, Cambridge, 1985).

Berry, E., 'Dio Chrysostom, the moral philosopher', *G&R* 30 (1983) pp. 70-80.

Bowersock, G.W., *Greek sophists in the Roman empire* (OUP, Oxford, 1969).

Bowie, E.L., 'Apollonius of Tyana: Tradition and reality', *ANRW* 2.16.2 (1978) pp. 1652-99.

Brancacci, A., *Rhetorike philosphousa. Dione Crisostomo nella cultura antica e bizantina* (Bibliopolis, Napoli, 1985).

Cahoon, J.W. (ed.), *Dio Chrysostom* vols I-V (Loeb Classical Library, 1932-34).

Edwards, M.J., 'Damis the Epicurean', *CQ* 41.2 (1991) pp. 563-6.

Flinterman, J-J., *Politiek, Paideia & Pythagorisme* (Styx, Groningen, 1993).

Häsler, F., *Favorin über die Verbannung* (Diss. Berlin, 1935).

Hense, O. (ed.), *C.Musonii Rufii Reliquiae* (Teubner, Leipzig, 1905).

Bibliography: Boethius

Harris, B.F., 'Stoic and Cynic under Vespasian', *Prudentia* 9 (1977) pp. 105-14.

Jagu, A., *Musonius Rufus, Entretiens et fragmenti*. Introd., trad & comm., *Stud. et Mater. zur Gesch. der Philos. Kl. R.V.* (Olms, Hildesheim, 1979).

Jones, C.P., *Philostratus, Life of Apollonius* (Penguin, Harmondsworth, 1970).

Jones, C.P., *The Roman world of Dio Chrysostom* (Harvard Univ. Press, Cambridge, Mass., 1978).

Jones, B.W., *Domitian and the exile of Dio of Prusa. PP* 45 (1990) pp. 348-57.

Kindstrand, J.F., *Homer in der Zweiten Sophistik. Studien zu der Homerlektüre und dem Homerbild bei Dion von Prusa, Maximos von Tyros und Ailios Aristeides* (Acta Universitatis Upsaliensis, 1973).

Koolmeister, R. & Tallmeister, T., *An index to Dio Chrysostomus* (UUP, Uppsala, 1981).

Lutz, C.E., 'Musonius Rufus, "the Roman Socrates" ', *YCIS* 10 (1947) pp. 3-147.

Macmullen, R., *Enemies of the Roman order* (Harvard UP, Cambridge, Mass., 1967).

Mead, G.R.S., *Apollonius of Tyana* (1901, repr. Ares, Chicago, 1980).

Mensching, E. (ed.), *Favorin von Arelate: Fragmenten: Memorabilien und Omnigena historia*, ed. & comm. (De Gruyter, Berlin, 1963).

Methy, N., 'Dion Chrysostome et la domination romaine', *AC* 63 (1994) pp. 173-92.

Moles, J.L., 'The career and conversion of Dio Chrysostom', *JHS* 98 (1978) pp. 79-100.

Moles, J., 'Dio Chrysostom: exile, Tarsus, Nero and Domitian', *LCM* 8 (1983) pp. 130-4.

Norsa, M. & Vitelli, G., *Il Papiro Vaticano Greco II: Favorinou peri fugês, Studi e testi* 53 (1931).

Nutton, V., 'Two notes on immunities *Digest* 27.1.6.10 & 11', *JRS* 61 (1971) pp. 52-63.

Puiggali, J., 'Maxime de Tyr et Favorinus', *AFLD* 10 (1980) pp. 47-62.

Puiggali, J., 'Dion Chrysostome et Maxime de Tyr', *Annales de la faculté des lettres et sciences humaines Univ. de Dakar* 12 (1982) pp. 9-24.

Quet, M.H., 'Rhétorique, culture et politique. Le fonctionnement du discours idéologique chez Dion de Pruse et dans les Moralia de Plutarque', *DHA* 4 (1978) pp. 51-119.

Rawson, E., 'Roman rulers and the philosophic adviser', in M. Griffin & J. Barnes (edd.), *Philosophia togata: essays on philosophy and Roman society* (Clarendon, Oxford, 1989) pp. 233-58.

Raynor, D.H., 'Moeragenes and Philostratus: two views of Apollonius of Tyana', *CQ* 34 (1984) pp. 222-6.

Schmitz, T., 'Trajan und Dion von Prusa. Zu Philostrat, *Vit. Soph.* 1, 7 (488)', *RhM* 139.3/4 (1996) pp. 315-19.

Sheppard, A.R.R., 'Dio Chrysostom, the Bithynian years', *AC* 53 (1984) pp. 157-73.

Sidebottom, H., 'Dio of Prusa and the Flavian dynasty', *CQ* 46 (1996) pp. 447-56.

Swain, S., 'Favorinus and Hadrian', *ZPE* 79 (1989) pp. 130-8.

Von Arnim, H., *Leben und Werk des Dio von Prusa* (Weidmann, Berlin, 1898).

Xenakakis, J., *Epictetus; philosopher-therapist* (The Hague, Nijhoff, 1969).

G. Boethius

Alfonsi, L., 'Boezio Poeta', *Antiquitas* 9 (1954) pp. 4-13.

Asztalos, M., 'Boethius as a transmitter of Greek logic to the Latin West: The Categories', *HSPh* 95 (1993) pp. 367-407.

Atkinson, J.K., *Boeces: De consolacion: éd. critique d'après le manuscrit 'Paris, Bibl. nationale, fr. 1096'* (M. Niemeyer Verlag, Tübingen, 1996).

Büchner, K., *Boethius: Philosophiae Consolationis Libri quinque* (Winter, Heidelberg, 1977).

Chadwick, H., *Boethius: the consolations of music, logic, theology and philosophy* (Clarendon, Oxford, 1981).

Chamberlain, D.S., 'Philosophy of music in the *Consolatio* of Boethius', *Speculum* 45 (1970) pp. 80-97.

Claassen, J.M., 'The *Consolatio Philosophiae* of Boethius: pagan tradition and Christian innovation', *UNISA Medieval Studies* 4 (1991b).

Courcelle, P., *La Consolation de Philosophie dans la tradition littéraire: Antécedents et posterité de Boèce* (Etudes Augustiniennes, Paris, 1967).

Bibliography: Boethius

Crabbe, A., 'Literary design in the *De Consolatione Philosophiae*', in M.T. Gibson (ed.), *Boethius: his life, thought and influence* (Oxford, 1981a).

Crabbe, A., 'Anamnesis and mythology in the *De consolatione Philosophiae*', in L. Obertello (ed.), *Atti Boeziani* (1981b) pp. 311-25.

Crocco, A., *Introduzione a Boezio* (Liguori, Naples, 1975).

Curley, T.F., 'The *Consolation of Philosophy* as a work of literature', *AJPh* (1987) pp. 108-367.

De Vogel, C.J., '*Amor quo coelum regitur*: Quel Amor et quel Dieu?', in L. Obertello (ed.), *Atti Boeziani* (1981) pp. 193-200.

Fuhrmann, M. & Gruber, J., *Boethius*, Wissenschaftliche Buchgesellschaft, Darmstadt, *Wege der Forschung* 483 (1984) pp. 323-49.

Fuhrmann, M., *Rom in der Spätantike: Porträt einer Epoche* (Artemis & Winckler, München, 1994).

Gegenschatz, E., 'Die Freiheit der Entscheidung in der *Consolatio Philosophiae* des Boethius', *MH* 15 (1958) pp. 110-29.

Gegenschatz, E. & Gigon, O. (edd.), *Trost der Philosophie* (Artemis, Zurich and Stuttgart, 1969).

Ghisalberti, A., 'L'ascesa a Dio nel II libro della consolatio', in L. Obertello (ed.), *Atti Boeziani* (1981) pp. 183-92.

Gibson, M.T. (ed.), *Boethius: his life, thought and influence* (Blackwell, Oxford, 1981).

Glei, R., 'Dichtung und Philosophie in der *Consolatio Philosophiae* des Boethius', *Würzburger Jahrbücher für die Altertumswissenschaft* NF 11 (1985) pp. 225-38.

Gruber, J., *Kommentar zu Boethius 'De consolatione Philosophiae'* (De Gruyter, Berlin, 1978).

Gruber, J., review of S. Lerer *Boethius and dialogue: literary method in 'The Consolation of Philosophy'* (Princeton UP, Princeton, 1985) in *Gymnasium* 95 (1988) pp. 445-7.

Hoenen, M.J.F.M. & Nauta, L., *Boethius in the Middle Ages: Latin and vernacular traditions of the* Consolatio Philosophiae (Brill, Leiden, 1997).

Kaylor, N.H., *The medieval Consolation of Philosophy* (New York, 1992).

Kirkby, H., 'The scholar and his public', in M.T. Gibson (ed.), *Boethius: his life, thought and influence* (Blackwell, Oxford, 1981).

Kopanos, V.A., *Symvole sten apokastase kai hermeneia tou ergon tou Boethiou 'De consolatione philosophiae'* (Aristoteleio Paneoistemio, Thessalonike, 1980).

Lerer, S., *Boethius and dialogue: literary method in 'The Consolation of Philosophy'* (Princeton UP, Princeton, 1985).

Matthews, J., 'Anicius Manlius Severinus Boethius', in M.T. Gibson (ed.), *Boethius: his life, thought and influence* (Blackwell, Oxford, 1981).

Mohrmann, C., 'Some remarks on the language of Boethius, *Consolatio Philosophiae*', *Festschrift Bieler* (Leiden, 1976) pp. 54-61.

Morton C.J., 'Boethius in Pavia: The tradition and the scholars', in L. Obertello (ed.), *Atti Boeziani* (1981) pp. 49-58.

Obertello, L., *Severino Boezio*, 2 vols (Genoa, 1974).

Obertello, L. (ed.), *Congresses Atti: Congrezzo internationale di Studi Boeziani, Pavia 5-8 Ottobre 1980* (Herder, Rome, 1981).

Obertello, L., 'La morte di Boezio e la verita storica', in L. Obertello (ed.), *Atti Boeziani* (1981) pp. 59-70.

O'Daly, G.J.P., *The poetry of Boethius* (Duckworth, London, 1991).

O'Daly, G.J.P., 'Sense-perception and imagination in Boethius *Philosophiae Consolatio* 5.m.4.4', in G.W. Most, H. Petersmann & A.M. Ritter, *Philanthropia kai eusebeia. Festschrift für Albrecht Dihle zum 70 Geburtstag* (Vandenhoeck & Ruprecht, Göttingen, 1993).

O'Donnell, J.J., *Boethius: Consolatio Philosophiae* (Bryn Mawr Commentaries, 1984).

Page, C., 'The Boethian metrum "*Bella bis quinis*": a new song from Saxon Canterbury', in M.T. Gibson (ed.), *Boethius: his life, thought and influence* (Blackwell, Oxford, 1981).

Patch, H.R., 'The beginnings of the legend of Boethius', *Speculum* 22 (1947) pp. 443-5.

Reiss, E., *Boethius* (Twayne, Boston, 1982).

Reitz, Ch., 'Beobachtungen zum fünften Buch der *Consolatio Philosophiae* des Boethius', *Würzburger Jahrbücher für die Altertumswissenschaft* NF 16 (1990) pp. 239-46.

Relihan, J.C., 'Agathias Scholasticus (A.P. 11.354), the philosopher Nicostratus and Boethius' Consolation', *Classica et Mediaevalia* 41 (1990) pp. 119-29.

Bibliography: Boethius

Samuels, A.E., review of R.W. Sharples, *Cicero, on Fate* (*De Fato*) and Boethius, *The consolation of philosophy IV.5-7* (*Philosophiae Consolationis*) in *CR* 43 (1993) pp. 56-8.

Shanzer, D.R., ' "*Me Quoque Excellentior*": Boethius, *De Consolatione* 4.6.38', *CQ* 33 (1983) pp. 277-83.

Starnes, C.J., 'Boethius and the development of Christian humanism', in L. Obertello (ed.), *Atti Boeziani* (1981) pp. 27-38.

Stewart, H.F. & Rand, E.K., *Boethius: 'The theological tractates' and 'The consolation of philosophy'*, with the English trans. of 'I.T.' 1609 (Loeb Classical Library, 1926).

Tester, S.J., *Fides quaerens intellectum: Medieval philosophy from Augustine to Ockham* (Bristol Classical Press, Bristol, 1989).

Tränkle, H., 'Ist die *Philosophiae Consolatio* des Boethius zum Vorgesehenen Abschluss gelangt?', *Vigiliae Christianae* 31 (1977) repr. *WDF* (Darmstadt, 1984) pp. 148-54.

Uhlfelder, M.L., 'The role of the liberal arts in Boethius' *Consolatio*', in M. Masi (ed.), *Boethius and the liberal arts* (Lang, Berne, 1981) pp. 17-30.

Watts, V.E., *Boethius, the Consolation of Philosophy* (Penguin, Harmondsworth, trans. 1969).

Index Locorum

Numbers in bold type refer to the pages of this book.

Subject Index

343